FINANCIAL ACCOUNTING

A Valuation Emphasis

FINANCIAL ACCOUNTING

A Valuation Emphasis

JOHN S. HUGHES
UCLA

FRANCES L. AYRES
University of Oklahoma

ROBERT E. HOSKIN
University of Connecticut

WILEY

John Wiley & Sons, Inc.

ACQUISITIONS EDITOR	Mark Bonadeo
SENIOR MARKETING MANAGER	Steven Herdegen
PROJECT EDITOR	Ed Brislin
ASSISTANT EDITOR	Brian Kamins
SENIOR PRODUCTION EDITOR	William A. Murray
MEDIA EDITOR	Allison Morris
SENIOR DESIGNER	Kevin Murphy
SENIOR ILLUSTRATION EDITOR	Anna Melhorn
INTERIOR DESIGN	Nancy Field
COVER DESIGN	David Levy
COVER PHOTO	Frank Whitney/The Image Bank/Getty Images

This book was set in Times Ten Roman by *The GTS Companies*/York, PA Campus and printed and bound by Donnelley/Willard. The cover was printed by Phoenix Color.

This book is printed on acid free paper. ∞

To order books or for customer service please, call 1-800-CALL WILEY (225-5945).

ISBN 0-471-20359-9

Printed in the United States of America.

10 9 8 7 6 5 4 3 2 1

Jack Hughes expresses his appreciation for the indulgence of his colleagues at UCLA and elsewhere for time spent away from academic research and for the support of his wife, Harriet, when the demands of the text intervened on their time together. Frances Ayres would like to thank her husband Tom for his patience and support and editorial assistance throughout the production of this book. She also wishes to thank her students who used earlier versions of this book and helped to improve it. Rob Hoskin thanks his wife Mary for her undying love and support in spite of the extra time devoted to producing this book.

About the Authors

Dr. John (Jack) S. Hughes holds the Ernst & Young Chair in Accounting at UCLA. He joined the UCLA faculty in 1999, having formerly been a member of faculties at Western New England College, Dartmouth College, Duke University, University of Minnesota, and University of British Columbia. He has won teaching awards in MBA programs at Duke and British Columbia and in undergraduate programs at Western New England, Purdue, and Minnesota.

Professor Hughes currently teaches in the MBA, Ph.D., and undergraduate programs. His present MBA course assignment is financial statement analysis, a course that emphasizes valuing equity from fundamental analysis. At the undergraduate level, Professor Hughes recently taught a course on Special Topics in Accounting that explored recent accounting scandals and their economic consequences and valuation implications. He serves as the accounting area Ph.D. advisor.

Professor Hughes has over 50 articles either published or forthcoming in major academic journals in accounting and economics, including *The Accounting Review, Journal of Accounting Research, Journal of Accounting and Economics, Review of Accounting Studies, Econometrica, Journal of Economic Theory, RAND Journal of Economics,* and *Journal of Law and Economics.* He is cofounder and a coeditor of the *Review of Accounting Studies.*

Professor Hughes's personal interests include cycling in the nearby Santa Monica mountains and rock climbing at his summer residence in British Columbia.

Dr. Frances L. Ayres, Ph.D., CPA is currently the Director of the School of Accounting and is the John W. Jr. and Barbara J. Branch Professor of Accounting at the University of Oklahoma. She received her Ph.D. in Accounting at the University of Iowa in 1982 and has taught at the University of Oklahoma for 22 years. Her teaching focus is in the financial accounting area. She has taught introductory financial accounting to undergraduates and MBAs, intermediate financial accounting, accounting theory, and financial statement analysis. Dr. Ayres has published in numerous academic and professional journals, including the *Journal of Accounting and Economics,* the *Journal of Accounting Research, The Accounting Review,* and *Management Accounting.* She serves as an ad hoc reviewer for several journals and serves on the editorial boards of *The Accounting Review* and *Journal of Accounting and Public Policy.* She is past editor of the *Journal of the American Taxation Association* and currently serves as president of the American Taxation Association. Her research interests focus on the impact of taxation and financial information and disclosures on managers and investors. She also serves on the Board of Directors of the Oklahoma City Chapter of the Financial Executives Institute and has served on the Business Advisory Board for Los Alamos National Laboratory.

Dr. Robert (Rob) E. Hoskin is currently Accounting Faculty and Director of Executive Programs at the School of Business, University of Connecticut. He received his Ph.D. from Cornell University in 1980 and taught for six years at the Fuqua School of Business, Duke University, before coming to the University of Connecticut. Dr. Hoskin has since served as Director of the Executive MBA Program and as Associate Dean prior to his current role. He spent six months with Price Waterhouse in 1990 as a faculty intern. He currently teaches primarily introductory Financial Accounting to MBAs, a course in Financial Services (Insurance and Banking) in the MS in Accounting Program, as well as several executive education programs in the insurance and banking arena.

Preface

PERSPECTIVE

We often hear that accounting is the language of business. Understanding this language has never been more important than it is today. Consider how accounting distortions and misstatements have so recently contributed to the downfall of several major corporations. The downfall of publicly traded corporations is manifested by a substantial decline in stock prices and the resultant aggregate loss of market value for those corporations. Understanding the connection between the firm's market value and its financial statements has become critical for all investors and creditors.

Today's CEOs are on the line to affirm the accuracy of reports generated by their firms for external users. The relevance and reliability of these reports are essential to smoothly functioning exchanges in capital markets. *Financial reports are the primary source of information that investors and potential investors use to make decisions about the value of firms in which they acquire ownership.* In this text, we emphasize the role of financial accounting reports in providing information useful to capital suppliers in making decisions about their investments in the firm.

We believe that accounting students should understand the valuation and income measurement issues inherent in the accounting system at a conceptual level. At the same time, they must also understand the accounting process to properly evaluate the relevance and reliability of financial statement information. The text, therefore, provides a solid underpinning in basic accounting procedures (the double-entry model) employed in the construction of those statements, as well as a rich exposure to accounting concepts.

UNDERLYING THEMES

Complemented by real-world examples throughout, the text illustrates how accounting disclosures interrelate with market values. Further, the text explores how parties observing those disclosures (e.g., investors, creditors, and managers) affect and are affected by their content. This contextual richness embodies two underlying themes: valuation and economic consequences. *Valuation* encompasses concepts and techniques for assessing not only the value of the firm as a whole, but also its specific resources and obligations. The text links accounting reports with stock market valuation through two well-known valuation models commonly used by financial analysts. *Economic consequences* speak to the real effects that financial reports and the policies governing the construction of those reports might have on a firm's efficiency in creating wealth and on the distribution of that wealth to the various stakeholders of the firm.

DISTINCTIVE FEATURES OF THE BOOK

In addition to the preceding themes, this text offers several distinctive pedagogical features:

- ◉ Early treatment of cash flow analysis serves to consolidate an understanding of the basic financial accounting model, by demonstrating how the principal financial statements contained in accounting reports relate to one another.
- ◉ Early exposure to financial ratios and basic valuation methods motivates consideration of asset and liability valuation and income measurement issues that follow in greater depth.
- ◉ A running example based on the health-products industry contributes to the coherence of content across chapters.
- ◉ Heavy reliance on excerpts from actual financial reports for illustration of key practices and as the source of data for end-of-chapter problems and cases connects the text to the real world of business.
- ◉ The text includes a significant number of real-world illustrations with margin notes that emphasize important points. We also illustrate the economic consequences of accounting choices, and incentives that may lead to those choices, with frequent margin references to the findings of academic research. We provide a complete listing of these references at the end of the book

DISTINCTIVE FEATURES OF EACH CHAPTER

At the beginning of each chapter, we provide a set of learning objectives focused on the major issues covered in the chapter. Following the learning objectives, each chapter has a real-world opening vignette designed to link valuation and financial statements with the real issues facing companies. In addition, each chapter has a significant

> **D**uring the day of August 25, 2000, the stock price of Emulex, a computer technology company, drastically dropped (see Exhibit 1.1) following an Internet story that it was under investigation by the Securities and Exchange Commission (SEC). The story also indicated that Emulex would restate its earnings downward as a result of the investigation. The stock quickly rebounded later that same day when investors learned that the story had been a hoax.
>   This event suggests that both earnings per se, and the credibility of that number are relevant to the stock market's assessment of a firm's value. Several questions come to mind: What are earnings? How are earnings linked to the market value of a company's stock? What role do the SEC and other institutions play in determining the reliability of reported earnings? These and many other questions pertaining to the construction of financial accounting information, and how that information relates to the value of the firm and the expectations of investors, lay at the heart of this text.

number of exhibits that feature real company illustrations of the topics discussed. These exhibits are labeled "The Real World." Many of the valuation and economic consequence issues are also highlighted in each chapter with margin notes designated with the ⧉ icon. Similar notes also accompany many of The Real World exhibits. In relevant places in the text, we also raise international

accounting issues through the use of "Thinking Globally" boxes ◉. Finally, in the end-of-chapter material we have also included some problems that focus on valuation issues relevant to the chapter.

Exhibit 3.13
Hasbro, Inc. and Subsidiaries

THE REAL WORLD
Hasbro, Inc.

Notes to Consolidated Financial Statements
(1) Summary of Significant Accounting Policies

Preparation of Financial Statements
The preparation of financial statements in conformity with generally accepted accounting principles requires management to make estimates and assumptions that affect the amounts reported in the financial statements and notes thereto. Actual results could differ from those estimates.
  Within GAAP, managers must make some significant estimates, such as the useful life and salvage value of a firm's property, plant, and equipment. Hasbro's disclosure reminds its financial statement readers that management makes and the impact of these estimates on those statements.

CHAPTER CONTENTS

The first two chapters provide the foundation on which financial accounting rests, describe the principal general-purpose financial statements, and comment on the potential economic effects of financial accounting choices. Chapters 3 and 4 develop the mechanics of financial accounting systems. Attention is given to the key concepts of duality between resources that the firm controls and claims to those resources held by creditors and owners (stockholders for corporations, the assumed firm type), and nominal accounts for explaining changes in resources and claims that evolve from profit-seeking activities. Chapter 5 focuses on cash flows and the operating, investing, and financing activities that give rise to those flows. This chapter completes the picture of the construction and content of financial statements by demonstrating how these various activities result in changes in a firm's financial position.

Chapter 6 transitions from the construction of financial statements to major valuation and income measurement issues crucial to statement interpretation. Consistent with a user perspective of financial reports, this chapter shows how ratios facilitate intertemporal and cross-sectional performance evaluation. In turn, assessing past performance leads naturally to forecasting, introduction of present value concepts, and the application of both of these to the valuation of a firm.

Although we believe that discussing both the cash flow statement and financial analysis early in financial accounting courses is highly desirable from a pedagogical standpoint, it is possible to assign Chapters 5 and 6 after the completion of the valuation and income measurement issues considered in Chapters 7 through 12.

Chapters 7 through 12 move systematically over major valuation and related income measurement issues pertaining to assets, liabilities, and stockholders' equity. The coverage in these chapters concisely addresses more substantive and representative topics for commercial and industrial enterprises.

Given the significance of intercorporate investments as a path to firm growth, Chapter 13 considers major classes of such investments. These range from temporary investments, where the investing firm's influence over the affairs of the firms in which an interest is acquired is fairly minimal, to those that are more permanent in nature, where the investing firm has some measure of influence or possibly full control.

While most first-level financial accounting texts conclude at this point, this text provides a bridge to standard courses in finance by introducing the two most commonly employed approaches for estimating the value of equity in Chapter 14. The chapter begins by presenting techniques for projecting future financial statements (i.e., pro forma statements) from forecasts of operating, investing, and financing activities. There may be no better method for aiding the internalization of financial accounting systems than to engage in such an exercise. Further, the method provides exposure to theory that seeks to assess the relationship between financial accounting information and market prices for the firm's stock.

END OF CHAPTER MATERIAL

Chapters conclude with key terms and a series of questions, exercises, and problems that test the understanding of chapter contents. The key terms are complemented by a glossary at the end of the book. The Review Questions section assesses understanding of essential terms and concepts. The Applying Your Knowledge section involves application of concepts and procedures to conventional text problems. The Using Real Data section brings actual financial statement disclosures into play for analysis designed to test facility in interpreting those disclosures. The Beyond the Book section prompts inquiries into financial reports outside the text. Completion of the end-of-chapter materials contributes to a working knowledge of financial accounting useful both in business pursuits and in personal investment.

END OF BOOK MATERIAL

Several appendixes are provided in the book. The first focuses on a more detailed look at adjusting entries and the second focuses on time value of money concepts and includes a set of problems. The remaining appendixes provide a complete set of references to the various FASB statements used in the book and the academic journal references made in many of the margin notes.

In the third appendix we have provided a case based on the 2002 financial statements of Chico's FAS, Inc. In this case, students have an opportunity to apply concepts they learned throughout the book to the data of a real company. We chose Chico's because their financial statements are straightforward and they are a competitor to the two firms that we analyzed in Chapter 6 of the book, AnnTaylor and Talbots. We selected the 2002 statements so that the data would be similar to that used in Chapter 6 and to make the valuation exercise more representative in that debt appears on the 2002 statements but disappears by the 2003 statements. Instructors will find the solutions to this case in the instructor manual and on the instructors' companion website for the book.

At the very end of the book is a complete glossary of the major terms used throughout the book and an index.

SUPPLEMENTS

FOR THE STUDENT

The Study Guide provides a comprehensive review of text content and contains detailed explanations of important chapter concepts. The Study Guide includes true/false statements, multiple choice questions, exercises, and demonstration problems with solutions. Each question was written to address a particular study objective in the text.

FOR THE INSTRUCTOR

Online Instructor Solutions Manual   The Solutions Manual contains sample syllabi and solutions to all end-of-chapter material.

Online Test Bank   The Test Bank offers questions consisting of true/false statements, multiple choice questions, short answers, analytical exercises, and essays. Suggested solutions are included.

Computerized Test Bank   The Test Bank is available in an electronic format to facilitate test preparation on Mac or IBM/PC-compatible computers.

PowerPoint Slides   Designed according to the organization of material in the textbook, the PowerPoint presentations will visually reinforce important concepts and help guide you through your lecture.

Acknowledgments

The authors wish to thank the following people at Wiley for their help in making this a successful textbook, particularly Mark Bonadeo, Senior Acquisitions Editor; Terry Ann Kremer, Freelance Development Editor; William Murray, Senior Production Editor; Brian Kamins, Assistant Editor; Ed Brislin, Project Editor; and Steven Herdegen, Senior Marketing Manager.

The authors also wish to acknowledge the faculty that participated in the manuscript review process at various times and in various ways throughout the course of development of this financial accounting textbook. They include:

Carleton Donchess at Bridgewater State University
Somnath Das at the University of Illinois, Chicago
Ron Davidson at Arizona State University West
Elliott Levy at Bentley College
Catherine Schrand at the University of Pennsylvania
James Ohlson at New York University
Michael Haselkorn at Bentley College
Gary Taylor at the University of Alabama
Burch Kealey at the University of Nebraska, Omaha
Anne Clem at Iowa State University
Robert Pinsker at Old Dominion University
Christine Schalow at California State University, Santa Barbara
Brandi Roberts at Southeastern Louisiana University
Kam Chan at Pace University
Margaret Shelton at the University of Houston
Ann Brooks at the University of New Mexico
Ginger Parker at Creighton University
Susan Young at Emory University
Charlene Abendroth at California State University, Hayward
James Wallace at the University of California, Irvine
Richard Frankel at the Massachusetts Institute of Technology
Wayne Shaw at Southern Methodist University
Carol Knapp at the University of Oklahoma
Rick Turpin at the University of Tennessee, Chattanooga
Darla Treece at Southern Illinois University
Brandi Roberts at Southeastern Louisiana University
David Aboody at the University of California, Los Angeles
A.J Potts at the University of Southern Maine
Jocelyn Kauffunger at the University of Pittsburgh
William Wrege at Ball State University

Kathleen Sevigny at Bridgewater State University
Russell Briner at the University of Texas, San Antonio
Chandra Seethamraju at Washington University, St. Louis
David Ryan at Temple University
Larry Walther at the University of Texas, Arlington
Bruce Swindle at McNeese State University
Jeffrey Harkins at the University of Idaho
Stephen Goldberg at Grand Valley State University
John Coulter at Western New England University
Charles Caliendo at the University of Minnesota
Paul Fischer at Pennsylvania State University
Harriet Griffin at North Carolina State University
James Largay at Lehigh University
Janet Greenlee at the University of Dayton
Sue Terzian at Wright State University
Larry Singleton at George Washington University
Merle Hopkins at the University of Southern California
Jack Cathey at the University of North Carolina, Charlotte
Paul Mason at the University of Kansas
Robert McGee at Seton Hall University
Gary Luoma at the University of South Carolina
Donna Philbrick at Portland State University
Obuela Persons at Rider University
Mark Lang at the University of North Carolina at Chapel Hill
Phillip Stocken at the University of Pennsylvania

Ancillary Authors
Molly Brown, James Madison University—Study Guide
Larry Falcetto, Emporia State University—Test Bank
Sarita Sheth, Santa Monica College—PowerPoint
Eileen Shifflem, James Madison University—Study Guide

Authors' Note

In writing this text, we have drawn on our experience in teaching financial accounting courses in the MBA and Executive MBA core and in initial undergraduate offerings. We believe that the presentation is well suited to high-quality graduate and undergraduate programs. Our intent is to provide coverage that is sufficiently complete and self-contained to serve the needs of students whose principal exposure to financial accounting is confined to a single course. However, we also believe that the text sets an appropriate foundation for professional accounting curricula. Our goals in designing this text include furthering an appreciation for the importance of financial accounting in the functioning of financial markets. We also seek to stimulate enthusiasm for financial accounting as an intellectual discipline on par with financial economics. The underlying themes of valuation and economic consequences help us achieve these goals, or so we perceive. Notwithstanding our best efforts to minimize mistakes and other forms of errata, we accept full responsibility for these and other shortcomings.

Brief Contents

Contents

CHAPTER 1

Financial Reporting: The Institutional Setting

LEARNING OBJECTIVES

After reading this chapter you should be able to:

1. Identify the types of business activities of publicly traded corporations reflected in financial accounting reports.

2. Explain the process governing the regulation of financial reporting and setting of Generally Accepted Accounting Principles (GAAP).

3. Describe the role of independent audits in monitoring compliance of financial reports with GAAP.

4. Recognize the economic consequences of accounting choices, and the link between owners' and managers' wealth and financial statement information.

5. Understand that a potential relationship exists between the value of a firm's stock and the information contained in financial reports, particularly the firm's statement of earnings.

During the day of August 25, 2000, the stock price of Emulex, a computer technology company, drastically dropped (see Exhibit 1.1) following an Internet story that it was under investigation by the Securities and Exchange Commission (SEC). The story also indicated that Emulex would restate its earnings downward as a result of the investigation. The stock quickly rebounded later that same day when investors learned that the story had been a hoax.

This event suggests that both earnings *per se*, and the credibility of that number are relevant to the stock market's assessment of a firm's value. Several questions come to mind: What are earnings? How are earnings linked to the market value of a company's stock? What role do the SEC and other institutions play in determining the reliability of reported earnings? These and many other questions pertaining to the construction of financial accounting information, and how that information relates to the value of the firm and the expectations of investors, lay at the heart of this text.

Exhibit 1.1

Emulex

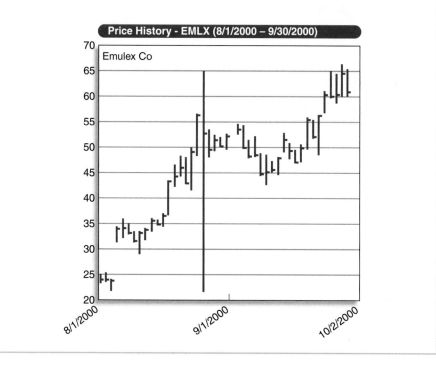

Emulex Stock Price Movement. The Vertical Bars Reflect the Range of Price Movement on the Day Shown. The Horizontal Bars Show the Closing Price for the Day.

In this book, we focus on the presentation of accounting information for business entities (firms) and its interpretation by external decision makers, such as investors, financial analysts, and government regulators. Firms prepare periodic reports that are made available to such external parties. A key component of these reports consists of financial information generated from the firm's accounting system. This information is summarized in a set of financial statements and related notes. The false report on Emulex referred to one of these statements, the Earnings Statement.

The **earnings statement** for a firm reports its revenues and expenses for a given period of time. **Revenues** are the amounts collected, or relatively certain to be collected, from customers in return for providing goods or services. **Expenses** are the amounts paid, or expected to be paid, to vendors in return for resources that go into the production and marketing of goods or services (such as materials, salaries, and utilities). You may also see earnings referred to as *profits* or *net income*.

$$\text{EARNINGS} = \text{REVENUE} - \text{EXPENSES}$$

Although all types of business entities prepare financial statements, we will focus on corporations in this text. **Corporations** are distinguished from other business types (we provide a more complete description of various business types in Chapter 2) by the issuance of shares of **stock,** which represent ownership in the company. When companies initially form, investors (owners) exchange cash for shares of stock in the company. As an example, when Jeff Bezos formed Amazon.com, Inc. in the state of Washington on July 5, 1994, he invested $10,000 in exchange for 1,700,000 shares. Owners then profit from their investment by increases in the value of their shares or by receiving dividends from the company. **Dividends** can typically only be paid if the company has positive earnings on a cumulative basis and may be viewed as returning part of the earnings of the company to the owners. In Amazon.com's case, the company has not produced a profit yet and therefore has paid no dividends. The value of the shares has, however, fluctuated considerably over the life of the company consistent with changes in investors' expectations of the future earnings of Amazon. At the time of this writing Amazon's share price was $40.21 a share. As of April 4, 2003, Jeff Bezos owned almost 108 million shares of Amazon.

Because of their significance in our economy, we specifically focus on **publicly traded corporations,** which are those corporations whose shares trade in a public stock exchange, such as the New York Stock Exchange. Emulex is one example of a publicly traded corporation. Some other more recognizable publicly traded corporations include Starbucks, Nike, and Coca Cola. For publicly traded corporations, financial analysts make buy-and-sell recommendations to investors wishing to purchase or sell shares of stock. These buy-and-sell recommendations may influence investors' purchases and sales, and indirectly, the price of stock. For example, the incorrect Emulex story prompted some analysts to recommend that investors sell their stock. The increase in investors wishing to sell their stock, along with the decrease in those willing to buy the shares, led to price declines. Upon learning of the false report, the situation reversed, causing the price to adjust upward.

As evidenced by investors and analysts' reaction to the news that Emulex would have to restate its earnings, information about a company's earnings plays a key role in assessing a firm's value. For this reason, companies periodically make announcements (typically on a quarterly basis) about their most recent performance. See the announcement of Pepsico in Exhibit 1.2. Further, analysts routinely report their forecasts of earnings and ratios related to earnings, such as the *price-to-earnings ratio (P/E ratio),* which factor significantly into their assessment of the firm's value. For example, in July 2003, the P/E ratio for Pepsico was approximately 21:1, based on the current estimate for the following

> Because the return on investment to a firm's owners (stockholders) comes from future dividends and changes in share value and estimates of both are often based on earnings, earnings are of considerable importance to investors as they make decisions about whether to buy or sell shares of stock.

PEPSICO Q1 EARNINGS PER SHARE INCREASES 17 PERCENT TO 45 CENTS

Worldwide volume grew 3 percent
Division net revenues grew 5 percent, and 6 percent on a currency neutral basis
Division operating profits grew 7 percent, and 8 percent on a currency neutral basis, following 14 percent growth in Q1 2002
Total net income grew 13 percent

Note the prominence of earnings in this disclosure. Also note that because Pepsico has worldwide operations, many of its accounting numbers are influenced by currency differences around the world. Therefore, the company includes data both as reported and after some adjustment for currency differences.

Exhibit 1.2
First Quarter 2003
Performance Announcement
by Pepsico

THE REAL WORLD

Pepsico

year's earnings and the current stock price at the time. The P/E ratio can be viewed as the amount investors are willing to pay for each dollar of forecasted earnings. When the earnings in the ratio are the forecasted earnings, the ratio is more specifically known as the *forward* P/E ratio. If, instead, the calculation is based on the last reported earnings (i.e., the actual earnings) then the ratio is called the *trailing* P/E. We will discuss the interpretation of the P/E ratio later in the book.

As will become clearer as you progress through the book, earnings provides a measure of the value added to the owners' wealth as a result of the firm's activities. We describe next those firm activities captured by the accounting process.

REPORTING ON THE ACTIVITIES OF THE FIRM

When assessing a firm's value, most analysts begin by reviewing the economic activities of the firm. All business firms engage in three basic kinds of activities: financing, investing, and operating. **Financing activities** are those activities directed at raising funds for the firm. Firms raise funds (sometimes called **capital**) from two basic sources: owners (*equity capital*) and lenders (*debt capital*). To raise funds from owners, corporations issue shares of stock. To raise funds from lenders, firms typically issue to the lenders a written promise indicating how the money will be repaid as well as the interest rate associated with the loan. There are many types of lenders, but one common lender would be a bank. For example, Skechers USA, Inc. was incorporated in 1992 and by the end of 2001 had $18,498,000 in loans payable to two banks.

A firm generally uses the funds obtained from its financing activities to engage in investing and operating activities. **Investing activities** typically consist of the firm's purchase of property and equipment to enable the company to make products or provide services. Firms may also purchase shares of stock of other companies. These purchases are also considered investing activities. **Operating activities** include those relatively short-term activities that the firm engages in to make and sell products and services. Representative of these activities are the collection of sales dollars from customers, the payment of salaries to employees, and the payment of utility costs.

The accounting process captures the financial effects of these activities. Individual economic events that affect the accounting system are called *transactions*. Financial statements are then constructed from the combined results of the transactions that occur during a particular period of time (e.g., a month, a quarter, a year). These statements reflect the transactions that have been recorded to date and, as such, form a historical record of the firm's activities. The challenge for analysts and investors is to utilize this historical record to assist in forecasting the future economic events that will, in turn, affect the firm's future earnings and hence its value.

Financial statement users make many significant decisions based on the information included in these reports. As a result, the information needs to be as accurate and comprehensive as possible. To ensure this, firms need to follow specific regulations when reporting their main activities. In the next section, we discuss the institutional environment in which accounting regulations are formulated and the key characteristics that are considered in setting accounting standards.

REGULATION OF FINANCIAL REPORTING

Many financial statement users lack the influence to force a company to release information that they might need to make effective decisions. For instance, in the United States, large publicly traded corporations are owned by numerous individuals. The shareholders in these large companies typically do not work for the company and thus have little firsthand information about its day-to-day activities. They therefore rely upon the periodic financial statements issued by the company's management to obtain knowledge about the firm's activities. To ensure that owners or potential owners of public companies get relevant, reliable, and timely information regarding those companies, laws and regulations dictate much of the content of these reports.

The ultimate authority for regulating financial reports of publicly traded companies in the United States rests with the **Securities and Exchange Commission (SEC).** Prompted by the 1929 stock market crash, the U.S. Congress established the SEC to administer the 1933 Securities Act and 1934 Securities and Exchange Act. That is, Congress empowered the SEC with the legal authority to set disclosure and accounting standards that all publicly traded firms are obliged to follow.

To provide adequate disclosure, the SEC created a reporting structure (SEC's Regulation S-X and S-K) that all public companies must follow. For example, the regulations require an annual report (10K), quarterly reports (10Q), and a report of significant events (8K). The 8K report is often used to disclose earning announcements or public meeting with analysts. For instance, on August 6, 2003, American Express issued an 8K report that contained the Chief Executive Officer's presentation to the financial community regarding the company's second quarter results. All of the reports filed with the SEC are available electronically via the electronic filing site of the SEC known as EDGAR.

Although the SEC retains its authority over the disclosures of publicly traded firms, it delegates the primary responsibility for creating accounting standards to the **Financial Accounting Standards Board (FASB).** The FASB consists of individuals from the private sector, principally professional accountants. Since its inception in 1973, the FASB has generated several *Statements of Financial Accounting Concepts (SFACs),* putting forth broad objectives for financial reports (known as the FASB's *conceptual framework*), and many **Statements of Financial Accounting Standards (SFASs)** that address specific valuation and income measurement issues.

On occasion, the SEC intervenes in setting standards, through two series of publications: *Financial Reporting Releases (FRRs)* and *Accounting and Auditing Enforcement Releases (AAERs).* In addition, SEC staff issue a series of bulletins, known as *Staff Accounting Bulletins (SABs),* that reflect their opinion and interpretation of other releases. Congress may also become involved when it deems necessary. Collectively, the body of accounting concepts, standards, guidelines, and conventions governing the construction of financial statements and related disclosures are referred to as **Generally Accepted Accounting Principles (GAAP).**

THINKING GLOBALLY

International Accounting Standards

The development of accounting standards has, in general, been a country-specific process. Each country has developed its own standards, which reflect its political, social, and economic environment. With the development of world markets for both products and capital, however, countries need a greater consensus with regard to financial reporting. To meet this need, the International Accounting Standards Committee (IASC) has been actively formulating international accounting standards.

The IASC is an independent, private-sector body that is funded by donations from accounting organizations around the world. Effective March 2001, a new organization emerged from the IASC, the International Accounting Standards Board (IASB). The IASB now establishes international accounting standards; as of 2002, the IASC/IASB issued 41 International Accounting Standards (IAS). The IASB will issue new standards known as International Financial Reporting Standards (IFRS). To promote the development of international accounting standards, the IASB developed relationships with the primary standard-setting bodies in numerous countries, including the FASB within the United States. In late 2002 the FASB and the IASB agreed to make their standards compatible with one another by January 1, 2005.

DETERMINING GENERALLY ACCEPTED ACCOUNTING PRINCIPLES

Recognizing that it cannot set accounting standards for every economic event that might occur, the FASB developed the conceptual framework (FASB, SFAC No. 2, 1980) that serves as a guide for both standard setting and practice. The conceptual framework seeks to define the desirable characteristics of accounting information. Qualitatively, a number of characteristics shape the financial statement disclosures required under GAAP. Some of the key characteristics are:

● **Relevance** The information is capable of making a difference in a decision. Relevant information may derive value from its role in predicting future performance (*predictive value*) or in assessing past performance (*feedback value*).

● **Reliability** The information faithfully represents the economic events it is intended to portray. Reliable information is accurate, neutral (unbiased), and verifiable (see *Verifiability*).

● **Verifiability** Independent measurers using the same methods reach the same results. Verifiable information allows independent observers to agree on what a reported amount represents.

● **Neutrality** The information conforms to standards that are independent of the interests of any particular constituency. Neutral information is not withheld or modified to serve the company's or users' objectives.

● **Comparability** The information can be compared across firms in a meaningful manner. Comparable information does not distort similarities or differences as a consequence of how the company uses accounting methods.

● **Consistency** The information is determined under the same accounting methods from one period to the next. Consistent information is free of the effects of changing methods in its determination.

Exhibit 1.3
Qualitative Characteristics of
Accounting Information

PRIMARY QUALITIES	
Relevance	Reliability
Understandability	Decision Usefulness
Predictive Value	Verifiability
Feedback Value	Neutrality
Timeliness	Representational Faithfulness
SECONDARY QUALITIES	
Comparability	Consistency

Exhibit 1.3
Qualitative Characteristics of
Accounting Information

Trade-offs exist when applying these qualities to a particular economic event. Two of the primary qualities highlighted in Exhibit 1.3, relevance and reliability, are often the focus of these trade-offs. For example, the most relevant information about a company that sells a product in high demand but limited supply may be the number of backorders of the product. This information may be very *relevant* to assessing current firm value as a forecast of future sales, but may not be a very *reliable* measure of future sales. For example, a competitor may be able to supply the same or similar product in a more timely manner which would result in the backorder being cancelled. As a case in point, in mid-2002, Palm, Inc. was having difficulties providing sufficient quantities of a very popular color model of its handheld product. The major distributors (those who had the backorders) found that their customers would not wait and sought alternative distribution channels to get the model. One distributor was quoted in a press release saying "if we can't support our customers in a timely manner, the customer goes and finds the product online." As a result of these trade-offs, in determining specific accounting standards, such as when to recognize backorder sales of a product, the FASB must consider all of the qualities of the information and seek to determine an acceptable solution. In general, backorders are not recognized as sales under GAAP because they generally fail to meet the reliability criteria. However, backorders are still a very relevant piece of information and are often disclosed by firms in their press releases.

An ill-defined concept that also influences the content of financial statements is **materiality.** Materiality means that firms can use a flexible accounting approach for insignificant amounts. For example, firms should account for the purchase of an electric stapler, office equipment, as a long-term asset. However, most firms simply treat the stapler as an expense rather than as an asset. GAAP allows this simpler accounting treatment because treating the stapler cost as an expense would not (materially) affect our view of the firm's assets or expenses.

Financial statement users need to monitor how firms handle the materiality concept when assessing a firm's value and compliance with GAAP. In recent years, the SEC has been concerned that some firms misuse the concept of materiality by deciding that as long as an item is less than a certain percentage of income or assets that it is immaterial (5 percent is often quoted as a rule of thumb). In response, the SEC issued SAB 99 (in 1999), which states that misstatements are not considered immaterial simply because they fall beneath a certain threshold. Firms must consider many other aspects of the misstatement in determining whether to correct it or not. For instance, in SAB 99 two other factors that must be considered are (1) whether the misstatement has the effect of increasing management's compensation say, by satisfying requirements for the award of bonuses or other forms of incentive compensation (see our discussion concerning economic consequences later in this chapter for more information about this factor) and (2) whether the misstatement involves concealment of an unlawful transaction.

Finally, although not a quality explicitly sought under GAAP, financial statements tend to reflect conservatism. **Conservatism** indicates a firm's tendency to anticipate losses, but not gains; carry assets at values that are often low by comparison with current market prices or appraisal values; recognize liabilities in anticipation of obligations that may or may not arise; and delay recognition of revenues until uncertainties have been resolved. For example, under current GAAP, many construction companies recognize the profits from a long-term construction project over the period of construction. However, if they anticipate that there will be a loss on the overall contract at the end of the construction period, they recognize the loss immediately. To illustrate, Foster Wheeler LTD (a construction company specializing in petroleum processing facilities) reported this type of policy in their annual report:

> The Company has numerous contracts that are in various stages of completion. Such contracts require estimates to determine the appropriate cost and revenue recognition. However, current estimates may be revised as additional information becomes available. If estimates of costs to complete long-term contracts indicate a loss, provision is made currently for the total loss anticipated.

Note, however, that the conceptual framework explicitly states that firms must avoid misusing conservatism to understate assets or overstate liabilities.

At times, however, the conceptual framework fails to provide enough guidance. The FASB then moves to adopt a more specific standard for a particular economic event. To do this, the FASB follows a very public process of determining a new standard, encompassing three main stages:

1. The FASB analyzes the issue using the conceptual framework and other relevant existing standards. It then prepares a Discussion Memorandum laying out the alternatives with their pros and cons. The FASB elicits feedback of the Discussion Memorandum from interested parties such as investors, financial analysts, government regulators, corporate executives, and professional accountants.

2. After assessing the responses to this document, the FASB deliberates on the alternatives and issues an Exposure Draft of its proposed pronouncement. The FASB makes the Exposure Draft available for further public comment.

3. In the last step, the FASB incorporates any additional comments and then issues its pronouncement in the form of a Statement of Financial Accounting Standards (SFAS).

The process the FASB uses to set accounting standards is essentially political and subject to override by the SEC or the U.S. Congress. For example, during the oil crisis in the 1970s, the FASB issued SFAS 19 that eliminated certain accounting practices used by oil and gas producers. The new standard would have resulted in more volatile reported earnings for smaller companies engaged in significant exploration activities. Some opponents of the new standard argued that with more volatile earnings, smaller producers might be unable to raise capital to continue exploration, inconsistent with the national interest in encouraging exploration. The political pressures subsequently brought to bear resulted in the FASB rescinding the pronouncement it had originally issued (SFAS 52).

GAAP provides the framework and the specific rules for how the various activities of the firm should be recorded in their accounting system. However, if the firm does not follow these rules or they apply them inappropriately, investors and other readers of the financial statements could be misled about the performance of the firm. For this reason all publicly traded firms are required to present audited statements in their reports. The auditors provide the reassurance that the firm has appropriately applied GAAP. In the next section, we discuss the nature of the audit.

INDEPENDENT AUDITS OF FINANCIAL STATEMENTS

All publicly traded companies must provide a report by independent auditors (see the report for Hasbro, Inc. in Exhibit 1.4). This report attests to the fairness of presentation (that the statements fairly represent the results of the

---

Exhibit 1.4
Hasbro, Inc. Auditors' Report

THE REAL WORLD

Hasbro, Inc.

The Board of Directors and Shareholders
Hasbro, Inc.:

We have audited the accompanying consolidated balance sheets of Hasbro, Inc. and subsidiaries as of December 29, 2002 and December 30, 2001 and the related consolidated statements of operations, shareholders' equity and cash flows for each of the fiscal years in the three-year period ended December 29, 2002. These consolidated financial statements are the responsibility of the Company's management. Our responsibility is to express an opinion on these consolidated financial statements based on our audits.

We conducted our audits in accordance with auditing standards generally accepted in the United States of America. Those standards require that we plan and perform the audit to obtain reasonable assurance about whether the financial statements are free of material misstatement. An audit includes examining, on a test basis, evidence supporting the amounts and disclosures in the financial statements. An audit also includes assessing the accounting principles used and significant estimates made by management, as well as evaluating the overall financial statement presentation. We believe that our audits provide a reasonable basis for our opinion.

In our opinion, the consolidated financial statements referred to above present fairly, in all material respects, the financial position of Hasbro, Inc. and subsidiaries as of December 29, 2002 and December 30, 2001 and the results of their operations and their cash flows for each of the fiscal years in the three-year period ended December 29, 2002 in conformity with accounting principles generally accepted in the United States of America.

As discussed in note 1 to the consolidated financial statements, effective December 31, 2001, the first day of the Company's 2002 fiscal year, the Company adopted the provisions of Statement of Financial Accounting Standards No. 142, "Goodwill and Other Intangibles."

/s/ KPMG LLP

Providence, Rhode Island
February 12, 2003

economic events that have affected the firm) and compliance of those statements with GAAP. **Auditors** are professional accountants who meet certification requirements set by states (i.e., Certified Public Accountants, or **CPA**s for short). Auditors must also follow procedures under the oversight of the American Institute of Certified Public Accountants (AICPA). The AICPA sets Generally Accepted Auditing Standards (GAAS) that define the auditor's responsibilities.

In addition to assessing compliance with GAAP, auditors also examine the firm's internal controls, verify its principal assets, review for unusual changes in its financial statements, inquire with outside parties concerning the firm's exposure to losses, and determine the firm's ability to continue as a going concern. The term **going concern** means that the auditor expects that the firm will continue to operate into the foreseeable future; in other words, they do not expect the company to go out of business or file for bankruptcy. Investors and others might view the value of a company quite differently if they assumed it would soon quit operating. Auditors also consider the existence or prospect of fraud, though the firm's management has primary responsibility for its detection.

> The auditor's opinion is important when using valuation techniques as it provides at least some level of assurance that the data being used to forecast future results are comparably prepared by companies.

Auditors also apply the concept of materiality in their work. They typically limit their responsibility to material items when they state in their audit opinions that financial statements "present fairly, *in all material respects,* the financial position, results of operations, and cash flows" of a client firm.

Finally, auditors issue one of several types of reports. In an *unqualified opinion* the auditor expresses no reservations concerning the fairness of the financial statements and conformance with GAAP. A *qualified opinion* includes an exception to the conclusion of fairness or conformance with GAAP. Exceptions commonly relate to a deviation from GAAP or a limitation in the scope of the auditor's procedures under GAAS. An *adverse opinion* states that the financial statements do not fairly present the company's financial position and results of operations in conformity with GAAP. Under a *disclaimer,* the auditor does not express an opinion on the financial statements.

Firms appoint auditors and pay their fees. As a result, controversy exists on the independence of auditors whose fees are paid by the client. To help resolve these concerns, the accounting profession devised the *AICPA Code of Conduct* and a *peer review* process to monitor compliance with performance standards. In 2002, the U.S. Congress passed the Sarbanes-Oxley Act (SOX) to address these and other concerns about the auditing profession, partly in response to the Enron failure and the subsequent demise of Arthur Andersen (see Exhibit 1.5). The SOX created a Public Company Accounting Oversight Board that monitors auditing, quality control, and independence standards, and rules. For example, oversight of the public accountant must be done through the firm's audit committee, which must be composed of members who are independent of the company.

Independent audits help to ensure that the financial statements reflect those qualities of accounting information we discussed earlier. Owners, lenders, and managers face economic incentives in their interaction with a firm that may influence accounting decisions. In the next section, we discuss the economic consequences to owners, lenders, and managers from the accounting choices made by the firm. As illustrated by the Enron example, these consequences can be very significant.

Exhibit 1.5

THE REAL WORLD

Enron

In October, 2001 the SEC requested information from Enron Corporation regarding a set of transactions with several related parties. The transactions had the approval of Enron's auditors, Arthur Andersen. By the end of the month, the inquiry had turned into a formal SEC investigation. In an 8K filing (recall that 8K filings detail the occurrence of any material events or corporate changes that should be reported to investors or security holders) with the SEC on November 8, 2001, Enron agreed to restate its financial statements for 1997 through 2001 to record the effects of the related party transactions. The net effect: Enron reduced its owners' equity section by $1.2 billion. On December 2, 2001, Enron filed for protection from its creditors under Chapter 11 of the U.S. bankruptcy laws. In its continuing investigation the SEC requested audit working papers from Arthur Andersen (AA). The SEC then discovered that several individuals at AA had shredded documents related to the Enron audit. The government eventually filed an indictment for obstruction of justice against AA, and the company suffered the loss of numerous clients. AA was ultimately found guilty of obstructing justice and agreed not to audit publicly traded companies.

The loss in credibility of Enron's reported earnings, both past and present, along with the revelation of losses and exposure of business risks led investors to conclude that the stock was overvalued. As a result, Enron suffered such severe declines in its stock price and future prospects that the company was forced to declare bankruptcy.

ECONOMIC CONSEQUENCES OF ACCOUNTING PRACTICES

Although GAAP places restrictions on accounting choices, firms still enjoy considerable flexibility in their selection and application of accounting methods. As a result, managers can and do affect the amounts reported in the financial statements. Allowing flexibility is a two-edged sword. On one hand, it makes it possible for financial statements to better reflect economic reality in the sense that one size does not fit all. On the other hand, it may provide the opportunity for firm owners or managers to manipulate information.

For example, lenders closely monitor a firm's activities to ensure that they will be repaid. One common way for owners to provide assurances to lenders and for lenders to protect themselves is to put restrictions into their lending contracts. These restrictions, called *covenants,* typically set minimums for certain accounting numbers or ratios that the firm must meet. The agreements typically state that the lender can make the loan immediately due if the firm violates these covenants. If a company found itself in danger of violating a covenant, there might be enough incentive to either change accounting methods or misreport transactions to avoid the violation. A mitigating factor on this behavior is that lenders often find it in their best interests to work with firms to restructure debt when violations occur (see Exhibit 1.6 regarding Cogent Communications Group).

As another example, compensation arrangements for a firm's management often include bonuses based on achieving a targeted amount of earnings. Under GAAP, managers commonly have sufficient discretion over accounting policies to significantly influence the recognition of revenues and expenses. In order to meet bonus targets, therefore, managers may advance the recognition of revenues or delay expenses as a means of reporting higher earnings. Other forms of discretion might include relaxing credit requirements customers must satisfy

Exhibit 1.6
Cogent Communications
Group, Inc.—10K Report, April,
2003

THE REAL WORLD

Cogent
Communications
Group

Breach of Cisco Credit Facility Covenant. We have breached the minimum revenue covenant contained in our credit facility from Cisco Systems Capital. This breach permits Cisco Capital, if it wishes, to accelerate and require us to pay approximately $262.7 million we owed to Cisco Capital as of March 28, 2003. Should Cisco Capital accelerate the due date of our indebtedness, we would be unable to repay it. If it accelerates the indebtedness, Cisco Capital could make use of its rights as a secured lender to take possession of all of our assets. In such event, we may be forced to file for bankruptcy protection. We are currently in active discussions with Cisco Capital to restructure the Company's debt.

 Note that violation of the covenant in this lending agreement had the potential to impose significant economic consequences to Cogent. You can imagine the pressure that this situation might exert on management to misstate revenues to be in compliance with the covenant. By June, however, Cogent had restructured its debt.

(to produce more revenues), postponing repairs and maintenance on equipment (to reduce expenses), and selling assets or retiring debt on which gains will be recorded (to increase income). These types of actions may actually reduce the firm's value. Although managers benefit by receiving a higher bonus, they do so at the expense of stockholders (lower firm value).

In compensation arrangements, firms try to design contracts that align the economic interests of managers with those of stockholders. One example is to provide some amount of a manager's compensation in the form of stock in the company. The idea is that managers will behave more like owners when managers' compensation includes stock. Stock could be awarded to managers directly. More frequently managers are given the option to buy shares of stock at a fixed price under what are called *stock option plans,* discussed later in the book. Often management compensation arrangements provide a combination of incentives, some based on earnings and some on stock price. For example, Intel compensates its executive managers with a combination of a base salary, a cash bonus tied to meeting an individual earnings performance target, a cash bonus tied to overall company earnings, and a stock option plan.

Other incentives to manipulate earnings may relate to lawsuits, labor negotiations, compliance with bank or insurance company regulations, and trade disputes with foreign rivals. For example, a firm facing litigation might prefer to ignore the likelihood of losing a lawsuit (by not recording a liability in advance of a settlement), thereby giving a false impression of the firm's value.

Many opportunities and incentives therefore exist for manipulating financial reports. One reason for allowing these opportunities to exist is that it may be too costly both to incorporate the level of detail required to set more stringent standards and to monitor compliance with those details. Another reason may be that allowing managers to select from a menu of accounting policies may provide an efficient means of communicating (*signaling*) information about the firm's future prospects when the economic consequences of a given policy depend on those prospects. For example, suppose that there are two companies in the same industry with similar debt agreements (including a restriction in their debt agreement that earnings must remain above $100,000). One firm has very good future sales prospects, and the other firm has very poor future sales prospects. If they both were faced with a decision about voluntarily (i.e., it was not a mandated change) adopting a new accounting policy that would reduce reported earnings in the future, the firm with good prospects would have little problem in adopting this policy as it expects to have good future earnings which would not force the company to violate its debt restrictions (even though it would reduce their future reported earnings due to the policy change). However, the firm with bad prospects would likely not adopt the new policy as it already is in a position to potentially violate the debt restriction (due to its poor future sales prospects) and the change in policy will make it even more likely. Therefore, by observing their decisions about the choice of accounting policy lenders might be able to infer the future prospects of companies and set the interest rates that they require accordingly.

Another economic consideration that managers face in the determination of accounting methods is the effect of the decision on the taxes paid by the company. All corporations pay taxes to the federal government (*Internal Revenue Service* or *IRS*) based on their earnings. The accounting rules for reporting earnings to the IRS are determined by the tax code and in some cases differ from GAAP. The company's objective in choosing its accounting policies for tax purposes is usually to minimize or delay its tax payments. In contrast, the company's objective in choosing its accounting policies for financial reporting purposes is to comply with GAAP. Although the norm is for firms to use different accounting methods for tax and financial reporting purposes, there is at least one case (LIFO inventory accounting) in which the method chosen for tax purposes is only permitted if that same method is used for reporting purposes. Accordingly, there may be a tax incentive that influences an accounting choice.

FINANCIAL REPORTING AND VALUATION

As the discussion in this chapter suggests, financial accounting disclosures, especially earnings, provide information upon which financial analysts and investors at large may project a firm's future cash flows that, in turn, determine firm value. The central role of earnings as an important factor in determining firm value is evidenced by the prominence of earnings forecasts by financial analysts in the financial press and a vast empirical literature by academics that documents stock price reactions to information conveyed by changes in those forecasts, earnings announcements *per se,* and other related disclosures.

In the chapters that follow, we will seek to further an appreciation of the role that financial statements play in arriving at estimates of firm value. Our efforts in this regard culminate in Chapter 14 with the presentation of two principal approaches for mapping information contained in what are called *pro-forma financial statements* (statements based on forecasts of future operating, investing, and financing activities) into value estimates; specifically, *discounted cash flow (DCF)* analysis and *residual income (RI)* analysis. At this point, it is sufficient for you to begin to think of a firm's financial accounting disclosures as a starting point in assessing its future cash flow prospects.

SUMMARY AND TRANSITION

As should be clear by now, accounting information, particularly earnings, plays a key role with investors in guiding their decisions to buy or sell stock. Analysts who advise investors also make significant use of accounting information in estimating the value of a share of stock as a basis for their buy or sell recommendations to investors. The reliability and relevance of accounting information are enhanced by a standard setting process involving both public (SEC) and private (FASB) sector bodies. Auditors provide additional assurance to investors that the accounting information is prepared in compliance with those standards.

Within the framework of generally accepted accounting principles, managers have considerable discretion over accounting policies adopted by the firm. Often managers' choices have economic consequences for themselves, their stockholders, and lenders. The nature of the consequences is driven by the contracts written between managers, stockholders, and lenders.

In the remainder of the book we will continue to visit valuation issues and to examine economic consequences issues as they arise. The next few chapters explain the construction of the financial statements contained in financial accounting reports and describe the major concepts underlying this construction. Considerable attention is given to the principal concepts used in the determination of earnings. These chapters are followed by an initial exposure to the techniques of financial analysis with a focus on the use of financial statements in assessing past performance and forecasting future performance. Later chapters consider a comprehensive set of valuation and income measurement issues in depth. The final chapter of the text provides basic introduction to the forecasting of financial statements and the two major approaches for valuing the firm based on components from those statements.

END OF CHAPTER MATERIAL

KEY TERMS

Auditors	Financial Accounting Standards Board (FASB)
Capital	Financing Activities
Conservatism	Generally Accepted Accounting Principles (GAAP)
Corporation	Going Concern
Dividends	Investing Activities
Earnings Statement	Materiality
Expenses	Operating Activities

Publicly Traded Corporations

Revenue

Securities and Exchange Commission (SEC)

Statement of Financial Accounting Standards (SFAS)

Stock

ASSIGNMENT MATERIAL

○ REVIEW QUESTIONS

1. Describe and illustrate the three major types of activities that firms engage in.

2. Discuss the meaning of Generally Accepted Accounting Principles, and describe the organizations that establish these principles.

3. What is the purpose of an auditor's opinion, and what types of opinions can auditors render?

4. Identify at least three major users of corporate financial statements, and briefly state how they might use the information from those statements.

5. List and briefly describe the major qualitative characteristics that accounting information should possess, according to the FASB concepts statements.

6. Discuss how materiality is used in the choice of accounting methods.

7. Describe what is meant by economic consequences of accounting practices and provide an example of how accounting choices can affect the welfare of parties with an interest in the firm.

8. How might differences in accounting standards across countries affect the analysis done by an analyst in predicting stock prices?

9. Describe what conservatism means in the construction of the financial statements of the firm.

○ APPLYING YOUR KNOWLEDGE

10. For a manufacturing company, list two examples of transactions that you would classify as financing, investing, and operating.

11. The AMAX Company purchased land several years ago for $60,000 as a potential site for a new building. No building has yet been constructed. A comparable lot near the site was recently sold for $95,000.

    a. At what value should AMAX carry the land on its balance sheet? Support your answer with consideration for the relevance and reliability of the information that would result.

    b. If AMAX wanted to borrow money from a bank, what information about the land would the bank want to know?

12. You are the accounting manager for a U.S. company that has just been acquired by a German company. Helmut, the CEO of the German company, has just paid you a visit and is puzzled why American companies report on two different bases, one for reporting to their stockholders and another to the taxing authority, because in Germany these are one and the same. Draft a memo explaining to Helmut why there are two different bases

and a brief explanation for why they might involve different accounting rules.

13. Harmonization of accounting standards has been proposed on a global basis. As a CEO of an American company, what would you see as advantages and disadvantages of having the same set of standards across countries?

14. Suppose that the FASB proposed that inventory be accounted for at its current market price (i.e., what you could sell it for) rather than its historical cost. Provide an argument that supports or opposes this change on the basis of relevance and reliability.

15. Suppose that you started your own company that assembles and sells laptop computers. You do not manufacture any of the parts yourself. The computers are sold through mail order. Make a list of the information that you consider relevant to assessing your firm's performance. When you are through, discuss how you would reliably measure that performance.

16. Suppose that you own and operate your own private company. You need to raise money to expand your operations, so you approach a bank for a loan. The bank loan officer has asked for financial statements prepared according to GAAP. Why would the loan officer make such a request and, assuming that your statements were prepared according to GAAP, how could you convince the banker that this was so?

17. In order for a company's stock to be listed (i.e., traded) on most stock exchanges, the company's financial statements are required to be audited by a CPA firm. Why?

18. As a manager, suppose that you are responsible for establishing prices for the products your division sells. Under GAAP your firm uses a method of inventory costing called LIFO that means that the costs of the last units purchased are the first ones that are reported in the statement of earnings. Consequently, the costs that remain in inventory are those associated with the first purchases. Because inventory can build up over the years, some of these costs may be very old. How relevant would these old costs attached to ending inventory be to you as you decide how to price inventory in the coming year? If they are not relevant, what piece of information would be more relevant to you?

19. From time to time there have been calls from the user community for management to disclose their own forecasts of future results such as net income. As an external user of the financial statements, discuss the relevance and the reliability of this type of information.

20. Suppose a company decides to change accounting methods such that it reports its revenues sooner than it previously did. Discuss how this might effect investors' evaluation of the company's stock.

○ USING REAL DATA

21. Amazon.com, Inc. has operated at a net loss since its formation, yet its stock has a positive value. Explain why investors would value the shares of Amazon at a positive value.

22. In early February 2001 Emulex Corporation revised its quarterly sales estimates downward. Prior to the revision Emulex had been expecting a 28 percent sales increase over the previous year and had shown 40 percent increases in sales annually for the last five years. Upon hearing this news, investors drove the price of Emulex down from $77.50 per share on a Friday to $40.25 on the following Monday. Explain why the valuation of Emulex dropped given this announcement.

23. In early February 2001 CISCO announced that it was missing its first quarter sales estimates. This was the first time since July 1994 that it had come in under its sales estimates, and it was the first time in more than three years that it had failed to beat its sales estimates. As an investor, how might you react to this news and how might this announcement affect the valuation of the company's shares?

○ BEYOND THE BOOK

The Beyond the Book problems are designed to force you to find and utilize resources found outside the book.

24. Familiarize yourself with the resources that are available at your university to acquire information about corporations. Most universities have an electronic database that contains financial statement information. The following is a short list of resources that may be available:

    LEXIS/NEXIS Database This is an incredibly large database that contains all sorts of news and financial information about companies. It contains all of the SEC filings including the 10-K, 20-F (foreign registrants), and Proxy Statements. The financial information is in full text form.

    CD-Disclosure This database contains full text financial footnote information for thousands of companies but does not contain full text of the major financial statements.

    EDGAR Filings The EDGAR filings are electronic forms of the SEC filings that are included in the Lexis/Nexis database but are also accessible through the internet (www.sec.gov).

    ABI Inform (UMI, Inc.) This database contains full text information from numerous business periodicals.

25. Go to the FASB's website (www.fasb.org), locate the project activities section, and list the titles of the projects on its projects update list.

26. For a publicly traded company of your choosing, answer the following questions:

    a. What are the products (or product lines) and/or services that your company sells? Please be as specific as possible.

    b. Who are the customers of your company? Please be as specific as possible.

    c. In what markets, domestic and global, does your company sell its products and/or services?

    d. Who are the major competitors of your company?

    e. What are the major inputs your company needs to manufacture its products? Who are the suppliers of these inputs?

f. Are any of the items listed in the questions above changing substantially? Use a two-year time span as a window to address this question.

g. What has happened to the stock price of your company over the last two years?

To answer these questions it will be useful to collect a series of articles concerning your company over the most recent two-year period. Try to find at least five reasonably sized articles. Use these as references to write a two- to three-page background paper about your company.

Financial Statements:
An Overview

LEARNING OBJECTIVES

After reading this chapter you should be able to:

1. Understand the differences in the major forms of business organization, as well as some of the relative pros and cons for choosing a particular form of business.

2. Identify the nature of information contained in the main general-purpose financial statements: Statement of Financial Position, Statement of Earnings, Statement of Cash Flows, and Statement of Changes in Stockholders' Equity.

3. Explain the connection between statements of financial position at points in time and changes in financial position over time.

4. Describe the types of supplemental disclosures accompanying financial statements in a firm's annual report.

On October 12, 2001, Polaroid Corporation filed for protection from creditors under Chapter 11 of the U.S. bankruptcy laws. This action resulted from the financial difficulties that Polaroid faced when its sales declined significantly, starting in the fourth quarter of 2000. As Exhibit 2.1 shows, the value of the company's stock began its downward slide late in the first quarter of 2000. Note that the S&P 500 (Standard and Poor's) is an index of how the stock market performed overall during this same period. This correspondence between declining quarterly sales and relative stock price suggests that investors rely on information contained in financial statements. In this chapter, we begin to explore this relationship by describing the contents of those statements.

Polaroid's stock price movement relative to the S&P Index and trading volume from March 1999 through April 2002.

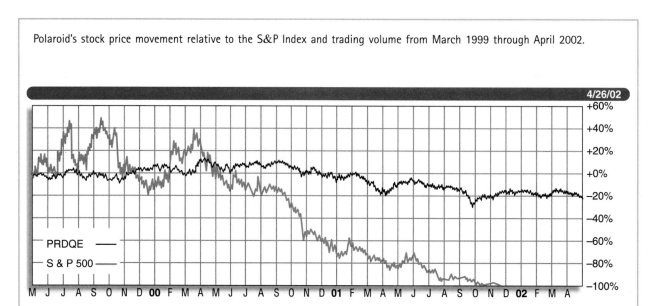

Exhibit 2.1

THE REAL WORLD

Polaroid

The changes in company value are very evident for a publicly traded corporation such as Polaroid since its stock price is published daily. This is not true for all forms of business. While we intend to focus on publicly traded corporations we would like to spend a little bit of time describing other forms of business so that you understand why the corporate form of business is the dominant one in the U.S. economy.

FORMS OF BUSINESS ORGANIZATION

The corporate form of business is by far the most popular for large publicly traded firms. This popularity stems from three principal features:

- Limited liability for its capital suppliers
- Ease of transferring ownership
- Ease of access to additional ownership funds

Limited liability means that investors in the firm's equity securities generally cannot lose more than the amounts that they invest, should the firm perform poorly. This feature can be compared to the unlimited liability of owners of **sole proprietorships** (single owners) and **partnerships** (multiple owners). If a sole proprietorship or partnership cannot meet its obligations to creditors, then creditors may seek satisfaction of their claims from the owner's or partners' personal assets, respectively. As a result, hybrid forms of organization have emerged, such as *limited liability companies (LLCs)* and *limited liability partnerships (LLPs),* which, as their name suggests, include the limited liability feature of corporations. Many public accounting firms are organized as LLPs, such as PricewaterhouseCoopers, LLP and KPMG, LLP. Some relatively well known businesses are also organized as LLCs, such as Orbitz, LLC (the web-based travel service) and BMW of North America, LLC (an importer of BMW products in North America).

Corporations, particularly large ones, are typically owned by a vast number of individuals. This ownership structure spreads the limited risk of ownership over many investors. In the case of a sole proprietorship, the single owner bears all the unlimited risk, whereas in partnerships, the partners share that risk. This difference in the distribution of risks appears to have played an important role in the rise of corporations as the preferred type of business organization.

Transfers of ownership in publicly traded corporations can be easily accomplished through the purchase and sale of investors' equity securities, in other words, the trading of stock. To trade stock, a corporation lists its stock on major stock exchanges, such as the *New York Stock Exchange* or *NASDAQ*. These exchanges attract large numbers of investors, as they can easily and quickly acquire or sell securities as needed to maximize their economic welfare. From the firm's perspective, stock exchanges provide relatively easy access to one type of capital needed to fund its investment and operating needs. In contrast, ownership of sole proprietorships is more difficult to transfer, as it requires finding buyers without benefit of stock exchange services. Transferring ownership of partnerships is also more difficult. If an existing partner leaves or a new partner enters the business, the existing partnership must first be dissolved and a new one then created.

The corporate form of business also allows the firm to increase its equity capital by offering additional shares for sale. In a publicly traded corporation, this means that many individual investors, other then the present owners, might become owners in the firm. The larger set of investors in the public stock markets allows the company access to a considerable amount of resources as it grows. Sole proprietorships, in comparison, have limited access to additional funds as they are constrained by the owner's wealth and ability to borrow. Partnerships also are at a disadvantage, as they usually only raise ownership funds through additional contributions of the partners or by admitting new partners to the business.

The corporate form does possess a potentially significant negative consideration: taxes. Corporations are subject to corporate income taxation, whereas sole-proprietorship and partnership income is taxed only at the individual level. Because individual investors are taxed on the income they receive from corporations (in the form of dividends and capital gains), the net result is that corporate income is taxed twice, once at the corporate level and a second time at the individual level. This tax structure may influence who chooses to invest in corporations and how corporations' securities are priced relative to holdings in other forms of business entities.

> The tax status of an entity has significant valuation implications, as taxes reduce cash flows.

Exhibit 2.2 summarizes some of the pros and cons of the main forms of business organization. Because of their dominance in the market, we focus on the reporting of publicly traded corporations in the remainder of the book. In the next section, we expand an understanding of corporations by discussing the nature of their financial statements.

Exhibit 2.2
Pros and Cons of Forms of
Business Organization

Form of Organization	Pros	Cons
Proprietorship	Income taxed once	Unlimited liability Ownership transfer difficult No sharing of risk Limited access to additional ownership funds
Partnership	Income taxed once Some sharing of risk Some access to additional ownership funds	Unlimited liability Ownership transfer difficult
Corporation	Limited liability Ease of transfer of ownership Relatively easy access to additional ownership funds	Double taxation

FINANCIAL ACCOUNTING REPORTS

As we discussed in Chapter 1, to conduct business, publicly traded corporations raise long-term funds from individuals and institutions through both lending agreements and the issuance of stock. Both lending agreements and stock represent claims on the resources (assets) that the corporation controls. Corporations also obtain short-term funds from other creditors; for example, suppliers often sell inventory to companies on credit. Such credit purchases are, in effect, short-term loans from the suppliers. Exhibit 2.3 shows the *balanced* relationship between the firm's resources on the one side, and claims to those resources on the other.

Financial statements provide information about the firm's resources and claims to resources at periodic points in time, and also about the changes to those resources and claims to resources from the firm's activities between those points in time. The major financial statements include the:

● Statement of Financial Position
● Statement of Earnings

Exhibit 2.3
Resources and Claims against
Resources

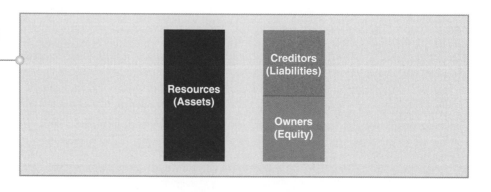

- Statement of Cash Flows
- Statement of Changes in Stockholders' Equity

Below we discuss each statement, as well as provide descriptions of many terms that each statement includes. In this chapter, we simply want to offer you a general sense of what each statement contains. We will provide more detailed explanations of the content in later chapters, so you need not try to fully understand them here.

STATEMENT OF FINANCIAL POSITION

The Statement of Financial Position describes the firm's resources and claims to those resources as seen in Exhibit 2.3. Accounting expressions for resources, creditors, and owners are, respectively, **assets, liabilities,** and **stockholders' equity** (or **common stockholders' equity** or simply **owners' equity**).

ASSETS

In simple terms assets are those resources owned by the company or those that the company has the right to use. From the accountant's point of view, assets are resources that have *probable future value* to the firm and are recognized under GAAP. Assets typically include *cash; accounts receivable* (amounts due from the firm's customers); *inventories* (for use in production or for sale); *plant, property, and equipment* (used to make products or provide services); and various *property rights* (the rights to use an economic resource such as a patent).

Accountants, however, do not consider some economic resources as assets because they fail to meet measurement criteria, such as the general criterion of reliability discussed in Chapter 1. For example, a brand image (e.g., the Coca Cola logo) created through advertising and customer satisfaction cannot be reliably valued and are not, therefore, recognized in the financial statements. Furthermore, the amounts at which resources are reflected as assets often differ from their current economic value. For example, the market or appraisal value of land some years after its acquisition might be greater than its recorded value (sometimes called the *carrying value*), as accounting standards stipulate that land be carried at its historical cost.

LIABILITIES

In simple terms, liabilities represent the amounts owed to others. From the accountant's point of view they represent *probable future sacrifices* of resources. Liabilities may include bank borrowings (*notes payable* or *mortgages payable*), borrowings that are done through publicly traded securities known as bonds (*bonds payable*), amounts due to suppliers (*accounts payable*), and amounts due to others providing goods or services to the company during production, such as utility companies and employees (*utilities payable* and *salaries payable,* respectively). Sometimes the word **accrued** appears with the liability titles (e.g., *accrued warranty liability, accrued expenses*), implying that the amounts have been estimated. Customers may also have some claim on resources if they have prepaid for goods and services that the company must deliver in the future. These types of claims, typically called *deferred revenue, unearned revenues,* or simply *deposits,* reflect items such as prepaid magazine subscriptions.

Similar to assets, accountants also do not consider all economic obligations as liabilities. For example, if a company contracts with another company to purchase goods that will be delivered at a future date at a fixed price, current accounting standards do not require the company to recognize the obligation to pay the supplier when the contract is signed. As neither company has satisfied its part of the contract, neither company recognizes the contract in its accounting records. In accounting jargon, this kind of contract is known as a *mutually unexecuted contract*. Also, some liabilities are so uncertain that they may not meet the criteria for recognition. For instance, potential legal liabilities associated with lawsuits are often excluded from liabilities because it is very uncertain as to whether the company will actually have to pay a settlement.

> As analysts try to predict the future cash flows of the firm, unrecorded liabilities may pose one of the more significant estimation challenges.

STOCKHOLDERS' EQUITY

Unlike creditor and customer claims that a firm settles within some specified time frame, equity claims have no specified time period for payment. Stockholders of a corporation are not assured a specific set of payments. Instead, they usually only receive cash payments when the company declares a *cash dividend* (when the firm generates positive earnings) or when stockholders elect to sell their shares. As a result, stockholders' equity is sometimes referred to as a **residual claim,** because owners can only claim what is left over after all creditor claims have been met. It can also be thought of as the residual claim on assets after deducting liabilities. In other words, owners can claim the difference between what the company owns and what it owes. **Net assets** (also referred to as **net book value**) can be calculated through the accounting equation that we discuss next.

THE ACCOUNTING EQUATION

As mentioned previously, the statement of financial position (often called a **balance sheet**) reports a firm's assets, liabilities, and stockholders' equity at a particular point in time. Further, a characteristic of a balance sheet is that the sum of assets equals the sum of liabilities and stockholders' equity (hence the word "balance"). This characteristic of the balance sheet is commonly referred to as the **accounting equation** (recall that Exhibit 2.3 illustrates this).

$$\text{Assets} = \text{Liabilities} + \text{Stockholders' Equity}$$

It follows from this equation that stockholders' equity equals assets less liabilities. That is:

$$\text{Stockholders' Equity} = \text{Assets} - \text{Liabilities}$$

Stockholders' equity is also called *net assets* or *net book value*. To illustrate a statement of financial position, based on the accounting equation, let's next look at a real company, Ross Stores.

STATEMENT OF FINANCIAL POSITION: ROSS STORES

Exhibit 2.4, Ross' 10K report, describes the company's business and operating goals. Reviewing this information first helps to provide insight into the information included in the financial statements.

Exhibit 2.5 shows Ross' Statement of Financial Position for the year ended February 1, 2003. Note that Ross presents two columns of data, one at the beginning of the year (2/2/2002) and the other at the end of the year (2/1/2003). The SEC requires two years of balance sheet data for annual reports. Further, the SEC requires firms to report the balance sheet data as of the end of their **fiscal** (financial) **year.** The fiscal year often ends on the same date as the calendar year, December 31. However, as with Ross, this need not be the case. Due to the seasonal nature of their business, many retail firms use year-ends other than December 31, for example, Tommy Hilfiger Corp (March 31), Wal-Mart (January 31), American Greetings (February 28), and Starbucks (September 30). Finally, note that the accounting equation is satisfied at both points in time. In fact, the accounting equation needs to be satisfied at all points in time in an accounting system.

Ross presents what is known as a **classified balance sheet.** This type of balance sheet lists assets in order of how quickly they can be converted into cash, sometimes referred to as **liquidity order.** In addition, a classified balance sheet also segregates assets into **current** and **noncurrent** categories. **Current assets** are cash and assets that are expected to be converted into cash or expire within one year or one operating cycle of the business, whichever is longer. For a manufacturing firm, the *operating cycle* is the time between the initial acquisition of raw materials and the collection on the sale of the inventory that is sold. Inventory is a current asset because it will be sold and converted into cash during the firm's current operating cycle, which, for most firms, is less than one year. Note that for certain kinds of inventory (e.g., any long-term construction project such as submarines and aircraft) the operating cycle could be longer than a year. This type of inventory would still meet the definition of a current asset as the inventory is sold within an operating cycle.

Ross Stores, Inc. ("Ross" or "the Company") operates a chain of off-price retail apparel and home accessories stores, which target value-conscious men and women between the ages of 25 and 54 primarily in middle-income households. The decisions of the Company, from merchandising, purchasing, and pricing, to the location of its stores, are aimed at this customer base. The Company offers brand-name and designer merchandise at low everyday prices, generally 20 percent to 60 percent below regular prices of most department and specialty stores. The Company believes it derives a competitive advantage by offering a wide assortment of quality brand-name merchandise within each of its merchandise categories in an attractive easy-to-shop environment.

Exhibit 2.4
Ross Stores Business
(from 10K)

THE REAL WORLD

Ross Stores

	2/1/2003	2/2/2002
ASSETS		
CURRENT ASSETS		
Cash and cash equivalents (includes $10,000 of restricted cash)	$ 150,649	$ 40,351
Accounts receivable	18,349	20,540
Merchandise inventory	716,518	623,390
Prepaid expenses and other	36,904	30,710
Total Current Assets	922,420	714,991
PROPERTY AND EQUIPMENT		
Land and buildings	54,772	54,432
Fixtures and equipment	412,496	351,288
Leasehold improvements	232,388	209,086
Construction-in-progress	61,720	24,109
	761,376	638,915
Less accumulated depreciation and amortization	358,693	307,365
	402,683	331,550
Other long-term assets	36,242	36,184
Total Assets	$1,361,345	$1,082,725
LIABILITIES AND STOCKHOLDERS' EQUITY		
CURRENT LIABILITIES		
Accounts payable	$ 397,193	$ 314,530
Accrued expenses and other	114,586	92,760
Accrued payroll and benefits	99,115	70,413
Income taxes payable	15,790	11,885
Total Current Liabilities	626,684	489,588
Long-term debt	25,000	—
Deferred income taxes and other long-term liabilities	66,473	48,682
STOCKHOLDERS' EQUITY		
Common stock, par value $.01 per share Authorized 300,000,000 shares Issued and outstanding 77,491,000 and 78,960,000 shares	775	790
Additional paid-in capital	341,041	289,734
Retained earnings	301,372	253,931
	643,188	544,455
Total Liabilities and Stockholders' Equity	$1,361,345	$1,082,725

Consistent with the nature of its business, Ross' assets include cash; accounts receivable, representing amounts due from its customers; merchandise inventories, representing costs of goods waiting to be sold; and property and equipment, representing the long-term investments in property and equipment that are necessary to its merchandising activities. In each case, these assets reflect an expected future benefit. For accounts receivable, it is the cash Ross expects to collect from customers. For merchandise inventories, it is the cash or receivables that Ross expects to arise from sales. For property and equipment, it is the sales that Ross expects to generate from their stores.

As with the asset section, the balance sheet classifies liabilities into a current and noncurrent section. Similar to current assets, **current liabilities** are liabilities that become due, or expected to be settled, within one year. Ross' liabilities are consistent with the nature of its business. They include accounts payable, principally representing amounts due to vendors of merchandise that it sells; accrued payroll, representing amounts owed to employees; accrued expenses, representing amounts owed to others for providing certain services, for example, utilities; and income taxes payable, representing amounts owed to the taxing authorities. Ross' liabilities also include long-term debt, representing amounts borrowed to finance its investment and operating activities.

As noted above, stockholders' equity represents the residual claim after liabilities have been met. **Common stock** and **additional paid-in capital** combined represent the amount contributed by stockholders when they purchased shares from the company. The remaining portion of stockholders' equity, **retained earnings,** represents the accumulated amount of net income less dividends distributed to stockholders since the company formed.

> The amount in the common stock accounts represents a par value assigned to the shares at issuance and has little economic significance. Par value should not be confused with market value of the firm's stock. Market value takes into account the entire equity of stockholders and is not limited to the portion of initial contribution labeled as par value.

As explained earlier, not all resources that Ross controls may be reported as assets on its balance sheet. GAAP restricts what items can appear on the balance sheet, as well as the values assigned to those items that do appear. For example, Ross' slogan "Dress for Less" may have value for its company recognition. However, difficulties in how to measure the economic benefits of slogans or brand names generally prevent their recognition as assets in an accounting sense. Going back to the example of Polaroid that started this chapter, Polaroid states that patents and trademarks are valued at $1 on its financial statements. This treatment recognizes that these assets have value, but by only recognizing them at $1 there is no material effect on the interpretation of the financial statements. Polaroid therefore indicates to its financial statement readers that these items have value even though the company cannot report them under GAAP.

> Market values are not used to value owners' equity in the financial statements as it would be circular logic to value stockholders' equity at market prices that, in principle, depend on the information contained in financial reports.

Recall that the accounting values for assets and liabilities may not reflect their current market values. Because stockholders' equity must equal assets less liabilities, it therefore follows that the book value of stockholders' equity does not necessarily equal its market value. For example, if we divide stockholders' equity from Ross' balance sheet ($643,188) by the number of shares of Ross' common stock outstanding (77,491), we obtain a **book value per share** of $8.35 at February 1, 2003. However, Ross' stock price during the year ended February 1, 2003 ranged from $32.76 to $46.88 a share.

FLOW STATEMENTS—CHANGES IN FINANCIAL POSITION

Changes in the firm's financial position from one point in time to another can be broadly classified into those related to *operating, investing,* and *financing activities.* Three statements describe these changes in the financial position of the firm: the Statement of Earnings, the Statement of Cash Flows, and the Statement

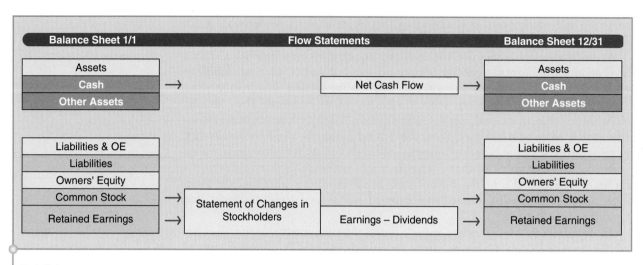

Exhibit 2.6
Financial Statement
Connections

of Changes in Stockholders' Equity. Exhibit 2.6 shows the relationships of the three flow statements to the balance sheet at the beginning and end of the period.

STATEMENT OF EARNINGS

The Statement of Earnings (sometimes called the *Statement of Income,* or *Income Statement*) explains changes in stockholders' equity arising from the firm's operating activities. It reports *revenues* from sales of goods and services to customers and the *expenses* of generating those revenues. Revenues are generally recognized at the point at which the company transfers the risks and benefits of ownership of the goods or services to the buyer. For most product firms, this happens at the date the product is delivered to the customer. Expenses are often classified into costs directly related to the goods sold **(cost of goods sold),** other operating expenses (including selling and administrative costs), financing costs (e.g., interest), and income taxes.

At the time revenues are recognized, the firm records the increase in assets that it has received in exchange for its goods or services. These assets are typically either cash or, if the customer is granted credit, accounts receivable. In some cases, a customer may pay for a product or service in advance of its receipt (e.g., school tuition). When this occurs, the firm cannot recognize the revenue from the sale until the product or service is delivered (as we will discuss in Chapter 4). Therefore, the receipt of cash results in the creation of a liability that represents this deferred revenue (the obligation of the firm to deliver the product or service in the future). Later, when revenue is recognized on the income statement, this liability account is reduced.

When expenses are recognized, they may be associated with decreases in assets (such as the decrease in inventory when cost of goods sold is recognized) or increases in liabilities (such as when salary expense is recognized before salaries are paid to employees).

Net income (loss) (also referred to as *net earnings*), then, is the excess of revenues (expenses) over expenses (revenues):

$$\text{Net Income} = \text{Revenues} - \text{Expenses}$$

Net income (loss) increases (decreases) owners' equity because it is added to the balance in retained earnings. Note that earnings can either be positive (income) or negative (loss).

Accounting recognition of the revenues and expenses that go into the determination of net income are governed by the **accrual concept** of accounting. As explained more fully in Chapter 4, under this concept, revenues are recorded as *earned,* not necessarily when cash is received, and expenses are recorded as *incurred,* not necessarily when cash is paid.

Let's look at the Statement of Earnings for Ross for three fiscal years (Exhibit 2.7). Ross prepares what is known as a single-step income statement. This type of income statement combines all revenues in one section and all expenses except income taxes in a second section. *Sales* are amounts charged to customers for merchandise. *Costs and Expenses* include *costs of goods sold, general and administrative costs,* and *interest expense.* As is the case for most retailers, costs of goods sold include costs associated with buying and distributing merchandise and building occupancy costs. General and administrative costs include salaries, wages, employee benefits, and other expense of managing the firm's activities. Interest expense pertains to the debt that appears on Ross' balance sheet and is therefore considered a nonoperating item. *Earnings before taxes* is then computed (subtracting all expenses from sales). The tax on this income is shown just prior to *Net earnings,* often referred to as the *bottom line.*

Net earnings summarizes the effect of Ross' operating activities on stockholders' equity. It is added to the balance of retained earnings at the end of the previous year in arriving at the balance at February 1, 2003. Because stockholders' equity equals net assets (assets less liabilities), net assets must also

> The accrual concept is very important to fully understand because analysts often use earnings as a starting point to forecast future cash flows of the firm.

Exhibit 2.7
Ross Stores—Statement of Earnings

THE REAL WORLD

Ross Stores

For the years ended (in thousands)	2/1/2003	2/2/2002	2/3/2001
SALES	$3,531,349	$2,986,596	$2,709,039
COSTS AND EXPENSES			
Cost of goods sold, including related buying, distribution, and occupancy costs	2,628,412	2,243,384	2,017,923
General, selling, and administrative	572,316	485,455	438,464
Interest expense, net	279	3,168	3,466
	3,201,007	2,732,007	2,459,853
Earnings before taxes	330,342	254,589	249,186
Provision for taxes on earnings	129,164	99,544	97,432
Net earnings	$ 201,178	$ 155,045	$ 151,754

reflect the results of operations. Intuitively, we can see that sales prices charged to customers not only increase net income (and hence owners' equity) in the form of revenues, but also increase assets by increasing either cash or accounts receivable. Likewise, salaries and wages of employees not only decrease net income (owners' equity) in the form of operating expenses, but either decrease assets by decreasing cash or increase liabilities by increasing accrued payroll. This two-sided effect of revenues or expenses is essential to preserve the relationship in the accounting equation. (This concept is discussed in detail in Chapters 3 and 4 so do not be concerned if it seems difficult to grasp at this point.)

STATEMENT OF CASH FLOWS

The Statement of Cash Flows also describes changes in financial position, specifically the changes in cash. This statement shows how investing, financing, and operating activities affect cash. Investment activities relate to the acquisition or disposal of long-term assets such as property and equipment. Financing activities relate to the issuance and repayment or repurchase of debt and equity. The operating activities section reports the cash inflows and outflows associated with the sales of goods and services to customers.

Under current accounting standards, the operating section of the statement can be presented in one of two forms: a **direct method,** under which the direct cash inflows and outflows are shown, or an **indirect method** (by far the most common), under which net income under the accrual concept is adjusted to its cash flow equivalent. Exhibit 2.8 illustrates the direct method of the Statement of Cash Flows for Rowe Companies (a group of companies that provides home furnishings). In contrast, Exhibit 2.9 shows the indirect method of the Statement of Cash Flows for Ross. Chapter 5 provides a more complete discussion of the differences in these two methods.

Looking at Exhibit 2.9, note how the operating section differs from the one presented in Exhibit 2.8. For the Ross Statement of Cash Flows, the operating section starts with net earnings, which is then adjusted to its cash flow equivalent (net cash provided by operating activities). Further note how the net earnings and the net cash provided by operating activities differ in each year. For instance, in 2003, net income was $201,178 (000s), whereas cash flow from operations was $332,445 (000s).

The investing section contains additions to property and equipment made during the year. Though not in Ross' case, this section may also include amounts invested in temporary investments or costs of acquiring the net assets of another firm. The financing section shows the proceeds and payments on long-term debt, the cash payments of dividends, the proceeds from the issuance of stock for employee stock plans (recall that we mentioned these in Chapter 1 as a common way to compensate certain managers), and repurchases of Ross' own shares.

Now that we have completed a look at three of the major financial statements for Ross, it is useful to revisit the diagram in Exhibit 2.6 that showed the connections among the balance sheet, income statement, and cash flow statement.

Exhibits 2.8
Statement of Cash Flows:
Direct Method

THE REAL WORLD

Rowe Companies

The Rowe Companies Annual Report 2003
CONSOLIDATED STATEMENTS OF CASH FLOWS

Year Ended (in thousands)	11/30/2003	12/1/2002	12/2/2001
Increase (Decrease) in Cash			
Cash flows from operating activities:			
Cash received from customers	$300,299	$336,853	$329,558
Cash paid to suppliers and employees	(287,266)	(317,217)	(331,014)
Income taxes received (paid), net	1,352	2,839	585
Interest paid	(5,225)	(4,028)	(2,397)
Interest received	225	347	480
Other receipts—net	942	1,340	1,109
Net cash and cash equivalents provided by (used in) operating activities	10,327	20,134	(1,679)
Cash flows from investing activities:			
Payments received on notes receivable	100	125	125
Increase in cash surrender value	(121)	(150)	(179)
Proceeds from sale of Mitchell Gold	39,573	–	–
Proceeds from sale of property and equipment	–	–	1,056
Capital expenditures	(3,995)	(3,323)	(3,317)
Payments under earn-out and related obligations (Note 2)	(15,759)	–	–
Net cash provided by (used in) investing activities	19,798	(3,348)	(2,315)
Cash flows from financing activities:			
Restricted cash released from (deposited to) collateral for letters of credit	264	(1,938)	–
Net borrowings (repayments) under line of credit	–	(9,368)	5,368
Draws under revolving loans	12,570	3,994	6,865
Proceeds from issuance of long-term debt	–	39,442	–
Repayments under revolving loans	(20,751)	(10,244)	(3,821)
Payments to reduce long-term debt	(18,759)	(47,874)	–
Payments to reduce loans on cash surrender value	(16)	–	–
Proceeds from loans against life insurance policies	–	–	3,014
Proceeds from issuance of common stock	3	38	27
Dividends paid	–	–	(1,379)
Purchase of treasury stock	(2)	(19)	(16)
Net cash provided by (used in) financing activities	(26,691)	(25,969)	10,058
Net increase (decrease) in cash and cash equivalents	3,434	(9,183)	6,064
Cash at beginning of year	274	9,457	3,393
Cash at end of year	$ 3,708	$ 274	$ 9,457

Exhibit 2.9
Ross Stores—Statement of
Cash Flows

Ross Stores

For the years ended (in thousands)	2/1/2003	2/2/2002	2/3/2001
CASH FLOWS FROM OPERATING ACTIVITIES			
Net earnings	$201,178	$155,045	$151,754
Adjustments to reconcile net earnings to			
net cash provided by operating activities:			
Depreciation and amortization of			
property and equipment	53,329	49,896	44,377
Other amortization	12,847	12,725	10,686
Deferred income taxes	17,375	12,633	10,015
Change in assets and liabilities:			
Merchandise inventory	(93,128)	(63,824)	(59,071)
Other current assets net	(4,003)	(16,901)	(980)
Accounts payable	81,958	54,064	5,751
Other current liabilities	54,541	34,384	(26,836)
Other	8,348	4,867	7,653
Net cash provided by operating activities	332,445	242,889	143,349
CASH FLOWS USED IN INVESTING ACTIVITIES			
Additions to property and equipment	(133,166)	(86,002)	(82,114)
Net cash used in investing activities	(133,166)	(86,002)	(82,114)
CASH FLOWS USED IN FINANCING ACTIVITIES			
Borrowings (repayments) under lines of credit	0	(64,000)	64,000
Proceeds from long-term debt	25,000	0	0
Issuance of common stock related			
to stock plans	50,863	54,581	14,303
Repurchase of common stock	(149,997)	(130,676)	(169,324)
Dividends paid	(14,847)	(13,595)	(12,389)
Net cash used in financing activities	(88,981)	(153,690)	(103,410)
Net increase (decrease) in cash and			
cash equivalents	110,298	3,197	(42,175)
Cash and cash equivalents:			
Beginning of year	40,351	37,154	79,329
End of year	$150,649	$ 40,351	$ 37,154
SUPPLEMENTAL CASH FLOW DISCLOSURES			
Interest paid	$ 409	$ 3,332	$ 3,352
Income taxes paid	$ 91,875	$ 61,433	$100,359

ARTICULATION OF THE FINANCIAL STATEMENTS

Exhibit 2.10 presents an update of Exhibit 2.6; we have now included the dollar amounts for the key components of these connections. Note how earnings and dividends affect the balance in retained earnings. However, in Ross' case, retained earnings is also affected by the repurchase of shares of its own stock. (We will discuss this type of transaction in Chapter 12.) Ross' Statement of

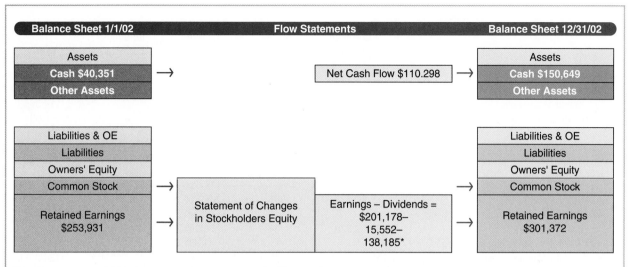

*Ross Stores has an additional adjustment to retained earnings ($138,185) in 2002 due to something called the "amortization of stock compensation." This adjustment will be discussed in Chapter 12. Note that most companies do not have this additional adjustment.

Exhibit 2.10
Financial Statement
Connections—Ross

THE REAL WORLD

Ross Stores

Changes in Stockholders' Equity, discussed next, provides these same direct connections between the beginning and ending balances in the accounts, as well as changes in those accounts.

STATEMENT OF CHANGES IN STOCKHOLDERS' EQUITY

The Statement of Changes in Stockholders' Equity provides details about all of the transactions that affect stockholders' equity, including such items as stock issuance, stock repurchases, net income, and dividends. Exhibit 2.11 shows Ross' Statement of Changes in Stockholders' Equity. Each column represents a particular account within stockholders' equity. The rows represent the balance and the transactions that have occurred over the most recent three years. Recall that retained earnings are increased by net income and decreased by dividends declared to stockholders (except for the adjustment for the repurchase of stock that we have already mentioned).

OTHER STATEMENT DISCLOSURES

A company's annual report to shareholders contains more than the financial statements themselves (see Exhibit 2.12). For example, footnotes describe significant accounting policies employed by the firm (see Exhibit 2.13), as well as elaborate on items that appear in the statements. The report of the firm's auditors attests to the fairness of the financial statements and their conformance

	Common Shares	Stock Amount	Additional Paid-In Capital	Retained Earnings	Total
BALANCE AT JANUARY 29, 2000	88,774	$888	$234,635	$237,908	$473,431
Common stock issued under stock plans, including tax benefit	1,854	18	14,285		14,303
Amortization of stock compensation			9,894		9,894
Common stock repurchased	(10,101)	(101)	(22,690)	(146,533)	(169,324)
Net earnings				151,754	151,754
Dividends declared				(12,511)	(12,511)
BALANCE AT FEBRUARY 3, 2001	80,527	805	236,124	230,618	467,547
Common stock issued under stock plans, including tax benefit	3,378	34	54,547		54,581
Amortization of stock compensation			11,881		11,881
Common stock repurchased	(4,945)	(49)	(12,818)	(117,809)	(130,676)
Net earnings				155,045	155,045
Dividends declared				(13,923)	(13,923)
BALANCE AT FEBRUARY 2, 2002	78,960	790	289,734	253,931	544,455
Common stock issued under stock plans, including tax benefit	2,341	23	50,840		50,863
Amortization of stock compensation			12,241		12,241
Common stock repurchased	(3,810)	(38)	(11,774)	(138,185)	(149,997)
Net earnings				201,178	201,178
Dividends declared				(15,552)	(15,552)
BALANCE AT FEBRUARY 1, 2003	77,491	$775	$341,041	$301,372	$643,188

Exhibit 2.11
Ross Stores—Statement of Changes in Stockholders' Equity (in thousands)

THE REAL WORLD

Ross Stores

with regulatory guidelines. Further, although not formally part of the company's financial statements, management provides its own assessment of the past year's operating results, liquidity, and capital expenditures, as well as financing strategies. Management provides this information through the management's discussion and analysis section of the annual report, commonly known as the *MD&A section*.

Exhibit 2.12
Typical Contents of an Annual Report

Message from Chief Executive Officer
Description of Principal Products or Services
Financial Highlights
Management's Discussion and Analysis
Statement of Financial Position
Statement of Earnings
Statement of Cash Flows
Statement of Changes in Stockholders' Equity
Notes to Financial Statements
Statement of Management's Responsibilities
Auditor's Report
Other Corporate Information

Merchandise Inventory. Merchandise inventory is stated at the lower of cost (determined using a weighted average basis) or net realizable value. The Company purchases manufacturer overruns and canceled orders both during and at the end of a season which are referred to as packaway inventory. Packaway inventory is purchased with the intent that it will be stored in the Company's warehouses until a later date, which may even be the beginning of the same selling season in the following year. Packaway inventory accounted for approximately 44 percent and 43 percent of total inventories as of February 1, 2003 and February 2, 2002, respectively.

Cost of Goods Sold. In addition to the product cost of merchandise sold, the Company includes its buying and distribution expenses as well as occupancy costs related to the Company's retail stores, buying, and distribution facilities in its cost of goods sold. Buying expenses include costs to procure merchandise inventories. Distribution expenses include the cost of operating the Company's distribution centers and freight expenses related to transporting merchandise.

Property and Equipment. Property and equipment are stated at cost. Depreciation is calculated using the straight-line method over the estimated useful life of the asset, typically ranging from five to 12 years for equipment and 20 to 40 years for real property. The cost of leasehold improvements is amortized over the useful life of the asset or the applicable lease term, whichever is less. Computer hardware and software costs are included in fixtures and equipment and are amortized over their estimated useful life generally ranging from five to seven years. Reviews for impairment are performed whenever events or circumstances indicate the carrying value of an asset may not be recoverable.

 Analysts must understand the accounting choices that firms make in order to interpret their financial statements and to make fair comparisons across firms. The summary of significant accounting policies footnote is very important in conveying this information about the choices the firm has made.

Exhibits 2.13
Ross Stores Footnotes:
Summary of Significant
Accounting Policies

THE REAL WORLD

Ross Stores

Beyond the annual report, additional financial information is made publicly available through filings with the SEC. These filings include prospectuses accompanying new stock issues, annual 10K reports (such as Exhibit 2.4), and 10Q reports (a 10Q reports contains quarterly financial statement information). These reports typically offer greater detail than the annual report. For example, these filings might include information on competition and risks associated with the firm's principal business, holdings of major stockholders, compensation of top executives, and announcements of various events.

THE INFLUENCE OF FINANCIAL STATEMENTS

Financial statements embody the standards by which other information is often constructed. For example, professional security analysts project revenues and estimate research and development spending. Given that such forecasts and projections pertain to information that will ultimately surface in financial statements (see the report for Archer Daniels in Exhibit 2.14), these reports are likely to reflect the same accounting principles. In other words, the influence of financial reports extends well beyond their contents

Exhibit 2.14
Archer Daniels Midland
Operating Earnings Up

THE REAL WORLD

Archer Daniels

January 19, 2001

DECATUR, Ill. Jan 14 (Reuters)—Archer Daniels Midland Co., the largest U.S. grain producer, said on Friday its fiscal second-quarter operating earnings rose 22 percent, beating forecasts, as sales in ethanol, feed, and cocoa products boosted results.

 This type of additional disclosure may potentially affect the company's stock valuation as it indicates changes in the expectations of future results ("beating forecasts"). How much the valuation changes depends, in part, on whether the increase in earnings is sustainable in the future. Although no obvious price reaction resulted on the day after this announcement, the price of ADMs stock rose from around $8 a share to $15 a share between October 2000 and February 2001. This clearly indicates the increased prospects of the company.

as such. There is a confirmation aspect to reports provided by the firm that becomes apparent as you look closely at financial information from other sources.

We opened the chapter relating how Polaroid suffered a drop off in sales, starting in the fourth quarter of 2000. Exhibit 2.15 shows the quarterly sales figures for Polaroid (taken from Polaroid's 10Q reports) over the period from the first quarter of 1998 through the second quarter of 2001. Notice the seasonal pattern of Polaroid's sales. That is, in a given year, Polaroid always realizes its highest sales in the fourth quarter, typically significantly up from the third quarter. However, in 2000, fourth-quarter sales are only slightly higher than those in the third quarter. This departure from the previous trend would be important to investors and analysts as they assessed the value of Polaroid's shares in the fourth quarter of 2001 and beyond. Note that sales then dramatically fell in the first and second quarters of 2001, leading up to Polaroid's declaration of bankruptcy in the third quarter of 2001. Sales are just one of the items that analysts would look at to understand earnings and the market value of Polaroid, but in this case perhaps, the most significant one.

Exhibit 2.15
Polaroid's Sales by Quarter

THE REAL WORLD

Polaroid

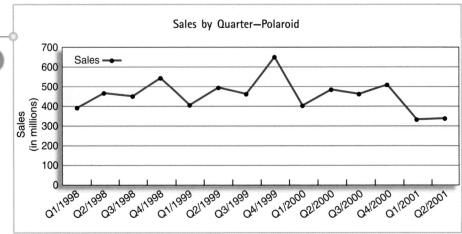

SUMMARY AND TRANSITION

In this chapter, we provided an overview of the corporate form of business and the major financial statements prepared under GAAP as a way to set the stage for examining the construction and use of financial accounting reports in the chapters that follow. As we described, corporations have become the dominant form of business entity due to such features as limited liability and the ease with which ownership can be transferred and capital can be raised.

The main general-purpose financial statements considered include a Statement of Financial Position, which describes the financial position in terms of its assets, liabilities, and stockholders' equity of the firm at a point in time; a Statement of Earnings, which describes the results of the firm's operations in terms of its revenues and expenses from one point in time to another; a Statement of Cash Flows, which describes the firm's investment, financing, and operating activities in terms of their effects on cash; and a Statement of Changes in Stockholders' Equity, which describes transactions affecting contributed capital and retained earnings in further detail.

Our description of these financial statements provides a first glimpse of the typical items comprising the resources that a firm may control (assets) and the claims to those resources held by creditors and owners (liabilities and stockholders' equity, respectively). We identified changes in assets and liabilities arising from the operating activities of the firm as composed of revenues and expenses, leading to the bottom-line number, net income or earnings. Other changes pertained to investment and financing activities. We also reviewed further details of changes in stockholders' equity. In Chapter 3, we describe the mechanics of the accounting system and how to analyze the effects of a particular transaction on these financial statements of the firm. Chapter 4 provides further detail on the measurement and reporting of revenues and expenses. Our coverage of the construction of financial statements then concludes with methods for distinguishing operating, investing, and financing cash flows.

END OF CHAPTER MATERIAL

KEY TERMS

Accounting Equation	Current Assets
Accrual Concept	Current Liabilities
Accrued	Direct Method
Additional Paid-in Capital	Fiscal Year
Assets	Indirect Method
Balance Sheet	Liabilities
Book Value per Share	Limited Liability
Classified Balance Sheet	Liquidity Order
Common Stock	Net Asset
Common Stockholders' Equity	Net Book Value
Cost of Goods Sold	Net income

Noncurrent Assets	Statement of Cash Flows
Owners' Equity	Statement of Changes in Stockholders' Equity
Partnership	Statement of Earnings
Residual Claim	Statement of Financial Position
Retained Earnings	Stockholders' Equity
Sole Proprietorship	

ASSIGNMENT MATERIAL

REVIEW QUESTIONS

1. Describe the pros and cons for organizing a business as a corporation rather than a partnership.

2. Describe and illustrate the three major categories of items that appear in a typical statement of financial position.

3. Describe the purpose of the four main financial statements that are contained in all annual reports.

4. What is the meaning of the term net assets?

5. Why might certain economic resources not be considered assets by accountants? Provide an example.

6. What is the accounting equation?

7. What is meant by a classified balance sheet?

8. How do accountants distinguish between current and noncurrent assets and liabilities?

9. Explain the meaning of retained earnings.

10. Why might the book value of a company be different from the market value of the company?

11. What is net income?

12. What are the two methods for reporting cash flow from operations that are allowed under GAAP?

13. What is comprehensive income?

14. How is other comprehensive income reported in the financial statements?

APPLYING YOUR KNOWLEDGE

15. Compare and contrast the statement of earnings and the cash flow statement.

Use the following abbreviations to respond to question 16:
CA—Current Assets
NCA—Noncurrent Assets
CL—Current Liabilities
NCL—Noncurrent Liabilities
CS—Capital Stock
RE—Retained Earnings

NI—Income statement item

CF—Cash flow statement item

16. Classify the following items according to where the item would appear in the financial statements:
    a. Inventory
    b. Taxes Payable
    c. Interest Expense
    d. Dividends
    e. Sales to customers
    f. Manufacturing Equipment
    g. New issuance of common stock
    h. Cash
    i. Bonds Payable (debt due in ten years)
    j. Employee's Wages

Use the following abbreviations to respond to question number 17:

O—Operating Item

F—Financing Item

I—Investing Item

17. Classify each of the following transactions as to whether they are operating, financing, or investing activities:
    a. Cash collected from customers
    b. Repayment of debt
    c. Payment of dividends
    d. Purchase of a truck (by a manufacturing company)
    e. Purchase of a truck (by a truck dealer)
    f. Purchase of shares of stock of another company
    g. Sale of a plant
    h. Utility expenses are incurred

18. Compute the missing balance sheet amounts in each of the following independent situations:

	A	**B**	**C**	**D**
Current Assets	?	$650,000	$230,000	$40,000
Noncurrent Assets	250,000	?	400,000	?
Total Assets	?	1,050,000	?	190,000
Current Liabilities	50,000	500,000	300,000	25,000
Noncurrent Liabilities	?	90,000	?	10,000
Owners' Equity	225,000	?	80,000	?
Total Liabilities and Owners' Equity	350,000	?	?	?

19. Compute the missing amounts in the reconciliation of retained earnings in each of the following independent situations:

	A	B	C	D
Retained Earnings Dec. 31, Year 1	$20,000	$100,000	?	$40,000
Net Income	15,000	?	400,000	22,000
Dividends Declared and Paid	6,000	35,000	250,000	?
Retained Earnings Dec. 31, Year 2	?	115,000	300,000	52,000

20. For each of the following companies, list at least two types of assets and one type of liability that you would expect to find on their balance sheet (try to include at least one item in your list that is unique to that business):

    a. The Washington Post Company—This is a company that is primarily in the newspaper business but also has operations in television stations, cable systems, *Newsweek* magazine, as well as some other smaller operations.

    b. International Paper—This is a company that is primarily in the forest products business, selling both paper and wood products.

    c. SBC—This is a telecommunications company.

    d. Hartford Financial Services Group—This is a multiline insurance company.

    e. Philip Morris Companies, Inc.—This is a company that is primarily in the tobacco business but has also diversified into foods, beer, financial services, and real estate.

    f. Citibank—This is a major commercial bank.

    g. Delta—This is a major airline.

21. For each of the companies listed in question number 20 list at least two line items that you would expect to find on their income statement (try to include at least one item in your list that is unique to that business).

22. For each of the companies listed in question number 20 list at least two line items that you would expect to find on their cash flow statement (try to include at least one item in your list that is unique to that business).

23. Suppose that your best friend wanted to start a new business providing desktop publishing services to customers. Your friend has some savings to start the business but not enough to buy all of the equipment that she thinks she needs. She has asked you for some advice about how to raise additional funds. Give her at least two alternatives and provide the pros and cons for each alternative.

24. Suppose that you and a friend form a partnership in which you both contribute the same amount of cash and you agree to share in profits on a 50–50 basis. Further suppose that you are responsible for running the day-to-day operations of the firm but your friend is a silent partner in the sense that he doesn't work in the business (he has another job). Because you have no other job, the partnership agrees to pay you $1,500 per month. How should the partnership treat this payment, as a distribution of profits or as an expense of doing business? What difference would it make to the distribution to you and your partner?

○ USING REAL DATA

Base your answer to problems 25–28 on the data from Polaroid provided here.

POLAROID CORP. Balance Sheet	12/31/1999	12/31/2000
Assets		
Current Assets		
Cash and cash equivalents	$ 92,000,000	$ 97,200,000
Receivables, less allowances of $23.9 in 1999 and $23.8 in 2000 (Note 6)	489,700,000	435,400,000
Inventories (Notes 5 and 6)	395,600,000	482,500,000
Prepaid expenses and other assets (Note 4)	130,800,000	103,500,000
Total Current Assets	1,108,100,000	1,118,600,000
Property, Plant, and Equipment:		
Land	14,700,000	6,900,000
Buildings	322,700,000	313,500,000
Machinery and equipment	1,620,100,000	1,597,500,000
Construction in progress	65,500,000	49,600,000
Total property, plant and equipment	2,023,000,000	1,967,500,000
Less accumulated depreciation	1,423,800,000	1,398,300,000
Net Property, Plant, and Equipment	599,200,000	569,200,000
Deferred Tax Assets (Note 4)	243,700,000	279,500,000
Other Assets	89,000,000	75,700,000
Total Assets	$2,040,000,000	$2,043,000,000
Liabilities and Stockholders' Equity		
Current Liabilities		
Short-term debt (Note 6)	$ 259,400,000	$ 363,700,000
Payables and accruals (Note 7)	338,000,000	334,100,000
Compensation and benefits (Notes 10 and 11)	138,100,000	76,700,000
Federal, state and foreign income taxes (Note 4)	14,700,000	18,800,000
Total Current Liabilities	750,200,000	793,300,000
Long-term debt (Note 8)	573,000,000	573,500,000
Accrued postretirement benefits (Note 11)	234,800,000	222,700,000
Other long-term liabilities	111,500,000	78,300,000
Total Liabilities	1,669,500,000	1,667,800,000
Preferred stock, Series A and D, $1 par value, authorized 20,000,000 shares; all shares unissued	–	–
Common stockholders' equity (Note 9)		
Common stock, $1 par value, authorized 150,000,000 shares (75,427,550 shares issued in 1999 and 2000)	75,400,000	75,400,000
Additional paid-in capital	395,200,000	363,100,000
Retained earnings	1,208,800,000	1,219,500,000
Accumulated other comprehensive income	(48,900,000)	(68,900,000)
Less: Treasury stock, at cost (30,811,263 and 29,895,578 shares in 1999 and 2000, respectively)	1,259,700,000	1,213,800,000
Deferred compensation	300,000	100,000
Total common stockholders' equity	370,500,000	375,200,000
Total Liabilities and Common Stockholders' Equity	$2,040,000,000	$2,043,000,000

POLAROID CORP. Income Statement

	12/31/1998	12/31/1999	12/31/2000
Net Sales	$1,845,900,000	$1,978,600,000	$1,855,600,000
Cost of goods sold	1,108,400,000	1,170,500,000	1,055,900,000
Marketing, research, engineering, and administrative expenses (Note 2)	736,500,000	700,500,000	696,400,000
Restructuring charges/(credits) (Note 2)	50,000,000	—	(5,800,000)
Total Costs	1,894,900,000	1,871,000,000	1,746,500,000
Profit/(Loss) from Operations	(49,000,000)	107,600,000	109,100,000
Other income/(expense):			
Interest income	2,900,000	2,700,000	5,500,000
Other	64,800,000	(19,500,000)	28,600,000
Total other income/(expense)	67,700,000	(16,800,000)	34,100,000
Interest expense	57,600,000	77,400,000	85,300,000
Earnings/(Loss) before Income Tax Expense	(38,900,000)	13,400,000	57,900,000
Federal, state and foreign income tax expense (Note 4)	12,100,000	4,700,000	20,200,000
Net Earnings/(Loss)	($51,000,000)	$8,700,000	$37,700,000

POLAROID CORP. Cash Flow

	12/31/1998	12/31/1999	12/31/2000
Cash Flows from Operating Activities			
Net earnings/(loss)	$ (51,000,000)	$ 8,700,000	$ 37,700,000
Depreciation of property, plant, and equipment	90,700,000	105,900,000	113,900,000
Gain on the sale of real estate	(68,200,000)	(11,700,000)	(21,800,000)
Other noncash items	62,200,000	73,800,000	22,900,000
Decrease/(increase) in receivables	79,000,000	(52,700,000)	41,800,000
Decrease/(increase) in inventories	(28,400,000)	88,000,000	(100,600,000)
Decrease in prepaids and other assets	39,000,000	62,400,000	32,900,000
Increase/(decrease) in payables and accruals	25,300,000	(16,500,000)	9,200,000
Decrease in compensation and benefits	(21,000,000)	(72,500,000)	(105,000,000)
Decrease in federal, state, and foreign income taxes payable	(29,900,000)	(54,000,000)	(31,500,000)
Net cash provided/(used) by operating activities	97,700,000	131,400,000	(500,000)
Cash Flows from Investing Activities			
Decrease/(increase) in other assets	(25,400,000)	16,500,000	4,500,000
Additions to property, plant, and equipment	(191,100,000)	(170,500,000)	(129,200,000)

	12/31/1998	12/31/1999	12/31/2000
Proceeds from the sale of property, plant, and equipment	150,500,000	36,600,000	56,600,000
Acquisitions, net of cash acquired	(18,800,000)	–	–
Net cash used by investing activities	(84,800,000)	(117,400,000)	(68,100,000)
Cash Flows from Financing Activities			
Net increase/(decrease) in short-term debt (maturities of 90 days or less)	131,200,000	(86,200,000)	108,200,000
Short-term debt (maturities of more than 90 days)			
Proceeds	73,000,000	41,800,000	–
Payments	(117,200,000)	(24,900,000)	–
Proceeds from issuance of long-term debt	–	268,200,000	–
Repayment of long-term debt	–	(200,000,000)	–
Cash dividends paid	(26,500,000)	(26,600,000)	(27,000,000)
Purchase of treasury stock	(45,500,000)	–	–
Proceeds from issuance of shares in connection with stock incentive plan	6,000,000	300,000	100,000
Net cash provided/(used) by financing activities	21,000,000	(27,400,000)	81,300,000
Effect of exchange rate changes on cash	3,100,000	400,000	(7,500,000)
Net increase/(decrease) in cash and cash equivalents	37,000,000	(13,000,000)	5,200,000
Cash and cash equivalents at beginning of year	68,000,000	105,000,000	92,000,000
Cash and cash equivalents at end of year	$105,000,000	$92,000,000	$ 97,200,000

25. Find the following amounts in the statements of Polaroid:
   a. Net sales in 2000
   b. Marketing, research, engineering, and administrative expenses incurred in 2000
   c. Interest expense in 2000
   d. Income tax expense in 1999
   e. Net income in 1999
   f. Inventories at the end of 2000
   g. Payables and accruals at the beginning of 2000
   h. Retained earnings at the end of 2000
   i. Accumulated other comprehensive income at the end of 2000
   j. Long-term borrowings at the beginning of 2000
   k. Cash produced from operating activities in 2000

l. Cash payments to acquire property, plant, and equipment in 2000

m. Dividends paid in 2000

n. Cash proceeds from new borrowings in 2000

o. Cash produced or used for investing activities in 2000

p. Amount of other comprehensive income in 2000

26. What is the trend in net income for the three years presented?

27. What is the trend in cash flow from operations for the three years presented?

28. What is the trend in net sales for the three years presented?

Base your answers to problems 29–35 on the data for Werner Enterprises provided here.

WERNER ENTERPRISES, INC.
CONSOLIDATED BALANCE SHEET
(In thousands, except share amounts)

	2000/12/31	1999/12/31
ASSETS		
Current assets:		
Cash and cash equivalents	$ 25,485	$ 15,368
Accounts receivable, trade, less allowance		
of $3,994 and $3,236, respectively	123,518	127,211
Receivable from unconsolidated affiliate	5,332	–
Other receivables	10,257	11,217
Inventories and supplies	7,329	5,296
Prepaid taxes, licenses, and permits	12,396	12,423
Current deferred income taxes	11,552	8,500
Other	10,908	8,812
Total current assets	206,777	188,827
Property and equipment, at cost		
Land	19,157	14,522
Buildings and improvements	72,631	65,152
Revenue equipment	829,549	800,613
Service equipment and other	100,342	90,322
Total property and equipment	1,021,679	970,609
Less accumulated depreciation	313,881	262,557
Property and equipment, net	707,798	708,052
Notes receivable	4,420	–
Investment in unconsolidated affiliate	5,324	–
Other noncurrent assets	2,888	–
	$ 927,207	$896,879
LIABILITIES AND STOCKHOLDERS' EQUITY		
Current liabilities:		
Accounts payable	$ 30,710	$ 35,686
Short-term debt	–	25,000
Insurance and claims accruals	36,057	32,993
Accrued payroll	12,746	11,846
Income taxes payable	7,157	926
Other current liabilities	14,749	14,755
Total current liabilities	101.419	121.206

	2000/12/31	1999/12/31
Long-term debt	105,000	120,000
Deferred income taxes	152,403	130,600
Insurance, claims, and other long-term accruals	32,301	30,301
Commitments and contingencies		
Stockholders' equity Common stock, $.01 par value, 200,000,000 shares authorized; 48,320,835 shares issued; 47,039,290 and 47,205,236 shares outstanding, respectively	483	483
Paid-in capital	105,844	105,884
Retained earnings	447,943	404,625
Accumulated other comprehensive loss	(34)	—
Treasury stock, at cost; 1,281,545 and 1,115,599 shares, respectively	(18,152)	(16,220)
Total stockholders' equity	536,084	494,772
	$ 927,207	$896,879

WERNER ENTERPRISES, INC.
CONSOLIDATED STATEMENTS OF INCOME
(In thousands, except per share amounts)

	2000/12/31	1999/12/31	1998/12/31
Operating revenues	$1,214,628	$1,052,333	$863,417
Operating expenses:			
Salaries, wages, and benefits	429,825	382,824	325,659
Fuel	137,620	79,029	56,786
Supplies and maintenance	102,784	87,600	72,273
Taxes and licenses	89,126	82,089	67,907
Insurance and claims	34,147	31,728	23,875
Depreciation	109,107	99,955	82,549
Rent and purchased transportation	216,917	185,129	139,026
Communications and utilities	14,454	13,444	10,796
Other	(2,173)	(11,666)	(11,065)
Total operating expenses	1,131,807	950,132	767,806
Operating income	82,821	102,201	95,611
Other expense (income):			
Interest expense	8,169	6,565	4,889
Interest income	(2,650)	(1,407)	(1,724)
Other	(154)	245	114
Total other expense	5,365	5,403	3,279
Income before income taxes	77,456	96,798	92,332
Income taxes	29,433	36,787	35,086
Net income	$ 48,023	$ 60,011	$ 57,246
Average common shares outstanding	47,061	47,406	47,667
Basic earnings per share	$ 1.02	$ 1.27	$ 1.20
Diluted shares outstanding	47,257	47,631	47,910
Diluted earnings per share	$ 1.02	$ 1.26	$ 1.19

WERNER ENTERPRISES, INC.
CONSOLIDATED STATEMENTS OF CASH FLOWS
(In thousands)

	2000/12/31	1999/12/31	1998/12/31
Cash flows from operating activities:			
Net income	$ 48,023	$ 60,011	$ 57,246
Adjustments to reconcile net income to net cash provided by operating activities:			
Depreciation	109,107	99,955	82,549
Deferred income taxes	18,751	22,200	14,700
Gain on disposal of operating equipment	(5,055)	(13,047)	(12,251)
Equity in income of unconsolidated affiliate	(324)	–	–
Tax benefit from exercise of stock options	130	663	389
Other long-term assets	(2,888)	–	–
Insurance, claims, and other long-term accruals	2,000	(500)	1,472
Changes in certain working capital items:			
Accounts receivable, net	3,693	(32,882)	(868)
Prepaid expenses and other current assets	(8,474)	(8,725)	(5,186)
Accounts payable	(4,976)	(12,460)	3,979
Accrued and other current liabilities	10,160	16,762	(4,090)
Net cash provided by operating activities	170,147	131,977	137,940
Cash flows from investing activities:			
Additions to property and equipment	(169,113)	(255,326)	(258,643)
Retirements of property and equipment	60,608	84,297	86,260
Investment in unconsolidated affiliate	(5,000)	–	–
Proceeds from collection of notes receivable	287	–	–
Net cash used in investing activities	(113,218)	(171,029)	(172,383)
Cash flows from financing activities:			
Proceeds from issuance of long-term debt	10,000	30,000	40,000
Repayments of long-term debt	(25,000)	–	–
Proceeds from issuance of short-term debt	–	30,000	20,000
Repayments of short-term debt	(25,000)	(15,000)	(20,000)
Dividends on common stock	(4,710)	(4,740)	(4,201)
Repurchases of common stock	(2,759)	(3,941)	(9,072)
Stock options exercised	657	2,188	1,335
Net cash provided by (used in) financing activities	(46,812)	38,507	28,062
Net increase (decrease) in cash and cash equivalents	10,117	(545)	(6,381)
Cash and cash equivalents, beginning of year	15,368	15,913	22,294
Cash and cash equivalents, end of year	$ 25,485	$ 15,368	$ 15,913
Supplemental disclosures of cash flow information:			
Cash paid during year for:			
Interest	$ 7,876	$ 7,329	$ 4,800
Income taxes	3,916	13,275	26,100
Supplemental disclosures of noncash investing activities:			
Notes receivable from sale of revenue equipment	$ 4,707	$ –	$ –

WERNER ENTERPRISES, INC.
CONSOLIDATED STATEMENTS OF STOCKHOLDERS' EQUITY
(In thousands, except share amounts)

	Common Stock	Paid–in Capital	Retained Earnings	Accumulated Other Comprehensive Loss	Treasury Stock	Total Stockholders' Equity
BALANCE, December 31, 1997	$387	$104,764	$296,533	$ —	($6,566)	$395,118
Purchases of 592,600 shares of common stock	—	—	—	—	(9,072)	(9,072)
Dividends on common stock ($.09 per share)	—	—	(4,428)	—	—	(4,428)
Five-for-four stock split	96	(96)	—	—	—	—
Exercise of stock options, 119,391 shares	—	670	—	—	1,054	1,724
Comprehensive income:						
Net income	—	—	57,426	—	—	57,246
BALANCE, December 31, 1998	483	105,338	349,351	—	(14,584)	440,588
Purchases of 302,600 shares of common stock	—	—	—	—	(3,941)	(3,941)
Dividends on common stock ($.10 per share)	—	—	(4,737)	—	—	(4,737)
Exercise of stock options, 198,526 shares	—	546	—	—	2,305	2,851
Comprehensive income:						
Net income	—	—	60,011	—	—	60,011
BALANCE, December 31, 1999	483	105,884	404,625	—	(16,220)	494,772
Purchases of 225,201 shares of common stock	—	—	—	—	(2,759)	(2,759)
Dividends on common stock ($.10 per share)	—	—	(4,705)	—	—	(4,705)
Exercise of stock options, 59,255 shares	—	(40)	—	—	827	787
Comprehensive income (loss):						
Net income	—	—	48,023	—	—	48,023
Foreign currency translation adjustments	—	—	—	(34)	—	(34)
Total comprehensive income	—	—	48,023	(34)	—	47,989
BALANCE, December 31, 2000	$483	$105,844	$447,943	($34)	($18,152)	$536,084

29. Verify that total assets equal total liabilities and owners' equity for Werner in 2000.

30. Find the following amounts in the statements of Werner:

   a. Revenues in 2000

   b. Salaries, wages, and benefits incurred in 2000

   c. Interest expense in 2000

   d. Income tax expense in 1999

    e. Net income in 1999

    f. Inventories at the end of 2000

    g. Accounts payable at the beginning of 2000

    h. Retained earnings at the end of 2000

    i. Long-term borrowings at the beginning of 2000

    j. Cash produced from operating activities in 2000

    k. Cash payments to acquire property, plant, and equipment in 2000

    l. Dividends paid in 2000

    m. Cash proceeds from new borrowings in 2000

    n. Cash produced or used for investing activities in 2000

31. Does Werner finance the firm mainly from creditors (total liabilities) or from owners (owners' equity) in 2000? Support your answer with appropriate data.

32. List the two largest sources of cash and the two largest uses of cash in 2000. (Consider operations to be a single source or use of cash.)

33. Suggest some reasons why income was $48,023 (000) in 2000, yet cash flow from operations was $170,147 (000).

34. What is the comprehensive net income for Werner in 2000?

35. On December 31, 2000, find the price of Werner's stock (use the library or the web) and compute the total market value of the company's stock that is outstanding based on the number of shares that were outstanding as of that date. Compare this value with the book value of owner's equity on Werner's balance sheet as of that date. If these numbers are different, offer an explanation for this discrepancy.

Base your answers to problems 36–42 on the data for Emulex Corporation provided here.

EMULEX CORP.: Balance Sheet	2001/07/01	2000/07/01
Assets		
Current assets:		
Cash and cash equivalents	$ 36,471,000	$ 23,471,000
Investments	148,204,000	128,234,000
Accounts and other receivables, less allowance for doubtful accounts of 1,298 in 2001 and 844 in 2000	40,239,000	24,332,000
Inventories, net	38,616,000	12,635,000
Prepaid expenses	2,527,000	1,021,000
Deferred income taxes	1,579,000	453,000
Total current assets	267,636,000	190,146,000
Property and equipment, net	18,379,000	6,927,000
Long-term investments	38,805,000	29,293,000
Goodwill and other intangibles, net	590,316,000	0
Deferred income taxes and other assets	2,878,000	3,629,000
Total Assets	$918,014,000	$229,995,000

	2001/07/01	2000/07/01
Liabilities and Stockholders' Equity		
Current liabilities:		
Accounts payable	$ 29,253,000	$ 17,869,000
Accrued liabilities	11,749,000	6,355,000
Income taxes payable and other current liabilities	300,000	320,000
Total current liabilities	41,302,000	24,544,000
Deferred income taxes and other liabilities	26,000	0
	41,328,000	24,544,000
Commitments and contingencies (note 9)		
Stockholders' equity:		
Preferred stock, $0.01 par value; 1,000,000 shares authorized (150,000 shares designated as Series A Junior Participating Preferred Stock); none issued and outstanding	0	0
Common stock, $0.10 par value; 120,000,000 shares authorized; 81,799,322 and 72,466,848 issued and outstanding in 2001 and 2000, respectively	8,180,000	7,247,000
Additional paid-in capital	861,461,000	155,190,000
Deferred compensation	(12,366,000)	0
Retained earnings	19,411,000	43,014,000
Total stockholders' equity	876,686,000	205,451,000
Total liabilities and stockholders' equity	$918,014,000	$229,995,000

EMULEX CORP.: Income Statement

	2001/07/01	2000/07/01	1999/07/01
Net revenues	$245,307,000	$139,772,000	$68,485,000
Cost of sales	120,812,000	73,346,000	40,138,000
Cost of sales—inventory charges related to consolidation	0	0	1,304,000
Total cost of sales	120,812,000	73,346,000	41,442,000
Gross profit	124,495,000	66,426,000	27,043,000
Operating expenses:			
Engineering and development	27,002,000	14,727,000	11,766,000
Selling and marketing	16,734,000	10,077,000	6,953,000
General and administrative	12,111,000	6,923,000	4,279,000
Amortization of goodwill and other intangibles	52,085,000	0	0
In-process research and development	22,280,000	0	0
Consolidation charges, net	0	0	(987,000)
Total operating expenses	130,212,000	31,727,000	22,011,000
Operating income (loss)	(5,717,000)	34,699,000	5,032,000
Nonoperating income	14,301,000	9,131,000	480,000
Income before income taxes	8,584,000	43,830,000	5,512,000
Income tax provision	32,187,000	11,016,000	247,000
Net income (loss)	($23,603,000)	$32,814,000	$5,265,000

EMULEX CORP.: Cash Flow

	2001/07/01	2000/07/01	1999/07/01
Cash flows from operating activities:			
Net income (loss)	($23,603,000)	$32,814,000	$5,265,000
Adjustments to reconcile net income (loss) to net cash provided by operating activities:			
Depreciation and amortization	4,801,000	1,814,000	1,648,000
Gain on sale of strategic investment	(1,884,000)	0	0
Stock-based compensation	1,756,000	0	0
Amortization of goodwill and other intangibles	52,085,000	0	0
In-process research and development	22,280,000	0	0
Loss (gain) on disposal of property, plant, and equipment	400,000	112,000	(750,000)
Deferred income taxes	(536,000)	(5,643,000)	0
Tax benefit from exercise of stock options	32,188,000	16,661,000	0
Impairment of intangibles	0	175,000	125,000
Provision for doubtful accounts	435,000	435,000	86,000
Changes in assets and liabilities:			
Accounts receivable	(15,714,000)	(7,679,000)	(5,033,000)
Inventories	(25,007,000)	(1,552,000)	(1,177,000)
Prepaid expenses and other assets	(111,000)	(701,000)	18,000
Accounts payable	5,882,000	6,474,000	4,486,000
Accrued liabilities	4,006,000	2,064,000	(2,987,000)
Income taxes payable	(37,000)	(32,000)	215,000
Net cash provided by operating activities	56,941,000	44,942,000	1,896,000
Cash flows from investing activities:			
Net proceeds from sale of property, plant, and equipment	0	30,000	2,999,000
Additions to property and equipment	(11,657,000)	(5,703,000)	(1,953,000)
Payment for purchase of Giganet, Inc., net of cash acquired	(15,530,000)	0	0
Purchases of investments	(524,091,000)	(637,892,000)	(115,380,000)
Maturity of investments	491,009,000	595,745,000	0
Proceeds from sale of strategic investment	5,484,000	0	0
Net cash used in investing activities	(54,785,000)	(47,820,000)	(114,334,000)
Cash flows from financing activities:			
Principal payments under capital leases	(12,000)	(18,000)	(76,000)
Net proceeds from issuance of common stock under stock option plans	9,742,000	4,083,000	184,000
Proceeds from note receivable issued in exchange for restricted stock	1,114,000	0	0
Net proceeds from stock offering	0	0	132,838,000
Net cash provided by financing activities	10,844,000	4,065,000	132,946,000
Net increase in cash and cash equivalents	13,000,000	1,187,000	20,508,000
Cash and cash equivalents at beginning of year	23,471,000	22,284,000	1,776,000
Cash and cash equivalents at end of year	$36,471,000	$23,471,000	$22,284,000

	2001/07/01	2000/07/01	1999/07/01
Supplemental disclosures:			
Noncash investing and financing activities			
Fair value of assets acquired	$ 7,832,000		
Fair value of liabilities assumed	8,136,000	$ 0	$ 0
Common stock issued and options			
assumed for acquired business	661,678,000	0	0
Cash paid during the year for:			
Interest	$ 352,000	$ 21,000	$ 60,000
Income taxes	221,000	32,000	53,000

36. What is Emulex's fiscal year-end date?

37. Find the following amounts in the statements of Emulex:

  a. Net sales in 2001

  b. Cost of sales in 2001

  c. Interest expense in 2001

  d. Income tax expense in 2001

  e. Amortization of goodwill in 2001 and in 2000

  f. Net income in 2001

  g. Inventories at the end of 2001

  h. Goodwill at the end of 2001

  i. Additional paid-in capital at the end of 2001

  j. Cash from operating activities for 2001

  k. Cash from investing activities for 2001

  l. Cash from financing activities for 2001

38. Does Emulex finance its business primarily from creditors or from owners? Support your answer with appropriate data.

39. In 2001 Emulex purchased a new business. How did Emulex pay for this acquisition?

40. What is the trend in sales and net income over the last three years, and can you provide an explanation for why there is a loss in 2001?

41. Does Emulex pay dividends on its stock?

42. On July 1, 2001 find the stock price of Emulex's stock (use the library or the web) and compute the total market value of the company's stock that is outstanding, based on the number of shares that were outstanding as of that date. Compare this value with the book value of owner's equity on Emulex's balance sheet as of that date. If these numbers are different, offer an explanation for this discrepancy.

○ BEYOND THE BOOK

43. For a company of your choosing, answer the following questions:

  a. What are the major sections included in your annual report?

  b. What are the three most important points made in the letter to the shareholders?

    c. What are the titles to the major financial statements included in the report?

    d. What are the total assets, total liabilities, and total stockholders' equity of the firm? What percent of the company's total assets are financed through liabilities?

    e. What were the net sales in the most recent year? Is this up or down from the prior year (answer in both dollar and percentage amounts)?

    f. What is the net income and earnings per share in the most recent year? Is this up or down from the prior year (answer in both dollar and percentage amounts)?

    g. Are any of the following items reported in the income statement: discontinued operations, extraordinary items, accounting method changes? If so, which ones?

    h. What is the net cash provided (used) by operating, financing, and investing activities for the most recent year?

    i. What is the last day of your company's fiscal year end?

    j. Who are the independent auditors, and what type of opinion did they give the company?

44. Refer to the footnotes that accompany the company you chose in 43.

    a. In the section "Summary of Significant Accounting Policies," what key policies are discussed?

    b. Does your company have long-term debt? If so, what is the interest rate?

    c. If your company has inventory, what do the footnotes tell you about the inventory?

    d. From the footnotes, does it appear that there are any obligations that the company may have that do not appear to be reflected as liabilities on the balance sheet? If so, what are they?

CHAPTER **3**

The Accounting Process

LEARNING OBJECTIVES

After reading this chapter you should be able to:

1 Recognize common business transactions and understand their impact on general-purpose financial statements.

2 Understand the dual nature of accounting transactions as reflected in the accounting equation.

3 Explain the basic construction of the Statement of Financial Position, the Statement of Earnings, and the Statement of Cash Flows.

4 Distinguish between economic events that are commonly recognized in accounting as transactions and those that are not.

5 Apply the concept of nominal or temporary accounts to record revenues and expenses, and identify their relationship to the Statement of Earnings and Statement of Financial Position.

6 Describe the accounting cycle and recognize the timing issues inherent in reporting financial results.

On March 2, 2001, investors reacted very favorably to an initial public offering (an Initial Public Offering or IPO is the first time a private company decides to issue shares to the public) from AFC Enterprises, Inc. The company operates and franchises quick-service restaurants, bakeries, and cafés (3618 in the United States and 27 in foreign countries) under the names Popeye's Chicken & Biscuits, Church's Chicken, Cinnabon, Seattle's Best Coffee, and Torrefazione Italia. The company also sells specialty coffees at wholesale and retail under the Seattle Coffee brand name. Sales totaled about $2.4 billion in 2000.

Although originally issued at $17, AFC shares opened at $19.50, climbed as high as $20.75, and ended the day at $20.38 on the Nasdaq Stock Market. The company had originally expected the shares to be offered at between $15 and $17. After the IPO, AFC had 29.5 million shares outstanding. You can see that with almost 30 million shares issued, AFC raised a substantial amount of money to fund its operations.

Investors and analysts use financial statements to guide their predictions and investment decisions. For example, when a company such as AFC Enterprises decides to issue stock to the public, it files information (in a document called a *prospectus*) containing past and projected financial performance. Investors, potential investors, managers, and other stakeholders rely on this financial statement information to help determine the company's value. As a result, these users must understand the process and assumptions underlying the construction of financial statements in order to make sound decisions based (in part) on these statements.

In the following pages, we present the fundamental aspects of the *double-entry accounting system* for constructing financial statements. The mechanical aspects of recording transactions are sometimes referred to as *bookkeeping*. You may well question why you should be concerned with this bookkeeping aspect of accounting, especially in light of today's computerized technology. The answer: You need to understand what the preparers are doing so that you can better interpret the output of their work, the financial statements. Let's start first with the balance sheet accounts, which underlie the financial statements.

BALANCE SHEET ACCOUNTS

Most of the balance sheet accounts are categorized as assets, liabilities, or stockholders' equity. Before examining specific transactions, let's review these in more detail.

ASSETS

The Financial Accounting Standards Board (FASB) Concepts Statement Number 6 (CON 6) defines an asset as follows (FASB, SFAC No. 6, 1985):

> Assets are probable future economic benefits obtained or controlled by a particular entity as a result of past transactions or events.

Probable future economic benefits means that a firm expects either future cash inflows or smaller cash outflows to result from the asset. For example, a prepaid expense, such as the premium on an insurance policy, is considered to be an asset because the coverage that the policy provides benefits future periods. However, as we noted in Chapter 2, some items have economic value but are not recognized as assets. For instance, if a firm faces uncertainty about future realization of cash flows, an item might not be recognized as an asset (e.g., research and development expenditures). Pepsico spends a significant amount of money each year for marketing its products. While this may create value for the business (brand recognition), they expense their advertising costs as they are incurred. Or, an item may be valuable to an entity but not owned or controlled by that entity, such as skilled employees.

Most assets originate as the result of a transaction with a party outside of the firm. A firm generally recognizes assets at the price it paid to acquire the assets. Exhibit 3.1 lists assets commonly found on a balance sheet:

Exhibit 3.1
Common Assets

Cash The amount of money that the firm has, including the amounts in checking and savings accounts.

Marketable Securities Short-term investments, such as stocks and bonds, in the securities of other companies.

Accounts Receivable Amounts owed to the firm that result from credit sales to customers.

Inventory Goods held for resale to customers.

Prepaid Expenses Expenses that have been paid for, but have not been used, such as rent paid in advance and insurance premiums.

Property, Plant, and Equipment (PP&E) Buildings, land, and equipment to be used for business operations over several years.

Intangible Assets Assets that have value, but do not have a physical presence, such as patents, trademarks, and goodwill.

Deferred Tax Assets Amounts of expected future tax savings.

LIABILITIES

In contrast to assets, liabilities are amounts recognized in accounting that result in expected future outflows of cash or delivery of goods or services. Exhibit 3.2 lists some of the more common balance sheet liabilities. Similar to assets, liability recognition also usually involves a transaction with an external party. FASB Con 6 defines liabilities as follows (FASB, SFAC No. 6, 1985):

Liabilities are probable future sacrifices of economic benefits arising from present obligations of a particular entity to transfer assets or provide services to other entities in the future as a result of past transactions or events.

Exhibit 3.2
Common Liabilities

Accounts Payable Amounts owed to suppliers from the purchase of goods on credit.

Notes Payable Amounts owed to a creditor (bank or supplier) that are represented by a formal agreement called a note. Notes payable can be either short-term (due in less than one year) or long-term (due more than one year in the future).

Accrued Liabilities Amounts that are owed to others relating to expenses that the company has incurred, but are not paid in cash as of the balance sheet date, such as interest payable or a warranty liability.

Taxes Payable Amounts currently owed to taxing authorities.

Deferred Taxes Amounts that the company expects to pay to taxing authorities in the future.

Bonds Payable Amounts owed to a creditor that are paid out over longer periods; they generally involve fixed interest payments as well as a large payment at the end of some specified period. Some bonds payable can be traded on exchanges in the same way as stock is traded. Bonds payable are generally long-term in nature, meaning that they are payable in a period more than one year from the date of issuance.

STOCKHOLDERS' EQUITY

Owners' or stockholders' equity is the last main category on the balance sheet. Stockholders' equity consists of two major components: contributed capital and retained earnings. **Contributed capital** reflects the amount of capital that a firm's owners have invested in the business. This amount is typically the sum of the **par** or **stated value** of stock issued, plus the amounts in excess of par, **additional paid-in-capital.** The sum of common stock plus additional paid-in-capital represents the total investment by shareholders at the time the company issued the stock.

> We would not expect a company to accumulate large amounts of cash, even if the company is very profitable. This is because cash as an asset does not generate high rates of return. Thus, management, seeking to maximize shareholders' wealth, generally keeps only as much cash as it requires to meet its operating needs and to make the repayment of its debt. Additional amounts may be held in anticipation of further investments.

Retained earnings is the total amount of earnings (revenues minus expenses) recorded in the accounting system to date, but not yet distributed to shareholders as dividends. Dividends are distributions of earnings to shareholders and are not considered an expense to the company. Remember that retained earnings are not cash. A company may have substantial earnings yet have no cash for at least two reasons. First, accounting rules require that earnings be recognized on an accrual basis. For example, firms sometimes recognize revenues before receiving cash (as in sales on account), and sometimes recognize expenses before paying cash out (as in wages owed to employees). Second, a company may use its cash to invest in noncash assets (e.g., a new computer system or repay debt).

NOMINAL ACCOUNTS

Balance sheet accounts (sometimes called **real** or **permanent accounts**) include a number of assets, liabilities, and stockholders' equity accounts such as those discussed in the previous sections. **Nominal accounts** (or **temporary accounts**) are accounts that a firm uses to determine its earnings. These accounts consist of revenue and expense accounts such as sales, cost of goods sold, wage and salary expenses, and selling and administrative expenses. Ultimately, these accounts affect a permanent account, namely retained earnings. (We'll discuss how this is accomplished later.) However, at this point, it is worth noting that the reason that revenue and expenses are considered to be temporary accounts is that the balances in these accounts are transferred (or *closed*) to retained earnings at the end of each accounting period. By closing revenue and expense accounts each period, the balances in these accounts reflect only the firm's operating performance for one period at a time. The retained earnings account contains cumulative earnings less dividends distributed to stockholders since the firm's inception.

Now that you have a good understanding of the types of accounts, let's see next how firms use them to record transactions.

ACCOUNTING FOR TRANSACTIONS

The starting point in constructing financial statements is the accounting recognition of **transactions,** or economic events. Most, but not all, transactions are triggered by an exchange between the firm and another party. Accounting recognition of these transactions take the form of an **entry,** which indicates the financial effects of that event on accounts that appear on the firm's financial statements.

Recall from Chapter 2 that the accounting equation states that

$$\text{Assets} = \text{Liabilities} + \text{Stockholders' Equity}$$

When firms record transactions in the accounting system, this equality must always be maintained.

To analyze transactions, you can use two approaches. The first approach is based on the accounting equation. Each transaction is analyzed in terms of how it affects assets, liabilities, and stockholders' equity (we'll illustrate this approach later in this chapter). The equation approach is only useful when first learning accounting, so you can more easily see how transactions affect the accounting equation and financial statements. However, this approach quickly becomes unwieldy and inefficient when dealing with a large number of transactions and accounts. As a result, most firms use the second approach, the double-entry accounting system.

DOUBLE-ENTRY ACCOUNTING SYSTEM

The **double-entry accounting system** expresses account balances and changes in account balances using terms called **debits** and **credits.** Although it requires some investment of your time and effort to be able to use debits and credits, having this skill is extremely useful. Once you understand the double-entry accounting system, you can efficiently assess the effects of a variety of types of transactions on a company's financial statements, as well as address valuation and income measurement issues.

The system of using debit and credits serves as the basis of virtually every accounting system worldwide. Further, the Sarbane's Oxley Act requires that top management certify to the fundamental accuracy of their company's financial statements. Such certification requires that management possess a basic understanding of the accounting process, in order to be able to communicate with the preparers of financial statements. Understanding the process of generating financial statements is an essential component of financial literacy.

T-ACCOUNTS

A debit means simply an entry or balance on the left-hand side of an account, and a credit is an entry or balance on the right-hand side of an account. Increases and decreases in specific accounts can be expressed by debit and credit entries following set conventions. The conventions that dictate the rules for debits and credits are structured so that all accounting transactions will maintain the equality of the accounting equation at all times. The basic form of an account can be represented using a so-called **T-account** of the following form (note that we have represented the balance on the debit side of the account but also recognize that the balance could appear on either side of the account):

Account Title	
Balance	
Debit	Credit
Balance	

A T-account shows the beginning and ending balance in an account, as well as the debit and credit entries for transactions affecting the account during a particular period of time. Whether an account is increased or decreased by a debit or credit depends on whether the account represents an asset, liability, or stockholders' equity, in other words, has a debit or a credit balance. As Exhibit 3.3 shows, assets are increased by debit entries and decreased by credit entries. Liabilities and stockholders' equity accounts (capital stock, additional paid in capital, and retained earnings) are increased by credits and decreased by debits.

As shown in Exhibit 3.3, we normally expect asset accounts to carry a debit balance, while liability and stockholders' equity accounts normally carry a credit balance. One way to think about these results is that the accounting equation shows assets on the left side (debit) and liabilities and stockholders' equity on the right (credit). An exception is retained earnings. A profitable company will have a credit balance in this account, but it can have a debit balance if it incurs a cumulative net loss. Finally, remember that to maintain the accounting equation, the sum of all debit account balances must equal the sum of all credit account balances.

JOURNAL ENTRIES

In a double-entry accounting system, firms typically track transactions as they occur in a chronological listing known as a **journal.** Each entry in the journal, known as a **journal entry,** summarizes both sides of a transaction (debit and

Exhibit 3.3
T-Accounts

T-Accounts for Assets, Liabilities, and Stockholders' Equity			
Assets		**Liabilities**	
Beginning balance Debits increase	Credits decrease	Debits decrease	Beginning balance Credits increase
Ending balance			Ending balance
Capital Stock (common stock + paid-in-capital)		**Retained Earnings**	
Debits decrease	Beginning balance Credits increase	Debits decrease	Beginning balance Credits increase
	Ending balance		Ending balance

credit). By convention, in a journal entry, the debit portion of the entry is shown first, followed by the credit portion. (See the sample journal entries that follow.) The credit entry is slightly indented from the debit to make the entry clear. The total debits for a transaction must equal the total credits for that transaction.

> Title of Account Debited   Amount Debited
>   Title of Account Credited   Amount Credited

For example, the journal entry to record the purchase of $100 of inventory for cash would appear as follows:

> Inventory   100
>   Cash   100

We will explain this transaction later, but for now just recognize the form of the journal entry.

After recording journal entries, they are then posted to the T-accounts. Posting simply means transferring the information in the journal entry to the appropriate T-accounts. (In this text, we will often simplify this two-step approach by recording the transaction directly to the T-account, bypassing the journal entry step.) The set of T-accounts that a company uses is collectively referred to as the **ledger.**

To illustrate the application of the accounting equation, journal entries, and T-accounts, assume that a company borrows $50,000,000 cash from a bank and signs a promissory note. This note specifies an interest rate and when the amount borrowed must be repaid. Using the accounting equation approach, we view this transaction as shown here (shown in millions of dollars):

> Assets = Liabilities + Stockholders' Equity
>   Notes
> Cash   Payable
> +50   = +50

Notice that the asset (Cash) is increased, and the liability (Notes Payable) is also increased. Observe also that we maintain the equality of the accounting equation. The journal entry for this transaction would appear as follows:

> Cash   50
>   Notes Payable   50

The debit to the Cash account means that cash (an asset) has increased by $50 and the credit to Notes Payable (a liability) means that account is increased as well. Posting this journal entry to the appropriate T-accounts, the transaction would be recorded as:

Cash		Notes Payable	
50			50

Observe that both the T-account and the journal entry maintain the equality of total debits and total credits. Note also that dollar signs ($) are generally omitted from journal entries and T-accounts. Journal entries are a useful way to represent individual transactions, while T-accounts illustrate the effect of a series of transactions on the accounts that comprise a company's financial statements.

COMPUTERIZED ACCOUNTING

The basic accounting process, still used today, has existed for centuries. Before computers, firms literally recorded accounting entries in paper journals, and then posted the individual components of those entries to paper ledger accounts. You can easily imagine the large amount of paperwork involved in a manual accounting system, even for a modestly sized business. Although today's accounting systems are computerized, they continue follow the same basic process. Transactions still give rise to entries in some form (a journal), from which summaries (ledger) by account can be created, which then serve as a foundation for the construction of financial statements.

Modern accounting systems are structured much differently than in the past and may be simply one part of a company's software system. These sophisticated systems provide a wide variety of management tools. For example, some systems may instantly determine the impact of a revenue or expense transaction on a company's income statement and balance sheet. There are several companies that provide very sophisticated systems, and Oracle is one of those companies. Exhibit 3.4 provides a description of Oracle's business.

Even though computers have eased the paperwork requirements of accounting systems, you still need to know how they work. Let's look at an example that illustrates the accounting process and the preparation of financial statements.

Exhibit 3.4
Oracle Corporation:
Description of Business
(Oracle 10-K, 2003)

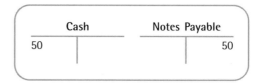

Oracle Corporation

We are the world's largest enterprise software company. We develop, manufacture, market, and distribute computer software that helps our customers manage and grow their businesses and operations. Our offerings include new software licenses, software license updates, and product support and services, which include consulting, advanced product services, and education. We also offer an integrated suite of business applications software and other business software infrastructure, including application server, collaborative software, and development tools.

AN ILLUSTRATION OF TRANSACTION ANALYSIS

Biohealth, Inc., is a hypothetical, wholesale health-products distributor (similar to an actual company in the health supply industry). As is often true for publicly traded companies, Biohealth is denoted by its *ticker symbol,* in this case BHT, used on the stock exchanges where the company's stock trades. BHT distributes (not manufactures) a wide variety of healthcare products and prescription medicines to hospitals, retail chains, and other health-related outlets. It also provides software solutions to a variety of businesses in the healthcare sector for managing their ordering and inventory. BHT was incorporated on December 20, 20X0 and began operations the following January.

The following economic events/transactions occurred in December prior to the start of BHT's operations:

1. BHT issued 250 million shares of common stock with a par value of $1 per share for $6.50 per share.
2. BHT acquired fixtures for $540 million. BHT estimates that the fixtures will be used for nine years.
3. The purchase of fixtures was partially financed with a $400 million note due in five years. The loan carries an interest rate of 7 percent.[1]

These transactions reflect BHT's start-up financing and investing activities. Let's look at them more closely.

ANALYSIS OF FINANCING AND INVESTING ACTIVITIES

Exhibit 3.5 summarizes the impact of these initial three transactions on the accounting equation. Notice how the accounts to the left of the equal (=) sign are added together, as well as the accounts to the right of the equal sign, to

	Assets		=	Liabilities			
#–Type	Cash	Fixtures	=	Notes payable	Common Stock	Paid–in Capital	Retained Earnings
Bal. 12/20/20X0	0	0	=	0	0	0	0
1-Financing	1,625		=		250	1,375	
2-Investing	(540)	540	=				
3-Financing	400		=	400			
Bal. 12/31/20X0	1,485	540	=	400	250	1,375	0

Exhibit 3.5
Impact of BHT's Financing and Investing Activities on the Accounting Equation (in millions of dollars)

[1]A note is a loan accompanied by a written promise to repay the amount owed. Interest on notes is always expressed in terms of an annual rate even if the note is for a period longer or shorter than one year. For example, the total interest on a six-month $1,000 note with an interest rate of 5 percent would be $1,000 × .05 × 6/12 = $25.

determine the ending balance. On each line of the exhibit, from individual transactions to ending balances, the accounting equation holds. Negative amounts, as shown in Exhibit 3.5, are enclosed in parentheses.

Issuing Stock (Transaction 1)

The first transaction increases Cash by $1,625 million (250 million shares × $6.50/share), increases Common Stock by $250 million (250 million shares × $1/share), and increases Additional Paid-In Capital by $1,375 million (the difference between cash and par value). We classify this transaction as a financing activity because it relates to how the company funds its operating and investing activities. Note that dollar figures are reported in millions, a common practice in financial statements.

Purchasing Fixtures (Transaction 2)

The second transaction increases assets (Fixtures) by $540 million, and decreases Cash by $540 million. This transaction is an investing activity. Investing activities involve purchase and sale of assets that are used over multiple periods such as property, plant, and equipment. Note that later in the chapter we classify fixtures under property, plant, and equipment (PPE).

Borrowing Funds (Transaction 3)

Although the third transaction relates to the investing activity in Transaction 2, it, by itself, is a financing activity. Here, the company borrows funds to finance its purchase of fixtures. Note that interest is not recognized yet on the loan as it is a charge that the firm incurs with the passage of time. Investing and financing activities often occur simultaneously. For example, America Online (AOL) acquired all of Time-Warner's common stock in January 2000. We classify AOL's stock acquisition of Time Warner as an investing activity because America Online now controls the assets of Time Warner. However, we also classify this as a financing activity, as AOL funded this transaction by issuing additional shares of AOL stock.

Using Journal Entries and T-Accounts to Record Transactions

We show the journal entries and T-accounts for the first three BHT transactions in Exhibits 3.6 and 3.7, respectively. The journal entry for Transaction 1 summarizes

Exhibit 3.6
Journal Entries for BHT's Financing and Investing Transactions (in millions of dollars)

Transaction #1		
Cash	1,625	
Common Stock		250
Additional Paid-in Capital		1,375
Transaction #2		
Fixtures	540	
Cash		540
Transaction #3		
Cash	400	
Notes Payable		400

Exhibit 3.7
T-Accounts for BHT's
Financing and Investing
Transactions (in millions of
dollars)

Cash				Fixtures		
Bal.	0			Bal.	0	
(1)	1,625	540	(2)	(2)	540	
(3)	400			Bal.	540	
Bal.	1,485					

Notes Payable		Common Stock	
	Bal. 0		Bal. 0
	400 (3)		250 (1)
	Bal. 400		Bal. 250

Additional Paid-In Capital	
	Bal. 0
	1,375 (1)
	Bal. 1,375

BHT's issuance of stock by showing an increase in BHT's Cash (debit to Cash) and increases in both Common Stock and Additional Paid-in Capital (credits to those accounts). The journal entry for Transaction 2 reflects an increase in assets (Fixtures) by a debit to Fixtures and a decrease in Cash by a credit to Cash. Finally, the journal entry for Transaction 3 shows an increase in Cash and an increase in Notes Payable by a debit to Cash and a credit to Notes Payable, respectively.

As Exhibit 3.7 shows, each T-account includes the sum of all transactions affecting the account to date. The beginning balances in the accounts are zero as the company just started business at the beginning of this period. Finally, note that the sum of the debit balances equals the sum of the credit balances.

Observe that the three investing and financing transactions had no effect on the retained earnings account because none of them involved the generation of revenues or concurrent expenses. Earlier in the chapter, we mentioned the notion of permanent and nominal accounts. However, no nominal accounts have been affected by transactions thus far.

Now that we've recorded the journal entries and posted them to the ledger (T-accounts), we can use this information to construct the financial statements.

CONSTRUCTING THE FINANCIAL STATEMENTS

Exhibit 3.8 shows BHT's Balance Sheet as of 12/31/20X0, summarizing the financial statement position of the firm. The balance sheet omits the beginning of the period, because the balances are all zero. Further, we don't need to prepare an income statement, as none of the initial three transactions produced revenue or expenses.

Exhibit 3.9 shows BHT's Statement of Cash Flows for the month ended 12/31/20X0. The statement indicates that the firm has not yet produced any cash flows from operating activities. Also, note that the total change in cash equals

Exhibit 3.8
Biohealth, Inc. (BHT) Balance
Sheet (in millions) as of
12/31/20X0

Assets	
Current Assets:	
Cash	$1,485
Property, Plant, and Equipment:	
Fixtures	540
Total Assets	$2,025
Liabilities and Stockholder's Equity	
Liabilities:	
Notes Payable	$ 400
Total Liabilities	400
Stockholders' Equity	
Common Stock	250
Additional Paid in Capital	1,375
Retained Earnings	0
Total Stockholders' Equity	$1,625
Total Liabilities and Stockholders' Equity	$2,025

Exhibit 3.9
Biohealth, Inc. (BHT)
Statement of Cash Flows (in
millions) for the Month
Ending 12/31/20X0

Cash Flow from Investing Activities	
Purchase Fixtures	($540)
Cash Flow from Financing Activities	
Proceeds from Issuance of Common Stock	1,625
Proceeds from Loan	400
Total Cash from Financing Activities	2,025
Net Change in Cash	$1,485
Cash Balance 12/20/20X0	0
Cash Balance 12/31/20X0	$1,485

the cash balance at the end of 12/31/20X0, because the company started with no cash on hand. Finally, the beginning cash balance is as of 12/20/20X0, the date the company formed. Normally, in a month-ending statement, the date would have been 12/1/20X0.

ANALYSIS OF OPERATING ACTIVITIES

Now that we've examined BHT's initial financing and investing activities, let's next look at a series of transactions occurring in BHT's first year of operation, starting on 1/1/20X1. The following events occurred during 20X1 (all figures are in millions of dollars).

4. BHT purchased inventory costing $34,340 on account.

5. BHT sold goods for $35,724 on account.

6. The cost of the inventory sold was $30,420.

7. BHT received $33,260 in customer payments on accounts receivable.

8. BHT paid $29,200 on its accounts payable.

9. BHT paid $4,800 to lease warehouse space for inventory storage for the year and for other miscellaneous selling and administrative costs.

10. Depreciation expense on the fixtures was $60 ($540/9 years).

11. BHT paid interest on the note payable of $28.

12. BHT declared and paid dividends of $150.

Most of these transactions are operating transactions because they relate to BHT's profit-generating activities. Operating transactions can involve revenue and expense accounts (nominal accounts), but they may also involve only asset or liability accounts. For example, Inventory and Accounts Payable accounts are affected when a company buys inventory on credit. While this acquisition of inventory might be viewed as an investing activity, accounting standards classify it as operating because the company holds the inventory for resale in the short term. We classify assets such as Accounts Receivable, Inventory, and Prepaid Expenses as operating assets in part because they are short-term or current in nature, and in part because they relate to the operating cycle of the business. In contrast, we do not regard marketable securities as operating assets.

Recall from Chapter 2 that classification as a current asset generally means that we expect the asset to be converted into cash or consumed within one year or within one operating cycle of the business, whichever is longer. Similarly, obligations such as accounts payable and other short-term payables are considered operating liabilities in part because they will be paid in less than one year (current liabilities) and in part because they relate to operating activities. However, debt may also be classified as current if it is to be repaid within a year. Thus, some but not all changes in various current assets and current liabilities are considered to be operating transactions.

Before examining how we recognize these operating transactions in the accounting system, we need to first discuss revenues and expenses in more detail.

Revenues and Expenses

Revenues reflect the sales value of goods or services sold by an enterprise. *Expenses* are the costs related to generating revenue, such as the cost of inventory sold and employee wages. Recall that net income is the difference between revenues and expenses. The cumulative amount of net income, minus dividends paid to shareholders over all accounting periods to date, appears on the balance sheet in the form of retained earnings. Exhibit 3.10 shows the changes of Retained Earnings in the balance sheet.

While we could immediately proceed to talk about the nominal accounts (revenue and expense accounts) and how to incorporate them into our entries,

Exhibit 3.10
Retained Earnings Flow
through the Balance Sheet

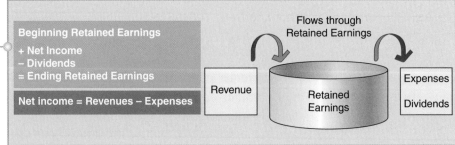

Net income = Revenues − Expenses

Beginning Retained Earnings
+ Net Income
− Dividends
= Ending Retained Earnings

Summary Impact of Operating Activities on the Accounting Equation

Transaction #– explanation	Cash	AR	Inventory	PPE	(AD)	=	AP	NP	CS CS	PIC PIC	Revenue − Expenses
			Assets			=	Liabilities		CS	PIC	Retained Earnings
Balance 12/31/20X0	1,485			540		=		400	250	1,375	
4. Purchase inventory			34,340			=	34,340				
5. Sales revenue		35,724				=					35,724
6. Cost of sales			(30,420)			=					(30,420)
7. Cash collection	33,260	(33,260)				=					
8. Payment for inventory	(29,200)					=	(29,200)				
9. S&A expenses	(4,800)					=					(4,800)
10. Depreciation expense					(60)	=					(60)
11. Interest expense	(28)					=					(28)
12. Dividend paid	(150)					=					(150)
Balance 12/31/20X1	567	2,464	3,920	540	(60)	=	5,140	400	250	1,375	266

Exhibit 3.11
Impact of BHT's Operating
Transactions on the Balance
Sheet

we take a two-step approach to analyzing operating transactions. In the section that follows, we will focus our attention on the permanent accounts as portrayed in the accounting equation to examine BHT's operating transactions. We will, therefore, portray revenue and expense events in terms of their (ultimate) impact on the Retained Earnings account (a permanent account) on the balance sheet. Accordingly, we treat revenues as direct increases (credits) to retained earnings and expenses as direct decreases (debits) to retained earnings as shown in Exhibit 3.11. It is important that you understand the ultimate effects on the permanent accounts, and it is often easier to focus on this effect first before we look more closely at nominal accounts. Following the accounting equation analysis of the transactions, we will present a more in-depth discussion of the nominal accounts and then illustrate the same transactions using journal entries and T-accounts, including the nominal accounts. If you prefer to consider the balance sheet equation effects and the journal entries simultaneously, then prior to reading about the transactions that follow, skip ahead to the section called "Nominal Accounts Revisited" and read about nominal accounts. You can then simultaneously follow the accounting equation effects in Exhibit 3.11 as well as the journal entry effects in Exhibit 3.15.

Using the Accounting Equation to Analyze Operating Activities

Exhibit 3.11 summarizes the effects of Transactions 4 through 12 using the accounting equation. We use the following abbreviations for the balance sheet accounts: AR, Accounts Receivable; PPE, Property, Plant, and Equipment; AD, Accumulated Depreciation; AP, Accounts Payable; NP, Notes Payable; CS, Common Stock; PIC, Paid-In Capital; and RE, Retained Earnings.

Purchasing Inventory on Account (Transaction 4)

Transaction 4 involves the credit (on account) purchase of inventory for resale. We consider this an operating activity because BHT expects to sell the inventory during the upcoming year for a price that exceeds its cost, generating profit for the company. The purchase is "on account," meaning that BHT pays for the inventory after its purchase. The result is that BHT has a liability, Accounts Payable, for the cost of the inventory purchased. The impact on the accounting equation is as follows:

4. Purchase of inventory on account

Assets					=	Liabilities		Stockholders' Equity		
Cash	AR	Inventory	PPE	(AD)	=	AP	NP	CS	PIC	RE
		34,340			=	34,340				

Purchasing inventory does not constitute an expense. The inventory holds future value and is owned by the firm. Therefore, it should be recorded as an asset. The cost of purchasing inventory eventually becomes an expense (cost of goods sold) at the time that BHT sells the inventory to a customer, that is, at the point when the firm no longer owns it (see Transactions 5 and 6).

Selling Inventory on Account (Transaction 5)

Transaction 5 involves the sale of inventory on account. "On account," in this context means that BHT did not collect cash at the time of the sale but expects to do so at some future date. The amount owed to BHT, accounts receivable, represents an asset. This new asset for BHT stockholders results in an increase in stockholders' equity. Further, BHT sells its inventory for more than its cost. We refer to the gross sales value of inventory sold as **sales revenue.** At the same time, the stockholders lost an existing asset (inventory). The cost of inventory sold is accounted for separately as an expense called **cost of goods sold** (see Transaction 6, which follows). The difference between the gross sales value of the inventory (sales revenue) and its cost (cost of goods sold) is **gross profit** to BHT. The gross profit amount affects BHT's stockholders' equity in the form of an increase in retained earnings. The impact of the sales revenue itself on the accounting equation is as follows:

5. Recognize sales revenue for sales on account

		Assets			=	Liabilities			Stockholders' Equity	
Cash	AR	Inventory	PPE	(AD)	=	AP	NP	CS	PIC	RE
	35,724				=					35,724

The recognition of revenues can often be a source of confusion and, potentially, manipulation. In some cases companies improperly recognize revenues and the SEC can force them to restate their earnings. Such an example is that of Lucent Technologies, as illustrated in Exhibit 3.12.

Recognizing Cost of Goods Sold (Transaction 6)

As previously mentioned, cost of goods sold is an expense related to generating the revenues recorded in Transaction 5. By accounting convention, a firm reports this expense in the same period as the related revenue. In this way, cost of goods sold is matched with the related revenue. An asset (inventory) was given up, so stockholders' equity also decreases. Specifically, this transaction decreases retained earnings. The impact on the accounting equation is shown as follows:

6. Recognize cost of goods sold

		Assets			=	Liabilities			Stockholders' Equity	
Cash	AR	Inventory	PPE	(AD)	=	AP	NP	CS	PIC	RE
		(30,420)			=					(30,420)

Exhibit 3.12

THE REAL WORLD

Lucent Technologies

In February 2001, Lucent Technologies, Inc. announced its cooperation with the SEC in a probe of the company's accounting practices. On November 21, 2000, Lucent had indicated that $125 million in improperly booked sales could reduce its results for the fourth quarter ended September 30, 2000. The announcement resulted in a 16 percent drop in the company's stock value. After an internal review, Lucent announced on December 21, 2000, that it was reducing previously reported fourth-quarter revenues by $679 million to $8.7 billion.

The fact that firms generally recognize revenues at the time of sale, rather than at the time of collection, could have important implications for the valuation of companies. Some companies may erroneously or fraudulently recognize sales by an accounting entry even when no legitimate sale has taken place. To minimize this type of opportunistic behavior, a firm's financial records are subject to examination by external auditors, internal control systems, and oversight by external members of a firm's board of directors. Further, legal sanctions apply to those firms that are found to have engaged in such behavior. However, as the Lucent example illustrates, none of these mechanisms are perfect.

Observe that neither the revenue or expense recognition for these transactions affected cash, due to accrual accounting. As we explain fully in Chapter 4, under this concept, a firm recognizes revenues when they have been earned. In this case, revenue recognition occurs when the inventory is delivered to the buyer and the firm can reasonably expect to collect cash in the future, not necessarily when BHT receives the cash. Similarly, a firm recognizes expenses not when it pays out cash, but when the cost (expenditure) can be matched to revenues (implying there is no future benefit to be received). Thus, a firm records inventory as assets upon purchase, and then records the cost of inventory sold as an expense when revenue is earned.

While some firms can calculate the cost of goods sold at the time of sale, many firms determine the cost of goods sold at the end of the period through the following calculation:

> Cost of Goods Sold Calculation:
>
> Cost of Goods Sold = Cost of Beginning Inventory + Purchases − Cost of Ending Inventory

Collecting Receivables (Transaction 7)

Transaction 7 indicates the collection of cash for sales on account. This transaction involves an exchange of one type of an asset (accounts receivable) for another (cash), and therefore has no effect on retained earnings. BHT already recognized the revenue from the sale when the sale took place.

7. Recognize collection of cash from past sales

	Assets				=	Liabilities		Stockholders' Equity		
Cash	AR	Inventory	PPE	(AD)	=	AP	NP	CS	PIC	RE
33,260	(33,260)				=					

Paying Accounts Payable (Transaction 8)

Transaction 8 records the payment for the inventory and other items that BHT purchased on account during the year.

8. Record payments on account

	Assets				=	Liabilities		Stockholders' Equity		
Cash	AR	Inventory	PPE	(AD)	=	AP	NP	CS	PIC	RE
(29,200)					=	(29,200)				

Paying Selling and Administrative Costs (Transaction 9)

Transaction 9 involves the payment of cash for rent and other selling and administrative expenses that BHT incurred during the year. Because these cash expenditures do not result in assets with future value, these costs immediately become expenses. These expenses affect the accounting equation as follows:

9. Payment of cash for rent and selling and administrative expenses

Assets					=	Liabilities			Stockholders' Equity	
Cash	AR	Inventory	PPE	(AD)	=	AP	NP	CS	PIC	RE
(4,800)					=					(4,800)

Depreciating Fixtures (Transaction 10)

When a firm purchases plant and equipment, it records these items as assets because they provide future benefits to the firm. Plant and equipment contribute to the production of products or services that can be sold in later periods. This productive capacity of plant and equipment, however, diminishes over time. As a result, for accounting purposes, the costs incurred in acquiring the plant and equipment should be expensed over the life of the plant and equipment. Specifically, accounting standards require that the costs incurred should be allocated to expense over the *useful life* of the asset using a rational and systematic method. We call these methods **depreciation methods,** and the expense that results **depreciation expense.** GAAP allows several depreciation methods, which we'll discuss in more detail in Chapter 9. These methods require several estimates. Exhibit 3.13 illustrates the disclosure made by Hasbro, Inc. regarding the use of estimates.

For example, the *straight-line depreciation* method assumes an equal amount of the cost of the asset is to be used up each year of its useful life. The method also factors in the possibility that the asset has some remaining estimated value

Exhibit 3.13
Hasbro, Inc. and Subsidiaries

THE REAL WORLD

Hasbro, Inc.

Notes to Consolidated Financial Statements

(1) Summary of Significant Accounting Policies

Preparation of Financial Statements

The preparation of financial statements in conformity with generally accepted accounting principles requires management to make estimates and assumptions that affect the amounts reported in the financial statements and notes thereto. Actual results could differ from those estimates.

Within GAAP, managers must make some significant estimates, such as the useful life and salvage value of a firm's property, plant, and equipment. Hasbro's disclosure reminds its financial statement readers of the estimates that management makes and the impact of these estimates on those statements.

at the end of its useful life, referred to as *salvage value*. A firm using this method therefore calculates depreciation expense dividing the original cost, less the salvage value, by the number of years of useful life. If BHT uses the straight-line method, with fixtures having a useful life of 9 years and a zero salvage value, its depreciation expense for the fixtures is [(Original Cost − Salvage)/Useful Life = ($540 − 0)/9 years = $60 million/year].

A firm records depreciation by an entry to Depreciation Expense (for the moment, retained earnings) and an entry to an account called Accumulated Depreciation. Accumulated Depreciation is a contra-asset account. **Contra-asset accounts** have credit balances and are an offset to a related asset account. In this case, the original cost of the fixtures is shown in the PP&E account. The entry shows Accumulated Depreciation as a direct reduction of this account. BHT reports the contra-asset on the balance sheet as a subtraction from the related asset account. The impact of recording depreciation on the accounting equation is shown as follows:

> The use of the accumulated depreciation account is helpful for analysis because it allows the financial statement user to observe the original cost of an asset from the asset account and then, using the information in the accumulated depreciation account, infer such information as the age of plant and equipment and how long before they may need to be replaced.

10. Recognition of depreciation expense

		Assets			=	Liabilities		Stockholders' Equity		
Cash	AR	Inventory	PPE	(AD)	=	AP	NP	CS	PIC	RE
				(60)	=					(60)

We show the Accumulated Depreciation account as a negative amount. On the balance sheet, after the first year's depreciation is recorded, the asset and related accumulated depreciation accounts for fixtures would appear on the balance sheet as follows:

Fixtures	$540
Less	
Accumulated depreciation	(60)
Net fixtures	$480

At the end of the second year, the accumulated depreciation account would show that two years of depreciation had been recognized, and fixtures and related accumulated depreciation on the balance sheet would appear as:

Fixtures	$540
Less	
Accumulated depreciation	(120)
Net Fixtures	$420

By keeping the accumulated depreciation separate from the original cost of the fixtures, the financial statement reader can estimate both how close assets are to being fully depreciated and the years remaining in the asset's estimated useful life. This information may be helpful predict when a firm will need to replace or upgrade equipment. For example, suppose a company discloses that its depreciation expense is $60 million, the asset is being depreciated using the straight-line method over nine years, and its accumulated depreciation is $300. We can then estimate that the asset's remaining useful life is 4 years (9 − (300/60) = 4). If a company does not list accumulated depreciation on the balance sheet, but instead shows property, plant, and equipment net of accumulated depreciation, a breakdown between the asset and related accumulated depreciation accounts is often provided in the firm's footnotes to the financial statements.

Paying Interest (Transaction 11)

When a firm borrows funds, it must pay for the use of the funds in the form of interest payments. In this case, we assume that the loan has simple interest at a rate of 7 percent per annum and is paid in cash. Thus, the interest on the loan is $28 million ($400 × .07) and affects the accounting equation as follows:

11. Payment of interest expense

	Assets				=	Liabilities		Stockholders' Equity		
Cash	AR	Inventory	PPE	(AD)	=	AP	NP	CS	PIC	RE
(28)					=					(28)

While we treat interest as an operating activity, others argue that interest expense should be considered a financing activity because it relates to borrowing funds. In fact, we employ this view in Chapter 14 when we consider valuing a firm. However, the FASB states that interest should be classified as an operating activity for cash flow purposes.

Dividends (Transaction 12)

Dividends return a certain amount of the profits to owners in the form of cash. A company's Board of Directors frequently declares dividends on a quarterly basis. However, a firm usually does not pay dividends at the date they are declared. Instead, a firm often pays them within the month following declaration. To deal with this delay, a firm creates a new liability, Dividends Payable. Dividends are not an expense of doing business and are not reported on the income statement. However, they do directly reduce retained earnings, as the owners are withdrawing a part of their profits from the firm. We will discuss dividends in more detail later in the text. Here, however, for simplicity, we assume that BHT pays dividends immediately in cash.

12. Declaration of dividends

	Assets				=	Liabilities		Stockholders' Equity		
Cash	AR	Inventory	PPE	(AD)	=	AP	NP	CS	PIC	RE
(150)					=					(150)

Now that we've examined how BHT's operating transactions affected the accounting equation, we're ready to look at the respective journal entries and T-accounting. However, before we can do that we need to provide more detail of the accounts used to record the firm's profit-measurement activities. In other words, we need to discuss nominal accounts.

Nominal Accounts Revisited

Recall that stockholders' equity consists of contributed capital and retained earnings. To record changes in retained earnings that result from a firm's operating activities, a firm uses *nominal accounts,* separate revenue and expense accounts, whose balances are transferred to retained earnings at the end of the accounting period. As mentioned earlier, the idea is to measure operating performance one period at a time, as retained earnings reflects *cumulative* revenues and expenses over all accounting periods. By using these nominal accounts, a firm can better analyze the inflows and outflows pertaining to the operating activities of the company for the accounting period just completed.

A firm uses separate accounts for each category of revenue and expense. A firm can then more easily determine the amounts to be included in the various line items on its income statement. Consistent with the usual effects of revenues increasing retained earnings and expenses decreasing retained earnings, revenues are increased by credits, while expenses are increased by debits. Accordingly, revenue accounts will normally have a credit balance, and expense accounts will normally have a debit balance. T-accounts for revenues and expenses are shown below:

T-Accounts for Revenues and Expenses

Revenues		Expenses	
Debits Decrease	Credits Increase	Debits Increase	Credits Decrease

Exhibit 3.14 summarizes the normal balance in each type of account and indicates how the account is affected by debit (left) and credit (right) entries.

With this improved understanding of nominal accounts, we're ready to resume analyzing BHT's operating transactions, now by using journal entries and T-accounts.

Exhibit 3.14
Normal Account Balances and
Debit and Credit Effects on
Accounts

Account Type	Normal Balance	Debit Entries	Credit Entries
Asset	Debit	Increase	Decrease
Liability	Credit	Decrease	Increase
Common Stock	Credit	Decrease	Increase
Paid-in-Capital	Credit	Decrease	Increase
Retained Earnings	Credit	Decrease	Increase
Revenue	Credit	Decrease	Increase
Expense	Debit	Increase	Decrease

Using Journal Entries and T-Accounts to Record Transactions

We show the journal entries and T-accounts for Transactions 4 through 12 in Exhibits 3.15 and 3.16, respectively. Note in Exhibit 3.16 that the beginning balances at the start of 20X1 carry forward from the end of the previous year (20X0). Further, note that the retained earnings account does not include entries other than the dividends declared at this point. This is because the nominal accounts, revenue and expense, have not yet been closed. These accounts will be closed and their balances moved to retained earnings after preparing the income statement. (We'll provide more details on the closing process in the next section.)

Exhibit 3.15
Journal Entries for Operating
Transactions

Transaction #4		
Inventory	34,340	
Accounts Payable		34,340
Transaction #5		
Accounts Receivable	35,724	
Sales		35,724
Transaction #6		
Cost of Sales	30,420	
Inventory		30,420
Transaction #7		
Cash	33,260	
Accounts Receivable		33,260
Transaction #8		
Accounts Payable	29,200	
Cash		29,200
Transaction #9		
S&A Expenses	4,800	
Cash		4,800
Transaction #10		
Depreciation Expense	60	
Accumulated Depreciation		60
Transaction #11		
Interest Expense	28	
Cash		28
Transaction #12		
Retained Earnings	150	
Cash		150

Exhibit 3.16
Added Operating Transactions
to BHT's T-Accounts

Cash			Account Receivable			Inventory		
Bal. 1,485			Bal. 0			Bal. 0		
	29,200 (8)		(5) 35,724			(4) 34,340	30,420 (6)	
(7) 33,260	4,800 (9)			33,260 (7)				
	28 (11)							
	150 (12)							
Bal. 567			Bal. 2,464			Bal. 3,920		

Fixtures			Accumulated Depreciation Fixtures			Note Payable		
Bal. 540				Bal. 0			Bal. 400	
				60 (10)				
				Bal. 60				

Account Payable			Capital Stock			Paid-in Capital		
	Bal. 0			Bal. 250			Bal. 1,375	
(8) 29,200	34,340 (4)							
	Bal. 5,140							

Retained Earnings			Sales Revenue			Cost of Sales		
	Bal. 0			Bal. 0		Bal. 0		
(12) 150				35,724 (5)		(6) 30,420		
				Bal. 35,724		Bal. 30,420		

S&A Expense			Depreciation Expense			Interest Expense		
Bal. 0			Bal. 0			Bal. 0		
(9) 4,800			(10) 60			(11) 28		
Bal. 4,800			Bal. 60			Bal. 28		

Note: Beginning account balances include the financing and investing activities prior to the start of 20X1.

CONSTRUCTING THE FINANCIAL STATEMENTS

Exhibit 3.17 shows a balance sheet for 12/31/20X1 compared to 12/31/20X0. Although total assets have dramatically increased, cash has decreased. Note also that the ending balance in retained earnings is determined using the closing entries discussed in the next section. An income statement and statement of cash flows follow in Exhibits 3.18 and 3.19, respectively. BHT provides an income statement only for the year ending 12/31/20X1, as the firm did not begin operations during 20X0. BHT provides cash flow statements for 20X0 and 20X1 for comparative purposes. As briefly discussed in Chapter 2, BHT, like most firms, prepares the cash flow statement using the *indirect approach* (we'll cover this in more depth in Chapter 5). That is, BHT determines its cash from operations

Exhibit 3.17
Balance Sheet for Biohealth, Inc. (BHT)

	As of 12/31/20X1	As of 12/31/20X0
Assets		
Current Assets:		
Cash	$ 567	$1,485
Accounts Receivable	2,464	0
Inventory	3,920	0
Total Current Assets	6,951	1,485
Property, Plant, and Equipment (Fixtures)	540	540
Less: Accumulated Depreciation	(60)	0
Net Property Plant and Equipment	480	540
Total Assets	$7,431	$2,025
Liabilities and Stockholders' Equity		
Liabilities:		
Current Liabilities:		
Accounts Payable	$5,140	$ 0
Long-Term Debt:		
Notes Payable	400	400
Total Liabilities	5,540	400
Stockholders' Equity		
Common Stock	250	250
Additional Paid-In Capital	1,375	1,375
Retained Earnings	266	0
Total Stockholders' Equity	1,891	1,625
Total Liabilities and Stockholders' Equity	$7,431	$2,025

Exhibit 3.18
Income Statement for Biohealth, Inc. (BHT)

	Year Ending 12/31/20X1
Sales Revenue	$35,724
Less: Cost of Goods Sold	(30,420)
Gross Profit	5,304
Selling and Administrative Expenses	(4,800)
Depreciation Expense	(60)
Interest Expense	(28)
Net Income	$ 416
Earnings per Share[2]	$ 1.66

[2]Earnings per share is the amount of earnings per share of common stock outstanding. There are some specific requirements regarding how this is computed that will be discussed later. However, in this case it is simply net income/shares of common stock outstanding, or $416,000,000/250,000,000.

	Year Ending 12/31/20X1	Year Ending 12/31/20X0
Cash from Operations:		
Net Income	$416	$ 0
Add: Noncash Expenses		
Depreciation	60	0
Less: Changes in Current Assets and Current Liabilities:		
Increase in Accounts Receivable	(2,464)	0
Increase in Inventory	(3,920)	0
Increase in Accounts Payable	5,140	0
Total Cash from Operations	(768)	0
Cash from Investing		
Purchase Fixtures	0	(540)
Total Cash from Investing	0	(540)
Cash from Financing		
Borrow on Long-Term Note	0	400
Dividend Payments	(150)	
Issue Stock	0	1,625
Total Cash from Financing	(150)	2,025
Total Change in Cash	($918)	$1,485

Exhibit 3.19
Statement of Cash Flows for the Years Ending 20X1 and 20X0 Biohealth, Inc. (BHT)

starting with net income and then adjusting for noncash operating transactions. Note that the activities in 20X0 were limited to financing and investing activities, as no BHT operations occurred during this start-up period.

The cash flow statement for 20X1 illustrates why cash decreased even though the company earned a profit. Although dividends somewhat reduced cash during the period, operations proved to be the primary driver of the decline in cash, as it had a negative cash flow of $768. This decrease was caused primarily by the increase in accounts receivable and inventory. Increasing inventory requires cash to buy or make the inventory, and the increase in accounts receivable reflects uncollected revenues, resulting in less cash. Offsetting this was the positive effect of the increase in accounts payable during the period. When a company buys things on credit (thereby increasing accounts payable), it conserves cash. Finally, depreciation also produced a minor effect. Depreciation expense is added back to net income. Although it is an expense and it decreases net income, it does not use cash.

CLOSING ENTRIES

After preparing the income statement, the balances in the temporary revenue and expense accounts must be transferred to the retained earnings account (a permanent account). This will reset the balance in each temporary account to zero, to start the next accounting period. For example, the accounting period for BHT was from 1/1/20X1 through 12/31/20X1. The entries that accomplish the transfer of balances from the revenue and expense accounts to retained earnings are called **closing entries.** We'll distinguish closing entries in this text by lettering the entries rather than numbering them.

Sometimes companies use a single temporary account, the **income summary account,** to accumulate balances from all the income statement accounts. Firms often find it useful to summarize the net of the revenues and expenses during the closing process to calculate taxes. Firms use the income summary account only during the closing process; it carries a zero balance at all other times. The balances from all the individual revenue and expense accounts are closed to this summary account. The balance in the income summary account is then closed to retained earnings. Exhibit 3.20 shows the journal entries and T-accounts to close the revenue and expense accounts for BHT. After making these closing entries, the balances in the revenues, expenses, and income summary accounts return to zero.

Exhibit 3.20
Closing Entries for BHT Revenue and Expense Accounts Period Ended 12/31/20X1

Journal Entries

Account Titles	Debit	Credit
a. Sales Revenue	35,724	
Income Summary		35,724
b. Income Summary	35,308	
Cost of Sales		30,420
S&A Expenses		4,800
Depreciation Expense		60
Interest Expense		28
c. Income Summary	416	
Retained Earnings		416

Closing Entries T-Accounts

Sales Revenue			Cost of Sales			S&A Expenses		
	Bal. 35,724		Bal. 30,420			Bal. 4,800		
(a) 35, 724				30,420 (b)			4,800 (b)	
	Bal. 0		Bal. 0			Bal. 0		

Depreciation Expense			Interest Expense			Retained Earnings		
Bal. 60			Bal. 28				Bal. 0	
	60 (b)			(28) (b)		(12) 150	416 (c)	
Bal. 0			Bal. 0				Bal. 266	

Income Summary		
	Bal. 0	
(b) 35,308	35,724 (a)	
(c) 416		
	Bal. 0	

Finally, just prior to making closing entries, a firm typically makes **adjusting entries.** Adjusting entries improve the accuracy of firm's financial statements, by enabling it to meet the accrual concept. For example, BHT's recording of depreciation is one type of adjusting entry. Other adjusting entries include the recognition of interest expense that has not been paid and wages that have been incurred but not paid. We'll discuss adjusting entries again in Chapter 4 and Appendix A covers adjusting entries in more detail.

THE ACCOUNTING CYCLE

The accounting cycle refers to the series of steps in the accounting process, which a firm repeats each time it prepares financial statements. While accounting systems may differ from very simple systems in a sole proprietorship, to multibillion-dollar systems in large companies, the process remains essentially the same:

1. *Identify transactions.* As we indicated earlier, some economic events are not recognized in accounting as transactions. For example, if Dell signed a contract with another company to furnish a large number of computers to the company over a period of time, this would be an event of economic consequence to Dell, but it would not be recorded as an accounting transaction.

2. *Journalize transactions.* A journal entry provides a summary of a particular event's impact on assets, liabilities, and stockholders' equity.

3. *Post journal entries to ledger accounts.* In this book, we use T-accounts to represent ledgers. In real accounting systems, ledger accounts can take many forms, but the key to thinking about the ledger is to realize that it carries forward all of the transactions that affect a particular account. In the case of permanent accounts as seen on the balance sheet (assets, liabilities, and various stockholders' equity accounts), the balances carry-forward over accounting periods. For example, the balance in accounts receivable at the end of 20X0 is the same as the balance at the beginning of 20X1. In contrast, the nominal or temporary accounts (revenues and expenses) will start each accounting period with a zero balance.

4. *Prepare period-end adjusting entries and then post them to ledger accounts.* An example would be recording depreciation.

5. *Prepare the income statement.*

6. *Close nominal accounts to retained earnings.*

7. *Prepare the balance sheet and cash flow statement.*

One final issue with regard to the accounting cycle is the frequency with which financial statements should be prepared. On one hand, a firm should prepare financial statements as often as necessary to provide timely information to management, stockholders, creditors, and others with an interest in the firm. On the other hand, a firm must balance the benefits of having up-to-date information with the cost of preparing the statements. In some businesses, management may need up-to-date information, in which case daily reports may be necessary. This is becoming more common as the cost of compiling timely information continues to decrease. In other businesses, a monthly statement may be sufficient.

Regardless of what time period a firm selects, firms will follow the same procedures as outlined in this chapter.

Companies whose stock is traded on a public exchange and who fall under the authority of the SEC are required to file financial statements quarterly, as well as on an annual basis. The frequency with which a firm prepares its financial statements is sometimes expressed in terms of how often the firm closes its books. If it closes its books monthly, the accounting cycle for the firm is one month, and the nominal (temporary) accounts are reset on a monthly basis. However, although a company may close its books more frequently than at year-end, annual financial statements require that revenues and expenses be accumulated over the entire year. Thus, firms do interim closings only for purposes of preparing interim statements.

ANALYZING FINANCIAL STATEMENTS

Understanding the accounting cycle will help you to use the information in the financial statements more effectively. To illustrate, as an investor or potential investor, you can obtain financial statements, but not information about the individual transactions that gave rise to those statements. However, by understanding the accounting process, you may be able to deduce some of the major transactions by analyzing the financial statements.

Say you looked at Exhibits 3.17, 3.18, and 3.19 without knowing BHT's transactions. By understanding the accounting process, you would be able to observe the following:

- Cash has declined for the year despite the fact that BHT reported a profit.
- The balance sheet shows an increase in Accounts Receivable, suggesting that cash collection from sales was less than the revenue recognized.
- The balance sheet shows an increase in Inventory, indicating that the company is purchasing more inventory than it is selling.
- Accounts Payable increased during the year, suggesting that the company is purchasing more inventory than it is paying to suppliers.

As BHT formed in 20X0, we would not be surprised by these findings, as they are typical of a new business. However, in an established company, significant changes in balance sheet accounts may signal information about the company's future cash flows. For example, if a company records large amounts of sales on account, and accounts receivable increases more rapidly than the sales, the company may not be collecting its accounts receivable on a timely basis or it may have relaxed its credit policies. This may signal future cash flow problems (defaults by customers). Similarly, increasing inventory coupled with decreasing (or less rapidly) increasing sales may signal that a company is having difficulty selling its inventory. In Chapter 6, we continue to consider how to assess past performance based on the information contained in financial statements, as well as to predict future performance.

As you progress through this text, you will appreciate more fully the power of the information conveyed about a company in its financial statements and the value to you of understanding the concepts underlying financial statement construction. Of particular importance is predicting transactions' impact on each of the major financial statements. For example, as a manager, you might consider generating additional sales by providing a more liberal credit policy (e.g., allowing customers with weaker credit to purchase goods on account). With a good knowledge of accounting, you could anticipate the effects of such a change in credit policies on the financial statements. In this particular case, you would likely see increased sales on the income statement, coupled with increased accounts receivable because weaker credit customers might pay more slowly or not at all. You might also see cash flows decline even if sales increased. This could occur due to a combination of two factors, slower sales collections and a need to purchase and pay for more inventory to sell to customers who have not yet paid. Thus, this business decision would impact all of the major financial statements.

SUMMARY AND TRANSITION

This chapter provided an overview of the accounting process used to generate financial statements. Understanding the framework of accounting allows you to readily determine the impact of economic events on the financial statements. This knowledge will allow you as a manager or investor to make sound decisions using information generated from the accounting process.

The accounting process contains two basic concepts: duality and the nominal (temporary) account. The concept of duality portrays accounting events in terms of the dual effects on the resources of the firm (its assets), the claims of creditors (its liabilities), and the owners' wealth (stockholders' equity). The duality concept is apparent in the accounting equation and the requirements that debits equal credits in the accounting representation of each transaction. Nominal accounts are used to describe changes in stockholders' equity that result from operating activities, principally revenues and expenses.

Understanding the accounting process is necessary to understanding the information conveyed in the financial statements that are the final product of that process. However, apart from the accounting process itself, there are many accounting choices and judgments that affect the implementation of that process and, thereby, shape the content of those statements. Chief among these are the recognition criteria which determine when an economic event should get recognized in the accounting system (such as the timing of recognizing revenues and expenses) and the valuation principles that determine the values of the assets and liabilities of the firm that meet the recognition criteria. These choices and judgments are addressed in the chapters that follow.

END OF CHAPTER MATERIAL

KEY TERMS

Additional Paid-In Capital	Contra-Asset Account
Adjusting Entries	Contributed Capital
Closing Entries	Cost of Goods Sold

Credits

Debits

Depreciation Expense

Depreciation Methods

Double-Entry Accounting System

Entry

Journal

Journal Entry

Ledger

Nominal Accounts

Par Value

Permanent Accounts

Retained Earnings

Sales Revenue

Stated Value

Summary Account

T-Account

Temporary Accounts

Transactions

ASSIGNMENT MATERIAL

REVIEW QUESTIONS

1. Explain what double-entry accounting means and provide an example.
2. Define an asset, according to GAAP.
3. Define a liability, according to GAAP.
4. Describe what owners' equity represents.
5. Discuss how retained earnings changes over time.
6. What is a permanent account?
7. What is a nominal or temporary account?
8. What is the proper form for a journal entry?
9. What is a ledger?
10. What is depreciation?
11. How is straight-line depreciation calculated?
12. What is a contra-asset account and how is it used in the context of depreciation?
13. "Expense accounts have debit balances, and debit entries increase these accounts." Reconcile this statement with the normal effects of entries on owners' equity accounts and the resulting balances.
14. Describe the closing process.
15. Discuss why one firm might close their books monthly and another might close them weekly.

APPLYING YOUR KNOWLEDGE

15. Explain why you agree or disagree with the following statement: "Retained earnings are like money in the bank; you can always use them to pay your bills if you get into trouble."
16. Respond to each of the following statements with a true or false answer:
    a. Debits increase liability accounts.
    b. Revenues are credit entries to owners' equity.

c. Cash receipts from customers are debited to accounts receivable.

d. Dividends declared decrease cash at the date of declaration.

e. Dividends are an expense of doing business and should appear on the income statement.

f. Selling goods on account results in a credit to accounts receivable.

g. Making a payment on an account payable results in a debit to accounts payable.

17. For each of the transactions below, indicate which accounts are affected and whether they increase or decrease.

a. Issue common stock for cash.

b. Buy equipment from a supplier on credit (short term).

c. Buy inventory from a supplier partly with cash and partly on account.

d. Sell a unit of inventory to a customer on account.

e. Receive a payment from a customer on his or her account.

f. Borrow money from the bank.

g. Declare a dividend (to be paid later).

h. Pay a dividend (that was previously declared).

18. For each of the following transactions, indicate how income and cash flow are affected (increase, decrease, no effect) and by how much:

a. Issue common stock for $1,000.

b. Sell, on account, a unit of inventory for $150 that cost $115. The unit is already in inventory.

c. Purchase equipment for $500 in cash.

d. Depreciate plant and equipment by $300.

e. Purchase a unit of inventory, on account, for $100.

f. Make a payment on accounts payable for $200.

g. Receive a payment from a customer for $75 on his or her account.

h. Declare a dividend for $400.

i. Pay a dividend for $400.

19. Show how each of the following transactions affects the balance sheet equation:

a. Borrow $1,500 from the bank.

b. Buy land for $20,000 in cash.

c. Issue common stock for $5,000. The par value of the stock is $1,500.

d. Buy inventory costing $3,000 on account.

e. Sell inventory costing $2,500 to customers, on account, for $3,500.

f. Make a payment of $250 to the electric company for power used during the current period.

g. Declare a dividend of $350.

h. Depreciate equipment by $500.

20. Show how each of the following transactions affects the balance sheet equation:

a. Issue common stock for $10,000. The stock has no par value attached to it.

b. Receive a payment from a customer on his or her account in the amount of $325.

c. Make a payment to the bank of $850. Of this amount, $750 represents interest and the rest is a repayment of principal.

d. Return a unit of inventory costing $200 that was damaged in shipment. You have already paid for the unit and have requested a refund from the supplier.

e. Dividends of $175 that were previously declared are paid.

f. Purchase equipment costing $1,800. You pay $600 in cash and give the supplier a note for the balance of the purchase price.

g. Sales on account of $15,000 are reported for the period.

h. A count of physical inventory at the end of the period indicates an ending balance of $575. The beginning balance was $485, and the purchases for the period were $11,500. Record the cost of goods sold.

21. For each of the following transactions, indicate how each immediately affects the balance sheet equation and what other effects there will be in the future as a result of the transaction:

a. Purchase equipment.

b. Borrow money from the bank.

c. Purchase inventory on account.

d. Sell inventory on account to customers.

e. Buy a patent for a new production process.

22. Indicate the effects of the following transactions on the balance sheet equation developed in the chapter. Assume that the fiscal year end of the firm is December 31.

a. Borrow $2,500 from the bank on 1/1/X1.

b. Pay interest on the bank loan on 12/31/X1. The interest rate is 10 percent.

c. Buy equipment on 1/1/X1 for $2,000. The equipment has an estimated useful life of five years and an estimated salvage value at the end of five years of $500.

d. Record the depreciation for the equipment as of 12/31/X1, assuming the firm uses the straight-line method.

e. Sales for the period totaled $5,500, of which $3,500 were on account. The cost of the products sold was $3,600.

f. Collections from customers on account totaled $2,800.

g. Purchases of inventory on account during 20X1 totaled $2,700.

h. Payments to suppliers totaled $2,900 during 20X1.

i. Dividends were declared and paid in the amount of $100.

23. Indicate the effects of the following transactions on the balance sheet equation developed in the chapter. Assume that the fiscal year end of the firm is December 31.

a. Issue common stock for $25,000, with a par value of $8,000.

b. Sales recorded for the period totaled $60,000, of which $25,000 were cash sales.

c. Cash collections on customer accounts totaled $37,000.

    d. Sign a contract to purchase a piece of equipment that costs $1,200, and put a downpayment of $100 on the purchase.

    e. Dividends of $1,300 are declared.

    f. Dividends of $1,150 that had previously been declared are paid.

    g. Depreciation of $3,300 was taken on the property, plant, and equipment.

    h. Purchase $31,350 of inventory on account.

    i. Inventory costing $35,795 was sold.

24. Indicate whether each of the following accounts normally has a debit or a credit balance:

    a. Accounts Receivable

    b. Accounts Payable

    c. Sales Revenue

    d. Dividends Declared

    e. Dividends Payable

    f. Depreciation Expense

    g. Common Stock (par value)

    h. Cost of Goods Sold

    i. Loan Payable

25. For each of the following accounts indicate whether the account would normally have a debit or a credit balance:

    a. Cash

    b. Accounts Payable

    c. Common Stock

    d. Sales Revenues

    e. Inventory

    f. Cost of Goods Sold

    g. Paid-In Capital

    h. Retained Earnings

    i. Accumulated Depreciation

26. For each of the following transactions construct a journal entry:

    a. Inventory costing $1,500 is purchased on account.

    b. Inventory costing $1,200 is sold on account for $1,800.

    c. Accounts receivable of $800 are collected.

    d. The firm borrows $10,000 from the bank.

    e. The firm issues common stock for $2,500 and $1,500 is considered par value.

    f. New equipment costing $3,500 is purchased with cash.

27. The T. George Company started business on 1/1/X2. Listed below are the transactions that occurred during 20X2.

    Required:

    a. Construct the journal entries to record the transactions of the T. George Company for 20X2.

b. Post the journal entries to the appropriate T-accounts.

c. Prepare a balance sheet and income statement for 20X2.

d. Prepare the closing entries for 20X2.

Transactions:

1. On 1/1/X2, the company issued 10,000 shares of common stock for $175,000. The par value of the stock is $10 per share.

2. On 1/1/X2, the company borrowed $125,000 from the bank.

3. On 1/2/X2, the company purchased (for cash) land and a building costing $200,000. The building was recently appraised at $140,000.

4. Inventory costing $100,000 was purchased on account.

5. An investment was made in Calhoun Company stock in the amount of $75,000.

6. Sales to customers totaled $190,000 in 20X2. Of these, $30,000 were cash sales.

7. Collections on accounts receivable totaled $135,000.

8. Payments to suppliers totaled $92,000 in 20X2.

9. Salaries paid to employees totaled $44,000. There were no unpaid salaries at year end.

10. A count of inventories at year end revealed $10,000 worth of inventory.

11. The building was estimated to have a useful life of 20 years and a salvage value of $20,000. The company uses straight-line depreciation.

12. The interest on the bank loan is recognized each month and is paid on the first day of the succeeding month; that is, January's interest is recognized in January and paid on February 1. The interest rate is 12 percent.

13. The investment in Calhoun Company paid dividends of $5,000 in 20X2. All of it had been received by year end.

14. Dividends of $15,000 were declared on 12/15/X2 and were scheduled to be paid on 1/10/X3.

28. The Hughes Tool Company started business on 10/1/X3. Its fiscal year runs through September 30 of the following year. Following are the transactions that occurred during fiscal year 19X4 (the year starting 10/1/X3 and ending 9/30/X4).

Required:

a. Construct the journal entries to record the transactions of the The Hughes Tool Company for fiscal year 20X4.

b. Post the journal entries to the appropriate T-accounts.

c. Prepare a balance sheet and income statement for fiscal year 20X4.

d. Prepare the closing entries for fiscal year 20X4.

Transactions:

1. On 10/1/X3, J. Hughes contributed $100,000 to start the business. Hughes is the sole proprietor of the business.

2. On 10/2/X3, Hughes borrowed $300,000 from a venture capitalist (a lender who specializes in start-up companies). The interest rate on

the loan is 11 percent. Interest is paid twice a year on March 31 and September 30.

3. On 10/3/X3, Hughes rented a building. The rental agreement was a two-year contract that called for quarterly rental payments of $20,000, payable in advance on January 1, April 1, July 1, and October 1. The first payment was made on 10/3/X3 and covers the period from October 1 to December 31.

4. On 10/3/X3, Hughes purchased equipment costing $250,000. The equipment had an estimated useful life of seven years and a salvage value of $40,000.

5. On 10/3/X3, Hughes purchased initial inventory with a cash payment of $100,000.

6. Sales during the year totaled $800,000, of which $720,000 were credit sales.

7. Collections from customers on account totaled $640,000.

8. Additional purchases of inventory during the year totaled $550,000, all on account.

9. Payments to suppliers totaled $495,000.

10. Inventory on hand at year end amounted to $115,000.

11. J. Hughes withdrew a total of $40,000 for personal expenses during the year.

12. Interest on the loan from the venture capitalist was paid at year-end, as well as $20,000 of the principal.

13. Other selling and administrative expenses totaled $90,000 for the year. Of these, $20,000 were unpaid as of year end.

29. The A.J. Smith Company started business on 1/1/X4. The company's fiscal year ends on December 31. Following are the transactions that occurred during 20X4.

Required:

a. Construct the journal entries to record the transactions of the The A.J. Smith Company for fiscal year 20X4.

b. Post the journal entries to the appropriate T-accounts.

c. Prepare a balance sheet and income statement for fiscal year 20X4.

d. Prepare the closing entries for fiscal year 20X4.

Transactions:

1. On 1/1/X4, the company issued 25,000 shares of common stock at $15 per share. The par value of each share of common stock is $10.

2. On 1/1/X4, the company purchased land and buildings from another company in exchange for $50,000 in cash and 25,000 shares of common stock. The land's value is approximately one-fifth of the total value of the transaction.

3. Equipment worth $100,000 was purchased on 7/1/X4, in exchange for $50,000 in cash and a one-year, 10 percent note, principal amount $50,000. The note pays semiannual interest, and interest was unpaid on 12/31/X4.

4. The equipment is depreciated using the straight-line method, with an estimated useful life of 10 years and an estimated salvage value of $0.

5. The buildings purchased in transaction 2 are depreciated using the straight-line method, with an estimated useful life of 30 years and an estimated salvage value of $40,000.

6. During the year, inventory costing $200,000 was purchased, all on account.

7. Sales during the year were $215,000, of which credit sales were $175,000.

8. Inventory costing $160,000 was sold during the year.

9. Payments to suppliers totaled $175,000.

10. At the end of the year, accounts receivable had a positive balance of $10,000.

11. On March 31, 20X4, the company rented out a portion of its building to Fantek Corporation. Fantek is required to make quarterly payments of $5,000 each. The payments are due on April 1, July 1, October 1, and January 1 of each year, with the first payment on 4/1/X4. All scheduled payments were made during 20X4.

12. Selling and distribution expenses amounted to $30,000, all paid in cash.

13. During the year, inventory worth $10,000 was destroyed by fire. The inventory was not insured.

14. The company calculates taxes at a rate of 30 percent. During the year, $3,000 was paid to the taxing authority.

15. Dividends of $4,000 were declared during the year, and $1,000 remained unpaid at year end.

30. The accounting system closing process takes some amount of time at the end of the accounting period in order to check for errors, make adjusting entries, and prepare the financial statements. In recent years there has been a real push to speed up this process for most firms. Discuss the incentives that companies might have to implement in order to make this a faster process.

31. During the year-end audit process, the auditing firm may find errors and omissions in the recording of transactions and will then ask management to make an adjusting entry to correct for these errors. In light of the purpose of the audit opinion, discuss plausible arguments that management might give to convince the auditor to waive making these suggested adjustments.

32. Suppose that a company has a bonus plan in which managers can earn a bonus if they meet certain net income targets. If the management team has discretion as to which depreciation method they might use, with the straight-line reporting the least amount of depreciation in the early years of the life of the asset, discuss the incentives that management would have in choosing a depreciation method. Also discuss how owners might protect themselves from any self-serving behavior on the part of management.

33. Discuss how creditors might protect their interests (relative to owners) when they negotiate their lending agreement with the firm.

USING REAL DATA

34. Base your answers to the following questions on the financial statements of Russ Berrie.

RUSS BERRIE & Co., Inc.:
Income Statement

	12/31/2001	12/31/2000	12/31/1999
Net sales	$294,291,000	$300,801,000	$287,011,000
Cost of sales	132,611,000	132,908,000	123,216,000
Gross profit	161,680,000	167,893,000	163,795,000
Selling, general and administrative expense	112,570,000	106,991,000	108,023,000
Information system write-off	0	0	10,392,000
Investment and other income net	(8,560,000)	(10,202,000)	(8,587,000)
Income before taxes	57,670,000	71,104,000	53,967,000
Provision for income taxes	17,496,000	23,163,000	17,531,000
Net income	$ 40,174,000	$ 47,941,000	$ 36,436,000

RUSS BERRIE & Co., Inc.:
Balance Sheet

	12/31/2001	12/31/2000
Assets		
Current assets		
Cash and cash equivalents	$148,872,000	$ 77,794,000
Marketable securities	94,181,000	141,032,000
Accounts receivable, trade, less allowance of $3,454 in 2001 and $3,460 in 2000	63,481,000	58,673,000
Inventories, net	37,374,000	47,430,000
Prepaid expenses and other current assets	4,550,000	5,508,000
Deferred income taxes	6,705,000	6,003,000
Total current assets	355,163,000	336,440,000
Property, plant, and equipment, net	24,623,000	26,745,000
Inventories—long-term, net	2,284,000	0
Other assets	4,574,000	3,824,000
Total assets	$386,644,000	$367,009,000
Liabilities and Shareholders' Equity		
Current liabilities		
Accounts payable	5,376,000	4,913,000
Accrued expenses	20,003,000	20,313,000
Accrued income taxes	6,848,000	7,192,000
Total current liabilities	32,227,000	32,418,000

	12/31/2001	12/31/2000
Commitments and contingencies		
Shareholders' equity		
Common stock: $0.10 stated value; authorized 50,000,000 shares; issued 2001, 25,682,364 shares; 2000, 25,413,626 shares	2,587,000	2,541,000
Additional paid-in-capital	73,794,000	63,103,000
Retained earnings	392,272,000	381,479,000
Accumulated other comprehensive loss	(4,165,000)	(4,310,000)
Unearned compensation	(75,000)	(149,000)
Treasury stock, at cost (5,632,014 shares at December 31, 2001 and 5,557,514 shares at December 31, 2000)	(109,996,000)	(108,073,000)
Total shareholders equity	354,417,000	334,591,000
Total liabilities and shareholders' equity	$386,644,000	$367,009,000

RUSS BERRIE & Co., Inc.:
Cash Flow

	12/31/2001	12/31/2000	12/31/1999
Cash flows from operating activities:			
Net income	$ 40,174,000	$47,941,000	$36,436,000
Adjustments to reconcile net income to net cash provided by operating activities:			
Depreciation and amortization	4,021,000	3,998,000	5,008,000
Information system write-off	0	0	10,392,000
Provision for accounts receivable reserves	1,828,000	2,298,000	2,534,000
Income from contingency reserve reversal	0	(2,544,000)	0
Other	415,000	390,000	(456,000)
Changes in assets and liabilities:			
Accounts receivable	(6,636,000)	414,000	(9,058,000)
Inventories, net	7,772,000	(3,123,000)	894,000
Prepaid expenses and other current assets	958,000	3,995,000	(197,000)
Other assets	(166,000)	78,000	(1,460,000)
Accounts payable	463,000	(1,315,000)	1,979,000
Accrued expenses	(310,000)	(631,000)	421,000
Accrued income taxes	(344,000)	1,086,000	(1,099,000)
Total adjustments	8,001,000	4,646,000	8,958,000
Net cash provided by operating activities	48,175,000	52,587,000	45,394,000
Cash flows from investing activities:			
Purchase of marketable securities	(97,335,000)	(48,959,000)	(46,365,000)
Proceeds from sale of marketable securities	144,331,000	45,567,000	60,017,000

	12/31/2001	12/31/2000	12/31/1999
Proceeds from sale of property, plant, and equipment	89,000	79,000	116,000
Capital expenditures	(2,405,000)	(4,087,000)	(8,435,000)
Net cash provided by (used in) investing activities	44,680,000	(7,400,000)	5,333,000
Cash flows from financing activities:			
Proceeds from issuance of common stock	10,737,000	2,155,000	2,416,000
Dividends paid to shareholders	(29,381,000)	(17,764,000)	(16,861,000)
Purchase of treasury stock	(1,923,000)	(15,619,000)	(44,292,000)
Net cash (used in) financing activities	(20,567,000)	(31,228,000)	(58,737,000)
Effect of exchange rate changes on cash and cash equivalents	(1,210,000)	(1,073,000)	(146,000)
Net increase (decrease) in cash and cash equivalents	71,078,000	12,886,000	(8,156,000)
Cash and cash equivalents at beginning of year	77,794,000	64,908,000	73,064,000
Cash and cash equivalents at end of year	$148,872,000	$77,794,000	$64,908,000
Cash paid during the year for:			
Interest	$ 196,000	$ 127,000	$ 118,000
Income taxes	17,841,000	22,077,000	18,630,000

a. Determine the amount of dividends declared during fiscal 2001.

b. Determine the amount of dividends paid during fiscal 2001.

c. Assuming that all sales were on account, determine the amount of cash collected from customers.

d. Assuming that the only transactions that flow through the accounts payable to suppliers and others are purchases of inventory and assuming that all additions to inventory were purchases of inventory, determine the cash payments to suppliers.

e. The other comprehensive income account reflects the translation of Russ Berrie's foreign subsidiaries. What has been the experience with these subsidiaries over time—have they resulted in net gains or net losses from translation?

f. In 1999, the company wrote off the cost of some of its information systems. How significant was this write-off (express your answer as a percent of income before the write-off)? How might an analyst factor this loss into his or her evaluation of the company's stock?

g. How does the company finance its business (use data to support your answer)?

h. How healthy is the company from a cash flow perspective?

35. Use the data from the financial statements of the GAP to answer the following questions:

   a. Determine the amount of dividends declared during the year ended 2/2/2002.

   b. Determine the amount of dividends paid during the year ended 2/2/2002.

   c. The GAP reports the ratio of each expense line item relative to net sales on its income statement. Use these data to discuss how profitable GAP has been over the last three years in selling its products.

   d. What has been the trend in revenues and earnings over the last three years (use data to support your answer)?

   e. How does the company finance its business (use data to support your answer)?

   f. How healthy is the company from a cash flow perspective?

   g. If you were an analyst, how might you react to the trends you see in income, debt, and cash flows over the years presented?

GAP, Inc. Income Statement
($ in thousands except share and per share amounts)

	52 Weeks Ended		53 Weeks Ended		52 Weeks Ended	
	Feb. 2, 2002	% to Sales	Feb. 3, 2001	% to Sales	Jan. 29, 2000	% to Sales
Net sales	$13,847,873	100.00%	$13,673,460	100.00%	$11,635,398	100.00%
Costs and expenses						
Cost of goods sold and occupancy expenses	9,704,389	70.1	8,599,442	62.9	6,775,262	58.2
Operating expenses	3,805,968	27.5	3,629,257	26.5	3,043,432	26.2
Interest expense	109,190	0.8	74,891	0.5	44,966	0.4
Interest income	(13,315)	(0.1)	(12,015)	(0.0)	(13,211)	(0.1)
Earnings before income taxes	241,641	1.7	1,381,885	10.1	1,784,949	15.3
Income taxes	249,405	1.8	504,388	3.7	657,884	5.6
Net earnings (loss)	($7,764)	(0.1%)	$877,497	6.4%	$1,127,065	9.7%

GAP, Inc. Balance Sheet

	Feb. 2, 2002	Feb. 3, 2001
Assets		
Current assets:		
Cash and equivalents	$1,035,749,000	$408,794,000
Merchandise inventory	1,677,116,000	1,904,153,000
Other current assets	331,685,000	335,103,000
Total current assets:	3,044,550,000	2,648,050,000
Property and equipment		
Leasehold improvements	2,127,966,000	1,899,820,000

	Feb. 2, 2002	Feb. 3, 2001
Furniture and equipment	3,327,819,000	2,826,863,000
Land and buildings	917,055,000	558,832,000
Construction-in-progress	246,691,000	615,722,000
	6,619,531,000	5,901,237,000
Accumulated depreciation and amortization	(2,458,241,000)	(1,893,552,000)
Property and equipment, net	4,161,290,000	4,007,685,000
Lease rights and other assets	385,486,000	357,173,000
Total assets	$7,591,326,000	$7,012,908,000
Liabilities and shareholders' equity:		
Current liabilities		
Notes payable	$ 41,889,000	$ 779,904,000
Current maturities of long-term debt	0	250,000,000
Accounts payable	1,105,117,000	1,067,207,000
Accrued expenses and other current liabilities	909,227,000	702,033,000
Total current liabilities	2,056,233,000	2,799,144,000
Long-term liabilities:		
Long-term debt	1,961,397,000	780,246,000
Deferred lease credits and other liabilities	564,115,000	505,279,000
Total long-term liabilities	2,525,512,000	1,285,525,000
Shareholders' equity:		
Common stock $.05 par value		
Authorized 2,300,000,000 shares; issued 948,597,949 and 939,222,871 shares; outstanding 865,726,890 and 853,996,984 shares	47,430,000	46,961,000
Additional paid-in capital	461,408,000	294,967,000
Retained earnings	4,890,375,000	4,974,773,000
Accumulated other comprehensive losses	(61,824,000)	(20,173,000)
Deferred compensation	(7,245,000)	(12,162,000)
Treasury stock, at cost	(2,320,563,000)	(2,356,127,000)
Total shareholders' equity	3,009,581,000	2,928,239,000
Total liabilities and shareholders' equity	$7,591,326,000	$7,012,908,000

GAP, Inc. Cash Flow			
Cash Flows from Operating Activities	52 Weeks Ended Feb. 2, 2002	53 Weeks Ended Feb. 3, 2001	52 Weeks Ended Jan. 29, 2000
Net earnings (loss)	($7,764,000)	$877,497,000	$1,127,065,000
Adjustments to reconcile net earnings (loss) to net cash provided by operating activities:			
Depreciation and amortization	810,486,000	590,365,000	436,184,000
Tax benefit from exercise of stock options and vesting of restricted stock	58,444,000	130,882,000	211,891,000
Deferred income taxes	(28,512,000)	(38,872,000)	2,444,000

	52 Weeks Ended Feb. 2, 2002	53 Weeks Ended Feb. 3, 2001	52 Weeks Ended Jan. 29, 2000
Change in operating assets and liabilities:			
Merchandise inventory	213,067,000	(454,595,000)	(404,211,000)
Prepaid expenses and other	(13,303,000)	(61,096,000)	(55,519,000)
Accounts payable	42,205,000	249,545,000	118,121,000
Accrued expenses	220,826,000	(56,541,000)	(5,822,000)
Deferred lease credits and other long-term liabilities	22,390,000	54,020,000	47,775,000
Net cash provided by operating activities	1,317,839,000	1,291,205,000	1,477,928,000
Cash flows from investing activities:			
Net purchase of property and equipment	(940,078,000)	(1,858,662,000)	(1,238,722,000)
Acquisition of lease rights and other assets	(10,549,000)	(16,252,000)	(39,839,000)
Net cash used for investing activities	(950,627,000)	(1,874,914,000)	(1,278,561,000)
Cash flows from financing activities:			
Net increase (decrease) in notes payable	(734,927,000)	621,420,000	84,778,000
Proceeds from issuance of long-term debt	1,194,265,000	250,000,000	311,839,000
Payments of long-term debt	(250,000,000)	0	0
Issuance of common stock	139,105,000	152,105,000	114,142,000
Net purchase of treasury stock	(785,000)	(392,558,000)	(745,056,000)
Cash dividends paid	(76,373,000)	(75,488,000)	(75,795,000)
Net cash provided by (used for) financing activities	271,285,000	555,479,000	(310,092,000)
Effect of exchange rate fluctuations on cash	(11,542,000)	(13,328,000)	(4,176,000)
Net increase (decrease) in cash and equivalents	$ 626,955,000	($41,558,000)	($114,901,000)
Cash and equivalents at beginning of year	408,794,000	450,352,000	565,253,000
Cash and equivalents at end of year	$1,035,749,000	$408,794,000	$ 450,352,000

36. Use the financial statements of Hasbro to answer the following questions:

a. Determine the amount of dividends declared during fiscal year 2001.

b. Determine the amount of dividends paid during fiscal year 2001.

c. Assuming that all sales were on account, determine the amount of cash collected from customers.

d. Assuming that the only transactions that flow through the accounts payable to suppliers and others are purchases of inventory, and assuming that all additions to inventory were purchases of inventory, determine the cash payments to suppliers.

e. What has been the trend in revenues and earnings over the last three years (use data to support your answer)?

f. How does the company finance its business (use data to support your answer)?

g. How healthy is the company from a cash flow perspective?

h. If you were an analyst, how might you react to the trends you see in income, debt, and cash flows over the years presented?

HASBRO, Inc. Income Statement

	12/30/2001	12/30/2000	12/30/1999
Net revenues	$2,856,339,000	$3,787,215,000	$4,232,263,000
Cost of sales	1,223,483,000	1,673,973,000	1,698,242,000
Gross profit	1,632,856,000	2,113,242,000	2,534,021,000
Expenses			
Amortization	121,652,000	157,763,000	173,533,000
Royalties, research and development	335,358,000	635,366,000	711,790,000
Advertising	290,829,000	452,978,000	456,978,000
Selling, distribution, and administration	675,482,000	863,496,000	799,919,000
Restructuring	(1,795,000)	63,951,000	64,232,000
Loss on sale of business units	0	43,965,000	0
Total expenses	1,421,526,000	2,217,519,000	2,206,452,000
Operating profit (loss)	211,330,000	(104,277,000)	327,569,000
Nonoperating (income) expense			
Interest expense	103,688,000	114,421,000	69,340,000
Other (income) expense, net	11,443,000	7,288,000	(15,616,000)
Total nonoperating expense	115,131,000	121,709,000	53,724,000
Earnings (loss) before income taxes and cumulative effect of accounting change	96,199,000	(225,986,000)	273,845,000
Income taxes	35,401,000	(81,355,000)	84,892,000
Net earnings (loss) before cumulative effect of accounting change	60,798,000	(144,631,000)	188,953,000
Cumulative effect of accounting change, net of tax	(1,066,000)	0	0
Net earnings (loss)	$ 59,732,000	($144,631,000)	$ 188,953,000

HASBRO, Inc. Balance Sheet

	12/30/2001	12/30/2000
Assets:		
Current assets		
Cash and cash equivalents	$ 233,095,000	$ 127,115,000
Accounts receivable, less allowance for doubtful accounts of $49,300 in 2001 and $55,000 in 2000	572,499,000	685,975,000
Inventories	217,479,000	335,493,000
Prepaid expenses and other current assets	345,545,000	431,630,000
Total current assets	1,368,618,000	1,580,213,000
Property, plant, and equipment, net	235,360,000	296,729,000
Other assets		
Goodwill, less accumulated amortization of $269,496 in 2001 and $225,770 in 2000	761,575,000	803,189,000
Other intangibles, less accumulated amortization of $398,183 in 2001 and $347,149 in 2000	805,027,000	902,893,000

	12/30/2001	12/30/2000
Other	198,399,000	245,435,000
Total other assets	1,765,001,000	1,951,517,000
Total assets	$3,368,979,000	$3,828,459,000
Liabilities and shareholders' equity:		
Current liabilities		
Short-term borrowings	$ 34,024,000	$ 226,292,000
Current installments of long-term debt	2,304,000	1,793,000
Accounts payable	123,109,000	191,749,000
Accrued liabilities	599,154,000	819,978,000
Total current liabilities	758,591,000	1,239,812,000
Long-term debt	1,165,649,000	1,167,838,000
Deferred liabilities	91,875,000	93,403,000
Total liabilities	2,016,115,000	2,501,053,000
Shareholders' equity		
Preference stock of $2.50 par value.	0	0
Authorized 5,000,000 shares; none issued		
Common stock of $.50 par value.		
Authorized 600,000,000 shares; issued		
209,694,630 shares in 2001 and 2000	104,847,000	104,847,000
Additional paid-in capital	457,544,000	464,084,000
Deferred compensation	(2,996,000)	(6,889,000)
Retained earnings	1,622,402,000	1,583,394,000
Accumulated other comprehensive earnings	(68,398,000)	(44,718,000)
Treasury stock, at cost, 36,736,156 shares		
in 2001 and 37,253,164 shares in 2000	(760,535,000)	(773,312,000)
Total shareholders' equity	1,352,864,000	1,327,406,000
Total liabilities and shareholders' equity	$3,368,979,000	$3,828,459,000

HASBRO, Inc. Cash Flow

	12/30/2001	12/30/2000	12/30/1999
Cash flows from operating activities:			
Net earnings (loss)	$59,732,000	($144,631,000)	$188,953,000
Adjustments to reconcile net earnings (loss) to net cash provided by operating activities:			
Depreciation and amortization of plant and equipment	104,247,000	106,458,000	103,791,000
Other amortization	121,652,000	157,763,000	173,533,000
Deferred income taxes	38,697,000	(67,690,000)	(38,675,000)
Compensation earned under restricted stock program	2,532,000	2,754,000	0
Loss on sale of business units	0	43,965,000	0
Change in operating assets and liabilities (other than cash and cash equivalents):			
Decrease (increase) in accounts receivable	99,474,000	395,682,000	(11,248,000)
Decrease (increase) in inventories	109,002,000	69,657,000	(44,212,000)

	12/30/2001	12/30/2000	12/30/1999
Decrease (increase) in prepaid expenses and other current assets	45,936,000	(84,006,000)	(26,527,000)
(Decrease) increase in accounts payable and accrued liabilities	(194,525,000)	(292,313,000)	193,626,000
Other, including long-term advances	(14,272,000)	(25,083,000)	(147,729,000)
Net cash provided by operating activities	372,475,000	162,556,000	391,512,000
Cash flows from investing activities:			
Additions to property, plant, and equipment	(50,045,000)	(125,055,000)	(107,468,000)
Investments and acquisitions, net of cash acquired	0	(138,518,000)	(352,417,000)
Other	(7,734,000)	82,863,000	30,793,000
Net cash utilized by investing activities	(57,779,000)	(180,710,000)	(429,092,000)
Cash flows from financing activities:			
Proceeds from borrowings with original maturities of more than three months	250,000,000	912,979,000	460,333,000
Repayments of borrowings with original maturities of more than three months	(250,127,000)	(291,779,000)	(308,128,000)
Net (repayments) proceeds of other short-term borrowings	(190,216,000)	(341,522,000)	226,103,000
Purchase of common stock	0	(367,548,000)	(237,532,000)
Stock option and warrant transactions	8,391,000	2,523,000	50,358,000
Dividends paid	(20,709,000)	(42,494,000)	(45,526,000)
Net cash (utilized) provided by financing activities	(202,661,000)	(127,841,000)	145,608,000
Effect of exchange rate changes on cash	(6,055,000)	(7,049,000)	(5,617,000)
Increase (decrease) in cash and cash equivalents	105,980,000	(153,044,000)	102,411,000
Cash and cash equivalents at beginning of year	127,115,000	280,159,000	177,748,000
Cash and cash equivalents at end of year	$233,095,000	$127,115,000	$280,159,000
Supplemental information			
Interest paid	$103,437,000	$ 91,180,000	$ 64,861,000
Income taxes paid (received)	($34,813,000)	$ 95,975,000	$108,342,000

○ BEYOND THE BOOK

37. Find the 10-K, proxy statement, and annual report of a typical company in the manufacturing business. Answer the following questions:

   a. From either the 10-K or annual report, discuss how important inventory is in relationship to other assets on the firm's balance sheet. Also address how important property, plant, and equipment is to the firm.

   b. How does the company finance its business?

   c. Compare the information provided in the 10-K and annual report and discuss at least five things that are in the 10-K that are not in the annual report. If you were a stockholder, would you want to know these things and why?

    d. From the proxy statement, what were the major issues (at least four) that were discussed at the annual meeting?

    e. What is the total compensation paid to the five highest-paid employees? Who was the highest paid? What percent of sales was the total paid? Does this seem reasonable and why?

    f. How many directors does the company have? How old are they and what percent of the board is female? How much do the directors get paid to attend meetings?

38. For the company you selected in problem 31, find at least three articles that discuss the nature of the markets for this company and the forecast of what the future may be for this sector of the economy. Write a one-page summary of your findings.

CHAPTER 4

Income Measurement and Reporting

LEARNING OBJECTIVES

After reading this chapter you should be able to:

1. Understand and apply the accrual basis of accounting and the related recognition and matching concepts.

2. Explain the operating cycle and its relation to accrual accounting.

3. Discuss revenue recognition methods and the reasons why revenue is recognized at different times for different economic events.

4. Identify links between accrual accounting and firm valuation.

5. Construct accrual entries for both revenue and expense transactions.

6. Explain how the income statement format reflects the concept of separating transitory items from operating earnings.

In late May 2001, ConAgra Foods announced that accounting and conduct matters at its United Agri Products Company (UAP) subsidiary would result in the restatement of its financial results. Certain accounting adjustments would also result in a restatement for fiscal 1998. The restatement reduced revenues and earnings for fiscal years 1998, 1999, and 2000, and increased revenues and earnings in fiscal year 2001. ConAgra restated its earnings due to accounting irregularities in its UAP subsidiary that related, in part, to its revenue recognition practices. In the days leading up to the announcement, ConAgra's stock price fell by approximately 6 percent. Clearly, as ConAgra's press release illustrates, investors and analysts pay close attention to the earnings reported by publicly traded companies.

To further your understanding of the earnings reported by companies, we examine the concepts of accrual-basis accounting in this chapter. Specifically, we examine the recognition criteria for revenues and expenses, and related implications for the recognition of assets and liabilities. We compare and contrast this accrual-basis recognition of revenues and expenses with the timing of the actual cash flows that result from these transactions.

You need to understand accrual accounting and how it differs from a cash basis for at least two reasons. First, investors and analysts often use forecasts of earnings to estimate future cash flows, which, in turn, affects their assessments of a firm's value. Second, owners often use earnings and stock prices (which may depend on earnings) to measure management performance. Accrual accounting, however, allows managers sufficient latitude to influence the performance measures upon which they are evaluated and paid. As a result, owners must understand this latitude in setting management compensation arrangements, and investors and analysts must do so in assessing firm value.

Let's begin with a discussion of the general concepts of accrual-based accounting.

ACCRUAL ACCOUNTING

In **accrual-basis accounting,** a firm recognizes revenues and expenses in the period in which they occur, rather than in the period in which the cash flows related to the revenues and expenses are realized. In contrast, **cash-basis accounting** recognizes revenues and expenses in the period in which the firm realizes the cash flow. For example, under the accrual basis, a firm that sells goods to customers on credit recognizes the sales revenue at the point of physical transfer of the goods. Under the cash basis, however, the firm waits to recognize the sale until it collects the cash. As the diagram in Exhibit 4.1 illustrates, this difference in timing of revenue recognition can have a significant impact on the period in which the revenues are reported if the date of delivery of the goods falls in a different accounting period than the collection of cash. Because the cash might be collected in an accounting period later than the period in which the goods were delivered, it is clear that the choice of when to recognize revenue may have a significant impact on the statement of earnings.

Firms use accrual-basis accounting because it provides information about future cash flows that is not available under the cash method. In our sales example, investors want to know the firm's sales, even if the cash has not been collected, in order to better predict the future cash flows upon which the value of the firm depends. Similarly, a company's expected future payments are also relevant information. However, accrual accounting, while more informative than the cash basis, also involves considerable judgment. As a result, accounting standard setters developed criteria to assure that firms use similar assumptions in

Exhibit 4.1
Revenue Recognition Timing

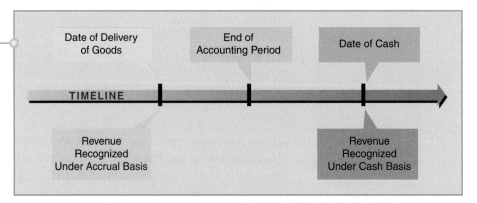

their judgments. In that way, the resulting revenue and expense numbers will be as consistent as possible with the qualitative characteristics of accounting information discussed in Chapter 1, such as neutrality, reliability, and verifiability.

The FASB's criteria are intended to guide all recognition decisions. These criteria detail what items should be recognized in the financial statements and when the items should be recognized. The following criteria apply to all financial statement components, including revenues, expenses, assets, liabilities, and stockholders' equity accounts:

Definition: The item meets the definition of an element of financial statements.

Measurability: The item has a relevant attribute measurable with sufficient reliability.

Relevance: The information about the item is capable of making a difference in user decisions.

Reliability: The information about the item is representationally faithful, verifiable, and neutral.

The above criteria include the concept of an attribute. *Attributes* are characteristics of financial statement items that we might choose to measure. For instance, inventory possesses several attributes. One of them is the cost the company incurs to either make or buy the inventory. A second attribute is the current selling price of the inventory. Whatever attribute we choose to measure, however, the recognition criteria require it to be "relevant." Often, accounting regulators must determine which attribute is the most relevant and reliable to report in the financial statements. We continue to address this issue as we progress through the text.

Recall in Chapter 3 that we defined assets, liabilities, and owners' equity. Later in this chapter we define revenues and expenses. All these definitions are based on the concepts of accrual accounting. Double-entry accounting links the recognition of revenues, expenses, assets, and liabilities. Let's look more closely at how revenue and expense recognition reflects these accrual-accounting concepts.

REVENUE RECOGNITION

Revenue recognition refers to the point in time at which revenue should be reported on the statement of earnings, a crucial element of accrual accounting. Typically, firms implement accrual accounting by first determining the revenues to be recognized and then matching the costs incurred in generating that revenue to determine expenses. It follows that the timing of revenue and expense recognition determines the earnings that are reported. Given that the information conveyed by earnings is a factor in estimating the value of the firm, revenue recognition is particularly important to analysts, investors, managers, and others with an interest in those estimates.

It is reasonable to imagine that these individuals desire earnings to be reported as early as possible in order to gain access to information upon which they can improve their estimates. However, this desire is likely to be tempered by an understanding that revenue recognized in advance of collecting the cash from customers implies some uncertainty that could be avoided if revenue recognition can be delayed until those collections are made. In other words, there is a trade-off between early access to information and the level of uncertainty contained in the revenue and related expenses reported on the statement of earnings. For example, an extreme view would argue that when a firm purchases inventory, it immediately adds value to the company because the goods can be sold later for a profit. Therefore, the firm should recognize the revenue (profit) upon inventory purchases, assuming that future sales will occur. The difficulty with this argument, of course, is the considerable uncertainty about both the timing and the amount of revenue that may be realized from future sales. For example, a company might purchase or manufacture inventory and be unable to sell it because of changing demand or excess supply.

Consider the electronic game industry in 2001. Three competitors, Microsoft, Sony, and Nintendo, sought industry dominance with the XBox, Playstation 2, and the Game-Cube, respectively. Manufacturers of these products needed to determine how many units to manufacture, set prices for the product, make arrangements with distributors (such as Toys Я Us, Wal-Mart, and Target), and ship the product in sufficient numbers to satisfy customers. Furthermore, the companies needed to consider the costs of product warranties and returns of unsold products. Finally, the three firms assumed that third-party software manufacturers would be able to offer a sufficient quality and variety of games on the different platforms to satisfy consumer demand. All of these factors worked to create substantial uncertainty about the profits from a particular product line. Thus, it would be difficult for any of these companies to argue that sales should have been recognized at the time they manufactured the products.

Because of the tension between the desire to recognize the value added by investment and production activities as early as possible, and the uncertainties involved in accurately portraying these results, accounting standard setters developed **revenue recognition criteria.** These criteria establish the requirements that must be met in order to recognize revenue on a company's books.

REVENUE RECOGNITION CRITERIA

At the time of this writing, the FASB is considering an approach for revenue recognition that is more closely linked to changes in assets and liabilities than the notions of realization and completion of the earnings process. Concerns with the present criteria for revenue realization are that they are sometimes in conflict with concepts of assets and liabilities, imprecisely defined, and difficult to consistently apply when the revenue generating process involves multiple steps.

GAAP requires that revenues be recognized at the earliest point in the firm's operating cycle, at which it meets the following criteria:

● Revenue is realized or realizable
● Revenue is earned by the enterprise

Realized or **realizable** means that an exchange of goods or services has taken place, the seller has either received cash or the right to receive cash, and collection is reasonably assured. **Earned** means that the goods or services have been delivered, and related obligations are substantially complete. In applying the earned criteria, a firm must apply judgment in determining whether the risks and rewards of ownership of the product have effectively been transferred to the buyer. That is, has there been substantial performance by both the seller and the buyer such that the earnings process is essentially complete? For instance, Werner Enterprises, a major trucking company, recognizes "operating revenues and related direct costs when the shipment is delivered." Because Werner is

Exhibit 4.2

THE REAL WORLD

Target Corporation

> **Target Corporation—Revenues**
>
> Revenue from retail sales is recognized at the time of sale. Leased department sales, net of related cost of sales, are included within sales and were $33 million in 2000, $31 million in 1999, and $29 million in 1998. Net credit revenues represent revenue from receivable-backed securities, which is comprised of finance charges and late fees on internal credit sales, net of the effect of publicly held receivable-backed securities. Internal credit sales were $5.5 billion, $5 billion, and $4.5 billion in 2000, 1999, and 1998, respectively.

responsible for transporting the goods of the customer, management judges that the earning process is only complete when the goods are ultimately delivered.

The revenue recognition criteria can be met at different points in a firm's operating cycle depending on the nature of the business. In the following sections, we illustrate some common points of revenue recognition used by various industries.

At Point of Delivery

A fairly common point of revenue recognition for manufacturing and retail firms is at the point when they deliver a product or service to a customer. As we noted previously, Werner, Inc. reports its revenue when the shipment is delivered. This is the point at which the customer accepts the risks and rewards of ownership of the asset, and at which point Werner ceases its obligation to the customer (the revenue has been earned). Further, the customer is now obligated to pay Werner for the delivery (the revenue is realizable).

Target's revenue recognition policy as shown in Exhibit 4.2 is more complex than that of Werner. Target derives its revenues not only from product sales but also from interest on credit sales to customers. However, for its product sales, the method of revenue recognition is at the time of delivery (which is also the time of sale). Target's 2000 income statement (shown later in Exhibit 4.11) reports sales of $36,362 million and net credit revenues of $541 million.

As Service Is Provided or Cost Incurred

For a firm that sells subscriptions, cash may be received in advance. The firm recognizes the revenue as it incurs costs in the fulfillment of those subscriptions. For example, Reader's Digest sells magazine subscriptions to individuals and newstands. In a footnote to its 2003 annual report, the company describes its revenue recognition methods as reported in Exhibit 4.3. As the footnote describes, Reader's Digest has three primary sources of revenue. It uses a

Exhibit 4.3

THE REAL WORLD

Readers Digest

> **Footnote on Revenue Recognition**
>
> Sales of our magazine subscriptions, less estimated cancellations, are deferred and recognized as revenues proportionately over the subscription period. Revenues from sales of magazines through the newsstand are recognized at the issue date, net of an allowance for returns. Advertising revenues are recorded as revenues at the time the advertisements are published, net of discounts and advertising agency commissions.

Because circulation numbers drive the rates that magazines charge to advertisers, magazine publishers sometimes overstate their sales. This practice of over-estimating monthly sales has led advertisers to be unwilling to pay the full cost for ads that are published or to demand refunds when new figures reveal that the estimated sales figures were missed. A publisher would need to recognize this reduction in revenues through an estimate of refunds. For instance, the following is the revenue recognition policy for Primedia, Inc. and it indicates that revenues are stated less an amount (provisions) for rebates, adjustments, and so forth.

"Advertising revenues for all consumer magazines are recognized as income at the on-sale date, net of provisions for estimated rebates, adjustments and discounts."

different recognition method for each type of revenue. The company recognizes subscriptions over the subscription period, newsstand sales at the issue date, and advertising revenues upon advertisement publication. The collection of cash does not determine the timing of revenue recognition. In the case of subscriptions, the revenue is earned as the goods are furnished to the purchaser. In the case of newsstand sales, the shipments are determined on a standing order (based on past sales), and newsstands pay only for the magazines that they sell. Thus, recognizing revenues at the issue date means that accurate estimation of the number of magazines to issue and of returns is critical to accurate revenue recognition. Finally, advertising revenues are recognized when the magazine is published (which constitutes providing the service to those purchasing advertisements).

Based on Contractual Agreements

Firms sometimes retain a substantial financial interest in the product or service, even after the initial sale. For example, Krispy Kreme, a typical franchiser, provides a significant amount of service related to establishing the business between the time of signing the agreement and the opening of the business. The company typically provides financing to the purchaser, allowing franchise fees to be paid in installments. Krispy Kreme defers revenues from the initial franchise fee until the opening of the new store is complete (i.e., the revenue has been earned).

Retail land sales also pose unique accounting problems. Retail land sales involve the sale of undeveloped land. Sales contracts may offer buyers below-market interest rates and attractive financing terms, with the land serving as collateral for the sale (sometimes called a *collateralized sale*). Because of uncertainties regarding the future costs of developing the land as well as the collectibility of the receivable (particularly when there are low down payments), accounting regulators established criteria to determine the conditions under which revenue from a retail land sale could be recognized at the signing of a sales contract. For example, footnotes to Amrep Corporation's annual report (reported in Exhibit 4.4) illustrate a typical disclosure in the case of retail land sales.

At Time of Production

When both the value and the assurance of sale can be estimated at the time of production, such as in certain agricultural and mining operations, a firm recognizes revenue at that point. Often, the company has a supply contract with

Exhibit 4.4

THE REAL WORLD

Amrep Corporation

Revenue Recognition Footnote

Land sales are recognized when the parties are bound by the terms of the contract, all consideration (including adequate cash) has been exchanged, and title and other attributes of ownership have been conveyed to the buyer by means of a closing. Profit is recorded either in its entirety or on the installment method depending on, among other things, the ability to estimate the collectibility of the unpaid sales price. In the event the buyer defaults on the obligation, the property is taken back and recorded in inventory at the unpaid receivable balance, net of any deferred profit, but not in excess of fair market value less estimated cost to sell.

a buyer that establishes the price of the commodity to be delivered and a time schedule for its delivery. For example, Kinross Gold Corporation (Kinross Annual Report 2000) notes that "Gold and Silver in inventory, in transit and at refineries, are recorded at net realizable value and included in accounts receivable with the exception of Kubaka bullion. The estimated net realizable value of Kubaka bullion is included in inventory until it is sold."

As Cash Is Collected

In most cases, revenue recognition criteria are met prior to collection. Firms can reasonably estimate collections at the time of sale, and the revenue is thus realizable. However, for some circumstances, collection of the receivable is sufficiently in doubt that revenue cannot be recognized at the time of sale. Recognition prior to collection would therefore not reflect the underlying economic reality. In these cases firms can use two methods to recognize revenue and related expenses as cash is collected: the installment method and the cost recovery method.

With the **installment method,** a firm recognizes gross profits in proportion to cash payments received. With the **cost recovery method,** a firm defers gross profit recognition until enough cash is collected to recover the costs. For example, assume that Wilson Land Company sells a home site for $100,000 that cost Wilson $60,000. The purchaser agrees to pay Wilson for the land in three payments of $40,000, $30,000, and $30,000. Exhibit 4.5 shows the amount of gross profit recognized each year under the installment method and the cost recovery method.

Either method results in the same total gross profit over three years. How, then, to determine the appropriate method of revenue recognition in a particular case? Firms generally use the cost recovery method only when considerable uncertainty exists about ultimate collection of the total sales price (so no profit is recognized until the costs have been covered). The decision, then, becomes whether to recognize a real estate sale under the installment method or at the time of sale. As a rule, retail land sales should only be recognized at the time of sale if both collection is assured and the seller has no remaining obligations to the buyer.

During Construction

In the long-term construction industry, major projects can take years to complete. Thus the operating cycle in this industry is very long, requiring special income recognition methods: the completed contract method and the percentage completion method. Under the **completed contract method,** a firm waits to recognize revenues and expenses until the project is complete. Under the **percentage**

Exhibit 4.5
Installment Method versus Cost Recovery Method

Profit % = ($100,000 − 60,000)/$100,000 = 40%

Year	Installment method gross profit	Cost recovery method gross profit
1	40% × $40,000 = $16,000	$0 ($40,000 cost recovered)
2	40% × $30,000 = $12,000	$10,000 ($20,000 cost recovered)
3	40% × $30,000 = $12,000	$30,000
Total	$40,000	$40,000

Exhibit 4.6
Revenue Recognition Using Percentage of Completion Method (dollars in billions)

Year	Degree of Completion	Revenue Recognized	Expenses Recognized	Gross Profit Recognized
1	$8/$15 = 53.33%	.533 × $20 = $10.67	$8	$2.67
2	$4/$15 = 26.67%	.267 × $20 = $5.33	$4	$1.33
3	$3/$15 = 20.00%	.20 × $20 = $4.00	$3	$1.00
Total	100.00%		$20.00	$15	$5.00

of completion method, a firm recognizes revenues and expenses in proportion to the degree of completion of the project. Degree of completion is typically measured by the cost incurred to date relative to the total estimated cost. For example, assume that Horning Construction agrees to build a casino. The purchaser agrees to pay $20 billion to Horning for the project. Horning expects to spend three years building the casino and estimates the following costs: Year 1, $8 billion; Year 2, $4 billion; Year 3, $3 billion. Exhibit 4.6 shows the amount of revenue and expenses recognized each year under percentage of completion.

Under the completed contract method, Horning Construction would recognize all of the revenue and expense at the end of year 3, at contract completion. Typically, though, firms use the completed contract method for short construction periods. However, to use the percentage completion method, firms must be able to accurately estimate costs to obtain reliable profit forecasts. As a result, if there is a high degree of cost uncertainty, the completed contract method may be used even for long-term contracts.

Although the percentage of completion and completed contract methods are the more common, firms sometimes use other methods of accounting for long-term construction contracts, such as the installment and cost recovery methods described earlier. Firms will likely use the installment method when the uncertainty pertains largely to assurance of collection (buyer's performance) rather than the reliability of future cost estimates (seller's performance). The cost recovery method is especially conservative and appropriate in cases where considerable uncertainty exists about collection and future costs.

Now that we have reviewed several aspects of revenue recognition, let's turn to the related issue of expense recognition.

EXPENSE RECOGNITION

The **matching concept** requires that firms recognize both the revenue and the costs required to produce the revenue (expenses) at the same time. The implications of this are two-fold. First, it means that firms must defer some costs on the balance sheet until they can be matched with sales. In some cases, though, direct matching with sales is not practical. In these cases, firms often expense the deferred costs based on the passage of time. Second, firms will not incur some costs at the time of the sale (e.g., warranty costs). Firms will thus need to estimate these costs, and accrue an expense to give proper matching with the revenue reported.

Perhaps the best example of direct matching is when a retail or wholesale company recognizes revenue at the time of delivery. Here, a related expense, **cost of goods sold,** which represents the cost of inventory that the company had on its balance sheet as an asset prior to the sale, must also be recognized. Target provides an example of such a company. Its cost of goods sold can be seen in Exhibit 4.11 (later in the chapter).

Matching is applied differently depending on the type of cost. Some costs, such as costs of goods sold, can be matched directly with sales. However, other costs, such as executive salaries, insurance, and depreciation of various assets used in the business, can be more difficult to directly link to revenue. In this case, firms usually either charge the costs to income as incurred (e.g., salaries and various administrative costs) or allocate the costs systematically over time periods (e.g., depreciation, interest, insurance). Werner, Inc. (the trucking company mentioned earlier) provides a service to its customers, so it has no cost of goods sold. However, if you review the income statement for Werner, you would see sales-related expenses such as salaries, fuel costs, and depreciation on its trucks, which are related to the delivery service it provides to its customers.

With expense recognition, GAAP guidelines focus on whether or not a cost should be treated as an asset (a **deferred expense**) or as an expense. For example, Prepaid Legal Services pays its sales force an advance of up to three years' worth of commissions on new customer sales. In the years prior to 2001, Prepaid treated these prepayments as deferred expenses (assets) and then expensed these deferred expenses over time to match them with revenues from the provided legal services. However, in 2001 the SEC concluded that Prepaid's accounting methods were not in accordance with GAAP arguing that the future revenue from these sales was highly uncertain. Effective in its third quarter 10-Q filing with the SEC as shown in Exhibit 4.7, Prepaid changed its accounting

---

Exhibit 4.7

THE REAL WORLD

Prepaid Legal Services

In the November 14, 2001, 10–Q filing of Prepaid Legal Services, the following disclosure was made:

As previously reported, in January 2001 and May 2001, the staff of the Division of Corporation Finance of the Securities and Exchange Commission (SEC) reviewed the Company's 1999 and 2000 Forms 10-K, respectively. On May 11, 2001, the Company received a letter from the staff of the Division of Corporation Finance advising that, after reviewing the Company's Forms 10-K, it was the position of the Division that the Company's accounting for commission advance receivables was not in accordance with GAAP. The Company subsequently appealed this decision to the Chief Accountant of the SEC. On July 25, 2001, the Company announced that the Chief Accountant concurred with the prior staff opinion of the Division of Corporation Finance. The Company subsequently announced that it would not pursue any further appeals and that it would amend its previously filed SEC reports to restate the Company's financial statements to reflect the SEC's position that the Company's advance commission payments should be expensed when paid. As previously discussed, the change in accounting treatment reduced total assets from $247 million at December 31, 2000 to $93 million, reduced total liabilities from $100 million to $48 million (due to the elimination of deferred taxes related to the receivables) and therefore reduced stockholders' equity from $147 million to $45 million. The elimination of the receivables reduced 2000 net income from $43.6 million, or $1.92 per diluted share, to $20.5 million, or $.90 per diluted share. The Company expects to amend its 2000 Annual Report on Form 10-K in the near future to reflect the change in accounting for commission of advance receivables and restate all periods included in the 2000 Form 10-K. The financial statements and the explanation thereof contained in this Form 10-Q reflect the change in the accounting treatment for advance payments made to associates.

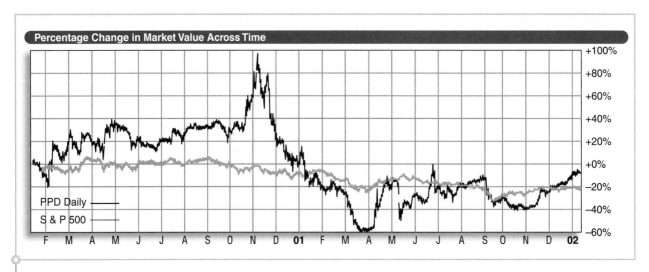

Exhibit 4.8
Prepaid Legal Services Inc.

methods to conform with the SEC ruling. The company now expenses the commissions in the period in which they were paid.

The concern over Prepaid's accounting methods stemmed back to December 2000, when a research report questioned the firm's economic viability. The graph in Exhibit 4.8 demonstrates the changes in value that took place between the issuance of this report and the change of policy in late 2001.

Now that we've discussed accrual-accounting concepts, let's next look at how firms put into practice these revenue and expense recognition criteria.

RECORDING ACCRUAL ENTRIES

In this section, we use four common types of economic events to illustrate how accrual accounting is applied and how the cash flow timing differs for each event. Exhibit 4.9 summarizes these revenue and expense events, and provides a simple example of each. Let's look more closely at each of these transactions.

REVENUES THAT ARE RECEIVED IN CASH BEFORE THEY ARE EARNED

In this situation the firm must record the cash received as an asset. However, as the firm cannot yet treat the transaction as earned revenue, it must postpone the recognition of revenue. The firm will, therefore, record a liability, **deferred revenue** (or *unearned revenue* or *customer deposits*), that represents an obligation to provide goods or services to the customer in the future. This obligation clearly meets the definition of a liability in that it most definitely represents a future sacrifice of resources to the firm. Recall our earlier illustration of Reader's Digest and its revenue recognition of subscriptions.

To illustrate the entries to be made for this type of transaction, let's return to our BHT example from Chapter 3. Suppose that BHT receives $20 million

Exhibit 4.9
Common Accrual Accounting
Events

Revenue Events	Example
Cash that is received in advance before the revenues are recognized as having been earned	Magazine subscriptions are usually paid in advance and earned when the publisher delivers the magazines.
Revenues that are recognized as having been earned before the revenues are received in cash	Sales on account, interest revenue on notes is earned with the passage of time and paid at regular intervals.

Expense Events	Example
Expenses that are paid in advance before they are recognized as having been incurred	Insurance is generally paid in advance to cover a future period. The expense is incurred with the passage of time as dictated by the policy.
Expenses that are recognized as having been incurred before they are paid in cash	Salary expense is incurred when the employees work, even though they may be paid later, such as once every two weeks.

in cash from customers for goods to be delivered in the future. BHT would make the following journal entry at the time cash is received:

```
Cash                    20
    Deferred Revenue             20
```

Later, when BHT earns the revenues (likely at delivery), the firm would make the following entry:

```
Deferred Revenue        20
    Revenue                      20
```

REVENUES THAT ARE EARNED BEFORE THEY ARE RECEIVED IN CASH

For most firms, revenue recognition criteria are most often met before the firms collect the cash. Here, the firm records revenues on its income statement and also an asset (accounts receivable). Accounts receivable meets the definition of an asset as the firm has probable future value in the right to receive cash from the customer at some point in the future. Recall in Chapter 3 that we showed you this type of transaction for BHT, as follows:

```
Accounts Receivable     35,724
    Sales                        35,724
```

As another example, consider interest accrued on a note receivable. A firm earns revenue (interest) on the note with the passage of time, periodically receiving cash. If the cash hasn't yet been received, the firm would record interest revenue and an asset (typically called interest receivable). To illustrate, suppose that BHT allows a customer to pay its bill over a longer period than normal by issuing a note receivable for the amount of the sale (say $100). Further, suppose that this note specifies that the customer pays 5 percent interest. At the end of the first year, the customer would owe an additional $5 for the interest ($100 × 5%). BHT records this earned revenue (assuming it hadn't been paid yet) as follows:

Interest Receivable	5	
Interest Revenue		5

When BHT collects the interest, it makes the following entry:

Cash	5	
Interest Receivable		5

EXPENSES THAT ARE PAID IN CASH BEFORE THEY ARE INCURRED

Cash payment often precedes the incurrence of an expense, such as with prepaid insurance. Insurance companies usually require payment of insurance policy premiums in advance of the coverage. If the firm has just paid its premium, then it should record the reduction in cash and the creation of an asset, typically called prepaid insurance. Prepaid insurance meets the definition of an asset: the insurance provides probable future value in terms of coverage (protection from risk) over the remaining period of the policy. The firm will then convert the prepaid insurance into an expense with the passage of time. For example, if BHT pays $150 for an insurance policy covering its plant, property, and equipment for the following year, it records the following entry at the date of payment:

Prepaid Insurance	150	
Cash		150

As time passes, the insurance is consumed as coverage expires. If six months have passed and half of the coverage, or $75 worth of the amount prepaid, has been consumed, BHT would make the following entry:

Insurance Expense	75	
Prepaid Insurance		75

EXPENSES THAT ARE INCURRED BEFORE THEY ARE PAID IN CASH

Salary expense is often incurred prior to it being paid, as most firms issue checks to employees after services have been received. If employees have worked for the firm, but haven't been paid, the firm should record an expense and a liability (salaries payable) indicating its obligation to pay the employees at a later date. To illustrate, if BHT employees earned $25 during the last week of December but will not be paid until the end of the first week in January, BHT would make the following entry on December 31:

Salaries Expense	25	
Salaries Payable		25

When BHT pays the employees, it would make the following entry:

Salaries payable	25	
Cash		25

Note that the initial entry in each of the previous four examples results in the creation of an asset or liability. These accrual-based assets and liabilities would not exist under the cash basis. In fact, most assets and liabilities that exist on a GAAP-prepared balance sheet, except cash, arise as a consequence of accrual-based accounting. These include receivables (revenue recognized before cash is received), inventories, prepaid expenses, property and equipment, intangible assets (cash paid before expense is recognized), payables and accrued liabilities (expense recognized before cash is paid), and deferred revenues (cash received before revenue is recognized).

Almost all of the transactions we have just discussed involve the use of an adjusting entry. Recall from our discussion in Chapter 3 that adjusting entries are made at the end of the period for transactions that do not involve an exchange with an external party. For example, when BHT recorded its deferred revenue, this entry was triggered by the receipt of cash. However, the later recognition of deferred revenue on the income statement was not accompanied by an exchange event and therefore was recorded via an adjusting entry. Similarly, the recording of prepaid insurance was triggered by the cash payment of the premium, while the recognition of insurance expense was recorded via an adjusting entry by the accountant after it was determined how much of the insurance coverage had expired. For a more detailed discussion of various adjusting entries refer to Appendix A.

The flexibility within GAAP as it relates to accrual entries might allow management to understate discretionary or estimated expenses or overstate estimated revenues in order to meet analysts' forecasts or internal performance targets. Considerable attention has been given to the implications of management's discretion within GAAP on earnings forecasts, estimates of firm value, and management compensation.

VALUATION IMPLICATIONS OF INCOME RECOGNITION

Reported net income plays an important role in determining a company's value. Simply put, net income from an accrual-accounting is informative about future cash flows to the business that, in turn, implies future potential cash flows to investors. The stream of future cash flows to investors determines the value of a company (as we describe more fully in Chapter 14). A company must generate positive cash flows for investors either in the form of dividends or an increased stock price in order to remain a viable business.

Both revenue and expense recognition involve assumptions and estimation. Accounting standards seek to provide relevant and timely information about a company to assist in forecasting its future while at the same time assuring the reliability of the information in the face of estimation and uncertainty. The criteria for revenue and expense recognition seek to balance these desired attributes in providing guidelines for the determination of earnings. Nevertheless, the link between current income and future cash flows remains uncertain. To improve our understanding of the imprecise relation between current earnings and future cash flows, let's look at the income statement more closely.

INCOME STATEMENT FORMAT

Financial statements should provide information that helps current and potential investors, creditors, and other users to assess the amount, timing, and uncertainty of prospective net cash flows to the firm. The income statement reports on a company's financial performance and provides information about future expected cash flows.

GAAP does not specify the format of the income statement in detail. As a result, the degree to which specific line items are combined into the aggregate line items that appear on the statement (sometimes referred as the degree of aggregation), as well as the labels used for the aggregate items, vary widely across firms. Because this can make statement interpretation challenging for the novice financial statement user, let's take a closer look at the line items.

LINE ITEM DEFINITIONS

When looking at the income statement, you should first determine which items relate to the core operations of the business, or are *persistent,* and which are *transitory,* or unrelated to the company's core operations. Investors value persistent profits more highly than transitory ones as they are more likely to continue in the future. For example, a business might report a loss from a lawsuit that involves a substantial cash outlay. However, this one-time cost has different implications for the value of the firm than a loss caused by operations (e.g., when product's costs exceed its sales). Thus, proper classification of items as continuing/recurring or noncontinuing/nonrecurring provides investors and financial statement users with more accurate forecasts of future cash flow.

To this end, the FASB provides direction in its definition (FASB Concepts No. 6, "Elements of Financial Statements") of revenues and expenses (FASB, SFAC No. 6, 1985):

● *Revenues:* "inflows or other enhancements of assets of an entity or settlements of its liabilities (or a combination of both) from delivering or producing goods, rendering services, or other activities that constitute the entity's ongoing major or central operations."

● *Expenses:* "outflows or other using up of assets or incurrences of liabilities (or a combination of both) from delivering or producing goods, rendering services, or carrying out other activities that constitute the entity's ongoing major or central operations."

● *Gains:* "increases in equity (net assets) from peripheral or incidental transactions of an entity and other events and circumstances affecting the entity except those that result from revenues or investments by owners."

● *Losses:* "decreases in equity (net assets) from peripheral or incidental transactions of an entity and from all other transactions and other events and circumstances affecting the entity except those that result from expenses or distributions to owners."

INCOME STATEMENT LABELS

The degree of aggregation and labeling of income statement items varies widely across companies. For example, some companies will explicitly list items such as gross profit, income from continuing operations, and other subcategories, while others simply list all revenues and subtract all costs. Income statements that provide greater detail and breakdown of costs by category are referred to as **multiple step.** Those that simply list revenue and expenses in two broad categories are called **single step.** Because valuing companies requires the ability to estimate future cash flows to owners, financial disclosures that help users to discern which revenues and costs are related to core continuing activities are most useful to financial statement users.

In general, multiple-step income statements include the following categories:

● Gross Profit
● Income from Continuing Operations
● Nonrecurring Items
● Extraordinary Items
● Accounting Changes and Errors

Let's look at each of the categories in more detail.

Income from Continuing Operations

Income from continuing operations is the difference between a company's operating revenues and its operating expenses. It does not include revenues from nonoperating sources nor from operations that a company discontinues. For example, Exhibit 4.10 shows the income statement for Albertson's, Inc., a large national grocery store chain. Note the line "Operating Profit," which reflects income from continuing operations. However, while Albertson's expects most of the operating items to continue from period to period, the company also lists several items that might not be considered recurring: "Merger-Related and Exit Costs," "Litigation Settlement," and "Impairment Store Closures." Albertson's separately discloses these one-time or limited-term items to allow analysts to adjust these charges out of the operating profits before trying to use the historical data to forecast future operating profits.

Exhibit 4.11 shows an income statement for Target for 2000 including comparative results for 1999 and 1998. Note that a complete income statement also includes earnings per share information (described later in the chapter). Target

Exhibit 4.10
Albertson Corporation
Consolidated Statement of
Earnings (millions except per
share data)

THE REAL WORLD

Albertson Corporation

In millions except per share data	52 weeks 02/01/2001	52 weeks 02/01/2000	52 weeks 01/28/1999
Sales	$36,762	$37,478	$35,872
Cost of sales	26,336	27,164	26,156
Gross profit	10,426	10,314	9,716
Selling, general, and administrative expenses	8,740	8,641	7,846
Merger-related and exit costs	24	396	195
Litigation settlement		37	
Impairment-store closures			24
Operating profit	1,662	1,240	1,651
Other (expense) income:			
Interest, net	(385)	(353)	(337)
Other, net	(3)	12	24
Earnings before taxes and extraordinary items	1,274	899	1,338
Income taxes	509	472	537
Earnings before extraordinary items	765	427	801
Extraordinary loss on extinguishment of debt, net of tax benefit of $7		(23)	
Net earnings	$ 765	$ 404	$ 801

Exhibit 4.11
Target Corporation
Consolidated Results of
Operations (millions except
per share data)

THE REAL WORLD

Target Corporation

	2000	1999	1998
Sales	$36,362	$33,212	$30,203
Net credit revenues	541	490	459
Total revenues	36,903	33,702	30,662
Cost of sales	25,295	23,029	21,085
Selling, general, and administrative expenses	8,190	7,490	6,843
Depreciation and amortization	940	854	780
Interest expense	425	393	398
Earnings before income taxes and extraordinary charges	2,053	1,936	1,556
Provision for income taxes	789	751	594
Net earnings before extraordinary charges	1,264	1,185	962
Extraordinary charges from purchase and redemption of debt, net of tax	—	41	27
Net earnings	$ 1,264	$ 1,144	$ 935
Earnings before extraordinary charges	$ 1.40	$ 1.32	$ 1.07
Extraordinary charges	—	(.04)	(.03)
Basic earnings per share	$ 1.40	$ 1.28	$ 1.04
Earnings before extraordinary charges	$ 1.38	$ 1.27	$ 1.02
Extraordinary charges	0	(.04)	(.03)
Diluted earnings per share	$ 1.38	1.23	.99

reports cost of sales; selling, general, and administrative expenses; depreciation; and amortization and interest expense. These reflect typical categories for a retail or wholesale company that sells products. However, Target's income statement does not explicitly show operating earnings. Thus Target's income statement readers must determine from the account titles, placement on the financial statement, and the disclosures provided in Target's footnotes which items represent Target's operating income.

Note that Target shows "Net Credit Revenues" in its total revenue section. This is interest income that represents income from Target's financing operations. Financing is one of Target's core operations, so analysts would probably classify this as a part of operating revenues. If, however, firms report interest income primarily from investment activities, the revenue would be classified as nonoperating or other revenue.

Nonrecurring Items

In addition to separating operating from nonoperating items, investors also want to identify recurring versus nonrecurring items. Unusual or infrequent revenues and/or expenses should be highlighted to signal financial statement users that the items do not have the same kind of information about future cash flows as do normal recurring ones. Some firms simply label unusual items as such. In other cases, accounting standard setters provide specific guidelines for how to report such items.

GAAP requires three items to be shown after the computation of tax expense: **discontinued operations, extraordinary items,** and the **cumulative effect of changes in accounting principles.** Because these items appear below both operating and nonoperating items and after the computation of tax expense, they are often referred to as "below the line" items. Because they are shown after the tax computation, firms show these items on a net of tax basis. For example, Target reported an extraordinary charge of $41 million in 1999. This $41 million represents the net amount after subtracting the tax effect.

Discontinued Operations

Results from discontinued operations represent amounts related to a line of business, such as a product, that a company decides to discontinue. The income statement items related to discontinued operations include (1) any gain or loss from operations of the discontinued business after the decision is made to discontinue and prior to actual termination of operations, and (2) any gain or loss on disposal of the business. In December, 2002, H.J. Heinz decided to spin off its pet snacks, U.S. tuna, U.S. retail private label soup and private label gravy, College Inn broths, and its U.S. infant feeding businesses. The income statement for Heinz in Exhibit 4.12 reflects the discontinued operations.

Extraordinary Items

Extraordinary items are both unusual in nature and infrequent in occurrence. These gains and losses are not expected to recur, and hence are segregated from operations. Because management may have an incentive to classify all bad news as extraordinary, the FASB developed guidelines that specify when a firm may classify an item as extraordinary. For example, the "unusual" nature criteria guidelines specify that the item must be unusual within the existing context of

Note that analysts often consider certain items as nonrecurring beyond those specified for GAAP purposes when they are valuing the firm. For instance, if a firm recorded a restructuring charge during the period, it wouldn't earmark this item as extraordinary but it is nonrecurring. If an item is less than likely to recur, then an analyst would put less weight on this item when determining value.

Exhibit 4.12
H.J. HEINZ Co. Income
Statement

THE REAL WORLD

H.J. Heinz

52 Weeks Ended (in 000s):	Apr-30-03	May-1-02	May-2-01
Sales	$8,236,836	$7,614,036	$6,987,698
Cost of products sold	5,304,362	4,858,087	4,407,267
Gross profit	2,932,474	2,755,949	2,580,431
Selling, general, and administrative expenses	1,758,658	1,456,077	1,591,472
Operating income	1,173,816	1,299,872	988,959
Interest income	31,083	26,197	22,597
Interest expense	223,532	230,611	262,488
Other expense/(income), net	112,636	44,938	(5,358)
Income from continuing operations before income taxes and cumulative effect of change in accounting principle	868,731	1,050,520	754,426
Provision for income taxes	313,372	375,339	190,495
Income from continuing operations before cumulative effect of change in accounting principle	555,359	675,181	563,931
Income/(loss) from discontinued operations, net of tax	88,738	158,708	(70,638)
Income before cumulative effect of change in accounting principle	644,097	833,889	493,293
Cumulative effect of change in accounting principle	(77,812)	–	(15,281)
Net income	$ 566,285	$ 833,889	$ 478,012

The issues surrounding extraordinary items highlight the difficulties involved in determining operating earnings or income from continuing operations. Management has an incentive to classify losses as extraordinary and to suggest that the losses will not persist into the future, and to move nonoperating and one-time gain items to revenues to make them appear as if they will recur. Accounting and auditing standards are intended to minimize these opportunities.

the business. Tornado damage in Oklahoma City, Oklahoma, would likely not be considered extraordinary because these storms frequently occur in Oklahoma. The possibility of tornado damage would therefore be considered a normal business risk of locating in Oklahoma. However, tornado damage in New Hampshire might meet these criteria.

GAAP also occasionally specifies extraordinary-item treatment for transactions that would not normally meet the criteria. For example, from 1975 through 2001, when companies retired debt early and incurred a book gain or loss, they reported these items as extraordinary. These gains and losses had no future cash flow implications. However, early retirements of debt have become so common that the FASB recently concluded that gains and losses on debt retirements should no longer be classified as extraordinary.

The FASB concluded that events related to the terrorist attack on the World Trade Center on September 11, 2001 were not extraordinary. The event would clearly be classified as unusual and infrequent, but the FASB was not convinced that the costs associated with this event were easily measurable. Further, the FASB was concerned that managers of poorly performing firms (particularly in the airline industry) would be tempted to classify all of their operating losses as extraordinary. Firms can still give significant footnote disclosure to explain any event that they believe significantly impacted their operations during the fiscal year. The obvious difficulty for analysts is to sort out which of the firm's results are expected to continue and which were related to this one-time event.

Accounting Changes and Errors

Accounting changes and errors comprise a third category of item that can result in separate disclosure. Accounting changes can occur from a change in accounting principle or from a change in estimate. Changes in accounting estimates do not require any restatements and may not even be disclosed. However, voluntary changes in accounting principle require firms to provide an adjustment for the effects of the change in prior years. In the year of the change, there will be a catch-up adjustment, known as the *cumulative effect* of the accounting principle change. Firms report this catch-up adjustment in a matter similar to that used for disposal of a segment of a business and extraordinary items. Accounting errors in prior period do require the restatement of prior periods through an adjustment to the beginning balance of the retained earnings account. These are called **prior period adjustments.**

PRO-FORMA EARNINGS

Recently, the SEC increased its focus on companies' misuse of accounting to mislead investors. One area of concern has been the presentation of pro forma earnings that represent a company in a more favorable light than actual earnings. **Pro forma earnings,** also called "as if" earnings, are earnings restated to reflect certain assumptions different from those in the actual earnings statement. For example, Waste Management, Inc. reported net income of $30 million for the third quarter of 2001. However, in its press release announcing its third quarter earnings, Waste Management reported pro forma earnings of $225 million. Items that the company eliminated from the pro forma earnings included consulting fees and truck painting.

In the November 2001 press release, Waste Management, Inc. announced financial results for its third quarter ended September 30, 2001. Revenues for the quarter were $2.90 billion as compared to $3.12 billion in the one-year-ago period. Included in the third quarter revenues was $203 million from operations which have since been sold. Net income reported for the quarter was $30 million, or $.05 per diluted share, for the third quarter 2000. On a pro forma basis, after adjusting for unusual costs and certain other items, including a charge related to the agreement to settle the class action lawsuit, third quarter 2001 net income was $225 million, or $.36 per diluted share as compared with $208 million or $33 per diluted share, in the one-year-ago period. Note that this disclosure offers significant information about which items are nonrecurring (e.g., sold operations and the lawsuit settlement). Also note that the company failed to include these items in its pro-forma disclosure.

EARNINGS PER SHARE

GAAP requires firms to disclose **earnings per share** in the income statement. (See the disclosure of Target in Exhibit 4.11.) There are two components of earnings per share, basic earnings per share and fully-diluted earnings per share. **Basic**

Analysts often focus on per share earnings when forecasting earnings and, as we discussed, the ability to meet earnings forecasts can significantly affect a company's share price.

earnings per share is simply net income divided by the weighted average number of shares of common stock outstanding for a company. Hence, it measures the per share earnings accruing to shareholders. A company reports **fully-diluted earnings per share** when it has stock options and other instruments that are convertible into shares of common stock that could potentially reduce the common shareholder's proportionate share of earnings if the instruments were converted. For example, when a company provides an executive stock option plan, more shares outstanding will occur if and when the executives exercise their options. This will reduce the proportionate equity in earnings of current shareholders. The fully-diluted earnings per share figure provides an estimate of this type of dilution. It calculates how low earnings per share might become if everything is converted. We'll provide a more detailed discussion of earnings per share and its computation in Chapter 12.

COMPREHENSIVE INCOME

FASB Concepts Statement 6 (FASB, SFAC No. 6, 1985) defines **comprehensive income** as the change in equity of a firm due to transactions and other events and circumstances from nonowner sources. It includes all changes in equity except those resulting from investments by owners and distributions to owners. At first glance, this appears to be a definition of earnings. The difference is that accounting standards allow for some items that affect owners' equity to bypass the income statement and be recorded directly in stockholders' equity.

Primarily, these transactions relate to holding gains and losses on certain investments in equity securities and the balance sheet effects of foreign currency translations. Foreign currency translation gains and losses occur when a company has a subsidiary in another country whose accounting records are maintained in a currency other than the U.S. dollar. When the results of this subsidiary are combined to produce the consolidated financial statements of the company, they must be translated from the currency in which they are kept to U.S. dollars by applying various exchange rates. This translation produces gains and losses in dollar terms that must be accounted for and reported. In many circumstances, these gains and losses bypass the income statement and end up in comprehensive income. Accounting standards require that comprehensive income be reported separately from earnings, usually disclosed in the Statement of Shareholders' Equity.

SUMMARY AND TRANSITION

Understanding the basis for recognition of revenues and expenses, as well as how those are presented, is critical to analyzing and using financial statements for decision making. The income statement provides useful information about future cash flows, but that information must also be both timely and reliable. In some cases, the trade-offs for more timely information may reduce the certainty of the information presented. As we saw in this chapter, a firm might wait and recognize revenues on long-term construction contracts until it receives cash. However, months or even years may lapse between the time construction begins and the contract price is fully collected. This lag reduces the usefulness of the information. Financial accounting standards are not intended to eliminate uncertainty, but they are intended to balance the conflict between the goals of providing relevant and timely information with information that is reliable and accurate.

At a conceptual level, accrual accounting seeks to recognize revenues as earned, rather than as the cash is received, and expenses as incurred, rather than as the cash is paid. To implement this concept, those who set the standards have devised criteria for revenue and related expense recognition that identify where in the operating cycle recognition is appropriate.

The usefulness of earnings in valuing the firm is enhanced by separating continuing/recurring operating items from more transitory noncontinuing/nonrecurring ones, such as profits or losses from discontinued operations, restructuring charges, and extraordinary items. The effects of accounting changes should also be identified to improve estimates of future earnings numbers.

END OF CHAPTER MATERIAL

KEY TERMS

Accrual-Basis Accounting	Deferred Revenue
Cash-Basis Accounting	Multiple-Step Income Statement
Revenue Recognition	Single-Step Income Statement
Revenue Recognition Criteria	Income from Continuing Operations
Realized/Realizable	Discontinued Operations
Earned	Extraordinary Items
Installment Method	Cumulative Effect of Changes in Accounting Principles
Cost Recovery Method	Prior Period Adjustment
Completed Contract Method	Pro Forma Earnings
Percentage Completion Method	Earnings per Share
Matching Concept	Basic Earnings per Share
Cost of Goods Sold	Fully-Diluted Earnings per Share
Deferred Expense	Comprehensive Income

ASSIGNMENT MATERIAL

REVIEW QUESTIONS

1. What advantages and disadvantages do you see in using the cash basis of accounting rather than the accrual basis?

2. Respond to each of the following statements with a true or false answer:

   a. Dividends declared decrease cash immediately.

   b. The cash basis recognizes expenses when they are incurred.

   c. There is no such thing as a prepaid rent account on the cash basis.

d. Dividends are an expense of doing business and should appear on the income statement.

e. On the accrual basis, interest should only be recognized when it is paid.

3. Explain how a prepaid expense (such as rent) gets handled under accrual basis accounting.

4. Explain how an accrued expense (such as interest) gets handled under accrual basis accounting.

5. Suppose that a firm's accounting policy was to recognize warranty expense only when warranty service was provided. Discuss whether this meets the matching concept under accrual basis accounting and other ways that this transaction might be handled.

6. Diagram a typical operating cycle of a manufacturing firm and briefly explain what assets and liabilities are likely to be created as a result of this operating cycle.

7. List the two major revenue recognition criteria that exist under GAAP.

8. Describe the concept of revenue being "earned" and contrast it with the concept of revenue being "realized."

9. Explain the difference between the percentage completion method and the completed contracts method.

10. Explain the difference between the installment method and the cost recovery method.

11. Explain the meaning of the matching concept.

◉ APPLYING YOUR KNOWLEDGE

12. Brickstone Construction Company signs a contract to build a building in four years for $40,000,000. The expected costs for each year are:

Year 1:	$ 9,750,000
Year 2:	12,025,000
Year 3:	6,500,000
Year 4:	4,225,000
Total	$32,500,000

The building is completed in year 4. Compute for each year, the total revenue, expenses, and profit under:

a. The Percentage of Completion Method

b. The Completed Contract Method

13. Sandra Carlson sold her house, which cost her $210,000, to Bob Fletcher for $300,000. Bob agreed to pay $60,000 per year for a period of five years. Compute the revenue, expense, and profit for each of the five years (ignoring interest):

a. The Installment Method

b. The Cost-Recovery Method

14. Imperial Corporation purchases a factory from Superior Manufacturing Company for $1,500,000. The cost of the factory on Superior's book is $975,000. The terms of agreement are that yearly installment payments of $705,000, $505,000, $455,000, and $255,000 will be made over the next four years. Each of these payments includes an interest payment of $105,000 per year. Compute the revenue, expense, and profit for each of the four years accruing to Superior Manufacturing Company as per:

   a. The Installment Method

   b. The Cost Recovery Method

15. Cruise Shipping, Inc. agreed to rebuild the *Santa Marice;* an old cargo ship owned by the Oceanic Shipping Company. Both parties signed the contract on November 28, Year 1, for $120 million which is to be paid as follows:

   $12 million at the signing of the contract
   $24 million on December 30, Year 2
   $36 million on June 1, Year 3
   $48 million at completion, on August 15 Year 4.

   The following cost were incurred by Cruise Shipping, Inc. (in millions):

Year 1:	$19.2
Year 2:	38.4
Year 3:	24.0
Year 4:	14.4
Total	$96.0

   a. Compute the revenue, expense, and profit for each of the four years (ignoring interest) for Cruise Shipping, Inc. as per:

      1. The Installment Method

      2. The Cost-Recovery Method

      3. The Percentage of Completion Method

      4. The Completed Contract Method

   b. Which method do you think should be employed by Cruise Shipping, Inc. to show the company's performance under the contract? Why?

16. Computronics Corporation received a contract on March 3, Year 1 for setting up a central communication and pricing center for a small university. The contract price was $1,000,000 which is to be paid as follows:

$150,000	at the signing of the contract
$ 60,000	on July 1, Year 1
$ 30,000	on December 31, Year 1
$ 80,000	on March 25, Year 2
$100,000	on August 25, Year 2
$180,000	on December 31, Year 2
$400,000	on June 30, Year 3

The system was completed on June 30, Year 3.
Estimated and actual costs were:

$150,000   for the six months ending June 30, Year 1
$225,000   for the six months ending December 31, Year 1
$262,500   for the six months ending June 30, Year 2
$75,000   for the six months ending December 31, Year 2
$37,500   for the six months ending June 30, Year 3

Total $750,000

a. Compute the revenue, expense, and profit for each of the six months as per:

  1. The Percentage of Completion Method

  2. The Completed Contract Method

  3. The Installment Method

  4. The Cost-Recovery Method

b. Which method should be used by Computronics Corporation? Why?

17. Forte Builders, a construction company, recognizes revenue from its long-term contracts using the percentage completion method. On March 29, 20X3, the company signed a contract to construct a building for $500,000. The company estimated that it would take four years to complete the contract and would cost the company an estimated $325,000. The expected costs in each of the four years are as follows:

Year	Cost
20X3	$113,750
20X4	97,500
20X5	81,250
20X6	32,500
Total	$325,000

On December 31, 20X4, the date Forte closes its books, the company revised its estimates for the cost in 20X5 and 20X6. It estimated that the contract would cost $200,000 in 20X5 and $100,000 in 20X6 to complete the contract. Compute the revenue, expense, and profit/loss for each of the four years.

18. Samson Industries purchased furniture and appliances from the Metal and Wood Company for $75,000 under the following payment plan which called for semiannual payments over two years:

Payment	Amount
1	$33,600
2	16,800
3	22,400
4	11,200
Total	$84,000

Each payment contains interest (assume that the proportionate share of interest in each payment is the same as the proportion of that payment to the total payments). Assuming that the cost of the furniture and appliances is $60,000, compute the revenue, expense, and profit that Metal and Wood Company would report for each of the installment payments under:

a. The Installment Method

b. The Cost-Recovery Method

19. On June 21, 20X1, Tristar Electric Company signed a contract with Denton Power, Incorporated to construct a small hydroelectric generating plant. The contract price was $10,000,000, and it was estimated that the project would cost Tristar $7,850,000 to complete over a three-year period. On June 21, 20X1, Denton paid Tristar $1,000,000 as a default-deposit. In the event that Denton backed out of the contract, Tristar could keep this deposit. Otherwise the default-deposit would apply as the final payment on the contract (assume for accounting purposes that this is treated as a deposit until completion of the contract). The other contractual payments are as follows:

Date	Amount
10/15/X1	$3,150,000
4/15/X2	1,350,000
12/15/X2	1,800,000
3/15/X3	1,755,000
8/10/X3	945,000
Total	$9,000,000

Estimated costs of construction were as follows:

Year	Amount
1	$3,532,500
2	2,747,500
3	1,570,000

The contract was completed on January 10, 20X4. Tristar closes its books on December 31 each year. Compute the revenue, expense, and profit to be recognized in each year using:

a. The Installment Method

b. The Cost-Recovery Method

c. The Percentage Completion Method

d. The Completed Contracts Method

20. Financial analysts frequently refer to the quality of a firm's earnings. Discuss how the quality of two firms' earnings might differ depending on the revenue recognition method that the two firms use.

21. Suppose that a firm is currently private but is thinking of going public (i.e., issuing shares in a publicly traded market). Discuss the incentives that the

firm might have to misstate its income statement via its revenue recognition policies.

22. Suppose that you are the sales manager of a firm with an incentive plan that provides a bonus based on meeting a certain sales target. Explain how meeting your sales target is influenced by the revenue recognition principles of the firm.

23. Suppose that you are a sales manager of a U.S.-based firm that sells products in Israel, which has traditionally had a high inflation rate. This means that the exchange rate of shekels per dollar typically increases dramatically from year to year. If your compensation is a function of sales as measured in dollars, what risks do you face in meeting your targets and how might you mitigate the risks that you face in meeting those targets?

24. Explain the incentives that a firm has in choosing its revenue recognition method for both financial reporting and tax purposes.

25. In the toy industry it is common to allow customers to return unsold toys within a certain specified period of time. Suppose that a toy manufacturer's year end is December 31 and that the majority of its products are shipped to customers during the last quarter of the year in anticipation of the Christmas holiday. Is it appropriate for the company to recognize revenue upon shipment of the product? Support your answer citing references to revenue recognition criteria.

26. Suppose that an importer in Seattle buys goods from a supplier in Hong Kong. The goods are shipped by cargo vessel. For goods that are in transit at year end, what recognition should the Seattle importer make of these goods in its financial statements? Support your answer based on revenue recognition criteria.

27. Suppose that a company recognizes revenues at the time that title passes to its inventory and that it ships its inventory FOB (free on board) shipping point (i.e., title passes at the shipping point). Suppose at year end that it has loaded a shipment of goods on a truck that is parked on the grounds of the company based on a firm purchase order from a customer. How should the firm treat this inventory in its financial statements at year end?

28. Firms often sell their accounts receivable to raise cash to support their operations. Suppose that a firm sells its accounts receivable with recourse. Recourse means that the buyer can return the account receivable to the selling company if it cannot collect on the receivable. How should this transaction be treated in the financial statements of the selling company?

29. Suppose that ESPN (the sports channel) sells $10,000,000 in advertising slots to be aired during the games that it broadcasts during the NCAA basketball tournament. Suppose further that these slots are contracted for during the month of September with a downpayment of $2,000,000. The ads will be aired in March. If the fiscal year end of ESPN is December 31, how should ESPN recognize this revenue in its financial statements?

30. Suppose that The GAP (a clothing retailer) sells gift certificates for merchandise. During the Christmas holiday period, suppose that it issues $500,000 in gifts certificates. If the firm's fiscal year end is December 31, how should it recognize the issuance of these gift certificates in its financial statements at year end?

31. Suppose that the XYZ Software company produces an inventory tracking software that it sells to manufacturing companies. Further suppose that the software sells for $100,000 each and it requires the company to provide customization to the buyers' operations, which can take several months. If the fiscal year end is September 30 and the company sells ten units of the product in August, how should it recognize these "sales" in the financial statements at year end?

32. Suppose that you are the auditor of ABC Manufacturing Company and during your audit of the firm's inventory you observe a significant amount of inventory that appears to be extremely old. How would you recommend that the firm deal with this inventory and how will it affect the revenues and expenses recognized during the period? Explain the incentives that the management of the firm might have for keeping the inventory in its warehouse.

33. Assume that a company is discontinuing a line of products due to lack of profitability. It is not sure whether this discontinuance meets the criteria for separate recognition as a discontinued line of business. The alternatives are to incorporate the losses from this line within normal operations or report them as a separate line item called "discontinued operations." As a stock analyst, discuss how the alternatives might affect your analysis of the company's stock.

○ USING REAL DATA

34. Zale Corporation sells fine jewelry and giftware in a chain of stores nationwide. The following footnotes appeared in the 2001 annual report along with the income statement below:

Revenue Recognition

The Company recognizes revenue in accordance with the Securities and Exchange Commissions Staff Accounting Bulletin No. 101, Revenue Recognition in Financial Statements (SAB 101). Revenue related to merchandise sales is recognized at the time of the sale, reduced by a provision for returns. The provision for sales returns is based on historical evidence of the Company s return rate. Repair revenues are recognized when the service is complete and the merchandise is delivered to the customers. Net Sales include amortized extended service agreements (ESA) which are amortized over the two-year service agreement period. ESA revenue and related expenses were previously netted in selling, general, and administrative expenses. Prior periods sales and cost of sales have been restated to reflect ESA revenue. The amortized ESA revenues were $25.0 million, $20.8 million, and $16.8 million for the years ended July 31, 2001, 2000, and 1999, respectively, and related ESA costs were $12.5 million, $10.8 million, and $9.5 million for the years ended July 31, 2001, 2000, and 1999, respectively.

Advertising Expenses are charged against operations when incurred and are a component of selling, general, and administrative expenses in the consolidated income statements. Amounts charged against operations were $78.5 million, $66.4 million, and $49.0 million for the years ended July 31, 2001, 2000, and 1999, respectively, net of amounts contributed by vendors to the Company. The amounts of prepaid advertising at July 31, 2001 and 2000, are $6.0 million and $6.4 million, respectively, and are classified as components of other assets in the Consolidated Balance Sheet.

Unusual Charges—Executives

Effective September 6, 2000, Robert J. DiNicola retired as Chairman of the Board but remained as a nonemployee member of the Board. In connection with his severance arrangement, the Company agreed to pay certain benefits of approximately $1.9 million consisting principally of an amount equivalent to one year of salary and bonus and other severance-related benefits including the accelerated vesting of certain options held by Mr. DiNicola.

Additionally, the Board approved the provision to Mr. DiNicola by the Company of a full recourse, $2.2 million interest-bearing loan at 8.74 percent for the sole purpose of purchasing 125,000 stock options prior to their expiration. The Company also extended the exercise period on an additional 500,000 stock options set to expire on September 6, 2002 to the earlier of the original ten-year term (to expire July 9, 2007), the maximum term pursuant to the Company's stock option plan, or two years after Mr. DiNicola leaves the Board of Directors. Based on the intrinsic value of these stock options on the modification date, no compensation charge was recorded by the Company.

Effective February 12, 2001, Beryl B. Raff resigned as Chairman of the Board and Chief Executive Officer. In connection with her resignation, the Company agreed to pay certain benefits of approximately $2.5 million consisting principally of an amount equivalent to three years of salary and other severance-related benefits including accelerated vesting of certain options and restricted stock.

Robert J. DiNicola was reappointed as Chairman of the Board and Chief Executive Officer, effective February 21, 2001, under a three-year contract with terms substantially consistent with his previous contract when he held the same position. In August 2001, the Company entered into a five-year employment agreement with Mr. DiNicola effective upon Mr. DiNicola's reelection as Chairman of the Board and Chief Executive Officer, replacing the earlier employment agreement. In April 2001, the Company extended a $2.1 million, three-year interest bearing loan at 7.25 percent to Mr. DiNicola for the purpose of purchasing a home. In August 2001, the loan was modified and extended with the entire principal amount to be repaid in August 2006.

Nonrecurring Charge

Upon the return of Robert J. DiNicola as Chairman and Chief Executive Officer on February 21, 2001, the Company performed an in-depth review to determine the inventory that was not of a quality consistent with the strategic direction of the Company's brands. As a result of that review, the Company recorded a nonrecurring charge in Cost of Sales of $25.2 million to adjust the valuation of such inventory and provide for markdowns to liquidate or sell-through the inventory.

ZALE CORP.: Income Statement			
	07/31/2001	07/31/2000	07/31/1999
Net sales	$2,068,242,000	$1,814,362,000	$1,445,634,000
Cost of sales	1,034,970,000	930,826,000	746,663,000
Nonrecurring charge	25,236,000	0	0
Gross margin	1,008,036,000	883,536,000	698,971,000
Selling, general, and administrative Expenses	804,780,000	630,687,000	509,570,000
Depreciation and amortization expense	58,290,000	42,431,000	29,478,000
Unusual item—executive transactions	4,713,000	0	0
Operating earnings	140,253,000	210,418,000	159,923,000
Interest expense, net	6,857,000	32,178,000	30,488,000
Earnings before income taxes	133,396,000	178,240,000	129,435,000
Income taxes	51,348,000	66,726,000	48,503,000
Net earnings	$ 82,048,000	$ 111,514,000	$ 80,932,000

a. Provide support for Zale's revenue recognition policy for its extended service agreements.

b. From an analyst's point of view, discuss why the change in reporting ESA's as part of revenue rather than as an offset to expenses would be important.

c. From an analyst's point of view, discuss why the disclosure of advertising costs by year might be important.

d. From an analyst's point of view, discuss how you might use the disclosures concerning the unusual and nonrecurring charges to assist you in predicting the stock price for Zale.

35. Lands' End, Incorporated is a direct merchant of clothing and other cloth products that are sold primarily through catalog mailings. The cost of catalog production and mailing is fairly substantial for a company such as Lands' End. Discuss how the costs associated with catalog production and mailing should be treated for accounting purposes. Frame your answer in terms of the revenue recognition criteria and the matching concept discussed in this chapter.

36. Many consumer electronics retailers have offered extended warranty contracts to their customers. These contracts typically provide warranty coverage beyond the manufacturer's warranty period, usually anywhere between 12 and 60 months from the date of purchase. The cost of these contracts is generally collected at the time of the purchase of the product. The following is the revenue recognition Disclosure for Best Buy, Inc.:

Revenue Recognition

We recognize revenues from the sale of merchandise at the time the merchandise is sold. We recognize service revenues at the time the service is provided, the sales price is fixed or determinable, and collectibility is reasonably assured.

We sell extended service contracts, called Performance Service Plans, on behalf of an unrelated third party. In jurisdictions where we are not deemed to be the obligor on the contract at the time of sale, commissions are recognized in revenues at the time of sale. In jurisdictions where we are deemed to be the obligor on the contract at the time of sale, commissions are recognized in revenues ratably over the term of the service contract.

Discuss why Best Buy's revenue recognition policy, with regard to commissions on Performance Service Plans, is different in different jurisdictions. Base your defense on the nature of the transaction and the revenue recognition criteria found in GAAP. In jurisdictions in which they are the obligor, what might happen to them should the third party not be able to live up to this agreement?

37. In the early 1990s a new business emerged to help individuals deal with the financial burdens of terminal illnesses, such as AIDS. If a terminally ill person has a life insurance policy, an investor group of companies could buy the insurance policy from the individual for a lump sum settlement amount. The seller could then use the proceeds to pay their bills. The buyer agrees to continue to make the premium payments until the individual dies and then collects the proceeds of the insurance policy upon death. These types of agreements are called viatical settlements. Depending on the estimated life span of the individual and the creditworthiness of the insurance company, the buyer might offer somewhere between 25 to 80 percent of the face value of the policy.

a. If you were an investor, how would you decide how much to pay for a given viatical agreement?

b. Having agreed on a price, how would you recognize revenue from this agreement (assume for the purposes of this question that there is more than one year from the inception of the agreement to the death of the seller) over the life of the contract?

c. Given your revenue recognition method outlined in part b, how would you treat the payment of premiums over the life of the contract?

d. Discuss any ethical dilemmas that the buyers of viatical agreements might face in the conduct of their business.

BEYOND THE BOOK

38. Using an electronic database, search for a company that has changed its revenue recognition methods during the last three years. Answer the following questions:

a. Describe the method that was used before the change as well as the new method.

b. Does the company give a reason for the change? If so, describe the change; if not, speculate on why the change occurred.

c. How significant an effect did the change have on the firm's financial statements? As an investor, how would you view this change?

d. Did the auditor agree with the change? Do you agree and why?

Prepare a short two- to three-page paper to respond to these questions.

CHAPTER 5

Financial Statements: Measuring Cash Flow

LEARNING OBJECTIVES

After reading this chapter you should be able to:

1. Understand and interpret the information about operating, investing, and financing activities found in the cash flow statement.

2. Explain the relationship between the cash flow statement and changes in balance sheet accounts.

3. Construct a cash flow statement using the indirect method.

4. Define free cash flows and explain how they can be determined from the Statement of Cash Flows.

Moody's Investor Service announced it was reviewing the debt rating for Georgia-Pacific (GP), citing concerns with Georgia-Pacific's weakening cash flow. Mark Gray, an analyst with Moody's said, "We looked at the company's position and we were concerned about the scope of the asset sales to Willamette and the weakening cash flow over the near term that would limit their debt reduction ability."

The announcement of Moody's review of Georgia-Pacific's debt rating highlights the importance of strong cash flows to a company's value. A downgrade in debt raises the cost of borrowing for Georgia-Pacific as well as lowers equity values. In this chapter we discuss the content and meaning of the information contained in the statement of cash flows.

Broadly speaking, the statement of cash flows reflects the operating, investing, and financing activities of the firm described in Chapter 1. As such, the statement of cash flows provides different information than the income statement that focuses on changes in stockholders' equity arising from operations. The cash flow statement explains changes in cash in terms of changes in noncash accounts appearing on successive balance sheets. These changes are not limited to those involving operations, but include those involving investing and financing.

Further, with respect to operating activities, the cash flow statement offers a different perspective than reflected on the income statement. As we discussed in Chapter 4, firms determine net income on an accrual basis by the application of revenue and expense recognition criteria. Recall that under the accrual basis of accounting, revenue may be earned and expenses incurred before or after the cash flows to which they relate. Net income, therefore, reflects the revenues earned and the expenses incurred by the firm as a result of its operating activities during the period, *not* the operating cash inflows and outflows. Operating cash flows may precede or follow the recognition of revenues or expenses on the income statement. Timing issues thus separate the recognition of income from the actual cash flows of the firm.

For example, if a firm's sales grow rapidly but a significant lag exists between the cash outflows to make the company's product and the inflows from the sales collections, the firm may experience a severe liquidity crisis. In other words, a firm may possess insufficient available cash to make the required payments for items such as salaries and accounts payable. This liquidity crisis may then spark the need to obtain additional financing to pay bills and to support the company's growth. If analysts focused on only the income statement, they would miss the liquidity crisis. Further, as the income statement does not report on the investing and financing activities of the firm, analysts would not see any attempts made by the firm to address the liquidity crisis (e.g., through additional financing or a slowdown in investing). The cash flow statement not only makes any liquidity crisis transparent, it also indicates how a firm addresses the crises. Because it contains such crucial data, let's take a closer look at the information a typical cash flow statement provides.

CASH FLOW STATEMENT COMPONENTS

SFAS 95 (FASB, SFAS No. 95, 1987) requires that all companies issue a cash flow statement and provides guidelines regarding its format. The Statement of Cash Flows provides information about changes in cash flows from all sources: operating, investing, and financing activities of an entity.

CASH FLOW FROM OPERATING ACTIVITIES

Cash flow from operations includes cash inflows from sales of goods and services to customers, and cash outflows from expenses related to the sales of goods and services to customers, such as cost of goods sold and selling and administrative expenses. In fact, cash from operations can be viewed as a measure of cash-basis

TECH DATA CORP.: Cash Flow	01/31/2002	01/31/2001	01/31/2000
Cash flows from operating activities:			
Cash received from customers	$17,511,511,000	$20,114,486,000	$16,788,960,000
Cash paid to suppliers and employees	(16,406,265,000)	(20,047,551,000)	(16,684,316,000)
Interest paid	(55,871,000)	(94,823,000)	(69,554,000)
Income taxes paid	(72,745,000)	(62,048,000)	(34,176,000)
Net cash provided by (used in) operating activities	976,630,000	(89,936,000)	914,000
Cash flows from investing activities:			
Acquisition of businesses, net of cash acquired	(183,000)	(19,198,000)	(42,898,000)
Expenditures for property and equipment	(28,466,000)	(38,079,000)	(59,038,000)
Software development costs	(20,719,000)	(22,705,000)	(18,381,000)
Net cash used in investing activities	(49,368,000)	(79,982,000)	(120,317,000)
Cash flows from financing activities:			
Proceeds from the issuance of common stock, net of related tax benefit	36,432,000	35,539,000	19,663,000
Net (repayments) borrowings on revolving credit loans	(1,118,167,000)	248,712,000	99,447,000
Proceeds from issuance of long-term debt, net of expense	284,200,000	0	0
Principal payments on long-term debt	(634,000)	(557,000)	(162,000)
Net cash (used in) provided by financing activities	(798,169,000)	283,694,000	118,948,000
Effect of change in year end of certain subsidiaries (Note 3)	0	0	23,626,000
Effect of exchange rate changes on cash	(10,091,000)	(6,637,000)	0
Net increase in cash and cash equivalents	119,002,000	107,139,000	23,171,000
Cash and cash equivalents at beginning of year	138,925,000	31,786,000	8,615,000
Cash and cash equivalents at end of year	$ 257,927,000	$ 138,925,000	$ 31,786,000

Exhibit 5.1
Direct Method Cash Flow Statement

THE REAL WORLD

Tech Data Corp.

earnings because it measures the cash inflows from sales in the period of collection and the cash outflows for expenses in the period of payment.

There are two approaches to presenting cash flow from operations, the **direct method** and the **indirect method.** Under the direct method, a firm first reports cash received from revenue-producing activities, and then subtracts its cash payments for expenses. Exhibit 5.1 illustrates this type of statement (see the shaded operating section). Notice that the company shown (Tech Data, a distributor of hardware and software products) combined its operating cash outflows to employees and suppliers into a single line item.

In contrast, the indirect method starts with net income and shows the adjustments necessary to arrive at cash flows from operations. Exhibit 5.2 shows this method in the statements of Tofutti Brands, Inc. (a producer of soy-based products).

FASB 95 allows the use of either method, as both methods produce identical results of cash from operations. However, most firms use the indirect approach. As a result, FASB 95 requires firms that report under the direct

Exhibit 5.2
Indirect Method Cash Flow
Statement

Tofutti Brands

TOFUTTI BRANDS, Inc.: Cash Flow

	12/29/2001	12/29/2000	12/30/1999
Cash flows from operating activities:			
Net income	$ 1,150,000	$ 956,000	$ 850,000
Adjustments to reconcile net income to net cash flows from operating activities:			
Provision for bad debts	40,000	60,000	60,000
Accrued interest on investments	0	(34,000)	(3,000)
Deferred taxes	(119,000)	(176,000)	332,000
Change in assets and liabilities:			
Accounts receivable	(625,000)	(105,000)	64,000
Inventories	92,000	(342,000)	17,000
Prepaid expenses	(1,000)	(1,000)	5,000
Accounts payable and accrued expenses	9,000	17,000	(51,000)
Accrued compensation	0	175,000	115,000
Income taxes payable	(144,000)	209,000	103,000
Net cash flows from operating activities	402,000	759,000	1,492,000
Cash flows from investing activities:			
Proceeds from redemption of investments	269,000	0	(250,000)
Other assets	(144,000)	(22,000)	(22,000)
Net cash flows from investing activities	125,000	(22,000)	(272,000)
Cash flows from financing activities:			
Notes payable	(8,000)	(22,000)	(18,000)
Issuance of common stock	35,000	50,000	84,000
Purchase of treasury stock	(436,000)	(247,000)	0
Net cash flows from financing activities	(409,000)	(219,000)	66,000
Net change in cash and equivalents	118,000	518,000	1,286,000
Cash and equivalents, at beginning of period	2,211,000	1,693,000	407,000
Cash and equivalents, at end of period	$ 2,329,000	$2,211,000	$1,693,000
Supplemental cash flow information:			
Interest paid		$ 2,000	$ 5,000
Income taxes paid	$ 750,000	$ 579,000	$ 151,000

method to also disclose the operating section data prepared under the indirect method (see Exhibit 5.3). Compare the net cash from operations in both Exhibits 5.1 and 5.3, and note how the amounts are identical. However, you can see that the indirect method disclosure (Exhibit 5.3) provides more information about investments in current operating assets net of operating liabilities than the direct method (Exhibit 5.1).

TECH DATA CORP.: Cash Flow	01/31/2002	01/31/2001	01/31/2000
Reconciliation of net income to net cash provided by (used in) operating activities:			
Net income	$ 110,777,000	$177,983,000	$127,501,000
Adjustments to reconcile net income to net cash provided by (used in) operating activities:			
Depreciation and amortization	63,488,000	63,922,000	57,842,000
Provision for losses on accounts receivable	40,764,000	41,447,000	40,877,000
Special charges (Note 13)	27,000,000	0	0
Deferred income taxes	(11,848,000)	(1,789,000)	1,306,000
Changes in assets and liabilities:			
Decrease (increase) in accounts receivable	314,000,000	(313,197,000)	(202,790,000)
Decrease (increase) in inventories	702,219,000	(146,093,000)	(220,585,000)
(Increase) in prepaid and other assets	(6,248,000)	(11,603,000)	(25,430,000)
(Decrease) increase in accounts payable	(264,722,000)	11,863,000	136,748,000
Increase in accrued expenses	1,200,000	87,531,000	85,445,000
Total adjustments	865,853,000	(267,919,000)	(126,587,000)
Net cash provided by (used in) operating activities	$976,630,000	($89,936,000)	$ 914,000

Exhibit 5.3
Indirect Method Disclosure under Direct Method

THE REAL WORLD

Tech Data

CASH FLOW FROM INVESTING ACTIVITIES

Investing activities involve the cash flow effect of transactions related to a company's long-term assets and investments. Examples include cash paid or received to purchase or sell property, plant, and equipment; investments in securities of other companies; and acquisitions of other companies. The investing activities section provides information about how a company uses its cash to generate future earnings. Investments represent opportunities for future earnings growth. For a growth company, we would normally expect cash from investing activities to be a net outflow, although this depends on the company's growth strategy.

For example, in Tech Data's cash flow statement (Exhibit 5.1), you see significant annual investments in property and equipment, and software development. Contrast this with Tofutti's cash flow statement (Exhibit 5.2), which includes little activity in the investing section. The company primarily leases its facilities (the cash flows from leasing would appear in the operating section) and therefore does not have significant investments in plant and equipment.

The investment section of the cash flow statement is where you would also see investments in other companies including acquisitions. You can see this kind of activity in Tech Data's statements. Note that in most acquisitions the investment cash flow occurs on the date of acquisition. Subsequent to the date of acquisition, the cash flows from operating the newly acquired company will start to appear in the operating section. At the date of acquisition, the firm reports new assets and liabilities from the acquisition (e.g., receivables, inventory, PP&E, accounts payable) that would appear in the firm's balance sheet as of the acquisition date. If a firm acquired a new company mid-year, then the net change in certain asset accounts (such as inventories) would include the changes due to operations and the changes due to the acquisition.

CASH FLOW FROM FINANCING ACTIVITIES

This section of the cash flow statement provides information about transactions with owners and creditors. Financing activities include issuance and repayment of debt such as loans, bank advances, and bonds payable, as well as issuances and repurchases of stock and payments of dividends.

Tofutti (Exhibit 5.2) shows relatively minor outflows of cash to repay notes payable. The remaining transactions relate to issuance of stock and repurchase of shares that are held in its treasury account. Tech Data's statements (Exhibit 5.1) show significantly more activity related to long-term debt.

Now that you can identify the components of the cash flow statement, how do you use its information? One of the best ways is by understanding the mechanics of preparing a cash flow statement. Going through the preparation process can shed light on how a firm generates and uses cash. Additionally, reconciling a firm's cash flow statement to its balance sheet and income statement can be a useful tool for financial statement analysis.

PREPARATION OF THE STATEMENT OF CASH FLOWS

In this section, we'll show how to prepare a cash flow statement (indirect method) using Biohealth, Inc. (BHT), the fictitious wholesale company we discussed in previous chapters. Exhibit 5.4 shows the balance sheets for BHT at 12/31/20X2 and 12/31/20X1. Exhibit 5.5 shows the income statement for BHT for the year ending 12/31/20X2.

We use a T-account worksheet to determine the net effects of the transactions for BHT for 20X2 on the cash account, as shown in Exhibit 5.6. Note that we use this worksheet only to assist in the construction of the cash flow statement. Do not confuse this worksheet with the firm's accounting system that contains the actual entries made to the system. In fact, you can also use a simple spreadsheet instead of a T-account worksheet.

The first step is to place the beginning and ending balances of all of the accounts from the balance sheet in the T-accounts, as shown in Exhibit 5.6. Then, we analyze the changes in the various accounts on the balance sheet and classify them into operating, investing, and financing activities. In order to do this, we rely on information from the income statement as well as any additional information provided about the company's operating, financing, and investing transactions. For example, the following additional information applies to the transactions of BHT for the year ending 12/31/20X2:

Exhibit 5.4
BHT Balance Sheet

Biohealth, Inc. (BHT)
Balance Sheet ($ in millions)

	As of 12/31/20X2	As of 12/31/20X1
Assets		
Current assets:		
Cash	$ 1,510	$ 567
Accounts receivable	3,650	2,464
Inventory	4,400	3,920
Prepaid expenses	360	0
Total current assets	9,920	7,101
Property, plant, and equipment (PPE)	950	540
Less: accumulated depreciation	(210)	(60)
Net property plant and equipment	740	480
	$10,660	$7,581
Liabilities and Stockholders' Equity		
Liabilities:		
Current liabilities:		
Accounts payable	$ 6,671	$5,140
Long-term debt:		
Notes payable	950	400
Total liabilities	7,621	5,540
Stockholders' equity		
Common stock	300	250
Additional paid-in capital	1,950	1,375
Retained earnings	789	266
Total stockholders' equity	3,039	2,041
	$10,660	$7,581

Exhibit 5.5
BHT Income Statement

Biohealth, Inc. (BHT)
Income Statement

	Year ending 12/31/20X2
Revenues	$43,850
Less: Cost of goods sold	(37,272)
Gross profit	6,578
Selling and administrative expenses	5,320
Depreciation expense	150
Interest expense	85
Net income	$1,023

Exhibit 5.6
BHT Cash Flow T-Account
Worksheet

BHT Cash Flow T-Account Worksheet Set Up

	Cash			Accumulated Depreciation—PPE	
Bal.	567			60	Bal.
Operating:					
Investing:				210	Bal.
				Accounts payable	
Financing:				5,140	Bal.
Bal.	1,510			6,671	Bal.
	Accounts receivable			**Notes payable**	
Bal.	2,464			400	Bal.
				950	Bal.
Bal.	3,650				
	Inventory			**Common Stock**	
Bal.	3,920			250	Bal.
Bal.	4,400			300	Bal.
	Prepaid Expenses			**Additional Paid-in capital**	
Bal.	0			1,375	Bal.
Bal.	360				
				1,950	Bal.
	PPE			**Retained Earnings**	
Bal.	540			266	Bal.
Bal.	950			789	Bal.

1. All inventory is purchased on credit from suppliers.
2. All sales to customers are for credit.
3. Borrowed $550 million during 20X2.
4. Issued 50 million shares of $1 par stock at $12.50 per share during 20X2.
5. Declared and paid $500 million in dividends to shareholders during 20X2.

Items 1 and 2 simply summarize common assumptions and need not correspond to the transactions that actually occurred. Items 3 through 5 provide information that you would find in the Statement of Stockholders' Equity and Notes to the Financial Statements.

We are now ready to create the worksheet entries for the cash flow statement. The basic approach is to examine each balance sheet account (other than cash) that changed and then assess its effect on cash. Next, we create a worksheet entry to show this effect on cash along with the corresponding change in the balance sheet account. Once we analyze all of the balance sheet accounts and complete the worksheet entries, we should have the basis of our cash flow statement. Let's start now with determining the worksheet entries for the operating section and then proceed through the investing and financing sections.

WORKSHEET ENTRIES FOR CASH FROM OPERATIONS

The starting point typically begins with analyzing the change in retained earnings. In the indirect approach, we record net income in the Cash account of the worksheet (as well as in the Retained Earnings account, to ensure that debits equal credits) as if it increased cash. We know, however, that not all revenues increase cash and not all expenses use cash. Therefore, subsequent entries will make adjustments to correct for the noncash components of earnings.

We obtain net income from the income statement in Exhibit 5.5, giving us the first entry:

| (1) | Cash | 1,023 | |
| | Retained Earnings | | 1,023 |

We now need to correct our "mistake" of reporting net income as if it were all cash. We start with adjustments to correct the revenue portion of net income.

Adjusting Net Income

Changes in current assets and liabilities in the operating section serve to correct line items in the net income number to their cash flow equivalent. For revenues, these adjustments serve to undo the effects of recognizing revenues when earned rather than as the cash is received, and for expenses the effects of recognizing them when incurred rather than when paid. We can thus view increases in current operating assets as requiring cash (and decreases providing cash) and increases in current operating liabilities as providing cash (and decreases requiring cash). Exhibit 5.7 summarizes the effects of these changes. With this understanding of adjustments, let's return now to our BHT example.

Exhibit 5.7
Adjustments to Net Income
Using the Indirect Method

Positive adjustments to income to determine cash from operations result from:

Decreases in current operating assets (A/R, inventory, prepaid assets, etc.)
Increases in current operating liabilities (A/P, Salaries Payable, etc.)*

Negative adjustments to income to determine cash from operations result from:

Increases in current operating assets other than cash
Decreases in current operating liabilities

*Notes Payable and the Current Portion of Long-Term Debt are typically not considered to be a part of operating liabilities even though they are generally classified as current liabilities. Also, there are instances where operating liabilities are classified as noncurrent and changes in those liabilities are included in the operating section of the cash flow statement.

Revenue Adjustments to Net Income

Because sales revenue is recorded on an accrual basis, not when cash is collected, we need to adjust income for the difference between sales revenue recognized and cash collected on accounts receivable (AR). This difference can be found in the change in the accounts receivable balance. In the case of BHT, accounts receivable increased, meaning that cash collections on account were less than the amount of sales recognized. Recall that we assume that all sales are on account. Therefore, we calculate cash collections on accounts receivable as follows:

$$\text{Cash Collections} = \text{Beginning AR} + \text{Sales} - \text{Ending AR}$$
$$= \text{Sales} - (\text{Ending AR} - \text{Beginning AR})$$
$$= \text{Sales} - \text{Change in AR}$$

For BHT, cash collections for 20X1 are therefore:

$$\text{Cash Collections} = \$2{,}464 + \$43{,}850 - \$3{,}650$$
$$\text{Cash Collections} = \$43{,}850 - (\$3{,}650 - \$2{,}464)$$
$$= \$43{,}850 - \$1{,}186 = \$42{,}664$$

Management could possibly report fraudulent earnings by reporting nonexistent sales and accounts receivable. Note however that the increase in sales that result from this behavior would be offset by the increase in receivables in the determination of operating cash flows; i.e., operating cash flows are unaffected by accruals per se. It would be far more difficult to implement fraud that affected cash flows.

Because cash collections are less than sales, when we reported net income in the cash account, we overstated the effect of sales on cash. As a result, we need to adjust by reducing cash for the increase in accounts receivable. A simpler alternative to the previous calculation would be to identify the change in the accounts receivable account. With a net debit to the accounts receivable account, by default, we would need to credit the Cash account for this difference, thereby reducing the amount reported in net income in the Cash account from Transaction 1. The entry to record this is:

(2)	Accounts receivable	1,186	
	Cash		1,186

This negative adjustment to cash matches the increase in the current operating asset, accounts receivable.

Cost of Goods Sold Adjustment to Net Income

After revenues, cost of goods sold is typically the first expense that appears on the income statement. Understanding the cash flow impact of the cost of inventory sales requires considering two separate timing relationships: (1) the relationship between the purchase of inventory (INV) and its recognition as a cost when sold, and (2) the relationship between the purchase of inventory and the payment for that inventory.

Recall from Chapter 3 the cost of goods sold equation:

$$
\begin{aligned}
\text{Cost of Goods Sold} &= \text{Beginning Inventory} + \text{Purchases} - \text{Ending INV} \\
&= \text{Purchases} - (\text{Ending INV} - \text{Beginning INV}) \\
&= \text{Purchases} - \text{Change in INV}
\end{aligned}
$$

Because we assume that all inventory is purchased on accounts payable (AP), we therefore calculate cash paid for purchases as:

$$
\begin{aligned}
\text{Payments} &= \text{Beginning AP} + \text{Purchases} - \text{Ending AP} \\
&= \text{Purchases} - (\text{Ending AP} - \text{Beginning AP}) \\
&= \text{Purchases} - \text{Change in AP}
\end{aligned}
$$

The difference between the expense (cost of goods sold) on the income statement and the cash paid to suppliers can be explained by the change in accounts payable less the change in inventory:

$$
\begin{aligned}
&\text{Cost of Goods Sold} - \text{Payments} \\
&= (\text{Purchases} - \text{Change in INV}) - (\text{Purchases} - \text{Change in AP}) \\
&= \text{Purchases} - \text{Purchases} - \text{Change in INV} + \text{Change in AP} \\
&= \text{Change in AP} - \text{Change in INV}
\end{aligned}
$$

The cost of goods sold for BHT was \$37,272 during the current year. We can apply the above equations to calculate the purchases for the period as \$37,752 (= CGS + Ending INV − Beginning INV = 37,272 + 4,400 − 3,920). Then we can use the purchases to calculate the payments for the period as \$36,222 (= Purchases + Beginning AP − Ending AP = 37,752 + 5,140 − 6,671). The difference between the cost of goods sold reported in income and the payments is therefore \$1,051 (\$37,272 − 36,222). Notice that this amount equals the difference between the change in AP (1,531) and the change in INV (480).

Again, we can avoid calculations by recording an entry that explains the change in the balance of both inventory and accounts payable with the corresponding entry to the operating section of the cash account, as follows:

(3)	Inventory	480	
	Cash		480

The change in accounts payable is:

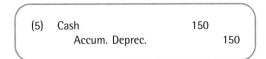

Depreciation Adjustment to Net Income

Depreciation is a noncash expense that a firm recognizes for financial reporting. It represents the allocation of the cost of plant and equipment over its useful life. Because depreciation expense is noncash, the amount of expense is added back to earnings to arrive at cash from operations. Sometimes depreciation is mistakenly thought of as a source of cash. This is incorrect in that depreciation does not generate cash for a business. Rather, it is an expense that does not require the use of cash (beyond the amount previously reported as an investment activity on earlier cash flow statements).

For many companies, depreciation is a large expense. Hence, cash from operations may be considerably larger than net income. However, because BHT is a wholesaling company and it leases its warehouses, it does not have proportionately as much depreciation as companies with large amounts of plant and equipment (e.g., in Exhibit 5.3 you can see a fairly substantial adjustment for depreciation for Tech Data Corp.). The entry to add back the depreciation expense to net income is:

Prepaid Expense Adjustment to Net Income

BHT also had an increase in its prepaid expenses account. While we could calculate the differences between expenses related to this prepayment and the actual cash flows as we did with inventory, we can again avoid this. Instead, we simply determine how the balance in this operating asset account changes and record the appropriate entry, as follows:

(6)	Prepaid Expenses	360	
	Cash		360

This completes the adjustments for the operating activities for BHT, as there are no other operating asset or liability accounts to consider. Other companies might also have accrued expenses, such as salaries payable, that would require adjustment. Further, GAAP requires firms to recognize all interest and tax cash flows in the operating section, so we might also have to adjust for changes in accounts such interest payable, taxes payable, and deferred taxes.

WORKSHEET ENTRIES FOR CASH FROM INVESTING

Only one investing activity occurred for BHT for the year ending 20X2: the acquisition of property, plant, and equipment. The entry is:

(7)	Property, Plant, and Equipment	410	
	Cash		410

Analyzing the cash from investing, however, may be more complex for a company that acquires or disposes of multiple groups of assets during a period. When a company disposes of a long-term asset such as property, plant, and equipment, it may report a gain or loss in the income statement from that transaction. Notice that the cash inflow from this sale should appear in the investing section. However, the gain or loss will appear in net income (and therefore will have been included in the cash account as part of net income in Transaction 1). Should this occur, we would need to remove the gain or loss from the operating section as the cash flows associated with these transactions should appear in the investing section. To remove a gain, we would credit the cash account; to remove a loss, we would debit the cash account.

WORKSHEET ENTRIES FOR CASH FROM FINANCING

BHT had several financing transactions during 20X2, including payment of dividends of $500 million. Recall that dividends are a distribution to shareholders, and as such are not an expense to the company. Hence, dividends are considered a financing transaction. When the board of directors declares dividends, an entry is made debiting retained earnings and crediting dividends payable. Later, when the dividend is actually paid to stockholders, dividends payable is debited and cash is credited. Because there is no dividends payable account, we know that all declared dividends have also been paid. Thus, the aggregate entry to record this in the worksheet is:

(8)	Retained earnings	500	
	Cash		500

BHT also issued a note payable. This is also a financing activity that increases the amount of cash available to BHT to fund its operations. The entry is:

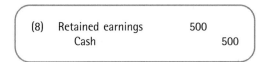

(9)	Cash	550	
	Note payable		550

		Cash							Accumulated Depreciation—PPE		
Bal.		567								60	Bal.
Operating:										150	(5)
Net Income	(1)	1,023	1,186	(2)	AR Increase						
Increase in AP	(4)	1,531	480	(3)	Inventory Increase						
Depreciation Expense	(5)	150	360	(6)	Increase in Prepaid Expenses					210	Bal.
Investing:											
			410	(7)	Purchase PPE						
									Accounts Payable		
Financing:										5,140	Bal.
Issue note payable	(9)	550								1,531	(4)
Issue common stock	(10)	625	500	(8)	Pay Dividends						
										6,671	Bal.
Bal.		1,510									

		Accounts Receivable				Notes Payable		
Bal.		2,464					400	Bal.
	(2)	1,186					550	(9)
							950	Bal.
Bal.		3,650						

		Inventory				Common Stock		
Bal.		3,920					250	Bal.
	(3)	480					50	(10)
Bal.		4,400					300	Bal.

		Prepaid Expenses				Additional Paid-In Capital		
Bal.		0					1,375	Bal.
	(6)	360					575	(10)
Bal.		360					1,950	Bal.

		PPE					Retained Earnings		
Bal.		540						266	Bal.
	(7)	410			(8)	500		1,023	(1)
Bal.		950						789	Bal.

Exhibit 5.8
T-Account Worksheet
Entries for BHT

Exhibit 5.9
Statement of Cash Flows for
the Years Ending 20X2 and
20X1 Biohealth, Inc (BHT)

	Year ending 12/31/20X2	Year ending 12/31/20X1
Cash from operations:		
Net income	$1,023	$416
Add: noncash expenses		
Depreciation	150	60
Changes in current assets and liabilities		
Increase in accounts receivable	(1,186)	(2,464)
Increase in inventory	(480)	(3,920)
Increase in prepaid expenses	(360)	
Increase in accounts payable	1,531	5,140
Total cash from operations	678	(768)
Cash from investing		
Purchase fixtures (PPE)	(410)	(0)
Total cash from investing	(410)	(0)
Cash from financing		
Issuance of long-term note	550	0
Issuance of common stock	625	
Dividends	(500)	(150)
Total cash from financing	675	(150)
Total change in cash	943	(918)
Cash balance 1/1/20X2	567	1,485
Cash balance 12/31/20X2	$1,510	$567

The final financing transaction affecting cash is the issuance of common stock.
We record this as follows:

(10) Cash	625	
Common Stock		50
Additional Paid-In Capital		575

At this point, we have analyzed all of the changes in the balance sheet
accounts other than cash and, therefore, also explained all of the changes in
cash. Exhibit 5.8 shows our completed worksheet entries. We can now construct
the cash flow statement from the information contained within the Cash account
in Exhibit 5.8. Exhibit 5.9 shows our completed cash flow statement for 2002,
along with the cash flow statement from the prior year (which we presented in
Chapter 3).

SUMMARY OF CASH FLOW STATEMENT PREPARATION—INDIRECT METHOD

To summarize, the preparation of the cash flow statement involves the following steps:

Cash from operations:
   Net income
   Add:

         Depreciation and amortization
         Losses on sales of noncurrent assets and liabilities
         Decreases in current operating assets other than cash
         Increases in operating liabilities

   Deduct:

         Gains on sales of noncurrent assets and liabilities
         Increases in current operating assets other than cash
         Decreases in current operating liabilities

Cash from investing:
   Add:

         Proceeds from sales of noncurrent assets and nonoperating current assets
         Proceeds from sales of other companies

   Deduct:

         Purchases of noncurrent assets and nonoperating current assets
         Acquisitions of other companies

Cash from financing:
   Add:

         Issuance of debt (borrowings)
         Issuance of stock

   Deduct:

         Debt repayments
         Dividends
         Stock repurchases

ARTICULATION OF THE CASH FLOW STATEMENT

As we said earlier, reconciling a firm's cash flow statement to its balance sheet and income statement can be a useful analytical tool. In simple cases, such as for Tofutti, the adjustments for changes in the various assets and liabilities that appear on the cash flow statement **articulate** with (are the same as) the corresponding changes in the balance sheet of the company. Exhibit 5.10 shows the balance sheet of Tofutti and includes a column that shows the net changes in the assets and liabilities of the firm. The operating items are highlighted. To demonstrate the articulation, look at the net change in inventories, accounts payable, and accrued expenses, and compare these changes with the net adjustments on the cash flow statement in Exhibit 5.2. Note that both the decrease in inventory and the increase in accounts payable result in a positive adjustment to net income consistent with the information in Exhibit 5.10.

The one account that does not appear to articulate is accounts receivable, where you will observe a change on the balance sheet of $585,000 and a change

TOFUTTI BRANDS, Inc.: Balance Sheet	12/29/2001	12/29/2000	Net Change
Assets			
Current assets:			
Cash and equivalents	$2,329,000	$2,211,000	$ 118,000
Short-term investments	0	269,000	(269,000)
Accounts receivable, net of allowance for doubtful accounts of $325,000 and $270,000, respectively	1,461,000	876,000	585,000
Inventories	816,000	908,000	(92,000)
Prepaid expenses	10,000	9,000	1,000
Deferred income taxes	478,000	359,000	119,000
Total current assets	5,094,000	4,632,000	462,000
Other assets:			
Other assets	325,000	181,000	144,000
	$5,419,000	$4,813,000	$606,000
Liabilities and stockholders' equity			
Current liabilities:			
Notes payable	$ 0	$ 8,000	($8,000)
Accounts payable and accrued expenses	155,000	146,000	9,000
Accrued compensation	375,000	375,000	0
Income taxes payable	187,000	331,000	(144,000)
Total current liabilities	717,000	860,000	(143,000)
Commitments and contingencies			
Stockholders' equity:			
Preferred stock—par value $.01 per share; authorized 100,000 shares, none issued	0	0	0
Common stock—par value $.01 per share; authorized 15,000,000 shares, issued and outstanding 6,091,267 shares at December 29, 2001 and 6,354,567 shares at December 30, 2000	61,000	64,000	(3,000)
Less: Treasury stock, at cost (18,100 shares and 122,400 shares at December 29, 2001 and December 30, 2000, respectively)	(38,000)	(247,000)	209,000
Additional paid-in capital	3,156,000	3,763,000	(607,000)
Accumulated earnings	1,523,000	373,000	1,150,000
Total stockholders' equity	4,702,000	3,953,000	749,000
Total liabilities and stockholders' equity	$5,419,000	$4,813,000	$606,000

of ($625,000) on the cash flow statement. However, the adjustment for the provision for bad debts in the cash flow statement also affects the accounts receivable account, because accounts receivable is reported net of the effects of bad debts on the balance sheet. Therefore, if you net the $40,000 adjustment for bad debts on the cash flow statement with the change in accounts receivable of ($625,000), you get the same change in net accounts receivable of $585,000

Although not all countries require preparation of a cash flow statement, cash flows are increasingly important in international markets. Many companies voluntarily disclose cash flow statements. International accounting standards (IAS Number 7) state that the cash flow statement is a basic financial state- ment that explains the change in cash and cash equivalents during a period. In some countries, a funds flow statement is presented. The funds statement is similar to the cash flow statement, but it reconciles changes in total working capital rather than cash.

reported on the balance sheet. We will revisit the issue of accounting for bad-debts in Chapter 7. The cash statement will not always articulate with the balance sheet primarily due to acquisitions and foreign currency translation, both of which are beyond the scope of this book.

SUPPLEMENTAL DISCLOSURES TO THE CASH FLOW STATEMENT

Companies often report supplemental disclosures on the cash flow statement. For example, GAAP requires firms to report all interest cash flows in the operating section. However, because users might want to view these amounts as financing cash flows, GAAP requires that firms disclose the dollar amount of interest cash flows that exist in the operating section. Many firms (like Tofutti) do this by providing supplemental cash flow information at the bottom of the statement, as shown in Exhibit 5.2. Other firms provide this information in a footnote to the financial statements. GAAP also requires all tax cash flows to be reported in the operating section, even though you could argue that they apply to all three sections. As a result, GAAP requires supplemental disclosure of the tax cash flows (again, see Exhibit 5.2).

In addition, a firm may engage in transactions that do not directly affect cash. However, if a transaction is considered a significant noncash activity, GAAP requires the firm to disclose this type of transaction as supplemental information. For example, Polaroid disclosed that, in 2000, it recorded noncash items of $22.9 million in cash flow from operating activities that consisted primarily of $12.0 million for the issuance of shares relating to their Retirement Savings Plan.

INTERPRETING THE CASH FLOW STATEMENT

The cash flow statement provides both insights into the effectiveness with which a company manages its cash flows, as well as signals of the underlying quality of its earnings flows. Management of cash flows is an important activity in a business. If a company's operating cash inflows are insufficient to meet operating cash outflow demands, a company may be forced to engage in additional borrowing or issuance of stock, or sale of long-term assets to meet cash needs. If the firm cannot raise sufficient cash from these sources, it may be forced into bankruptcy. For example, Kmart Corporation filed Chapter 11 bankruptcy following a slow holiday season in 2001. One source of the company's problem was the inability to pay suppliers on a timely basis due to the declining sales.

In the case of Tofutti (Exhibit 5.2), you can see that net income increased each year over the most recent three-year period of time. However, you also can observe that cash from operating activities has declined over this same period. To understand why, look to the adjustments to net income. Observe that in 2000 the three largest negative adjustments were for inventories, deferred taxes, and accounts receivable.

Although we discuss deferred taxes in greater depth later in Chapter 10, the simple explanation for now is that federal tax laws often allow or require different accounting methods to be used in calculating taxable income than those methods used to report under GAAP. In the case of depreciation, for example, the tax code provides a benefit to businesses in the form of allowing for more rapid depreciation write-offs for tax purposes than firms use for financial reporting. As a result, tax payments are deferred because taxable income (i.e., income reported for tax purposes) is usually less than income before taxes reported for financial accounting purposes. Hence, tax payments are less than the tax expense reported on net income. The difference between the actual tax liability and the tax expense reported for financial reporting is reported as an account called "deferred taxes." Notice for Tofutti that the adjustment for deferred taxes goes in different directions in different years. Negative adjustments mean that there were net, noncash, income-improving effects during the year as a result of deferred taxes, and vice versa for positive adjustments.

While taxes are a difficult item to fully explain at this point, we can provide interpretation for the other two items. The negative adjustments for both the inventory and accounts receivable balance mean that they are increasing over the year. One explanation might be an increase in the firm's sales. Looking at the income statement for Tofutti (Exhibit 5.11), sales did significantly increase in 2000 over 1999. In fact, Tofutti's sales showed a growth of approximately

Exhibit 5.11
Income Statement

THE REAL WORLD

Tofutti Brands, Inc.

TOFUTTI BRANDS, Inc.:
Income Statement

	12/29/2001	12/29/2000	12/30/1999
Net sales	$16,254,000	$13,343,000	$11,912,000
Cost of sales	10,550,000	8,192,000	7,349,000
Gross profit	5,704,000	5,151,000	4,563,000
Operating expenses:			
Selling	1,896,000	1,724,000	1,521,000
Marketing	391,000	277,000	199,000
Research and development	483,000	397,000	376,000
General and administrative	1,381,000	1,288,000	1,043,000
	4,151,000	3,686,000	3,139,000
Operating income	1,553,000	1,465,000	1,424,000
Other income	268,000	103,000	12,000
Income before income tax	1,821,000	1,568,000	1,436,000
Income taxes	671,000	612,000	(586,000)
Net income	$1,150,000	$956,000	$850,000

12 percent. However, the net change in inventories of $342,000 (see the cash flow statement, Exhibit 5.2) to bring the balance in inventories to $908,000 (see the balance sheet, Exhibit 5.10) seems to be approximately a 60 percent increase in inventories. This seems out of line with the growth in sales. You would want to, therefore, seek a better explanation for what happened to inventories during 2000. Tofutti explains in its 10-K that part of this increase in inventory was the result of introducing new products (as well as an increase in sales).

In 2001 the largest single adjustment ($625,000) is in accounts receivable, while inventories actually show a decline. Again, looking at the income statement, you can see that sales grew substantially in 2001. This provides some explanation for the growth in accounts receivable, but the growth in accounts receivable is much higher (67 percent) than the annual sales growth (22 percent). If you read Tofutti's annual report, you will see that management indicates that sales increased significantly in the last quarter of the year that led to the high level of accounts receivable at year end. This is obviously good news in terms of future prospects as sales are going up significantly.

However, notice that in the current period this immense growth is starting to put a strain on cash from operations. This is not unusual for a rapid-growth company, but is something that the company must take into consideration in its planning to make sure that it does not end up in a cash crisis. Because Tofutti has a significant balance in its cash account (which has also been increasing over this period of time), it seems to be in no immediate danger of a cash crisis.

Interestingly, Tofutti reported a smaller amount of bad debt expense in 2001 than in 2000 despite a considerable increase in accounts receivable. Bad debt expense reported in 2001 was $40,000 compared to $60,000 in 2000 and 1999. In Tofutti's statement, the provision for bad debts (sometimes called bad debt expense) is a deduction in arriving at net income, for the company's estimate of the sales made during the period that it does not expect to collect (customers who never pay their bill). As such it is a noncash expense.

Further, as the balance sheet shows, although Tofutti's allowance for uncollectible accounts increased about 20 percent from 2000 to 2001, it did not increase proportionately to the increase in accounts receivable. This is a potential concern because a relationship usually exists between sales, accounts receivable, and the amount of estimated bad debt expense recognized (we discuss this in more depth in Chapter 7). If Tofutti underestimated its bad debt expense during 2001, the reported net accounts receivable may be too high, leading to overstated assets and earnings for Tofutti. The fact that a significant portion of Tofutti's increased earnings has not been collected may be a red flag, signaling to investors that future cash flows may not be as strong as the income statement alone suggests.

In summary, cash from operations can provide important information about a company's current and future prospects. GAAP guidelines for revenue and expense recognition are intended to result in earnings that, in part, reflect expected future cash flows, but both revenue and expense recognition rules, even if appropriately applied, involve significant estimation. Furthermore, managers may manage earnings to meet targeted earnings numbers or analyst's forecasts. As a result, careful study of cash from operations, together with the other financial statement information, may provide clues about a company's performance not evident from either statement alone. A company with increasing receivables, inventory, and payables may show positive earnings. However, if the company fails to generate cash and pay its creditors, the company may have financial distress regardless of the earnings reported.

VALUATION IMPLICATIONS OF THE CASH FLOW STATEMENT

Cash flows can have significant implications for the valuation of firms, and firms like Procter & Gamble often refer to cash flow in their announcements of performance as shown in Exhibit 5.12.

The cash flow statement provides information not directly available from either the income statement or the balance sheet. In order for a company to retain and grow in value, it must not only earn a profit, it must also generate cash that can be used to invest in growing the business or paying dividends to shareholders. The cash flow statement provides insights not only into the sources of a company's cash, but how it uses that cash. Analysts look at both sources of information to help determine the company's ultimate profit potential.

Many companies even report performance in terms of cash flows as well as earnings. Cemex reported the following information about its 2001 fourth-quarter results (the term EBITDA stands for Earnings Before Interest, Taxes, Depreciation, and Amortization): "Cash earnings increased 11% to US$446 million, compared to US$400.5 million in the fourth quarter of 2000; lower interest expense enabled cash earnings to outpace EBITDA growth." Note that the "cash earnings" referred to in the Cemex disclosure is close to the cash from operations a firm would report on its cash flow statement except that it is before taxes and there are no adjustments for the changes in the working capital accounts (i.e., accounts receivable, inventories, accounts payable).

Analysts' estimates of the market value of firm typically rely on projections of free cash flows to equity holders as the principal input. **Free cash flows** to equity holders are the cash flows from operating activities, less cash flows used for investing activities, plus cash flows from debt financing activities, and less the increase in cash needed to sustain operations. Equivalently, if the entire increase in cash is required by operations, then free cash flows to equity holders

---

Exhibit 5.12

THE REAL WORLD

Procter & Gamble

CINCINNATI, January 31, 2002—The Procter & Gamble Company today reported that it exceeded consensus expectations for second quarter results. P&G delivered on the high end of its financial guidance for the October–December quarter, behind record quarter unit volume. For the quarter ended December 31, 2001, unit volume grew five percent versus the prior year led by double-digit growth in the health and beauty care businesses. Excluding acquisitions and divestitures, unit volume increased four percent. Net sales were $10.40 billion, up two percent versus one year ago. "We are seeing clear improvements in our results, and we're pleased to have met our commitments once again," said P&G President and Chief Executive A. G. Lafley. "We're continuing our unyielding focus on delivering better consumer value on our brands, building core categories, reducing the company's cost structure, and improving our cash flow."

are cash distributions to stockholders (dividends and stock repurchases), net of cash proceeds from stock issues. The concept is that these are cash flows that would be available to stockholders each period to provide a return to them.

To illustrate the calculation of free cash flows, consider the calculation of the free cash flows for our BHT example (refer back to Exhibit 5.11 for the line items on the cash flow statement):

Cash from operations:	$678
Cash from investing:	(410)
Cash from borrowing:	550
Change in cash:	(943)
Total free cash flows to equity:	($125)

Observe that the total free cash flows to equity (stockholders) can also be determined by subtracting proceeds from the issuance of stock from dividends ($500 − $625 = −$125). Note that we are assuming the entire change in cash ($943) is needed to support operations.

SUMMARY AND TRANSITION

In order to help determine firm value, earnings must provide a signal of future cash flows. This means that earnings should be indicative of the firm's ability to generate future cash flows. This does not imply a one-to-one correlation between the pattern of operating cash flows and earnings, but it does suggest that revenues should reflect cash inflows in a systematic manner and that expenses should likewise reflect operating cash outflows. One way to think about earnings is as a smoothing of cash flows. The cash flow statement makes the association between earnings and operating cash flows more apparent than it might be otherwise.

Cash flows from investing activities are also important. In order to grow, companies must generally invest in long-term assets. The cash flow statement provides information about asset replacements as well as investments in new assets. The difference between operating cash flows and investing cash flows is a measure of the extent to which the company is able to finance its growth internally.

Cash flows from financing activities show amounts raised externally from creditors and stockholders, net of repayments and dividends. Careful analysis of this section provides indications of the company's debt commitments and dependency of stockholders in obtaining the cash necessary to sustain operating and investing activities.

We will return to an analysis of the information contained in the cash flow statement in the next chapter. As is probably evident from reading this chapter, full understanding of the cash flow statement can be daunting. While the cash flow statement can be complex, an investment in understanding its information is worth the time for anyone with a serious interest in interpreting and using financial statements. The cash flow statement can be a useful tool to help filter the information provided in the balance sheet and income statement in order to get a more complete view of a company's past and future expected performance.

END OF CHAPTER MATERIAL

KEY TERMS

Articulate

Direct Method

Free Cash Flows

Indirect Method

ASSIGNMENT MATERIAL

REVIEW QUESTIONS

1. Discuss why it is important for firms to prepare a cash flow statement in addition to an income statement.

2. Discuss how a firm's receivables, inventory, and payables policies affect cash flow relative to the income produced in a given period.

3. What is meant by a lead/lag relationship in terms of the cash flow statement?

4. For a firm with a cash flow problem, list at least three potential reasons for the problem, and suggest a possible solution for each of these reasons.

5. Describe the three major categories of cash flows that are required to be disclosed by SFAS 95.

6. Discuss the difference between the direct and indirect (reconciliation) methods for constructing the operation section of the cash flow statement.

7. Depreciation is a source of cash. Explain your reasons for agreeing or disagreeing with this statement.

APPLYING YOUR KNOWLEDGE

8. In what section of the cash flow statement (operating, investing, or financing) would each of the following items appear?

   a. Purchase of net plant, property, and equipment

   b. Proceeds from a bank loan

   c. Collections from customers

   d. Dividends to stockholders

   e. Proceeds from the sale of marketable securities (stocks and bonds)

   f. Retirements of debt

   g. Change in accounts receivable

   h. Net income

   i. Gain/loss from the sale of plant, property, and equipment

   j. Cash proceeds from the sale of plant, property, and equipment

9. Explain why a high sales growth rate can create significant cash flow problems for a company.

10. Explain the timing of the cash flows related to the purchase, use, and ultimately the sale of property, plant, and equipment.

11. Discuss the classification of interest cash flows in the statement of cash flows under SFAS No. 95 and discuss why you believe this is either appropriate or not.

12. For each of the transactions listed below,

a. Indicate the effect on balance sheet categories in the following format:

Trans. #	Cash	Other Current Assets	Noncurrent Assets	Current Liabilities	Noncurrent Liabilities	Owners' Equity

b. State, for the transactions affecting cash, whether they relate to an operating, investing, or financing activity.

Transactions:

1. Credit purchases, $10,000
2. Cash paid to suppliers, $8,000
3. Credit sales, $25,000
4. Cost of goods sold, $15,000
5. Cash payments received on accounts receivable, $18,000
6. Salaries accrued, $1,500
7. Salaries paid (previously accrued), $1,000
8. Machine purchased for $800 in cash
9. Depreciation expense, $200
10. Borrowed (long-term) $5,000 to purchase plant
11. Interest of $50 is accrued and paid on the amount borrowed for the purchase of the plant
12. Debentures worth $1,000 are issued
13. Equipment having book value of $700 is sold for $700 cash
14. Dividends declared, $350
15. Dividends paid, $200
16. Insurance premium for the next year paid, $175
17. 1000 shares of stock issued at $1 per share
18. Rent received for building, $250
19. Income taxes accrued and paid, $325

13. For each of the transactions listed below,

a. Indicate the effect on balance sheet categories in the following format:

Trans. #	Cash	Other Current Assets	Noncurrent Assets	Current Liabilities	Noncurrent Liabilities	Owners' Equity

b. State, for the transactions affecting cash, whether they relate to an operating, investing, or financing activity.

Transactions:

1. 5,000 shares of common stock are issued at $10 per share.
2. Plant, property, and equipment worth $120,000 is purchased for $50,000 in cash and the balance in common stock.

3. Rent payments of $5,000 are received in advance.

4. Sales contracts for $100,000 are signed and a $25,000 deposit is received in cash.

5. Merchandise inventory worth $85,000 is purchased on account.

6. Goods worth $15,000 were found defective and returned to suppliers. These goods had been purchased on account.

7. Sales were $175,000 of which $100,000 was on account.

8. Cash is paid to suppliers in the amount of $60,000.

9. Equipment recorded at $10,000 was destroyed by fire.

10. The company purchased 500 shares of X Company stock at $5 per share for short-term investment purposes.

11. The company purchased 2,000 shares of Z Company at $8 per share in an effort to buy a controlling interest in the company (a supplier).

12. Interest expense for the year amounted to $2,500 and was paid in cash.

13. The sales contract in question 4 was cancelled. $10,000 of the deposit was returned and the rest was forfeited.

14. A bank loan for $75,000 was taken out and is due in five years.

15. Equipment with a cost of $50,000 was sold for $60,000. The $60,000 was in the form of a note.

16. During the year, warranty services costing $3,500 were provided to customers. A provision for warranty services was provided in a separate transaction.

17. Depreciation for the year totaled $20,000.

18. Dividends of $10,000 were declared and $5,000 remained unpaid at year end.

19. Patents on a new manufacturing process were purchased for $5,000.

20. Research and development expenses amounted to $15,000 and were charged to expense as incurred.

14. Compute the cash flow from operations in each of the following cases:

	I	II	III
Sales Revenues	$25,000	$35,000	$65,000
Depreciation Expense	3,000	5,000	20,000
Cost of Goods Sold	15,000	38,000	41,000
Other Expenses	1,500	700	1,200
Dividends Paid	3,000	–	1,000
Increase (Decrease) in:			
Inventories	5,000	(10,000)	15,000
Accounts Receivable	3,500	1,000	(2,000)
Prepayments	(500)	(1,000)	1,800
Salaries Payable	(10,000)	5,000	(15,000)
Interest Payable	(5,000)	(500)	5,000
Other Current Liabilities	8,000	(10,000)	800

15. Compute the cash flow from operations in each of the following cases:

	I	II	III
Sales Revenues	$175,000	$200,000	$225,000
Cost of Goods Sold	100,000	185,000	195,000
Depreciation	20,000	15,000	10,000
Interest Expense	5,000	25,000	15,000
Dividends Paid	8,000	—	5,000
Profit (Loss) on Sale of PP&E	—	(10,000)	25,000
Increase (Decrease) in:			
Common Stock	10,000	5,000	—
Bonds Payable	20,000	(30,000)	(15,000)
Interest Payable	(25,000)	(5,000)	10,000
Accounts Payable	(25,000)	10,000	15,000
Accounts Receivable	50,000	(40,000)	35,000
Inventories	(10,000)	(15,000)	25,000
PP&E	100,000	(50,000)	—

16. Financial statement data for Dennison Corporation for 20X8 is as follows:

Dennison Corporation
Comparative Balance Sheets

	12/31/X7	12/31/X8
Assets		
Cash	$25,500	$4,400
Accounts Receivable	59,000	35,000
Inventories	30,000	50,000
Total Current Assets	114,500	89,400
Property, Plant, and Equipment	165,000	180,000
Accumulated Depreciation	(61,900)	(80,400)
Total Noncurrent Assets	103,100	99,600
Total Assets	$217,600	$189,000
Liabilities and Owners' Equity		
Accounts Payable	$38,600	$28,500
Salaries Payable	24,000	12,000
Total Current Liabilities	62,600	40,500
Bank Loan	50,000	40,000
Total Liabilities	112,600	80,500
Common Stock	100,000	100,000
Retained Earnings	5,000	8,500
Total Liabilities and Owners' Equity	$217,600	$189,000
Income Statement		
Sales		$185,500
Expenses:		
Cost of Goods Sold	87,500	
Salaries Expense	48,000	
Depreciation Expense	23,500	
Interest Expense	8,000	
Loss on Sale of PP&E	5,000	
Total Expenses		172,000
Net Income		$13,500

Additional Information:

1. Equipment originally costing $35,000 was sold for $25,000.
2. Dividends declared and paid during the year were $10,000.

Required:

Prepare a statement of cash flows for Dennison Corporation for the year ended 12/31/X8, supported by a T-account worksheet. Use the indirect approach to prepare the operating section.

17. Financial statement data for Matrix, Incorporated is as follows:

Matrix, Incorporated Balance Sheets	12/31/X3
Assets	
Cash	15,500
Accounts Receivable	10,000
Trade Notes Receivable	5,000
Inventories	20,500
Total Current Assets	51,000
Property, Plant, and Equipment	160,000
Accumulated Depreciation	(35,500)
Total Noncurrent Assets	124,500
Total Assets	$175,500
Liabilities and Owners' Equity	
Accounts Payable	5,000
Salaries Payable	18,000
Total Current Liabilities	23,000
Bonds Payable	50,000
Total Liabilities	73,000
Common Stock	100,000
Retained Earnings	2,500
Total Liabilities and Owners' Equity	$175,500

Matrix, Incorporated Trial Balance for the Year Ended 12/31/X4	Debits	Credits
Cash	$2,900	
Accounts Receivable	12,500	
Prepaid Rent	6,000	
Inventories	18,900	
Cost of Goods Sold	275,500	
Depreciation Expense	10,000	
Rent Expense	12,000	
Interest Expense	15,000	
Salaries Expense	24,000	
Property, Plant, and Equipment	160,000	
Accumulated Depreciation		$ 45,500
Accounts Payable		13,800

	Debits	Credits
Interest Payable		9,000
Salaries Payable		6,000
Bonds Payable		10,000
Common Stock		100,000
Retained Earnings		2,500
Sales		350,000
Totals	$536,800	$536,800

Required:

a. Prepare an income statement and a reconciliation of retained earnings for the year ended 12/31/X4.

b. Prepare a balance sheet for the year ended 12/31/X4.

c. Prepare a statement of cash flows for the year ended 12/31/X4 supported by a T-account worksheet. Use the indirect approach to prepare the operating section.

18. The financial statement data for Crescent Manufacturing Company is as follows:

Crescent Manufacturing Company Comparative Balance Sheets	12/31/X0	12/31/X1
Assets		
Cash	17,800	12,800
Marketable Securities	125,000	25,000
Accounts Receivable	38,600	69,600
Prepaid Insurance	6,000	—
Inventories	43,300	93,300
Total Current Assets	230,700	200,700
Property, Plant, and Equipment	225,000	300,000
Accumulated Depreciation	(36,300)	(86,300)
Total Noncurrent Assets	188,700	213,700
Total Assets	$419,400	$414,400
Liabilities and Owners' Equity		
Accounts Payable	12,600	15,000
Interest Payable	8,000	5,600
Dividends Payable	20,000	30,000
Total Current Liabilities	40,600	50,600
Mortgage Payable	100,000	75,000
Bonds Payable	75,000	75,000
Total Liabilities	215,600	200,600
Common Stock	250,000	250,000
Treasury Stock	(50,000)	(60,000)
Retained Earnings	3,800	23,800
Total Owners' Equity	203,800	213,800
Total Liabilities and Owners' Equity	$419,400	$414,400

	12/31/X0	12/31/X1
Income Statement		
Sales	$508,000	
Interest Revenue	12,500	
Gain on Sale of Marketable Securities	25,000	
Total Revenues		$545,500
Expenses:		
Cost of Goods Sold	330,000	
Depreciation Expense	50,000	
Insurance Expense	12,000	
Interest Expense	43,500	
Salaries Expense	60,000	
Total Expenses		495,500
Net Income		$ 50,000

Additional Information:

1. 10,000 shares of Sigma Company, which were purchased at a cost of $10 per share, were sold at a price of $12.50 per share.

2. Dividends declared during the year amounted to $30,000 and remained unpaid at year end.

Required:

Prepare a statement of cash flows for Crescent Manufacturing Company for the year ended 12/31/X1 supported by a T-account worksheet. Use the indirect method to prepare the operation section.

19. The Balance Sheet for Simco Corporation as of the beginning and the end of the 20X1 appears below. During the year, no dividends were declared or paid, there was no sale of PP&E and no debt repaid. Net Income for the period was $35,000 and included $25,000 in depreciation expenses. Prepare a statement of cash flows for Simco Corporation for the current year and also prepare a T-account worksheet supporting the cash flow statement. Use the cash reconciliation approach.

SIMCO CORPORATION
Balance Sheet

	12/31/X0	12/31/X1
Assets		
Current Assets		
Cash	$ 10,000	$ 8,000
Accounts Receivable	86,000	100,000
Inventories	102,000	112,000
Total Current Assets	198,000	220,000
Property, Plant, and Equipment	485,000	600,000
Less: Accumulated Depreciation	125,000	150,000
Total PP&E	360,000	450,000
Total Assets	$558,000	$670,000

	12/31/X0	12/31/X1
Liabilities and Owners' Equity		
Current Liabilities		
Accounts Payable	$ 78,000	$ 95,000
Wages Payable	30,000	40,000
Total Current Liabilities	108,000	135,000
Long-Term Debt		
Bonds Payable	100,000	125,000
Total Liabilities	208,000	260,000
Owners' Equity		
Common Stock	150,000	175,000
Retained Earnings	200,000	235,000
Total Liabilities and Owners' Equity	$558,000	$670,000

20. Comparative Balance Sheets of Marvel Cosmetics Company for 20X2 are as follows:

MARVEL COSMETICS COMPANY
Comparative Balance Sheet

	12/31/X1	12/31/X2
Assets		
Current Assets		
Cash	$ 188,000	$ 200,000
Accounts Receivable	133,000	120,000
Trade Notes Receivable	61,000	70,000
Inventory	326,000	439,000
Total Current Assets	708,000	829,000
Noncurrent Assets		
Land	500,000	525,000
Machinery	238,000	483,000
Accumulated Depreciation	(97,500)	(143,000)
Total Noncurrent Assets	640,500	865,000
Total Assets	$1,348,500	$1,694,000
Liabilities and Owners' Equity		
Current Liabilities		
Accounts Payable	$ 158,000	$ 145,000
Interest Payable	10,000	17,500
Total Current Liabilities	168,000	162,500
Noncurrent Liabilities		
Debentures	200,000	350,000
Total Liabilities	368,000	512,500
Owners' Equity		
Common Stock	550,000	650,000
Retained Earnings	430,500	531,500
Total Owners' Equity	980,500	1,180,500
Total Liabilities and Owners' Equity	$1,348,500	$1,694,000

Additional Information:

a. Net Income is $151,000 and includes depreciation expenses of $105,500.

b. Dividends declared and paid during the year were $50,000.

c. A machine costing $80,000 was sold at its book value of $20,000.

d. There was no Repayment of long-term debt.

Prepare a Statement of Cash Flows for Marvel Cosmetics Company for the year ended 12/31/X2, supported by a T-account worksheet.

21. The financial statement data for Pharmex Pharmaceutical Company for 20X5 is as follows:

PHARMEX PHARMACEUTICAL COMPANY	12/31/X4	12/31/X5
Comparative Data		
Debits		
Cash	80,000	50,000
Accounts Receivable	185,000	235,000
Inventories	296,000	325,000
Machinery	545,000	555,000
Total	1,106,000	1,165,000
Credits		
Accumulated Depreciation	122,500	172,500
Accounts Payable	97,500	82,500
Bonds Payable	150,000	175,000
Common Stock	350,000	400,000
Retained Earnings	386,000	335,000
Total	1,106,000	1,165,000
Income Statement Data		
Sales		1,052,000
Gain on Sale of PP&E		15,000
Cost of Goods Sold		878,000
Depreciation Expense		75,000
Interest Expenses		60,000
Rent Expense		85,000

Additional Information:

Acquisition cost of new machinery is $135,000. Old machinery having an original cost of $125,000 was sold at a gain of $15,000. Dividends of $20,000 were declared and paid.

a. Prepare an income statement including a reconciliation of retained earnings for the year ended 12/31/X5.

b. Prepare a statement of cash flows for Pharmex Pharmaceuticals Company for the year ended 12/31/X5 supported by a T-account work sheet.

22. From the perspective of a bank loan officer, discuss why the cash flow statement may or may not be more important in your analysis of a company that is applying for a loan.

23. From the perspective of a stock analyst, discuss why the cash flow statement may or may not be more important in your analysis of a company for which you must make a recommendation.

24. Use the data in the cash flow statement for Amazon.Com, Inc. to answer the questions that follow.

Amazon.com, Inc.
Consolidated Statements of Cash Flows
(in thousands)
Years Ended December 31,

	2001	2000	1999
Cash and cash equivalents, beginning of period	$822,435	$ 133,309	$ 71,583
Net loss	(567,277)	(1,411,273)	(719,968)
Adjustments to reconcile net loss to net cash used in operating activities:			
Depreciation of fixed assets and other amortization	84,709	84,460	36,806
Stock-based compensation	4,637	24,797	30,618
Equity in losses of equity-method investees, net	30,327	304,596	76,769
Amortization of goodwill and other intangibles	181,033	321,772	214,694
Noncash restructuring-related and other	73,293	200,311	8,072
Loss (gain) on sale of marketable securities, net	(1,335)	(280)	8,688
Other losses (gains), net	2,141	142,639	—
Noncash interest expense and other	26,629	24,766	29,171
Cumulative effect of change in accounting principle	10,523	—	—
Changes in operating assets and liabilities:			
Inventories	30,628	46,083	(172,069)
Prepaid expenses and other current assets	20,732	(8,585)	(54,927)
Accounts payable	(44,438)	22,357	330,166
Accrued expenses and other current liabilities	50,031	93,967	95,839
Unearned revenue	114,738	97,818	6,225
Amortization of previously unearned revenue	(135,808)	(108,211)	(5,837)
Interest payable	(345)	34,341	24,878
Net cash used in operating activities	(119,782)	(130,442)	(90,875)
Investing Activities:			
Sales and maturities of marketable securities	370,377	545,724	2,064,101
Purchases of marketable securities	(567,152)	(184,455)	(2,359,398)
Purchases of fixed assets, including internal use software and web-site development	(50,321)	(134,758)	(287,055)

	2001	2000	1999
Investments in equity-method investees and other investments	(6,198)	(62,533)	(369,607)
Net cash provided by (used in) investing activities	(253,294)	163,978	(951,959)
Financing Activities:			
Proceeds from exercise of stock options and other	16,625	44,697	64,469
Proceeds from issuance of common stock, net of issuance costs	99,831	–	–
Proceeds from long-term debt and other	10,000	681,499	1,263,639
Repayment of long-term debt and other	(19,575)	(16,927)	(188,886)
Financing costs	–	(16,122)	(35,151)
Net cash provided by financing activities	106,881	693,147	1,104,071
Effect of exchange-rate changes on cash and cash equivalents	(15,958)	(37,557)	489
Net increase (decrease) in cash and cash equivalents	(282,153)	689,126	61,726
Cash and cash Equivalents, end of period	$540,282	$ 822,435	$ 133,309
Supplemental cash flow information:			
Fixed assets acquired under capital leases	$ 4,597	$ 4,459	$ 25,850
Fixed assets acquired under financing agreements	1,000	4,844	5,608
Equity securities received for commerical agreements	331	106,848	54,402
Stock issued in connection with business acquisitions and minority investments	5,000	32,130	774,409
Cash paid for interest	112,184	67,252	30,526

a. Why is net cash provided by operating activities less negative than net income for the three years presented?

b. What specific items contributed most to the greater net loss in 2000 than in the other two years?

c. How were investment activities in 1999 financed?

d. What trend do you observe for debt and related cash paid for interest over the three years presented?

e. What general concerns do you have about the future operating activities of the company based on your review of the cash flow statement for the three years presented?

25. Use the data in the cash flow statement for Barnes Group, Inc. to answer the questions that follow.

BARNES GROUP, Inc.: Cash Flow

	12/31/2001	12/31/2000	12/31/1999
Operating activities:			
Net income	$19,121,000	$35,665,000	$28,612,000
Adjustments to reconcile net income to net cash provided by operating activities:			
Depreciation and amortization	37,045,000	35,871,000	30,602,000
Loss (gain) on disposition of property, plant, and equipment	2,093,000	(1,960,000)	(857,000)
Changes in assets and liabilities:			
Accounts receivable	11,378,000	1,087,000	(1,731,000)
Inventories	(3,629,000)	(7,631,000)	1,980,000
Accounts payable	13,634,000	(5,415,000)	17,356,000
Accrued liabilities	(5,552,000)	1,026,000	(9,524,000)
Deferred income taxes	6,510,000	5,863,000	3,655,000
Other	(13,700,000)	(12,649,000)	(7,296,000)
Net cash provided by operating activities	66,900,000	51,857,000	62,797,000
Investing activities:			
Proceeds from disposition of property, plant, and equipment	1,093,000	2,744,000	1,929,000
Capital expenditures	(22,365,000)	(26,575,000)	(27,222,000)
Business acquisitions, net of cash acquired	(1,036,000)	(104,935,000)	(92,239,000)
Redemption of short-term investments	–	–	2,566,000
Other	(4,286,000)	(5,776,000)	(2,019,000)
Net cash used by investing activities	(26,594,000)	(134,542,000)	(116,985,000)
Financing activities:			
Net (decrease) increase in notes payable	(1,583,000)	(5,201,000)	5,249,000
Payments on long-term debt	(28,000,000)	(60,000,000)	(70,000,000)
Proceeds from the issuance of long-term debt	22,765,000	150,000,000	159,000,000
Proceeds from the issuance of common stock	2,845,000	3,920,000	1,486,000
Common stock repurchases	(8,798,000)	(9,197,000)	(22,351,000)
Dividends paid	(14,806,000)	(14,677,000)	(14,564,000)
Proceeds from the sale of debt swap	13,766,000	–	–
Net cash (used) provided by financing activities	(13,811,000)	64,845,000	58,820,000
Effect of exchange rate changes on cash flows	(930,000)	(2,489,000)	(1,206,000)
Increase (decrease) in cash and cash equivalents	25,565,000	(20,329,000)	3,426,000
Cash and cash equivalents at beginning of year	23,303,000	43,632,000	40,206,000
Cash and cash equivalents at end of year	$48,868,000	$23,303,000	$43,632,000

a. What changes in assets and liabilities contributed most to the increase in net cash provided by operating activities in 2001 over that in 2000?

b. How were business acquisitions financed in 1999 and 2000?

c. What changes in financing activities do you observe in 2001 by comparison to the two previous years?

d. What is your general assessment of the company's ability to finance its investing activities from operating cash flows beyond 2001?

26. Use the data in the cash flow statement for GAP, Inc. to answer the questions that follow.

GAP, Inc.: Cash Flow	52 Weeks Ended Feb. 2, 2002	53 Weeks Ended Feb. 3, 2001	52 Weeks Ended Jan. 29, 2000
Cash flows from operating activities:			
Net earnings (loss)	$ (7,764,000)	$877,497,000	$1,127,065,000
Adjustments to reconcile net earnings (loss) to net cash provided by operating activities:			
Depreciation and amortization	810,486,000	590,365,000	436,184,000
Tax benefit from exercise of stock options and vesting of restricted stock	58,444,000	130,882,000	211,891,000
Deferred income taxes	(28,512,000)	(38,872,000)	2,444,000
Change in operating assets and liabilities:			
Merchandise inventory	213,067,000	(454,595,000)	(404,211,000)
Prepaid expenses and other	(13,303,000)	(61,096,000)	(55,519,000)
Accounts payable	42,205,000	249,545,000	118,121,000
Accrued expenses	220,826,000	(56,541,000)	(5,822,000)
Deferred lease credits and other long-term liabilities	22,390,000	54,020,000	47,775,000
Net cash provided by operating activities	1,317,839,000	1,291,205,000	1,477,928,000
Cash flows from investing activities:			
Net purchase of property and equipment	(940,078,000)	(1,858,662,000)	(1,238,722,000)
Acquisition of lease rights and other assets	(10,549,000)	(16,252,000)	(39,839,000)
Net cash used for investing activities	(950,627,000)	(1,874,914,000)	(1,278,561,000)
Cash Flows from financing activities:			
Net increase (decrease) in notes payable	(734,927,000)	621,420,000	84,778,000
Proceeds from issuance of long-term debt	1,194,265,000	250,000,000	311,839,000
Payments of long-term debt	(250,000,000)	–	–
Issuance of common stock	139,105,000	152,105,000	114,142,000
Net purchase of treasury stock	(785,000)	(392,558,000)	(745,056,000)
Cash dividends paid	(76,373,000)	(75,488,000)	(75,795,000)
Net cash provided by (used for) financing activities	271,285,000	555,479,000	(310,092,000)
Effect of exchange rate fluctuations on cash	(11,542,000)	(13,328,000)	(4,176,000)
Net increase (decrease) in cash and equivalents	626,955,000	(41,558,000)	(114,901,000)
Cash and equivalents at beginning of year	408,794,000	450,352,000	565,253,000
Cash and equivalents at end of year	$1,035,749,000	$408,794,000	$ 450,352,000

a. What trend do you observe in net income for the three years presented?

b. Why does net cash provided by operating activities not display the same trend as noted in your answer to a.?

c. What other information from the cash flow statements can be used to explain the substantial increase in depreciation and amortization from 2001 to 2002?

d. How would you describe the events pertaining to debt that occurred in 2002?

27. Use the data in the cash flow statement for Polaroid Corporation to answer the questions that follow.

POLAROID CORP.: Cash Flow	12/31/1998	12/31/1999	12/31/2000
Cash flows from operating activities:			
Net earnings/(loss)	$ (51,000,000)	$ 8,700,000	$37,700,000
Depreciation of property, plant, and equipment	90,700,000	105,900,000	113,900,000
Gain on the sale of real estate	(68,200,000)	(11,700,000)	(21,800,000)
Other noncash items	62,200,000	73,800,000	22,900,000
Decrease/(increase) in receivables	79,000,000	(52,700,000)	41,800,000
Decrease/(increase) in inventories	(28,400,000)	88,000,000	(100,600,000)
Decrease in prepaids and other assets	39,000,000	62,400,000	32,900,000
Increase/(decrease) in payables and accruals	25,300,000	(16,500,000)	9,200,000
Decrease in compensation and benefits	(21,000,000)	(72,500,000)	(105,000,000)
Decrease in federal, state, and foreign income taxes payable	(29,900,000)	(54,000,000)	(31,500,000)
Net cash provided/(used) by operating activities	97,700,000	131,400,000	(500,000)
Cash flows from investing activities:			
Decrease/(increase) in other assets	(25,400,000)	16,500,000	4,500,000
Additions to property, plant, and equipment	(191,100,000)	(170,500,000)	(129,200,000)
Proceeds from the sale of property, plant, and equipment	150,500,000	36,600,000	56,600,000
Acquisitions, net of cash acquired	(18,800,000)	–	–
Net cash used by investing activities	(84,800,000)	(117,400,000)	(68,100,000)
Cash flows from financing activities:			
Net increase/(decrease) in short-term debt (maturities 90 days or less)	131,200,000	(86,200,000)	108,200,000
Short-term debt (maturities of more than 90 days)			
Proceeds	73,000,000	41,800,000	–
Payments	(117,200,000)	(24,900,000)	–
Proceeds from issuance of long-term debt	–	268,200,000	–
Repayment of long-term debt	–	(200,000,000)	–
Cash dividends paid	(26,500,000)	(26,600,000)	(27,000,000)
Purchase of treasury stock	(45,500,000)	–	–
Proceeds from issuance of shares in connection with stock incentive plan	6,000,000	300,000	100,000
Net cash provided/(used) by financing activities	21,000,000	(27,400,000)	81,300,000
Effect of exchange rate changes on cash	3,100,000	400,000	(7,500,000)
Net increase/(decrease) in cash and cash equivalents	37,000,000	(13,000,000)	5,200,000
Cash and cash equivalents at beginning of year	68,000,000	105,000,000	92,000,000
Cash and cash equivalents at end of year	$105,000,000	$92,000,000	$97,200,000

a. Why is the upward trend in net earnings/(loss) not reflected in net cash provided/(used) by operating activities for the three years presented?

b. How were net additions to property, plant, and equipment in 2000 principally financed?

c. What would be a reasonable estimate of the change in property, plant, and equipment during 2000?

d. What indications are there that the company will need to seek external financing in 2001?

28. Use the data in the cash flow statement for Tech Data Corporation to answer the questions that follow.

TECH DATA CORP.: Cash Flow	01/31/2002	01/31/2001	01/31/2000
Cash flows from operating activities:			
Cash received from customers	$17,511,511,000	$20,114,486,000	$16,788,960,000
Cash paid to suppliers and employees	(16,406,265,000)	(20,047,551,000)	(16,684,316,000)
Interest paid	(55,871,000)	(94,823,000)	(69,554,000)
Income taxes paid	(72,745,000)	(62,048,000)	(34,176,000)
Net cash provided by (used in) operating activities	976,630,000	(89,936,000)	914,000
Cash flows from investing activities:			
Acquisition of businesses, net of cash acquired	(183,000)	(19,198,000)	(42,898,000)
Expenditures for property and equipment	(28,466,000)	(38,079,000)	(59,038,000)
Software development costs	(20,719,000)	(22,705,000)	(18,381,000)
Net cash used in investing activities	(49,368,000)	(79,982,000)	(120,317,000)
Cash flows from financing activities:			
Proceeds from the issuance of common stock, net of related tax benefit	36,432,000	35,539,000	19,663,000
Net (repayments) borrowings on revolving credit loans	(1,118,167,000)	248,712,000	99,447,000
Proceeds from issuance of long-term debt, net of expense	284,200,000	–	–
Principal payments on long-term debt	(634,000)	(557,000)	(162,000)
Net cash (used in) provided by financing activities	(798,169,000)	283,694,000	118,948,000
Effect of change in year end of certain subsidiaries (Note 3)	–	–	23,626,000
Effect of exchange rate changes on cash	(10,091,000)	(6,637,000)	–
Net increase in cash and cash equivalents	119,002,000	107,139,000	23,171,000
Cash and cash equivalents at beginning of year	138,925,000	31,786,000	8,615,000
Cash and cash equivalents at end of year	$ 257,927,000	$ 138,925,000	$ 31,786,000

TECH DATA CORP.: Cash Flow	01/31/2002	01/31/2001	01/31/2000
Reconciliation of net income to net cash provided by (used in) operating activities:			
Net income	$ 110,777,000	$177,983,000	$127,501,000
Adjustments to reconcile net income to net cash provided by (used in) operating activities:			
Depreciation and amortization	63,488,000	63,922,000	57,842,000
Provision for losses on accounts receivable	40,764,000	41,447,000	40,877,000

	01/31/2002	01/31/2001	01/31/2000
Special charges (Note 13)	27,000,000	–	–
Deferred income taxes	(11,848,000)	(1,789,000)	1,306,000
Changes in assets and liabilities:			
Decrease (increase) in accounts receivable	314,000,000	(313,197,000)	(202,790,000)
Decrease (increase) in inventories	702,219,000	(146,093,000)	(220,585,000)
(Increase) in prepaid and other assets	(6,248,000)	(11,603,000)	(25,430,000)
(Decrease) increase in accounts payable	(264,722,000)	11,863,000	136,748,000
Increase in accrued expenses	1,200,000	87,531,000	85,445,000
Total adjustments	865,853,000	(267,919,000)	(126,587,000)
Net cash provided by (used in) operating activities	$976,630,000	$ (89,936,000)	$ 914,000

a. How does the format of the cash flow statements for this company differ from the format used by most companies?

b. What changes do you note in the reconciliation of net income to net cash provided by (used in) operating activities that most explain the dramatic increase in net cash provided by those activities?

c. How did the company finance its investing activities in 2000 and 2001?

d. Where were the funds obtained to repay borrowings on revolving credit loans in 2002?

e. What evidence is there that the company has reversed its growth during 2002 from what it was during the previous two years?

◉ BEYOND THE BOOK

29. For a company of your own choosing, answer the following questions related to its cash flow statement:

a. What is the trend in net income for the three years presented?

b. What is the trend in cash from operations for the three years presented?

c. In the most recent year, explain why the cash from operations differs from net income.

d. What other cash needs did the firm have in the most recent time period outside of operations?

e. Where did the company get the cash to cover the needs identified in part (d)?

f. What concerns do you have about the financial health of the company from your analysis of the cash flow statement?

Financial Statement Analysis

LEARNING OBJECTIVES

After studying this chapter students should be able to:

1 Understand how to adjust financial statements to give effect to differences in accounting methods.

2 Be able to calculate and interpret common financial ratios.

3 Evaluate a firm's short-term and long-term debt repayment abilities and its profitability.

4 Have a basic understanding of methods of forecasting future revenues or earnings.

5 Understand the concept of present value and its application to valuing free cash flows and residual earnings.

In late 2001 Starbucks Corp. announced that it had beat analysts' expectations and reported a first quarter profit (for the quarter ended September 30, 2001) of 25 cents a share. The analysts' previous estimate was 23 cents a share. In the same announcement Starbucks also reported record revenues of $667 million, up 26 percent from $529 million in the same period a year ago. Earnings were $49 million, up 41% over the same period a year ago of $34.7 million. Starbucks also indicated that it had raised its own projections of the year's fiscal earnings by a penny per share.

Despite the very sizeable increase in revenues and earnings over the previous year for Starbucks, note that analysts' forecasts nearly matched Starbucks' reported amounts and thus we would expect very little adjustment to Starbucks' market value as a result of this disclosure. The prominence of revenues in this earnings release is consistent with analysts viewing changes in revenues as a measure of growth and, hence, as a key factor in forecasting future performance.

In virtually all cases, financial statement users are concerned with predicting future outcomes of a firm. However, these forecasts usually begin with an assessment of the firm's *past performance.* In this chapter, we'll show you how financial statement analysis provides this link from evaluating past performance to forecasting future expectations.

OVERVIEW OF FINANCIAL STATEMENT ANALYSIS

Financial statement analysis refers to a set of procedures for transforming past data from a firm's published financial statements into information useful for future decisions. Many different types of decisions are based on financial statement analysis, such as whether to extend credit, buy or sell securities, or reward managers for their performance.

Financial statement analysis typically involves making **inter-temporal** (across time) and **cross-sectional** (across firms) comparisons. Inter-temporal comparisons help to identify trends in past data as well as reveal areas of concern that may warrant special attention. Cross-sectional comparisons (of a firm with its main rivals) indicate relative performance that may have a bearing on future market share. One complication in making both types of comparisons using raw financial statement data is the effect of changes or differences in firm size. For instance, if we were analyzing the pizza business and wanted to compare Domino's, Sbarro, and Bertucci's, they are very different in size with revenues of $1,275 million, $360 million, and $162 million, respectively. Analysts commonly adjust for such differences by using financial ratios in making these comparisons.

Another complication is that accounting policies may vary across time or across firms. When this occurs, analysts may need to adjust for these variations by restating financial statements in order to place them on a common basis. Such restatements answer the question of what the firm's financial statements would look like "as if" they had been prepared under the same set of accounting policies.

Once analysts transform the data into ratios and understand the trends that may be present, they next assess future prospects by constructing **operating forecasts,** for example, the forecast of net income from operations. A formal approach to forecasting extrapolates past operating data through statistical models that take advantage of inter-temporal relationships present in that data (these models are often called *time-series models*). Less formal approaches rely more on analysts' subjective judgments of future trends. Regardless of the approach used, operating forecasts should factor in the outlook for the industry and the economy as a whole, the company's business plan, and the nature of competition.

	02/01/2003	02/01/2002	02/01/2001
Net sales	$1,380,966,000	$1,299,573,000	$1,232,776,000
Cost of sales	633,473,000	651,808,000	622,036,000
Gross margin	747,493,000	647,765,000	610,740,000
Selling, general, and administrative expenses	612,479,000	576,584,000	501,460,000
Amortization of goodwill	–	11,040,000	11,040,000
Operating income	135,014,000	60,141,000	98,240,000
Interest income	3,279,000	1,390,000	2,473,000
Interest expense	6,886,000	6,869,000	7,315,000
Income before income taxes	131,407,000	54,662,000	93,398,000
Income tax provision	51,249,000	25,557,000	41,035,000
Net income	$ 80,158,000	$ 29,105,000	$ 52,363,000

Exhibit 6.1
Consolidated Statements of Income

THE REAL WORLD

AnnTaylor Stores Corporation

We're now ready to take a closer look at financial statement analysis. We'll use the data from AnnTaylor Stores Corporation (see Exhibits 6.1 and 6.2) to illustrate the process of financial statement analysis. Our first step is to review the financial statements to determine if they need to be restated.

CREATING COMPARABLE DATA FOR FINANCIAL STATEMENT ANALYSIS

Analysts must often consider how a firm's financial statements would appear if it used a different accounting method. For example, analysts may seek to undo the effects of overly aggressive income recognition ("as if" restatements), assess the effects of an impending change in accounting policy, or compare the performance of firms that employ different accounting methods. These adjustments can be quite complex in some situations. A full understanding of restatements requires a level of understanding of accounting that is beyond the scope of this book. However, a basic knowledge of accounting is sufficient to understand the idea of restatements and how to make basic restatements. Here we provide examples of some common restatements. Let's review how analysts create comparable data for each of these situations.

"AS IF" RESTATEMENTS

A useful technique in restating revenues, expenses, or income is to determine first how balances of related accounts appearing on comparative balance sheets would be affected; then, adjust the item in question by the change in the difference between the beginning and ending balances. For example, suppose a company recognized revenue for sales of goods or services at the time of delivery, despite considerable uncertainty about future collections from customers. Analysts determine the effect on the company's revenues, if it

Exhibit 6.2
Consolidated Balance Sheets

AnnTaylor Stores
Corporation

	02/01/2003	02/01/2002
Current assets:		
Cash and cash equivalents	$ 212,821,000	$ 30,037,000
Accounts receivable, net	10,367,000	65,598,000
Merchandise inventories	185,484,000	180,117,000
Prepaid expenses and other current assets	46,599,000	50,314,000
Total current assets	455,271,000	326,066,000
Property and equipment, net	247,115,000	250,735,000
Goodwill, net	286,579,000	286,579,000
Deferred financing costs, net	4,170,000	5,044,000
Other assets	17,691,000	14,742,000
Total assets	$1,010,826,000	$883,166,000
Liabilities and stockholders' equity:		
Current liabilities		
Accounts payable	$ 57,058,000	$ 52,011,000
Accrued salaries and bonus	27,567,000	12,121,000
Accrued tenancy	10,808,000	10,151,000
Gift certificates and merchandise credits redeemable	25,637,000	21,828,000
Accrued expenses	30,125,000	37,907,000
Current portion of long-term debt		1,250,000
Total current liabilities	151,195,000	135,268,000
Long-term debt, net	121,652,000	118,280,000
Deferred lease costs and other liabilities	23,561,000	17,489,000
Stockholders' equity common stock, $.0068 par value; 120,000,000 shares authorized; 48,932,860 and 48,275,957 shares issued, respectively	332,000	328,000
Additional paid-in capital	500,061,000	484,582,000
Retained earnings	296,113,000	218,600,000
Deferred compensation on restricted stock	(3,968,000)	(9,296,000)
	792,538,000	694,214,000
Treasury stock, 4,050,972 and 4,210,232 shares, respectively, at cost	(78,120,000)	(82,085,000)
Total stockholders' equity	714,418,000	612,129,000
Total liabilities and stockholders' equity	$1,010,826,000	$883,166,000

adopted the less-aggressive procedure of delaying recognition until cash was received, as follows:

Revenue (as if recognized at time of collection) =
Revenue (as Reported) + Decrease (−Increase) in Accounts Receivable

Consider the data from AnnTaylor. From Exhibit 6.1 we find reported revenues of $1,381.0 (all numbers in millions, rounded to the nearest hundred thousand). From Exhibit 6.2, we compute a decrease in accounts receivable of $55.2 ($10.4 − $65.6). Thus, if AnnTaylor recognized revenue as it collected cash from customers, revenues would equal $1,436.2 ($1,381.0 + $55.2).

Inventories provide another illustration. Different firms often value inventories under different methods, such as the "first-in, first-out" (FIFO) and "last-in, first-out" (LIFO) methods. For instance, Ford Motor Company uses LIFO, whereas Dell Computer uses FIFO. As discussed in more detail in Chapter 8, LIFO usually results in higher costs of goods sold and lower inventory levels on the balance sheet than FIFO. However, GAAP requires firms that apply the LIFO method to include a disclosure explaining the net difference in inventory values as a result of applying these two methods. Firms often report this difference, known as the LIFO reserve, in a footnote. Using these data, you can calculate what the cost of goods sold would have been under FIFO using the following calculation:

> Cost of goods sold (as if FIFO had been used) =
> Cost of goods sold (as reported, LIFO) + Decrease (−Increase) in LIFO Reserve

One last illustration of the adjustment process relates to a company's accounting treatment of warranty expenses. Most companies, for example Ford Motor Company, recognize warranty costs (on an estimated basis) as expenses at the time of sale rather than when paid. Suppose, however, that an analyst wants to determine a company's warranty settlement cost. In this case, we adjust the expense under the former treatment to determine the amount of claims settled as follows:

> Warranty Expense (as if recorded when settled) =
> Warranty Expense (as reported) + Decrease (−Increase) in Warranties Payable

Thinking Globally

International Accounting Issues

Because countries employ different accounting standards, analysts frequently need to make adjustments before conducting a cross-sectional analysis across countries. For example, Canadian companies selectively capitalize (record as assets) research and development (R&D) costs at the time these costs are incurred, while U.S. companies are required by GAAP to write off (record as expenses) those costs immediately.

If research and development (R&D) costs were initially recorded as an asset (as they might be under Canadian standards) and subsequently amortized as an expense, then one could calculate what R&D expense would be reported under the U.S. policy (which requires immediate recognition as an expense when the expenditures are made) as shown below:

> R&D Expense (U.S.) = R&D Amortization Expense (Canadian)
> + Increase (−Decrease) in Unamortized R&D Costs (Canadian)

Note that adjustments made to the income statement might also affect the calculation of income taxes, and therefore all as-if adjustments should also include adjustments for the tax effects.

Note that all of these adjustments focus on the income statement. In each case, however, to maintain the accounting equation, an impact also occurs on the balance sheet through an adjustment of an asset or a liability account. Further, because these adjustments affect net income, a change also occurs in retained earnings. For example, if a company begins accruing an expense that it previously recognized only when paid, then the balance in accrued liabilities increases, expenses on the income statement also increase, and the balance in retained earnings decreases by the reduction in net income.

Finally, note that some changes in the timing of revenue and expense recognition materially affect only the balance sheet. For example, as mentioned, Canadian companies are allowed to capitalize (record as an asset) some research and development (R&D) costs and then later amortize the costs to income. Suppose that a particular Canadian company capitalized costs in an amount equal to its amortization expense in the year you are analyzing. If you were to adjust the statements to conform to U.S. GAAP (where the firm must expense all R&D as incurred), the adjusted expense would be the same as the original expense and therefore there would be no effect of this adjustment on the income statement. However, the balance sheets would still differ as both assets and retained earnings would be lower if no R&D costs had ever been capitalized. In other words, balance sheet restatements reflect the cumulative effects (the effects of applying the new method in all prior years) of differences in accounting methods, whereas income statement restatements reflect only the current year effect.

MANDATED ACCOUNTING CHANGES

Accounting rule changes by the FASB and the SEC frequently occur. Accordingly, analysts need to be aware of the consequences of these changes on the financial statements. However, analysts are assisted with this task as follows:

● The FASB and the SEC typically specify how firms must handle these mandated changes within the financial statements.

● Firms usually document these changes in the footnotes of the financial statements in the period in which the change is made.

● The FASB and the SEC often require that firms also restate past financial statements to give effect to the mandated change in question.

● In some cases, these changes require that the cumulative effects on income of applying the new rules be shown as a separate line item in the income statement for the year in which the change is made.

● Auditors call attention to accounting rule changes in their report to stockholders.

Hence, a question seldom arises as to whether a change has occurred.

The greater challenge for analysts in dealing with mandated accounting changes is to evaluate the economic consequences of the change. For example, suppose a firm previously issued debt containing a covenant (a contractual restriction) that requires net worth (stockholders' equity) determined under GAAP to stay above a specified level. Now suppose that the FASB changes a rule governing revenue recognition, with the result of reducing the firm's net income to the point where it violates the covenant. To avoid this, the firm might have to cut its dividend. This might cause the value of the company's stock to fall due to an increase in risk, because of the reduction of cash flows (dividends) to shareholders.

Another consequence of a change to a more conservative method of revenue recognition might be to alter the incentives (often earnings-based bonuses) to managers provided by compensation contracts. For example, consider an executive who receives a bonus if reported income exceeds a certain level. If the accounting change makes it highly unlikely that this level will be reached in the year of change, no matter how much effort the executive applies, he or she may decide to postpone initiatives until the following year when it is more likely that he or she would receive the bonus. This reduced effort may negatively affect firm value.

DISCRETIONARY ACCOUNTING CHANGES

Within the GAAP framework, managers have considerable discretion in their choices of accounting treatments. Further, evidence suggests that managers make use of their discretion in responding to incentives and furthering the interests of shareholders (when their incentives are aligned). Beyond the consideration of the comparability of the data that result when the change occurs, the bigger issues for analysts are the motivation of the firm's management and the potential for significant economic consequences.

For example, consider firms in an industry that seeks trade relief. These firms must show they have been injured by the anticompetitive practices of foreign rivals. Managers in these companies would have an incentive to make accounting decisions that lower their reported income, in order to demonstrate such injury. Evidence (Lenway and Rayburn, *Contemporary Accounting Research,* 1992) does indicate that in the mid-1980s, U.S. semiconductor producers generally had higher negative accruals coincident with petitions alleging dumping by Japanese producers.

Accounting treatments may also influence real investment and financing decisions. For example, firms generally do not recognize changes in the market value of debt (sometimes referred to as unrealized holding gains and losses) that result when interest rates in the economy change. However, a company seeking to increase or decrease its reported income for reasons mentioned above might decide to retire its debt early, causing the recognition of the gain or loss.

Finally, note that accounting decisions might serve as signaling devices, whereby a firm may be able to persuade investors that it has more favorable future cash flow prospects. For example, as we will see in Chapter 8, if a firm uses the LIFO method of valuing inventories for tax purposes, it must also use this same method for reporting to its shareholders (in periods of rising prices, LIFO results in lower reported net income and therefore lower tax payments). Theorists suggest that firms choosing to forego the tax benefits of LIFO by using FIFO for reporting purposes (and hence for tax purposes) may be signaling that they have stronger cash flow prospects than comparable firms that use LIFO.

Once analysts complete reviewing a firm's financial statements, and restating as necessary, calculating ratios can lead to more meaningful information. In the next section, we'll see how to use ratios to analyze a firm's past performance, which is the next step in financial statement analysis.

> Firms using LIFO could mimic the firms with stronger cash flow prospects by also choosing FIFO. However, they may find the loss of tax benefits to outweigh the benefits of not having investors learn that they have weaker cash flow prospects.

USING FINANCIAL RATIOS TO ASSESS PAST PERFORMANCE

To assess a firm's past performance from periodic financial statements, analysts must first adjust the contents for inter-temporal changes or cross-sectional variations in firm size. For example, it does not mean much when assessing operating efficiency to compare income either over time for a firm that is changing in size or between small and large firms. Analysts remove effects of scale (size) by employing financial ratios. Financial ratios are often broadly organized into those that assess profitability and those that assess debt-repayment ability.

ASSESSING PROFITABILITY

From an investor's perspective, **rate of return on equity (ROE)** presents a comprehensive accounting measure of a firm's performance. For a company with only common stock outstanding (we consider other types of stock in Chapter 12), we determine ROE as follows:

$$\text{ROE} = \frac{\text{Net Income}}{\text{Average Stockholders' Equity}}$$

Because a firm earns net income over a period of time, the denominator of this ratio also reflects the level of stockholders' investment over this same period of time. Hence, it makes sense to calculate the average amount invested during the period in the denominator. Most analysts compute the average as simply the sum of the beginning and ending balances of stockholders' equity, divided by two. The implicit assumption in this computation is that the change in balances remained uniform over the period. If the change in balances varied over the period, analysts might then use more sophisticated averaging techniques.

ROE is an accounting measure of the profitability of the firm's past investments. We can compare this measure to the expected rate of return investors require in order to buy the firm's stock, called the cost of equity. Investors measure returns on the firm's stock from market data such as dividends and changes in market prices. The expected rate of return on the firm's stock depends on the risks that equity holders cannot eliminate through holding a well-diversified portfolio (in other words, a portfolio of a wide variety of stocks); something that we discuss further in Chapter 14. An ROE greater than the cost of equity suggests that the firm has been successful in finding projects to invest in whose returns exceed investors' expectations. However, a firm's ability to consistently find projects that result in an ROE in excess of its cost of equity is likely to be limited by competitors attracted to the same projects. Accordingly, in the long run we would anticipate that ROE would converge toward the cost of equity and that the ROE of firms in the same industry would converge to the industry average.

ROE can be decomposed into both a measure of the efficiency with which a firm uses its assets to generate income and of the capital structure of the firm.

$$\text{ROE} = \frac{\text{Net Income}}{\text{Average Assets}} \times \frac{\text{Average Assets}}{\text{Average Stockholders' Equity}}$$

The first component is commonly referred to as **rate of return on assets (ROA),** and the second component is commonly referred to as **financial leverage.** Thus, a shorthand expression for ROE is:

$$ROE = ROA \times Leverage$$

ROA can be further decomposed into profit margin and asset turnover:

$$ROA = \frac{Net\ Income}{Sales} \times \frac{Sales}{Average\ Assets}$$

or:

$$ROA = Profit\ Margin \times Total\ Asset\ Turnover$$

This decomposition allows us to distinguish between operating strategies that emphasize profit per dollar of sales (profit margin) versus sales per dollar of investment in assets (total asset turnover).

For AnnTaylor, we calculate ROE and ROA as follows:

$$ROE = \frac{80.2}{(714.4 + 612.1)/2} = 12.1\%$$

$$ROA = \frac{80.2}{1,381} \times \frac{1,381}{(1,010.8 + 883.2)/2} = 8.5\%$$

$$ROA = 5.8\% \times 1.46 = 8.5\%$$

ROA, as a measure of return on investment on assets, is complicated by employing a numerator (net income) that includes the return to debtholders in the form of interest expense. An alternative measure, more focused on the efficiency of assets employed in the firm's operating activities, is the **rate of return on capital (ROC).** Here, the numerator of ROC uses operating income. Operating income can be obtained by adding back interest expense, net of taxes, to net income. Because this ratio is an after-tax ratio, we must adjust for taxes related to interest expense. In the denominator, debt and stockholders' equity replace total assets, to represent the net assets contributed by the firm's capital suppliers (total assets less operating liabilities, i.e., liabilities other than debt).

$$ROC = \frac{Net\ Income + Interest\ Expense \times (1 - tax\ rate)}{Average\ Debt + Average\ Stockholders'\ Equity}$$

We calculate ROC for AnnTaylor as follows:

$$ROC = \frac{80.2 + 6.9 \times (1 - 51.2/131.4)}{((121.7 + 23.6 + 1.3 + 118.3 + 17.5)/2 + (714.4 + 612.1)/2)} = 10.3\%$$

We obtain the tax rate by comparing the tax expense reported by AnnTaylor ($51.2) with the income before tax ($131.4), resulting in a tax rate of 39 percent (51.2/131.4). We determine the total debt by adding together the long-term debt and the deferred lease cost and other liabilities on the balance sheet (including the current portion of long-term debt from the current liability section). We can then compare the above measure to the composite market return required by the suppliers of both debt and equity capital, commonly referred to as the company's **weighted average cost of capital (WACC).** However, this calculation is beyond the scope of this book. We will provide more discussion on estimating the cost of equity capital in Chapter 14.

Shareholders of a firm leverage their investment by borrowing additional funds from debtholders to invest in additional assets. **Trading on equity** refers to the use of leverage to generate a higher ROE for shareholders. Because ROC provides a measure of the return to investments in assets (before distributions to any capital suppliers), shareholders can generate higher returns to themselves (ROE) as long as ROC on assets financed through debt exceeds the after-tax interest rate charged by debtholders, in other words, the cost of debt capital. Whether stockholders will benefit from trading on equity in the long run depends on the trade-off between the added risk of their position and the added expected return. Note that AnnTaylor generated a ROE of 12.1 percent, versus a ROA of 8.5 percent and a ROC of 10.3 percent. This indicates that they have used leverage to their shareholders' advantage, as ROE is greater than either ROA or ROC.

Recall from the decomposition of ROA that we calculate profit margin by dividing net income by sales. To further explore factors that influence profit margin, we can prepare a common size income statement. A **common size income statement** expresses each component of net income as a percent of sales. Exhibit 6.3 presents common size income statements for AnnTaylor.

The advantage of a common size statement is that it allows analysts to identify factors responsible for changes in profit margin. For example, rising product costs that are not passed on to customers might be reflected in higher cost of sales, as a percent of sales, and lower gross profit margins. Similarly, holding unit costs constant, a change in pricing policy might be evident from a comparison of gross profit margins. Administrative and marketing efficiencies may

Exhibit 6.3
Common Size Income
Statement

THE REAL WORLD

AnnTaylor Stores
Corporation

	02/01/2003	02/01/2002	02/01/2001
Net sales	100.0%	100.0%	100.0%
Cost of sales	45.9%	50.2%	50.5%
Gross margin	54.1%	49.8%	49.5%
Selling, general, and administrative expenses	44.4%	44.4%	40.7%
Amortization of goodwill	0.0%	0.8%	0.9%
Operating income	9.8%	4.6%	8.0%
Interest income	0.2%	0.1%	0.2%
Interest expense	0.5%	0.5%	0.6%
Income before income taxes	9.5%	4.2%	7.6%
Income tax provision	3.7%	2.0%	3.3%
Net income	5.8%	2.2%	4.2%

also become more apparent when the direct effects of growth in sales are removed.

In Exhibit 6.3, Net Income (as a percent of sales in 2003) is 5.8 percent, the same amount we calculated in the Profit Margin Ratio component of ROA. Net Income in 2003 presents a significant improvement as indicated by the increase in profit margin to 5.8 percent from the 2.2 percent in 2002. Reviewing the common size income statement, we identify this change as a direct result of a significant improvement in the cost of sales relative to sales revenues (50.5 percent to 45.9 percent), as well as a decline in the amortization of goodwill (which disappeared in 2003).

As another example of how to interpret the common size income statement, in Exhibit 6.4 find the common size income statement for Amazon.com for the years 2000 through 2002. Note that Amazon was able to maintain its gross profit percentage at approximately 25 percent over the three years. However, it cut its total operating expenses from 55 percent of sales to 24 percent of sales over

Amazon.com, Inc.
Common Size Income Statement

	12/31/2002	12/31/2001	12/31/2000
Net sales	100%	100%	100%
Cost of sales	75%	74%	76%
Gross profit	25%	26%	24%
Operating expenses:	0%	0%	0%
Fulfillment	10%	12%	15%
Marketing	3%	4%	7%
Technology and content	5%	8%	10%
General and administrative	2%	3%	4%
Stock-based compensation	2%	0%	1%
Amortization of goodwill and other intangibles	0%	6%	12%
Restructuring-related and other	1%	6%	7%
Total operating expenses	24%	39%	55%
Loss from operations	2%	−13%	−31%
Interest income	1%	1%	1%
Interest expense	−4%	−4%	−5%
Other income (expense), net	0%	0%	0%
Other gains (losses), net	−2%	0%	−5%
Net interest expense and other	−5%	−4%	−9%
Loss before equity in losses of equity method investees	−4%	−17%	−40%
Equity in losses of equity-method investees, net	0%	−1%	−11%
Loss before change in accounting principle	−4%	−18%	−51%
Cumulative effect of change in accounting principle	0%	0%	0%
Net loss	−4%	−18%	−51%

Exhibit 6.4
Amazon.com, Inc. Common Size Income Statement

THE REAL WORLD

Amazon.Com, Inc.

this same period. Note further that this resulted in the conversion of an operating loss of 31 percent from operations in 2000 to a gain of 2 percent from operations in 2002. While Amazon has still shown a net loss, this analysis implies that it has demonstrated significant progress in trying to achieve profitability from its operations.

ASSESSING TURNOVER RATIOS

Total asset turnover, as depicted in the decomposition of ROA, equals sales divided by total assets. The concept of a turnover is that we invest in assets to sell goods and services. We then expect that our investment in assets will be converted (or turned over) into sales. For AnnTaylor this ratio is 1.46, indicating that the investment in total assets is converted or turned over into sales 1.46 times a year. This ratio reflects significant averaging, as property and equipment turns over much less than 1.46 times a year and merchandise inventories turn over much more frequently. As a result, analysts seeking a better understanding of the company's performance in managing its operating assets may find it useful to consider more specific asset turnover ratios, including accounts receivable and inventory turnovers.

We calculate accounts receivable turnover and inventory turnover as follows:

$$\text{Receivables Turnover} = \frac{\text{Sales}}{\text{Average Receivables}}$$

$$\text{Inventory Turnover} = \frac{\text{Cost of Goods Sold}}{\text{Average Inventories}}$$

This type of ratio provides a measure of how many times a firm converts a particular asset into a sale (inventory turnover) or how much a firm needs a particular type of asset to support a given level of sales (accounts receivable turnover). In effect, asset turnover ratios reflect the ability of the company to efficiently use its assets to generate sales.

Often, we convert turnover ratios into an alternative form to represent the number of days that a firm, in a sense, holds an asset, as follows:

$$\text{Days Receivables} = \frac{\text{Average Receivables}}{\text{Average Sales per day}}$$

or:

$$\text{Days Receivables} = \frac{365}{\text{Receivables Turnover}}$$

$$\text{Days Inventory} = \frac{\text{Average Inventories}}{\text{Average Cost of Goods Sold per day}}$$

or:

$$\text{Days Inventory} = \frac{365}{\text{Inventory Turnover}}$$

Decreases in receivables and inventory turnover ratios, or increases in days receivables and inventory, may indicate collection and sales problems, respectively.

Similarly, accounts payable turnover reflects the efficiency with which a firm manages its credit from its suppliers, or alternatively, how much credit the firm needs in support of its sales efforts. We calculate this ratio as follows:

$$\text{Payables Turnover} = \frac{\text{Cost of Goods Sold}}{\text{Average (Accounts) Payable}}$$

$$\text{Days Payables} = \frac{\text{Average (Accounts) Payable}}{\text{Average Cost of Goods Sold per day}}$$

or:

$$\text{Days Payables} = \frac{365}{\text{Payables Turnover}}$$

Other turnover ratios consider various asset groupings such as:

$$\text{Working Capital Turnover} = \frac{\text{Sales}}{\text{Average Current Assets} - \text{Average Current Liabilities}}$$

$$\text{Capital Assets Turnover} = \frac{\text{Sales}}{\text{Average Plant, Property, and Equipment}}$$

Here again, lower turnover ratios may indicate deterioration in operating efficiency. We calculate the applicable turnover ratios for AnnTaylor as follows:

$$\text{Receivables Turnover} = \frac{1,381}{(10.4 + 65.6)/2} = 36.3$$

$$\text{Days Receivables} = \frac{365}{36.3} = 10$$

$$\text{Inventory Turnover} = \frac{633.5}{(185.5 + 180.1)/2} = 3.4$$

$$\text{Days Inventory} = \frac{365}{3.4} = 107.3$$

$$\text{Payables Turnover} = \frac{633.5}{(57.1 + 52.0)/2} = 11.6$$

$$\text{Days Payables} = \frac{365}{11.6} = 31.4$$

$$\text{Working Capital Turnover} = \frac{1,381}{(455.3 + 326.1)/2 - (151.2 + 135.3)/2} = 5.6$$

$$\text{Capital Assets Turnover} = \frac{1,381}{(247.1 + 250.7)/2} = 5.5$$

Looking at these ratios, we can make several observations about AnnTaylor. The days in receivables seems to be relatively small. However, recognize that many of AnnTaylor's sales are for cash. Therefore, by including total sales in the numerator of the turnover ratio we have overstated the sales that result in receivables. This results in an understatement of the days to collect from credit sales. Further recognize that AnnTaylor's credit sales are typically via a nonproprietary credit card and those are immediately converted into cash. Inventory turns over more than three times a year. For a clothing retailer such as AnnTaylor, this makes sense as its product line changes from one season to the next. It also appears that AnnTaylor receives approximately 30 days of credit from their suppliers as the days of payables is slightly over 30 days.

In addition to turnover ratios, we can prepare a common size balance sheet to assess the investments being made in asset categories as well as the amounts and forms of financing. A **common size balance sheet** expresses each line item as a percent of total assets. Exhibit 6.5 presents common size balance sheets for AnnTaylor.

Exhibit 6.5
Common Size Balance Sheet

THE REAL WORLD

AnnTaylor Stores
Corporation

	02/01/2003	02/01/2002
Current assets		
Cash and cash equivalents	21.1%	3.4%
Accounts receivable, net	1.0%	7.4%
Merchandise inventories	18.3%	20.4%
Prepaid expenses and other current assets	4.6%	5.7%
Total current assets	45.0%	36.9%
Property and equipment, net	24.4%	28.4%
Goodwill, net	28.4%	32.4%
Deferred financing costs, net	0.4%	0.6%
Other assets	1.8%	1.7%
Total assets	100.0%	100.0%
Liabilities and stockholders' equity:		
Current liabilities		
Accounts payable	5.6%	5.9%
Accrued salaries and bonus	2.7%	1.4%
Accrued tenancy	1.1%	1.1%
Gift certificates and merchandise credits redeemable	2.5%	2.5%
Accrued expenses	3.0%	4.3%
Current portion of long-term debt	0.0%	0.1%
Total current liabilities	15.0%	15.3%
Long-term debt, net	12.0%	13.4%
Deferred lease costs and other liabilities	2.3%	2.0%
Stockholders' equity common stock, $.0068 par value; 120,000,000 shares authorized; 48,932,860 and 48,275,957 shares issued, respectively	0.0%	0.0%
Additional paid-in capital	49.5%	54.9%
Retained earnings	29.3%	24.8%
Deferred compensation on restricted stock	−0.4%	−1.1%
	78.4%	78.6%
Treasury stock, 4,050,972 and 4,210,232 shares, respectively, at cost	−7.7%	−9.3%
Total stockholders' equity	70.7%	69.3%
Total liabilities and stockholders' equity	100.0%	100.0%

In looking at this common size balance sheet, a couple of questions arise. For example, why have accounts receivable and inventory declined? If production costs have declined as shown on the income statement, perhaps the carrying value of inventory has also declined. This, however, does not explain the change in accounts receivable. As sales have actually increased during the year, we would have to investigate further to understand this change. By reading the details of the 10-K report for AnnTaylor, we discover that the firm sold the receivables associated with its proprietary credit card in fiscal year 2003 (we will refer to the fiscal year as the year in which the fiscal year ended, e.g., AnnTaylor ended fiscal year 2003 on February 1, 2003). This resulted in the much lower level of receivables at the end of 2003.

> Analysts are often led to search other sources of information to answer the questions that are raised by financial statement analysis such as the changes in accounts receivable for AnnTaylor.

In terms of its financing, the common size balance sheet indicates that AnnTaylor finances its assets with approximately 12 percent long-term debt and 70 percent equity (relative to total assets). This leads us to the next section in which we focus on the ability of the company to pay its long-term debt.

ASSESSING DEBT REPAYMENT ABILITY

Analysts assessing a company's debt-paying ability often separate short-term and long-term debt-paying ability. While this distinction may be somewhat arbitrary, a qualitative difference exists in how we measure the ability of a firm to repay debt that either matures before cash flows are generated by future operations or concurrently with those flows.

SHORT-TERM DEBT

Measures of the firm's ability to meet current obligations from existing assets include:

$$\text{Current Ratio} = \frac{\text{Current Assets}}{\text{Current Liabilities}}$$

$$\text{Quick Ratio} = \frac{\text{Cash, Marketable Securities, and Receivables}}{\text{Current Liabilities}}$$

$$\text{Cash Ratio} = \frac{\text{Cash and Cash Equivalent Investments}}{\text{Current Liabilities}}$$

These ratios primarily differ by the ease and speed with which assets included in the numerator can be converted to cash. Inventories are the furthest removed, as sales of inventory often give rise to receivables before producing cash. Receivables are closer to being converted to cash but are less easily converted than marketable securities. Low ratios may suggest future problems in repaying short-term liabilities as they become due.

The following ratios reflect AnnTaylor's short-term debt-repayment ability:

$$\text{Current Ratio} = \frac{455.3}{151.2} = 3$$

$$\text{Quick Ratio} = \frac{212.8 + 10.4}{151.2} = 1.5$$

$$\text{Cash Ratio} = \frac{212.8}{151.2} = 1.4$$

Due to the significant changes in cash and receivables that we noted earlier, these ratios may differ somewhat in the current year. In fact, when we compute them for the prior year, the ratios are 2.4, 0.7, and 0.2, respectively.

LONG–TERM DEBT

In the long term, a firm's ability to meet obligations is closely related to its ability to generate cash flows from operations. Interest coverage ratios consider the ability of the firm either to earn sufficient income or produce sufficient cash to make interest payments on the long-term debt.

$$\text{Interest Coverage} = \frac{\text{Income before Interest and Tax Expenses}}{\text{Interest Expense}}$$

The interest coverage ratio is based on net income, a long-run predictor of cash from operations but is not a cash flow measure itself. Some analysts also compute the cash equivalent ratio as follows:

$$\text{Interest Coverage} = \frac{\text{Cash from Operations before Interest and Tax Payments}}{\text{Interest Payments}}$$

Why do we compute income or cash before taxes? Recall that a firm meets its interest requirements before taxes are assessed. Low interest coverage ratios imply a greater risk of being unable to service debt as a consequence of fluctuations in operating results.

A different perspective on repayment ability focuses on debt capacity as measured by balance sheet leverage ratios:

$$\text{Debt Equity Ratio} = \frac{\text{Short-term Debt} + \text{Long-term Debt}}{\text{Stockholders' Equity}}$$

The debt-equity ratio predominantly measures the financial risk when assessing the risk/expected return trade-off relevant to investors. The more debt a company has, the more interest payments the company will be obligated to pay before common stock investors can earn a return on their investment.

The following ratios reflect AnnTaylor's long-term debt repayment ability and financial risk:

$$\text{Interest Coverage} = \frac{151.4 + 6.9}{6.9} = 20$$

$$\text{Debt Equity Ratio} = \frac{121.6}{714.4} = .2$$

We calculate the cash flow measure of interest coverage from information contained in the cash flow statement (not included here). In the statement, we see that cash from operations equaled $155.5 in 2003. In the supplemental disclosure to the statement, we find interest payments of $1.3 and tax payments of $40.1 (all figures in millions). We therefore calculate the cash measure as 151.5 (($155.5 + 1.3 + 40.1)/1.3). This amount is primarily due to a large portion of the company's interest expense being noncash expenses.

We have reviewed many financial ratios and how to compute them. Exhibit 6.6 provides a summary listing. Next, let's review how we can use this information

Exhibit 6.6
Summary Table of Ratios

$$\text{ROE} = \frac{\text{Net Income}}{\text{Average Stockholders' Equity}}$$

$$\text{ROA} = \frac{\text{Net Income}}{\text{Sales}} \times \frac{\text{Sales}}{\text{Average Assets}}$$

$$\text{ROC} = \frac{\text{Net Income} + \text{Interest Expense} \times (1 - \text{tax rate})}{\text{Average Debt} + \text{Average Stockholders' Equity}}$$

$$\text{Receivables Turnover} = \frac{\text{Sales}}{\text{Average Receivables}}$$

$$\text{Days Receivables} = \frac{365}{\text{Receivables Turnover}}$$

$$\text{Inventory Turnover} = \frac{\text{Cost of Goods Sold}}{\text{Average Inventories}}$$

$$\text{Days Inventory} = \frac{365}{\text{Inventory Turnover}}$$

$$\text{Payables Turnover} = \frac{\text{Cost of Goods Sold}}{\text{Average (Accounts) Payable}}$$

$$\text{Days Payables} = \frac{365}{\text{Payables Turnover}}$$

$$\text{Working Capital Turnover} = \frac{\text{Sales}}{\text{Average Current Assets} - \text{Average Current Liabilities}}$$

$$\text{Capital Assets Turnover} = \frac{\text{Sales}}{\text{Average Plant, Property, and Equipment}}$$

$$\text{Current Ratio} = \frac{\text{Current Assets}}{\text{Current Liabilities}}$$

$$\text{Quick Ratio} = \frac{\text{Cash, Marketable Securities, and Receivables}}{\text{Current Liabilities}}$$

$$\text{Cash Ratio} = \frac{\text{Cash and Cash Equivalent Investments}}{\text{Current Liabilities}}$$

$$\text{Interest Coverage} = \frac{\text{Income Before Interest and Tax Expenses}}{\text{Interest Expense}}$$

$$\text{Debt/Equity Ratio} = \frac{\text{Short-term Debt} + \text{Long-term Debt}}{\text{Stockholders' Equity}}$$

to get a better understanding of a firm's past performance as well as make more accurate forecasts of the future.

USING FINANCIAL RATIOS TO ASSESS COMPARATIVE PERFORMANCE

Ratios can be used to assess comparative performance. To do so, the analyst typically would look for trends in the data both across time (*inter-temporal* comparisons) and across firms (*cross-sectional* comparisons).

INTER-TEMPORAL COMPARISONS

We use inter-temporal comparisons of financial ratios to help reveal changes in performance as well as identify causes for those changes. For example, AnnTaylor's ROE increased from 4.9 percent $(29.1/(612.1 + 574)/2)$ in fiscal year 2002 to 12.1 percent in 2003. From the common-size income statements (Exhibit 6.3), we find that the major cause of this improvement results from the change in profit margins (from 2.2 percent to 5.8 percent). Further investigation points to a reduction in cost of sales as a percent of sales (from 50.2 percent to 45.9 percent). In turn, from management's discussion and analysis (not included here but available in the 10-K report), we note that the higher percent cost of sales in 2001 is a consequence of an inventory write-down (inventory values written down resulting in a loss) in that year.

Another significant change pertains to AnnTaylor's short-term debt-paying ability. The current ratio, quick ratio, and cash ratio all increased significantly during fiscal year 2003. Most of the change in these ratios relates to an increase in cash, as reflected in the cash ratio that went from 0.2 at the end of fiscal year 2002 to 1.4 at the end of fiscal year 2003. Offsetting some of the increase in the current and quick ratios due to cash is the decline in the accounts receivable. Again, management's discussion and analysis provide an explanation: the company sold its proprietary credit card receivables during fiscal year 2003. Further, we observe that the company's receivables turnover increased from 21 $(1,299.6/(65.6 + 58)/2)$ to 36.3 during that year.

CROSS-SECTIONAL COMPARISONS

Another dimension in the use of financial ratios to evaluate performance lies in cross-sectional comparisons with other companies, especially those in the same industry. In order to illustrate, we calculated similar ratios from the Talbots' financial statements (Exhibits 6.7 and 6.8). Talbots, like AnnTaylor, is also a women's clothing retailer specializing in classic styles.

Exhibit 6.9 provides a comparison of the ratios for AnnTaylor and Talbots. Looking first at profitability:

	AnnTaylor	Talbots
ROE	12.1%	21.3%
ROA	8.5%	14.2%
ROC	10.3%	18.0%

Exhibit 6.7
Statement of Net Income

THE REAL WORLD

Talbots

	02/01/2003	02/01/2002	02/01/2001
Net sales	$1,595,325,000	$1,612,513,000	$1,594,996,000
Costs and expenses:			
Cost of sales, buying, and occupancy	963,501,000	967,163,000	936,009,000
Selling, general, and administrative	435,757,000	435,334,000	467,324,000
Operating income:	196,067,000	210,016,000	191,663,000
Interest			
Interest expense	3,262,000	6,102,000	7,706,000
Interest income	409,000	927,000	3,364,000
Interest expense, net	2,853,000	5,175,000	4,342,000
Income before taxes	193,214,000	204,841,000	187,321,000
Income taxes	72,455,000	77,840,000	72,119,000
Net Income	$120,759,000	$127,001,000	$115,202,000

	02/01/2003	02/01/2002	02/01/2001
Net sales	100.0%	100.0%	100.0%
Costs and expenses:			
Cost of sales, buying, and occupancy	60.4%	60.0%	58.7%
Selling, general, and administrative	27.3%	27.0%	29.3%
Operating income:	12.3%	13.0%	12.0%
Interest			
Interest expense	0.2%	0.4%	0.5%
Interest income	0.0%	0.1%	0.2%
Interest expense, net	0.2%	0.3%	0.3%
Income before taxes	12.1%	12.7%	11.7%
Income taxes	4.5%	4.8%	4.5%
Net Income	7.6%	7.9%	7.2%

Talbots surpasses AnnTaylor on all the above measures of profitability. We can trace a major cause of this higher performance to selling, general, and administrative expenses from a common size income statement (shown in Exhibit 6.7). These expenses are only 27.3 percent for Talbots as compared to 44.3 percent for AnnTaylor. Total asset turnover provides another contributing factor to the difference in these rates of return (1.9 for Talbots versus 1.5 for AnnTaylor). AnnTaylor does a better job of collecting on its receivables but is less efficient with regard to its inventory turnover.

From a debt-repayment point of view, Talbots also has an advantage in the long-run in that its interest coverage ratio is 60. However, it does have a slightly higher debt-to-equity ratio at 0.28 and its current, quick, and cash ratios are all less favorable than AnnTaylor's at 2.95, 1.4, and 0.17, respectively.

Exhibit 6.8
Balance Sheet

THE REAL WORLD

Talbots

	02/01/2003	02/01/2002
Current assets:		
Cash and cash equivalents	$ 25,566,000	$ 18,306,000
Customer accounts receivable, net	181,189,000	172,183,000
Merchandise inventories	175,289,000	183,803,000
Deferred catalog costs	5,877,000	8,341,000
Due from affiliates	8,793,000	9,618,000
Deferred income taxes	10,255,000	8,222,000
Prepaid and other current assets	28,929,000	29,089,000
Total current assets	435,898,000	429,562,000
Property and equipment, net	315,227,000	277,576,000
Goodwill, net	35,513,000	35,513,000
Trademarks, net	75,884,000	75,884,000
Deferred income taxes	0	3,595,000
Other assets	9,403,000	8,934,000
Total Assets	$871,925,000	$831,064,000
Current liabilities:		
Accounts payable	$ 48,365,000	$ 49,645,000
Accrued income taxes	11,590,000	1,019,000
Accrued liabilities	87,986,000	79,628,000
Total current liabilities	147,941,000	130,292,000
Long-term debt	100,000,000	100,000,000
Deferred rent under lease commitments	20,688,000	19,542,000
Deferred income taxes	2,921,000	0
Other liabilities	32,699,000	13,354,000
Commitments		
Stockholders equity:		
Common stock, $0.01 par value; 200,000,000 authorized; 75,270,013 shares and 74,935,856 share issued, respectively, and 57,505,802 shares and 60,382,406 shares outstanding, respectively	753,000	749,000
Additional paid-in capital	389,402,000	378,955,000
Retained earnings	572,741,000	472,594,000
Accumulated other comprehensive income (loss)	(15,437,000)	(5,508,000)
Restricted stock awards	(78,000)	(697,000)
Treasury stock, at cost:17,764,211 shares and 14,553,450 shares, respectively	(379,705,000)	(278,217,000)
Total stockholders' equity	567,676,000	567,876,000
Total liabilities and stockholders' equity	$871,925,000	$831,064,000

While the assessment of past performance is useful, analysts are primarily concerned with forecasting the future. To that end, analysts often use their analysis of past performance to assist them in the forecasting of the future results of the firm. We now turn to a discussion of forecasting.

Ratio	Ann Taylor	Talbots
ROE	12.1%	21.3%
ROA	8.5%	14.2%
Profit Margin	5.8%	7.6%
Total Asset Turnover	1.46	1.90
ROC	10.3%	18.0%
Receivables Turnover	36.3	9.0
Days of Receivables	10.0	40.4
Inventory Turnover	3.4	5.4
Days of Inventory	107.3	68.0
Accounts Payable Turnover	11.6	19.7
Days of Accounts Payable	31.4	18.6
Working Capital Turnover	5.6	5.4
Capital Asset Turnover	5.5	5.4
Current Ratio	3	2.95
Quick Ratio	1.5	1.4
Cash Ratio	1.4	0.17
Interest Coverage	20	60
Debt/Equity	0.2	0.28

Exhibit 6.9
Ratio Comparison of Ann Taylor and Talbots

THE REAL WORLD

Ann Taylor and Talbots

FORECASTING

The financial analyst's principal stock-in-trade lies in forming estimates of firm values based on forecasts of future earnings or cash flows. In developing forecasts, analysts may use their understanding of markets for the firm's products or services to model supply and demand, formal statistical methods to exploit past observations in characterizing time series behavior, experience and judgment to determine future trends, or some combination of these approaches. The value of a forecast ultimately is derived from improved decision making based on the estimates that the forecast produces.

Forecasting future operating performance usually begins with predicting sales. There are many ways in which to approach this task. An economist might form a set of equations that models industry supply and demand (called *structural* equations as they describe the structure of market supply and demand conditions faced by the firm). Economists may then use estimates of these equations to predict the future price of a firm's output, which, when combined with projected production, would lead to a forecast of sales. The data required by such a model might include wages of workers and income of consumers, implying the need to forecast these factors.

An alternative modeling approach looks for a functional relationship between sales and time. By examining past observations of sales, analysts may detect a systematic relationship between sales and the passage of time that can be reasonably portrayed by a mathematical equation. For example, sales might be growing at a fixed rate such as 2 percent a year or it might be growing at a certain percentage of another variable, such as population growth.

Evidence indicates that the market may react differentially to whether a firm meets or fails to meet analysts' forecasts, although the evidence is mixed as to the direction. See Skinner and Sloan, *Review of Accounting Studies* (2002) and Payne and Thomas, *The Accounting Review* (2003).

Less-formal approaches to forecasts rely on analysts' intuition and judgment. The simplest approach would be to predict that next period's sales would equal this period's sales. Another approach might be to portray future sales as a weighted average of current sales and the previous forecast. Last, but not least, rather than rely on economic or mathematical models or simply intuition, we can instead build a statistical model of time series behavior from an analysis of past observations based only on the data. In other words, an analyst might statistically examine the properties of the data themselves to specify a forecasting model. Let's look at this approach in more detail.

TIME SERIES ANALYSIS

Time series analysis basically estimates a model of the process generating the variable of interest (in our case, sales) from past observations. Typically, the initial step in identifying such a model is to estimate the *statistical correlations* (how one variable behaves relative to another) between lagged observations. For example, current sales might be correlated with sales of the previous period, sales of two periods ago, sales of three periods ago, and so on. These correlations allow analysts to determine a tentative model. For example, some firms display seasonal variations in quarterly sales such that, say, fourth quarter sales are more highly correlated with fourth quarter sales of the previous year than with third quarter sales of the current year (e.g., holiday-season sales for toy manufacturers). Accordingly, a suitable forecasting model of quarterly sales would likely take that correlation information into account.

Once we formulate a model, we then check how well the estimated model captures the time series behavior of the data. This might involve a measure of *forecast errors* (deviations between actual sales and sales predicted by the model). If necessary, we repeat the process until the measure used to check the model indicates that it fits the data sufficiently well.

However, analysts want to forecast earnings, so providing a sales forecast using time series analysis is only half the battle. Analysts must also forecast expenses for the firm, usually by relating them to sales. For example, analysts might employ common-size ratios under the assumption that expenses would remain a constant percentage of sales. Some expenses may also depend on planned investments in working capital and long-term assets, such as plant, property, and equipment. Thus, a comprehensive approach toward forecasting earnings or cash flows often involves projecting a full set of financial statements including successive balance sheets. These forecasted financial statements are called the **pro forma statements.**

PRO FORMA STATEMENTS

Firms sometimes prepare pro forma statements to depict the consequences of a future financing event. For example, an initial public offering (IPO) of stock for sale to the public requires the preparation of a *prospectus* (a document filed with the SEC) containing financial statements that reflect the disposition of the anticipated proceeds from the sale of stock and the pro forma changes to assets, liabilities, and stockholders' equity that would result.

Exhibit 6.10
Intel Corporation

THE REAL WORLD

Intel Corporation

Pro forma information is required by SFAS No. 123 as if the company had accounted for its employee stock options (including shares issued under the Stock Participation Plan, collectively called "options") granted subsequent to December 31, 1994 under the fair value method of that statement.

For purposes of pro forma disclosures, the estimated fair value of the options is amortized to expense over the options' vesting periods. The company's pro forma information follows:

(In millions-except per share amounts)	2001	2000	1999
Net income	$254	$9,699	$6,860

To judge the significance of these adjustments, note that the reported net income for Intel was $1,291, $10,535, and $7,314 (in millions) for the years 2001, 2000, and 1999, respectively. Therefore, the effect of this adjustment was less than 10 percent of net income in 1999 and 2000 but was an 80 percent decline in income in 2001. This could have a significant influence on an analyst's forecast of the future income on the company.

Firms also use pro forma statements to depict the consequences of an alternative accounting treatment when more than one method is allowed. For example, accounting rules for employee stock options (considered in Chapter 12) allow firms to either recognize compensation expense associated with those options or not recognize compensation expense but disclose pro forma net income as if the compensation expense had been recorded. Exhibit 6.10 illustrates the disclosure for Intel.

Although our principal perspective in developing forecasts of operating data is at the firm level, analysts must also characterize the future prospects of the industry and economy at large. Business cycles and industry trends often factor prominently in forming predictions regarding the outlook for firms susceptible to the influence of those factors. In such cases, we might begin to build a forecast for the firm by first developing or obtaining forecasts at an industry- or economy-wide level. An integrated approach might involve joint analyses of firm, industry, and economy data with the objective of improving estimates at the firm level.

A risk to forecasting models that focus only on time series data is that analysts might be ignoring changes in competitive strategy and changes in organizational structure. For example, how would analysts handle a firm's merger with another company? This event might fundamentally alter the basic statistical properties of a the firm's sales or earnings. In this case, analysts can capture this change with a more encompassing model. Or, analysts might modify pre-merger operating data as if both firms had always been a single entity (an example of employing pro forma statements) and then apply one of the forecasting approaches described above.

TIME VALUE OF MONEY

Analysts utilize forecasts of future results to help them value the stock of a company today. Before we explain more fully how analysts incorporate their forecasts of future results to arrive at these value estimates, it is important to talk about the concepts of the time value of money, specifically the *present value* of money.

A standard question in an effort to convey the concept of time value of money is to ask whether you would prefer to receive a dollar today or a dollar tomorrow. Most people will respond by saying that they would prefer to receive the dollar today. When asked why, many observe that if they had the dollar today then they would be at least as well off as if they waited until tomorrow because they could always choose to hold the dollar rather than spend it. Moreover, they would have the option not to hold the dollar and spend it if they so chose, which implies more value. It often occurs to at least some that if they had the dollar today, then they could immediately deposit it in their bank and, given that their bank pays interest on a daily basis, they would have more than a dollar tomorrow. In other words, there is a time value to money.

There are many familiar examples of the time value of money. TV ads for automobiles often present prospective buyers with a low interest rate on funds borrowed to pay for a car or a lump sum reduction in the purchase price if they pay in cash. Bank statements may show interest earned on funds held on deposit, copies of information returns filed by insurance companies and brokerage houses also report interest earned, while similar filings by mortgage companies report interest paid. It is hard to escape some exposure to the notion of interest and a time value to money.

In virtually all of the situations where time value of money is relevant, the problem is to somehow compare a dollar amount today, known as **present value,** with an amount in the future, known as **future value.** The calculations that we often employ to compare values at different points in time are referred to as **time value of money** calculations and they all involve the time value of money being expressed as an **interest rate** or **discount rate.** Next we consider the process of converting a present value into a future value and vice versa.

FUTURE VALUE

A useful way to approach the concept of the present value of a future value (sometimes referred to as a **future sum**) is to turn the issue around and ask what an investment of cash today would yield in terms of cash in the future if, in the interim, that investment earned interest. Suppose that one could invest $1,000 in a bank savings account that pays interest at a rate of 5 percent for one year. At the end of the year, the account would contain $1,050, the initial investment of $1,000 plus interest of $50 ($1,000 × 0.05). Now, suppose that the $1,050 was left in the savings account for a second year and the interest was allowed to also earn interest (called **compounding of interest**). At the end of that year the account would contain $1,102.50 ($1,050 + $1,050 × 0.05 or $1,000 × (1 + 0.05)^2). Note that the $50 of interest earned in the first year then earned $2.50 of interest in the second year, reflecting the compounding of interest. Mathematically, the future value of C dollars at the end of two years at an interest rate of r, compounded annually, can be expressed as follows (where **FV** is referred to as a **future value factor**):

$$\text{Future Value}(2) = C + rC + r(C + rC) = C + 2rC + r^2C = C(1 + r)^2 = C \times \text{FV}_{2r}$$

Generalizing in the above to n years at rate r, we obtain

$$FV_{n,r} = (1 + r)^n$$
$$\text{Future Value}(n) = C \times FV_{n,r}$$

Note that many books, this one included, contain a table of such future value factors arranged by the number of periods (n) and the interest rate per period (r). Such tables are often referred to as **future value of \$1** tables. Functions that calculate these factors are also incorporated into handheld financial calculators and spreadsheet programs such as Microsoft Excel™.

PRESENT VALUE

The concept of present value reverses the exercise by posing the question: what is an amount to be received in the future worth now? Intuitively, one would expect present value to be less than the future amount because, if we had the cash now, then it could be invested, earn interest, and be worth more in the future.

In the numerical example above, the present value of \$1,050 to be received in one year given an interest rate (discount rate) of 5 percent and annual compounding would be \$1,050 ÷ 1.05 or \$1,000. Similarly, the present value of \$1,102.50 to be received two years hence would be \$1,102.50 ÷ $(1.05)^2$, or \$1,000 again. It should be fairly clear that mathematically, the present value of C dollars to be received in two years at a discount rate of r, compounded annually, can be expressed as follows (where **PV** is the **present value factor**):

$$\text{Present Value}(2) = \frac{C}{(1 + r)(1 + r)} = \frac{C}{(1 + r)^2} = C \times PV_{2,r}$$

Again, generalizing to n years, results in:

$$PV_{n,r} = \frac{1}{(1 + r)^n}$$
$$\text{Present Value}(n) = C \times PV_{n,r}$$

ADJUSTING FOR UNCERTAINTY

In applying time value of money concepts to an investor's decisions, the interest rate (discount rate) that the investor would use should reflect their own personal time preference for money. Typically this rate will be a function of the other opportunities available to the investor for return on investment and some adjustment for the risk or uncertainty associated with the investment opportunity. The issue of risk is that if one waits until tomorrow to receive the dollar, then something may happen between today and tomorrow such that tomorrow's dollar (or some portions of the dollar) might not materialize. All else held constant, the interest rate required by an investor when there is uncertainty about the outcome of the investment might be higher than the interest rate on a sure thing, depending on the risk preferences of the investor. If the investor is risk averse, then the discount rate employed by that investor would likely be higher to compensate for bearing the risk. By risk averse we mean that the individual strictly prefers a sure thing to a gamble for which the expected payoff is the same as the payoff on the sure thing. For example, risk averse individuals often buy insurance. They prefer to pay a certain premium to an insurance company for coverage of a possible loss when the expected loss is less than the premium.

MODELS FOR VALUING EQUITY

One application of both forecasting and the time value of money is to estimate the value of the equity of a firm. The two basic approaches used by analysts for estimating the value of equity are the **discounted cash flow (DCF)** and **residual income (RI)** models. Both approaches begin with forecasts of operating results. In the DCF approach, forecasting techniques are used to estimate future free cash flows to equity (discussed in Chapter 5); in the RI approach, a quantity known as *future abnormal earnings* is estimated rather than cash flows.

DCF APPROACH

Under the DCF approach, operating income is transformed into cash from operations by adding back noncash expenses including depreciation and amortization of operating assets, and subtracting changes in operating working capital. This is the same format used in the cash flow statement to produce cash from operations under GAAP. Cash from operations is then reduced by cash used in investment activities and increased by net borrowings (or reduced by net repayments of borrowings) to arrive at an amount known as **free cash flow** to equity holders (i.e., stockholders). Free cash flows must then be forecasted over the future life of the firm. Typically, DCF analysis also establishes a **time horizon** for the analysis, and the firm's value at the end of that time period (known as the **terminal value**) is estimated. This terminal value is then discounted along with the estimates of free cash flow, using the present value techniques described earlier, to obtain the estimate of the value for the firm's stock. The discount rate employed reflects the rate of return investors require in order to buy the firm's stock. This rate is sometimes called the firm's equity **cost of capital.**

To illustrate, let FCF_1, FCF_2, and FCF_n denote free cash flows received at the end of future periods 1, 2, and so forth, up to the end of the life of the firm in period n. The terminal period is n, and let TV_n be the estimated terminal value. We can calculate the present value of the firm and the estimated value of stockholders' equity as follows:

$$\text{Value of Stockholders' Equity} = \frac{FCF_1}{(1 + r)} + \frac{FCF_2}{(1 + r)^2} + \cdots\cdots + \frac{FCF_n}{(1 + r)^n} + \frac{TV_n}{(1 + r)^n}$$

Exhibit 6.11 provides condensed financial data for a hypothetical firm in the form of pro forma financial statements over an assumed remaining firm life (investment horizon) of four years. The initial balance sheet at time 0 reflects

Exhibit 6.11
Pro forma Financial
Statements Hypothetical Firm

Balance Sheet Period	0	1	2	3	4
Equipment, Net	1,000	750	500	250	0
Total Assets	1,000	750	500	250	0
Common Stock	1,000	1,000	1,000	1,000	0
Retained Earnings	0	−250	−500	−750	0
Total Liability and Owners' Equity	1,000	750	500	250	0

Income Statement Period	1	2	3	4
Revenue	500	500	500	500
Depreciation	−250	−250	−250	−250
Net Income	250	250	250	250

Cash Flow Statement Period	1	2	3	4
Net Income	250	250	250	250
Depreciation	250	250	250	250
Operating Cash Flow	500	500	500	500
Dividends	−500	−500	−500	−500
Change in Cash	0	0	0	0

equipment of $1,000 purchased from the proceeds of a common stock issue for that amount. The equipment will last four years, at which point it becomes valueless. To keep the calculation simple we will assume that the terminal value is zero at that point in time. Revenues are forecasted to be $500 per year. The only expense is depreciation, which we assume is $250 per year. All available cash each year is distributed in the form of a dividend to common stockholders. The cost of equity is assumed to be 10 percent.

In this example, free cash flows are equivalent to cash from operations on the cash flow statement as there are no investment or debt cash flows. Because free cash flow is the same in all four years, the present value of those cash flows, our estimate of equity value, can be calculated as follows:

$$
\begin{aligned}
&\text{Value of Stockholders' Equity} \\
&= 500 \times \left(\frac{1}{1 + .10} + \left(\frac{1}{1 + .10} \right)^2 + \left(\frac{1}{1 + .10} \right)^3 + \left(\frac{1}{1 + .10} \right)^4 \right) \\
&= 500 \times \left(\frac{1 - (1 + .10)^{-4}}{.10} \right) = 1,585
\end{aligned}
$$

where the last term contained in parentheses is a shorthand way of expressing the present value factor for a series of constant amounts received each year. This stream of cash flows (the four $500 payments) is called an **annuity,** and the factor in the last equation would be called a *present value of an annuity factor.* A more detailed description of present value and annuities, along with related tables of present value factors, is provided in Appendix B.

Observe that the value of stockholders' equity derived from the free cash flows of $1,585 is also the present value of the stream of future dividends. Thus, a value of stockholders' equity of $1,585 makes sense when one looks at firm value from an investor's perspective. The interpretation would be that if you purchased the stock in this company for $1,585 and received the four dividends of $500 each, you would have received a return of 10 percent on your investment, due to the fact that we used a discount rate of 10 percent to present value the cash flows.

RI APPROACH

Under the RI approach, a quantity known as **abnormal earnings** is calculated. Abnormal earnings are simply those earnings that are above or below the earnings currently expected by investors, given their investment in the firm and their required (expected) rate of return. Abnormal earnings are calculated by deducting a charge for the use of capital provided by stockholders from net income. This **capital charge** is determined by multiplying the book value of stockholders' equity at the start of the year by cost of equity capital (rate). The present value of abnormal earnings projected over the life of the firm is then added to the initial book value of stockholders' equity to arrive at an estimate of the value of stockholders' equity. To put this in simple terms, if the firm issued stock for $1,000 and invested the proceeds in operating assets and stockholders expected to earn 10 percent on their investment, then they would expect $100 in earnings every period. If earnings were above or below $100 then they would be viewed as abnormal earnings.

Let AE_1, AE_2 and AE_K denote abnormal earnings for future periods 1, 2, k, and so on over the remaining life of the firm. The value of stockholders' equity is then:

$$\text{Value of Stockholder's Equity} = \text{Book Value of Stockholder's Equity} + \frac{AE_1}{(1 + r)}$$

$$+ \frac{AE_2}{(1 + r)^2} + \cdots\cdots\cdots + \frac{AE_k}{(1 + r)^k} + \cdots\cdots\cdots$$

Using the data from Exhibit 6.11, the cost of capital charge is calculated by multiplying stockholders' equity at the beginning of each period by the cost of capital (10 percent). Abnormal earnings are then calculated as the reported net income minus the capital charge:

Year 1: $150 = $250 − (10% × $1,000)
Year 2: $175 = $250 − (10% × $750)
Year 3: $200 = $250 − (10% × $500)
Year 4: $225 = $250 − (10% × $250)

The book value of stockholders' equity is the $1,000 of common stock at the start of the forecast horizon. Accordingly, the value of stockholders' equity can be determined from accounting numbers as follows:

$$\text{Value of Stockholders' Equity} = 1,000 + 150 \times \left(\frac{1}{1.10}\right) + 175 \times \left(\frac{1}{1.10}\right)^2$$
$$+ 200 \times \left(\frac{1}{1.10}\right)^3 + 225 \times \left(\frac{1}{1.10}\right)^4 = 1,585$$

Not surprisingly, the value of stockholders' equity is the same under both a DCF and an RI approach. It should also not be surprising that this asset is worth more than the $1,000 paid to acquire it given that the investor is expecting a 10 percent return. If you just consider the first year, the asset would be expected to return only $100 in income, yet it returns $250 or $150 more than expected. This is true in each of the four years of the asset's life, as shown in the calculation of abnormal earnings. Therefore, the $1,000 asset is worth more ($1,585) than its cost.

SUMMARY AND TRANSITION

Financial statement analysis encompasses many dimensions. Because companies often employ different methods of accounting, it may be necessary to transform financial statements to reflect common accounting practices when making cross-sectional comparisons. Fortunately, accounting reports often contain sufficient information, either in the statements themselves or in accompanying footnotes and supporting schedules, to make these transformations.

A further problem in working from data contained in financial statements for purposes of both time series and cross-sectional comparisons is adjusting for differences in size. To remedy this problem, analysts construct financial ratios that place accounting numbers on a common scale. Besides controlling for differences in size, financial ratios are useful in assessing operating performance. Two broad classes of financial ratios for use in this respect are ratios that measure profitability and ratios that measure debt-repayment ability.

One of the more common ratios for assessing profitability from the stockholders' perspective is rate of return on equity (ROE), determined by dividing net income by stockholders' equity. ROE can be usefully broken down into rate of return on assets (ROA) and leverage, as measured by the ratio of total assets-to-debt. In turn, ROA can be broken down into profit margin and asset turnover, measures of the company's efficiency in converting sales into profits and assets into sales, respectively. The company's ability to generate a higher return on stockholders' equity through the use of financial leverage can be determined by comparing ROE to the rate of return on capital (ROC), where capital is defined as debt plus stockholders' equity, and interest, net of taxes, is added to net income in the numerator of this ratio.

Indicators of a company's short-term debt repayment ability include liquidity ratios, such as the current ratio (current assets divided by current liabilities), quick ratio (current assets other than inventories and prepaid expenses divided by current liabilities), and cash ratio (cash divided by current liabilities). Common ratios for assessing long-term debt-repayment ability include interest coverage (income before interest expense and taxes divided by interest expense) and debt to total debt and equity.

Financial analysts are principally concerned with predicting future performance. This typically begins with a forecast of sales. Sales forecasts might be based on economic models of supply and demand facing the firm, mathematical models that relate sales to time, models based on subjective judgment, and statistical models that extrapolate past sales behavior. Projections of future operating expenses often involve common-size ratios and an assumption that costs will remain proportional to sales. Industry- and economy-wide data may also be useful in forming predictions concerning how the company will fare. The company's strategies in meeting its competition may be relevant as well.

Analysts may then use the forecasted data to provide an estimate of the market value of equity using time value of money techniques. Two basic models are used in this process: the discounted cash flow model and the residual income model.

At this point in the book, we have provided an overview of the basics of financial reporting and financial statement analysis. In the next several chapters, we will return to the balance sheet and focus on more detailed accounting issues related to each of the major types of assets, liabilities, and owners' equity accounts.

END OF CHAPTER MATERIAL

KEY TERMS

Abnormal Earnings	Interest Rate
Annuity	Inter-temporal
Capital Asset Turnover	Inventory Turnover
Capital Charge	Operating Forecasts
Cash Ratio	Present Value
Common Size Balance Sheet	Present Value Factor
Common Size Income Statement	Pro Forma Statements
Compounding of Interest	Profit Margin
Cost of Capital	Quick Ratio
Cross-sectional	Receivables Turnover
Current Ratio	Residual Income Model (RI)
Debt/Equity Ratio	Return on Assets (ROA)
Discount Rate	Return on Capital (ROC)
Discounted Cash Flow Model (DCF)	Return on Equity (ROE)
Financial Leverage	Terminal Value
Financial Statement Analysis	Time Horizon
Free Cash Flow	Time Value of Money
Future Sum	Total Asset Turnover
Future Value	Trading on Equity
Future Value Factor	Weighted Average Cost of Capital (WACC)
Interest Coverage	Working Capital Turnover

ASSIGNMENT MATERIAL

REVIEW QUESTIONS

1. Compare and contrast inter-temporal and cross-sectional analysis.
2. For each of the following ratios, reproduce the formula for their calculation:
   a. ROA
   b. ROC
   c. ROE
   d. Receivable Turnover
   e. Inventory Turnover
   f. Payables Turnover
   g. Current
   h. Quick
   i. Debt/Equity
   j. Interest Coverage
3. Describe leverage and explain how it is evidenced in the ROA, ROC, and ROE ratios.
4. Explain, using the profit margin and total asset turnover ratios, how two companies in the same industry can earn the same ROA, yet may have very different operating strategies.
5. What is the advantage of preparing common-size statements in financial statement analysis?
6. Explain why the current ratio is subject to manipulation as a measure of liquidity.
7. Explain how as-if restatements might be used in financial statement analysis.
8. Explain how mandated and discretionary accounting method changes can affect financial statement analysis.
9. What is the purpose of adjusting for scale?
10. Describe the discounted cash flow approach to estimating the value of stockholders' equity.
11. Describe how free cash flow would be calculated.
12. Describe the residual income approach to estimating the value of stockholders' equity.

APPLYING YOUR KNOWLEDGE

13. Discuss the implications that different country accounting standards have for the statement analysis of foreign competitor companies.
14. Suppose that you are analyzing two competitor companies, one a U.S. company and the other a company in the United Kingdom, whose statements are expressed in pounds. Discuss whether it is necessary to convert the statements of the UK company into U.S. dollars before computing ratios.

15. Auditors typically conduct a preliminary review of a firm's financial statements using analytical procedures, which include ratio analysis. As an auditor, why would ratio analysis be useful in auditing the financial statements?

16. Contracts with lenders, such as bonds, typically place restrictions on the financial statement ratios. Two commonly used ratios are the current ratio and the debt/equity ratio. Explain why these might appear as restrictions; in other words, do they protect the lender?

17. Management compensation plans typically specify performance criteria in terms of financial statement ratios. For instance, a plan might specify that management must achieve a certain level of return on investment (e.g., ROA). If management were trying to maximize their compensation, how could they manipulate the ROA ratio to achieve this maximization?

18. The financial data for Nova Electronics Company and Pulsar Electricals for the current year is as follows:

	Annual Sales	Accounts Receivable Jan 1	Accounts Receivable Dec 31
Nova Electronics	3,893,567	1,103,879	1,140,251
Pulsar Electricals	1,382,683	357,934	243,212

a. Compute the Accounts Receivable Turnover for each company.

b. Compute the average number of days required by each company to collect the receivables.

c. Which company is more efficient in terms of handling its accounts receivable policy?

19. Information regarding the activities of Polymer Plastics Corporation is as follows:

	Year 1	Year 2	Year 3	Year 4	Year 5
Cost of Goods Sold	363,827	411,125	493,350	579,686	608,670
Average Inventory	60,537	76,560	107,338	156,672	202,895

a. Do a time series analysis for the inventory turnover for each year and also compute the average number of days that inventories are held for the respective years.

b. Is Polymer Plastics Corporation efficiently managing its inventories?

20. The following financial information relates to Delocro Mechanical, Inc. (amounts in thousands):

	Year 1	Year 2	Year 3	Year 4
Sales	2,000	2,200	2,420	2,662
Average Total Assets	1,111	1,222	1,344	1,479
Average Owners' Equity	620	682	750	825
Net Income	200	230	264	304
Interest Expense	50	55	61	67
Tax Rate	40%	40%	40%	30%

For each year calculate:

a. Return on Owners' Equity (ROE)

b. ROI

   i. Profit Margin Ratio

   ii. Total Asset Turnover

c. Comment on the profitability of Delocro Mechanical, Inc.

21. Empire Company's balance sheet is as follows:

Total Assets	$500,000	Liabilities	$100,000
		Owner's Equity	400,000
	$500,000		$500,000

The interest rate on the liabilities is 10 percent, and the income tax rate is 30 percent.

a. If the ROE is equal to the ROI, compute the Net Income.

b. Compute the ROE, taking the Net Income determined in part a.

c. Compute the income before interest and taxes for the net income derived in part a.

d. Assume that total assets remain the same (i.e., at $500,000) and that loans increase to $300,000, while Owners' Equity decreases to $200,000. The interest rate is now 8 percent, and the income tax rate remains at 30 percent. What is the ROE if you require the same ROA as calculated in part b?

e. Compare the ROE in both situations and comment.

22. Spectrum Associates' financial data is as follows (amounts in thousands):

		Year 1	Year 2	Year 3	Year 4
Current Assets					
	Accounts Receivable	$ 700	$ 800	$ 600	$ 650
	Cash	200	100	200	150
	Other Current Assets	100	100	250	100
	Inventories	500	1,000	1,450	2,100
		$1,500	$2,000	$2,500	$3,000
Current Liabilities					
	Accounts Payable	$ 600	$ 700	$ 825	$ 800
	Accrued Salaries	300	400	495	400
	Other Current Liabilities	100	150	165	300
		$1,000	$1,250	$1,475	$1,500

a. Compute the current and quick ratios for years 1 through 4.

b. Comment on the short-term liquidity position of Spectrum Associates.

23. Artscan Enterprises' financial data is as follows:

	Year 1	Year 2	Year 3
Income before Interest and Taxes	$ 400	$ 600	$ 800
Interest	70	100	135
Current Liabilities	375	475	750
Noncurrent Liabilities	625	1,125	1,600
Owners' Equity	$1,000	$1,500	$2,000

a. Compute the Debt/Equity and Times Interest Earned Ratio.

b. Comment on the long-term liquidity position of Artscan Enterprises.

24. State the immediate effect (increase, decrease, no effect) of the following transactions on:

a. Current Ratio

b. Quick Ratio

c. Working Capital

d. ROE

e. Debt/Equity Ratio

Transaction:

1. Inventory worth $25,000 is purchased on credit.

2. Inventory worth $125,000 is sold on account for $158,000.

3. Payments of $65,000 are made to suppliers.

4. A machine costing $120,000 is purchased. $30,000 is paid in cash, and the balance will be paid in equal installments for the next three years.

5. Shares of common stock worth $100,000 are issued.

6. Equipment costing $80,000 with accumulated depreciation of $50,000 is sold for $40,000 in cash.

7. Goods worth $35,000 were destroyed by fire. Salvage value of some of the partly burnt goods was $3,000, which is received in cash. The goods were not insured.

25. Calculate the present value of $10,000 to be received ten years from now at 12 percent assuming that interest is compounded:

a. annually

b. quarterly

c. monthly

26. Calculate the present value of an annuity of $100 each year for the next ten years at 12 percent assuming that interest is compounded once a year.

27. Suppose that the free cash flows for a firm are estimated to be $500 per year in each of the next ten years and that the terminal value at the end of the ten years is expected to be $2,000. If your desired rate of return given the risk of this investment was 15 percent, using the DCF approach, what would be the maximum price you would be willing to pay for the entire firm?

28. Suppose that the abnormal earnings of the firm are estimated to be $200 a year for each of the next ten years and that it has a current book value of

$1,500. Using the residual income approach, what would be the maximum amount you would pay for the entire firm if your desired rate of return given the risk of this investment were 12 percent?

○ USING REAL DATA

29. Use the data from the financial statements of Dell and Gateway to answer the following questions.

DELL COMPUTER CORP. Balance Sheet	01/31/2003	01/31/2002
Current assets:		
Cash and cash equivalents	$ 4,232,000,000	$ 3,641,000,000
Short-term investments	406,000,000	273,000,000
Accounts receivable, net	2,586,000,000	2,269,000,000
Inventories	306,000,000	278,000,000
Other	1,394,000,000	1,416,000,000
Total current assets	8,924,000,000	7,877,000,000
Property, plant, and equipment, net	913,000,000	826,000,000
Investments	5,267,000,000	4,373,000,000
Other noncurrent assets	366,000,000	459,000,000
Total assets	$15,470,000,000	$13,535,000,000
Liabilities and stockholders' equity		
Current liabilities:		
Accounts payable	$ 5,989,000,000	$ 5,075,000,000
Accrued and other	2,944,000,000	2,444,000,000
Total current liabilities	8,933,000,000	7,519,000,000
Long-term debt	506,000,000	520,000,000
Other	1,158,000,000	802,000,000
Commitments and contingent liabilities (Note 6)		
Total liabilities	10,597,000,000	8,841,000,000
Stockholders equity:		
Preferred stock and capital in excess of $.01 par value; shares issued and outstanding: none	—	—
Common stock and capital in excess of $.01 par value; shares authorized: 7,000; shares issued: 2,681 and 2,654, respectively	6,018,000,000	5,605,000,000
Treasury stock, at cost; 102 and 52 shares, respectively	(4,539,000,000)	(2,249,000,000)
Retained earnings	3,486,000,000	1,364,000,000
Other comprehensive income (loss)	(33,000,000)	38,000,000
Other	(59,000,000)	(64,000,000)
Total stockholders' equity	4,873,000,000	4,694,000,000
Total liabilities and stockholders' equity	$15,470,000,000	$13,535,000,000

DELL COMPUTER CORP. Income Statement

	01/31/2003	01/31/2002	01/31/2001
Net revenue	$35,404,000,000	$31,168,000,000	$31,888,000,000
Cost of revenue	29,055,000,000	25,661,000,000	25,445,000,000
Gross margin	6,349,000,000	5,507,000,000	6,443,000,000
Operating expenses:			
Selling, general, and administrative	3,050,000,000	2,784,000,000	3,193,000,000
Research, development, and engineering	455,000,000	452,000,000	482,000,000
Special charges	–	482,000,000	105,000,000
Total operating expenses	3,505,000,000	3,718,000,000	3,780,000,000
Operating income	2,844,000,000	1,789,000,000	2,663,000,000
Investment and other income (loss), net	183,000,000	(58,000,000)	531,000,000
Income before income taxes and cumulative effect of change in accounting principle	3,027,000,000	1,731,000,000	3,194,000,000
Provision for income taxes	905,000,000	485,000,000	958,000,000
Income before cumulative effect of change in accounting principle	2,122,000,000	1,246,000,000	2,236,000,000
Cumulative effect of change in accounting principle, net	–	–	59,000,000
Net income	$ 2,122,000,000	$ 1,246,000,000	$ 2,177,000,000

DELL COMPUTER CORP. Cash Flow Statement

	01/31/2003	01/31/2002	01/312/001
Cash flows from operating activities:			
Net income	$2,122,000,000	$1,246,000,000	$2,177,000,000
Adjustments to reconcile net income to net cash provided by operating activities:			
Depreciation and amortization	211,000,000	239,000,000	240,000,000
Tax benefits of employee stock plans	260,000,000	487,000,000	929,000,000
Special charges	–	742,000,000	105,000,000
(Gains)/losses on investments	(67,000,000)	17,000,000	(307,000,000)
Other, primarily effects of exchange rate changes on monetary assets and liabilities denominated in foreign currencies	(410,000,000)	178,000,000	135,000,000
Changes in:			
Operating working capital	1,210,000,000	826,000,000	642,000,000
Noncurrent assets and liabilities	212,000,000	62,000,000	274,000,000
Net cash provided by operating activities	3,538,000,000	3,797,000,000	4,195,000,000
Cash flows from investing activities:			
Investments:			
Purchases	(8,736,000,000)	(5,382,000,000)	(2,606,000,000)
Maturities and sales	7,660,000,000	3,425,000,000	2,331,000,000
Capital expenditures	(305,000,000)	(303,000,000)	(482,000,000)
Net cash used in investing activities	(1,381,000,000)	(2,260,000,000)	(757,000,000)

	01/31/2003	01/31/2002	01/312/001
Cash flows from financing activities:			
Purchase of common stock	(2,290,000,000)	(3,000,000,000)	(2,700,000,000)
Issuance of common stock under employee plans	265,000,000	298,000,000	395,000,000
Net cash used in financing activities	(2,025,000,000)	(2,702,000,000)	(2,305,000,000)
Effect of exchange rate changes on cash	459,000,000	(104,000,000)	(32,000,000)
Net increase (decrease) in cash	591,000,000	(1,269,000,000)	1,101,000,000
Cash and cash equivalents at beginning of period	3,641,000,000	4,910,000,000	3,809,000,000
Cash and cash equivalents at end of period	$4,232,000,000	$3,641,000,000	$4,910,000,000

GATEWAY, INC. Balance Sheet

	12/31/2003	12/31/2002
ASSETS		
Current assets:		
Cash and cash equivalents	$ 349,101,000	$ 465,603,000
Marketable securities	739,936,000	601,118,000
Accounts receivable, net	210,151,000	197,817,000
Inventory	114,136,000	88,761,000
Other, net	250,153,000	602,073,000
Total current assets	1,663,477,000	1,955,372,000
Property, plant, and equipment, net	330,913,000	481,011,000
Intangibles, net	13,983,000	23,292,000
Other assets, net	20,065,000	49,732,000
	$2,028,438,000	$2,509,407,000
Liabilities and equity		
Current liabilities:		
Accounts payable	$ 415,971,000	$ 278,609,000
Accrued liabilities	277,455,000	364,741,000
Accrued royalties	48,488,000	56,684,000
Other current liabilities	257,090,000	240,315,000
Total current liabilities	999,004,000	940,349,000
Other long-term liabilities	109,696,000	127,118,000
Total liabilities	1,108,700,000	1,067,467,000
Commitments and contingencies (Note 5)		
Series C redeemable convertible preferred stock, $.01 par value, $200,000 liquidation value, 50 shares authorized, issued and outstanding in 2003 and 2002	197,720,000	195,422,000
Stockholders' equity:		
Series A convertible preferred stock, $.01 par value, $200,000 liquidation value, 50 shares authorized, issued and outstanding in 2003 and 2002	200,000,000	200,000,000
Preferred stock, $.01 par value, 4,900 shares authorized; none issued and outstanding	—	—
Class A common stock, nonvoting, $.01 par value, 1,000 shares authorized; none issued and outstanding	—	—

	12/31/2003	12/31/2002
Common stock, $.01 par value, 1,000,000 shares authorized; 324,392 shares and 324,072 shares issued and outstanding in 2003 and 2002, respectively	3,244,000	3,240,000
Additional paid-in capital	734,550,000	732,760,000
Retained earnings (Accumulated deficit)	(218,571,000)	307,379,000
Accumulated other comprehensive income	2,795,000	3,139,000
Total stockholders' equity	722,018,000	1,246,518,000
	$2,028,438,000	$2,509,407,000

GATEWAY, INC. Income Statement

	12/31/2003	12/31/2002	12/31/2001
Net sales	$3,402,364,000	$4,171,325,000	$ 5,937,896,000
Cost of goods sold	2,938,800,000	3,605,120,000	5,099,704,000
Gross profit	463,564,000	566,205,000	838,192,000
Selling, general, and administrative expenses	974,139,000	1,077,447,000	2,022,122,000
Operating loss	(510,575,000)	(511,242,000)	(1,183,930,000)
Other income (loss), net	19,328,000	35,496,000	(94,964,000)
Loss before income taxes and cumulative effect of change in accounting principle	(491,247,000)	(475,746,000)	(1,278,894,000)
Provision (benefit) for income taxes	23,565,000	(178,028,000)	(271,683,000)
Loss before cumulative effect of change in accounting principle	(514,812,000)	(297,718,000)	(1,007,211,000)
Cumulative effect of change in accounting principle, net of tax	–	–	(23,851,000)
Net loss	(514,812,000)	(297,718,000)	(1,031,062,000)
Preferred stock dividends and accretion	(11,138,000)	(11,323,000)	–
Net loss attributable to common stockholders	$ (525,950,000)	$ (309,041,000)	$(1,031,062,000)

GATEWAY, INC. Cash Flow

	12/31/2003	12/31/2002	12/31/2001
Cash flows from operating activities:			
Net loss	$(514,812,000)	$(297,718,000)	$(1,031,062,000)
Adjustments to reconcile net loss to net cash provided by (used in) operating activities:			
Depreciation and amortization	163,973,000	159,458,000	199,976,000
Provision for uncollectible accounts receivable	11,297,000	11,139,000	23,151,000
Deferred income taxes	6,000,000	257,172,000	(27,282,000)
Loss on investments	808,000	30,272,000	186,745,000
Write-down of long-lived assets	66,397,000	52,975,000	418,304,000
Gain on settlement of acquisition liability	–	(13,782,000)	–
Loss on sale of property	6,052,000	–	–
Cumulative effect of change in accounting principle	–	–	23,851,000
Gain on extinguishment of debt	–	–	(6,890,000)
Other, net	1,941,000	(1,929,000)	(1,707,000)
Changes in operating assets and liabilities:			
Accounts receivable	(23,633,000)	11,020,000	301,630,000

	12/31/2003	12/31/2002	12/31/2001
Inventory	(25,375,000)	31,505,000	194,799,000
Other assets	306,258,000	(76,975,000)	21,729,000
Accounts payable	137,716,000	(59,856,000)	(442,312,000)
Accrued liabilities	(95,117,000)	(103,868,000)	(87,714,000)
Accrued royalties	(8,196,000)	(79,014,000)	(2,747,000)
Other liabilities	39,382,000	54,924,000	(40,810,000)
Net cash provided by (used in) operating activities	72,691,000	(24,677,000)	(270,339,000)
Cash flows from investing activities:			
Capital expenditures	(72,978,000)	(78,497,000)	(199,493,000)
Proceeds from sale of investment	–	11,100,000	–
Purchases of available-for-sale securities	(530,323,000)	(614,023,000)	(638,869,000)
Sales of available-for-sale securities	401,109,000	436,316,000	356,071,000
Proceeds from the sale of financing receivables	–	9,896,000	569,579,000
Purchase of financing receivables, net of repayments	–	–	(28,476,000)
Proceeds from notes receivable	20,045,000	–	50,000,000
Other, net	–	–	189,000
Net cash provided by (used in) investing activities	(182,147,000)	(235,208,000)	109,001,000
Cash flows from financing activities:			
Proceeds from issuance of notes payable	–	–	200,000,000
Principal payments on long-term obligations and notes payable	–	–	(3,984,000)
Proceeds from stock issuance	–	–	200,000,000
Payment of preferred dividends	(8,840,000)	(5,878,000)	–
Stock options exercised	1,794,000	367,000	9,431,000
Net cash provided by (used in) financing activities	(7,046,000)	(5,511,000)	405,447,000
Foreign exchange effect on cash and cash equivalents	–	–	2,893,000
Net increase (decrease) in cash and cash equivalents	(116,502,000)	(265,396,000)	247,002,000
Cash and cash equivalents, beginning of year	465,603,000	730,999,000	483,997,000
Cash and cash equivalents, end of year	$ 349,101,000	$ 465,603,000	$ 730,999,000

a. Calculate the following ratios:

ROE, ROC, ROA, Profit Margin, Total Asset Turnover, Receivable Turnover, Inventory Turnover, Payables Turnover Current, Quick, Debt/Equity

b. Calculate the common-size balance sheet and income statement.

c. Comment on the financial health of the two organizations from the point of view of a lender who has been asked to make a $200 million loan to each of the companies.

d. Estimate Dell's and Gateway's 2003 net sales if sales were recognized as cash is collected rather than on the accrual basis. Comment on the significance of the difference between your estimate and reported sales.

e. Suppose you are interested in forecasting future sales for Dell and Gateway. Describe methods that can be used. Forecast Dell's and Gateway's sales for 2006. Justify your answer.

30. Use the data from the financial statement of Home Depot and Lowes to answer the following questions.

HOME DEPOT, INC. Balance Sheet

	02/01/2004	02/01/2003
Assets		
Current assets:		
Cash and cash equivalents	$ 2,826,000,000	$ 2,188,000,000
Short-term investments, including current maturities of long-term investments	26,000,000	65,000,000
Receivables, net	1,097,000,000	1,072,000,000
Merchandise inventories	9,076,000,000	8,338,000,000
Other current assets	303,000,000	254,000,000
Total current assets	13,328,000,000	11,917,000,000
Property and equipment, at cost:		
Land	6,397,000,000	5,560,000,000
Buildings	10,920,000,000	9,197,000,000
Furniture, fixtures, and equipment	5,163,000,000	4,074,000,000
Leasehold improvements	942,000,000	872,000,000
Construction in progress	820,000,000	724,000,000
Capital leases	352,000,000	306,000,000
	24,594,000,000	20,733,000,000
Less accumulated depreciation and amortization	4,531,000,000	3,565,000,000
Net property and equipment	20,063,000,000	17,168,000,000
Notes receivable	84,000,000	107,000,000
Cost in excess of the fair value of net assets acquired, net of accumulated amortization of $54 at February 1, 2004 and $50 at February 2, 2003	833,000,000	575,000,000
Other assets	129,000,000	244,000,000
Total assets	$34,437,000,000	$ 30,011,000,000
Liabilities and stockholders' equity		
Current liabilities:		
Accounts payable	$ 5,159,000,000	$ 4,560,000,000
Accrued salaries and related expenses	801,000,000	809,000,000
Sales taxes payable	419,000,000	307,000,000
Deferred revenue	1,281,000,000	998,000,000
Income taxes payable	175,000,000	227,000,000
Current installments of long-term debt	509,000,000	7,000,000
Other accrued expenses	1,210,000,000	1,127,000,000
Total current liabilities	9,554,000,000	8,035,000,000

	02/01/2004	02/01/2003
Long-term debt, excluding current installments	856,000,000	1,321,000,000
Other long-term liabilities	653,000,000	491,000,000
Deferred income taxes	967,000,000	362,000,000
Stockholders' equity		
Common stock, par value $0.05; authorized: 10,000 shares, issued and outstanding 2,373 shares at February 1, 2004 and 2,362 shares at February 2, 2003	119,000,000	118,000,000
Paid-in capital	6,184,000,000	5,858,000,000
Retained earnings	19,680,000,000	15,971,000,000
Accumulated other comprehensive income (loss)	90,000,000	(82,000,000)
Unearned compensation	(76,000,000)	(63,000,000)
Treasury stock, at cost, 116 shares at February 1, 2004 and 69 shares at February 2, 2003	(3,590,000,000)	(2,000,000,000)
Total stockholders' equity	22,407,000,000	19,802,000,000
Total liabilities and stockholders' equity	$34,437,000,000	$30,011,000,000

HOME DEPOT, INC. Income Statement

	02/01/2004	02/01/2003	02/01/2002
Net sales	$64,816,000,000	$58,247,000,000	$53,553,000,000
Cost of merchandise sold	44,236,000,000	40,139,000,000	37,406,000,000
Gross profit	20,580,000,000	18,108,000,000	16,147,000,000
Operating expenses:			
Selling and store operating	12,502,000,000	11,180,000,000	10,163,000,000
Pre-opening	86,000,000	96,000,000	117,000,000
General and administrative	1,146,000,000	1,002,000,000	935,000,000
Total operating expenses	13,734,000,000	12,278,000,000	11,215,000,000
Operating income	6,846,000,000	5,830,000,000	4,932,000,000
Interest income (expense):			
Interest and investment income	59,000,000	79,000,000	53,000,000
Interest expense	(62,000,000)	(37,000,000)	(28,000,000)
Interest, net	(3,000,000)	42,000,000	25,000,000
Earnings before provision for income taxes	6,843,000,000	5,872,000,000	4,957,000,000
Provision for income taxes	2,539,000,000	2,208,000,000	1,913,000,000
Net earnings	$ 4,304,000,000	$3,664,000,000	$3,044,000,000

HOME DEPOT, INC. Cash Flow

	02/01/2004	02/01/2003	02/01/2002
Cash flows from operations:			
Net earnings	$4,304,000,000	$3,664,000,000	$3,044,000,000
Reconciliation of net earnings to net			
Cash provided by operations:			
Depreciation and amortization	1,076,000,000	903,000,000	764,000,000
Decrease (increase) in receivables, net	25,000,000	(38,000,000)	(119,000,000)
Increase in merchandise inventories	(693,000,000)	(1,592,000,000)	(166,000,000)
Increase in accounts payable and accrued liabilities	790,000,000	1,394,000,000	1,878,000,000
Increase in deferred revenue	279,000,000	147,000,000	200,000,000
(Decrease) increase in income taxes payable	(27,000,000)	83,000,000	272,000,000
Increase (decrease) in deferred income taxes	605,000,000	173,000,000	(6,000,000)
Other	186,000,000	68,000,000	96,000,000
Net cash provided by operations	6,545,000,000	4,802,000,000	5,963,000,000
Cash flows from investing activities:			
Capital expenditures, net of $47, $49, and $5 of noncash capital expenditures in fiscal 2003, 2002 and 2001, respectively	(3,508,000,000)	(2,749,000,000)	(3,393,000,000)
Purchase of assets from off-balance sheet financing arrangement	(598,000,000)	–	–
Payments for businesses acquired, net	(215,000,000)	(235,000,000)	(190,000,000)
Proceeds from sales of businesses, net	–	22,000,000	64,000,000
Proceeds from sales of property and equipment	265,000,000	105,000,000	126,000,000
Purchases of investments	(159,000,000)	(583,000,000)	(85,000,000)
Proceeds from maturities of investments	219,000,000	506,000,000	25,000,000
Other	0	0	(13,000,000)
Net cash used in investing activities	(3,996,000,000)	(2,934,000,000)	(3,466,000,000)
Cash flows from financing activities:			
Repayments of commercial paper obligations, net	–	–	(754,000,000)
Proceeds from long-term debt	–	1,000,000	532,000,000
Repayments of long-term debt	(9,000,000)	–	–
Repurchase of common stock	(1,554,000,000)	(2,000,000,000)	–
Proceeds from sale of common stock, net	227,000,000	326,000,000	445,000,000
Cash dividends paid to stockholders	(595,000,000)	(492,000,000)	(396,000,000)
Net cash used in financing activities	(1,931,000,000)	(2,165,000,000)	(173,000,000)
Effect of exchange rate changes on cash and cash equivalents	20,000,000	8,000,000	(14,000,000)
Increase (decrease) in cash and cash equivalents	638,000,000	(289,000,000)	2,310,000,000
Cash and cash equivalents at beginning of year	2,188,000,000	2,477,000,000	167,000,000
Cash and cash equivalents at end of year	2,826,000,000	2,188,000,000	2,477,000,000
Supplemental disclosure of cash payments made for:			
Interest, net of interest capitalized	70,000,000	50,000,000	18,000,000
Income taxes	$2,037,000,000	$1,951,000,000	$1,685,000,000

Lowe's Companies, Inc.
Consolidated Balance Sheets
(In Millions, Except Par Value Data)

	Jan-30-04	Jan-31-03
Assets		
Current assets:		
Cash and cash equivalents	$ 1,446,000,000	$ 853,000,000
Short-term investments (note 3)	178,000,000	273,000,000
Accounts receivable, net (note 1)	131,000,000	172,000,000
Merchandise inventory (note 1)	4,584,000,000	3,968,000,000
Deferred income taxes (note 13)	59,000,000	58,000,000
Other current assets	289,000,000	244,000,000
Total current assets	6,687,000,000	5,568,000,000
Property, less accumulated depreciation (notes 4 and 5)	11,945,000,000	10,352,000,000
Long-term investments (note 3)	169,000,000	29,000,000
Other assets (note 5)	241,000,000	160,000,000
Total assets	$19,042,000,000	$16,109,000,000
Liabilities and shareholders' equity		
Current liabilities:		
Short-term borrowings (note 6)	$ —	$ 50,000,000
Current maturities of long-term debt (note 7)	77,000,000	29,000,000
Accounts payable	2,366,000,000	1,943,000,000
Employee retirement plans (note 12)	74,000,000	88,000,000
Accrued salaries and wages	335,000,000	306,000,000
Other current liabilities (note 5)	1,516,000,000	1,162,000,000
Total current liabilities	4,368,000,000	3,578,000,000
Long-term debt, excluding current maturities (notes 7, 8, and 11)	3,678,000,000	3,736,000,000
Deferred income taxes (note 13)	657,000,000	478,000,000
Other long-term liabilities	30,000,000	15,000,000
Total liabilities	8,733,000,000	7,807,000,000
Shareholders' equity (note 10):		
Preferred stock $5 par value, none issued	—	—
Common stock —$.50 par value; shares issued and outstanding January 30, 2004 — 787 January 31, 2003 — 782	394,000,000	391,000,000
Capital in excess of par value	2,237,000,000	2,023,000,000
Retained earnings	7,677,000,000	5,887,000,000
Accumulated other comprehensive income	1,000,000	1,000,000
Total shareholders' equity	10,309,000,000	8,302,000,000
Total liabilities and shareholders' equity	$19,042,000,000	$16,109,000,000

Lowe's Companies, Inc.
Consolidated Statements of Earnings

Years Ended on	Jan-30-04	Jan-31-03	Feb-1-02
Net sales	$30,838,000,000	$26,112,000,000	$21,714,000,000
Cost of sales	21,231,000,000	18,164,000,000	15,427,000,000
Gross margin	9,607,000,000	7,948,000,000	6,287,000,000
Expenses:	–	–	–
Selling, general, and administrative (note 5)	5,543,000,000	4,676,000,000	3,857,000,000
Store opening costs	128,000,000	129,000,000	140,000,000
Depreciation	758,000,000	622,000,000	513,000,000
Interest (note 15)	180,000,000	182,000,000	174,000,000
Total expenses	6,609,000,000	5,609,000,000	4,684,000,000
Pre-tax earnings	2,998,000,000	2,339,000,000	1,603,000,000
Income tax provision (note 13)	1,136,000,000	880,000,000	593,000,000
Earnings from continuing operations	1,862,000,000	1,459,000,000	1,010,000,000
Earnings from discontinued operations, net of tax (note 2)	15,000,000	12,000,000	13,000,000
Net earnings	$ 877,000,000	$ 1,471,000,000	$ 1,023,000,000

LOWES COMPANIES, INC. Cash Flow

	01/30/2004	01/30/2003	01/30/2002
Cash Flows from operating activities:			
Net earnings	$1,877,000,000	$1,471,000,000	$1,023,000,000
Earnings from discontinued operations, net of tax	(15,000,000)	(12,000,000)	(13,000,000)
Earnings from continuing operations	1,862,000,000	1,459,000,000	1,010,000,000
Adjustments to reconcile net earnings to net cash provided by operating activities:			
Depreciation and amortization	781,000,000	641,000,000	530,000,000
Deferred income taxes	178,000,000	208,000,000	42,000,000
Loss on disposition/write-down of fixed and other assets	31,000,000	18,000,000	39,000,000
Stock-based compensation expense	41,000,000	–	–
Tax effect of stock options exercised	31,000,000	29,000,000	35,000,000
Changes in operating assets and liabilities:			
Accounts receivable, net	2,000,000	(9,000,000)	(5,000,000)
Merchandise inventory	(648,000,000)	(357,000,000)	(326,000,000)
Other operating assets	(45,000,000)	(41,000,000)	(37,000,000)
Accounts payable	423,000,000	228,000,000	1,000,000
Employee retirement plans	(14,000,000)	40,000,000	114,000,000
Other operating liabilities	399,000,000	461,000,000	193,000,000

	01/30/2004	01/30/2003	01/30/2002
Net cash provided by operating activities from continuing operations	3,041,000,000	2,677,000,000	1,596,000,000
Cash flows from investing activities:			
Decrease (increase) in investment assets:			
Short-term investments	139,000,000	(203,000,000)	(30,000,000)
Purchases of long-term investments	(381,000,000)	(24,000,000)	(1,000,000)
Proceeds from sale/maturity of long-term investments	193,000,000	–	3,000,000
Increase in other long-term assets	(95,000,000)	(33,000,000)	(14,000,000)
Fixed assets acquired	(2,444,000,000)	(2,359,000,000)	(2,196,000,000)
Proceeds from the sale of fixed and other long-term assets	45,000,000	44,000,000	42,000,000
Net cash used in investing activities from continuing operations	(2,543,000,000)	(2,575,000,000)	(2,196,000,000)
Cash flows from financing activities:			
Net decrease in short-term borrowings	(50,000,000)	(50,000,000)	(150,000,000)
Long-term debt borrowings	–	–	1,087,000,000
Repayment of long-term debt	(29,000,000)	(63,000,000)	(63,000,000)
Proceeds from employee stock purchase plan	52,000,000	50,000,000	38,000,000
Proceeds from stock options exercised	97,000,000	65,000,000	77,000,000
Cash dividend payments	(87,000,000)	(66,000,000)	(60,000,000)
Net cash provided by (used in) financing activities from continuing operations	(17,000,000)	(64,000,000)	929,000,000
Net cash provided by discontinued operations	112,000,000	16,000,000	14,000,000
Net increase (decrease) in cash and cash equivalents	593,000,000	54,000,000	343,000,000
Cash and cash equivalents, beginning of year	853,000,000	799,000,000	456,000,000
Cash and cash equivalents, end of year	$1,446,000,000	$ 853,000,000	$ 799,000,000

a. Calculate the following ratios:

   ROE, ROC, ROA, Profit Margin, Total Asset Turnover, Receivable Turnover, Inventory Turnover, Payables Turnover Current, Quick, Debt/Equity

b. Calculate the common-size balance sheet and income statement.

c. Comment on the financial health of the two organizations from the point of view of a lender who has been asked to make a $200 million loan to each of the companies.

d. Estimate Lowe's and Home Depot's sales for the year ending February 1, 2004 if sales had been recorded as cash is collected rather than on the accrual basis. Comment on the significance of the difference between your estimate and reported sales.

   Suppose you are interested in forecasting future sales for Lowes and Home Depot. Describe methods that can be used. Forecast Lowe's and Home Depot's sales for 2006. Justify your answer.

Assuming that the amount forecast for 2006 will continue indefinitely into the future, estimate the market value of Lowes and Home Depot using the free cash flow and residual income approaches. Assume a required rate of return of 10 percent. Hint: The present value of a stream of cash flows that continues into infinity is computed as the amount divided by the required rate of return. For example, the present value of $10 to be received annually forever is $10/.1 = \$100$ (assuming a 10 percent required rate of return).

BEYOND THE BOOK

31. Prepare a comparative ratio analysis of two competitor companies. At the direction of your instructor, pick either two domestic or one domestic and one foreign competitor. At a minimum, use the set of ratios discussed in the text and at least three years of data. Use any additional ratios that might be commonly used in the industry that you select (you may also need to drop some of the ratios discussed in the book if they are not relevant).

    Required: Prepare a written report summarizing your comparative analysis. For the purpose of this report, assume some sort of decision perspective; for instance, you might assume that you are a bank loan officer evaluating the two competitors to decide which has the best lending risk profile.

Valuing Receivables

LEARNING OBJECTIVES

After reading this chapter you should be able to:

1. Understand why firms anticipate doubtful accounts from customers and recognize bad debt expense.

2. Describe the estimation methods used to determine the provision for doubtful accounts and the balance in the allowance for doubtful accounts.

3. Explain the relationship between revenue recognition, and the concept of net realizable value applied to receivables.

4. Discuss the conversion of receivables into cash through factoring and securitization and the disclosure requirements associated with this activity.

The stock price of MicroStrategy, a data-mining and customized information delivery company, experienced a one-day stock price drop of 50 percent (see Exhibit 7.1) when it announced a restatement of revenues due to a change in its accounting treatment of software sales (for which the company performs significant subsequent services). The change shifts revenue from recognition at the time of software delivery to a percentage of completion basis over the software contract's life. Further, the company reclassified an accounts receivable to a short-term investment, as a result of a software transaction that involved receiving shares of the customer's common stock. The impact of these accounting changes on net income reduced earnings per share from $0.15 per share to a loss of between $0.43 and $0.51 per share.

This event points to the potential importance of policies for both the timing of revenues and the classification of assets as receivables in valuing the firm. While the stock market may have reacted to the reporting effects of the accounting change *per se*, it is also possible that the market interpreted the change as new information about the nature of the company's operations. In fact, upon reviewing the company's stock price over the past two years, we see that it corresponds to the behavior of Internet stocks at large. These changes reflect a revision of investor expectations concerning growth in this sector. The short history of Internet companies such as MicroStrategy suggests that recent accounting information concerning sales and related receivables may have played a significant role in forming those expectations.

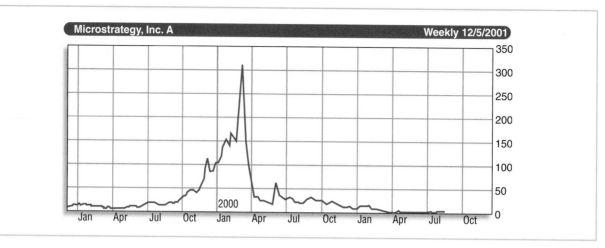

Exhibit 7.1
MicroStrategy Stock
Price Movement

THE REAL WORLD

MicroStrategy Inc.

As we described in detail in Chapter 4, receivables are created at the point of revenue recognition if cash has not yet been received. Receivables are amounts owed to the firm, by parties at arm's length from the firm (e.g., not a firm's employee). **Accounts receivables,** also called **trade receivables,** typically arise from sales of goods or services to customers on credit. **Financing receivables** generally arise from lending money to others. Accounts receivable are commonly short-term in nature and generally do not bear explicit interest, in contrast to **notes receivable,** a type of financing receivable. Notes take the form of written promises to pay specific amounts, including interest, at given future due dates. A firm may convert accounts receivable to notes receivable when it becomes necessary or desirable to extend the payment period and require that interest be included.

In this chapter, we discuss both types of receivables in more detail, beginning with accounts receivable.

ACCOUNTS RECEIVABLE

For accounting purposes, firms value accounts receivables at their **net realizable value.** Net realizable value represents the amount that the firm expects to collect. The amounts that the firm expects it will not collect due to customers' inability to pay are called **uncollectible accounts, doubtful accounts,** or **bad debts.** The amounts that the firm expects it will not collect due to its policy of allowing customers to return goods or to receive a reduction in the original sales price are called **sales returns** and **sales allowances,** respectively.

A firm faces difficulty in determining net realizable value, however, as it must estimate doubtful accounts, sales returns, and sales allowances. Further, once a firm makes these estimates, how should the firm best reflect them in the financial statements? Finally, how does a firm deal with the differences between these estimates and the actual amounts, as these differences become known to the firm over time? Let's begin to address these questions by first describing alternative methods of accounting for doubtful accounts, setting aside for the moment how to determine estimates.

DOUBTFUL ACCOUNTS RECOGNITION

Firms might use two approaches for accounting for doubtful accounts: the direct write-off method and the allowance method. For the **direct write-off method,** a firm simply reduces accounts receivable and records bad debt expense when accounts actually become uncollectible and are written off. All firms set a policy that dictates when collection efforts will end on an account. For instance, if the policy states that a firm will write off accounts more than 120 days overdue, then the firm will remove the account from its books after 120 days and perhaps turn it over to a collection agency.

Although simple, this method contains several flaws. The most significant flaw is that the method may fail to recognize bad debt expense in the same accounting period as the credit sales that gave rise to those receivables. This is critical because it means that sales that are recognized are, in effect, overstated. That is, the sales on account reflect sales that will not actually be realized through cash collection. This error is corrected in a future period when the firm writes off the account in an accounting period subsequent to the original sale. However, this timing difference can mislead market participants who respond to the earnings at the time they are reported. Another flaw with the direct write-off method is that the accounts receivable account is not stated at its net realizable value. Current disclosure standards are moving toward more emphasis on balance sheet valuations, and overstatement of assets is not consistent with GAAP.

A second approach, called the **allowance method,** avoids these flaws by using estimates of doubtful accounts to determine bad debt expense at the time of sale. By recognizing an expense in the same accounting period as the sale, the firm satisfies the matching concept of expense recognition. The method also states accounts receivable at its net realizable value through the use of a contra-asset account, called the **allowance for doubtful accounts.** This account contains the amount of receivables that the firm estimates is uncollectible. The advantage of this treatment is that the balance sheet reports both the full amount due from customers (accounts receivable) and the amount that the firm expects not to collect (allowance for doubtful accounts).

Only the allowance method is consistent with GAAP. The direct write-off method, however, is required for tax reporting. The reason for the difference is that for tax purposes, the allowance method may lead to an overstatement of expenses, and management incentives for tax purposes are generally to reduce taxes, while for financial accounting the incentives usually are to report higher earnings. This represents one of several accounting areas where a timing difference exists between tax and financial reporting (we'll discuss this further in Chapter 10). As a result, because firms may use both methods, let's look at them in more detail.

ILLUSTRATION OF DOUBTFUL ACCOUNTS METHODS

We illustrate both the direct write-off and allowance methods using BHT, the hypothetical company we've used in earlier chapters. Following are the balance sheet and income statement for 20X2 of BHT (from Chapter 5). Note that BHT has made no adjustments for bad debts in these financial statements.

Biohealth, Inc. (BHT)
Balance Sheet
($ in millions)

	As of 12/31/20X2	As of 12/31/20X1
Assets		
Current Assets:		
Cash	$ 1,510	$ 567
Accounts receivable	3,650	2,464
Inventory	4,400	3,920
Prepaid expenses	360	0
Total current assets	9,920	7,101
Property, plant, and equipment (PPE)	950	540
Less: accumulated depreciation	(210)	(60)
Net property, plant, and equipment	740	480
	$10,660	$7,581
Liabilities and Stockholders' Equity		
Liabilities:		
Current liabilities:		
Accounts payable	6,671	5,140
Long-term debt:		
Note payable	950	400
Total liabilities	7,621	5,540
Stockholders' equity		
Common stock	300	250
Additional paid-in capital	1,950	1,375
Retained earnings	789	266
Total stockholders' equity	3,039	2,041
	$10,660	$7,581

Biohealth, Inc. (BHT)
Income Statement

	Year ending 12/31/20X2	Year ending 12/31/20X1
Revenues	$43,850	$35,724
Less: Cost of goods sold	(37,272)	(30,420)
Gross profit	6,578	5,304
Selling and administrative expenses	5,320	(4,800)
Depreciation expense	150	(60)
Interest expense	85	(28)
Net income	$ 1,023	$416

Suppose we estimate bad debts for BHT to be approximately 1 percent of revenues in both 20X1 and 20X2, leading to bad debt expense estimates of $357 in 20X1 and $438 in 20X2 (20X1 revenues of $35,724 and 20X2 revenues $43,850 are shown in the income statement). We further assume that BHT wrote off bad debts of $240 in 20X1 and $510 in 20X2. Let's examine how the accounting would proceed under the two methods beginning with the direct write-off method. We assume that the cash collections on accounts receivable remain unchanged from those that produced the balances in the 20X1 and 20X2 financial statements.

Direct Write-Off Method

Recall that under this method we delay accounting recognition of doubtful accounts until such accounts are actually written off. Accordingly, the only accounting entries would be to record the actual write-offs in both years:

```
To record bad debt expense in 20X1:

    Bad Debts Expense               240
        Accounts Receivable                 240
```

```
To record bad debt expense in 20X2:

    Bad Debts Expense               510
        Accounts Receivable                 510
```

Under this treatment, Accounts Receivable at the end of 20X1 would be 2,224 (2,464 − 240). This would change the beginning balance in 20X2 to 2,224 and with the additional writeoffs of 510 the ending balance in 20X2 would be 2,900 (3,650 − 240 − 510). Net income would be 176 (416 − 240) in 20X1 and 513 (1,023 − 510) in 20X2.

Allowance Method

As described previously, the allowance method provides for recognition of doubtful accounts based on estimates in advance of actual write-off, with the offsetting credit to a contra-asset account, Allowance for Doubtful Accounts. In this case, the actual write-offs reduce both Accounts Receivable and Allowance for Doubtful Accounts as shown:

```
To record the provision in 20X1:

    Provision for Doubtful Accounts       357
        Allowance for Doubtful Accounts           357

To record the write-offs in 20X1:

    Allowance for Doubtful Accounts       240
        Accounts Receivable                       240
```

To record the provision in 20X2:

Provision for Doubtful Accounts	438	
Allowance for Doubtful Accounts		438

To record the write-offs in 20X2:

Allowance for Doubtful Accounts	510	
Accounts Receivable		510

Note that the balance in the allowance account at the end of 20X1 would be 117 (357 − 240) and 45 (117 + 438 − 510) at the end of 20X2.

The change in terminology, from bad debts expense to **provision for doubtful accounts,** reflects the fact that under the allowance method, the amount recorded as an expense is an estimate, while under the direct write-off method, the amount recognized is the actual bad debt amount. The term provision describes various expenses that a firm estimates, such as income taxes, the costs of fulfilling warranties, and bad debts.

Because the beginning balance in the allowance account reflects estimates of bad debts previously recorded as an expense, it would be double counting to also record actual write-offs of bad debts as an expense. Instead, actual write-offs offset earlier estimates by reducing the balance in the allowance account.

Let's now compare the effects of the two methods on the reported value of Accounts Receivable. Under the allowance method, the balance in Allowance for Doubtful Accounts would be deducted from Accounts Receivable to arrive at a net asset of 2,224 − 117 = 2,107 in 20X1 and 2,900 − 45 = 2,855 in 20X2. The lower net balances of Accounts Receivable using this method reflect the amounts that BHT expects to collect, not the amounts due from customers, that is, the net realizable value. Let's continue to compare the two methods, this time using a real company.

> The allowance method should provide more useful information to analysts as they attempt to estimate the future cash flows of the firm as management is providing their own estimate of how much of the revenues reported in the period they actually expect to collect.

REAL COMPANY ILLUSTRATION OF DOUBTFUL ACCOUNTS

Exhibit 7.2 shows the relevant data regarding doubtful accounts from Wickes, Inc. for the year ended December 30, 2000. Note that we could also use the information contained in the financial statements of Wickes (as shown in Exhibit 7.3) because Wickes uses the allowance method. The balance sheet shows the balances in the allowance account and the income statement shows the provision. We can then calculate the write-offs knowing the other three amounts, as the account must balance.

Exhibit 7.2
Wickes, Inc. Data on Doubtful Accounts for the Year Ended December 30, 2000

THE REAL WORLD

Wickes, Inc.

Allowance for Doubtful Accounts, 12/25/99	4,105
Provision for Doubtful Accounts	983
Write-offs of Accounts Receivable	(2,297)
Allowance for Doubtful Accounts, 12/30/00	2,791

Exhibit 7.3
Partial Financial
Statements from Wickes'
2000 Annual Report

THE REAL WORLD

Wickes, Inc.

Consolidate Balance sheet on
Dec 31, 2000 (partial)

	December 30, 2000	December 25, 1999
Assets		
Current assets:		
Cash	$ 243	$ 72
Account receivable, less allowance for doubtful account of $2,791 in 2000 and $4,105 in 1999	76,659	110,103
Notes receivable from affiliate	201	481
Inventory	117,910	120,705
Deferred tax asset	6,692	7,184
Prepaid expenses	3,405	2,663
Total current assets	205,110	241,208

Consolidated statement of operation
for year 2000 (partial)

	December 30, 2000	December 25, 1999	December 26, 1998
Net sales	$1,027,604	$1,087,402	$912,190
Cost of sales	804,512	862,798	717,071
Gross profit	223,092	224,604	195,119
Selling, general, and administrative expenses	199,889	185,884	166,420
Depreciation, goodwill, and trademark amortization	5,877	5,295	4,513
Provision for doubtful accounts	983	1,724	2,915
Restructuring and unusual items		5,932	
Other operating income	(3,292)	(4,932)	(6,017)
	203,457	187,971	173,793
Income from operations	19,635	36,633	21,326

Consolidated statement of cash flows (partial)

	December 30, 2000	December 25, 1999	December 26, 1998
Cash flows from operating activities:			
Net income(loss)	$ 2,854	$ 7,588	($965)
Adjustments to reconcile net income (loss) to net cash from operating activities	(6,806)		
Extraordinary gain	6,507	5,852	4,785
Depreciation expense	222	222	222
Amortization of goodwill	621	399	246
Amortization of deferred financing costs	1,274	1,510	1,447
Provision for doubtful accounts	983	1,724	2,915
Gain on sale of assets	(146)	(1,458)	(1,834)
Deferred tax (benefit) provision	(2,116)	4,460	(330)
Change in asset and liabilities:			
Decrease/(increase) in account receivable	32,461	(16,904)	(14,053)
Decrease/(increase) in inventory	2,795	(15,831)	(1,010)
(Decrease)/increase in accounts payable and accrued liabilities	(22,150)	3,539	10,814
Increase in prepaids and other assets	(1,830)	(666)	(1,715)
Net cash provided by/(used in) operating activities	14,669	(9,565)	522

We now have enough information to summarize the entries that likely would have been recorded by Wickes under the two methods. First, the following entry would have been made under the direct write-off method:

Direct Write-off Method

Bad Debts Expense	2,297	
Accounts Receivable		2,297

Remember that with this method, the potential exists for a mismatching of sales during 2000 with bad debts expense. That is, we assume some of the accounts written off in the above entry arose from credit sales in the previous fiscal year. Further, we expect that some of the accounts receivable at the end of the present fiscal year may turn out to be uncollectible in the next year. Note that accounts receivable on December 30, 2000 would not have been presented at net realizable value given that no allowance for doubtful accounts is created under this method. In comparison with net realizable value at year end 2000, Wickes' accounts receivable would have been overstated by $2,791. Hence, it is not surprising that this method is not permitted under GAAP.

Now let's view the journal entries for Wickes using the allowance method:

Allowance Method

Provision for Doubtful Accounts	983	
Allowance for Doubtful Accounts		983
Allowance for Doubtful Accounts	2,297	
Accounts Receivable		2,297

Exhibit 7.3 shows partial balance sheets, income statements, and cash flow statements from Wickes' 2000 annual report. If Wickes had used the direct write-off method of accounting for bad debts, then accounts receivable on the balance sheet would not have been reduced by an allowance account, implying that accounts receivable would have been reported at the full amount due from customers rather than the amount Wickes expects to collect from those customers, thus overstating accounts receivable. The effect on the income statement would have been for actual bad debts of 2,297 to replace the provision for doubtful accounts of 983 as the amount recorded as an expense. This would lower income from operations by the difference of 1,314 (6.7 percent of net income).

Further, net income on the cash flow statement also would have been reduced by 1,314, and the adjustment of net income for the provision for doubtful accounts (now an adjustment for actual bad debts) would have changed to 2,297, or a net increase of 1,314. The change in accounts receivable would remain at 32,461 because this is the actual change in the total amount due from customers before the allowance is deducted. Hence, there would have been no net effect on cash provided by operating activities. More generally, it is important to note that changes in accounting methods such as from the allowance method to the direct write-off method do not alter cash flows, even though they typically do affect balance sheet values and operating income.

ESTIMATING DOUBTFUL ACCOUNTS

If analysts are to have an accurate estimate of future cash flows, management must provide an accurate estimate of the company's doubtful accounts. One method used to estimate provisions for doubtful accounts is based on the percentage relationship between amounts written off and credit sales, referred to as the **percentage of sales method.** Adjustments of past percentage estimates may be necessary to reflect changes in a company's credit policies and clientele. The more liberal those policies, in the sense of easier credit-granting criteria such as longer payment periods or lower down payments, the higher the percentage of credit sales that may become uncollectible. Looking at the percentages of the provision for doubtful accounts to net sales over the past three years for Wickes in Exhibit 7.3, we can calculate a decrease from 0.320 percent (2,915/912,190) in 1998 to 0.096 percent in 2000, or a 70 percent decrease over the three years. This change could be the result of a tightening of credit policy or a favorable shift in creditworthiness of customers.

An alternative to the percentage of sales method is the **aging of receivables method.** This method involves determining accounts receivable that are not expected to be collected as of the end of the period. The provision for doubtful accounts is then determined to be the amount needed to bring the allowance for doubtful accounts to the required balance. Under an aging of receivables, individual account balances are classified into groupings based on how many days a balance has been outstanding. For instance the following table might represent such an aging schedule:

Age	Amount	% Estimated to Be Uncollectible	Required Balance in Allowance
Less than 30 days	$300,000	3%	$ 9,000
31–60 days	50,000	12%	6,000
61–90 days	30,000	20%	6,000
91–120 days	10,000	35%	3,500
Required Balance at Year End			$24,500

The basic idea is that the longer an account balance has been outstanding, the lower the likelihood of payment and the larger should be the amount in the allowance account to cover that expectation.

The aging of receivables approach thus emphasizes the relationship of the allowance account to accounts receivable. For Wickes, the allowance account shows a 32 percent decline that can be largely explained by a 30 percent decrease in accounts receivable. Another measure might be to compute the ratio of the allowance to the balance in accounts receivable. For Wickes this ratio declined from 3.73 percent to 3.64 percent. This may indicate that Wickes believes that the quality of its receivables at the end of the current year are slightly higher than the previous year; therefore the balance in the allowance can be a lower fraction of the balance in the receivables.

Another way to view an adjustment of the balance in the allowance account is as a consequence of errors in previous estimates of the provision for doubtful accounts made on a percentage of sales basis. If the percentage used in applying the percent of sales method was too low (high) relative to actual write-off experience, then the balance in the allowance account would tend to be low (high) relative to accounts receivable. Accordingly, adjustments in the allowance account due to an aging of receivables may also imply an adjustment in the percentage used to estimate the provision for doubtful accounts in the future. The offsetting entries for adjustments to the allowance for doubtful accounts are usually made to the provision for doubtful accounts.

Over time, basing bad debt estimation on the percentage of credit sales deemed to be uncollectible or on the percentage of accounts receivable should even out. However, in any given period, differences in estimates will exist depending on whether a firm uses sales or accounts receivable to determine bad debt expense. In the case where a firm estimates bad debts as a percentage of sales, the firm emphasizes the matching principle. That is, the expense associated with bad debts is matched to sales. In contrast, when a firm determines bad debts using the aging accounts receivable method, the emphasis is on accurate balance sheet estimation of receivables net of the allowance for doubtful accounts (i.e., expected net realizable value). As a matter of practice, even if a firm uses the percentage of sales method, this should not result in net accounts receivable being carried at more than its expected net realizable value on the balance sheet.

Exhibit 7.4 provides a further example of changes in collection experience and receivables-management procedures that led to reductions in provisions for doubtful accounts by Sears & Roebuck. Looking at the partial financial statements in the exhibit, we see a decline in both the provision for doubtful accounts from the income statement and the allowance for doubtful accounts from the balance sheet, despite fairly constant levels of sales and accounts receivable.

For a company like Sears that has significant credit card receivables, we typically find significant additional disclosure in the footnotes of the financial statements as illustrated in Exhibit 7.5.

SALES RETURNS AND ALLOWANCES

Accounts receivable may also be decreased for the estimated value of goods returned or found to be defective by customers, for which the company has agreed to reduce the amount owed. The accounting treatment of sales returns and allowances is similar to that for uncollectible accounts. A firm establishes an allowance for sales returns and allowances and then estimates a provision for sales returns and allowances based on past experience. Unlike the provision

Exhibit 7.4
Partial Financial Statements
from Sears & Roebuck's 1999
Annual Report

THE REAL WORLD

Sears & Roebuck

Consolidated statements of Income (partial)

	1999	1998	1997
Revenues			
Merchandise sales and services	$36,728	$36,957	$36,649
Credit revenues	4,343	4,618	4,925
Total revenues	41,071	41,575	41,574
Costs and expenses			
Cost of sales, buying, and occupancy	27,212	27,444	26,985
Selling and administrative	8,418	8,384	8,394
Provision for uncollectible accounts	871	1,287	1,532
Depreciation and amortization	848	830	785
Interest	1,268	1,423	1,409
Reaffirmation charge			475
Restructuring and impairment costs	41	352	
Total cost and expenses	38,658	39,720	39,580
Operating income	2,413	1,855	1,994

Consolidated Balance Sheets (partial)

	1999	1998
Assets		
Current assets	$ 729	$ 495
Retained interest in transferred credit and card receivables	3,144	4,294
Credit card receivables	18,793	18,946
Less allowance for uncollectible accounts	760	974
Net credit card receivables	18,033	17,972
Other receivables	404	397
Merchandise inventories	5,069	4,816
Prepaid expenses and deferred charges	579	506
Deferred income taxes	709	791
Total current assets	28,667	29,271

Exhibit 7.5
Sears & Roebuck, Footnote to
Financial Statements

THE REAL WORLD

Sears & Roebuck

Credit Card Receivables

Credit card receivables arise primarily under open-end revolving credit accounts used to finance purchases of merchandise and services offered by the company. These accounts have various billing and payment structures, including varying minimum payment levels and finance charge rates. Based on historical payment patterns, the full receivable balance will not be repaid within one year.

Credit card receivables are shown net of an allowance for uncollectible accounts. The company provides an allowance for uncollectible accounts based on impaired accounts, historical charge-off patterns, and management judgment.

In 1997 and 1998 under the company's proprietary credit system, uncollectible accounts were generally charged off automatically when the customer's past due balance was eight times the scheduled minimum monthly payment, except that accounts could be charged off sooner in the event of customer bankruptcy. However, in the fourth quarter of 1998,
(Continued)

Exhibit 7.5
(Continued)

the company converted 12 percent of its managed portfolio of credit card receivables to a new credit processing system. The remaining 88 percent of accounts on the proprietary credit system were then converted to the new system in the first and second quarters of 1999. Under the new system, the company charges off an account automatically when a customer has failed to make a required payment in each of the eight billing cycles following a missed payment. Under both systems, finance charge revenue is recorded until an account is charged off, at which time uncollected finance charge revenue is recorded as a reduction of credit revenues.

Credit

Credit selling and administrative expense increased 9.0 percent in 1999 from the 1998 amount. This increase was primarily attributable to increased investment in credit collection efforts, enhanced risk management systems, the TSYS conversion costs, and the launch of the Sears Premier Card. In 1998, selling and administrative expenses increased 7.7 percent from the 1997 level primarily due to increased collection and risk management activities and litigation costs.

Domestic provision for uncollectible accounts and related information, as well as the delinquency rates for accounts that had been converted to TSYS were as follows on a quarterly basis through 1999:

Millions	1999	1998	1997
Provision for uncollectible accounts	$ 837	$ 1,261	$ 1,493
Net credit charge-offs to average managed credit card receivables	6.44%	7.35%	6.48%
Delinquency rates at year end	7.58%	6.82%	7.00%
Owned credit card receivables	$17,068	$17,443	$19,386
Allowance for uncollectible owned account	$ 725	$ 942	$ 1,077
January 2, 1999 (12% converted)			9.28%
April 3, 1999 (50% converted)			8.07%
July 3, 1999 (100% converted)			7.29%
October 2, 1999 (100% converted)			7.57%
January 2, 2000 (100% converted)			7.58%

In 1999, the domestic provision for uncollectible accounts decreased $424 million to $837 million. The decrease is attributable to lower average owned credit card receivable balances and improvement in portfolio quality during the year. As shown in the table, delinquency rates on a TSYS basis declined from year end of 1999. In addition, the net charge-off rate for 1999 decreased to 6.44 percent from 7.35 percent in 1998. The allowance for doubtful accounts at year end is $725 million, or 4.26 percent of on-book receivables as compared to 5.44 percent at the prior year end.

 Note that the costs of administering Sears' plan have escalated dramatically (7.7 percent and 9 percent) over the last two years. This would have a definite negative impact on the company's valuation. However, offsetting this would be the improvement in the charge-offs to receivables ratio which has declined, indicating better experience in collecting receivables. The improvement in the percentage of the allowance to the balance in accounts receivable also should be a good sign indicating higher quality receivables.

for doubtful accounts, firms typically treat the provision for sales returns and allowances as a direct reduction of sales in arriving at net sales.

However, Land's End, a major catalog clothing retailer, uses a somewhat different treatment for potential returns. Rather than establish an allowance for returns to be subtracted from accounts receivable, the firm sets up a liability by

Reserve for returns, January, 1999	7,193
Reserve for returns, January, 2000	7,869

Exhibit 7.6
Data Based on Land's End's
Annual Report for the Year
Ended January, 2000

THE REAL WORLD

Land's End

debiting a provision for returns, an expense, and crediting reserve for returns, a liability. Later actual returns lead to reductions of accounts receivable (assuming the customers hasn't yet paid their bill; otherwise the entry would be to cash) and reserve for returns, much the same as write-offs of uncollectible accounts lead to reductions in accounts receivable and the allowance for doubtful accounts.

Let's illustrate this treatment of sales returns by using data from Land's End's annual report, embellished by a hypothetical provision for returns ($35,000) and implied actual returns (all amounts in thousands). Using the data in Exhibit 7.6 and a hypothetical provision of $35,000, journal entries summarizing the changes in Land's End's Reserve for returns during the year ended January 2000 would be as follows:

Provision for returns	35,000	
Reserve for returns		35,000
Reserve for returns	34,324	
Accounts Receivable		34,324

Exhibit 7.7 shows how these accounts would appear on the balance sheet and income statement. One financial statement analysis issue to be aware of when analyzing Land's End's statements would be that Land's End would have a higher total asset balance compared to a firm that treats the allowance as a contra-asset because they have treated their "reserve" for returns as a liability. This will have an effect on any ratio that uses total assets in its calculation (such as the ROA ratio).

Now that you understand the accounting methods for accounts receivable, we turn to a consideration of the connection between accounts receivable recognition and revenue recognition because analysts often focus on the income statement (and, hence, revenues) in their forecasts of future results.

Exhibit 7.7
Partial Financial Statements
from Land's End's Annual
Report

THE REAL WORLD

Land's End

Consolidated Balance Sheets (in thousands)	January 28, 2000	January 29, 1999
Assets		
Current assets:		
Cash and cash equivalents	$ 76,413	$ 6,641
Receivables, net	17,753	21,083
Inventory	162,193	219,686
Prepaid advertising	16,572	21,357
Other prepaid expenses	5,816	7,589
Deferred income tax benefits	10,661	17,947
Total current assets	$289,408	$294,303

Exhibit 7.7
(Continued)

	January 28, 2000	January 29, 1999
Current liabilities:		
Lines of credit	$ 11,724	$ 38,942
Accounts payable	74,510	87,922
Reserve for returns	7,869	7,193
Accrued liabilities	43,754	54,392
Accrued profit sharing	2,760	2,256
Income taxes payable	10,255	14,578
Total current liabilities	$150,872	$205,283

Consolidated statement of cash flow (in thousands)

	January 28, 2000	January 29, 1999	January 30, 1998
Cash flows from (used for) operating activities:	$48,034	$31,185	$64,150
Net income			
Adjustments to reconcile net income to net cash flows from operating activities			
Nonrecurring charge (credit)	(1,774)	12,600	
Depreciation and amortization	20,715	18,731	15,127
Deferred compensation expense	158	653	323
Deferred income taxes	8,270	(5,948)	(1,158)
Pretax gain on sale of subsidiary			(7,805)
Loss on disposal of fixed assets	926	586	1,127
Change in assets and liabilities excluding the effects of divestitures:			
Receivables, net	3,330	(5,640)	(7,019)
Inventory	57,493	21,468	(104,545)
Prepaid advertising	4,785	(2,844)	(7,447)
Other prepaid expenses	1,773	(2,504)	(1,366)
Accounts payable	(13,412)	4,179	11,616
Reserve for returns	676	1,065	944
Accrued liabilities	(7,664)	6,993	8,755
Accrued profit sharing	504	(2,030)	1,349
Income taxes payable	(4,323)	(5,899)	(1,047)
Other	3,387	1,665	64
Net cash flows from (used for) operating activities	122,878	74,260	(26,932)

ACCOUNTS RECEIVABLE AND REVENUE RECOGNITION

Recall from Chapter 4 that firms base revenue recognition on the realization concept. That is, firms realize revenue upon completion of the company's performance, in the sense of an arm's-length transaction whereby the company provides goods or services to customers. The point of delivery of those goods or services is commonly considered the critical event in that process. However, complications can arise in determining what constitutes such delivery.

Exhibit 7.8
Intel (from Notes to Its 2000
Annual Report)

THE REAL WORLD

Intel

Revenue Recognition

The company generally recognizes net revenues upon the transfer of title. However, certain of the company's sales are made to distributors under agreements allowing price protection and/or right of return on merchandise unsold by the distributors. Because of frequent sales price reductions and rapid technological obsolescence in the industry, Intel defers recognition of revenues on shipments to distributors until the distributors sell the merchandise. Management believes that the company's revenue recognition policies are in accordance with the Securities and Exchange Commission Staff Accounting Bulletin No. 101, "Revenue Recognition in Financial Statements" (SAB 101).

 Intel has come under criticism for this policy. Some investors believe that such a policy allows a company considerable discretion as to the timing of revenue recognition, in a sense, making it possible to shift operating income to future periods when operating performance is weaker. In general, this approach may reflect some companies' attempts to smooth reported income. Smoothing reported income avoids episodes of negative earnings as well as creates an impression of lower earnings volatility.

For example, say that a manufacturing company sets a liberal returns policy that allows its customers (intermediaries such as wholesalers or retailers) to reverse sales if they cannot sell the goods. Should the company recognize the initial sale as revenue and corresponding accounts receivable at the time the company ships the goods, subject to a suitable allowance for potential sales returns? Or should the company delay the recognition of sales and corresponding receivables until the goods are resold to final customers? A third possibility would be to recognize accounts receivable pursuant to the initial sale to the intermediary, but delay the recognition of revenue until the goods are resold, by crediting a liability account called **deferred or unearned revenue.** The disclosure for Intel in Exhibit 7.8 illustrates this type of recognition along with concerns for how Intel may have used its discretion in estimating amounts to be deferred.

As discussed in Chapter 4, some companies employ a **percentage of completion method** of accounting for long-term contracts with customers to deliver goods or services. This method of accounting requires that the company periodically assess both the costs to complete projects under contract and the prospect of collection of the contract price from customers. Tenfold, a provider of large-scale e-business software applications, uses the percentage of completion method and provides an example that shows the significance of these assessments. From a schedule summarizing changes to its allowance for doubtful accounts from the company's 2000 annual report (see Exhibit 7.9), we see a dramatic increase in the company's allowance for doubtful accounts resulting from such an assessment. During 2000, Tenfold experienced significant delays in completing several major projects and this ultimately resulted in customer dissatisfaction to the point that it was unlikely that Tenfold was going to be able to collect. This had major implications for the value of the company, and the stock price dropped from approximately $55 per share in early April, 2000 to $1.50 per share by year end.

Advancing revenue recognition through percentage of completion may be suitable when a firm expects both collection from the customer and no major uncertainties regarding future costs. However, when these criteria cannot be

Schedule II
TENFOLD CORPORATION
Valuation and Qualifying Accounts
for the Years Ended December 31, 2000,
1999, and 1998 (in thousands)

Allowances for doubtful accounts (billed and unbilled)	Balance at beginning of period	Additions charged to costs and expenses	Deductions*	Balance at end of period
Year ended December 31, 1998	$ 0	$ 500	$ 0	$ 500
Year ended December 31, 1999	$500	$ 763	($ 538)	$ 725
Year ended December 31, 2000	$725	$12,722	($3,160)	$10,287

*Represents write-offs of accounts receivable.

Exhibit 7.9
Disclosure for Tenfold's 10K
Report

THE REAL WORLD

Tenfold Corporation

Academic researchers have documented evidence of investor reactions to the likelihood that new conservative rules concerning revenue recognition might be adopted (Hughes and Ricks, *Journal of Accounting and Economics,* 1984). The reaction has been to decrease stock price if there is a higher likelihood of adoption.

met, the company may delay sales revenue and accompanying cost of sales recognition until it actually receives the cash. For example, firms often sell consumer durable goods, such as appliances, on an installment basis. Under the installment sales method of accounting, the firm defers a portion of the gross profit on the sale and then later recognizes income as it receives payments.

Revenue recognition can prove to be a controversial issue for both firms and analysts, for example, revenue recognition concerning retail land sales. In order to curb what the SEC and AICPA felt at the time were abuses in the form of overly aggressive recognition practices, the latter organization produced an industry guide. The guide caused many retail land sales companies to switch to more conservative accounting methods, such as the installment basis of accounting.

While accounts receivable are typically short-term receivables, various types of businesses generate receivables that are collected over much longer periods of time. The long-term nature of these receivables requires some additional considerations that we explore in the next section.

FINANCING RECEIVABLES

Financing receivables may arise from loans made to customers or other parties outside the firm, or from the reclassification of accounts receivables pursuant to allow a customer a longer repayment period. One form of financing receivables is notes receivables. Notes receivables are commonly interest bearing, meaning that they include provisions for periodic interest payments. If the dates that interest becomes due differ from the company's report date, then the firm makes an entry to accrue the interest earned by the company on the note, but not yet paid by the customer. (Recall such an entry included among the period-end adjustments we made in Chapter 3.) Some firms report this **accrued interest receivable** as an asset in the current assets section of the balance sheet. However, more commonly, firms include accrued interest as part of the balance of the notes themselves. In other words, notes receivables are valued at principal

Exhibit 7.10
ILX Resorts Notes
Receivable Data

THE REAL WORLD

ILX Resorts

| Notes Receivable, net, at 12/31/2000 | $26,619,583 |
| Interest Income for the year ended 12/31/2000 | $ 3,087,403 |

plus accrued interest. For example, Exhibit 7.10 contains excerpts from ILX Resorts' 2000 annual report pertaining to notes receivable. These notes arose from financing provided to customers of ILX Resorts' sales of ownership interests in vacation properties.

A journal entry summarizing the recognition of interest for the year ended December 31, 2000 might appear as follows:

| Notes Receivable | 3,087,403 | |
| Interest Income | | 3,087,403 |

If interest received as cash amounted to $3,000,000, then the entry to reflect this would appear as follows:

| Cash | 3,000,000 | |
| Notes Receivable | | 3,000,000 |

Some manufacturing companies maintain a separate financial services division. For example, General Motors supplies financing for its customers through its subsidiary, General Motors Acceptance Corporation. As Exhibit 7.11 illustrates, the income statement for General Motors presents both revenues and expenses for the company as a whole as well as a breakdown that separates financing and insurance activities from automotive and other activities of a nonfinancial nature.

Exhibit 7.11
Statement of Income
from GM Corporation's
Annual Report

THE REAL WORLD

General Motors
Corporation

Consolidated Statements of Income (Dollars in millions, except per share amounts) Years ended December 31,	2000	1999	1998
General Motors Corporation and Subsidiaries			
Total net sales and revenues	$184,632	$176,558	$155,445
Cost of sales and other expenses	145,664	140,708	127,785
Selling, general, and administrative expenses	22,252	19,053	16,087
Interest expense	9,552	7,750	6,629
Total costs and expenses	177,468	167,511	150,501
Income from continuing operations before income taxes and minority interests	7,164	9,047	4,944
Income tax expense	2,393	3,118	1,636
Equity income/(loss) and minority interests	(319)	(353)	(259)
Income from continuing operations	4,452	5,576	3,049
Income (loss) from discontinued operations	–	426	(93)
Net income	4,452	6,002	2,956

Exhibit 7.11
(Continued)

(Dollars in millions) Years ended December 31, Automotive, Communications Services, and Other Operations	2000	1999	1998
Total net sales and revenues	$160,627	$156,107	$137,161
Cost of sales and other expenses	138,303	134,111	121,491
Selling, general, and administrative expenses	16,246	14,324	11,918
Total costs and expenses	154,549	148,435	133,409
Interest expense	815	828	786
Net expense from transactions with Financing and Insurance Operations (Note 1)	682	308	82
Income from continuing operations before income taxes and minority	4,581	6,536	2,884
Income tax expense	1,443	2,167	1,018
Equity income/(loss) and minority interests	(299)	(327)	(239)
Income from continuing operations	2,839	4,042	1,627
Income (loss) from discontinued operations	—	426	(93)
Net income—Automotive, Communications Services, and Other Operations	$ 2,839	$ 4,468	$ 1,534

(Dollars in millions) Years ended December 31, Financing and Insurance Operations	2000	1999	1998
Total revenues	$ 24,005	$ 20,451	$ 18,284
Interest expense	8,737	6,922	5,843
Depreciation and amortization expense	5,982	5,445	4,920
Operating and other expenses	5,805	4,595	4,067
Provisions for financing and insurance losses	1,580	1,286	1,476
Total costs and expenses	22,104	18,248	16,306
Net income from transactions with Automotive, Communications Services, and Other Operations	(682)	(308)	(82)
Income before income taxes and minority interests	2,583	2,511	2,060
Income tax expense	950	951	618
Equity income/(loss) and minority interests	(20)	(26)	(20)
Net income—Financing and Insurance Operations	$ 1,613	$ 1,534	$ 1,422

In all cases, whether the receivables are short-term or long-term, the firm must wait for some amount of time to collect the cash. In managing the firm's cash position, some firms need to shorten the period of time to collection even further. One method of doing this is to sell the receivables to another company, which is discussed in the next section.

SELLING RECEIVABLES

A firm seeking to raise cash in advance of when it might collect amounts due from customers might sell its receivables to other institutions. Or, a company might sell its receivables because it may prefer not to bear the risk of noncollection or incur the costs of credit management. We refer to sales of receivables as **factoring receivables.**

Receivables may be sold either *with recourse* or *without recourse.* Recourse means that if the party to whom the company sells its receivables cannot collect the amounts due from the customers on their accounts, then the company agrees to be responsible for payment. That is, the company selling the receivables remains contingently liable for payment if the customer defaults. When receivables are sold with recourse, the seller must disclose that fact and the amount of its liability exposure. There are also situations where the sale of receivables with recourse is such that the transaction does not constitute a sale at all but a borrowing that is collateralized by the receivables. In this case, the firm records a liability for the obligation to pay back the factoring company for the loan and then segregates the receivables that the firm uses to repay this loan on its balance sheet.

Recently, another form of selling receivables, **securitization,** has become quite popular. Securitization transactions are those in which a firm sells its receivables to another entity, often through entities known as *trusts.* The selling company often retains some residual ownership interest in the receivables. Typically the entity's assets consist of pools of such receivables, not necessarily limited to receivables from one firm. The entity purchasing the receivables obtains the necessary financing by issuing securities (hence the word securitization) that are either privately placed or sold through public offerings to institutions, such as insurance companies, mutual funds, or even individuals.

The composition of securities sold in this fashion can be quite varied. The face value of receivables held generally exceeds the face value of securities issued, with the difference representing a residual equity interest of the companies selling the receivables. This equity interest may be reported with receivables that have not been sold in the financial statements of those companies. Depending on the nature of the credit risk involved in the securitized receivables, some entities also obtain additional security protection for the investors through a guarantee by a third party.

Pier 1's securitization disclosure provides a useful illustration. The diagram in Exhibit 7.12 helps to illustrate the relationships in the Pier 1 arrangement. In this arrangement, we find no evidence that a Third-Party Guarantor exists, but we have included it in the diagram to illustrate how it might be structured in other such arrangements. However, as we pointed out earlier, many securitizations do

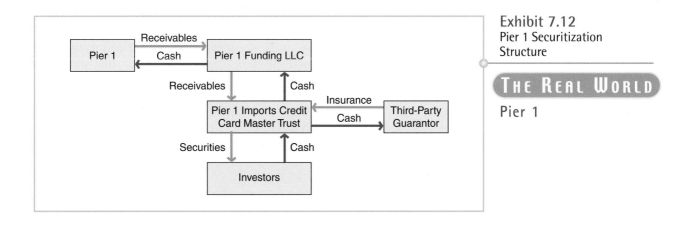

Exhibit 7.12
Pier 1 Securitization
Structure

THE REAL WORLD

Pier 1

Exhibit 7.13
Pier 1 Footnotes

THE REAL WORLD

Pier 1

Securitization

In February 1997, the Company securitized its entire portfolio of proprietary credit card receivables (the "Receivables"). The Company sold all existing Receivables to a special purpose wholly-owned subsidiary, Pier 1 Funding, Inc., predecessor to Pier 1 Funding, LLC ("Funding"), which transferred the Receivables to the Pier 1 Imports Credit Card Master Trust (the "Master Trust"). The Master Trust issues beneficial interests in the Master Trust that represent undivided interests in the assets of the Master Trust consisting of the Receivables and all proceeds of the Receivables. On a daily basis, the Company sells to Funding for transfer to the Master Trust all newly generated Receivables, except those failing certain eligibility criteria, and receives as the purchase price payments of cash (funded from the amount of undistributed principal collections from the Receivables in the Master Trust) and residual interests in the Master Trust. The Company has no obligation to reimburse Funding, the Master Trust, or purchasers of any certificates issued by the Master Trust for credit losses from the Receivables. Funding was capitalized by the Company as a special purpose wholly-owned subsidiary that is subject to certain covenants and restrictions, including a restriction from engaging in any business or activity unrelated to acquiring and selling interests in receivables. Neither Funding nor the Master Trust is consolidated with the Company.

In the initial sale of the Receivables, the Company sold $84.1 million of the Receivables and received $49.6 million in cash and $34.1 million in beneficial interests in the Master Trust. The Master Trust sold to third parties $50.0 million of Series 1997-1 Class A Certificates, which bear interest at 6.74 percent and mature in May 2002. Funding retained $14.1 million of Series 1997-1 Class B Certificates, which are currently non-interest bearing and subordinated to the Class A Certificates. Funding also retained the residual interest in the Master Trust. As of February 26, 2000 and February 27, 1999, the Company had $53.8 million and $41.0 million, respectively, in beneficial interests in the Master Trust. Beginning in October 2001, unless prefunded through a new series of certificates, principal collections of Receivables allocable to Series 1997-1 Certificates will be used to amortize the outstanding balances of the Series 1997-1 Certificates and will not be available to fund the purchase of new receivables being transferred from the Company.

provide some amount of insurance coverage so that the master fund can finance the purchase of receivables at a lower interest rate, as the risk to the investors is less. The footnote disclosure for Pier 1 provides more details about the securitization transaction, as illustrated in Exhibit 7.13.

Agencies such as Moody's or Standard & Poor's sometimes rate trust securities. Regulated holders of trust securities may have to satisfy restrictions with respect to the ratings of the securities they hold. Third-party guarantors may provide insurance to holders of trust securities that enhances their ratings. Appraisals by rating agencies and guarantors may serve to reduce the information asymmetries between the companies that seek to sell their receivables and investors in trust securities. The extent to which they perform this function efficiently could help to explain the emergence of securitization as a means for redistributing the risks and returns associated with receivables.

Accounting for sales and securitization of receivables and other financial assets requires that companies keep financial assets on their books as well as maintain control over the assets. After a transfer of financial assets, such as selling or securitizing accounts receivables, a company must recognize the assets for which it maintains control and any liabilities that it has incurred as a result of the transaction (SFAS No. 140, FASB, 2000). For example, Pier 1's 2003 balance sheet reports as an asset "Beneficial Interest in Securitized Receivables," of $40,538,000.

SUMMARY AND TRANSITION

In this chapter, we focused on accounting for receivables and related issues of revenue recognition. Under GAAP, non-interest–bearing and relatively short-term receivables such as those that arise from sales to customers in the ordinary course of business are valued at net realizable value. Net realizable value is the amount that the firm expects to collect. The allowance method of accounting for uncollectible accounts makes it possible to implement this valuation principle by creating a contra-asset account that is deducted from receivables on the balance sheet, while recognizing a provision for doubtful accounts that is deducted as an expense in determining net income. Similar accounting procedures were described for anticipated sales returns and allowances.

The realization concept that governs revenue recognition requires that we identify the point at which revenue can be said to have been earned. Often this is the point at which delivery of the goods or services has been made. However, in appropriate circumstances, revenue could be recognized in advance of completion of a long-term project for customers or subsequent to delivery or completion. The key judgments are whether performance by the firm and that by the customer are reasonably assured, and the absence of any major uncertainties affecting profits from the sale.

We also considered accounting for financing receivables that bear interest and are relatively long-term in nature. Net realizable values are now expressed in present value terms. Interest on financing receivables is recognized on an accrual basis.

Sometimes firms sell receivables to accelerate the receipt of cash. These sales may be with recourse, in which case the firm remains responsible for payment if the customer from whom receivables are due fails to pay. An increasingly common form of selling receivables is securitization. Securitization involves selling receivables to an entity that specializes in this type of investment.

Financial reporting of receivables and related revenues can be an important determinant of a firm's value. Often receivables comprise a significant portion of a company's assets. A change in accounting principles governing selection of accounting methods in the retail land sales industry provides a useful illustration of the economic consequences that may accompany such events.

END OF CHAPTER MATERIAL

KEY TERMS

Accounts Receivable

Accrued Interest Receivable

Aging of Receivables Method

Allowance for Doubtful Accounts

Allowance Method

Bad Debts

Deferred Revenue

Direct Write-Off Method

Doubtful Accounts

Factoring Receivables

Financing Receivable

Net Realizable Value

Notes Receivable

Percentage of Completion Method

Percentage of Sales Method

Provision for Doubtful Accounts

Sales Allowances

Sales Returns

Securitization

Trade Receivable

Uncollectible Accounts

ASSIGNMENT MATERIAL

○ REVIEW QUESTIONS

1. Briefly describe how accounts receivable meet the criteria of probable future value and ownership to qualify as assets.

2. Describe and compare the direct write-off method and the allowance method for determining bad debt expense. Is one more consistent with GAAP than the other?

3. Explain what factoring of accounts receivable is and what the term recourse means.

4. Explain how accounts and notes receivable differ.

5. Explain what the term securitization means.

6. What events need to be considered in establishing the net realizable value of accounts receivable?

7. Describe the nature of the account called deferred revenue.

○ APPLYING YOUR KNOWLEDGE

8. The trial balance of Peters & Scot, Inc. shows a $50,000 outstanding balance in the accounts receivable account at the end of its first year of operations. During the year, 75 percent of the total credit sales had been collected and no accounts had been charged off as uncollectible. The company estimated that 1.5 percent of the credit sales would be uncollectible. During the following year, the account of James Cordon, who owed $500, was judged uncollectible and was written off. At the end of the year, the amount previously written off was collected in full from Mr. Gordon.

a. Prepare the necessary journal entries to record all of the preceding transactions in the books of Peters & Scot.

b. Determine the amount reported on Peters & Scot's balance sheet to represent net realizable value as of the end of the year.

c. What is the impact on Peters & Scot's reported earnings and the carrying value of accounts receivable if the estimated uncollectible accounts are underestimated?

9. The Sabre Razor Company's accounts receivable show the following balances:

Age of Accounts	Balance Receivable
Not yet due	$500,000
1–30 days past due	300,000
31–60 days past due	100,000
61–90 days past due	50,000
91–120 days past due	10,000

The credit balance in the allowance for uncollectibles account is now $25,000. After a thorough analysis of the collection history, the company estimates that the following percentages of receivables will eventually prove uncollectible:

Age of Accounts	Percent Uncollectible
Not yet due	0.5%
1–30 days past due	2.5%
31–60 days past due	10.0%
61–90 days past due	50.0%
91–120 days past due	90.0%

a. Prepare an aging schedule for the accounts receivable and give the journal entry to record the necessary change in the allowance for uncollectibles.

b. Determine the amount reported on Sabre Razer's balance sheet to represent net realizable value as of the end of the year.

c. What is the impact on Sabre Razer's reported earnings and the carrying value of accounts receivable if the estimated uncollectible accounts are underestimated?

10. On March 1, the Gamma Company receives a note from the Moon Company in settlement of its account. The nine-month, 15 percent note for $10,000 is valued at its face amount. On August 31, the Gamma Company endorses the note to Varian Company to settle an account payable. The note is endorsed with recourse. The note is valued at its face amount, plus accrued interest. On December 7, the Varian Company notifies Gamma Company that the note was honored.

a. Prepare the journal entries for these transactions on:

1. the books of the Gamma Company

2. the books of the Varian Company

b. Would your answers to section a differ if the note from Moon Company was endorsed to Varian company without recourse? Explain.

11. The Ace Company's credit sales during the first year of its operations (20X1) were $925,000. On December 31, 20X1, the accounts receivables had a debit balance of $125,000. The management estimated that 2 percent of all credit sales would probably be uncollectible. The company wrote off accounts worth $5,650 at the end of the first year.

On December 31, 20X2, the unadjusted trial balance showed the following:

	Debit	Credit
Accounts Receivable	138,000	
Allowance for Uncollectibles	6,350	
Credit Sales		1,250,000
Bad Debt Expense		

The company, on advice of its auditor, decided to change its method of accounting for bad debts. It decided to adopt the aging method for estimating uncollectibles and estimated that $28,850 of the accounts receivable may eventually be uncollectible.

a. Give the necessary journal entries, and prepare T-accounts for 20X1 and 20X2.

b. What is the bad debt expense in 20X2? Give the journal entry for recording bad debt expense.

c. Why might the auditor make the recommendation to change from the percentage of sales to the aging method for bad debts?

12. Suppose that a retail company that currently only allows its customers to pay cash or use a credit card decides to offer its customers its own form of credit card. How would this decision be reflected on the company's balance sheet and reported earnings? What would be the primary effects of the implementation of new transactions on the cash flows of the firm? From a shareholder's point of view, do you think this would have a positive or a negative effect on the valuation of the company's stock? Explain the logic of your answer.

USING REAL DATA

13. Use the data in the following table for Hartmarx, Inc. to answer the questions below.

Date	Sales	Accounts Receivable Gross	Allowance Balance	Bad Debt Expense	Write-offs	Additions due to Acquisitions
11/30/2003	561,849	128,382	10,604	4,714	3,094	—
11/30/2002	570,300	135,205	8,984	3,649	4,850	—
11/30/2001	600,200	150,348	10,185	3,688	1,586	463
11/30/2000	680,647	143,121	7,700	1,493	2,362	—
11/30/1999	726,805	153,560	8,639	1,769	1,926	586
11/30/1998	725,002	139,552	8,210			

a. Reconstruct the journal entries made during 2003 to record sales and the related adjustments for bad debts.

b. Calculate the accounts receivable turnover ratios for the most recent five years.

c. Discuss the collection experience of Hartmarx over the last five years and support your conclusions with appropriate data.

14. In its 2003 annual report, American Greetings (a manufacturer of greeting cards) reported sales revenues of $1,995,860. Its fiscal year ends on February 28. The following information was gathered from the quarterly reports of the company:

For the Quarter Ended	Accounts Receivable Balance (in thousands)
11/30/2001	538,546
2/28/2002	288,986
5/31/2002	335,304
8/31/2002	337,817
11/30/2002	513,922
2/28/2003	309,967

a. Calculate the A/R turnover ratio using the accounts receivable balances that would appear on the annual report for the year ended February 28, 2003.

b. Calculate the A/R turnover ratio that would result if American Greetings ended its fiscal year on November 30 rather than February 28. The sales revenue that would have been reported for the year ended November 30, 2002 would have been $2,032,063.

c. Calculate the A/R turnover ratio using the quarterly data to compute an average (rather than just the beginning and end of the year figures).

d. Comment on which of the ratios calculated in parts a through c best represents the turnover of the company and why.

15. Use the data in the financial statements of True North Communications, Inc. to answer the questions that follow.

TRUE NORTH COMMUNICATIONS, INC.
10-K 2000–12–31: Balance Sheet

	12/31/2000	12/31/1999
Current assets:		
Cash and cash equivalents	$ 136,322,000	$ 118,265,000
Short-term investments	0	16,858,000
Marketable securities	180,000	2,076,000
Accounts receivable, net of allowance for doubtful accounts of $20,795 in 2000 and $15,292 in 1999	1,048,793,000	1,020,701,000
Expenditures billable to clients	58,422,000	69,512,000
Other current assets	39,877,000	19,529,000
Total current assets	1,283,594,000	1,246,941,000

	12/31/2000	12/31/1999
Property and equipment:		
Land and buildings	917,000	1,009,000
Leasehold improvements	103,070,000	90,132,000
Furniture and equipment	241,698,000	246,635,000
	345,685,000	337,776,000
Less accumulated depreciation and amortization	(179,609,000)	(180,977,000)
Total property and equipment	166,076,000	156,799,000
Other assets:		
Intangible assets, net of accumulated amortization of $141,592 in 2000 and $117,373 in 1999	458,747,000	443,956,000
Investment in affiliated companies	92,803,000	33,312,000
Other assets	62,070,000	83,145,000
Total other assets	613,620,000	560,413,000
Total assets	$2,063,290,000	1,964,153,000
Liabilities and stockholders' equity		
Current liabilities:		
Accounts payable	$1,160,974,000	$1,034,980,000
Short-term bank borrowings	45,540,000	117,847,000
Income taxes payable	39,117,000	22,642,000
Current portion of long-term debt	11,736,000	9,036,000
Accrued expenses	229,143,000	210,283,000
Total current liabilities	1,486,510,000	1,394,788,000
Noncurrent liabilities:		
Long-term debt	26,730,000	36,632,000
Liability for deferred compensation	75,459,000	67,723,000
Other noncurrent liabilities	69,608,000	139,761,000
Total noncurrent liabilities	171,797,000	244,116,000
Stockholders' equity:		
Preferred stock, $1.00 par value, authorized 100 shares, none issued	0	0
Common stock, 33 1/3 CENTS par value, authorized 90,000 shares, 50,120 issued in 2000 and 48,881 in 1999	16,656,000	16,295,000
Paid-in capital	342,404,000	293,435,000
Retained earnings	69,704,000	37,970,000
Unrealized gain on marketable securities	89,000	1,179,000
Cumulative translation adjustment	(21,017,000)	(20,786,000)
Less treasury stock, at cost: 1 in 2000; 24 in 1999	(35,000)	(983,000)
Less deferred compensation	(2,818,000)	(1,861,000)
Total stockholders' equity	404,983,000	325,249,000
Total liabilities and stockholders' equity	$2,063,290,000	$1,964,153,000

TRUE NORTH COMMUNICATIONS, INC.
10-K 2000-12-31:
Income Statement

	12/31/2000	12/31/1999	12/31/1998
Commissions and fees	$1,556,843,000	$1,439,414,000	$1,274,284,000
Operating expenses:			
Salaries and benefits	914,889,000	871,433,000	806,602,000
Office and general	448,661,000	421,733,000	364,524,000
Restructuring and other charges	16,910,000	75,354,000	3,278,000
Total operating expenses	1,380,460,000	1,368,520,000	1,174,404,000
Operating income	176,383,000	70,894,000	99,880,000
Other income (expense):			
Interest income	5,910,000	7,300,000	6,118,000
Interest expense	(17,211,000)	(18,128,000)	(22,242,000)
Loss on involuntary conversion of affiliate investment	0	0	(12,616,000)
Gains on sales of marketable securities and other	3,454,000	11,172,000	17,810,000
Total other income (expense)	(7,847,000)	344,000	(10,930,000)
Income before taxes, minority interest, and equity income	168,536,000	71,238,000	88,950,000
Provision for income taxes	75,755,000	41,289,000	56,066,000
Income before minority interest and equity income	92,781,000	29,949,000	32,884,000
Minority interest expense	(2,986,000)	(4,161,000)	(4,044,000)
Equity in earnings (loss) of affiliated companies	(28,192,000)	2,434,000	5,427,000
Net income	$ 61,603,000	$ 28,222,000	$ 34,267,000

a. Calculate the accounts receivable turnover ratio for True North.

b. What proportion of total assets is concentrated in the accounts receivable?

c. In a disclosure in the 10-K report, True North indicates that the top ten clients of the company represent 21 percent of the accounts receivable balance. How does this information affect your assessment of the risk of investing in True North?

16. Use the financial statements of Clayton Homes, Inc. to answer the questions that follow.

CLAYTON HOMES, INC. 10-K405 2001-06-30:
Balance Sheet

	06/30/2001	06/30/2000
Assets		
Cash and cash equivalents	$ 47,763,000	$ 43,912,000
Trade receivables	14,683,000	21,796,000
Other receivables, principally installment contracts, net of reserves for credit losses and unamortized discounts of $20,560 in 2001 and $4,217 in 2000	657,224,000	500,942,000
Residual interests in installment contract and mortgage receivables	170,122,000	150,329,000
Inventories, net	185,695,000	222,431,000
Securities available-for-sale	30,956,000	47,734,000

	06/30/2001	06/30/2000
Restricted cash	111,060,000	96,904,000
Property, plant, and equipment, net	309,438,000	305,479,000
Deferred income taxes	22,710,000	24,284,000
Other assets	104,519,000	92,567,000
Total assets	$1,654,170,000	$1,506,378,000
Liabilities and shareholders' equity		
Accounts payable and accrued liabilities	$ 118,057,000	$ 122,760,000
Debt obligations	141,862,000	99,216,000
Other liabilities	246,773,000	248,027,000
Total liabilities	506,692,000	470,003,000
Shareholders' equity		
Preferred stock, $.10 par value, authorized 1,000 shares, none issued	0	0
Common stock, $.10 par value, authorized 200,000 shares, issued 137,991 at June 30, 2001, and 137,499 at June 30, 2000	13,799,000	13,750,000
Additional paid-in capital	43,593,000	39,500,000
Retained earnings	1,081,137,000	983,806,000
Accumulated other comprehensive income (loss)	8,949,000	(681,000)
Total shareholders' equity	1,147,478,000	1,036,375,000
Total liabilities and shareholders' equity	$1,654,170,000	$1,506,378,000

CLAYTON HOMES, INC. 10-K405 2001-06-30:
Income Statement

	06/30/2001	06/30/2000	06/30/1999
Revenues			
Net sales	$849,157,000	$993,916,000	$1,040,668,000
Financial services	227,916,000	228,642,000	233,848,000
Rental and other income	73,883,000	70,787,000	69,767,000
	1,150,956,000	1,293,345,000	1,344,283,000
Costs and expenses			
Cost of sales	562,267,000	660,429,000	705,128,000
Selling, general, and administrative	374,628,000	384,067,000	367,430,000
Financial services interest	706,000	1,032,000	7,981,000
Provision for credit losses	42,500,000	20,800,000	12,459,000
	980,101,000	1,066,328,000	1,092,998,000
Operating income	170,855,000	227,017,000	251,285,000
Interest expense	(5,561,000)	(5,749,000)	(11,995,000)
Interest revenue/other	4,057,000	7,357,000	6,678,000
Income before income taxes	169,351,000	228,625,000	245,968,000
Provision for income taxes	(62,700,000)	(84,600,000)	(91,000,000)
Net income	$106,651,000	$144,025,000	$154,968,000

CLAYTON HOMES, INC. 10-K405 2001-06-30:
Cash Flow

	06/30/2001	06/30/2000	06/30/1999
Cash flows from operating activities			
Net income	$106,651,000	$144,025,000	$154,968,000
Adjustments to reconcile net income to net cash provided by operating activities			
Depreciation and amortization	20,600,000	20,422,000	17,795,000
Amortization of residual interests, net of gain on sale	14,205,000	3,256,000	(15,089,000)
Provision for credit losses	42,500,000	20,800,000	12,459,000
Realized loss on securities available-for-sale	488,000	1,218,000	0
Deferred income taxes	(4,082,000)	(3,861,000)	(8,267,000)
Decrease (increase) in other receivables, net	1,200,000	5,720,000	(93,014,000)
Decrease (increase) in inventories	36,736,000	(37,987,000)	(17,331,000)
Increase (decrease) in accounts payable, accrued liabilities, and other	(55,766,000)	(60,184,000)	14,631,000
Cash provided by operations	162,532,000	93,409,000	66,152,000
Origination of installment contract receivables	(815,546,000)	(983,090,000)	(1,085,484,000)
Proceeds from sales of originated installment contract receivables	660,802,000	886,040,000	1,030,442,000
Principal collected on originated installment contract receivables	40,686,000	48,040,000	80,610,000
Net cash provided by operating activities	48,474,000	44,399,000	91,720,000
Cash flows from investing activities			
Acquisition of installment contract receivables	(321,711,000)	(206,154,000)	(253,625,000)
Proceeds from sales of acquired installment contract receivables	225,654,000	229,412,000	389,866,000
Principal collected on acquired installment contract receivables	23,154,000	19,836,000	73,200,000
Proceeds from sales of securities available-for-sale	29,527,000	37,733,000	0
Acquisition of property, plant, and equipment	(24,559,000)	(34,398,000)	(47,749,000)
Decrease (increase) in restricted cash	(14,156,000)	3,223,000	(13,951,000)
Net cash provided by (used in) investing activities	(82,091,000)	49,652,000	147,741,000
Cash flows from financing activities			
Dividends	(9,320,000)	(9,335,000)	(9,606,000)
Net borrowings (repayment) on credit facilities	45,800,000	0	(227,873,000)
Proceeds from (repayment of) long-term debt	(3,154,000)	2,739,000	76,759,000
Issuance of stock for incentive plans and other	4,624,000	3,553,000	3,602,000
Repurchase of common stock	(482,000)	(49,776,000)	(81,394,000)
Net cash provided by (used in) financing activities	37,468,000	(52,819,000)	(238,512,000)
Net increase in cash and cash equivalents	3,851,000	41,232,000	949,000
Cash and cash equivalents at beginning of year	43,912,000	2,680,000	1,731,000
Cash and cash equivalents at end of year	$ 47,763,000	$ 43,912,000	$2,680,000
Supplemental disclosures for cash flow information			
Cash paid during the year for interest	$ 6,267,000	$ 6,781,000	$ 19,976,000
Income taxes	$ 76,723,000	$ 97,903,000	$ 95,931,000

a. When Clayton sells a home, it provides a certain amount of financing that is represented by the "other receivables" line on its balance sheet. It estimates credit losses on these long-term receivables. Given the information in the statements, recreate the entries made to record the credit losses and the reserve during 2001.

b. Clayton also securitizes some of its installment receivables and sells them to a special purpose entity. It retains a certain amount of ownership interest in these receivables in the line item called "residual interests." It recognizes income from the receivables in the line item called "financial services." What proportion of the firm's revenues come from this activity? How does this income compare to the investment in receivables?

c. How have credit losses changed relative to revenues over the last three years?

d. How does net income compare to cash from operations? There are two line items that refer to cash from operations. Explain what the difference between these two items represents.

● BEYOND THE BOOK

17. Choose a company as directed by your instructor and answer the following questions:

a. Prepare a quick analysis of the accounts receivable (gross) and the allowance for doubtful accounts by listing the beginning and ending amounts in these accounts and calculating the net change in both dollar and percentage terms for the most recent year.

b. Compute the following ratios for the most recent two years:

- Bad debt expense divided by net sales
- Allowance for doubtful accounts divided by gross accounts receivable
- Accounts receivable turnover (in times and days)

Comment on both the reasonableness of these ratios and on any significant changes in these ratios.

CHAPTER **8**

Valuing Inventories

LEARNING OBJECTIVES

After reading this chapter you should be able to:

1 Explain how merchandising and manufacturing companies value inventory and determine costs of goods sold.

2 Understand the periodic and perpetual methods for recording inventory transactions.

3 Recognize the implications of alternative inventory costing methods for income measurement, cash flows, and asset valuation.

4 Read and interpret inventory footnote disclosures.

During the first quarter of 2001, Cisco Systems (the dominant U.S. data networking company) announced inventory changes that totaled $4.1 billion. Cisco wrote down an astonishing $2.5 billion worth of parts, a sum equal to the inventory the company was carrying at the end of 2000. On top of that, Cisco expected inventory at the end of the current quarter to be higher by $1.6 billion. As the following graph indicates, the market reacted unfavorably to Cisco's disclosure. From the end of December 2000 through the first quarter of 2001 the company lost almost 70 percent of its market value.

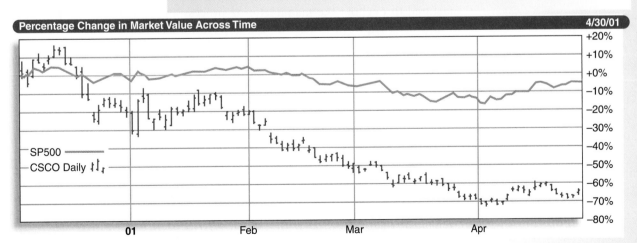

Percentage Change in Market Value Across Time — 4/30/01

As is evident from Cisco's situation, inventory valuation plays an important role in assessing a firm's performance. **Inventories** represent costs of goods awaiting sale to customers, or further processing prior to being offered for sale. The manner in which companies determine inventory costs, the behavior of market prices for inventory replacement or subsequent sale, and the management of inventory levels can significantly affect asset values and net income.

From an accrual accounting standpoint, inventories are costs to be recognized in future periods, when they can be matched with revenues. In this chapter, our treatment of inventories includes describing various methods of valuing inventories, procedures for recording changes in inventories, tax implications of accounting methods chosen, and effects of management decisions regarding inventory on asset values and income. Let's begin by discussing what inventory is and what it costs.

MERCHANDISE AND MANUFACTURING INVENTORIES

Wholesale and retail companies generally purchase inventory in a form that is ready for sale. For example, the retail company Limited Brands' inventory includes clothing items offered for sale by its different retail outlets (e.g., Express, Lerner, Limited Stores, Structure, and Victoria's Secret). On the balance sheet, retailers such as Limited Brands report a single line item for its inventories.

The companies that furnish inventory to Limited Brands are manufacturing companies. Manufacturing companies make inventories for sale using materials, labor, and other production costs. For example, Levi Strauss makes clothing that Limited Brands buys. As illustrated in Exhibit 8.1, its inventory consists of raw materials, work-in-process, and finished goods. **Raw materials inventory** represents goods purchased from outside that have not yet entered the manufacturing process. **Work-in-process inventory** is inventory that is partially manufactured, but not yet complete. The inventory that a firm sells to its customers is the **finished goods inventory.**

Inventory costing for a manufacturing company is more complex than for a wholesale or retail company because a firm must track the costs of goods manufactured throughout the manufacturing process and assign costs to the goods as they are completed. Let's take a closer look at inventory costs.

Exhibit 8.1
From the Balance Sheet of
Levi Strauss

THE REAL WORLD

Levi Strauss &
Company

	11/24/2001	11/25/2002
Inventories:		
Raw materials	98,987	97,261
Work-in-process	74,048	50,499
Finished goods	418,679	462,417
Total inventories	591,714	610,177

Exhibit 8.2
Inventory Cost Flows in a
Manufacturing Environment

Cost of Goods Sold

Beginning Inventory Finished Goods

+ Cost of Goods Manufactured

− Ending Inventory Finished Goods

= Cost of Goods Sold

Cost of Goods Manufactured

Beginning Inventory Work-in-Process

+ Direct Labor Costs Incurred

+ Direct Material Applied to Production

+ Factory Overhead Costs Incurred

− Ending Inventory Work-in-Process

= Cost of Goods Manufactured

INVENTORY COSTS

For a merchandising company, inventory costs include the purchase price plus any shipping costs, packaging costs, and other costs necessary to get the inventory ready for sale. For a manufacturing company, however, determining costs for goods in process, or completed and available for sale, is more involved.

Inventory costs for a manufacturing firm (see Exhibit 8.2) include raw materials used; the cost of labor applied in the production process, referred to as *direct labor;* and factory overhead costs. Factory overhead costs include labor that is related to manufacturing but not directly traceable to a product (such as a factory foreman or custodial staff), and various manufacturing costs such as tools, utility consumed, and an allocation of the cost of the manufacturing facility (depreciation).

All costs that relate directly or indirectly to manufacturing the product, including raw materials, direct labor, and factory overhead, are considered **product costs.** This means that these costs are capitalized as part of the cost of inventory until the finished goods are sold.

All manufactured goods contain some costs that will not vary with the level of production, such as some labor costs or equipment depreciation, referred to as **fixed costs.** As a result of fixed costs, the cost per unit of product will vary if the level of production varies. That is, fixed costs allocated to products make the cost per unit lower (higher) as production rises (falls). For example, assume a factory has a manufacturing capacity of 20 million units of product, and incurs fixed factory overhead costs of $40 million. If the plant operates at capacity, the fixed cost allocated per unit is $2 ($40/20). However, if the plant produces only 15 million units, the fixed cost allocated per unit will be $2.67 ($40/15).

This feature of manufacturing firms has implications for earnings management. Suppose that the company expects that customer demand will allow for the sale of only 15 million units. Management may therefore choose to manufacture more products than they can sell to reduce the per-unit cost that must be charged for each unit of product sold and thereby increase reported profits. Careful reading of the financial statements may reveal if this has occurred, as such a practice will lead to increasing inventory balances relative to the level of sales (i.e., a decline in the inventory turnover ratio).

INVENTORY-LEVEL MANAGEMENT

Companies seek to make a profit by selling inventory at an amount that exceeds the cost paid to acquire or manufacture the inventory. For example, various manufacturing companies sell inventory to Limited Brands at an amount in excess of what it costs them to manufacture the inventory. In turn, Limited Brands then sells the goods to consumers at a higher amount than it paid for those goods. As suggested by the news release for Cisco, careful inventory management is critical in determining a company's profitability. Inventory does not make money while it is sitting in stores or factories. Businesses must have enough inventory to meet current demands of customers, but not so much that the company ties up funds in inventory that might otherwise be more profitably employed in other investments.

VALUING INVENTORY

A firm initially records inventory as an asset on the balance sheet at its *acquisition cost.* However, GAAP requires that a firm *value* its inventory at **lower of cost or market.** This means that if inventory declines in value so that it cannot be sold at or above its acquisition cost, then it must be written down (i.e., the cost must be removed from inventory) and a corresponding loss recognized in the determination of net income. GAAP states that market value should be the **replacement cost** unless the estimated proceeds from the sale of the inventory, or **net realizable value,** is less than replacement cost. In that case, inventory must be written down to net realizable value.

To illustrate the application of the lower of cost or market requirement, assume that Limited Brands has a large stock of sweaters in various stores, costing a total of $43 million. Assume that the $43 million approximates the replacement cost of the sweaters to Limited Brands. However, the firm hopes to sell the sweaters for a retail price of $86 million. At the end of the year, management determines that the amount that can be realized on the sale of the sweaters is only $30 million. At the time that management makes this determination, the company must then record a loss of $13 million ($43–30) and mark the inventory down to $30 million. Note that the firm cannot consider the original retail price ($86 million) in determining the loss. This is because accounting conservatism requires that Limited Brands not recognize the income from the sale of the sweaters until the sweaters are actually sold. The decline in value must be recognized when it occurs.

Apart from how to apply the lower of cost or market rule, there is the matter of assessing when a writedown might be necessary. Exhibit 8.3 describes a similar approach taken by Chico's to assess the need to write down its inventories.

In general, the lower of cost or market rule is applied to groups or pools of inventory items rather than on an item by item basis. Some companies provide more detailed disclosures explaining the application of the lower of cost or market rule, but this is not typical.

Exhibit 8.3
Chico's FAS, Inc. and
Subsidiaries, 2001 Annual
Report

THE REAL WORLD

Chico's

1. Business Organization and Significant Accounting Policies: Inventory Valuation

The company identifies potentially excess and slow-moving inventory by evaluating turn rates and inventory levels in conjunction with the Company's overall growth rate. Excess quantities are identified through evaluation of inventory agings, review of inventory and historical sales experiences, as well as specific identification based on fashion trends. Further, exposure to inadequate realization of carrying value is identified through analysis of gross margins and markdowns in combination with changes in the fashion industry.

This disclosure indicates that the company takes a systematic approach to evaluating its inventory values and recognizing write-downs on a timely basis.

ACCOUNTING FOR INVENTORY

Inventory, whether merchandise for resale or manufactured goods, remains as an asset until sold. At this point, the company recognizes revenue for the sales price of the inventory and an expense (cost of good sold) for the cost of inventory sold, as shown in Exhibit 8.4.

What happens, though, when companies sell products with the right to return the product? According to GAAP, revenue and related cost of goods sold should not be recognized when right of return exists unless returns can be reasonably estimated. When analyzing the earnings of a company that offer customers the right of return, the analyst must therefore estimate the probability that transfers of goods will actually take place and result in bona fide sales (and hence, produce earnings).

Further, some companies experience inventory shrinkage due to theft, lost items, or waste. Periodic physical inspections and counts serve to reveal inventory shrinkage, prompting the company to recognize losses in inventory that affect income. Physical counts allow the company to match the inventory on hand with the inventory records to determine the shrinkage that may have occurred. Chico's, in its 2001 annual report, discusses its estimation of inventory shrinkage:

> The company estimates its expected shrinkage of inventory between physical counts by assessing the chain-wide average shrinkage experience rate, applied to the related periods' sales value. Such assessments are updated on an annual basis to reflect the most recent physical inventory shrinkage experience rates.

Some companies have shipped unordered goods or goods on consignment to customers and reported these shipments as sales revenue to help managers achieve profit goals. This practice, called channel stuffing, not only overstates sales but also misreports cost of sales and inventory.

Exhibit 8.4
Excerpt from Limited Brands'
2001 Income Statement

THE REAL WORLD

Limited Brands

Limited Brands, Inc. Consolidated Statements of Income (in millions)			
	2001	2000	1999
Net sales	$9,363	$10,105	$9,766
Cost of goods sold, buying, and occupancy	($6,110)	($6,668)	($6,443)
Gross income	$3,253	$ 3,437	$3,323

Exhibit 8.5
Rite-Aid 10-K (Restated) 2000

THE REAL WORLD

Rite-Aid

> **Inventory/Cost of Goods Sold**
>
> The restated financial statements reflect adjustments to inventory and cost of goods sold related primarily to reversals of unearned vendor allowances previously recorded as a reduction to cost of goods sold, to correctly apply the retail method of accounting, record write-downs for slow moving and obsolete inventory, recognize certain selling costs including promotional markdowns and shrink in the period in which they were incurred, accrue for inventory cut-off, and to reflect unearned vendor allowances in the inventory balances.
>
> Rite Aid was required to restate its financial statements for 1998 through 2000 due to a number of accounting errors. The effect of the restatement was that earnings for this period were reduced by $1.6 billion.

The magnitude of inventories and the potential effects of shifting costs between costs of goods sold and inventories may, in some cases, result in management misuse of the discretion available in estimating components of cost of goods sold to intentionally misrepresent earnings. Without the auditors help, this kind of activity is very difficult to detect from reported financial data. Auditors play a significant role in trying to detect this kind of potentially fraudulent activity. Exhibit 8.5 shows the disclosure that Rite-Aid made when it was required to restate its financial statements in 2000.

Now that you have a good sense of what constitutes inventory and cost of goods sold, let's review how firms record and track these items.

INVENTORY RECORDING PROCEDURES

Firms can follow two broad approaches for allocating costs between inventory and cost of goods sold: the **periodic method** and the **perpetual method.** The former defers the determination of this allocation until the end of the accounting period, while the latter allocates costs as sales are made during the course of the period.

PERIODIC METHOD

For the periodic method, firms use the following equation to determine the cost of inventory sold:

> Beginning Inventory + Purchases of Inventory − Ending Inventory
> = Cost of Goods Sold

This method seems very straightforward and if costs are known, it is. Firms simply track purchases in the accounting system but not the costs of units sold. Instead, firms periodically take a physical count of inventory, and then determine cost of goods sold for the period by subtracting the cost of ending inventory from the cost of beginning inventory plus purchases.

As such, the periodic system is low cost and easy to implement. However, it has some distinct disadvantages. First, it does not provide an ongoing record of items that have been sold. As a result, reordering must be triggered by physical observation of inventory levels. This can lead to lost sales if insufficient inventory is on hand. Second, a periodic inventory system does not provide a direct measure of the distinction between goods sold and goods stolen or lost. Firms must therefore estimate stolen goods by comparing the actual gross profit on sales to that anticipated, given the level of sales.

At one time, almost all companies used a periodic inventory system because of the high cost of tracking actual units sold. However, technological advances (e.g., barcode scanning equipment) have greatly lowered the cost of tracking inventory, allowing more firms to switch to the perpetual method.

PERPETUAL METHOD

Today, even many small businesses use a barcode system that tracks and even automatically reorders inventory as it is sold. Such systems track both the physical units sold and the cost assigned to the unit. As a result, many companies have the ability to know immediately the gross profit earned as sales are generated.

Under the perpetual method, firms make an accounting entry to record the transfer of costs from inventories to cost of goods sold as sales are made. This procedure makes it possible to know the status of inventories without needing a physical count. However, firms still need to perform a physical count to measure inventory shrinkage (e.g., due to theft) and otherwise maintain internal control.

Regardless of whether a company uses a periodic or perpetual method of determining cost of goods sold, the company must assign a particular unit cost to each sale. Sometimes the cost of a particular item is easily known; for instance, when a car is sold, the dealer has a specific invoice detailing the cost of the car. Other cases, however, prove more difficult. For example, think of a grocery store that sells a large variety of items that are purchased at different times with different costs. In these cases, a company must typically make an assumption about how to assign the unit costs to its inventory (cost flow). We'll review these cost flow assumptions next.

INVENTORY COST FLOW ASSUMPTIONS

U.S. companies use four common inventory cost flow methods, each of which can be applied on either a periodic or perpetual basis: (1) **first-in, first-out (FIFO)**; (2) **last-in, first-out (LIFO)**; (3) **weighted average**; and (4) **specific identification.** If all units are the same and there are no cost changes, then all inventory methods will result in identical costs. However, when costs change, different inventory methods result in different costs and different balance sheet carrying amounts for inventory.

FIRST-IN, FIRST-OUT

The FIFO inventory method usually most closely follows the physical flow of goods, assuming that a company sells the units in the order in which it purchased them. Costs of inventory purchased first are assumed to be the first costs charged to cost of goods sold. Thus, the inventory on the balance sheet

Exhibit 8.6
FIFO Inventory Flow

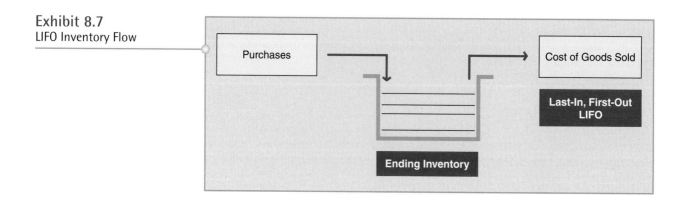

represents the cost of the most recent inventory purchased that has not yet been sold. Limited Brands uses FIFO. One way to envision this flow is to think of inventory as entering a pipeline as shown in Exhibit 8.6. As new items are added, they push other items ahead in the pipeline and when units are sold, they are removed from the opposite end of the pipeline.

LAST-IN, FIRST-OUT

Firms using the LIFO method of inventory charge costs in reverse order of acquisition. That is, firms charge the most recent costs to cost of goods sold. Inventory on the balance sheet thus represents the cost of the earliest inventory purchased. In reality, this physically seldom occurs, as most companies rotate stock and try to sell older items first. Why, then, do firms use LIFO? The primary motivation for using LIFO reflects tax considerations.

Under LIFO, the most recent unit costs go first to the income statement. If prices rise, charging the more recent costs to costs of goods sold results in lower operating income and, hence, lower taxes. Note, however, that if inventory levels decrease after several years of using LIFO to value inventories, then old costs would be assigned to goods sold, thereby reversing the tax benefits of LIFO.

The diagram in Exhibit 8.7 illustrates how LIFO works. The concept is that inventory acts like a bucket in that purchases are added on top of the bucket and when a unit is sold its cost is picked off the top of the pile in the bucket to end up in cost of goods sold. Note that Exhibits 8.6 and 8.7 refer to *cost* flows, not to the physical flow of goods. Regardless of the cost flow assumption, the physical flow of goods normally follows a FIFO pattern.

Exhibit 8.7
LIFO Inventory Flow

Exhibit 8.8
Sherwin-Williams Company,
2001 Annual Report
Note 3—Inventories

Inventories are stated at lower of cost or market with cost determined primarily on the last-in, first-out (LIFO) method, which provides a better matching of costs and revenues. The following presents the effect on inventories, net income, and net income per share had the company used the first-in, first-out (FIFO) inventory valuation method adjusted for income taxes at the statutory rates and assuming no other adjustments. This information is presented to enable the reader to make comparisons with companies using the FIFO method of inventory valuation.

	2001	2000	1999
Percentage of total inventories on LIFO	88%	89%	90%
Excess of FIFO over LIFO	$112,669	$110,124	$97,953
Decrease in net income due to LIFO	(1,567)	(7,916)	(894)
Decrease in net income per share due to LIFO	(.01)	(.05)	(.01)

THE REAL WORLD

Sherwin-Williams
Company

When Congress allowed the use of LIFO, it also implemented a rule known as the LIFO conformity rule. This rule dictates that if a firm uses LIFO for tax reporting, then it also must use LIFO for financial reporting. The LIFO conformity rule represents a rare instance of federal tax law dictating financial reporting practices.

The financial accounting rationale for LIFO contends that LIFO achieves a better matching of current costs with current revenues, and hence a more accurate picture of continuing profit margins. However, because LIFO charges the most recent costs to cost of goods sold, amounts reported as inventory on the balance sheet represent old unit costs. Over a period of time, the gap between the costs at which a firm carries inventory on the balance sheet and the replacement cost of the inventory can become very large if prices change significantly. In recognition of this, GAAP requires that companies that use LIFO provide footnote disclosure regarding the current cost of inventories. This footnote allows users to determine the effect on assets, cost of goods sold, and earnings of using LIFO rather than current costs. Exhibit 8.8 provides an illustration of this type of disclosure for Sherwin-Williams.

Sherwin-Williams goes further than the GAAP requirement and shows the earnings impact as well as the difference in inventories from using LIFO. Note also that Sherwin-Williams does not use LIFO for all of its inventories. Companies can use multiple cost flow assumptions depending on the nature of their inventories. Finally, note that many companies provide much less detailed disclosures than Sherwin-Williams.

WEIGHTED AVERAGE

The weighted average inventory method uses average costs for both balance sheet inventories and cost of goods sold. The weighted average method is often

THINKING GLOBALLY

The LIFO inventory method is predominantly a U.S. phenomenon and is not allowed in most other countries. Therefore, a U.S.-based company that has foreign subsidiaries is likely to have multiple inventory flow assumptions reported in its financial statements. The typical situation would be for the company to reports its U.S. inventories using LIFO and its foreign inventories using FIFO or average costing.

Accounting Policies

c) Inventory

Inventory, which is primarily electronic fuel management systems and related components, is valued at the lower of cost, determined on a weighted average basis, and net realizable value. Inventory is classified as a current asset because management anticipates using it in a normal business cycle.

During the year ended December 31, 2001, the company's provision for inventory write-down related primarily to the discontinuance of a product line. Inventory related to early versions of the "Eagle" dual fuel engine management system was written off to reflect obsolescence in the technology and a commercial market for this product not materializing.

 Note also that AFS wrote off inventory that declined in value. This write-down was reported as a separate expense line in the income statement. The materiality concept dictates that small write-downs of inventory may be considered to be part of cost of goods sold, but major write-downs should be separately disclosed.

used for firms that have large numbers of low-cost items where it is not really worth it to keep track of individual units of inventory. The financial effects of this method fall in between the effects of LIFO and FIFO. The lower of cost or market rule applies for weighted average inventories as well as for FIFO and LIFO. The disclosure in Exhibit 8.9 illustrates the use of the weighted average method for Alternative Fuel Systems.

SPECIFIC IDENTIFICATION

Firms using specific identification track the cost of specific units of inventory sold. Firms generally use this method only with either very expensive or unique inventory items. For example, First Cash Financial Services operates pawn stores which have unique items in inventory. As part of its business, it sells specific items of inventory that it acquired through its pawn business when the customer defaults or fails to return to claim the item. In this case, using the specific identification method is feasible because First Cash can identify the specific cost of the item in inventory and there is no need to make an assumption about cost flow. A car dealership would be an example of a type of company that also uses the specific identification method. In this case, each item in inventory is very expensive and the dealership may use the invoice price of the car or truck to negotiate a price with the buyer.

ILLUSTRATION OF COST FLOW ASSUMPTIONS

Let's now return to our hypothetical example, BHT (used in previous chapters), to illustrate the differences in methods and resulting costs depending on the choice of inventory method. Recall that BHT is a wholesale supplier of pharmaceuticals and medical supplies. BHT buys from pharmaceutical and manufacturing companies, and then resells the supplies to hospitals, drug stores, and other health care providers.

Exhibit 8.10
BHT's Inventory

Date	Explanation	Units (100 Tablets/Unit)	Cost/Unit
01/01/20X1	Beginning Inventory	900	$610
02/05/20X1	Sell 500 units	(500)	
03/15/20X1	Purchase 500 Units	500	$624
04/21/20X1	Sell 600 units	(600)	
06/25/20X1	Purchase 700 units	700	$650
08/26/20X1	Sell 600 units	(600)	
10/27/20X1	Purchase 600 units	600	$660
12/31/20X1	Ending Inventory	1,000	

For simplicity, let's assume that BHT prices its inventory equally at the beginning of the period (20X1) for all inventory methods. As a further simplification, let's focus on only one BHT product. Exhibit 8.10 shows BHT's inventory of 500-mg Levaquin Tablets for 20X1 (Levaquin is an anti-infective drug produced by Ortho-McNeil Pharmaceutical).

The cost assigned to the units sold depends on the cost flow assumption used as well as whether BHT tracks the inventory on a periodic or a perpetual basis. Let's begin by assuming that BHT tracks its inventory using a periodic system, and determine costs using the three main costing methods.

PERIODIC INVENTORY COMPUTATIONS

Recall that firms using the periodic method do not track individual units sold at the time of sale. Instead, a firm determines the amount of inventory sold at the end of an accounting period by physically counting inventory on hand at that time.

Periodic FIFO

In order to determine the cost of units sold, we must first determine how many units were sold. We can see that BHT sold 1,700 units during the year (500 + 600 + 600), with 900 units in beginning inventory and 1,000 units in ending inventory.

Under the FIFO method, recall that the first inventory acquired is the first sold. Therefore:

Periodic FIFO cost of goods sold is:

$$900 \times \$610 + 500 \times \$624 + 300 \times \$650 = \$1,056,000$$

Periodic FIFO ending inventory is:

$$400 \times \$650 + 600 \times \$660 = \$656,000$$

Periodic LIFO

In the case of LIFO, the most recently purchased inventory is the first charged to cost of goods sold. When using periodic LIFO, the specific time of purchase is not considered. Instead, the most recently purchased units are assumed sold, regardless of the actual time of the acquisition. Therefore:

Periodic LIFO cost of goods sold is:

$$600 \times \$660 + 700 \times \$650 + 400 \times \$624 = \$1,100,600$$

Periodic LIFO ending inventory is:

$$900 \times \$610 + 100 \times \$624 = \$611,400$$

Periodic Weighted Average

For the weighted average method, we calculate the average cost of inventory and then use this cost to determine both cost of goods sold and ending inventory. We determine the average cost of inventory for Levaquin as follows:

Total cost of inventory on hand plus inventory purchased:

$$900 \times \$610 + 500 \times \$624 + 700 \times \$650 + 600 \times \$660 = \$1,712,000$$

Total units on hand plus units acquired:

$$900 + 500 + 700 + 600 = 2,700 \text{ units}$$

Average cost/unit = $1,712,000/2,700 = $634.0741

We can now compute the cost of goods sold and inventory (note that we have extended the computation of the unit cost to four decimal places in order to avoid rounding errors in the dollar amount of the ending inventory and cost of goods sold):

Periodic weighted average cost of good sold is:

$$1,700 \times \$634.0741 = \$1,077,926$$

Periodic weighted average ending inventory is:

$$1,000 \times \$634.0741 = \$634,074$$

PERPETUAL INVENTORY COMPUTATIONS

Using the perpetual method to track costs is a bit more complex. Perpetual LIFO requires tracking of the timing of purchases and sales. Similarly, weighted average requires computation of a moving average cost that depends on the inventory on hand at the time of sale. Let's look at these computations in more detail.

Perpetual FIFO

FIFO results remain the same whether using a perpetual or periodic system. Because FIFO assumes that the oldest units on hand are the next sold, the timing does not affect cost of sales computations. Therefore, the FIFO perpetual calculations are the same as the FIFO periodic ones shown previously.

Perpetual LIFO

For perpetual LIFO, we must determine cost of goods sold at the time of each sale using the inventory on hand. For BHT, the computations would be as follows:

2/05/20X1 sale of 500 units:

$$\text{Cost of goods sold: } 500 \times \$610 = \$305,000$$

4/21/20X1 sale of 600 units:

$$
\begin{array}{rl}
\text{Cost of goods sold: } 500 \times \$624 = & \$312,000 \\
100 \times \$610 = & \underline{61,000} \\
& \$373,000
\end{array}
$$

8/26/20X1 sale of 600 units:

$$\text{Cost of goods sold } 600 \times \$650 = \$390,000$$

Therefore:

Perpetual LIFO cost of goods sold is:

$$\$305,000 + \$373,000 + \$390,000 = \$1,068,000$$

Perpetual LIFO ending inventory is:

$$300 \times \$610 + 100 \times \$650 + 600 \times \$660 = \$644,000$$

Perpetual Weighted Average

As with perpetual LIFO, we must determine cost as inventory is sold. After each purchase, we must therefore recalculate the weighted average cost (WAC) as follows:

2/05/20X1 sale of 500 units:

$$
\begin{array}{l}
\text{WAC} = \$610 \\
\text{Cost of goods sold} = 500 \times \$610 = \$305,000
\end{array}
$$

4/21/20X1 sale of 600 units:

$$
\begin{array}{l}
\text{WAC} = (400 \times \$610 + 500 \times \$624)/900 = \$556,000/900 = \$617.7778 \\
\text{Cost of goods sold} = 600 \times \$617.7778 = \$370,667.
\end{array}
$$

8/26/20X1 sale of 600 units:

> WAC = (300 × \$617.7778 + 700 × \$650)/1000 = \$640,334/1000 = \$640.3333.
> Cost of goods sold = 600 × \$640.3333 = \$384,200.

Therefore:

Perpetual weighted average cost of sales is:

> \$305,000 + \$370,667 + \$384,200 = \$1,059,867.

Perpetual weighted average ending inventory is:

> WAC = (400 × \$640.33 + 600 × \$660)/1000 = \$652,132/1000 = \$652.1333.
> Ending Inventory = 1,000 × \$652.132 = \$652,133

COMPARISON OF INVENTORY METHODS

Exhibit 8.11 summarizes the results of the computations for FIFO, LIFO, and weighted average using the periodic and perpetual methods. Because of rising prices and inventory levels, LIFO resulted in the highest cost of goods sold and the lowest ending inventory. (With falling prices, LIFO results in the lowest cost of goods sold and the highest ending inventory.) Using the perpetual method produces a lower cost of goods sold for both LIFO and weighted average than the periodic methods (due to rising prices). Finally, note that weighted average produces results between LIFO and FIFO using either the periodic or perpetual methods.

INVENTORY METHOD CHOICES AND FIRM VALUE

As Exhibit 8.11 illustrates, management's choice of inventory methods can significantly affect both cost of sales and the balance sheet value of inventory. These differences affect key ratios such as the gross profit ratio, the taxes paid, and the reported earnings. Clearly, inventory method choice impacts firm valuation.

Exhibit 8.11
Inventory Method
Comparison

Method	Cost of Goods Sold	Ending Inventory
Periodic		
FIFO	\$1,056,000	\$656,000
LIFO	1,100,000	611,400
Weighted Average	1,077,926	634,074
Perpetual		
FIFO	1,056,000	656,000
LIFO	1,068,000	644,000
Weighted Average	1,059,867	652,133

How, then, do firms select which inventory method to use? Some of the factors that can influence management's choice of inventory methods follow:

○ *Taxes* The primary motive for using LIFO is to lower or at least postpone payment of taxes. As the example from Sherwin-Williams indicates, LIFO can result in substantial tax savings.

○ *Industry practice* Many companies choose to follow the prevalent method used in their industry to provide more meaningful comparisons across companies.

○ *Bookkeeping costs* While LIFO can reduce taxes, it is substantially more complex to implement than FIFO or weighted average inventory methods.

○ *Managerial opportunism* In some cases, management may seek to use an inventory method that results in higher net income in order to avoid violation of debt covenants, earn bonuses, or meet performance targets.

○ *Signaling to Financial Markets* Companies that might benefit from LIFO choose not to utilize it as a means of signaling that they have better future cash flow prospects (see Fellingham, Hughes, and Schwartz, *Journal of Accounting Research*, 1988).

> Another possible reason for not using LIFO is that it reduces earnings during a time of rising prices. Some companies may be reluctant to use an accounting method that lowers earnings even to save taxes.

Given that use of LIFO may save or delay payment of substantial taxes, the cash flow approach to firm valuation would seem to suggest that firms that are subject to rising prices should use the LIFO method of inventory and that capital markets should reward these firms higher market values. However, if the firm has debt covenants based on accounting numbers, then the reduced earnings from LIFO may place the firm in violation of these covenants, and lead to costly re-contracting costs. The choice of whether to adopt LIFO must therefore take into account numerous factors. In the next section, we look at LIFO's effect on the financial statements.

LIFO'S EFFECT ON FINANCIAL STATEMENTS

Because under LIFO the costs charged to inventory represent the most recent purchases, management can make inventory purchase decisions that substantially affect the amount of cost of goods sold (and hence net income) reported under LIFO. Let's look at some of these discretionary decisions.

LATE PURCHASES

If prices are changing at the end of a period, management can alter income simply by purchasing more inventory at the end of an accounting period. Consider our previous example regarding BHT's inventory of Levaquin tablets. Suppose that the price of Levaquin increased sharply at the end of December due to an unexpected increase in demand, to $750 per unit of 100 tablets. Suppose further that on December 31, BHT purchases 1000 additional units. Under FIFO, this purchase would have no effect on cost of goods sold. However, under the LIFO periodic method, cost of goods sold would now be:

$$1000 \times \$750 + 600 \times \$660 + 100 \times \$650 = \$1,211,000.$$

This amount compares to the previously computed amount of $1,100,000 for the same number of units sold.

Now, suppose that prices dramatically fell for Levaquin and that the price on December 31 was $500 per unit. If BHT purchased an additional 1000 units on December 31 at this price, LIFO cost of goods sold would be:

$$1000 \times \$500 + 600 \times \$660 + 100 \times \$650 = \$961,000.$$

The above amount is lower than the amount we previously calculated for LIFO of $1,100,000, but note that it is also lower than the amount calculated for FIFO of $1,056,000. This effect results solely from the timing of inventory purchase. Management may exploit this feature of LIFO to alter year-end earnings. If the only purpose of the late purchase is to allow management to alter reported earnings, such behavior is likely to raise red flags from audit committees and regulators concerned with the fairness of financial reporting. Further, note that the additional purchases also carry some additional costs for the firm, such as additional storage space and insurance, which would need to be factored into the decision.

While management does have a choice among accounting methods, using these options to manage reported earnings is an example of the type of transaction being closely scrutinized by the SEC. This is particularly the case if the effect is to raise reported earnings and management bonuses. However, if the late purchase decreases earnings to reduce taxes, then it may be considered a legitimate tax-planning technique.

LIFO LIQUIDATIONS

A **LIFO liquidation** occurs when more inventory is sold than was purchased during a period for a firm using LIFO. When a LIFO liquidation occurs, the firm charges inventory costs to cost of goods sold from inventory acquired in prior periods. If inventory has been growing over time and prices have been increasing, the LIFO costs remaining on the balance sheet reflect much lower costs than the current cost of inventory. As a result, a LIFO liquidation shows a much larger profit margin for those units liquidated. This, in turn, increases operating income and, hence, taxes. Exhibit 8.12 illustrates Omnova's LIFO liquidation during 2001.

	November 30,	
	2001	2000
(Dollars in millions)		
Raw materials and supplies	$22.2	$22.0
Work-in-process	2.9	4.6
Finished products	61.1	66.4
Approximate replacement cost of inventories	86.2	93.0
LIFO reserve	(18.1)	(25.0)
Other reserves	(11.4)	(8.7)
Inventories	$56.7	$59.3

Inventories using the LIFO method represented approximately 75 percent and 76 percent of the total replacement cost of inventories at November 30, 2001 and 2000, respectively. During 2001, LIFO inventory quantities were reduced resulting in a partial liquidation of LIFO bases in Decorative and Building Products, the effect of which increased segment operating profit by $1.2 million. The net loss in 2001 was favorably impacted by $0.7 million. During 2000, LIFO inventory quantities were reduced as well, which increased segment operating profit of Decorative & Building Products and Performance Chemicals by $4.3 million and $1.1 million, respectively. Net income was favorably impacted by $3.2 million in 2000.

Exhibit 8.12
Omnova, 2001 Annual Report
Note J—Inventories

THE REAL WORLD

Omnova LIFO
Liquidation

The amount referred to in the Omnova note (in Exhibit 8.12) as the "LIFO reserve" is the difference between LIFO and FIFO carrying amounts of inventory. Note that the LIFO reserve fell consistent with LIFO increasing earnings. In some cases, such as Omnova, the effect of a LIFO liquidation is clearly explained, while in other cases it is not so obvious. However, the required footnote disclosures are sufficient to calculate the earnings effect of using LIFO, and to re-create the inventory and cost of goods sold on a FIFO basis. In the next section, we illustrate how to calculate this conversion.

FINANCIAL ANALYSIS AND INVENTORY: CONVERTING FROM LIFO TO FIFO

Because different inventory methods result in substantially different amounts, both on the income statement and the balance sheet, comparison of companies using different methods will not result in meaningful information. However, because GAAP requires that companies that use LIFO provide current values of inventories (often, though not always, based on FIFO), we can convert values for a LIFO firm to those that would approximate the results if the firm used those current values.

For example, Blair Corporation's footnote disclosure regarding inventory (from its 2001 annual report) is as follows:

Inventories are valued at the lower of cost or market. Cost of merchandise inventories is determined principally on the last-in, first-out (LIFO) method. If the FIFO method had been used, inventories would have increased by approximately $5,366,000 and $6,717,000 at December 31, 2001 and 2000, respectively.

Exhibit 8.13
Blair Corporation Effect of
Using LIFO 2001

Blair Corporation

	LIFO	FIFO	FIFO–LIFO (LIFO Reserve)
Inventory 1/1/20X1	$109,572,639	$116,289,639	$6,717,000
+ Purchases	271,762,691	271,762,691	0
− Inventory 12/31/20X1	95,412,144	100,778,144	5,366,000
= Cost of goods sold	285,923,186	287,274,186	1,351,000

Note that Blair Corporation reports a smaller difference between LIFO and FIFO at the end of 2001 than at the beginning. This reflects either a decline in costs or a liquidation of a portion of the firm's LIFO reserves. It also means that FIFO will result in lower earnings and taxes than LIFO for 2001.

We can calculate the difference in earnings using the data provided in the financial statements. Exhibit 8.13 summarizes the results of that calculation. We found the LIFO inventory figures on Blair's 2000 and 2001 balance sheets, and the FIFO inventory amounts are computed from the LIFO reserve amounts given in the footnote. Blair reports its cost of goods sold on a LIFO basis in its 2001 income statement. From the LIFO data, we can then calculate purchases under LIFO. The purchases are the same under either inventory method. By using the ending inventory amounts and the purchases, we can then compute the FIFO cost of goods sold.

We compute the inventory balance on January 1, 2001 using FIFO as the LIFO inventory plus the increase had FIFO been used, or $109,572,639 + $6,717,000 = $116,289,639. The ending balance inventory as of December 31, 2001 on a FIFO basis is $95,412,144 + $5,366,000 = $100,778,144. LIFO cost of goods sold is reported on Blair's 2001 income statement. We determine purchases by using the cost of goods sold equation (Beginning Inventory + Purchases − Ending Inventory = Cost of Goods Sold).

While we determined the cost of goods sold for both LIFO and FIFO, as well as purchases for illustrative purposes, such a calculation is unnecessary to determine the effect of using LIFO on cost of goods sold. Note that the difference in cost of goods sold as a result of using LIFO equals the change in the difference between LIFO and FIFO inventories for 2001. In other words, the cost of goods sold using FIFO ($287,274,186) is the cost of goods sold using LIFO ($285,923,186) adjusted for the change in the LIFO reserves ($285,923,186 + $1,351,000).

RATIO ANALYSIS IMPLICATIONS

LIFO can also affect financial ratios in a way that makes the ratios difficult to interpret. This is because the balance sheet levels of inventory do not match with the inventory costs charged to cost of goods sold. This problem can become quite severe when firms use LIFO over a long period of time.

For example, we use the inventory turnover ratio to analyze the performance of inventory. Recall that the formula for inventory turnover is:

$$\text{Inventory Turnover} = \frac{\text{Cost of Goods Sold}}{\text{Average Inventories}}$$

Calculating for Blair, its inventory turnover using LIFO is:

$$\$285,923,186/(\$109,572,639 + \$95,412,144)/2 = 2.78$$

On a FIFO basis, inventory turnover would be:

$$\$287,274,186/(\$116,289,639 + \$100,778,144)/2 = 2.64$$

This results in about a 5 percent difference in the number of days of inventory. While this doesn't sound very large, a real fluctuation in the amount of inventory to produce this kind of change would have resulted in a reduction of approximately $5.5 million in inventory.

Another approach sometimes used for LIFO firms is to compute the inventory turnover using LIFO cost of goods sold and FIFO inventories. This method provides the closest match of costs between the numerator and the denominator because both are based on the most recent prices of inventory.

Using this method, Blair's inventory turnover would be:

$$\$285,923,186/(\$116,289,639 + \$100,778,144)/2 = 2.63$$

In this case, the results are not much different than the FIFO numbers. This is because although FIFO cost of goods sold is based on older numbers than LIFO, the inventory turnover indicates that they are not significantly older. The differences between LIFO and FIFO are the greatest when the LIFO reserve is very large.

TRANSITION AND SUMMARY

For most companies, inventories are a significant asset. They pose challenges to the company in terms of physical management and control, as well as reporting issues. There are a number of different allowable methods of accounting for inventory, and no clear answer as to which is the best method in any situation. Management, analysts, corporate boards, and other users of financial statements need to understand the importance of inventory recognition methods and their impact on reported profits and balance sheet valuations in order to make informed decisions.

Under GAAP, inventories are valued at the lower of cost or market. Cost can be determined using alternative cost flow assumptions: FIFO, LIFO, and weighted average. LIFO is the least intuitive, calling for the newest costs to be assigned to goods sold and the oldest costs to inventory. The motivations for LIFO include tax advantages and better matching of current costs and revenues. LIFO also affords managers opportunities to manipulate earnings through year-end purchases or the deferral of purchases of inventory.

Inventory is one of the most important current assets of the firm. In the next chapter we turn our focus to the long-term assets of the firm and their effects on the financial statements.

END OF CHAPTER MATERIAL

KEY TERMS

Finished Goods Inventory

First-In, First-Out Method (FIFO)

Fixed Costs

Inventories

Last-In, First-Out Method (LIFO)

LIFO Liquidation

Lower of Cost or Market

Net Realizable Value

Periodic Method

Perpetual Method

Product Costs

Raw Materials Inventory

Replacement Cost

Specific Identification Method

Weighted Average Method

Work-in-Process Inventory

ASSIGNMENT MATERIAL

REVIEW QUESTIONS

1. Describe the valuation methods for inventory allowed under U.S. GAAP.

2. Describe how the lower of cost or market rule is applied to inventory under GAAP and how GAAP defines "market" for the purpose of this rule.

3. Describe the basic differences between the periodic and perpetual methods of tracking inventory.

4. Discuss the advantages and disadvantages of using the periodic method versus the perpetual method.

5. Describe the three major cost flow assumptions that are allowed under GAAP.

6. Discuss the incentives that a firm may have for choosing one cost flow assumption over another. Be sure to include a discussion of the choice for both reporting and tax purposes.

7. Describe the effects of a LIFO liquidation on the income of a firm. Discuss the effects of year-end purchasing behavior on reported income with the three major cost flow assumptions.

8. Describe the effects the choice of LIFO or FIFO may have on the ratios related to inventory. Specifically, discuss the inventory turnover and current ratios.

9. Describe how the choice of inventory may affect investors' perceived value of the firm.

APPLYING YOUR KNOWLEDGE

10. The Halo Company, a manufacturer of soaps and cosmetics, had raw material inventory worth $30,000 at a unit cost of $15 on March 31. The purchases during the month of April are as follows:

Date	Units Purchased	Total Cost
4/3	3,000	$45,000
4/10	1,000	18,000
4/14	4,000	80,000
4/23	2,500	55,000
4/29	1,000	30,000

A physical count of inventory showed that 2,500 units were still left on March 31. Compute the cost of inventory on March 31 using each of the following cost flow assumptions:

a. Periodic FIFO

b. Periodic LIFO

c. Periodic weighted average

11. The following information relates to the merchandise inventory of Apen Corporation for the month of May:

Date	Transaction	Units	Amount
5/1	Beginning Inventory	6,000	$60,000
5/3	Purchased	3,000	36,000
5/7	Sold	4,000	
5/15	Sold	2,000	
5/23	Purchased	1,000	18,000
5/29	Sold	3,500	

a. Compute the cost of goods sold and ending inventory as of May 31 using the following inventory systems and cost flow assumptions:

1. Periodic FIFO

2. Perpetual FIFO

3. Periodic LIFO

4. Perpetual LIFO

5. Periodic Weighted Average

6. Perpetual Weighted Average

b. Assume that Apen has a marginal tax rate of 35 percent. What is the amount of difference in tax expense for the month of May between periodic FIFO and periodic LIFO? Assume that the same method is used for tax and financial reporting in each case.

c. Refer to part b: Which method would be expected to result in the highest value for Apen Corporation? Explain your answer.

12. In mid-September, Trojan, Incorporated is faced with a decision as to how many units it should produce for the balance of the accounting year, which

ends on December 31. The company began its operations in the current year with an inventory of 35,000 units at a cost of $15 per unit. During the year, it produced 65,000 units at a unit cost of $18. The annual capacity of the plant is 200,000 units. It is estimated that the unit cost of producing additional units (for the remaining part of the year) will be $25. The company, after doing time-series and cross-sectional analyses, expects the annual sales to be $125,000 units at a selling price of $28 per unit. The company uses a periodic LIFO inventory system.

Assume that the company has been performing poorly prior to this year and that it is under constant pressure from the shareholders to improve performance. How many additional units should the company produce to maximize net income? Identify any problems associated with this strategy.

Assume that the company's profits have been unusually large during the year as a result of some unexpected gains, and it is necessary that the profits for the remainder of the year be minimal so that the company may pay a smaller amount of taxes. How many additional units should the company produce to minimize net income? Identify any problems associated with this strategy.

13. The following data relates to the inventory valuations of Aurora, Inc. using different inventory methods (the company started operations in 20X1):

Period	LIFO	FIFO	Lower of FIFO Cost or Market
12/31/X1	$ 65,000	$ 60,000	$ 55,000
12/31/X2	135,000	125,000	120,000
12/31/X3	150,000	143,000	130,000
12/31/X4	100,000	125,000	125,000

There was no beginning balance of inventory in 19X1.

a. For 20X1, state whether the prices went up or down.

b. For 20X4, state whether the prices went up or down.

c. Which method would show the highest income in each year?

d. Which method would show the income for the four years combined?

14. Discuss the implications that different international accounting standards, with respect to inventory, have for the statement analysis of foreign competitor companies.

15. Describe the concerns that you might have for the ratio analysis of inventories when comparing a U.S. company with a foreign competitor.

16. As an auditor, what concerns might you have about the measurement of inventories at year end and what effects might misstatements in these amounts have on the financial statements of the company?

17. Suppose that a firm has used LIFO since it began business and that prices have generally risen from that point to the present. In one of the company's debt agreements there is a restrictive covenant that the company must maintain a current ratio of 2; otherwise it is in violation of the debt agreement and it immediately becomes due. If you represent the lender, what reaction would you have if the firm wanted to change its inventory method

from LIFO to FIFO? How would your answer change if you knew that the company was already financially distressed?

18. Suppose that your firm has always used LIFO and that prices have been rising over the years. In order to become more efficient, you have recommended that the firm change its manufacturing processes and adopt a just-in-time process which will either eliminate or significantly reduce inventory levels. What are the financial statement implications of your decision and what might be the financial trade-offs that you should consider in implementing your decision?

19. Suppose that you are a manager of a division and your company uses LIFO to measure inventories. Prices have been rising fairly rapidly during the last quarter and you expect this to increase during at least the next quarter. On the last day of the year, you have an opportunity to buy a significant amount of inventory at a price that you know you will not be able to duplicate next quarter but it is still significantly higher than the prices you paid for goods earlier in the year. Part of your compensation is based on exceeding a net income target which you project that you will just meet without this year-end purchase.

   a. How will net income and your compensation be affected by this year-end purchase?

   b. What ethical dilemma do you face in making the decision as to whether to purchase this additional inventory?

   c. Suppose that the amount of inventory that you need to purchase is beyond what the company normally carries in stock. What additional costs should you consider in making this decision?

USING REAL DATA

20. Effective January 1, 1970, Chrysler Corporation changed its method of accounting for its inventories from LIFO to FIFO. The LIFO reserve account had a balance of approximately $110 million at the time of the change. General Motors and Ford were using the FIFO method at the time of the change by Chrysler. Shortly thereafter, GM and Ford changed their method from FIFO to LIFO. GM and Ford continued to use LIFO, and Chrysler switched back to LIFO effective January 1, 1984.

   The following data were obtained from the 1994 annual reports of Chrysler, GM, and Ford (amounts in millions):

Company	Account	1994	1993
Chrysler	Inventory—LIFO	$3,356.0	$3,629.0
	LIFO reserve	328.0	259.0
	Cost of goods sold	38,032.0	
GM	Inventory—LIFO	10,127.8	8,615.1
	LIFO reserve	2,535.9	2,519.0
	Cost of goods sold	117,220.5	
Ford	Inventory—LIFO	6,487.0	5,538.0
	LIFO reserve	1,383.0	1,342.0
	Cost of goods sold	96,180.0	

a. Describe the effects on the financial statements of Chrysler of the 1970 switch from LIFO to FIFO. Speculate on the motives that Chrysler might have had for making this switch.

b. Calculate the inventory turnover ratios for all three companies in 1994 on both a LIFO and a FIFO basis.

c. Explain your reasoning for which set of ratios in part b you think best portrays the difference in turnover that exists among the three companies.

21. Lindsay Manufacturing Company uses LIFO to account for the majority of its inventory, and its income statement follows. This information was available in footnote F of the firm's 2002 annual report:

$ IN THOUSANDS	2002	AUGUST 31, 2001
First-in, first-out (FIFO) inventory	$14,461	$11,989
LIFO reserves	(3,153)	(2,551)
Obsolescence reserve	(359)	(629)
Weighted average inventory	4,634	1,303
Total inventories	$15,583	$10,112

LINDSAY MANUFACTURING CO.
Income Statement

	08/31/2002	08/31/2001	08/31/2000
Operating revenues	$145,890,000	$126,669,000	$129,785,000
Cost of operating revenues	112,963,000	98,739,000	98,189,000
Gross profit	32,927,000	27,930,000	31,596,000
Operating expenses:			
Selling expense	8,804,000	7,200,000	5,660,000
General and administrative expense	8,630,000	7,885,000	7,446,000
Engineering and research expense	2,377,000	2,301,000	2,064,000
Restructuring charges	0	899,000	0
Total operating expenses	19,811,000	18,285,000	15,170,000
Operating income	13,116,000	9,645,000	16,426,000
Interest income, net	1,647,000	1,754,000	2,599,000
Other income, net	551,000	2,000	118,000
Earnings before income taxes	15,314,000	11,401,000	19,143,000
Income tax provision	4,650,000	3,440,000	5,935,000
Net earnings	$ 10,664,000	$ 7,961,000	$ 13,208,000

a. What cost of goods sold would Lindsay have reported if it used FIFO in 2002? Does the direction of the difference between LIFO and FIFO make sense? Explain your reasoning.

b. Assuming that the marginal tax rate for Lindsay was 30 percent in 2002, what would net income have been in 2002 using FIFO?

c. Assuming that tax rates prior to 2002 average 35 percent, estimate the cumulative tax savings for Lindsay from using LIFO.

d. Compute the inventory turnover ratio using LIFO and FIFO figures. Which rate best represents the physical inventory turnover for Lindsay and why?

e. Lindsay also reports an obsolescence reserve. Explain the nature of this type of reserve and provide evidence as to whether the amount of obsolescence has increased or decreased during 2002.

22. Deere & Company reports the majority of its inventory using the LIFO method, and its income statement follows. This information is provided in footnote 13 to its 2002 annual report:

> Most inventories owned by Deere & Company and its United States equipment subsidiaries are valued at cost, on the last-in, first-out (LIFO) basis. Remaining inventories are generally valued at the lower of cost, on the first-in, first-out (FIFO) basis, or market. The value of gross inventories on the LIFO basis represented 72 percent and 70 percent of worldwide gross inventories at FIFO value on October 31, 2002 and 2001, respectively. If all inventories had been valued on a FIFO basis, estimated inventories by major classification at October 31 in millions of dollars would have been as follows (in millions of dollars):

	2002	2001
Raw materials and supplies	$ 515	$ 516
Work-in-process	361	376
Finished machines and parts	1,444	1,618
Total FIFO value	2,320	2,510
Adjustment to LIFO value	948	1,004
Inventories	$1,372	$1,506

DEERE & CO. Income Statement	10/31/2002	10/31/2001	10/31/2000
Net sales and revenues:			
Net sales	$11,702,800,000	$11,077,400,000	$11,168,600,000
Finance and interest income	1,339,200,000	1,445,200,000	1,321,300,000
Health care premiums and fees	636,000,000	585,000,000	473,700,000
Other income	269,000,000	185,300,000	173,200,000
Total	13,947,000,000	13,292,900,000	13,136,800,000
Costs and expenses:			
Cost of sales	9,593,400,000	9,376,400,000	8,936,100,000
Research and development expenses	527,800,000	590,100,000	542,100,000
Selling, administrative, and general expenses	1,657,300,000	1,716,800,000	1,504,900,000
Interest expense	637,100,000	765,700,000	676,500,000
Health care claims and costs	518,400,000	476,000,000	380,500,000
Other operating expenses	410,300,000	392,700,000	319,200,000
Total	13,344,300,000	13,317,700,000	12,359,300,000

	10/31/2002	10/31/2001	10/31/2000
Income (loss) of consolidated group before income taxes:	602,700,000	(24,800,000)	777,500,000
Provision for income taxes	258,300,000	17,700,000	293,800,000
Income (loss) of consolidated group	344,400,000	(42,500,000)	483,700,000
Equity in income (loss) of unconsolidated affiliates credit	(3,800,000)	(3,300,000)	600,000
Other	(21,400,000)	(18,200,000)	1,200,000
Total	(25,200,000)	(21,500,000)	1,800,000
Net income (loss)	$ 319,200,000	($64,000,000)	$ 485,500,000

a. What cost of goods sold would Deere have reported if it used FIFO in 2002? Does the direction of the difference between LIFO and FIFO make sense? Explain your reasoning.

b. Assuming that the marginal tax rate for Deere was 43 percent in 2002, what would net income have been in 2002 using FIFO?

c. Assuming that tax rates prior to 2002 average 35 percent, estimate the cumulative tax savings for Deere from using LIFO.

d. Compute the inventory turnover ratio using LIFO and FIFO figures. Which rate best represents the physical inventory turnover for Deere and why?

23. During the third quarter (ended December 31, 2004), Casey's General Stores (CGS) announced that it had changed its method of accounting for its inventory of gasoline from LIFO to FIFO. CGS's gasoline sales typically represent 61 percent of total sales for the period. During the third quarter, gasoline profit margins eroded with the margin down 2.8 cents per gallon relative to a historical average of 10.5 cents per gallon. In the third quarter, this equated to an erosion of profit margin of $6.8 million. Following are the financial statements for the fiscal year that ended April 30, 2003.

CASEY'S GENERAL STORES, INC. Balance Sheet

	04/30/2003	04/30/2002
Assets		
Current assets		
Cash and cash equivalents	$ 40,544,000	$ 18,946,000
Short-term investments	—	10,000
Receivables	5,742,000	5,127,000
Inventories (Note 1)	63,009,000	60,498,000
Prepaid expenses (Note 5)	4,590,000	3,816,000
Income taxes receivable	2,989,000	9,222,000
Total current assets	116,874,000	97,619,000
Other assets	808,000	992,000
Property and equipment, at cost (Note 2)		
Land	166,262,000	155,794,000
Buildings and leasehold improvements	386,552,000	366,328,000
Machinery and equipment	463,240,000	429,012,000
Leasehold interest in property and equipment (Note 6)	9,712,000	10,446,000

	04/30/2003	04/30/2002
	1,025,766,000	961,580,000
Less accumulated depreciation and amortization	368,123,000	324,936,000
Net property and equipment	657,643,000	636,644,000
Total assets	$775,325,000	$735,255,000
Liabilities and shareholders' equity		
Current liabilities		
Note payable to bank (Note 2)	$ 0	$5,275,000
Current maturities of long-term debt (Note 2)	19,897,000	9,648,000
Accounts payable	64,880,000	69,912,000
Accrued expenses		
Property taxes	8,011,000	7,470,000
Other (Note 9)	24,550,000	19,768,000
Total current liabilities	117,338,000	112,073,000
Long-term debt, net of current maturities (Note 2)	162,394,000	173,797,000
Deferred income taxes (Note 5)	86,871,000	75,786,000
Deferred compensation (Note 7)	4,484,000	4,380,000
Total liabilities	371,087,000	366,036,000
Shareholders' equity (Note 3)		
Preferred stock, no par value, none issued	—	—
Common stock, no par value, 49,669,112 and 49,623,812 shares		
issued and outstanding at April 30, 2003 and 2002, respectively	40,008,000	39,562,000
Retained earnings	364,230,000	329,657,000
Total shareholders' equity	404,238,000	369,219,000
Total liabilities and shareholders' equity	$775,325,000	$735,255,000

CASEY'S GENERAL STORES, INC. Income Statement

	04/30/2003	04/30/2002	04/30/2001
Net sales	$2,155,606,000	$2,032,226,000	$1,904,899,000
Franchise revenue	2,451,000	3,059,000	3,767,000
	2,158,057,000	2,035,285,000	1,908,666,000
Cost of goods sold	1,743,971,000	1,658,511,000	1,558,147,000
Operating expenses	290,801,000	268,766,000	241,444,000
Depreciation and amortization	47,299,000	44,702,000	41,492,000
Interest, net (Note 2)	13,030,000	12,756,000	11,998,000
	2,095,101,000	1,984,735,000	1,853,081,000
Income before income taxes	62,956,000	50,550,000	55,585,000
Provision for income taxes (Note 5)	23,420,000	18,805,000	20,584,000
Net income	$ 39,536,000	$ 31,745,000	$ 35,001,000

a. Discuss CGS's motivation to change methods from LIFO to FIFO.

b. In CGS's footnotes to the financial statements dated April 30, 2003, the company indicated that its inventories were accounted for using the LIFO method and that the inventory value was $17,800,000 and $17,670,000 below replacement cost as of April 30, 2003 and 2002, respectively. Calculate the cost of goods sold that would have been reported using FIFO in the year ended April 30, 2003.

c. Using the cost of goods sold calculated in part b, calculate the inventory turnover and days of inventory using both the LIFO and the FIFO data for the year ended April 30, 2003.

d. How do you think the stock market might have reacted to CGS's announcement of its decision to change its inventory method?

24. Following are the financial statements of Allegheny Technologies. The company uses LIFO to account for its inventories. You will also find the inventory footnote from Allegheny's 2003 annual report.

ALLEGHENY TECHNOLOGIES, INC. Income Statement			
	12/31/2003	12/31/2002	12/31/2001
Sales	$1,937,400,000	$1,907,800,000	$2,128,000,000
Costs and expenses:			
Cost of sales	1,873,600,000	1,744,500,000	1,862,300,000
Selling and administrative expenses	248,800,000	188,300,000	198,800,000
Restructuring costs	62,400,000	42,800,000	74,200,000
Loss before interest, other income, and income taxes	(247,400,000)	(67,800,000)	(7,300,000)
Interest expense, net	27,700,000	34,300,000	29,300,000
Other income (expense), net	(5,100,000)	(1,700,000)	200,000
Loss before income tax provision (benefit) and cumulative effect of change in accounting principle	(280,200,000)	(103,800,000)	(36,400,000)
Income tax provision (benefit)	33,100,000	(38,000,000)	(11,200,000)
Net loss before cumulative effect of change in accounting principle	(313,300,000)	(65,800,000)	(25,200,000)
Cumulative effect of change in accounting principle, net of tax	(1,300,000)	—	—
Net Loss	$ (314,600,000)	$ (65,800,000)	$ (25,200,000)

ALLEGHENY TECHNOLOGIES, INC.
Balance Sheet

	12/31/2003	12/31/2002
Assets		
Cash and cash equivalents	$ 79,600,000	$ 59,400,000
Accounts receivable, net	248,800,000	239,300,000
Inventories, net	359,700,000	392,300,000
Income tax refunds	7,200,000	51,900,000
Deferred income taxes	—	20,800,000
Prepaid expenses and other current assets	48,000,000	32,000,000
Total current assets	743,300,000	795,700,000
Property, plant, and equipment, net	711,100,000	757,600,000
Cost in excess of net assets acquired	198,400,000	194,400,000
Deferred pension asset	144,000,000	165,100,000
Deferred income taxes	34,300,000	85,400,000
Other assets	53,800,000	95,000,000
Total assets	$1,884,900,000	$2,093,200,000
Liabilities and stockholders' equity		
Accounts payable	$ 172,300,000	$ 171,300,000
Accrued liabilities	194,600,000	161,000,000
Short-term debt and current portion of long-term debt	27,800,000	9,700,000
Total current liabilities	394,700,000	342,000,000
Long-term debt	504,300,000	509,400,000
Accrued postretirement benefits	507,200,000	496,400,000
Pension liabilities	220,600,000	216,000,000
Other long-term liabilities	83,400,000	80,600,000
Total liabilities	1,710,200,000	1,644,400,000
Stockholders' equity:		
Preferred stock, par value $0.10: authorized—50,000,000 shares; issued—none	—	—
Common stock, par value $0.10: authorized—500,000,000 shares; issued 98,951,490 at 2003 and 2002; outstanding—80,654,861 shares at 2003 and 80,634,344 shares at 2002	9,900,000	9,900,000
Additional paid-in capital	481,200,000	481,200,000
Retained earnings	483,800,000	835,100,000
Treasury stock: 18,296,629 shares at 2003 and 18,317,146 shares at 2002	(458,400,000)	(469,700,000)
Accumulated other comprehensive loss, net of tax	(341,800,000)	(407,700,000)
Total stockholders' equity	174,700,000	448,800,000
Total liabilities and stockholders' equity	$1,884,900,000	$2,093,200,000

Note 2 Inventories (in millions)	December 31, 2003	December 31, 2002
Raw materials and supplies	$ 37.5	$ 32.7
Work-in-process	356.2	358.5
Finished goods	84.9	80.4
Total inventories at current cost	478.6	471.6
Less allowances to reduce current cost values to LIFO basis	−111.7	−74.7
Progress payments	−7.2	−4.6
Total inventories	$359.7	$392.3

Inventories, before progress payments, determined on the last-in, first-out method were $292.4 million at December 31, 2003 and $327.0 million at December 31, 2002. The remainder of the inventory was determined using the first-in, first-out and average cost methods. These inventory values do not differ materially from current cost.

During 2003 and 2002, inventory usage resulted in liquidations of last-in, first-out inventory quantities. These inventories were carried at the lower costs prevailing in prior years as compared with the cost of current purchases. The effect of these last-in, first-out liquidations was to decrease cost of sales by $7.9 million in 2003 and by $3.7 million in 2002.

a. Calculate the cost of goods sold that would have been reported in 2003 had Allegheny used the FIFO method.

b. Calculate the inventory turnover and day of inventory under both the LIFO and FIFO methods.

c. What was the effect of LIFO liquidations on income in 2003?

d. What would you expect this impact to be on Allegheny's stock value? Explain your answer.

○ BEYOND THE BOOK

25. Use a company database that contains news reports to identify a company that uses the LIFO inventory method. Next use an SEC document retrieval service such as EDGAR (or EDGARSCAN) to retrieve the most recent financial statement of the company. Use the data to answer the following questions:

a. Calculate the cost of goods sold that would have been reported in the most recent year had the company used the FIFO method.

b. Calculate the inventory turnover and day of inventory under both the LIFO and FIFO methods.

c. Did the company experience any LIFO liquidations during the year? If so, calculate the effect of the liquidations on income.

CHAPTER **9**

Valuing Long-Lived Assets

LEARNING OBJECTIVES

After studying this chapter you should be able to:

1. Determine whether expenditures should be capitalized as assets or expensed.

2. Understand the process of depreciation and amortization for allocating costs, as firms realize the benefits of using up assets.

3. Identify the economic incentives and consequences of alternative accounting treatments for long-term assets.

4. Understand the accounting treatments of certain intangible assets.

On June 22, 2002, Worldcom, Inc. announced that it would restate its earnings for 2001 and the first quarter of 2002. The company had improperly capitalized over $3.8 billion of expenditures. Instead of recording charges to local telephone networks (to complete calls) as an expense, the company erroneously capitalized the costs as an asset. Less than a month after the startling news of the earnings misstatement, Worldcom filed for bankruptcy court protection on July 21. Subsequently, Nasdaq delisted Worldcom's stock (which meant that Worldcom could no longer trade on the exchange). Prior to this, the stock had traded at nearly $40 per share (in 2000).

(1) Summary of significant accounting policies

Property, Equipment, and Depreciation

Additions and improvements to property and equipment are capitalized at cost, while maintenance and repair expenditures are charged to operations as incurred. If equipment is traded rather than sold, the cost of new equipment is recorded at an amount equal to the lower of the monetary consideration paid plus the net book value of the traded property or the fair value of the new equipment.

Depreciation is calculated based on the cost of the asset, reduced by its estimated salvage value, using the straight-line method. Accelerated depreciation methods are used for income tax purposes. The lives and salvage values assigned to certain assets for financial reporting purposes are different than for income tax purposes. For financial reporting purposes, assets are depreciated over the estimated useful lives of 30 years for buildings and improvements, five to ten years for revenue equipment, and three to ten years for service and other equipment.

 Note that Werner states that it uses a different depreciation method for tax purposes than for financial accounting, which is a common practice. Later in this chapter, we will discuss the differences in methods for tax and financial accounting purposes, and the impact that these differences have on financial statements.

As the Worldcom scandal shows, capitalization of a cost that should properly have been an expense can mislead investors and lead to significant financial statement restatement. To avoid this situation, GAAP provides guidelines so firms may properly determine which costs should be treated as assets, how to treat the costs subsequent to recognition as an asset, and when to record write-downs. These guidelines, although not precise in all cases, dictate whether an expenditure should be considered an asset. Charges paid by Worldcom for the use of local phone lines clearly benefit only the current period and are directly tied to the production of the current period's revenues. Hence, they should have been expensed.

In this chapter we consider accounting for long-lived assets, both tangible (e.g., buildings, equipment, and furniture and fixtures) and intangible (e.g., computer software, oil and gas exploration costs, and patents). Outlays for such assets are called **capital expenditures,** that is, items that firms place on the balance sheet as assets. Having been capitalized, firms then allocate these costs as **depreciation** or **amortization** expenses over the useful lives of the assets, based on management's estimate of the time period over which the company is likely to benefit from them. Companies generally discuss the method of depreciation used, as well as provide some information about asset lives, in footnote disclosures. The disclosure for Werner Enterprises, Inc. in Exhibit 9.1 illustrates a typical disclosure for tangible assets. In the next section, we start by considering which costs should be included in the initial acquisition of tangible assets.

CAPITALIZATION CRITERIA

Generally, firms should capitalize all costs necessary to acquire a long-lived asset and prepare it for its intended use. As a simple example, assume that BHT (our hypothetical company from previous chapters) purchases equipment used in its warehouse operations for a cost of $4 million. In addition, BHT incurs set-up and assembly costs for the equipment of $250,000. BHT should capitalize the equipment at a cost of $4,250,000. However, many capitalization situations require consideration of other expenses such as:

● Cash or other assets given up to acquire the asset
● Installation costs
● Transportation costs
● Legal costs
● Taxes
● Interest cost (for self-constructed assets)

Determining the specific costs to be capitalized with respect to a particular asset acquisition requires management judgment and knowledge of standard practices. However, management should consider two critical questions in determining the amounts and items to be capitalized related to long-term assets. First, are the costs directly related to the asset? Costs that are incidental to a particular asset, or administrative costs that would be incurred regardless of whether the firm acquires an asset, should not be capitalized. Second, do the capitalized costs exceed the value of the asset? A firm should not capitalize an asset at an amount that exceeds the present value of future cash flows expected to be realized from the asset.

What happens when management exercises poor judgment involving capitalization costs? Waste Management, Inc. for example, needed to restate its financial statements from 1992 through 1997 after discovering errors related to depreciation expense and capitalized interest (see Exhibit 9.2). Such restatements decrease investor confidence in management. However, note that not all errors requiring restatements result from intentional decisions. They may relate to erroneous interpretations of GAAP, or simply a disagreement between management and the SEC regarding the appropriate accounting to be used with respect to a specific item. The SEC reviews filings by public companies and may request clarification or require restatements if it disagrees with management's interpretation of GAAP.

Managers may have incentives for manipulating capitalization decisions. For example, some market observers speculated that Worldcom's capitalized line-access charges were a means of meeting financial analysts' expectations regarding its earnings.

Note 1—Restatements and Reclassifications

In its 1997 Report on Form 10-K, the Company has restated and reclassified its previously reported financial results for 1992 through 1997. Unaudited quarterly financial data for 1996 and the first three quarters of 1997 have also been restated and reclassified. Except as otherwise stated herein, all information presented in this Report on Form 10-Q/A includes all such restatements and reclassifications.

As a result of a comprehensive review begun in the third quarter of 1997, the Company determined that certain items of expense were incorrectly reported in previously issued financial statements. These principally relate to vehicle, equipment and container depreciation expense, capitalized interest, and income taxes. With respect to depreciation, the Company determined that incorrect vehicle and container salvage values had been used, and errors had been made in the expense calculations. The Company also concluded that capitalized interest relating to landfill construction projects had been misstated. On January 1, 1995, the Company changed its accounting for capitalized interest, but the cumulative "catch-up" charge was not properly recorded in the 1995 financial statements, and errors were made in applying the new method in subsequent years. Accordingly, capitalized interest for the interim periods from 1995 through the third quarter of 1997 has been restated.

Exhibit 9.2
Waste Management, Inc.
Quarterly Report, June 9,1998

THE REAL WORLD

Waste Management, Inc.

We began this section with a simple example of capitalized costs. Next, we'll turn to more complex situations: interest costs, basket purchases, equipment improvements and repairs, and asset exchanges.

INTEREST CAPITALIZATION

One of the more subtle capitalization issues pertains to interest cost, associated with funds tied up in the self-construction of long-lived assets. In most cases, a firm *expenses* the interest it pays over time as the interest accrues. However, a firm *capitalizes* interest under certain circumstances, dictated by FASB Statement No. 34. Accordingly, firms must capitalize interest for assets that require an extended period of time to construct (such as facilities or buildings) and that are constructed for a company's own use or for discrete projects intended for sale or lease, such as real estate projects. On the other hand, firms expense interest for short-term investments, such as in manufactured inventories produced on a regular or routine basis.

The amount of interest a firm capitalizes is an allocation of a company's interest cost over the time needed to construct the assets, or if there is a specific loan for the project, the actual interest incurred. Requiring interest capitalization provides greater consistency between the cost of self-constructing assets and purchasing assets. For example, if a company purchases a building constructed by an outside contractor, the cost of the interest to the contractor will be priced into the cost of the building.

Determining when interest should be capitalized and the appropriate amount to include often requires management judgment. For example, suppose that a company builds and sells prefabricated homes. Would the company capitalize interest on this type of construction? It would not, because this type of home is built rapidly and repetitively manufactured. However, if a company constructs cruise ships or customized sailboats, and sells them to another party, the interest involved in construction would appropriately be capitalized. The key issue here is whether or not an identifiable asset is constructed over a period of time, such that the firm incurs material interest cost on the asset.

Firms compute capitalized interest based on the average amount invested in the asset under construction and the interest rate attached to the specific borrowing associated with the construction. If no specific borrowing for the construction exists, then the firm uses its average interest rate on its long-term borrowings. However, the amount of interest that can be capitalized is limited. Firms can only capitalize interest to the extent that funds have been invested in the asset being constructed. Furthermore, firms cannot capitalize a greater amount of interest cost than that actually incurred.

Let's return to our BHT example. Suppose that BHT constructs a new corporate headquarters. The facility costs $120,000,000 and requires two years to complete. BHT finances the project with a two-year, 7 percent note. Exhibit 9.3 shows the timing of events related to the project and the amount of interest that BHT capitalizes each year.

BASKET PURCHASES

Basket purchase describes the acquisition of a group of assets for an amount assigned to the entire asset group. Such purchases may occur when a company purchases facilities that include building, land, and equipment. In the case of a

Exhibit 9.3
Computing Capitalized
Interest Costs

Costs Related to BHT's Construction of New Headquarters:

Year 1: Weighted average construction cost: $90,000,000
Year 2: Weighted average construction cost: $115,000,000

Funds Borrowed:

1/1/Year 1—Took out $100,000,000 loan
12/31/Year 1—Paid interest on loan (7 percent)
12/31/Year 2—Paid interest and principal on loan
12/31/Year 2—Headquarters completed

Year 1, Interest capitalized:

Because the average construction cost is less than the loan, the capitalized interest is limited to interest on the average cost of construction during year 1. Hence capitalized interest is:

$90,000,000 × .07 = $6,300,000

Year 2, Interest capitalized:

The amount of interest cannot exceed the interest paid. As BHT borrowed $100,000,000, interest paid is 7 percent of this amount. So, interest capitalized in year 2 is:

$100,000,000 × .07 = $7,000,000.

Note in this case, BHT borrowed specifically to fund the project. If BHT had long-term borrowings not specifically for this project, then interest would still be capitalized but at the rate of BHT's average long-term borrowing rate.

basket purchase, a company must determine a way to assign costs to the individual assets acquired. The appropriate method is to assign costs to the individual assets in proportion to their fair market values. Determination of these values often requires obtaining appraisals or other verifiable estimates of the fair value of the individual assets. Exhibit 9.4 illustrates an example of a basket purchase allocation.

Exhibit 9.4
Basket Purchase

Assume that BHT acquires land, a building, and manufacturing equipment for a total price of $2,400,000. BHT obtained the following independent estimates of market values of these assets:

Land	$1,000,000
Building	1,200,000
Equipment	800,000
Total	$3,000,000

BHT should assign the following initial carrying values to the assets:

Land ($1,000,000/$3,000,000) × $2,400,000 = $800,000
Building ($1,200,000/$3,000,000) × $2,400,000 = $960,000
Equipment ($800,000/$3,000,000) × $2,400,000 = $640,000

> Accounting conservatism dictates that while it is inappropriate to systematically understate assets, generally when an issue is ambiguous, the accounting treatment should favor expensing over capitalization.

IMPROVEMENTS AND REPAIRS

Companies with long-term assets often incur costs to maintain, improve, or extend the life of the assets. In general, if these costs substantially add to the asset's value or its useful life, a firm should capitalize them. Costs to repair an asset and maintain it in working condition should be expensed. For example, suppose the BHT owns a fleet of trucks used in its wholesale operations. BHT would expense normal repair costs, such as oil changes and brake relinings, but capitalize any costs to extend the life of a truck, such as rebuilding an engine.

The difference between the incentives for tax reporting and financial reporting is striking when it comes to capitalizing expenses as assets. For tax purposes, companies prefer to expense items as rapidly as possible, even though IRS regulations require companies to capitalize costs that benefit multiple periods. In contrast, for financial reporting purposes, management may try to treat items as assets that do not benefit future periods and that should be expensed. Both incentives are in conflict with principles that govern the proper treatment.

ASSET EXCHANGES

An exception to the cost principle lies in the area of asset exchanges. Just as you might trade in an old car when purchasing a new one, firms sometimes replace assets by exchanging one asset for a similar one. Commonly, a company pays cash for the difference between the cost of the new asset and the market or trade-in value of the old asset.

Exhibit 9.5
Similar Asset Exchanges

Example 1:

BHT exchanges a truck with a cost of $22,000 and accumulated depreciation of $15,000 for a new truck. The market value of the new truck is listed at $25,000. BHT pays an additional $19,000 in cash as part of the exchange. BHT records the new truck at a price of $22,000 and recognizes a loss of $1,000 on the exchange.

New truck	$25,000	
Loss on exchange	1,000	
Accumulated depreciation (old truck)	15,000	
Old truck		$22,000
Cash		19,000

Example 2:

Assume the same data as in Example 1 except that BHT pays an additional $17,000 in the exchange (hence incurring a gain on the exchange). BHT records the new truck at $24,000 and does not recognize the gain.

New truck	$24,000	
Accumulated depreciation (old truck)	15,000	
Old truck		$22,000
Cash		17,000

APB Opinion No. 29 covers the accounting requirements for asset exchanges. In general, if the exchange is for a similar asset and the transaction results in a gain, the gain is not recognized. The firm simply records the new asset at the book value of the old asset plus the additional cash paid. If the transaction results in a loss, however, then the firm immediately recognizes the loss. Exhibit 9.5 reviews both cases using the BHT example.

The area of asset exchanges can lead to manipulations of earnings because management has the discretion as to whether it wants to sell assets and buy new assets or trade in assets for new assets. For tax purposes, management has an incentive to sell assets where a tax loss can be taken (thus reducing taxes), and exchange assets when a sale would result in a taxable gain (thus avoiding the gain). The situation can be more complex in practice if a company receives cash in an asset exchange, or if the asset has a different cost basis for tax purposes than for financial accounting purposes.

This completes our review of capitalizing costs for long-lived tangible assets. As we mentioned in the beginning of the chapter, after a firm capitalizes the costs, it then begins to allocate them as a depreciation expense over the asset's useful life. Let's turn next to the methods firms use to do this.

DEPRECIATION

Firms acquire assets, such as buildings and equipment, with the intent that they be used for an extended period. When a firm uses an asset over multiple periods, the firm depreciates the cost of the asset over the asset's useful life. The matching principle directs that, when possible, costs should be matched to the revenues generated by the costs. In the case of long-term assets, however, direct matching often proves difficult, if not impossible. As a result, GAAP dictates that firms systematically allocate the cost of the asset over its estimated useful life.

Recorded depreciation expense thus does *not* represent the actual decline in value of an asset over a period, or even the cost of using the asset. Instead, depreciation expense serves as a reminder that a company incurred past costs, and provides information about how the company will charge those costs to future periods. In addition, information about the balance in accumulated depreciation, and the length of the depreciation period being used, often provides useful information about the likely need for future expenditures for plant and equipment.

DEPRECIATION METHODS

There are many ways that a firm could systematically allocate the costs of acquisition of its assets to future periods. In this section we cover the two depreciation methods that are most commonly used in practice: straight-line and declining balance methods. The declining balance method is an accelerated form of depreciation in that more depreciation is expensed in the early years of the asset's life relative to the straight-line method. We also discuss depreciation methods used for tax purposes and the rationale for the choices that firms make in choosing depreciation methods.

Straight-Line Depreciation

The simplest method of depreciation is **straight-line depreciation.** The basic formula for straight line depreciation is:

$$\text{Depreciation Expense} = \frac{(\text{Asset Cost} - \text{Estimated Salvage Value})}{\text{Estimated Useful Life}}$$

The difference between the cost and the salvage value is sometimes referred to as the **depreciable cost** of the asset. Accountants sometimes refer to the "straight-line rate," which is the percentage of the depreciable cost that is expensed each year. In simpler terms, we can actually calculate the straight-line rate as *1/N,* where *N* represents the useful life of the asset. For example, if the asset has a five-year life, the straight-line rate is $1/5 = 0.2$ or 20 percent. The notion of "straight-line" is probably best conveyed by viewing the change in the asset's carrying value over its life, as illustrated in the graph in Exhibit 9.6 (a $100,000 asset depreciated straight-line over ten years):

Note that even this relatively straightforward computation requires a number of calculations. First, a firm must determine the correct cost of the asset. As discussed earlier, this cost includes all costs to acquire or build the asset and prepare it for its intended purpose. Second, a firm must obtain an estimate of the asset's **salvage value** (i.e., its value at the end of its useful life). Firms often obtain this information by using estimates from prior asset retirements or sales. The salvage value assumed in Exhibit 9.6 was $10,000. Finally, a firm must estimate the asset's useful life. The useful life should represent the shorter of the physical life of the asset or the period over which a company plans to use it.

For example, if a company routinely sells a fleet of vehicles used by the business every three years, the depreciation period for the vehicle should be three

Exhibit 9.6
Straight-line Depreciation

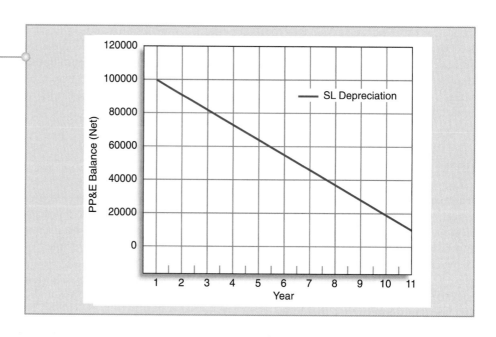

Exhibit 9.7
Straight-Line Depreciation

Asset Cost	$18,000		
Estimated Useful Life	5 years		
Estimated Salvage	$ 3,000		

Depreciation Expense Computations:	Depreciation Expense	Ending Net Book Value
Year 1: ($18,000 − $3,000)/5 =	$3,000	$15,000
Year 2: (18,000 − 3,000)/5 =	3,000	12,000
Year 3: (18,000 − 3,000)/5 =	3,000	9,000
Year 4: (18,000 − 3,000)/5 =	3,000	6,000
Year 5: (18,000 − 3,000)/5 =	3,000	3,000

years. The salvage value in this case should be the estimated salvage for three-year-old vehicles of the type used. Avis documents in its 10-K report that it depreciates its fleet of vehicles straight-line at rates between 10 percent and 29 percent. Exhibit 9.7 provides an illustration of the straight-line method. Note that by the end of year 5, the book value will be the estimated salvage value of $3,000.

Exhibit 9.8 provides a typical disclosure of a firm's depreciation policies from the Arch Chemicals Annual Report.

Declining Balance Methods

The **declining balance methods** are so called because firms compute depreciation on the asset's net book value, which declines over time. The most commonly used declining balance method for financial reporting is the *double-declining balance*. As Exhibit 9.9 shows, under this method, firms use twice the depreciation rate (hence the word "double") of the straight-line rate. Note that the declining balance method ignores salvage value in computing depreciation. However, once an asset approaches estimated salvage value, firms can only record depreciation expense equal to the amount that would bring the asset to its salvage value.

Exhibit 9.8
Arch Chemicals, Inc.
and Subsidiaries 2001
Annual Report

THE REAL WORLD

Arch Chemicals

Notes to the financial Statements

Property, Plant, and Equipment
Property, plant, and equipment are recorded at cost. Depreciation is computed on a straight-line basis over the following estimated useful lives:

Improvements to land	10 to 20 years
Building and building equipment	5 to 25 years
Machinery and equipment	3 to 12 years

Leasehold improvements are amortized over the term of the lease or the estimated useful life of the improvement, whichever is less. Start-up costs are expensed as incurred.

Estimates of useful lives provide an area where management may opportunistically seek to "manage" earnings by using unrealistically long lives. In order to allow investors and other users to assess the reasonableness of asset lives used, companies disclose information about the useful lives used for various classes of assets.

Exhibit 9.9
Double-Declining Balance
Depreciation

			Depreciation Expense	Ending Book Value
Asset Cost	$18,000			
Estimated Useful Life	5 years			
Estimated Salvage	$ 3,000			

The depreciation rate is 40 percent per year computed as the straight-line rate times 2.

Depreciation Expense Computations			Depreciation Expense	Ending Book Value
Year 1:	$18,000 × .4	=	$7,200	$10,800
Year 2:	10,800 × .4	=	4,320	6,480
Year 3:	6,480 × .4	=	2,592	3,888
Year 4:	(3,888 − 3,000)/2 =		444	3,444
Year 5:	(3,888 − 3,000)/2 =		444	3,000

Looking at the example in Exhibit 9.9, note what occurs in Years 4 and 5. If a company follows the straight application of declining balance method, the company would only be able to take $888 of depreciation in Year 4 and no depreciation in Year 5. However, many companies choose to adopt straight-line depreciation once the declining balance depreciation reaches the level where further charges would reduce the asset below its salvage value.

Exhibit 9.10 provides an example of footnote disclosure for depreciation calculated under the declining balance method using the Wellco Energy Services annual report.

Tax Depreciation

For tax purposes, firms follow depreciation guidelines set by the Internal Revenue Code. Tax depreciation for property placed in service after 1986 is based on the **Modified Accelerated Cost Recovery System (MACRS).** Key features of

Exhibit 9.10
Wellco Energy Services, Inc.
2001 Annual Report

THE REAL WORLD

Wellco Energy
Services, Inc.

1. Summary of significant accounting practices

Capital Assets

Capital assets are recorded at cost less accumulated amortization. Amortization is provided on a declining balance basis based on the estimated useful lives of the assets at the following annual rates:

Computer hardware and software	30%
Trucks and trailers	30%
Office furniture and equipment	30%
Directional drilling equipment	20%
Oilfield rental equipment	20%
Wellsite office and accommodation trailers	20%

  Firms may use a variety of rates with the declining balance method. Here, Wellco uses different declining balance rates for different assets. Also note that Wellco uses the term "amortization" instead of "depreciation." In the United States, firms typically use amortization to refer to the write-off of intangible assets, and depreciation to refer to tangible assets.

the MACRS system are as follows:

- Asset lives are shorter than their economic lives.
- Depreciation methods are more rapid than straight-line (based on either 150-percent or 200-percent declining balance methods).
- No salvage value is assumed.

MACRS defines certain classes of assets based on their depreciable lives. Property falling into the three-to-ten-year classes uses 200 percent declining balance, while property in the 15-to-20-year classes uses 150 percent declining balance.

The use of MACRS results in assets being depreciated both over shorter lives and usually at a faster rate than for financial reporting. A company may also use an accelerated method for financial reporting, but if the asset lives differ between the two methods, the amount of depreciation recognized will also differ. However, in accounting for long-lived tangible assets, there is no required conformity between tax and financial reporting. Management can and often does use different depreciation methods and useful lives for tax and financial reporting purposes.

> Tax laws are intended to stimulate investment. Allowing firms to write-off assets more rapidly than the economic life would allow encourages new investment.

CHOICE OF DEPRECIATION METHODS

What factors influence the choice of depreciation methods? For financial reporting, firms commonly use the straight-line method. One reason for this may be that the straight-line method results in higher reported earnings than accelerated methods. However, some companies may use an accelerated depreciation method to provide greater consistency between tax and financial reporting. Significantly large gaps between tax and financial reporting can lead to penalty taxes known as the *alternative minimum tax* (*AMT*).

Management may use the choice of depreciation methods and useful lives to systematically manage reported earnings. For example, selecting a longer useful life than management expects will increase earnings in the short run. Of course, if useful lives are unreasonably long, it is more likely that when the firm sells the assets, they will not be fully depreciated and it will be necessary to recognize a loss on the sale. However, the net effect of this is that management may be able to move this loss to an unusual or infrequent expense. Losses on sales of noncurrent assets may be classified as "other" or unusual expenses. While these losses still constitute part of "income from continuing operations," management may exclude these items from so-called "pro forma" earnings if separately disclosed in the income statement.

As you can see, management has significant discretion when it comes to depreciation expense. These choices exist, in part, because calculations involving depreciation expense rely on estimates and assumptions, such as an asset's useful life and its salvage value. Besides the initial selection of assumptions, management may decide to change these assumptions at some point later in the asset's life. In the next section, we examine how changes in depreciation estimates are reported.

EFFECT OF CHANGES IN ESTIMATES

Depreciation requires an estimate of the useful life and salvage value of assets in advance. Therefore, in some cases, management may need to change these estimates at a later date. Reasons for changes in estimates may relate to technological changes or other economic changes unknown to the company at the time it acquired the assets.

For example, the useful lives of personal computers have changed rapidly since the early 1980s, when they first became commonly used in business. In the early years, estimated lives were fairly long as management did not anticipate the speed of change in personal computing. Then, in the late 1980s and 1990s, firms replaced computers so often that some companies simply expensed them when purchased. More recently, as technological innovation has slowed, personal computer useful lives need to be adjusted once again to reflect expected replacement dates.

Firms record any changes in estimated useful lives or salvage value of assets *prospectively*. This means that a firm adjusts the current year's and future years' depreciation to account for any changes in estimates, but does not restate prior years' depreciation. To illustrate, assume that a company depreciates an asset costing $18,000 over a five-year period, using straight-line depreciation with no salvage value. At the beginning of the third year, management decides that the asset will be used for six years rather than five. Depreciation expense for years 1 and 2 would be $18,000/5 or $3,600 per year. The change in estimate at the beginning of year 3 will change the depreciation expense to $2,700 per year ($18,000 − $3,600 − $3,600)/4 for the remaining four years.

In this case, the change in estimate reduces depreciation expense, thereby increasing reported earnings. The external audit committee, corporate audit boards, and internal auditors must carefully scrutinize such changes to assure that the changes are appropriate and are not undertaken simply to meet earnings targets or to mislead investors. When a firm makes material changes in estimates, the firm's financial footnotes should provide information about the reason for the change. Exhibit 9.11 provides an example of the disclosure provided when such a change is made from the annual report of Blockbuster.

Exhibit 9.11
Blockbuster, 2001
Annual Report

THE REAL WORLD

Blockbuster

Notes to the Financial Statements

Note 4—Change in Accounting Estimates for Rental Library
In connection with the strategic re-merchandising plan discussed in Note 3, Blockbuster reevaluated and changed the accounting estimates related to its rental library, including residual values and useful lives. Effective July 1, 2001, the residual value of VHS rental products was reduced from $4 to $2, and the residual value of game rental products was reduced from $10 to $5. In addition, the Company reduced its estimate of the useful life of its base stock VHS rental library from 36 months to 9 months. These changes in estimate reflect the impact of changes in the Company's rental business, such as an increase in DVD rental revenues, a decrease in VHS rental revenues and trends affecting games, which have led to a reduction in the average selling value of the Company's previously rented VHS and game products and a reduction in the average life of VHS rental products. As a result of these changes in estimate, cost of rental revenues was $141.7 million higher, net loss was $90.1 million higher, and net loss per share was $0.51 higher for the year ended December 31, 2001.

 In response to the increasing popularity of DVD media in comparison to VHS, Blockbuster reduced the residual value and useful life of its VHS media. The effect of these changes increased Blockbuster's cost of rental revenues and resulted in its net loss.

ASSET IMPAIRMENTS

Even when firms systematically depreciate assets, it is possible that for some reason the asset will decline in value such that its recoverable value is less than its book value (cost minus accumulated depreciation). SFAS No. 121 (FASB, SFAS No. 121, 1995) addresses this possibility. SFAS 121 requires that long-lived tangible and intangible assets be reviewed for impairment when economic events suggest that a firm may not recover the carrying amount of an asset. The review for recoverability requires that the firm estimate the expected future cash flows from the use of the asset. If the sum of the expected future cash flows (without discounting or interest) is less than the carrying value, then an impairment charge must be recognized. The impairment loss should be an amount needed to reduce the asset to its fair value. Exhibit 9.12 provides a sample disclosure of asset impairment.

While, theoretically, firms may recognize impairment charges at any time, the type of events and circumstances leading to an impairment review suggest that companies are more likely to recognize impairment charges when they are having financial difficulties and may be incurring losses. As a result, care needs to be taken to assure that impairments are not recorded prematurely as a means to improve future performance. In some cases, companies experiencing an economic downturn may seek to find all sources of losses and bundle them in order to improve future earnings. This is called a *big bath*. The impact: reporting a high return on investment is easier in future years because the asset basis is lower.

Managers find the notion of a big bath appealing for several reasons. First, while the market responds negatively to losses, its reaction may not be proportionate to the response to positive earnings or to the size of the loss. Furthermore, if the firm incurs the loss during a general economic downturn, the negative market response to the loss may be even less. Second, management compensation is often based on meeting certain earnings growth and market performance

Note 2—Significant Accounting Policies

(f) Impairment of Long-lived Assets: Long-lived assets are reviewed for impairment whenever events or changes in circumstances indicate that the carrying amount of the asset may not be recoverable. Recoverability of assets to be held and used is measured by a comparison of the carry amount of an asset to its undiscounted future net cash flows expected to be generated by the asset. If such assets are considered to be impaired, impairment is measured by comparing the carrying amount to the fair value or undiscounted cash flow.

During Fiscal year 1999, the Company continued to operate at a loss, continued to downsize its operations, and was not using certain plant assets at their full capacity, which triggered a review of its long-lived assets. Based on the Company's business plan for fiscal 2000, the trend in the apparel industry to move production off-shore and the age and condition of the Company's distribution facility in the United States, the Company determined that certain of its plan assets were impaired. The Company calculated the present value of expected cash flows of certain plant assets consisting of land, buildings, machinery, and equipment to be held and used to determine the fair value of the assets. Accordingly, in the fourth quarter of fiscal 1999, the Company recorded an impairment charge of $1,415.

Exhibit 9.12
Delta Apparel, Inc., 2001
Annual Report

THE REAL WORLD

Delta Apparel, Inc.

targets. If management is aware that the targets will be missed, they have an incentive to maximize losses in the current period. Doing so makes it easier to meet targets in the future.

What's wrong with this? Such behavior interjects biases into financial statements and misleads investors. Further, it may lead management to prematurely recognize impairment losses.

INTANGIBLE ASSETS

In addition to long-lived tangible assets (i.e., property, plant, and equipment) either purchased or manufactured, businesses also have intangible resources that provide long-term value. *Internally created intangibles* relate to expenditures that create value over multiple periods. In general, internally created intangible assets are not capitalized as assets. Instead, these types of expenditures are considered current period expenses. However, when intangible assets are purchased, they are measured and treated as assets. Examples of intangible assets include the following:

- Research and development
- Computer software
- Goodwill
- Trademarks
- Patents

The accounting treatment of intangible resources varies with the type of resource. Let's take a closer look at some of these intangible resources.

RESEARCH AND DEVELOPMENT

GAAP requires that research and development costs be expensed as incurred. As a result, companies that invest heavily in research and development will tend to have fewer assets, with a higher rate of return on them, than companies that invest more heavily in physical facilities. This also suggests that, if the research and development is successful, companies with heavy investments in research and development should have higher market-to-book ratios than comparable companies that invest in physical assets.

COMPUTER SOFTWARE

Interestingly, although the development of computer software is similar to research and development, the software industry successfully lobbied the FASB for separate treatment. During the early 1980s, the software industry grew rapidly, and firms in this industry argued that writing off all software development costs would be detrimental to economic development. In response to this concern, the FASB issued SFAS No. 86 (FASB, SFAS No. 86, 1985).

FASB No. 86 specifies that a firm should expense its costs of creating computer software until it establishes the software's technological feasibility. At that time, the firm capitalizes software production costs, reporting them at the lower of unamortized cost or net realizable value. The amortization period is the estimated economic life of the product.

This treatment is unique to the software industry. For example, a pharmaceutical company engages in research and development, and subsequently in product development. However, pharmaceutical companies only capitalize the actual manufacturing costs. This peculiarity caused political problems for pharmaceutical companies, who are often criticized for high margins on their profitable products (e.g., Bristol Myers Squibb, 65 percent; Eli Lilly, 80 percent; and Schering Plough, 75 percent). One reason that these margins appear to be so high is that the firms expensed their biggest cost (the research and development leading to the development of the drugs) in years prior to the actual sale.

OIL AND GAS EXPLORATION COSTS AND RESERVES

The oil and gas industry also has unique issues relating to long-term assets. Oil and gas are natural resources discovered by drilling in a number of locations. Geologists determine that drilling in certain areas is likely to uncover oil. However, a significant number of these drillings prove unsuccessful.

Most companies use one of two methods of accounting for oil exploration development costs: **successful efforts** and **full cost.** Under successful efforts accounting, a firm only capitalizes the costs of drilling for areas where it finds oil, and expenses any costs related to unsuccessful drilling. Under the full cost method of accounting, a firm capitalizes all drilling costs, whether successful or not. Under either method, a firm writes off the capitalized costs over the period during which it removes oil or gas from the ground.

Because the full cost method results in more costs being capitalized, it also results in higher earnings, as long as companies continue to grow and find new oil. This is because exploration costs do not reduce current period's earnings as much as they would under successful efforts.

As a result of a more favorable and less-volatile earnings effect, smaller companies tend to use the full cost method, while larger diversified companies most often use successful efforts. The FASB, however, preferred the successful efforts method for displaying the risks associated with exploration activities. As a result, in 1977 the FASB issued SFAS No. 19 (FASB, SFAS No. 19, 1977), mandating that all firms use successful efforts.

This standard proved highly controversial. Small oil and gas producers lobbied Congress, arguing that successful efforts accounting made it impossible for them to raise capital and would therefore significantly reduce oil exploration. At that time, many expressed significant concerns about a worldwide oil shortage and rising costs due to dependence on foreign oil. These conditions prompted congressional involvement, leading the SEC to nullify the SFAS requirement for SEC filings. Consequently, the FASB suspended SFAS No. 19 in 1979 (FASB, SFAS No. 25, 1979). Today companies continue to have a choice of methods.

The SEC then pushed for a method of accounting known as reserve recognition accounting. Under reserve recognition accounting, oil and gas reserves and changes in their value would be recognized as assets. This method was not accepted due to the large errors inherent in estimating reserves. However, in 1982 the FASB issued SFAS No. 69 (FASB, SFAS No. 69, 1982), requiring oil and gas companies to provide supplemental disclosures of the value of oil and gas reserves and changes in the reserves. For oil and gas companies, the value of reserves, while off the balance sheet, is one of their most important economic resources.

One final issue related to oil and gas accounting is worth mentioning. Writing off the capitalized costs of oil and gas production is called **depletion.** The most common method of depletion is called **units-of-production.** Under this method, firms estimate the amount of oil available and then recognize depletion in proportion to the amount pumped each year. Exhibit 9.13 provides an illustration of a typical press release for an oil and gas company.

GOODWILL

Goodwill is an intangible asset that a company recognizes primarily when it buys another company in its entirety. While a company may develop internally

---

Exhibit 9.13

THE REAL WORLD

Anadarko Petroleum
Corporation

July 25, 2002—Anadarko Petroleum Corporation today reported net income available to common stockholders of $239 million, or 93 cents per share (diluted) for the second quarter of 2002. For the second quarter of 2001, the company reported net income available to common stockholders of $401 million, or $1.50 per share (diluted).

In January 2002, Anadarko discontinued the amortization of goodwill in accordance with the Statement of Financial Accounting Standards No. 142 "Goodwill and Other Intangible Assets." Stated without amortization of goodwill, net income for the second quarter of 2001 would have been $420 million, or $1.57 per share (diluted).

"This quarter, Anadarko achieved volumes of 50 million barrels of oil equivalent and reported several nice discoveries, which puts us on track to deliver on our goal of 199 million BOE by year-end," said John Seitz, Anadarko president and chief executive officer. "Our progress to date will help us build momentum to grow production by at least 5 percent in 2003," Seitz added. "We have a deep portfolio of attractive prospects ready to drill. A number of high-potential wells that we're planning should contribute to growth in production and reserves for many years to come."

 Note that the press release addresses not only Anadarko's earnings, but also its volume of oil, discoveries of oil during the past year, and management's assessment of future prospects. The disclosure also discusses Anadarko's accounting for goodwill, a class of intangible assets considered in this chapter.

Before the cumulative effect of the adoption of FAS 142, the Company reported a net loss of $1 million, or break-even per basic common share in the first quarter of 2002 (which includes certain nonrecurring items totaling $688 million of pretax losses). This compares to a reported net loss of $1.4 billion, or $0.31 loss per basic common share, in the same quarter of 2001 (which includes certain nonrecurring items totaling $691 million of pretax losses, and goodwill and intangible amortization of approximately $1.8 billion, which did not recur in 2002 due to the adoption of FAS 142).

The first-quarter adoption of FAS 142 resulted in a one-time, noncash charge that reduced the carrying value of the Company's goodwill by approximately $54 billion. After the effect of this accounting change, the Company incurred a net loss of $54.2 billion for the quarter, or a loss of $12.25 per basic common share.

Exhibit 9.14
AOL Time Warner
(press release)
Q1 2002, April 24, 2002
Consolidated Reported
Results

THE REAL WORLD

AOL Time Warner

generated goodwill, a company does not recognize such goodwill as an asset. Until recently, goodwill was considered to be a wasting asset and was amortized over periods ranging from ten to forty years. SFAS No. 142 (FASB, SFAS No. 142, 2001), enacted in 2001, substantially changed the accounting treatment of goodwill and other purchased intangibles (patents, trademarks, etc.).

Under SFAS No. 142, goodwill is not amortized but firms annually test goodwill and other intangibles for impairment using a two-step process. The first step screens for impairment, and the second step measures the amount of the impairment that results in an impairment loss on the income statement. One of the largest goodwill write-offs ever recognized was by AOL Time Warner in the first quarter of 2002. Exhibit 9.14 includes an excerpt from AOL's press release regarding its first quarter of 2002 annual earnings statement. An important consideration regarding purchased patents or other capitalized legal rights is that subsequent amortization should be over economic lives that may at times be shorter than their legal lives (economic lives could not be longer than legal lives).

TRANSITION AND SUMMARY

Long-lived assets reflect capital expenditures expected to contribute to the generation of future cash flows. The determination of what costs to capitalize as long-lived assets often requires judgment, thereby affording management discretion that may affect reported income. Further, the economic value to the company of such assets is difficult to measure. As a result, firms account for long-lived assets on a depreciated historical cost basis. In the event that depreciated cost is greater than market value (impairment), long-lived assets must be written down to market value. The net effect of these requirements means that the balance sheet values of long-lived assets are normally less than their fair market value.

Firms also possess economic resources that are not recognized as assets. Most notable of these are internally created goodwill and research and development assets. However, specific unrecognized economic resources vary by industry. For example, in the petroleum industry, the market value of oil and gas reserves is a major value driver and is disclosed as an asset but not specifically recorded in the financial statements.

END OF CHAPTER MATERIAL

KEY TERMS

Capital Expenditures

Depreciation

Amortization

Interest Capitalization

Basket Purchase

Straight-Line Depreciation

Depreciable Cost

Salvage Value

Declining Balance Methods

Modified Accelerated Cost Recovery System (MACRS)

Successful Efforts

Full Cost

Depletion

Units-of-Production Method

ASSIGNMENT MATERIAL

● REVIEW QUESTIONS

1. Describe what is meant by tangible and intangible assets.

2. Discuss the types of costs that should be capitalized for a piece of plant or equipment.

3. Describe the procedure under GAAP to allocate the cost of a basket purchase of assets to the individual assets.

4. Describe how interest can be capitalized as a part of the construction costs of an asset.

5. Discuss the purpose of depreciation expense and the various patterns of depreciation that might be taken by a firm.

6. Discuss the motivations that a firm might have for choosing one depreciation method over another for both book and tax purposes.

7. Describe how salvage value and useful life are used in the calculation of depreciation under the two primary methods: straight-line and declining balance.

8. Describe the advantages that MACRS offers firms and why Congress provided this advantage.

9. Discuss the nature of full cost versus successful efforts methods of accounting for drilling costs.

10. Under GAAP, describe the conditions under which intangible assets can be recorded on the books of a firm and the rules under which that value can then be expensed over the life of the asset. Specifically discuss goodwill, research and development, and patents.

11. Discuss the conditions under which a firm is required to write down its long-term assets.

● APPLYING YOUR KNOWLEDGE

12. Suppose that a firm decides to discontinue a line of business. Describe what you think would be the most appropriate valuation basis for the property,

plant, and equipment for this discontinued operation. As an investor in the stock of the company, discuss what disclosure might be most useful to you in this circumstance.

13. As a lender, discuss how much comfort you might get from the existence of long-term assets, specifically plant and goodwill, in making a long-term loan to a firm.

14. As an auditor, discuss how you might evaluate a firm's property, plant, and equipment to assess whether it should write down the value of these assets.

15. In some countries (such as the United Kingdom) firms can write off goodwill at the date of acquisition by directly reducing owners' equity; in other words, the write-off does not pass through net income. Suppose that a U.S. company and a UK company agreed to purchase the same company for the same amount of money. As a stock analyst, describe how the balance sheet and income statement would differ for the two companies after the acquisition. Discuss whether this provides any differential advantage to either of the two companies.

16. Suppose that you are the accounting manager of a division of a large firm and your compensation is partly based on meeting a net income target. In the current year it seems unlikely that your division will meet its target. You have some property, plant, and equipment that have been idle for a while but have not yet been written off. What incentives do you have to write its value off during the current year and if you do write it off, how will it impact your future ability to meet the income targets for your division?

17. Forest product companies that buy timberland face a basket purchase situation. The purchase of timberland involves both the land that is purchased as well as the timber that stands on the land. If you are the accounting manager, how would you attempt to allocate the purchase price of the timberland between the land and the timber? What incentives might you have to allocate a disproportionate amount to either the land or the timber?

18. In evaluating the liquidity of a firm, what effect does the capitalization of interest have on your analysis (how does it affect the ratios that you might compute to evaluate liquidity)?

19. As a stock analyst, discuss any inadequacies that you might find with the financial statements (as prepared under GAAP) of a firm that is predominantly a research and development company.

20. In some countries, firms are permitted to revalue property, plant, and equipment to current replacement cost. The gain/loss that results is typically reported as a direct adjustment to owners' equity; in other words, it does not pass through income. As a stock analyst comparing a U.S. company with a foreign competitor that is allowed to revalue assets, how would this affect your analysis and how might you adjust the financial statements to make a fair comparison between the two companies?

21. Suppose that you have been asked to provide an analysis of a potential acquisition candidate by your firm. Which long-term assets that exist on the financial statements are the most likely to be misstated by their book values and why? Discuss the long-term assets of the candidate firm that might not be represented at all on the financial statements of the firm.

22. On June 30, 20X5, Sherman Bros. purchased a new machine for $20,000. A useful life of ten years and a salvage value of $500 were estimated. On September 30, 20X6, another machine was acquired for $50,000. Its useful life was estimated to be 15 years and its salvage value $2,000. On April 30, 20X7, the first machine was sold for $17,000. Sherman Bros. closes its books on December 31 each year and uses the straight-line method of depreciation.

Required: Give the necessary journal entries for the years 20X5 through 20X7.

23. On March 31, 20X4, Hammer & Holding, Inc. purchased new machinery. The company acquired the new machinery by trading in its old machine, paying $22,975 in cash and issuing a 12 percent note for $5,000. The old machinery was acquired on June 30, 20X1, for $30,000. At that time, its estimated useful life was ten years, with a $1,000 salvage value. The asset's market value was approximately the same as its book value at the date of trade-in. The new machinery's estimated life is five years, and its salvage value is $2,500. The company uses a straight-line method of depreciation and closes its books on December 31.

Required:

a. Give the necessary journal entries for 20X4.

b. On March 31, 20X9, the machinery acquired in 20X4 could not be sold, and the company decided to write it off. Give the necessary journal entries for 20X9.

24. On October 31, 20X3, the Steelman Cupboard Company acquired a new machine for $85,000. The company estimated the useful life to be ten years and expected a salvage value of $1,000. On December 31, 20X5, the company decided that the machine was to be used for another ten years beyond that date and that the salvage value would be $800. On June 30, 20X8, the machine was sold for $45,000. The company uses the straight-line method of depreciation and closes its books on December 31.

Required: Give the necessary journal entries for 20X3, 20X6, and 20X8.

25. The Vector Company builds its own machinery, which it later uses for the production of its products. On January 1, 20X4, the company borrowed $5 million at an annual interest rate of 9 percent for a period of six years. Interest is paid on January 1 for the interest incurred in the previous year. The company borrowed the money specifically to finance the construction of this necessary machinery. On July 1, 20X4, the company initiated its production process for building a machine. An average amount of $3.5 million was invested in making the machine in 20X4. On January 1, 20X5, the company borrowed another $5 million for general purposes, not strictly related to construction of the equipment, at an interest rate of 10 percent for a period of five years. On average, an additional amount of $2 million was invested in the manufacture of the equipment in 20X5. The construction process was completed on March 31, 20X6. The additional average amount of construction costs incurred in 20X6 was $75,000. The Vector Company makes all its interest payments on time and closes its books on December 31.

Required: Give the necessary journal entries for 20X4, 20X5, and 20X6.

26. A machine is purchased on January 1, 20X3, for $50,000. It is expected to have a useful life of eight years and a salvage value of $2,000. The asset

qualifies as a five-year asset for tax purposes. The company closes its books on December 31.

Required:

a. Compute the amount of depreciation to be charged each year using each of the following methods:

   1. Straight-line method

   2. Double-declining balance method

b. Under what circumstances might management have an incentive to over-estimate the asset's expected useful life?

c. What are the valuation implications of systematically overestimating assets' useful lives for financial reporting purposes?

27. The Pure Oil Company estimated that the new oil field that it acquired has 5 million barrels of oil. The company extracted 500,000 barrels in year 1, 600,000 barrels in year 2, and 1 million barrels in year 3. The costs capitalized for the oil field total $25 million. The company uses the depletion method.

Required: Compute the depletion expense for each year.

READING AND INTERPRETING PUBLISHED FINANCIAL STATEMENTS

28. The asset section of the balance sheet of McCormick & Company, Inc. from its 1996 annual report is shown below. McCormick & Company produces and markets spices and other food products.

MCCORMICK & CO., INC.
Balance Sheet

	11/30/1996	11/30/1995
Current assets		
Cash and cash equivalents	$ 22,418,000	$ 12,465,000
Receivables, less allowances of $3,527 for		
1996 and $2,545 for 1995	217,495,000	223,958,000
Inventories	245,089,000	383,222,000
Prepaid expenses	15,648,000	17,093,000
Deferred income taxes	33,762,000	33,980,000
Total current assets	534,412,000	670,718,000
Property, plant, and equipment, net	400,394,000	524,807,000
Goodwill, net	165,066,000	180,751,000
Prepaid allowances	149,200,000	183,357,000
Investments and other assets	77,535,000	54,706,000
Trademarks, formulae, etc.	1,000	1,000
Human relations	1,000	1,000
	$1,326,609,000	$1,614,341,000

Required:

a. Listed among the assets of McCormick are "Trademarks, formulae, etc." and "Human relations." Discuss the nature of these assets and why you think they should or should not be recorded on the books of the company.

b. Does the presence of the assets discussed in Part a change the analysis of the company in any way?

29. Here are the third-quarter income statement results for Nicor, Inc. Nicor is the parent company of Nicor Gas. During the third quarter of 2003, Nicor changed its method of allocating depreciation expense to its quarterly financial statements. Nicor calculates its depreciation expense on a straight-line basis, but prior to the change had allocated the annual amount of this straight-line depreciation to its quarterly statements on the basis of what it referred to as the "level of weather-normalized gas deliveries." Therefore, the allocation was driven in part by quarterly sales. In the third quarter, this was changed to allocate the depreciation using a straight-line method; in other words, an equal amount was allocated to each quarter.

Nicor, Inc.
Condensed Consolidated Statements of Operations (unaudited)
(millions, except per share data)

	Three months ended Sep. 30		Nine months ended Sep. 30	
	2003	2002	2003	2002
Operating revenues				
Gas distribution (includes revenue taxes				
of $11.4, $9.1, $98.3, and $66.0, respectively)	$223.4	$172.7	$1,699.6	$ 971.2
Shipping	63.8	66.6	197.4	191.6
Other	7.6	13.1	21.9	29.8
	294.8	252.4	1,918.9	1,192.6
Operating expenses				
Gas distribution				
Cost of gas	117.6	65.4	1,221.5	527.3
Operating and maintenance	51.4	48.2	164.5	143.4
Depreciation	35.6	17.0	107.6	96.2
Taxes, other than income taxes	14.4	13.4	108.4	77.1
Mercury-related costs (recoveries)	–	(19.7)	(17.8)	(19.5)
Property sale (gains) losses	–	–	(0.4)	(3.4)
Shipping	60.8	62.2	183.8	179.2
All other	10.8	12.3	26.9	30.0
	290.6	198.8	1,794.5	1,030.3
Operating income	4.2	53.6	124.4	162.3
Equity investment income (loss), net	4.8	(2.6)	12.9	(7.5)
Other income (expense), net	0.4	0.7	1.5	2.5
Interest expense, net of amounts capitalized	8.8	9.7	27.8	28.4
Income before income taxes and cumulative effect of				
accounting change	0.6	42.0	111.0	128.9
Income taxes	0.1	12.2	36.3	40.1
Income before cumulative effect of accounting change	0.5	29.8	74.7	88.8
Cumulative effect of accounting change, net of				
3.0 income tax benefit	–	–	(4.5)	–
Net income	$ 0.5	$ 29.8	$ 70.2	$ 88.8

a. From a conceptual point of view, discuss which of the two methods seems most appropriate to report quarterly depreciation.

b. Nicor disclosed that its third-quarter net income fell by approximately 95 percent because of this change. Estimate what the net income would have been had the previous method been followed.

c. Nicor also disclosed the pro forma effects of this change on the prior year's (2002) results. On a pro forma basis, the depreciation would have been $36.2 million for the three months ended September 30, 2002. How would this have affected reported net income for that quarter?

d. What effect will this change have on the yearly depreciation expense reported by Nicor?

30. Nicor, Inc. (see the description in the previous problem) operates gas distribution, transmission, and storage facilities. In accordance with industry practice, it has recognized its obligation associated with the ultimate closing of those facilities over time. Until 2003, Nicor recognized those costs as additional depreciation expense, arguing that these costs ultimately affected the salvage value of the asset. If taken to the end of the life of the asset, this would imply that the asset would ultimately have a negative value on the company's books, reflective of these additional accrued costs. Discuss whether you believe this is the appropriate accounting to follow for these costs and if it is not, suggest an appropriate alternative.

31. Teekay Shipping Corporation is incorporated under the laws of the Republic of the Marshall Islands but trades shares on a U.S. exchange (ticker TK) and prepares its statements under U.S. GAAP. On December 9, 2003, the International Maritime Association (IMO) announced stricter regulations governing the tanker industry such that the phase-out of single hull tankers would be accelerated due to the environmental concerns for potential oil spills resulting from the rupture of single hull tankers. Twenty-two out of 86 of Teekay's owned fleet (its total fleet, including leased vessels, numbers 150) would be affected. The net effect on Teekay's affected vessels would be to shorten their estimated life from 25 years to 21 years as well as to affect the total future revenue stream that would be produced from these vessels. Teekay uses the straight-line method to depreciate its vessels.

a. Discuss what potential effects these events would have on Teekay's balance sheet and income statement.

b. What effect would these events have on the cash flow statement of Teekay?

c. If the effect of the regulations is to reduce the worldwide fleet of tankers, discuss what you think might be the valuation impact on Teekay's stock price.

○ BEYOND THE BOOK

32. Choose a company as directed by your instructor and answer the following questions:

a. Prepare a quick analysis of the noncurrent asset accounts by listing the beginning and ending amounts in these accounts and calculating the net change in both dollar and percentage terms for the most recent year. If your company does not prepare a classified balance sheet, you will need to determine which assets are noncurrent.

b. If any of the accounts change by more than 10 percent, give an explanation for this change.

c. What percentage of the company's total assets are invested in property, plant, and equipment? Has this percentage changed significantly over the last year?

d. What depreciation method(s) does the company use for its financial statements?

e. Use the following formulas to examine the property, plant, and equipment for the company:

Average Age of PP&E = Total Accumulated Depreciation/Total Depreciation Expense

Average Useful Life of PP&E = Total Gross PP&E/Total Depreciation Expense

Note: Remember that depreciation expense may not be disclosed in the income statement but will usually appear in the statement of cash flows. Compare your results to any information disclosed in the footnotes. Do these results make sense?

f. Does the company have any significant intangible assets? If so, describe each of them.

g. Compare the company you selected with at least two other companies in the same industry. How does your company compare in terms of its accounting for long-term assets? What are the potential implications of any differences?

CHAPTER 10

Operating Liabilities: Recognition and Disclosure

After reading this chapter you should be able to:

1. Determine when to recognize a liability for accounting purposes.

2. Understand the accounting treatment of account payables, accrued liabilities, deferred revenue, and restructuring charges.

3. Recognize the disclosure requirements for contingent liabilities.

4. Explain the concept of income tax and financial reporting timing differences and related deferrals of income taxes.

5. Identify the main accounting issues and disclosure requirements associated with company-provided pension and other post-retirement benefits.

During 2001 Shigeo Watanabe, President, Chairman of the Board, and Chief Executive Officer of the Bridgestone Corporation, announced the following: "Net earnings declined 80% in the past year, to 17.7 billion yen ($164 million). That decline is attributable mainly to a special charge in connection with the tire recall in the United States. We have recorded a charge at Bridgestone/Firestone of $754 million (81.4 billion yen) for costs already incurred in replacing the recalled tires and for potential liabilities and other legal costs in connection with the problems that led to the recall. That provision is consistent with generally accepted accounting principles."

As the CEO of Bridgestone indicates, the widely publicized recall of Firestone tires in 2001 gave rise to the recognition of a sizeable provision for losses and related liability. The provision included estimates of the direct costs of the recall, as well as of the projected settlements of product liability suits and claims, net of insurance recoveries. Accounting decisions such as this often involve considerable judgment as to what constitutes a liability that should be recognized under generally accepted accounting principles.

The treatment of liabilities is equally as important as that of assets in the valuation of the firm. While assets represent future cash inflows to the firm, liabilities represent future cash outflows. An important issue in assessing the financial health of a firm is the consideration of liabilities that have not been recognized on the firm's financial statements. In this chapter, we begin by addressing the issue of when to recognize liabilities, including the treatment of contingencies, such as the prospect of future losses from the settlement of a lawsuit. Next, we review accounting treatments of various classes of operating liabilities. Operating liabilities considered in this chapter include amounts owed to vendors (who supply inputs to production or goods for resale), accruals of wages and other expenses yet to be paid, obligations to deliver goods and services to customers who have paid in advance, estimated costs of future claims related to product warranties, deferred income taxes, and pensions and other post-retirement benefits. We consider liabilities related to a firm's financing activities, such as bonds, in Chapter 11.

LIABILITY RECOGNITION

Recall that in previous chapters we reviewed recognition criteria for assets, revenues, and expenses. Here, we consider the general recognition criteria associated with liabilities. The FASB's Statement of Financial Accounting Concepts No. 6 (FASB, SFAC No. 6, 1985) discusses the basic characteristics of liabilities as follows:

● A liability is a probable future sacrifice of resources.
● The entity that is obligated has little or no discretion to avoid the future sacrifice.
● The transaction or event that gives rise to the obligation has already occurred.

The probable future sacrifice criterion is similar to the probable future value criterion for assets. However, the rules for recognition of liabilities often require recognition of liabilities earlier than that of assets, due to accounting conservatism. In general, accounting conservatism requires greater certainty with respect to recognition of assets and revenues than it does with respect to liabilities and expenses.

BALANCE SHEET CLASSIFICATION

Firms classify balance sheet liabilities as either current or noncurrent. Current liabilities include those that come due in less that one year (or, more rarely, one operating cycle, if longer). Noncurrent liabilities include long-term debt and other obligations due in more than one year. While we consider both long-term

	05/25/2003	05/25/2002
Notes payable	26,900,000	30,900,000
Current installments of long-term debt	508,700,000	209,000,000
Accounts payable	1,277,000,000	2,103,900,000
Advances on sales	351,300,000	374,800,000
Accrued payroll	282,700,000	291,100,000
Other accrued liabilities	1,210,400,000	1,161,800,000
Current liabilities of discontinued operations	146,400,000	141,900,000
Total current liabilities	3,803,400,000	4,313,400,000

Exhibit 10.1
Current Liability Section of the Balance Sheet

THE REAL WORLD

ConAgra Foods

and short-term debt as financing activities, liabilities that occur in the course of normal operations are referred to as operating liabilities. Most, but not all, operating liabilities are classified as current liabilities, while most, but not all, financing liabilities are long-term.

The balance sheet of ConAgra Foods as shown in Exhibit 10.1 illustrates this type of classification. ConAgra's current liabilities include debt (notes payable and the current installments of long-term debt) as well as operating liabilities. **Notes payable** represent ConAgra's formal promise to repay an amount in the future. Here, the firm classifies notes payable as current liabilities if the amount is due in one year or less (and noncurrent otherwise). The **current installments of long-term debt** relate to that portion of long-term debt that is also due in one year or less. This classification highlights to users the portion of long-term debt that has matured. We will consider both notes payable and long-term debt in more detail in Chapter 11. Note also that ConAgra reports the current liabilities of discontinued operations in a single line item. In Chapter 4 we had discussed the income statement treatment of discontinued operations. On the balance sheet, firms are required to also segregate the assets and liabilities of discontinued operations from those of continuing operations. ConAgra's remaining current liabilities all relate to operations, which we look at next.

ACCOUNTS PAYABLE

Accounts payable occur when a firm buys goods or services on credit. Because payment is generally deferred for a relatively short period of time, such as 30 to 60 days, these accounts generally do not carry explicit interest charges. Under some agreements, there can be either a penalty for late payment or a discount provision for early payment. The penalty and the difference between the discounted payment and the full payment can both be viewed as interest charges for delayed payments on these liabilities.

To illustrate, let's return to our example from previous chapters, Biohealth Inc. (BHT). BHT purchases goods from a pharmaceutical company with terms of 2/10 net 30. This means that BHT receives a discount of 2 percent off the invoice price if it pays the balance within ten days. The full invoice price is due within 30 days. Suppose that BHT orders drugs with an invoice price of $6,200,000 from the supplier. The discount for paying within ten days is $124,000,

Exhibit 10.2

THE REAL WORLD

Fleming Company

An article in the *Wall Street Journal* (Zimmerman, *Wall Street Journal,* 2002) on September 5, 2002 criticized the Fleming Company's policy of deducting amounts from its payments to suppliers. Some vendors argued that this deduction policy led to Fleming underpaying its accounts. In response, Fleming held a press conference in which the company claimed that it simply followed standard industry practice. Mark Hanson, Chairman of the Board and CEO of Fleming, wrote an open letter to Fleming associates in which he stated, "Deductions are an accepted, industry-wide practice that allow buyers such as Fleming to capture all vendor dollars we are entitled to receive but haven't been reflected on vendor invoices." The market response to the news of the disputed discounts was not positive. Fleming's stock price dropped from $8 per share on September 4 to $4.55 a share on September 20 as the market revised its expectations. Fleming filed for bankruptcy in 2003.

> Taking or not taking a discount on purchases can have a significant impact on the cash flows of the firm from operations because the implicit interest rate for such transactions is often very high, making the option of not taking the discount very expensive.

so the net price of the drugs is $6,076,000. If BHT fails to take the discount, it would pay $124,000/$6,076,000 = 2.041 percent for the use of $6,076,000 for 20 days (30 − 10). On an annualized basis, this interest rate amounts to over 37 percent. As a result, because of the costs involved, firms usually take any purchase discounts offered. Many companies follow a practice of recording the cost of purchases net of the discount (in this case at $6,076,000) to reflect the expectation that the purchase discount will be taken.

In most cases, recognition of accounts payable is straightforward. However, as the Fleming Company disclosure in Exhibit 10.2 illustrates, even accounts payable can be subject to dispute regarding the correct amount of the liability to recognize. The effect of the deductions that Fleming was alleged to have taken were discounts off of the bills presented to them by vendors. These deductions were then used to reduce the expenses reported in the current period, thus increasing reported net income. In one class action lawsuit filed against Fleming, the magnitude of the discounts under dispute had reached $100 million which exceeded the company's first quarter net income in 2001.

ADVANCES ON SALES AND UNEARNED REVENUE

> A common measure of a young firm's ability to service its debt is a crude measure of operating cash flows known as EBITDA (earnings before interest, taxes, depreciation, and amortization). Sometimes this measure is further refined to include increases in unearned revenue that arise from receiving more cash from customers than amounts recognized as revenue.

Advances on sales represent amounts received from customers, but not yet earned, as determined by the revenue recognition concepts introduced in Chapter 4. A similar item is **unearned revenues,** defined as revenues that have been collected but for which the company has not yet provided the goods or services. For example, magazine subscriptions are generally paid in advance. When a company sells a subscription, it records a debit to cash (or accounts receivable) and a credit to unearned revenue. As the company earns the revenue by sending out the magazine, unearned revenue is debited and revenues are credited.

For example, Reader's Digest reports unearned revenues of $291.6 million and $289.4 million in the current liabilities section of its balance sheet at fiscal year ends 2001 and 2000, respectively, and magazine revenues of $652.5 million for fiscal year 2001. (A footnote discusses its method of revenue recognition policy, noting that it defers sales and recognition of magazine subscriptions until delivery to subscribers.) We can reconstruct hypothetical journal entries (in millions) to summarize Reader's Digest's new subscriptions and revenue recognized in 2001 as follows (the 654.7 can be calculated since you know the beginning and ending balance in the unearned revenue account as well as the amount earned during the year [291.6 + 652.5 − 289.4]):

Cash or Accounts Receivable	654.7	
Unearned Revenue		654.7
Unearned Revenue	652.5	
Revenues		652.5

Note that the company initially records magazine subscriptions as unearned revenue. Upon delivery of the magazine subscription, the company then recognizes the revenues by reducing the unearned revenue account and booking the revenue.

ACCRUED LIABILITIES

Accrued liabilities are expenses that have been incurred but not yet paid. Recognition of accrued liabilities is important because at the cut-off date the balance sheet should include all items that meet the definition of liabilities.

Accrued payroll or wages payable provide a common example. Such an item consists of salaries and wages that have been earned by employees but not yet paid, due to delays in timing between financial reporting dates and the completion of payroll periods. The wage expense to be recorded is the amount earned by employees during the time period covered by the financial statements. If the wage payment date does not coincide with the ending period of the financial statements, an accrued payroll must be established. Other accrued liabilities represent amounts for which accruals have been recorded because they meet the definition of a liability but no cash has been paid. Examples of these types of accrued liabilities include warranty liabilities, taxes payable, and accrued interest payable.

Warranty liabilities represent an amount that must be estimated. To properly match costs with revenues, a firm records estimated warranty costs as expenses and related liabilities at the time it sells the products. Settlements of warranty claims are then charged against the liability as they are paid. For products sold repetitively over long periods of time, a firm can estimate warranty costs fairly easily. However, new products' warranty costs often prove less predictable. In cases of highly uncertain future costs, a company may instead elect to delay the recognition of revenue until these costs are actually incurred as an alternative way of fulfilling the matching concept.

> In some cases, unexpected events occur that lead to much larger charges than estimated by the warranty (such as Firestone's tire recall). These events may prompt the recognition of a further loss and related liability or reduction in cash. Analysts can be expected to monitor such events and adjust their projections of future cash flows possibly in advance of their accounting recognition.

In the case where warranty claims can be reasonably estimated in advance, a useful analogy can be made to accounting for bad debts. Both involve estimating a provision based on past experience. While the credit side of the entry to record a provision for bad debts is made to a contra-asset account deducted from accounts receivable, the credit side of the entry to record a provision for warranties is to an accrued liability. Exhibit 10.3 illustrates balance sheet disclosures of warranty liabilities and other accruals for Winnebago Industries.

While warranty expense does not appear as a line item on Winnebago's 2003 income statement, there was a disclosure in their 10-K report that indicated the company recorded an expense of $13,085,000 as well as reductions in the liability account of $11,481,000 for their actual payments. We can reconstruct

Exhibit 10.3
Winnebago Industries 2003
Balance Sheet

Winnebago Industries

	8/30/2003	8/31/2002
Accrued expenses		
Accrued compensation	15,749,000	18,673,000
Product warranties	9,755,000	8,151,000
Insurance	5,087,000	5,967,000
Promotional	4,599,000	4,499,000
Other	4,969,000	4,471,000

summary journal entries (in thousands) based on this information if we assume that the firm settles its warranty claims in cash (though other possibilities might include the reduction of the customer's account receivable or a reduction of inventory to provide replacements).

Warranty Expense	13,085	
Accrued Product Warranties		13,085
Accrued Product Warranties	11,481	
Cash		11,481

Another type of accrued liability, similar to product warranties, arises when companies self-insure against losses that might be incurred as a result of accidents to property or to individuals. For example, some trucking companies such as Werner Enterprises self-insure their fleets based on the view that they can control their loss exposure to the extent that the expected losses amount to less than the premiums they would otherwise have to pay to insurance companies. Werner reports a liability (both current and non-current) whose title is "insurance and claims accruals."

CONTINGENCIES

Contingencies occur when realization of a revenue (gain) or expense (loss) depends on an uncertain future event. Firms typically do not recognize gain contingencies in accounting, because they often fail to meet the criteria for revenue recognition. In contrast, firms do recognize **loss contingencies** under certain circumstances. The lack of symmetry between the accounting treatment of contingent gains and losses is generally due to conservatism.

Firms can experience many different types of contingent losses as follows:

● A pending lawsuit, in which the firm may or may not report a liability, depending on management's expectation of the ultimate judgment and/or settlement in the case.

● Negotiations with various regulatory bodies such as the Internal Revenue Service, the Environmental Protection Agency, and the Justice Department can create contingent losses such as costs of land reclamation at a superfund site. A superfund site is a physical site that has been contaminated with pollutants from multiple sources and meets certain size criteria. All companies that contributed to the contamination are ultimately held accountable for reclaiming the land at the site.

The Company is involved in certain claims and pending litigation arising in the normal course of business. Management believes the ultimate resolution of these matters will not have a material effect on the consolidated financial statements of the Company.

Under GAAP (FASB, SFAS No. 5, 1975), a firm should recognize a contingent loss in its financial statements only if the loss meets both the following criteria:

- Information available prior to the issuance of the financial statements indicates that it is probable that an asset has been impaired or that a liability has been incurred.
- The amount of the loss can be reasonably estimated.

Disclosure of loss contingencies is required when there is a reasonable possibility of a loss. However, GAAP provides very little guidance on how to apply this standard. As a result, practices differ across firms. For example, if no contingent loss is recognized but some loss is possible, then SFAS 5 calls for footnote disclosures of the contingency. Many companies provide a sort of boilerplate disclosure regarding loss contingencies. To illustrate, Werner Enterprises provides very little detail about its contingencies in its 2003 Annual Report notes, as shown in Exhibit 10.4 due primarily to the fact that they are not expected to be material.

In contrast to the disclosure of Werner, Microsoft provides extensive disclosure for their heavily publicized lawsuit with the U.S. Department of Justice, as shown in Exhibit 10.5.

Notes to the Financial Statement

Contingencies

The Company is a defendant in *U.S. v. Microsoft*, a lawsuit filed by the Antitrust Division of the U.S. Department of Justice (DOJ) and a group of eighteen state Attorneys General alleging violations of the Sherman Act and various state antitrust laws. After the trial, the District Court entered Findings of Fact and Conclusions of Law stating that Microsoft had violated Sections 1 and 2 of the Sherman Act and various state antitrust laws. A judgment was entered on June 7, 2000 ordering, among other things, the breakup of Microsoft into two companies. The judgment was stayed pending an appeal. On June 28, 2001, the U.S. Court of Appeals for the District of Columbia Circuit affirmed in part, reversed in part, and vacated the judgment in its entirety and remanded the case to the District Court for a new trial on one Section 1 claim and for entry of a new judgment consistent with its ruling. In its ruling, the Court of Appeals substantially narrowed the bases of liability found by the District Court, but affirmed some of the District Court's conclusions that Microsoft had violated Section 2. On September 6, 2001, the plaintiffs announced that on remand they will not ask the Court to break Microsoft up, that they will seek imposition of conduct remedies, and that they will not retry the one Section 1 claim returned to the District Court by the Court of Appeals. On August 7, 2001, Microsoft petitioned the Supreme Court for a writ of certiorari to review the appellate court's ruling concerning its disqualification of the District Court judge. Microsoft may petition the Supreme Court to review other aspects of the appellate court's decision after final judgment is entered.

Exhibit 10.6
Footnotes of Dow Chemical
(2003)

THE REAL WORLD

Dow Chemical
Company

Environmental Matters

Accruals for environmental matters are recorded when it is probable that a liability has been incurred and the amount of the liability can be reasonably estimated, based on current law and existing technologies. The Company had accrued obligations of $394 at December 31, 2002, for environmental remediation and restoration costs, including $43 for the remediation of Superfund sites. At December 31, 2003, the Company had accrued obligations of $381 for environmental remediation and restoration costs, including $40 for the remediation of Superfund sites. This is management's best estimate of the costs for remediation and restoration with respect to environmental matters for which the Company has accrued liabilities, although the ultimate cost with respect to these particular matters could range up to twice that amount. Inherent uncertainties exist in these estimates primarily due to unknown conditions, changing governmental regulations and legal standards regarding liability, and evolving technologies for handling site remediation and restoration.

The following table summarizes the activity in the Company's accrued obligations for environmental matters for the years ended December 31, 2003 and 2002:

Accrued Obligations for Environmental Matters	2003	2002
Balance at January 1	$394	$444
Additional accruals	68	52
Charges against reserve	(77)	(108)
Adjustments to reserve	(4)	6
Balance at December 31	$381	$394

The amounts charged to income on a pretax basis related to environmental remediation totaled $68 in 2003, $52 in 2002, and $47 in 2001. Capital expenditures for environmental protection were $132 in 2003, $147 in 2002, and $179 in 2001.

Finally, the disclosure for Dow Chemical Company in Exhibit 10.6 from its 2003 annual report illustrates the accrual of environmental liabilities.

Some companies may also use contingencies to create so-called "cookie jar" reserves, by recording large expenses and reserves for **contingent liabilities** (particularly tax liabilities). These reserves are then adjusted downward by managers (i.e., take something out of the cookie jar) seeking to increase (i.e., manage) earnings.

Some contingencies such as those arising from loan guarantees and sales of receivables with recourse are sufficiently complex that the FASB has issued separate accounting pronouncements related to their treatment. Discussion of these in detail is beyond the scope of this book. However, an important notion to keep in mind is that, in general, disclosure requirements are moving toward requiring that any type of liability be recorded at its fair value. Present accounting standards have focused on recording at fair value contingent liabilities that occur as a result of external transactions. An analyst or financial statement user should exercise caution in evaluating all contingent disclosures. In some cases, reference to additional SEC filings or public documents regarding lawsuits may be necessary to assess risks.

PURCHASE AND SALES COMMITMENTS

In the course of business, many firms sign agreements committing the firm to certain transactions. The obligation of the firm is contingent on the seller or the buyer performing their part of the contract. For the seller, performance is achieved by delivering the goods on time. For the buyer, performance is achieved by accepting delivery of the goods and remitting payment. If the seller fails to deliver goods, then the buyer is not obligated to pay. If the buyer fails to accept receipt of the goods or make payment, then the seller may have the right to recover the goods.

The signing of the contract creates what is known as a **mutually unexecuted contract.** Neither the buyer nor the seller has performed yet on their part of the contract. The seller has not delivered any inventory, and the buyer has neither taken receipt nor paid any cash. Commitments such as these can create a contingent loss that must be disclosed and recognized. As illustrated in Exhibit 10.7, Boston Beer Company has commitments to purchase hops (an ingredient in making beer). Note that Boston Beer provides disclosures regarding losses that have been recognized on purchase commitments, as well as a discussion of possible future losses.

Hops Purchase Commitments

The Company utilizes several varieties of hops in the production of its products. To ensure adequate supplies of these varieties, the Company enters into advance multi-year purchase commitments based on forecasted future hop requirements among other factors.

During the fourth quarter of 2001, the Company completed certain hop disposal transactions and cancelled certain hop future contracts. The total non-recurring pretax charge incurred during the fourth quarter 2001 related to the disposal of hop inventories was $3.2 million. The total pre-tax charge recorded during the fourth quarter 2001 related to the reserve for excess hops inventory and fees associated with the cancellation of contracts was approximately $1.1 million. The transactions were deemed necessary in order to bring hop inventory levels and future contracts into balance with the Company's current brewing volume and hop usage, as the Company did not believe that these hop inventories and future hop contracts would be used by the Company within the foreseeable future.

The Company recorded charges, net of recoveries, of $477,000, $530,000, and $1.1 million related to the reserve for excess hops inventory and fees associated with the cancellation of contracts during the years ended December 29, 2001, December 30, 2000, and December 25, 1999, respectively.

Recently, there has been a significant change in hop market conditions that appears to be non-temporary in nature. This has resulted in a decline in market prices ranging between 20% and 80% as compared to the Company's historical cost of hops for crops that were previously committed to. No losses have been recognized on hop inventories on hand since the difference between the spot price and the contracted price is more than offset by the margin on the ultimate sale of the Company's products.

The computation of the excess inventory and purchase commitment reserve requires management to make certain assumptions regarding future sales growth, product mix, cancellation costs and supply, among others. Actual results may materially differ from management's estimates. The Company continues to manage inventory levels and purchase commitments in an effort to maximize utilization of hops on hand and hops under commitment. The Company's accounting policy for hops inventory and purchase commitments is to recognize a loss by establishing a reserve to the extent inventory levels and commitments exceed forecasted needs. The Company will continue to manage hops inventory and contract levels, as necessary. The current levels are deemed adequate, based upon foreseeable future brewing requirements. The Company does not anticipate further material losses related to hop inventories or contract commitments within the foreseeable future. However, changes in management's assumptions regarding future sales growth, product mix, and hop market conditions could result in future material losses.

Exhibit 10.7
2001 Annual Report
The Potential Impact of Known Facts, Commitments, Events, and Uncertainties

THE REAL WORLD

Boston Beer Company

Disclosing commitments may allow a firm to gain a competitive advantage over their rivals; for example, by entering into a sales commitment a firm may capture market share before production occurs (Hughes, Kao, and Williams, *Review of Accounting Studies,* 2002).

> The hedging of risks with forward or futures contracts reduces the volatility of the firm's future cash flows. Although such risks may be diversifiable by investors through holding broad portfolios of securities, managers may engage in hedging activities as a means of reducing operating risks that impact on their compensation.

Closely related to purchase and sales commitments are forward contracts and futures contracts. These contracts involve promises to buy or sell a commodity at a specific price on a specified future date. Firms enter these contracts to ensure a supply of materials and to hedge the risk that the price will change before the purchase or sale is completed. Boston Beer provides one such example. As another, Hershey enters into forward contracts to buy cocoa for the future production of chocolate. The contract fixes the price it will pay. Otherwise, Hershey incurs the risk that the price of cocoa might rise before the firm needs to buy and take delivery. Accounting for hedges is complex. The FASB requires that hedges be accounted for at the fair market value of the assets and liabilities created from the hedge contract. Detailed discussion of this topic is complex and is beyond the scope of this book.

RESTRUCTURING CHARGES

In recent years, many companies have undertaken business restructurings. These restructurings may involve plant closings, employee severance costs, and other related expenses. Restructurings commonly involve a noncash charge in the year of the restructuring that establishes a liability or reserve for restructuring. In the year of the restructuring, a company may recognize a large loss with no cash flow effect but in subsequent years, when the cash is paid, no additional expense is recognized. Regulators have tightened requirements regarding disclosures of restructurings because of concerns that firms were inappropriately managing reported earnings using restructurings. To illustrate how a restructuring charge may work, assume that in year 2004 BHT decides to close a warehouse and consolidate operations. The decision is expected to cost BHT $20 million and will involve plant closing and layoffs over the next two years (2005 and 2006). In 2004 BHT will record the following:

Loss due to restructuring	$20,000,000	
Reserve for restructuring		$20,000,000

Then, assuming that the costs are evenly spread over 2005 and 2006, in each year BHT will record:

Reserve for restructuring	$10,000,000	
Cash, assets, etc.		$10,000,000

SFAS 146 (FASB, SFAS No. 146, 2002) requires that a restructuring cost be recognized only when an actual liability has been incurred. Prior to that time, companies often used restructurings to manage earnings by inappropriately recognizing large expenses in bad years (sometimes referred to as "taking a big bath") and then having the ability in future years to draw against the reserve

payments that would have been expenses in those years. Therefore, BHT could undertake the preceding transaction only if an actual liability had been incurred.

INCOME TAXES

Accounting for income taxes poses some unique problems and issues. Income tax reporting requirements can differ from financial reporting requirements. There are two sources of difference, permanent and timing. **Permanent differences** between tax and financial reporting occur when a firm records revenues and/or expenses at different amounts for tax and financial accounting purposes. For example, municipal bond interest income is tax exempt, yet a firm still records it as income for financial reporting purposes. Executive stock options provide another example. For financial reporting purposes, many firms do not currently recognize executive stock options expense. This is expected to change in the near future. The FASB has issued an exposure draft that would require that equity based compensation including options be accounted for at fair value as of the grant date. However, even with the proposed change, stock options will result in a different amount of compensation for financial accounting than for tax purposes. The proposed financial accounting rules require that compensation be recognized based on fair value of the option at the grant date, while IRS regulations allow tax-deductible expenses for the business (and taxable income to employees) at the exercise date.

Timing differences (also referred to as **temporary differences**) relate to differences as to when firms recognize income and expenses for tax and financial reporting not how much. There are a number of sources of timing differences. Among the most significant are those stemming from differences in the depreciable life and method of depreciation for tax and financial reporting purposes. Recall that statutes determine depreciation for tax purposes. The effect is that firms generally recognize depreciation more rapidly for tax purposes than for financial accounting.

Deferred taxes arise from timing differences because the firm uses different accounting methods for tax and book purposes. Permanent differences do not give rise to deferred taxes. Accounting for deferred taxes is covered by SFAS No. 109 (FASB, SFAS No. 109, 1992). This method required by SFAS No. 109, often referred to as the "liability method," focuses on the balance sheet and not the income statement. It attempts to measure the liability to pay taxes in the future based on a set of assumptions about future revenues and expenses. This requires that firms be able to forecast future earnings.

THINKING GLOBALLY

International activities can significantly reduce taxable income. These permanent differences result in a difference between the statutory tax rate and the effective tax rate on financial accounting income. Companies are required to disclose the major source of permanent differences in a reconciliation of their effective tax rate to the statutory rate.

Once a firm calculates the liability for these deferred taxes and establishes the liability for the amounts currently payable to the taxing authority, the tax expense to be reported to the stockholders is then arrived at by default and is often known as a "plug" figure that makes the journal entry balance. The liability method requires that a firm does a pro forma (as-if) calculation of the amounts of income tax that will be payable in the future, based on the timing differences that exist. The details on this can be quite complex because it requires estimation of the timing and amount of future revenues and expenses.

DEFERRED TAX LIABILITIES

When a firm anticipates future tax payments, it creates **deferred tax liabilities.** To illustrate, assume that BHT acquires an asset costing $20,000, and that it depreciates the asset over five years for both tax and financial accounting purposes. Assume that BHT acquired the asset on June 30 of year 1 (halfway through the year). For financial accounting, BHT uses the straight-line depreciation method for financial reporting, but MACRS (modified-accelerated-cost-recovery system) for taxes. Finally, no salvage value is assumed. Exhibit 10.8 shows the resulting depreciation schedules.

Assume that BHT anticipates that future income before taxes and depreciation and future taxable income will be sufficiently large that it can utilize its depreciation deductions fully. Looking at Exhibit 10.8, you can see that during the first two years of the asset's life, tax depreciation exceeds financial accounting depreciation. However, the reverse occurs in years 3 through 6. The depreciation taken for tax purposes in the early years of the asset's life thus creates a deferred tax liability. This liability is reversed or "paid" in the later years of the asset's life. Let's take a closer look at how this happens.

Assume that BHT reports income before depreciation and taxes of $10,000 in years 1 through 6, and that this asset is the only source of depreciation. Also assume a tax rate of 35 percent. Exhibit 10.9 shows the calculation of BHT's income taxes.

Taxes payable are calculated in the middle section of Exhibit 10.9 and are based on the income before taxes reported to the tax authority multiplied by the tax rate.

Exhibit 10.8
BHT's Deferred Tax Schedule

Year	Tax Depreciation Percentage[1]	Tax Depreciation	Financial Depreciation Percentage	Financial Depreciation
1	20.00%	$4,000	10%	$2,000
2	32.00%	6,400	20%	4,000
3	19.20%	3,840	20%	4,000
4	11.52%	2,304	20%	4,000
5	11.52%	2,304	20%	4,000
6	5.76%	1,152	10%	2,000

[1]Percentages are based on the IRS's MACRS tables using the half-year convention. This is a convention that allows for one-half year depreciation in the first year regardless of the date of asset purchase.

	Year 1	Year 2	Year 3	Year 4	Year 5	Year 6
TAX EXPENSE CALCULATION						
Income before taxes and depreciation	$10,000	$10,000	$10,000	$10,000	$10,000	$ 10,000
Depreciation expense	2,000	4,000	4,000	4,000	4,000	2,000
Income before taxes	8,000	6,000	6,000	6,000	6,000	8,000
Income tax expense, current	2,100	1,260	2,156	2,694	2,694	3,097
Income tax expense, deferred	700	840	(56)	(594)	(594)	(297)
Net income	$ 5,200	$ 3,900	$ 3,900	$ 3,900	$ 3,900	$5,200.00
TAX PAYABLE CALCULATION						
Income before taxes and depreciation	$10,000	$10,000	$10,000	$10,000	$10,000	$ 10,000
Depreciation	4,000	6,400	3,840	2,304	2,304	1,152
Income before taxes	6,000	3,600	6,160	7,696	7,696	8,848
Taxes payable (35%)	2,100	1,260	2,156	2,694	2,694	3,097
DEFERRED TAX CALCULATION						
Differences in depreciation expense		(2,400)	160	1,696	1,696	848
Taxes on difference (35%)		(840)	56	594	594	297
Sum of tax differences (DT Balance)	700					

Exhibit 10.9
Calculation of BHT's
Income Taxes

The deferred tax calculation is in the bottom section of the table. Notice that in Year 1, the deferred tax amount is calculated as the sum of all of the future amounts that will be paid based on the differences in the way depreciation is reported for tax and book purposes. These future differences are calculated by taking the differences in the depreciation expense in each subsequent period and then multiplying by the tax rate in those future years (here assumed to be 35 percent).

The tax expense that is then reported to shareholders is shown in the top section and it has two components, the current and the deferred amounts. The current amount is the amount of tax currently payable to the tax authority and the deferred amount is the same as the amount we calculated for the deferred tax for the period.

Deferred income tax liabilities may be very large in capital-intensive industries. For example, Union Pacific Corporation, a railroad company, has a deferred tax liability balance as of December 31, 2003 of $9.169 billion. This is 27 percent of Union Pacific's total assets of $33.46 billion, and 74 percent of Union Pacific's total equity of $12.354 billion.

DEFERRED TAX ASSETS

In addition to deferred tax liabilities, **deferred tax assets** may arise out of timing differences resulting from recognizing income more rapidly for tax than for financial reporting purposes. One such case arises from bad debt expense estimation. GAAP requires that bad debts be estimated for financial reporting purposes at the time of sale. However, for tax purposes bad debts can be recognized only when a specific account is written off. This means that firms recognize bad debts faster for financial accounting than for tax purposes, resulting in a deferred tax asset. Product warranties provide another example. Similar to bad debts, estimates are not deductible, only the actual claims. Again, this may result in a timing difference for which the deductions on the tax return lag provisions on the income statement.

To illustrate accounting for income taxes for a real company, we use data from a note to Werner Enterprises' 2003 financial statements (see Exhibit 10.10). Note that the timing differences for Werner include several that we discussed previously (uncollectibles as well as property and equipment). The amount reported as Total Income Tax Expense of $44,249 (thousand) is the amount that appears on Werner's income statement. The amounts reported as a current deferred tax

Exhibit 10.10

THE REAL WORLD

Werner Enterprises

Note 5—Income Taxes

Income tax expense consists of the following (in thousands):

	12/31/2003	12/31/2002	12/31/2001
Current:			
Federal	$ 46,072	$ 959	$(12,194)
State	3,657	127	(1,688)
	49,729	1,086	(13,882)
Deferred:			
Federal	(6,159)	31,692	37,358
State	679	4,199	5,171
	(5,480)	35,891	42,529
Total income tax expense	$ 44,249	$ 36,977	$ 28,647

At December 31, deferred tax assets and liabilities consisted of the following (in thousands):

	2003	2002
Deferred tax assets:		
Insurance and claims accruals	$ 48,081	$ 34,914
Allowance for uncollectible accounts	3,078	2,364
Other	3,743	3,358
Gross deferred tax assets	54,902	40,636
Deferred tax liabilities:		
Property and equipment	219,849	211,135
Prepaid expenses	42,174	38,763
Other	6,670	10,009
Gross deferred tax liabilities	268,693	259,907
Net deferred tax liability	$213,791	$219,271

These amounts (in thousands) are presented in the accompanying Consolidated Balance Sheets as of December 31 as follows:

	2003	2002
Current deferred tax liability	$ 15,151	$ 17,710
Noncurrent deferred tax liability	198,640	201,561
Net deferred tax liability	$213,791	$219,271

The company has not recorded a valuation allowance, as it believes that all deferred tax assets are likely to be realized as a result of the Company's history of profitability, taxable income, and reversal of deferred tax liabilities.

liability and a noncurrent deferred tax liability appear in the current and noncurrent liability sections of its balance sheet. From the data contained in this note, we can reconstruct a journal entry (in thousands), summarizing the recognition and payment of income taxes.

Income Tax Expense (Provision)	44,249	
Deferred Tax Liability (Current)	2,559	
Deferred Tax Liability (Noncurrent)	2,921	
Cash or Income Taxes Payable		4,972

Note that all current deferred tax assets and liabilities are netted out to produce either a net deferred tax asset or a deferred tax liability. Current deferred taxes are those that arise from timing differences in the accounting for items that are classified as current, such as the accounting for bad debts. Noncurrent deferred tax assets and liabilities are also netted, and they arise from timing differences that arise from noncurrent items such as depreciation.

Deferred tax asset and liability recognition becomes even more complex if a company incurs significant **net operating losses (NOLS)** over a period of time. NOLS result if, for tax purposes, the firm reports a loss before taxes. Under current tax law, NOLS can be used to offset taxes in prior periods (called **tax loss carrybacks**). If no positive income occurs in prior periods to offset the loss, then the company can carry forward the tax loss to future periods and offset future taxable income (to the extent it materializes). These are called **tax loss carryforwards.** NOLS are a source of deferred tax assets because they often result in future tax deductions. However, these assets are realizable only if the company has sufficient taxable income in the future that the NOLS results in a deduction.

In cases where a firm doubts that it will realize its deferred tax assets, FAS 109 requires that the deferred tax assets be reduced using a valuation allowance account.

> GAAP does not allow discounting of deferred tax liabilities, implying that the value of the deferred tax liability is overstated relative to other liabilities that are discounted. Also, if companies continue to show a positive growth rate and continue to invest in long-term assets, the deferred tax liability balance will simply grow larger over time and while some differences will reverse themselves, this reversal will be offset by new differences that give rise to additional deferred tax liabilities. Some analysts ignore or heavily discount deferred tax liabilities in considering a company's leverage because the timing of when these differences will result in actual cash outflows is in the very distant future, if at all.

REPORTING OF DEFERRED TAXES

As we discussed in the previous section and as illustrated by Werner Enterprises (Exhibit 10.10), SFAS 109 (FASB, SFAS No. 109, 1992) requires that for reporting purposes, all current deferred tax liabilities and assets be offset and presented as a single amount. Further, all noncurrent deferred tax liabilities and assets should be offset and presented as a single amount. In addition to the disclosure of the deferred tax differences, firms are required to present other disclosures regarding their income taxes. In Exhibit 10.11 there are excerpts from the tax footnotes for General Electric Company. One of the required disclosures is a reconciliation of the actual tax rate of the company (sometimes called the *effective rate*) with the statutory tax rate. Note that GE's actual reported tax rate is much lower than the statutory rate, due primarily to international activity resulting in earnings that are not required to be reported in the United States. GE has been successful in lowering its effective tax rate from the statutory rate of 35 percent to 21.7 percent in 2003, principally because of its international activities.

In addition to lowering its tax rate through the use of international activities, notice that GE also reports very significant deferred tax liabilities that amount to a total of $12.647 billion at the end of 2003. Disclosures in the tax footnote, while providing some information about timing and permanent differences, do not provide information that would allow a user to determine actual cash taxes paid. The closest number is the current tax expense, which GE reports as $3.188 billion. However, GE's cash flow statement reports for the same year that GE's actual cash payments for taxes were $1.539 billion in 2003. A large part of this difference is likely to the exercise of stock options, which create a tax deduction for GE but not an expense.

Exhibit 10.11
Excerpts from Tax Footnotes in General Electric's 2003 Annual Report

THE REAL WORLD

General Electric

Provision for Income Taxes
(In millions)

	2003	2002	2001
GE			
Current tax expense	$ 2,468	$ 2,833	$3,632
Deferred tax expense from temporary differences	389	1,004	561
	2,857	3,837	4,193
GECS			
Current tax expense (benefit)	720	−1,488	517
Deferred tax expense from temporary differences	738	1,409	863
	1,458	−79	1,380
Consolidated			
Current tax expense	3,188	1,345	4,149
Deferred tax expense from temporary differences	1,127	2,413	1,424
Total	$ 4,315	$ 3,758	$5,573

Reconciliation of U.S. Federal Statutory Tax Rate to Actual Tax Rate

	2003	2002	2001
Statutory U.S. federal income tax rate	35.00%	35.00%	35.00%
Increase (reduction) in rate resulting from:			
Amortization of goodwill	—	—	1.00
Tax-exempt income	(1.10)	(1.20)	(1.30)
Tax on international activities, including exports	(9.00)	(10.60)	(5.40)
Americom/Rollins goodwill	—	—	(1.10)
All other net	(3.20)	(3.30)	0.10
	(13.30)	(15.10)	(6.70)
Actual income tax rate	21.70%	19.90%	28.30%

Deferred Income Taxes
December 31 (In millions)

	2003	2002
Assets		
GE	$ 7,594	$ 6,817
GECS	9,948	7,584
	17,542	14,401
Liabilities		
GE	9,505	8,744
GECS	20,684	18,174
	30,189	26,918
Net deferred income tax liability	$12,647	$12,517

Reports from Other Countries

International accounting standards (IAS 12) recommend treatment similar to U.S. reporting for taxes. In some countries, such as Germany, Italy, Norway, and Chile, accounting practices follow the tax requirements of the country. Therefore, no deferred tax account is necessary as there are no differences between book and tax. In most other countries, such as Denmark, France, and Japan, the provision for income taxes is based on the taxable income and not on the book income reported to owners.

Therefore, in these countries, no deferred taxes will be shown either. A relatively small number of countries (including Canada and South Africa) follow the U.S. practice of computing deferred taxes on all timing (temporary) differences (excluding permanent differences). The United Kingdom follows the U.S. practice except that differences that will not reverse in the foreseeable future are not recorded as deferred taxes (treated like permanent differences).

PENSIONS AND OTHER POSTRETIREMENT BENEFITS

Pensions represent noncurrent liabilities because although employees earn pension benefits during their working years, the payments of the pensions occur in the future when they retire. There are two types of pension plans, defined benefit plans and defined contribution plans. The financial reporting requirements for pensions are covered in SFAS 87 (FASB, SFAS No. 87, 1985), Employers' Accounting for Pensions.

DEFINED BENEFIT PLANS

Defined benefit plans pay guaranteed amounts to employees based on a pension formula. The formula generally reflects a function of the years an employee has worked and the salary at the time of retirement (or an average of several years or the highest paid years). Most defined benefit plans are self-funded. The firm establishes a separate entity operated by an independent trustee. Payments are made into the fund during the period of time that employees work, and payments to retirees are paid from the fund. Because the company cannot easily utilize the assets that are invested with the independent trustee, GAAP allows the company to remove the liability from its books to the extent that it has funded this liability with payments to the trustee. As a result, most of the obligation for the defined benefit pension plan is not reflected on a company's balance sheet. Note, however, that the company still remains ultimately liable to the retiree for the benefits that are guaranteed. With certain limitations, the payments made to the trustee can also be deducted as expenses for tax purposes.

Companies with defined benefit plans must provide detailed disclosures regarding the value of pension plan assets and pension obligations. These disclosures include, among other things, the total pension liability of the plan and the fair value of the assets that are held in trust. If the assets are less than the liabilities, then the plan is said to be underfunded. For example, the U.S. pension plans for Ford Motor Company as of December 31, 2003 reflected pension obligations of $40.5 billion and assets with a fair value of $37.0 billion. Thus, this pension plan is underfunded. In contrast, the pension plan for General

Exhibit 10.12
General Electric Pension
Disclosures

General Electric

Projected Benefit Obligation (In millions)	2003	2002
Balance at January 1	$33,266	$30,423
Service cost for benefits earned (a)	1,213	1,107
Interest cost on benefit obligation	2,180	2,116
Participant contributions	169	158
Plan amendments	654	9
Actuarial loss (b)	2,754	1,650
Benefits paid	−2,409	−2,197
Balance at December 31 (c)	$37,827	$33,266

Fair Value of Assets (In millions)	2003	2002
Balance at January 1	$ 37,811	$45,006
Actual gain (loss) on plan assets	8,203	−5,251
Employer contributions	105	95
Participant contributions	169	158
Benefits paid	−2,409	−2,197
Balance at December 31	$43,879	$ 37,811

Electric as of December 31, 2003 listed pension obligations of $37.8 billion and assets of $43.9 billion, making it an overfunded plan.

Exhibit 10.12 shows the detailed disclosures for General Electric in 2003 for their pension plan assets and liabilities. Note in the top of the exhibit that the pension obligation is referred to as the *projected benefit obligation*. The changes in the obligation during the year are affected by new benefits earned by employees (service cost), interest on the benefit obligation (because the liability is carried at its net present value, interest must be recognized each year), employee contributions to their own plan, changes in the parameters of the plan (plan amendments), changes due to adjustments to the assumptions made in the calculation (actuarial losses), and the benefits paid to retirees during the period. Note further that the fair value of the assets in the plan exceeds the projected benefit obligation by $6,052 million at the end of 2003 ($43,879 million − $37,827 million).

The Pension Benefit Guarantee Corporation (PBGC) provides federal insurance for defined benefit plans. The PBGC can apply pressure to companies to live up to their pension obligations, but they also provide a backstop if the company should go into bankruptcy or otherwise go out of business and not be able to meet its pension obligations.

For defined benefit plans, the balance sheet reflects the net of pension liabilities recognized by the company, less the amounts set aside to fund those plans. In some cases, this is a net liability and in others it is a net asset depending on whether the fund is overfunded or underfunded. However, current accounting rules allow certain changes in the pension liabilities or assets to be deferred initially (i.e., not immediately recognized in the financial statements) and then amortized into the financial statement in the future. Therefore, the current balance sheet may not reflect the full funded status of the plans. For instance, while General Electric was net overfunded by $6.1 billion ($43.9 − $37.8) at the end of 2003, it reported a net pension asset on its books of $15.2 billion. The difference

Prepaid Pension Asset/(Liability) December 31 (In millions)	2003	2002
Funded status (a)	$ 6,052	$ 4,545
Unrecognized prior service cost	1,571	1,165
Unrecognized net actuarial loss	7,588	8,356
Net asset recognized	$15,211	$14,066

Exhibit 10.13
General Electric Pension Disclosure

THE REAL WORLD

General Electric

of $9.1 billion reflects losses that have not yet been amortized into GE's financial statements. Exhibit 10.13 provides the full disclosure that GE made of this difference in 2003. Note that "prior service cost" refers to costs associated with amendments to the plan's parameters and "actuarial losses" refer to changes in the assumptions used in the calculation of the liability.

While the balance sheet reflects the net of the assets and liabilities of the plan, the income statement reflects the net pension expense and pension revenues for the period. Therefore, revenues (income) from the investments in the pension are allowed to offset the expenses related to the pension liabilities. For instance, in 2003 General Electric reported net pension income of $1.0 billion because the income from its invested assets exceeded the expenses of its pension liabilities (remember that they are significantly overfunded as a plan). Exhibit 10.14 provides the full disclosure General Electric made in 2003 for its pension expense (or in GE's case, pension income). Note in the exhibit that the expenses of the plan (service costs, interest cost, etc.) are offset by the income earned on the plan assets resulting in net pension income rather than net pension expense in all three years reported.

DEFINED CONTRIBUTION PLANS

In a **defined contribution plan,** the employer agrees to make payments of a certain amount into a plan. However, the employer makes no guarantee as to the amount of retirement income. Instead, the employee's retirement income is a function of the value at the time of retirement of the contributions to the plan on his or her behalf. Thus, defined contribution retirement plans result in much less obligation to the employer. The plans, as a result, are often supplemented by 401(k) plans that allow employees to make tax-deferred contributions to their own retirement in addition to those made by the employer, as illustrated in Exhibit 10.15 for Finish Line.

Effect on Operations (In millions)	2003	2002	2001
Expected return on plan assets	$4,072	$4,084	$4,327
Service cost for benefits earned (a)	−1,213	−1,107	−884
Interest cost on benefit obligation	−2,180	−2,116	−2,065
Prior service cost	−248	−217	−244
Net actuarial gain recognized	609	912	961
Income from pensions	1,040	1,556	2,095

Exhibit 10.14
General Electric Pension Expense Disclosure

THE REAL WORLD

General Electric

Exhibit 10.15
Finish Line 2003 Annual Report

THE REAL WORLD

Finish Line

6. Retirement Plan

The Company sponsors a defined contribution profit sharing plan which covers substantially all employees who have completed one year of service. Contributions to this plan are discretionary and are allocated to employees as a percentage of each covered employee's wages. During 2001, the Company amended and restated the plan to add a 401(k) feature whereby the Company matches 100 percent of employee contributions to the plan up to 3 percent of an employee's wages. The Company's total expense for the plan in 2003, 2002, and 2001 amounted to $2,207,000, $1,603,000, and $1,036,000, respectively.

> One consequence of ERISA (in addition to pressures for companies to be more and more competitive) has been that many companies have moved away from offering defined benefit plans and into defined contribution plans. These plans often do not provide the same level of retirement benefits unless supplemented by substantial employee savings or 401(k) plans, but they do limit the employer's liability. Recently, former and current employees of firms affected by these changes have sued to recover lost benefits.

At one time, most pension plans were defined benefit plans. However, the liabilities created by these plans posed major problems for companies and in many instances, the companies did not set aside sufficient assets to cover the retirement benefits. This sometimes led to employees failing to receive pensions that they had earned. Some employers also terminated employees to avoid full vesting. *Vesting* means that if the benefits vest with the employee, even if the employee leaves the company they will still be entitled to receive the benefits at retirement. Most pension plans have some period of time (say five years) before the benefits vest with the employee. The Employee Retirement Income Security Act of 1974 (ERISA) was enacted to counter these abuses. ERISA requires that companies with defined benefit plans provide a minimal level of funding and defines participation and vesting requirements. Failure to meet ERISA requirements can result in a denial of tax deductions for pension plans or imposition of fines on companies offering such plans.

Other post-retirement benefits include employee medical costs and related expenses. Unlike pensions, most post-retirement obligations are not fully funded. Part of the reason for this is that there is no tax deductibility for contributions made to these types of funds. SFAS 106 (FASB, SFAS No. 106, 1990) requires that these costs be accrued and a liability recognized on the balance sheet for the unfunded portion of these costs in much the same way as pensions are recognized. General Electric reported health care obligations of $9.7 billion at the end of 2003 with only $1.6 billion in assets set aside to pay for these costs.

SUMMARY AND TRANSITION

In this chapter, we considered criteria for the recognition of liabilities. For many liabilities, the existence and amount of the firm's obligations are specified by invoices, as for accounts payable, or by contracts that specify future payments such as for notes payable. Other liabilities take the form of accruals. These include payroll, utilities, and warranties to name a few common classes. Accounting for warranties involves estimates of future claims, as would self-insurance accruals. A liability is established in advance of when actual claims may be received in order to match the expected costs to the sales to which they relate.

Loss contingencies may give rise to liabilities depending on whether the loss is probable and amenable to reasonable estimation. Contingencies not meeting those conditions are often disclosed in notes to the firm's financial statements.

They include possible loss exposure due to legal suits, environmental damages, and tax payments.

The determination of income for tax purposes may vary from reported income before taxes, due to permanent differences and timing differences. A common example of the latter would be cases in which a firm depreciates assets more rapidly for tax purposes than for reporting purposes. Another common example is bad debts, for which the expense for reporting purposes is an estimate based on sales, while the deduction for tax purposes is the amount actually written off. As a consequence, the amount of tax currently due may differ from the amount recognized as an expense. The difference is recorded as a change to either a deferred tax asset or a deferred tax liability.

There may often be liabilities associated with pension and health benefits provided to employees. These come about if the payments made by the sponsoring company to fund those benefits occur later than the period in which the employees work and the benefits are earned.

In the next chapter, we extend our discussion of liabilities to include non-operating liabilities involved in the financing of the firm. The two major liabilities we will focus on are long-term debt in the form of bonds payable as well as those related to the leasing of assets.

END OF CHAPTER MATERIAL

KEY TERMS

Accounts Payable	Net Operating Losses (NOLs)
Accrued Liabilities	Notes Payable
Advances on Sales	Other Post-Retirement Benefits
Contingent Liabilities	Pensions
Current Installments of Long-Term Debt	Permanent Differences
Deferred Tax Asset	Tax Loss Carrybacks
Deferred Tax Liability	Tax Loss Carryforwards
Deferred Taxes	Temporary Differences
Defined Benefit Plans	Timing Differences
Defined Contribution Plans	Unearned Revenue
Loss Contingencies	Warranty Liabilities
Mutually Unexecuted Contract	

ASSIGNMENT MATERIAL

◉ REVIEW QUESTIONS

1. List the three essential characteristics of a liability.
2. Explain how purchase commitments are reported under GAAP.

3. Describe the appropriate valuation method for liabilities under GAAP. Include a discussion of both current and noncurrent liabilities in your answer.

4. Describe the nature of an account called unearned revenues, and provide an example.

5. Explain how accrued wages would be recognized in the financial statements under GAAP.

6. Explain the circumstances under which a contingency would be recognized in the financial statements under GAAP.

7. Describe how deferred taxes are calculated in the liability method.

8. Describe/discuss the meaning of the following terms: timing differences, temporary differences, and permanent differences.

9. Some accountants do not believe that deferred taxes meet the criteria for recognition as a liability. Discuss deferred taxes in terms of the three criteria for a liability, and provide your own arguments for whether they meet the criteria.

10. Describe the nature of tax loss carrybacks and carryforwards.

11. Differentiate defined contribution pension plans from defined benefit plans.

12. Explain the following terms: overfunded, underfunded, and fully funded.

13. Explain the difference between pensions and other post-retirement benefits.

◎ APPLYING YOUR KNOWLEDGE

14. On April 10, 20X4, while looking for new furniture for his new home, Dr. Reliever, a surgeon, cut his right index finger because some of the nails on the table he was looking at were not hammered in properly. On June 10, 20X4, Dr. Reliever sued the furniture store for $50 million. The case came to trial on September 13, 20X4, and the jury reached a decision on December 13, 20X4, finding the store liable and awarding Dr. Reliever a sum of $35 million. On February 3, 20X5, the furniture store, dissatisfied by the judgment, appealed to a higher court. The higher court reheard the case beginning on July 18, 20X5. On November 25, 20X5, a jury again found the store liable and awarded $50 million to Dr. Reliever. On January 15, 20X6, the furniture store paid $50 million to Dr. Reliever.

Required:

Considering the stated events, explain when the furniture store should recognize a loss. Why?

15. The Air Cool Air Conditioning Company services air conditioners on a quarterly basis. It offers its customers a service plan that costs $500 per year and includes four service visits during the year. The company collects the entire $500 when the contract is signed and recognizes the revenue on a quarterly basis when each of the four service visits is completed. On January 1, 800 contracts were outstanding. Of these, 300 expired at the end of the first quarter, 200 at the end of the second quarter, 150 at the end of the

third quarter, and 150 at the end of the fourth quarter. Sales of contracts and expenses during the year are as follows:

Quarter	Contracts Sold	Expenses
1	300	$80,000
2	250	66,000
3	350	98,000
4	400	115,000

Assume that the sale of contracts takes place at the beginning of each quarter.

Required:

a. Give the necessary journal entries for each of the four quarters.

b. How many contracts were still outstanding at the end of the fourth quarter, and what is the value of these contracts?

16. On January 1, 20X2, the Fitwell Nuts & Bolts company purchased a new machine costing $8,000. The company uses straight-line depreciation for book purposes and MACRS for tax purposes. The machine has an estimated useful life of four years and zero salvage value. For tax purposes, the machine is in the three-year asset class, and the MACRS deduction percentages are: 33.33 percent, 44.45 percent, 14.81 percent, and 7.41 percent. The company is in the 40 percent marginal tax bracket and closes its books on December 31.

Required:

Calculate the amount of deferred tax each year and give the necessary journal entries for recording the tax expense for the years, assuming that income before depreciation and taxes is constant at $20,000 each year. Also, prepare a deferred tax T-account for each of the years using the liability method assuming that the tax rate of 40 percent remains constant throughout the life of the asset.

17. On July 1, 20X3, the Hudson Manufacturing Company signed a contract with Forte Turbine Company to purchase ten machines costing $20,000 each. The machines will be purchased one every year for ten years. Hudson estimates the useful life of the machines to be five years with zero salvage value. The company uses the straight-line method for book purposes and MACRS for tax purposes. The machines are in the five-year asset class, and the MACRS deduction percentages are: 20 percent, 32 percent, 19.2 percent, 11.52 percent, 11.52 percent, and 5.76 percent. The company closes its books on June 30.

Required:

a. Calculate the amount of deferred tax under the liability method for the first six years, assuming that the tax rate is 30 percent and that it remains constant throughout the ten-year period.

b. Calculate the balance in deferred tax at the end of the year.

c. Repeat parts a and b for year 7, and compare the balance in deferred tax at the end of year 7 with that of year 6. In what circumstances would the subsequent balances be constant?

18. On January 1, 20X4, the American Works Company purchased a new machine costing $15,000. The company estimated the useful life of the machine to be five years with zero salvage value. The company uses straight-line depreciation for book purposes, and the asset qualifies as a three-year asset (MACRS) for tax purposes. The MACRS deduction percentages are: 33.33 percent, 44.45 percent, 14.81 percent, and 7.41 percent. The company closes its books on December 31. The income before depreciation and taxes in 20X4 is $50,000.

    Required:

    Calculate the deferred tax amount, income tax expense, and tax payable for 20X4 using the liability method. Assume the tax rates to be 40 percent in 20X4, 35 percent in 20X5 and 20X6, and 30 percent in 20X7 and 20X8.

19. As a stock analyst, discuss how you might view the nature of deferred taxes and whether you would treat them the same way that you might treat a long-term bond.

20. Suppose that you have been asked by your company to evaluate a potential acquisition candidate. The company has been in the chemical business for more than 60 years and has several plants scattered throughout the United States. Describe what you might find in terms of disclosure in the firm's financial statements relative to environmental liabilities and what additional information you would like to have in assessing its liabilities.

21. Suppose that you are the sales manager for a construction company and you are responsible for securing contracts. As a part of your negotiations with customers, you offer a "sweetener" to your contracts, which is an agreement to supply raw materials to customers at a fixed price over an extended period of time. The price fixed in the contract is currently right at the fair market price for the raw materials.

    a. What does your accounting department need to know about these sweeteners to appropriately account for these agreements?

    b. How should the accounting department record these transactions?

    c. Under what circumstances might your answer to part b change?

    d. What should stockholders know about these agreements?

USING REAL DATA

22. In the 2002 annual report of National Service Industries, Inc. (a lighting equipment, textile rental, and specialty chemical firm), the following footnote appears:

    Self Insurance
    It is the Company's policy to self-insure for certain insurable risks consisting primarily of physical loss to property, business interruptions resulting from such loss, and workers' compensation, comprehensive general, and auto liability. Insurance coverage is obtained for catastrophic property and casualty exposures as well as those risks required to be insured by law or contract. Based on an independent actuary's estimate of the aggregate liability for claims incurred, a provision for claims under the self-insured program is recorded and revised annually.

The activity in the self-insurance liability for each of the years ended August 31 was as follows:

	2002	2001	2000
Accrual, beginning of period	$15,596	$21,934	$24,005
Expense	9,433	10,944	5,216
Payments	(9,986)	(17,282)	(7,287)
Accrual, end of period	$15,043	$15,596	$21,934

Required:

a. Evaluate the appropriateness of recording self-insured liabilities on the books of the firm using the criteria for a liability.

b. Reconstruct the entries that National made in 2002 to record the transactions associated with self-insurance.

23. The following tables disclose information regarding the pension and other post-retirement benefit plans for PPG Industries, Inc. in 2003.

(Millions)	Pensions		Other Post-Retirement Benefits	
	2003	2002	2003	2002
Projected benefit obligation, Jan 1	$2,719	$2,414	$ 993	$823
Service cost	60	54	23	17
Interest cost	173	165	65	58
Plan amendments	11	21	(37)	0
Actuarial losses	180	182	174	176
Benefits paid	(170)	(172)	(93)	(81)
Foreign currency translation adjustments	94	41	10	0
Other	(2)	14	0	0
Projected benefit obligation, Dec 31	$3,065	$2,719	$1,135	$993
Market value of plan assets, Jan 1	$2,030	$2,423		
Actual return on plan assets	480	(280)		
Company contributions	63	20		
Participant contributions	1	2		
Benefits paid	(158)	(159)		
Plan expenses and other, net	(3)	(3)		
Foreign currency translation adjustments	67	27		
Market value of plan assets, Dec 31	$2,480	$2,030		
Funded status	($585)	($689)	($1,135)	($993)
Accumulated unrecognized:				
Actuarial losses	1,275	1,459	527	376
Prior service cost	97	103	(16)	21
Additional pension liability	(1,095)	(1,318)	0	0
Net accrued benefit cost	($308)	($445)	($624)	($596)

(Millions)	Pensions			Other Post-Retirement Benefits		
	2003	2002		2003	2002	
Service cost	$60	$54	$48	$23	$17	$12
Interest cost	173	165	159	65	58	48
Expected return on plan assets	(173)	(224)	(279)	0	0	0
Amortization of transition assets	0	(4)	(5)	0	0	0
Amortization of prior service cost	18	18	17	1	3	3
Amortization of actuarial losses	98	45	7	26	13	1
Net periodic benefit cost (income)	$ 176	$ 54	($53)	$ 115	$ 91	$64

The following assumptions were used by PPG in calculating their pension and other post-retirement liabilities:

	2003	2002	2001
Discount rate	6.50%	7.00%	7.30%
Expected return on assets	8.40%	9.50%	10.90%
Rate of compensation increase	4.10%	4.10%	4.10%

Respond to the following questions:

a. What is the funded status of the pension plans at the end of 2003?

b. What has been the experience with return on plan assets over the past three years? Use data from the tables to support your conclusions.

c. What net amount of pension asset or liability is reported by PPG as of the end of 2003?

d. What effect does the change in discount rate have on both the balance sheet valuation of the pension liabilities as well as the net periodic benefit cost (income) over the last two years?

24. In 1998 Sealed Air Corporation (the makers of bubblewrap), through a complex transaction, sold a subsidiary known as Cryovac to W.R. Grace Company (Grace). The terms of the transaction were such that Grace supposedly assumed all liabilities of Cryovac, including those that related to asbestos. However, subsequently W.R. Grace entered bankruptcy and asbestos claimants brought suit against Sealed Air alleging that the liabilities for asbestos were "fraudulently transferred" in the sale to Grace. In 2002, Sealed Air reached an agreement with these claimants to settle this suit that would result in cash payments and stock issuance (of Sealed Air stock) to the claimants once the bankruptcy plan for Grace was approved. Following are the financial statements for Sealed Air as reported in the 2003 10-K.

SEALED AIR CORP. Income Statement

	12/31/2003	12/31/2002	12/31/2001
Net sales	$3,531,900,000	$3,204,300,000	$3,067,500,000
Cost of sales	2,419,100,000	2,146,700,000	2,077,200,000
Gross profit	1,112,800,000	1,057,600,000	990,300,000
Marketing, administrative, and development expenses	574,100,000	542,500,000	513,100,000
Goodwill amortization	–	–	57,000,000
Restructuring and other (credits) charges	(500,000)	(1,300,000)	32,800,000
Operating profit	539,200,000	516,400,000	387,400,000
Interest expense	(134,300,000)	(65,300,000)	(76,400,000)
Asbestos settlement and related costs	(2,800,000)	(850,100,000)	(12,000,000)
Loss on debt repurchase	(33,600,000)	–	–
Other income (expense), net	8,400,000	7,100,000	(1,500,000)
Earnings (loss) before income taxes	376,900,000	(391,900,000)	297,500,000
Income tax expense (benefit)	136,500,000	(82,800,000)	140,800,000
Net earnings (loss)	$ 240,400,000	($309,100,000)	$ 156,700,000

SEALED AIR CORP. Balance Sheet

	12/31/2003	12/31/2002
Assets		
Current assets:		
Cash and cash equivalents	$ 365,000,000	$ 126,800,000
Notes and accounts receivable, net of allowances for doubtful accounts of $17.9 in 2003 and $18.7 in 2002	615,200,000	546,800,000
Inventories	371,200,000	329,400,000
Prepaid expenses and other current assets	18,800,000	11,700,000
Deferred income taxes	57,600,000	41,600,000
Total current assets	1,427,800,000	1,056,300,000
Property and equipment, net	1,042,400,000	1,013,000,000
Goodwill	1,939,500,000	1,926,200,000
Deferred income taxes	85,000,000	84,300,000
Other assets	209,400,000	181,000,000
Total Assets	$4,704,100,000	$4,260,800,000
Liabilities, Preferred Stock, and Shareholders' Equity		
Current liabilities:		
Short-term borrowings	$18,200,000	$ 53,400,000
Current portion of long-term debt	2,400,000	2,000,000
Accounts payable	191,700,000	167,000,000
Deferred income taxes	5,800,000	4,300,000
Asbestos settlement liability	512,500,000	512,500,000
Other current liabilities	459,800,000	413,600,000
Total current liabilities	1,190,400,000	1,152,800,000

	12/31/2003	12/31/2002
Long-term debt, less current portion	2,259,800,000	868,000,000
Deferred income taxes	34,900,000	31,000,000
Other liabilities	95,400,000	69,000,000
Total Liabilities	3,580,500,000	2,120,800,000
Commitments and contingencies (Note 18)		
Authorized 50,000,000 preferred shares. Series A convertible preferred stock, $50.00 per share redemption value, no shares authorized in 2003 and 27,365,594 shares authorized in 2002, no shares outstanding in 2003 due to redemption of all outstanding shares on July 18, 2003 and 26,540,099 share	0	1,327,000,000
Shareholders' equity:		
Common stock, $.10 par value per share. Authorized 400,000,000 shares; issued 85,547,227 shares in 2003 and 84,764,347 shares in 2002	8,600,000	8,500,000
Cost of treasury common stock, 461,785 shares in 2003 and 723,415 shares in 2002	(19,600,000)	(31,100,000)
Common stock reserved for issuance related to asbestos settlement, 9,000,000 shares, $.10 par value per share in 2003 and 2002	900,000	900,000
Additional paid-in capital	1,046,900,000	1,037,100,000
Retained earnings	243,700,000	31,900,000
Deferred compensation	(16,300,000)	(9,900,000)
	1,264,200,000	1,037,400,000
Minimum pension liability	(1,600,000)	(2,200,000)
Accumulated translation adjustment	(147,000,000)	(222,200,000)
Unrecognized gain on derivative instruments	0	8,000,000
Accumulated other comprehensive loss	(140,600,000)	(224,400,000)
Total Shareholders' Equity	1,123,600,000	813,000,000
Total Liabilities, Preferred Stock, and Shareholders' Equity	$4,704,100,000	$4,260,800,000

SEALED AIR CORP. Cash Flow	12/31/2003	12/31/2002	12/31/2001
Cash flows from operating activities:			
Net earnings (loss)	$240,400,000	($309,100,000)	$156,700,000
Adjustments to reconcile net earnings (loss) to net cash provided by operating activities:			
Depreciation and amortization of property and equipment	154,100,000	144,100,000	141,700,000
Other amortization, including goodwill in 2001	19,100,000	20,900,000	78,900,000
Amortization of bond discount	900,000	700,000	600,000

	12/31/2003	12/31/2002	12/31/2001
Amortization of terminated treasury lock agreements	(500,000)	—	—
Noncash portion of restructuring and other charges (credits)	—	—	7,300,000
Noncash portion of asbestos settlement	—	321,500,000	—
Deferred tax provisions	(23,400,000)	(257,200,000)	(9,100,000)
Net loss on long-term debt repurchased	33,600,000	—	—
Net loss (gain) on disposals of property and equipment	2,300,000	100,000	(200,000)
Changes in operating assets and liabilities, net of businesses acquired:			
Change in the Receivables Facility	—	(95,600,000)	95,600,000
Change in notes and accounts receivable, net of Receivables Facility	(20,300,000)	(22,700,000)	27,100,000
Inventories	(11,600,000)	(32,600,000)	16,500,000
Other current assets	(5,400,000)	(2,100,000)	(1,700,000)
Other assets	(900,000)	(20,000,000)	(3,900,000)
Accounts payable	9,200,000	23,700,000	(5,700,000)
Income taxes payable	4,000,000	12,700,000	35,700,000
Asbestos settlement liability	—	512,500,000	—
Other current liabilities	57,500,000	25,100,000	40,300,000
Other liabilities	10,700,000	1,900,000	(1,100,000)
Net cash provided by operating activities	469,700,000	323,900,000	578,700,000
Cash flows from investing activities:			
Capital expenditures for property and equipment	(124,300,000)	(91,600,000)	(146,300,000)
Proceeds from sales of property and equipment	3,400,000	5,200,000	4,400,000
Businesses acquired in purchase transactions, net of cash acquired	(2,500,000)	(10,500,000)	(36,000,000)
Net cash used in investing activities	(123,400,000)	(96,900,000)	(177,900,000)
Cash flows from financing activities:			
Proceeds from long-term debt	1,582,000,000	281,400,000	482,400,000
Payment of long-term debt	(276,700,000)	(240,000,000)	(631,500,000)
Payment of senior debt issuance costs	(19,500,000)	—	(2,200,000)
Net proceeds from the termination of interest rate swap agreements	700,000	2,700,000	—
Net proceeds from the termination of treasury lock agreements	13,900,000	—	—
Net payments of short-term borrowings	(37,300,000)	(77,100,000)	(163,800,000)
Repurchases of preferred stock	(36,700,000)	(28,800,000)	(18,800,000)
Redemption of preferred stock	(1,298,100,000)	—	—
Dividends paid on preferred stock	(41,900,000)	(40,500,000)	(69,200,000)
Proceeds from stock option exercises	4,700,000	800,000	500,000
Net cash used in financing activities	(108,900,000)	(101,500,000)	(402,600,000)
Effect of exchange rate changes on cash and cash equivalents	800,000	(12,500,000)	4,400,000
Cash and cash equivalents:			
Net change during the period	238,200,000	113,000,000	2,600,000
Balance, beginning of period	126,800,000	13,800,000	11,200,000
Balance, end of period	$365,000,000	$126,800,000	$13,800,000

Respond to the following questions:

a. Determine how much of the $850,100,000 expense on the income statement was actually a cash outflow during 2002.

b. Reconstruct as best you can the journal entry that was made in 2002 to record this estimated loss.

c. Discuss how this liability might be affected were the bankruptcy plan for Grace not to be approved.

d. The recorded liability for asbestos settlement accrues interest at a rate of 5.5 percent and is recorded by Sealed Air as a part of interest expense, and the liability appears in other current liabilities. Discuss the magnitude of this additional expense to Sealed Air and how it affects the firm's cash flows.

25. In 2001 Sealed Air Corporation decided to do some restructuring of its operations and announced a restructuring program that resulted in a $32.8 million charge to operations in 2001 (see the income statement in problem 24). Following is the disclosure regarding these restructuring plans as of the end of 2003.

During 2001, based primarily on weakening economic conditions, especially in the United States, the Company conducted a review of its business to reduce costs and expenses, simplify business processes and organizational structure, and to refine further the Company's manufacturing operations and product offerings. As a result of this review, which the Company completed in the fourth quarter of 2001, the Company announced and began implementing a restructuring program that resulted in charges to operations of $32.8 million for 2001. These charges consisted of the following (amounts in millions):

	Year Ended December 31, 2001
Employee termination costs	$23.9
Facility exit costs	1.6
Long-lived asset impairments	7.3
Total	$32.8

The portion of this restructuring charge related to the Company's food packaging segment was $21.1 million, and the portion applicable to the protective and specialty packaging segment was $11.7 million.

The Company originally expected to incur $25.5 million of cash outlays to carry out this restructuring program. These cash outlays primarily consisted of severance and other personnel-related costs as well as lease and other contractual arrangement termination costs. As of December 31, 2003, the Company had made total cash payments of approximately $22.9 million ($5.3 million in 2003, $11.8 million in 2002, and $5.8 million in 2001). In 2003 and 2002, the Company adjusted the 2001 cash restructuring accrual for net credits of $0.5 million and $1.3 million, respectively, as discussed below. After these cash outlays and the net credits, the restructuring accrual at December 31, 2003 was $0.8 million, representing cash outlays expected to be made in 2004 and future years, primarily for severance-related costs.

Required:

a. What effect did the restructuring plan have on cash in each of the three years from 2001 through 2003?

b. Reconstruct the entry that was made in 2001 to record the effects of the restructuring plan.

c. Explain what you think the company means by "credits" in 2002 and 2003 and how this affects the balance in the accrual.

26. Following you will find the financial statements of National Service Industries, Inc. for 2002. In 2003 the company merged with National Service Acquisition Company, which then went private.

NATIONAL SERVICE INDUSTRIES, INC. Income Statement	08/31/2002	08/31/2001	08/31/2000
Sales and Service Revenues:			
Service revenues	$319,669,000	$334,820,000	$321,522,000
Net sales of products	212,761,000	228,462,000	225,190,000
Total sales and service revenues	532,430,000	563,282,000	546,712,000
Costs and Expenses:			
Cost of services	191,534,000	192,664,000	183,867,000
Cost of products sold	164,285,000	183,357,000	177,359,000
Selling and administrative expenses	173,868,000	182,106,000	157,121,000
Amortization expense	1,853,000	2,807,000	2,411,000
Interest expense	385,000	1,770,000	1,578,000
Gain on sale of corporate headquarters building	(7,966,000)	–	–
Gain on sale of businesses	(1,052,000)	(2,359,000)	(356,000)
Restructuring expense, asset impairments, and other charges	22,693,000	26,073,000	–
Other expense (income), net	(2,161,000)	1,135,000	(3,165,000)
Total costs and expenses	543,439,000	587,553,000	518,815,000
(Loss) income before income tax (benefit) expense	(11,009,000)	(24,271,000)	27,897,000
Income tax (benefit) expense	(4,074,000)	(8,980,000)	10,824,000
(Loss) income from continuing operations	(6,935,000)	(15,291,000)	17,073,000
Discontinued Operations:			
Income from discontinued operations, net of income taxes of $7,066 in 2002, $26,848 in 2001, and $52,494 in 2000 (Note 2)	11,534,000	42,304,000	82,797,000
Costs associated with effecting the spin-off, net of tax benefit of $717	(19,069,000)	–	–
Total discontinued operations	(7,535,000)	42,304,000	82,797,000
Cumulative effect of change in accounting principle, net of tax benefit of $10,830	(17,602,000)	–	–
Net (Loss) Income	($32,072,000)	$ 27,013,000	$ 99,870,000

NATIONAL SERVICE INDUSTRIES, INC.
Balance Sheet

	08/31/2002	08/31/2001
Assets		
Current Assets:		
Cash and cash equivalents	$ 20,969,000	$ 0
Receivables, less allowance for doubtful accounts of $1,173 in 2002 and $1,798 in 2001	52,198,000	60,406,000
Inventories, at the lower of cost (on a first-in, first-out basis) or market	16,037,000	19,195,000
Linens in service, net of amortization	51,806,000	56,910,000
Deferred income taxes	0	9,138,000
Prepayments	5,086,000	11,300,000
Insurance receivable (Note 6)	42,024,000	28,616,000
Other current assets	693,000	804,000
Total Current Assets	188,813,000	186,369,000
Property, Plant, and Equipment, at cost:		
Land	5,715,000	12,775,000
Buildings and leasehold improvements	49,867,000	57,433,000
Machinery and equipment	259,730,000	258,344,000
Total Property, Plant, and Equipment	315,312,000	328,552,000
Less accumulated depreciation and amortization	167,356,000	157,507,000
Property, Plant, and Equipment, net	147,956,000	171,045,000
Other Assets:		
Goodwill (Note 1)	0	28,432,000
Other intangibles (Note 1)	8,357,000	8,629,000
Insurance receivable (Note 6)	140,831,000	66,574,000
Prepaid benefit cost	30,644,000	34,465,000
Other	2,497,000	2,584,000
Total Other Assets	182,329,000	140,684,000
Net assets of discontinued operations (Note 2)	0	400,296,000
Total Assets	$519,098,000	$898,394,000
Liabilities and Stockholders' Equity		
Current Liabilities:		
Current maturities of long-term debt	$ 1,093,000	$ 1,011,000
Notes payable	0	1,999,000
Accounts payable	16,569,000	28,164,000
Accrued salaries, commissions, and bonuses	7,007,000	7,050,000
Current portion of self-insurance accrual	5,785,000	3,119,000
Environmental accrual (Note 6)	5,777,000	7,291,000
Litigation accrual (Note 6)	41,288,000	30,453,000
Deferred income taxes	8,811,000	0
Other accrued liabilities	19,506,000	19,561,000
Total Current Liabilities	105,836,000	98,648,000
Long-term debt, less current maturities	984,000	1,990,000
Deferred income taxes	7,853,000	32,431,000
Self-insurance accrual, less current portion	9,258,000	12,477,000
Litigation accrual (Note 6)	166,844,000	82,917,000
Other long-term liabilities	7,690,000	7,303,000

	08/31/2002	08/31/2001
Commitments and contingencies (Note 6)		
Stockholders' equity:		
Series A participating preferred stock, $.05 stated value, 500,000 shares authorized, none issued		
Preferred stock, no par value, 500,000 shares authorized, none issued		
Common stock, $1 par value, 120,000,000 shares authorized, 14,478,500 shares issued in 2002 and 14,479,745 shares in 2001	14,479,000	14,480,000
Paid-in capital	11,570,000	72,860,000
Retained earnings	552,302,000	995,537,000
Unearned compensation on restricted stock (Note 5)	(4,092,000)	(880,000)
Accumulated other comprehensive income items	(2,350,000)	(43,000)
	571,909,000	1,081,954,000
Less Treasury stock, at cost (3,510,515 shares in 2002 and 4,173,299 shares in 2001)	351,276,000	419,326,000
Total Stockholders' Equity	220,633,000	662,628,000
Total Liabilities and Stockholders' Equity	$519,098,000	$898,394,000

a. Identify all of the accounts on the balance sheet that are related to the asbestos litigation accruals, including any insurance recoverable.

b. Assuming that there were not actually cash flows related to the litigation during 2002, reconstruct the entry(ies) that was made during the period to record additional accruals and related recoveries.

c. In the company's footnotes describing the litigation, the company indicated that its current year might range as high as $139 million but because no estimate was more likely than any other, the company accrued at the low end of the range. If the company were to accrue at the high end of the range, what effect would this have on the income statement and balance sheet in 2002?

● BEYOND THE BOOK

27. Use a database such as Lexis-Nexis to search for a company that disclosed a significant contingency over the last two years (lawsuit, environmental liability, etc.) and then use EDGAR to determine how the effects of that contingency were reported in the 10-K.

28. For a company of your own choosing (or one assigned by your instructor), use a database such as EDGAR to find its most recent 10-K and then respond to the following questions:

a. What type of retirement plans does the company have?

b. What contributions did the company make to those plans in the most recent year?

    c. For defined benefit plans:

       1. What is the funded status of the plan?

       2. What was the experience with the return on plan assets over the most recent two years?

       3. What net amount is reported on the balance sheet for pension assets or liabilities at the end of the most recent period?

       4. What assumptions did the company make in computing its pension liabilities over the last three years?

29. For a company of your own choosing or one assigned by your instructor, use a database such as EDGAR to find its most recent 10-K or annual report and respond to the following questions.

    a. What is the company's effective tax rate as reported in the footnotes? What are major sources of difference between the effective tax rate and the statutory rate?

    b. Does the company have employee stock option plans? If so, what was the dollar value of stock exercised in the current year? Find the tax savings as a result of stock options exercised.

CHAPTER 11

Debt: Pricing, Covenants, and Disclosure

LEARNING OBJECTIVES

After reading this chapter, you should be able to:

1. Understand how to apply present value techniques to price debt.

2. Explain how interest is recognized on debt and the related effect of the amortization of debt discounts and premiums.

3. Identify the role of debt covenants in resolving incentive conflicts between debtholders and stockholders.

4. Describe the treatment of gains and losses on early debt retirement.

5. Distinguish between capital leases and operating leases.

6. Appreciate incentives for structuring leases as operating.

7. Understand the nature of special purpose entities and the controversy over off-balance sheet liabilities.

During 2001 the financial markets closely watched Enron, a large energy producing and trading company. The company had filed for bankruptcy protection, the largest such case in U.S. history. From an accounting standpoint, several factors contributed to Enron's collapse including inadequate disclosure for transactions, financial misstatements, and massive off-balance sheet liabilities. As a consequence, Enron investors may not have fully understood their exposure to risks associated with affiliates of Enron (called *special purpose entities*), implied by loan guarantees provided by Enron to debt holders and others providing capital to those affiliates. Revelation of Enron's responsibility for such debt, along with losses in those entities, are widely viewed as having precipitated the company's bankruptcy.

As a result of Enron's collapse, the SEC and FASB began to revise GAAP to forestall similar collapses in the future. The AICPA responded with a statement of position to improve financial reporting and auditing systems. Finally, the five largest auditing firms issued a joint statement, reflecting the seriousness of the issues involved. Enron's auditor, Arthur Andersen, has also been forced out of business due to this situation.

The Enron case points toward a larger issue of transparency regarding obligations that do not rise to the level of debt to be formally recognized on companies' balance sheets. As we will bring out in this chapter, the distinction between what constitutes liabilities for balance sheet purposes is sometimes arbitrary and unclear.

In this chapter, we consider various types of debt including notes, bonds, and lease obligations. *Debt* refers to those interest-bearing liabilities that are less directly linked to operating activities than those described in Chapter 10. That is, debt is part of the "capitalization" of the firm. Debt, along with stockholders' equity, provides financing for the firm's investments in working capital and long-lived assets.

NOTES PAYABLE

In general, **notes payable** take the form of contracts (often called *financial instruments*) that commit the firm to future payments of principal and interest. For example, the firm might borrow funds from a bank or other financial institution by issuing a written promise to repay the amount borrowed (the *principal*), plus some compensation to the lender for use of the funds (the *interest*). To reduce the risk to the lender from default, the firm might pledge assets as collateral. For example, firms may secure some notes by accounts receivables, inventories, or property. Firms usually repay principal and interest through periodic and/or lump-sum payments over the life of the loan.

The accounting in the case where interest is paid periodically and principal is repaid at maturity is straightforward. The issuing firm records a liability, notes payable, at the time it issues the note, recognizes the periodic interest payments as an expense, and eliminates the liability at maturity. To illustrate, recall the borrowing of $400 million at a 7 percent interest rate by BHT, our hypothetical company from previous chapters. In this instance, BHT would make the following journal entry (in millions) to record the issuance of the debt:

Cash	400	
Notes Payable		400

One year later, BHT would record interest paid as follows (note that this same entry is made every year up to the maturity date):

Interest Expense	28	
Cash		28

When BHT repays the note at maturity, it would make the entry:

Notes Payable	400	
Cash		400

Exhibit 11.1
Mattel Corporation

THE REAL WORLD

Mattel Corporation

> **6-3/4 percent Senior Notes**
>
> . . . the Company issued $100.0 million aggregate principal amount of 6-3/4 percent Senior Notes maturing May 15, . . . Interest is payable semiannually on the fifteenth day of May and November.

Let's look at a more complex example. Exhibit 11.1 includes an excerpt from Mattel's annual report (Mattel's fiscal year end is December 31). Observe from the exhibit that the company pays interest on the notes semiannually, at dates that do not correspond to the company's December 31 fiscal year-end date. Accordingly, each year the company needs to accrue interest from the last semiannual interest payment date to the fiscal year-end date. A likely year-end adjusting entry to record interest accrued between November 15 and December 31 would then be (Yearly Rate × Fraction of Year × Principal = .0675 × (1.5/12) × 100,000,000 = 843,750):

Interest Expense	843,750	
Accrued Interest Payable		843,750

Later, on May 15 of the following year, the company might make the following journal entry, to record the next semiannual interest payment (Payment = .0675 × (6/12) × 100,000,000 = 3,375,000):

Interest Expense	2,231,250	
Accrued Interest Payable	843,750	
Cash		3,375,000

Here, part of the interest payment retires the accrued liability created by the earlier year-end adjusting entry. Mattel charges the rest to interest expense because it relates to use of borrowed funds for the year in which the firm makes the payment.

One issue firms face in recording notes payable is how to determine the value at which the note should initially be recorded. In the next section, we discuss how notes are valued or priced in the marketplace.

PRICING OF DEBT

A firm typically arranges notes payable with private lenders such as banks and other financial institutions. The lender typically loans an amount (often called the *issue* or *selling price*) that the firm then repays through a combination of periodic payments (an annuity) and a large lump-sum payment on the maturity date of the note (commonly known as the **maturity value, par value,** or **face value**).

In many cases a firm issues (sells) notes at par that prescribe periodic interest payments based on the interest rate required by the lender. This specified interest rate (known as the **contract rate** or **coupon rate**) is then the rate of return earned by the lender (often referred to as the **yield** or the **effective rate**) on the note. Because the notes were issued at par, the periodic payments in this situation exactly equal the interest expense that the borrowing firm incurs.

The term *coupon rate* is used when the debt instrument includes coupons that are detachable and are submitted to the borrower for payment by the lender (investor). The contract thus fixes the payments to the lender. If the lender agrees to lend the firm the par value of the note, then the lender's yield rate would equal the contract rate. However, the lender may decide it needs to earn a different rate of return than that specified by the contract rate, usually because the prevailing market rate for debt involving similar risk is greater or less than the contract rate. In this case, the lender agrees to lend the firm either more than the par value (for a lower effective rate) or less than the par value (for a higher effective rate). As a result, the price at which the firm sells the note to the lender essentially adjusts the contract rate to the lender's required rate of return or yield.

Lenders use present value techniques (remember that we first introduced these techniques in Chapter 6 when we discussed the major valuation methods) to determine the price that they will pay for such a note. They take into consideration the maturity payment, the periodic contract or coupon payments, and the time to maturity as well as their own required rate of return for these types of contracts. Let's illustrate using our BHT example. Suppose that the notes, still with a par value of $400 (in thousands) and contract rate of 7 percent, had a four-year life to maturity and the lender priced the notes to yield 8 percent. Exhibit 11.2 depicts the cash flows over the life of the notes and the calculation of the price using present value factors from Appendix B. Note that because the lender requires a higher rate of return than the contract rate, the amount received by the issuer ($386.75) at the beginning is less than the par value ($400).

Exhibit 11.3 provides a real-world example of notes issued at a price below par value. Here, observe that Champion Home Builders, like most firms, states the price for notes as a percent of maturity value. In Exhibit 11.3, the issue price

Exhibit 11.2
Calculation of Present Value
of BHT Notes (in thousands)

Yearly Interest Payments = Face Value × Contract Rate = $400 × 7% = $28
Maturity Payment = $400

Year	Payment
1	$28
2	28
3	28
4	28 + 400

Discount Rate = 8 percent

Present Value = PV(annuity of $28 for 4 years)
                   + PV(lump sum $400 at end of 4 years)
Present Value = $28 × 3.31213 + $400 × 0.73503 = $386.75

Exhibit 11.3

THE REAL WORLD

Champion Home
Builders

Champion Home Builders Co., a wholly owned subsidiary of Champion Enterprises, Inc., a maker of prefabricated homes, announced that it had sold $150 million of five-year senior notes in the private placement market. The facts related to the borrowing are:

Borrower: Champion Home Builders Co.
Amount: $150 Million
Coupon: 11.25%
Maturity: 4/15/2007
Type: Senior Notes
Issue Price: 99.066
First Pay Date: 10/15/2002
Last Moody's Rating: B2
Yield: 11.50%
Pay Frequency: Semiannual

is 99.066. This means that lenders paid 99.066 percent of the maturity value ($150 million) or $148.6 million. Note that this implies that the yield or effective interest rate on these bonds is higher than the coupon rate because Champion Home Builders received less than the par value of the debt even though they must pay the full amount. Differences between the coupon rate and the yield interest rate occur because the price of the debt will vary as market interest rates change.

Unlike our BHT example, Champion makes its coupon payments semiannually. Therefore, the rate for calculating semiannual coupon payments is one-half the coupon rate, or $(1/2) \times 11.25\% = 5.625\%$. We can see from Exhibit 11.3 that the future cash flows to service the above debt include ten (10) semiannual coupon payments of $8.4375 million ($150 million $\times$ 5.625%) starting on October 15, 2002 and a payment of the principal of $150 million at the end of five (5) years.

The issue price stated (99.066) provides lenders an annual yield of 11.50 percent or semiannual yield of 5.75 percent, which is higher than the contract rate. (Note that the price is lower than the maturity value, as will always be the case when the yield required by lenders is higher than the contract rate.) Lenders arrive at this price by applying present value techniques to the payments in the contract and their own required yield. The note provides a ten-payment annuity of $8.4375 million for ten semiannual periods and a lump sum of $150 million at the end of the ten semiannual periods. Using the present value techniques described in Appendix B, lenders add together the present value of the annuity and the lump sum, using their required yield rate of 5.75 percent (note that the semiannual periods would be used for compounding purposes; i.e., interest is assumed to compound twice a year). The net result is a present value of $148.6 million, or 99.066 percent of the $150 million maturity value.

Generalizing, we say that debt is issued at **par,** at a **discount,** or at a **premium.** *Issued at par* means the price equals the maturity value (price = 100). If the issue price is less than the maturity value (price < 100), then the debt is *issued at a discount.* Finally, if the issue price is greater than the maturity value (price > 100), the debt is *issued at a premium.* You can see how the pricing reflects a comparison of the yield to the contract rate. If the yield equals the contract rate, then the debt is issued at par. If the yield is higher than the contract rate, the debt is issued at a discount, and vice versa for debt issued at a premium. Because notes issued at a premium rarely occur, in the next section, we discuss the accounting issues for the debt issued at a discount.

ACCOUNTING FOR DISCOUNTS ON DEBT

How do firms record the issuance of debt issued at a discount, as in the BHT and Champion examples? For BHT, the issue price of $386.75 implies a discount of $13.25 ($400 − 386.75). One way to think about the discount is to view it as prepaid interest; i.e., BHT borrowed $400 but immediately gave the lender back $13.25 (to increase its yield on the loan). However, because the yield is spread out over the life of the loan, the prepaid interest should be recognized as an expense (amortized) over the life of the notes. This treatment thus matches the costs of borrowing the funds with the benefits that follow from the use of the funds.

However, if we record the discount as an asset, then the liability account will not be stated at its net present value, the required valuation method under GAAP. Therefore, under GAAP, we instead record the discount as a contra-liability to the note payable account. This treatment results in reporting the debt on the balance sheet at the present value of future payments of principal, and measuring interest in terms of the effective interest rate at the date of issue. (Note that firms frequently suppress disclosure of an unamortized discount on the balance sheet by showing the notes net of the discount.)

Let's now review the accounting steps involved in amortizing a discount on debt. The first step is to determine interest expense by multiplying the net book value at the start of the period by the effective interest rate. In the BHT example, interest expense for the first year would be $386.75 × .08 = $30.94. The next step is to calculate the difference between that amount and the cash payment of interest based on the contract rate. For BHT, that amount equals $2.94 ($30.94 − 28.00). This reduces the balance of the unamortized discount, thereby increasing the net book value of the debt.

Journal entries depicting the issuance of the notes at the discount and the first annual interest payment (in thousands) would be as follows:

At issuance:

Cash	386.75	
Discount on Notes Payable	13.24	
Notes Payable		400.00

At the first interest payment:

Interest Expense	30.94	
Cash		28.00
Discount on Notes Payable		2.94

Year	Beginning Balance	Balance in Discount	Interest Expense	Interest Payment	Amortization of Discount
1	386.75	13.25	30.94	28	2.94
2	389.69	10.31	31.18	28	3.18
3	392.87	7.13	31.43	28	3.43
4	396.29	3.71	31.70	28	3.70
5	400.00	0.00			

Exhibit 11.4
Amortization Table
for BHT Note

The net book value (par value − unamortized discount) at the end of the first year would be $400 − ($13.25 − $2.94) = $389.69. Exhibit 11.4 depicts the full schedule of interest payments, interest expense, discount amortization, and net book value of the notes. This is often referred to as an *amortization table.*

Let's look at another example. For the Champion case, the difference between the maturity value ($150 million) and the issue price ($148.6 million) is the discount ($1.4 million). Similar to the BHT example, the following summary journal entries depict the issuance of Champion's notes and the first two semiannual interest payments and related amortization. The journal entry at issuance is:

Cash	148,600,000	
Discount on Notes Payable	1,400,000	
Notes Payable		150,000,000

Recall from our calculation earlier that the cash payments at the end of each six months are $8,437,500. We then calculate interest expense for the first six months as $148,600,000 × 5.575% = $8,544,500, resulting in the following entry:

Interest Expense	8,544,500	
Cash		8,437,500
Discount on Notes Payable		107,000

The net book (also called carrying) value of the debt then increases at the end of the first six months by the amount of the discount, bringing it to $148,707,000 ($148,600,000 + $107,000). We then calculate interest expense in the second six months to be $8,550,652 ($148,707,000 × 5.575%), resulting in the following entry:

Interest Expense	8,550,652	
Cash		8,437,500
Discount on Notes Payable		113,152

Again, the balance in Discount on Notes Payable is reduced with each entry to recognize interest expense. In turn, this treatment increases the net book value of the notes payable. The book value represents the sum of the proceeds

Exhibit 11.5

IDEC Pharmaceuticals
Corporation and
Subsidiary

(in thousands)		
	2001	2000
Zero coupon subordinated convertible notes, due 2019 at 5.5%	$135,977	$128,888

received when the notes were issued and the cash saved by paying interest at the coupon rate of 5.625 percent (rather than the 5.750 percent that investors require). By the date that the notes mature, all of the discount would have been amortized. This brings the net book value just before the notes are retired to their par value of $150 million.

ZERO-COUPON DEBT

An extreme example of notes issued at a discount would be so-called **zero-coupon** notes. As the term suggests, the coupon rate specified in its contract is zero (0), meaning that there are no coupon payments. The only payment on such notes is the payment of par value at maturity. Hence, for these notes, the entire yield is contained in the discount at which the firm issues the notes.

For example, Exhibit 11.5 shows an excerpt from notes to IDEC Pharmaceuticals' financial statements for 2001 (note that IDEC has since merged with Biogen). Interest expense related to these notes explains the change in the book value shown ($7,089 = $135,977 − 128,888), resulting in the following journal entry (note: we can also determine this amount by applying the effective rate to the beginning book value (5.5% × $128,888 = $7,089):

Interest Expense	7,089
Notes Payable	7,089

In this case, we show the credit entry directly adding to the notes payable account, as IDEC reports the notes on the balance sheet net of their discount. The credit entry could just as easily have been to the discount account. This would have the same net effect of raising the net balance in the notes payable account from the end of 2000 to the end of 2001.

FAIR VALUE OF DEBT

Subsequent changes in market conditions, or future firm cash flow prospects of the firm, may cause the **fair value** of debt to deviate from its book value. By fair value we mean the price at which the debt would likely trade between investors. In turn, the price at which investors trade the debt equals the present value of the future payments of interest and principal determined using the market interest rate demanded by investors for this company's debt. If the market interest rate increases above the effective rate after issuing the debt, then the present value of the debt using the market rate would be lower than the book

	December 26, 1999		December 27, 1998	
	Carrying Value	Fair Value	Carrying Value	Fair Value
Medium-term notes	$ –	$ –	$ 40,000	$ 40,000
Senior notes	100,000	99,000	100,000	101,000
Industrial development bonds	5,000	5,000	5,000	5,000
Total	105,000	104,000	145,000	146,000
Less current portion	–	–	40,000	40,000
	$105,000	$104,000	$105,000	$106,000

Fair values were determined using discounted cash flows at current interest rates from similar borrowings.

Exhibit 11.6
Adolph Coors
Long-Term Debt Consists of the Following (in thousands):

THE REAL WORLD

Adolph Coors

The disclosure of the "fair values" of debt allows investors to determine unrealized holding gains and losses induced by changes in the market's interest rate for debt of similar duration and risk. Such gains (losses) are real in the sense that the issuer could, in principle, repurchase the debt at less (more) than its book value or continue to pay lower (higher) interest than the market currently requires.

value (and vice versa if market rates decline). The difference between this market value and the book value of debt would be an unrealized gain or loss. Such an unrealized gain or loss would not be recognized under current GAAP. However, GAAP does require that fair value be disclosed for the benefit of investors (FASB, SFAS No. 107, 1991). Exhibit 11.6 provides this type of disclosure for Adolph Coors. Observe that the fair value of the Senior Notes was greater than the book value in 1998, but less than the book value in 1999. As a result, we infer that interest rates for similar debt must have increased during the year.

EARLY DEBT RETIREMENT

Sometimes a firm retires debt before its maturity date. Such early debt retirement can occur because an issuer exercises a contractual provision allowing it to *redeem* (repurchase) its debt at a prespecified *redemption price.* Or, the issuer repurchases its own debt (on the market, if it is publicly traded, or from private lenders through subsequent negotiations). As suggested by the previous fair value discussion, early debt retirement often gives rise to a gain or loss in the form of a difference between the redemption price and the debt's book value.

Prior to 2002, GAAP required that gains and losses on early debt retirement be treated as extraordinary items for income reporting purposes (FASB, SFAS No. 4, 1995). The classification of gains and losses on early debt retirement did not depend on whether they met the general conditions for extraordinary items, as we described in Chapter 4. Instead, gains and losses on early debt retirements were classified as extraordinary, even if such retirements are not unusual or infrequent events. Exhibit 11.7 illustrates this prior treatment by Tenet Healthcare Corporation. In 2002 the FASB rescinded SFAS 4 in SFAS 145 (FASB, SFAS No. 145, 2002). The reason given by the FASB was that debt extinguishment is now part of the risk management strategy for many companies, and the classification of gains and losses that are part of an entity's risk management strategy does not meet the requirements for an extraordinary item. GAAP was changed such that the early retirement of debt must meet the same criteria for extraordinary item treatment as all other items. Therefore, in most circumstances the early retirement of debt will not be treated as extraordinary.

Exhibit 11.7
Tenet Healthcare Corporation

THE REAL WORLD

Tenet Healthcare
Corporation

> In May 2001 the Company repurchased an aggregate of $514 million of its Senior and Senior Subordinated Notes. In connection with the repurchase of debt and the refinancing of its bank credit agreement, the Company recorded an extraordinary charge from early extinguishment of debt in the amount of $35 million, net of tax benefits of $21 million, in the fourth quarter of the year ended May 31, 2001.

Using the data in Exhibit 11.7, we can reconstruct the journal entry made by Tenet (in millions) to reflect the retirement itself before income tax effects:

Notes Payable	514	
Loss on Retirement of Notes Payable	56	
Cash		570

Note that the market price of the Tenet bonds is greater than the carrying value. This implies that interest rates have fallen since the debt has been issued. As a result, Tenet would record a loss in retiring the debt. Conversely, if interest rates has risen, the price of the debt would have fallen and Tenet would have recorded a gain if the debt had been retired. In effect, Tenet had a choice between paying more than the book value to retire the debt or paying higher than market interest rates over the remaining life of the debt. In either event, Tenet has suffered an economic loss with the reduction of interest rates subsequent to when the debt was issued. If the market interest rate had risen after the debt was issued, then the price of the debt would have fallen and Tenet could either have paid less than the book value to retire the debt or enjoyed lower interest rates over the debt's remaining life.

DEBT COVENANTS

It has been suggested that through a combination of earnings-based debt covenants and conservative accounting policies, a firm may be able to signal higher expected future cash flows to lenders, thereby achieving lower interest rates on the debt than would otherwise be obtained (see Levine and Hughes, *Journal of Corporate Finance*, 2004).

Debt covenants generally serve to restrict the investment and financing policies of the issuing firm. However, even though covenants reduce debt holders' risk through these restrictions, the issuing firm also receives advantages. Because of the reduced risk to debt holders, the issuer may receive better terms such as a reduction in interest rates.

Covenants limit opportunistic behavior by management of the issuing firm. For example, covenants commonly restrict future dividend distributions to stockholders to a maximum percentage of net income. To appreciate why such a restriction might be useful, imagine the incentives of managers once the funds have been obtained from the debt holders. If no limitations on the dividends that could be declared existed, management might distribute all available funds to stockholders, leaving debt holders at greater risk of not being repaid. Of course, debt holders would likely anticipate this possibility (if no limitations existed) and, therefore, require a higher interest rate. In fact, if the risk of being left with nothing becomes too great, investors may be unwilling to buy the debt at any price. Thus, in order to obtain a lower interest rate or even find takers for the debt, management may find it in the best interests of the firm to restrict its future dividend policy.

Often debt covenants require the firm to maintain certain financial ratios. In the case of dividend covenants, the company may be restricted from distributing dividends if they are in excess of a percent of net income or if they would reduce net worth below a percentage of total assets. Other covenants may require the company to maintain interest coverage and leverage ratios (described in Chapter 6). Non-accounting covenants may restrict management from issuing further debt, investing in very risky projects, or acquiring other businesses. The disclosures for several companies in Exhibit 11.8 illustrate how ratios may be incorporated into the covenant requirements.

In general, debt covenants do not require firms to use specific accounting methods or dictate how firms determine accounting accrual estimates. This flexibility provides management with some scope to manipulate accounting inputs

Exhibit 11.8

THE REAL WORLD

Use of Ratios in Covenants

Primedia, Inc. and Subsidiaries

Under the most restrictive covenants as defined in the bank credit facility agreement, the Company must maintain a minimum interest coverage ratio, as defined, of 2.0 to 1 and a minimum fixed charge coverage ratio, as defined, of 1.05 to 1. The maximum allowable debt leverage ratio, as defined, is 6.0 to 1. The maximum leverage ratio decreases to 5.75 to 1, 5.5 to 1, 5.0 to 1, and 4.5 to 1, respectively, on July 1, 2004, January 1, 2005, January 1, 2006, and January 1, 2007. The minimum interest coverage ratio increases to 2.25 to 1 and 2.5 to 1, respectively, on January 1, 2004, and January 1, 2005. The Company is in compliance with all of the financial and operating covenants of its financing arrangements.

Hasbro, Inc.

The agreement contains certain restrictive covenants setting forth minimum cash flow and coverage requirements, and a number of other limitations, including restrictions on capital expenditures, investments, acquisitions, share repurchases, incurrence of indebtedness, and dividend payments. The Company was in compliance with all covenants as of and for the year ended December 28, 2003.

International Game Technology and Subsidiaries

We are required to comply with certain covenants contained in these agreements, including restrictions on our ability to:

● incur indebtedness
● grant liens on our assets
● enter into sale/leaseback transactions
● make investments, acquisitions, dispositions
● pay dividends
● make certain other restricted payments without the written consent of the lenders

If we are unable to maintain the financial ratios required under our bank revolving line of credit, the lenders could terminate their commitments and declare all amounts borrowed, together with accrued interest and fees, to be immediately due and payable. If this happened, other indebtedness that contains cross-default or cross-acceleration provisions, including the senior notes, may also be accelerated to become due and payable immediately.

We were in compliance with all applicable covenants at September 30, 2003.

Academic studies show that firms facing potential violation of accounting-based debt covenants tend to exercise discretion over accounting accruals to reduce the prospect of violation. Managers of firms facing the prospect of violating debt covenants tend to make income-increasing accounting choices (see Sweeney, *Journal of Accounting and Economics*, 1994.)

to the ratios employed. Debt holders should anticipate that management may use this flexibility to minimize the prospects of violating covenants in pricing the debt. For example, management might employ aggressive accounting techniques to meet an interest coverage ratio limitation.

CREDIT AGREEMENTS

Firms often arrange a **line of credit** with financial institutions or corporate lenders in order to ensure that they can borrow as short-term needs arise. Sometimes these lines of credit are set up on a *revolving basis,* such that the firm may borrow, repay, and reborrow without need of a new agreement each time. These agreements may specify the maximum amount that the firm can borrow as well as how the interest rate will be determined.

Interest rates on lines of credit are often based on the *London Interbank Offer Rate (LIBOR),* plus *basis points.* Basis points refer to interest rates times 100. For example, the borrowing rate might be set at the current LIBOR rate plus 200 basis points. If the LIBOR rate at the time of borrowing is 2.50 percent, then the interest rate would be set at 4.50 percent. Borrowing under lines of credit may also involve collateral and debt covenants. The disclosure for Boise Cascade in Exhibit 11.9 illustrates this type of borrowing.

BONDS PAYABLE

Firms, especially larger well-established ones, sometimes issue publicly traded bonds (although these may also be called notes). Typically, bonds sold to the investing public include the following characteristics:

● A **bond indenture,** which gives the terms of the agreement between the issuer and investors. This agreement specifies the coupon rate and dates of payment, the maturity date and amount to be paid at that time, any collateral and name of a **trustee** (who holds title to that collateral), and covenants that restrict certain company policies, such as the amount of dividends that may be distributed to stockholders.

● A *registrar* and *disbursing agent,* such as a bank, to receive interest and principal payments and distribute them to bond holders.

● Engraved *bond certificates,* often in denominations of $1,000. Some bonds, referred to as *coupon bonds,* have coupons attached that represent periodic interest payment promises. More often bonds are *registered,* which means that the issuer records the bond holders' names and addresses and sends the periodic payments to those parties.

Exhibit 11.9

THE REAL WORLD

Boise Cascade

In March 2002, we entered into a three-year, unsecured revolving credit agreement with fourteen major financial institutions. The agreement permits us to borrow as much as $560 million at variable interest rates based on either the London Interbank Offered Rate (LIBOR) or the prime rate. The borrowing capacity under the agreement can be expanded to a maximum of $600 million. Borrowings under the agreement were $210 million at December 31, 2003.

Exhibit 11.10
Archer Daniels Midland
Company, 2003 Annual
Report

THE REAL WORLD

Archer Daniels
Midland Company

Note 5—Debt and Financing Arrangements
(In thousands)

	2003	2002
5.935% Debentures $500 million face amount, due in 2032	$ 493,013	0
7.0% Debentures $400 million face amount, due in 2031	397,380	$ 397,285
7.5% Debentures $350 million face amount, due in 2027	348,009	347,980
8.875% Debentures $300 million face amount, due in 2011	298,823	298,722
6.625% Debentures $300 million face amount, due in 2029	298,634	298,614
8.125% Debentures $300 million face amount, due in 2012	298,593	298,489
8.375% Debentures $300 million face amount, due in 2017	295,162	294,984
7.125% Debentures $250 million face amount, due in 2013	249,569	249,539
6.95% Debentures $250 million face amount, due in 2097	246,212	246,183
6.75% Debentures $200 million face amount, due in 2027	196,001	195,890
6.25% Notes $250 million face amount, paid in 2003	0	249,793
Other	781,779	539,605
Total long-term debt	3,903,175	3,417,084
Current maturities	−30,888	−305,790
	$3,872,287	$3,111,294

- Indenture agreements, which also specify any collateral associated with the bond to protect investors. *Mortgage bonds* carry a mortgage on real estate, *collateral trust bonds* commonly involve the issuer placing stocks or bonds in the hands of the trustee, and *debenture bonds* are secured by the general credit of the issuer rather than by specific assets.

- *Convertible,* meaning that bonds can be exchanged for common stock of the issuer at some prescribed exchange rate of shares for bond certificates. Bonds may also be *callable* or *redeemable,* meaning that the issuer may repurchase the bonds at a prespecified price.

Similar to notes, for pricing purposes a bond can be described by the future cash payments to be made to bondholders. The pattern of future payments can vary. For example, coupon bonds typically call for semiannual coupon payments at a stated rate (called the coupon rate) applied to the par value of the bond. *Serial bonds* call for periodic payments of principal as well as interest. *Zero-coupon bonds,* like zero-coupon notes, require a single payment of par value at maturity and no periodic payments before that point. The accounting treatment of bonds is essentially the same as that previously discussed for notes payable. Firms often have a large variety of notes and bonds that they have issued at various times as illustrated in Exhibit 11.10 for Archer Daniels Midland Company.

ACCOUNTING FOR COUPON BONDS

Coupon bonds can be issued at par value, at a premium, or at a discount. Coupon bonds have a fixed payment and maturity date. During the time that the bonds are outstanding, they can be bought and sold. The price of the bond will depend on the market yield rate for bonds of similar risk and duration (time to maturity). Cash interest payments are made either annually, semiannually, or quarterly. The cash interest payments are determined by the coupon rate, while the price is determined by the yield interest rate. Suppose that BHT issues $10,000,000 worth of $1,000 face value bonds that mature in five years and pay interest semiannually. The bonds have a coupon rate of 6 percent and are issued to yield 8 percent. The bond price is determined based on the cash flows as follows:

1. Semiannual interest payments $10,000,000 × .06 × 6/12 = $300,000
2. Number of payments = 10(5 years × 2 payments per year)
3. Present value of interest = Present value of an annuity in arrears of $300,000, for ten periods discounted at 4 percent (the yield rate times 6/12) as payments are semiannual = 8.11090 × 300,000 = $2,433,270.
4. Present value of principal repayment = Present value of $10,000,000 to be received in ten periods discounted at 4 percent = $10,000,000 × .67556 = $6,755,600.
5. Total present value is the sum of the interest plus the principal or $9,188,870 ($2,433,270 + 6,755,600).

The price of the bond is the sum of these two cash flows or $9,188,870. Note that if the bond had a yield rate that was less than the coupon rate, then similar to the earlier discussion of notes issued at a premium, the price would be greater than the par value, while if the yield rate exactly equaled the coupon rate, then the price would equal the bond par value. The journal entry to record the bond issuance would be as follows:

Cash	9,188,870	
Discount on Bonds Payable	811,130	
Bonds Payable		10,000,000

Interest expense would be recorded on the bond based on the yield rate of 8 percent compounded semiannually while the cash payments would be based on the coupon rate. The difference between the cash paid and the interest recorded would amortize the discount. The accounting entries are similar to those shown for BHT's note payable earlier in the chapter.

LEASES

Leases are contracts under which a **lessee** commits to make future payments to a **lessor** in return for the future use of the lessor's property. From the lessee's perspective, leases can take one of two possible forms, **operating leases** or **capital leases.** In the case of operating leases, the property is assumed to remain with the lessor. However, certain leases qualify as **capital leases** (FASB, SFAS No. 13, 1976). Capital leases convey most of the usual benefits and risks of ownership to the lessee. To be treated as a capital lease, a lease contract must be noncancelable and meet at least one of the following criteria:

○ Ownership is transferred to the lessee at the end of the lease term.
○ Transfer of ownership at the end of the lease term is likely because the lessee has a *bargain purchase option.* Such an option gives the right to purchase

the leased property at a specified future date for a price substantially less than the fair value of the property at that date.

- The lease extends for at least 75 percent of the property's useful life.
- The present value of the minimum contractual lease payments equals or exceeds 90 percent of the fair value of the property at the start of the lease.

Clearly, if the lessee owns the property at the end of the lease term, or the lessee is likely to acquire ownership by exercising an option to purchase, then it is reasonable to conclude that the usual benefits of ownership reside with the lessee. Similarly, if the lease runs for most of the useful life of the property, or involves payments with a present value that comes close to fair value of the property, then the principal benefits and risks of ownership have been transferred.

Basically, at some point a lease contract becomes indistinguishable from an installment purchase of property. For example, if a firm borrows funds under an installment note payable in order to finance the acquisition of property, the firm would recognize and record the borrowing of funds and the purchase of property. The result would be an asset to reflect the property acquired and a liability to reflect the obligation to repay the funds borrowed.

A capital lease is essentially similar. Here, a firm acquires an asset in the form of property rights that are equivalent to ownership (in the sense of who receives the benefits and assumes the risks). At the same time, the firm creates an obligation to make future payments much the same as under a loan agreement. In fact, when we break it down in this manner, it seems very clear that the accounting for a capital lease should parallel the accounting for the combination of a purchase of an asset and a borrowing of funds.

If a lease does not qualify as a capital lease, then it is classified as an **operating lease.** In many cases managers prefer operating leases because neither the lease obligations nor the leased assets are reported on the balance sheet.

Let's illustrate accounting for leases by lessees. Suppose that BHT leases fixtures (worth $540 million) for their useful life of nine (9) years. Assume that BHT makes lease payments of $86,443 (in thousands) per year. If we further assume that the appropriate discount rate to obtain a present value of these future payments is 8 percent (we will use the same rate we assumed for investors in our earlier discussion of BHT's notes), the present value of these payments is then $540 million. These assumptions make the "cost" of acquiring these fixtures the same whether BHT leases or purchases them.

Let's review the journal entries involved. The journal entry (in thousands) when BHT enters the lease is:

Fixtures	540,000	
Capital Lease Obligation		540,000

Each year after entering the lease, BHT needs to record the lease payments and depreciate the fixtures. The entry to record the first payment would be broken down into an interest component of $43,200 (in thousands) (i.e., 8% × $540 million) and a principal component of $43,243:

Interest Expense	43,200	
Capital Lease Obligation	43,243	
Cash		86,443

Note that the capital lease obligation would be $496,757 ($540,000 − $43,243) at the end of the first year. The entry to record depreciation on a straight-line basis with no salvage value would be:

Depreciation Expense	60,000	
Accumulated Depreciation		60,000

Exhibit 11.11 shows the balance sheet (in thousands) at the end of the first year.

Note that one consequence of depreciating the asset in a straight-line fashion while the interest is recognized under the effective interest method is that the net book value of the leased fixtures after the first year is less than the

Exhibit 11.11
Balance Sheet for Biohealth, Inc. (BHT)

		As of December 31, 20X1
Assets		
Current assets:		
Cash		$1,171
Accounts receivable		2,464
Inventory		3,920
Total current assets		7,555
Property, plant, and equipment (fixtures)	$540	
Less: accumulated depreciation	(60)	
Net property, plant, and equipment		480
Total assets		$8,035
Liabilities and stockholders' equity		
Liabilities:		
Current liabilities:		
Accounts payable		$5,140
Capital lease obligation		497
Notes payable		400
Total liabilities		6,037
Stockholders' Equity:		
Common stock		250
Additional paid-in capital		1,375
Retained earnings		373
Total stockholders' equity		1,998
Total liabilities and stockholders' equity		$8,035

remaining book value of the capital lease obligation. More generally, the method of depreciation is intended to match the cost of property rights conveyed by the lease to the benefits that unfold in the form of future revenues in a systematic way. The method of accounting for the capital lease obligation matches the cost of borrowing funds to the benefits that accrue to using debt as the means of financing assets. As the principal of the capital lease obligation is reduced, the firm has the use of less borrowed funds, implying that the costs of borrowing in the form of interest expense should also be reduced.

In the following year, BHT would base interest expense on the updated liability balance of $496,757 (in thousands), resulting in:

Interest Expense	39,741	
Capital Lease Obligation	46,702	
Cash		86,443

Interest expense each period diminishes as the principal upon which interest is based is also reduced. This process continues until the ninth year, when the asset would be fully depreciated and the capital lease obligation would be reduced to zero.

GAAP requires additional supplemental disclosures for firms that engage in lease transactions, to provide users with information about future payments that may not be reflected on the balance sheet, particularly for operating leases (FASB, SFAS No. 13, 1975). Exhibit 11.12 shows an example of the required

Exhibit 11.12

THE REAL WORLD

Nanogen

The Company leases its facilities and certain equipment under operating lease agreements that expire at various dates through 2010. Rent expense was $843,000, $927,000, and $783,000 in 2003, 2002, and 2001, respectively.

The Company leases certain equipment under capital lease obligations. Cost and accumulated amortization of equipment under capital leases were $16.1 million and $11.9 million at December 31, 2003, and $14.1 million and $9.7 million at December 31, 2002. Amortization of equipment under capital lease obligations is included in the depreciation expense.

Annual future minimum obligations for operating and capital leases as of December 31, 2003 are as follows (in thousands):

	Operating Leases	Capital Lease Obligations
2004	$ 989	$ 855
2005	1,086	494
2006	1,167	110
2007	1,179	0
2008	1,220	0
Thereafter	1,582	0
Total minimum lease payments	$7,223	1,459
Less amount representing interest		130
Present value of future minimum capital lease obligations		1,329
Less amounts due in one year		743
Long-term portion of capital lease obligations		$ 586

supplemental disclosures of lease commitments, including those related to both capital leases and operating leases.

Looking at Nanogen's disclosure about its capital lease obligations in Exhibit 11.12, we see that the principal component of minimum lease payments for 2004 is reflected in the amounts due in one year ($743). The gross amount of the payments due in 2004 ($855) includes both principal and interest. Accordingly, we can envision the following journal entry (in thousands) for capital lease payments in 2004:

Interest Expense	112	
Capital Lease Obligations	743	
Cash		855

Accounting for operating leases simply involves recording rent expense as a firm makes the lease payments. There is no accounting recognition of an asset nor a lease obligation at the start of the lease and, therefore, no depreciation nor reduction of a lease liability. In Nanogen's case, a suitable journal entry (in thousands) to record 2004 payments on operating leases might be:

Rent Expense	989	
Cash		989

The classification of leases as operating or capital is important in the sense of whether a firm includes a liability for the present value of future lease payments on its balance sheet. Some maintain that the present value of minimum future lease payments should be recognized as a liability on the balance sheet, irrespective of whether it meets the criteria established for capital leases. Others argue that the right to use leased property is an asset in that it gives rise to future benefits. Thus, we might view operating leases as off-balance sheet liabilities (as well as off-balance sheet assets). An interesting question becomes whether investors distinguish between footnote disclosures and formal recognition of leases within the financial statements. Note that Nanogen reports over $7 billion in undiscounted operating lease obligations. This is nearly five times as great as its capital leases. Consider what the impact on Nanogen's balance sheet would be if these were treated as capital leases. Also, in some cases operating leases may help companies to finance growth without violating existing debt covenants.

Academic studies suggest that lease obligations, including those associated with operating leases, are considered part of a firm's leverage and are relevant to the assessment of so-called systematic risk and, hence, pricing of the firm's stock (see Ely, *Journal of Accounting Research*, 1995).

SPECIAL PURPOSE ENTITIES

Special purpose entities (SPEs) (now part of what the FASB refers to as *variable interest entities*) are separate legal entities that are jointly financed by a parent company and independent investors. These entities may take many forms, including corporations, joint ventures, trusts, or partnerships. One purpose in creating such entities is to improve risk-sharing, by allowing firms to separate risky ventures from their other business activities. The idea is to achieve financing for risky ventures from investors better prepared to accept such risks than the stockholders of the parent company. Although specific accounting practices for SPEs are beyond the scope of this text, the recent attention given to the use of SPEs to keep debt off the balance sheet leads us to include some discussion of the various forms that SPEs may take.

Firms often form SPEs for the purpose of financing research and development activities (R&D). Such an arrangement may shield the stockholders and debt holders of the parent company from the risks associated with R&D. Instead, these risks are borne by those capital suppliers who have risk preferences or a tax status more conducive to R&D activities than the parent company's capital suppliers.

Firms also create SPEs to acquire assets that are then leased to the parent company, as illustrated by AOL Time Warner in Exhibit 11.13. Typically, the terms of the lease do not meet the criteria for capital leases. As a result, the parent company does not need to record a liability or related asset. Such *synthetic leases* represent a form of "off balance sheet" liabilities. These arrangements do, however, provide tax advantages to the parent company as they are viewed as owning the asset for tax purposes and are thus eligible for the depreciation deduction.

Securitizations, such as those described in Chapter 7, often take the form of an SPE. Recall that a securitization arrangement involves the creation of a separate entity (an SPE) in order to buy a company's accounts receivable. An alternative to transferring receivables to an SPE through a securitization arrangement would be to simply borrow needed funds and pledge the receivables as collateral. The differences are that an SPE is not consolidated, implying that less debt is reported on the parent company's balance sheet and that a different set of investors may provide the equity portion of the SPE's capital.

GAAP for SPEs is currently under consideration. One important issue is when to consolidate an SPE with the parent company. As we describe later in Chapter 13, consolidating an SPE with its parent company means combining the assets and liabilities of the two entities on the balance sheet. This treatment eliminates the prospect of off-balance sheet liabilities in the form of SPEs and the concerns that such arrangements have raised.

Exhibit 11.13

THE REAL WORLD

AOL Time Warner

Real Estate and Aircraft Operating Leases

AOL Time Warner has entered into certain arrangements for the lease of certain aircraft and property, including the Company's future corporate headquarters at Columbus Circle in New York City (the "AOL Time Warner Center") and a new productions and operations support center for the Turner cable networks in Atlanta (the "Turner Project"). Each of these properties will be funded through SPEs that are wholly owned by third parties, and these leasing arrangements will be accounted for by AOL Time Warner as operating leases. Pursuant to FASB Statement No. 13, "Accounting for Leases," and related interpretations for operating leases, the leased asset and the total obligation over the life of the lease are not reflected on the balance sheet. Instead, the lease payments are reflected as a charge to operating income generally as payments are made.

SUMMARY AND TRANSITION

In this chapter, we considered accounting for various forms of debt. Whether debt takes the form of notes payable, bonds, or capital lease obligations, part of the accountant's task is to distinguish between the interest and principal components of future payments. The principal component is the present value of those future payments discounted using the effective interest rate determined when the debt is issued. For some debt, interest is paid periodically and principal is repaid at maturity. If the debt is issued at par (i.e., the principal), then interest is simply recorded as an expense as incurred.

However, firms often issue debt at a price below its par value. The discount from par represents interest and must be amortized as interest expense over the life of the debt. Sometimes debt is retired before its maturity date. The repurchase price in order to retire the debt may differ from its book value. For example, if market interest rates have increased (decreased), since the debt was issued, then the book value would likely be higher than the repurchase price, giving rise to a gain (loss). Such gains or losses are only regarded as extraordinary for income reporting purposes if they meet the general criteria for such items.

Frequently, debt contracts contain covenants that restrict actions that the issuer may take. Common examples include limiting dividend payments to a constant percentage of net income or disallowing them completely unless net worth exceeds some lower bound. Other covenants limit investments, preclude issuing further debt, or restrict future business acquisitions. Covenants based on accounting numbers may create incentives for managers to manipulate accounting choices to avoid violating such covenants. Hence, the flexibility afforded managers by GAAP is an important consideration.

An indirect form of borrowing may be created through a special purpose entity. A common example of an SPE is a synthetic lease under which the SPE acquires property financed to a large extent by debt and leases that property to the parent company. Many market observers are critical of using SPEs as devices for keeping liabilities off the balance sheet. Currently, accounting policy makers are considering new rules to correct past abuses.

END OF CHAPTER MATERIAL

KEY TERMS

Bond Indenture	Fair Value
Capital Lease	Issued at a Discount
Contract Rate	Issued at a Premium
Coupon Rate	Issued at Par
Debt Covenants	Lessee
Early Retirement of Debt	Lessor
Effective Rate	Line of Credit
Executory Contracts	Notes Payable

Operating Lease
Securitization
Special Purpose Entities (SPEs)

Trustee
Yield
Zero-Coupon Notes

ASSIGNMENT MATERIAL

REVIEW QUESTIONS

1. Describe the following terms that relate to a bond: indenture agreement, bond covenants, face value, maturity date, coupon rate, coupon payments, and collateral.

2. Discuss how bonds are priced and how the price is affected by changes in market interest rates.

3. Describe the following terms as they relate to the issuance and sale of bonds: par, premium, and discount.

4. Discuss the meaning of the term bond discount and what is meant by the amortization of a bond discount.

5. Discuss the benefits of leasing from both the lessee's and the lessor's point of view.

6. List and discuss the criteria used to distinguish capital leases from operating leases for lessees.

7. Discuss how debt covenants provide protection for debt holders and give an example.

8. Discuss how the gains or losses on the early retirement of debt are handled under GAAP.

9. Discuss the nature of a special purpose entity and explain how it might be used to report liabilities off the balance sheet.

10. Explain how present value concepts affect the price of notes payable.

11. Explain the concept of a discount on a note or bond payable and discuss the accounting treatment of the discount.

12. Explain the concept of a premium on a note or bond payable and discuss the accounting treatment of the premium.

APPLYING YOUR KNOWLEDGE

13. The Standard Mills Company issues 100 bonds with a face value of $1,000 that mature in 30 years. The bonds carry a 10 percent coupon rate and are sold to yield 12 percent. Interest is paid semiannually.

    Required:

    a. Compute the issue price of the bonds and show the journal entry to record the issuance of the bonds.

    b. Compute interest expense for the first year and show the journal entries to record this expense and the corresponding coupon payments.

14. Emkay, Inc. issues a $1,000,000 12 percent note maturing in ten years. Interest is paid on the note semiannually over the term of the note and principal is due on the maturity date.

    Required:

    a. Compute the issue price of the note and give the journal entry to record the issuance.

    b. Compute the book value of the note five years after issuance, that is, the beginning of the sixth year.

    c. Compute the market value of the note five years after issuance if the market yield has increased to 14 percent.

    d. Compare the book value and the market value (calculated in part c) at the end of five years, and explain why a difference exists.

    e. If the note was to be retired at the market value computed in part c, compute the gain or loss on the retirement of the note.

15. The Spartan Tech Company issued 8 percent bonds with a face value of $100,000, maturing in three years. Interest on the bonds is paid semiannually. Prepare an amortization table for the three years under each of the following conditions:

    Required:

    a. Market yield at issuance is 8 percent.

    b. Market yield at issuance is 10 percent.

    c. Market yield at issuance is 6 percent.

16. On July 1, 20X3, the Turlotec Manufacturing Company leased one of its machines to Start Mechanical Company. The ten-year lease was classified as a capital lease for accounting purposes. The lease agreement required equal semiannual payments of $50,000, payable in advance on July 1 and January 1 each year, and an interest rate of 16 percent. Both companies close their books annually on December 31.

    Required:

    a. Show the necessary journal entries relating to the lease in the books of Start Mechanical Company during 20X3. Assume that the machine has a useful life of ten years and a zero salvage value and that Start Mechanical uses straight-line depreciation.

    b. Assume that Start Mechanical has total assets of $1,800,000 and total debt of $1,500,000 prior to the lease arrangement with Turlotec. How would the capital lease affect the Debt/Equity ratio of Start Mechanical?

    c. Explain why Start Mechanical might prefer to structure the lease as an operating lease.

17. Bagel Boys, Inc. has decided to lease a truck to deliver its bagels. The company signs an agreement on January 1, 20X1 to lease a truck for $350 per month for the next three years. The title to the truck reverts to the lessor at the end of the lease term. The lease calls for payments on the first of the month starting on February 1, 20X1. Bagel Boys, Inc. closes its books monthly and believes that 9 percent is an appropriate discount rate for the lease.

    Required:

    a. Assuming that the market value of the truck is $20,000 and that the lessor believes its useful life is five years, how should Bagel Boys account for this lease?

b. Show the appropriate accounting entries for the first two months of 20X1 for the lease under both the operating lease method and the capital lease method. Assume that Bagel Boys depreciates its assets using the double declining balance method.

18. Bagel Boys has a debt covenant that specifies it must maintain a leverage ratio defined as total debt to total equity of no more than 4 to 1. Bagel Boys currently has total assets of $100,000 and total debt of $80,000. Would treating the lease in question 17 as a capital lease put Bagel Boys in violation of its debt covenant? Explain.

USING REAL DATA

19. In 1979 IBM Corporation issued bonds in the public bond market for the first time in its history. At the time it was the largest single bond issue ever offered for $1 billion worth of debt. The issue date was October 16, 1979. The issue was split into two bonds, one of which carried a coupon rate of 9.5 percent and had a face value of $500 million. The offering price was 99.4 percent.

Required:

a. Show the issuance entry and the first two coupon payment (and interest recognition) entries that IBM would have made for the 9.5 percent notes issued. Assume the original issuance price stated above. The price implies a yield of 9.62 percent.

b. Suppose that the appropriate yield at issuance was 10 percent instead of 9.62 percent. What would have been the issuance price of the bonds?

c. Before all of the bonds could be sold in the public bond market, the Federal Reserve Board issued tough new credit restrictions in the economy. Due to these restrictions, interest rates in the economy increased and by the time the price of the bonds adjusted for this change, the price of each bond fell approximately $50 each (for each $1,000 face value bond). What would you estimate the yield of the bonds in part a to be?

20. In August 1990, USX Corporation issued $920 million of zero coupon bonds that were due in 2005. Zero coupon bonds pay no coupon payments and make a maturity payment of only the face value. Interest is still compounded semiannually as with an ordinary bond. Answer the following questions with regard to this offering:

Required:

a. If bond buyers demand a return of 8 percent from the investment in these bonds, what would be the issue price of the bonds? The following present-value factors may be useful:

Present value of $1:

15 periods @ 8 percent = 0.31524
30 periods @ 4 percent = 0.30831

Present value of an annuity in arrears:

15 periods @ 8 percent = 8.55948
30 periods @ 4 percent = 17.29199

b. The bonds were actually issued at a price of 31.393 percent, which implies a yield of 7.875 percent. Assuming the bonds were issued on August 1, 1990, construct the journal entries that would be made during 1990 to account for these bonds. Indicate the net book value of the bonds at the end of 1990. USX closes its books on December 31.

21. In July 1990, Johnson & Johnson announced the issuance of $250 million of 8.5 percent notes due on August 15, 1995. The price of the bonds was quoted as 100 percent. Assuming the bonds were issued on August 15, 1990, answer the following questions:

Required:

a. Construct the journal entry made on August 15, 1990, for the issuance of these bonds.

b. Johnson & Johnson closes its books on December 31. Reconstruct the entries that would be made during 1990 and 1991 to account for these bonds.

c. Suppose that after one year (August 15, 1991) Johnson & Johnson wants to pay off this debt early. It decides to buy back this issue at the current market price. If market rates have moved to 8 percent, compute the amount that the company will have to pay. In addition, construct the entry that Johnson & Johnson would make to account for this transaction.

22. On June 19, 1991, Columbia Gas System, Inc. had bonds outstanding that were due in 1996 and carried an 8.25 percent coupon rate. On that date, the bonds traded approximately at par value. On June 20, 1991, Columbia Gas System, Inc. announced that it was defaulting on a short-term bank note. The bonds were immediately downgraded by the credit-rating agencies to junk bond status.

Required:

a. Given that the bonds were trading at par on June 19, 1991, what discount rate were investors using to price Columbia's bonds?

b. Suppose that, because of the downgrade to junk bond status, investors now (on June 20, 1991) demand a 14 percent return on their investment in these bonds. Calculate the price that a single bond would trade at under these conditions. For the purposes of this question, assume that the bond is exactly five years from maturity (i.e., the bonds mature on June 20, 1996).

c. Regardless of your answer to part b, assume that Columbia issued these bonds for the first time on June 20, 1991, at a price of 81 percent. This corresponds to a yield of 13.6 percent. Show the journal entries that would be made upon the issuance of these bonds and at the first two coupon dates. Use a single bond to illustrate the entries.

23. On October 28, 2002, General Mills completed a private placement of zero coupon convertible debentures with a face value of approximately $2.23 billion. The bonds were priced to yield 2.00 percent. The bonds had 20 years to maturity.

Required:

a. Calculate the price of a single bond and then compute the proceeds from the total issue.

b. Construct the journal entry that would be made on October 28, 2002.

c. Construct the journal entry that would be made on April 28, 2003 (General Mills' fiscal year-end date is May 25, 2003).

d. The bond issue was convertible into shares of common stock and was also callable by General Mills; in other words, General Mills could buy back the bonds at a fixed price three years after their issuance. Discuss how these two features make the bonds either more or less attractive to investors.

24. The following table provides detailed information of the outstanding debt issues for Toys Я Us from their 2003 annual report. The 2003 fiscal year-end date for the company is January 31, 2004.

(In millions)	2003	2002
475 million Swiss franc note, due and paid on January 28, 2004 (a)	$ —	$ 348
500 million euro-denominated bond, due and paid on February 13, 2004 (b)	624	538
6.875% notes, due fiscal year 2006	265	267
Note at an effective cost of 2.23% due in semiannual installments through fiscal year 2008	135	158
7.625% notes, due fiscal year 2011	546	554
7.875% note, due fiscal year 2013	391	
7.375% note, due fiscal year 2018	397	
8 3/4% debentures, due fiscal year 2021, net of expenses (d)	199	198
Equity security units	408	408
Other	41	47
	3,006	2,518
Less current portion	657	379
Total	$2,349	$2,139

Required:

a. The Swiss franc note and the euro-denominated bond are debt instruments that must be paid in a currency different from the U.S. dollar (specifically francs and euros). What additional risks (beyond the risks of repayment) do such foreign currency denominated debts pose for the company?

b. The notes due in fiscal years 2011 and 2013 were issued during fiscal year 2003. If their coupon rates are reflective of the discount rate appropriate for the company in 2003, how would the market value for the company's 8¾ percent debentures compare with the carrying value of these debentures?

25. The following table provides information about the leases for Wal-Mart Stores. In addition, the balance sheet and income statement for Wal-Mart is also included.

Fiscal Year	Operating Leases	Capital Leases
2005	$ 665	$ 430
2006	651	427
2007	599	419
2008	553	411
2009	519	397
Thereafter	5,678	3,002
Total minimum rentals	$8,665	5,086
Less estimated executory costs		44
Net minimum lease payments		5,042
Less imputed interest at rates ranging from 4.2% to 14.0%		1,849
Present value of minimum lease payments		$3,193

WAL-MART STORES, INC. Income Statement

	01/31/2004	01/31/2003	1/31/2002
Revenues:			
Net sales	$256,329,000,000	$229,616,000,000	$204,011,000,000
Other income, net	2,352,000,000	1,961,000,000	1,812,000,000
	258,681,000,000	231,577,000,000	205,823,000,000
Costs and Expenses:			
Cost of sales	198,747,000,000	178,299,000,000	159,097,000,000
Operating, selling, general, and administrative expenses	44,909,000,000	39,983,000,000	35,147,000,000
Operating Profit	15,025,000,000	13,295,000,000	11,579,000,000
Interest:			
Debt	729,000,000	799,000,000	1,080,000,000
Capital leases	267,000,000	260,000,000	274,000,000
Interest income	(164,000,000)	(132,000,000)	(171,000,000)
	832,000,000	927,000,000	1,183,000,000
Income from continuing operations before income taxes and minority interest	14,193,000,000	12,368,000,000	10,396,000,000
Provision for Income Taxes:			
Current	4,941,000,000	3,883,000,000	3,625,000,000
Deferred	177,000,000	474,000,000	140,000,000
	5,118,000,000	4,357,000,000	3,765,000,000
Income from continuing operations before minority interest	9,075,000,000	8,011,000,000	6,631,000,000
Minority interest	(214,000,000)	(193,000,000)	(183,000,000)
Income from continuing operations	8,861,000,000	7,818,000,000	6,448,000,000
Income from discontinued operation, net of tax	193,000,000	137,000,000	144,000,000
Net income	$ 9,054,000,000	$ 7,955,000,000	$ 6,592,000,000

WAL-MART STORES, INC. Balance Sheet	01/31/2004	01/31/2003
Assets		
Current assets:		
Cash and cash equivalents	$5,199,000,000	$2,736,000,000
Receivables	1,254,000,000	1,569,000,000
Inventories	26,612,000,000	24,401,000,000
Prepaid expenses and other	1,356,000,000	837,000,000
Current assets of discontinued operation	0	1,179,000,000
Total Current Assets	34,421,000,000	30,722,000,000
Property, plant, and equipment, at cost:		
Land	12,699,000,000	11,202,000,000
Buildings and improvements	38,966,000,000	33,345,000,000
Fixtures and equipment	17,861,000,000	15,640,000,000
Transportation equipment	1,269,000,000	1,099,000,000
	70,795,000,000	61,286,000,000
Less accumulated depreciation	15,594,000,000	13,116,000,000
Property, plant, and equipment, net	55,201,000,000	48,170,000,000
Property under capital lease:		
Property under capital lease	5,092,000,000	4,814,000,000
Less accumulated amortization	1,763,000,000	1,610,000,000
Property under capital leases, net	3,329,000,000	3,204,000,000
Other assets and deferred charges:		
Goodwill	9,882,000,000	9,389,000,000
Other assets and deferred charges	2,079,000,000	2,594,000,000
Other assets of discontinued operation	0	729,000,000
Total assets	$104,912,000,000	$94,808,000,000
Liabilities and shareholders equity		
Current liabilities:		
Commercial paper	$3,267,000,000	$1,079,000,000
Accounts payable	19,332,000,000	16,829,000,000
Accrued liabilities	10,342,000,000	8,857,000,000
Accrued income taxes	1,377,000,000	748,000,000
Long-term debt due within one year	2,904,000,000	4,536,000,000
Obligations under capital leases due within one year	196,000,000	176,000,000
Current liabilities of discontinued operation	0	294,000,000
Total current liabilities	37,418,000,000	32,519,000,000
Long-term debt	17,102,000,000	16,597,000,000
Long-term obligations under capital leases	2,997,000,000	3,000,000,000
Deferred income taxes and other	2,288,000,000	1,859,000,000
Liabilities of discontinued operation	0	10,000,000
Minority interest	1,484,000,000	1,362,000,000
Shareholders equity:		
Preferred stock ($0.10 par value; 100 shares authorized, none issued)	0	0
Common stock ($0.10 par value; 11,000 shares authorized, 4,311 and 4,395 issued and outstanding in 2004 and 2003, respectively)	431,000,000	440,000,000
Capital in excess of par value	2,135,000,000	1,954,000,000

	01/31/2004	01/31/2003
Retained earnings	40,206,000,000	37,576,000,000
Other accumulated comprehensive income	851,000,000	(509,000,000)
Total shareholders' equity	43,623,000,000	39,461,000,000
Total liabilities and shareholders' equity	$104,912,000,000	$94,808,000,000

Required:

a. What is the average rate of interest that Wal-Mart pays for its capital leases?

b. If the operating leases have approximately the same timing as the capital leases, at what value might you estimate the present value of the operating leases?

c. Based on your calculation in part b, how would the debt/equity ratios of Wal-Mart be affected if the operating leases were to be capitalized?

26. The following is the balance sheet and lease footnote disclosure for CVS Corporation from its 2004 10-K report:

CVS CORP. Balance Sheet

	01/03/2004	01/03/2003
Assets:		
Cash and cash equivalents	$ 843,200,000	$ 700,400,000
Accounts receivable, net	1,349,600,000	1,019,300,000
Inventories	4,016,500,000	4,013,900,000
Deferred income taxes	252,100,000	216,400,000
Other current assets	35,100,000	32,100,000
Total current assets	6,496,500,000	5,982,100,000
Property and equipment, net	2,542,100,000	2,215,800,000
Goodwill	889,000,000	878,900,000
Intangible assets, net	403,700,000	351,400,000
Deferred income taxes	0	6,600,000
Other assets	211,800,000	210,500,000
Total assets	$10,543,100,000	$9,645,300,000
Liabilities:		
Accounts payable	$ 1,666,400,000	$1,707,900,000
Accrued expenses	1,499,600,000	1,361,200,000
Short-term debt	0	4,800,000
Current portion of long-term debt	323,200,000	32,000,000
Total current liabilities	3,489,200,000	3,105,900,000
Long-term debt	753,100,000	1,076,300,000
Deferred income taxes	41,600,000	0
Other long-term liabilities	237,400,000	266,100,000
Commitments and contingencies (Note 9)		
Shareholders' equity:		
Preferred stock, $0.01 par value	0	0

	01/03/2004	01/03/2003
Preference stock, series one ESOP convertible, par $1.00	242,700,000	250,400,000
Common stock, par value $0.01	4,100,000	4,100,000
Treasury stock, at cost	(428,600,000)	(469,500,000)
Guaranteed ESOP obligation	(163,200,000)	(194,400,000)
Capital surplus	1,557,200,000	1,546,600,000
Retained earnings	4,846,500,000	4,104,400,000
Accumulated other comprehensive loss	(36,900,000)	(44,600,000)
Total shareholders' equity	6,021,800,000	5,197,000,000
Total liabilities and shareholders' equity	$10,543,100,000	$9,645,300,000

The Company leases most of its retail locations and five of its distribution centers under noncancelable operating leases, whose initial terms typically range from 15 to 25 years, along with options that permit renewals for additional periods. The Company also leases certain equipment and other assets under noncancelable operating leases, whose initial terms typically range from three to ten years. Minimum rent is expensed on a straight-line basis over the term of the lease. In addition to minimum rental payments, certain leases require additional payments based on sales volume, as well as reimbursements for real estate taxes, maintenance, and insurance.

Following is a summary of the Company's net rental expense for operating leases for the respective years:

In millions	2003	2002	2001
Minimum rentals	$838.4	$790.4	$758.2
Contingent rentals	62.0	65.6	67.6
	900.4	856.0	825.8
Less: sublease income	(10.1)	(9.3)	(9.1)
	$890.3	$846.7	$816.7

Following is a summary of the future minimum lease payments under capital and operating leases as of January 3, 2004:

In millions	Capital Leases	Operating Leases
2004	$0.2	$855.9
2005	0.2	816.3
2006	0.2	757.7
2007	0.2	704.5
2008	0.2	661.6
Thereafter	0.3	6,992.9
	1.3	$10,788.9
Less: imputed interest	(0.4)	
Present value of capital lease obligations	$0.9	

The Company finances a portion of its store development program through sale-leaseback transactions. The properties are sold at net book value, and the resulting leases qualify and are accounted for as operating leases. The Company does not have any retained or contingent interests in the stores nor does the Company provide any guarantees, other than a corporate level guarantee of lease payments, in connection with the sale-leasebacks. Proceeds from sale-leaseback transactions totaled $487.8 million in 2003, $448.8 million in 2002, and $323.3 million in 2001. During 2001, the Company completed a sale-leaseback transaction involving five of its distribution centers. The distribution centers were sold at fair market value resulting in a $35.5 million gain, which was deferred and is being amortized to offset rent expense over the life of the new operating leases. The operating leases that resulted from these transactions are included in the above table.

Required:

a. The interest rate on CVS's long-term debt averaged approximately 6.0 percent. If we assume that the operating lease payments are spread evenly over the 15 years that would remain on the average life of the leases, what would the net present value of the operating leases be as of January 1, 2004?

b. If the operating leases in part a were to be capitalized, how would this affect the debt/equity ratio of the firm? Quantify your answer.

c. Sale/leaseback transactions are ones in which the company owns a property and then sells it to another entity but immediately leases the property back for an extended period of time. Assuming that the proceeds from the sales in 2001 were solely for the five distribution centers that are discussed in the footnote, construct the entry that would be made for these sale/leaseback transactions.

d. In years subsequent to the sale/leaseback described in part c, how would future financial statements be affected by these transactions?

27. In February 2004 Rayonier, Inc. (a forest products company) sold timberland for $25 million and recorded an $18.6 million profit from the sale. The buyer provided a 15-year installment note at a fixed interest rate of 5.17 percent and a letter of credit to secure the payments. In March 2004 Rayonier created a special purpose entity and transferred the note to that entity. The following was the disclosure of this transaction in the company's 10-Q report to the SEC:

> In March 2004, Rayonier monetized the installment note by contributing the note and the letter of credit to a bankruptcy-remote limited liability subsidiary that meets the requirements of a qualified special purpose entity (QSPE) as defined by SFAS No. 140, *Accounting for Transfers and Servicing of Financial Assets and Extinguishments of Liabilities.* As such, the QSPE is not consolidated in the Company's financial statements. Using the installment note and the letter of credit as collateral, the QSPE issued $22.5 million of 15-year Senior Secured Notes with a fixed interest rate of 5 percent and remitted cash of $22.5 million to the Company. At closing, the Company had an equity interest of $2.5 million in the QSPE and will receive cash flow from the QSPE in amounts equal to the excess of interest received on the installment note over the interest paid on the Senior Secured Notes. At March 31, 2004, the

Company computed the fair market value of its interest in the QSPE to be $2.8 million and recognized a gain of $0.3 million in the first quarter of 2004. In addition, the Company calculated and recorded a guarantee liability of $43 thousand per FIN 45, Guarantor's Accounting and Disclosure Requirements for Guarantees, Including Indirect Guarantees of Others, to reflect its obligation of up to $2.5 million under a make-whole agreement, pursuant to which it guaranteed certain obligations of the QSPE. This guarantee obligation is also collateralized by the letter of credit. Upon maturity of the Senior Secured Notes in 2019 and termination of the QSPE, Rayonier will receive the remaining $2.5 million balance of cash.

Required:

a. Construct the entry that Rayonier made for the sale of the timberland in February.

b. Construct the entry that Rayonier made for the transfer of the note to the special purpose entity in March.

c. Construct the entry that Rayonier made on March 31 to record the interest received from QSPE (assume that the transfer of the note had occurred on March 1).

d. Construct the entry that Rayonier made on March 31 to record the fair market value of the investment in QSPE.

e. Discuss the motivation for Rayonier to construct the special purpose entity.

f. What risk does Rayonier retain related to the note receivable that was transferred?

28. The following is a press release issued by Revlon indicating that it does not plan to consummate a planned refinancing plan.

Revlon, Inc. (NYSE: REV) and its wholly-owned subsidiary, Revlon Consumer Products Corporation ("RCPC"), together announced that, due to current unfavorable market conditions, RCPC does not intend to consummate its previously-announced refinancing transactions at this time. RCPC is terminating its tender offer and consent solicitation for its outstanding 12% Senior Secured Notes due 2005 and its tender offers for its outstanding $8\frac{1}{8}$% Senior Notes due 2006 and 9% Senior Notes due 2006 and does not intend, at this time, to redeem such notes. RCPC also announced that it has postponed its previously-announced proposed senior notes offering and its proposed new senior credit facilities in light of the recent unfavorable market conditions. The Company indicated that it will continue to monitor market conditions and continue to execute its growth plan.

In response to Revlon's announcement, Moody's revised its outlook for Revlon to "negative," citing expected difficulties for Revlon in meeting liquidity targets and debt covenants. Explain why Revlon's decision to terminate its planned redemption of the notes might be considered bad news by analysts.

○ BEYOND THE BOOK

29. Find a company that has significant operating leases (or use a company that your instructor assigns). An industry that typically uses a significant amount of operating leases is the consumer retail industry. From the

disclosures in the 10-K report of this company, respond to the following questions:

a. Does the company have both capital leases and operating leases?

b. If there are capital leases, what is the average rate of interest that the company pays for its capital leases?

c. If the operating leases have approximately the same timing as the capital leases, at what value might you estimate the present value of the operating leases? Alternatively, if there are no capital leases, estimate the present value of the operating leases using the average interest rate paid on the company's long-term debt.

d. Based on your calculation in part c, how would the debt/equity ratios of the company be affected if the operating leases were to be capitalized?

30. Find a company that has had a downgrade of its public debt during a recent period. Discuss what led to the downgrade, how its financial performance related to the downgrade, and what, if any, debt covenants were violated.

CHAPTER 12

Stockholders' Equity: The Residual Interest

LEARNING OBJECTIVES

After reading this chapter, you should be able to:

1. Construct the entries for stock issuance.

2. Understand the difference between common and preferred stock.

3. Distinguish between cash and stock dividends and understand accounting treatments for the latter.

4. Appreciate why firms repurchase stock and construct entries for such repurchases.

5. Understand disclosure requirements for employee stock options and related compensation expense.

6. Recognize the nature of convertible securities and associated accounting issues.

7. Understand the basic construction of earnings per share and its potential role in valuation.

At the end of fiscal year 2002, Cognos, Inc. (a Canadian corporation specializing in business intelligence software) reported a profit of $19.4 million (U.S.), based on U.S. accounting standards. The company's chief executive officer said (in a press release) that Cognos had a "great" fourth quarter, and its earnings handily beat analysts' expectations. However, upon further reading of the footnotes to the annual report, if the company had reported its employee stock options as a business expense, Cognos' net income would have been a $6.1 million loss.

A stock option gives the holder the right to purchase a share of stock at a specified price on or before a specified future date. Increasingly over the past decade, firms have granted stock options to officers and other key employees as a form of compensation. Yet generally accepted accounting standards do not require the recognition of the cost of employee stock options as an expense on the firm's income statement. Recent accounting scandals have focused attention on the incentive properties of stock options as a form of compensation and on the propriety of current accounting practices. The controversy over the treatment of stock options is part of larger concerns about the role of accounting in valuing the firm.

In this chapter, we consider the principal elements of stockholders' equity and transactions that produce changes in stockholders' equity. We begin with a description of the properties of preferred and common stock. We then review the accounting treatment of stock issues, stock repurchases, stock splits, stock dividends, stock rights, stock options, and convertible securities.

OVERVIEW OF STOCKHOLDERS' EQUITY

Stockholders' equity represents the claims of stockholders in the firm's assets. These claims can be further classified as contributed capital and undistributed income. **Contributed capital** includes the par or stated value of all types of stock whether it be common stock or preferred stock (discussed later in the chapter) and amounts paid by stockholders in excess of the stock's par or stated value. See the stockholders' equity section of Great Western Bancorporation, Inc. in Exhibit 12.1. Contributed capital is represented by the lines for Preferred Stock, Common Stock, and Additional Paid-In Capital. **Undistributed income** includes retained earnings and accumulated other comprehensive income. **Retained earnings** is accumulated net income less dividends distributed to stockholders. **Other comprehensive income** reflects various direct adjustments to stockholders' equity such as unrealized holding gains and losses on marketable securities (described in Chapter 13).

Exhibit 12.1

THE REAL WORLD

Great Western Bancorporation, Inc.

	06/30/2003	06/30/2002
Stockholders' equity		
Preferred stock, $100 par value; authorized 500,000 shares; issued and outstanding: 9,000 shares of 8% cumulative, nonvoting; 8,000 shares of 10% noncumulative, nonvoting; 100,000 shares of variable rate, noncumulative, nonvoting	$ 11,700,000	$ 11,700,000
Common stock, $1.00 par value, authorized 1,000,000 shares; issued and outstanding 2003—124,952 shares, 2002—125,132 shares	125,000	125,000
Additional paid-in capital	2,051,000	2,058,000
Retained earnings	106,433,000	92,285,000
Accumulated other comprehensive income	6,065,000	3,995,000
Total stockholders' equity	$126,374,000	$110,163,000

TYPES OF STOCK

As the disclosure for Great Western Bancorporation in Exhibit 12.1 illustrates, corporations often have more than one type of stock that they issue to owners. While all types of stock indicate some kind of ownership interest in the firm, there are often differences in the rights of the various types of stock. For instance, in Exhibit 12.1 you will notice that the preferred stock (there are actually three types of preferred issued by the company) is non voting, which means that preferred stockholders have no direct say in how the company is operated. In the following sections, we will cover the two most commonly issued types of stock: common and preferred.

COMMON STOCK

Common stock represents the residual interest in a firm's assets. **Residual interest** means that the claims of common stockholders to the firm's assets, met either through dividends or liquidation, are subordinate to the claims of creditors and preferred stockholders (described below). Dividends to common stockholders usually cannot exceed retained earnings. Distributions in liquidation (when the firm goes out of legal existence) are made to common stockholders only after debt has been repaid and preferred stockholders have recovered the par value of their holdings. This ensures a minimum safety margin on behalf of creditors and preferred stockholders, as common stockholders absorb losses before affecting the interests of the other two groups.

Common stockholders do exercise control over the firm's activities. Their voting rights enable them to elect a board of directors and to approve certain transactions. A **board of directors** appoints officers who oversee the conduct of the firm's affairs. A relatively small minority of stockholders may effectively control the firm by obtaining *proxies* that transfer voting rights from stockholders who prefer an inactive role in the firm's affairs.

A firm may issue stock through either a private placement (issued directly to a set of investors) or a public offering (issued through a public market). Public offerings are accompanied by a prospectus and made through intermediaries, such as investment banks, who provide underwriting services. A **prospectus** describes a firm's principal business activities, its exposure to risks, its major contractual relationships, as well as providing its pro forma financial statements.

Underwriting agreements often provide guarantees of the price the firm will receive from the shares; the underwriter accepts the risk of loss should the shares not sell at that price. In this case, the underwriter acts like an insurer. However, some underwriting agreements rely on the underwriters' "best efforts" to sell the shares of stock at the agreed-upon price. If the shares fail to sell at this price, then the issuing firm usually withdraws the shares or issues them at a reduced price.

When a firm issues stock, the price that it receives usually exceeds its par or stated value. A **par (or stated) value** represents a nominal value assigned to a share of stock, to ensure a minimum level of equity participation in the capitalization of the firm. In most states, firms are not allowed to pay a dividend to stockholders out of the par value of the stock, thus protecting the debt holders to some degree. However, par value is commonly set well below the price at which the firm initially sells its stock.

From an accounting standpoint, par value merely serves to determine how much of the sales price of newly issued stock a firm records in its stock account. A firm typically records the excess of the price over par as **paid-in capital.** For example, recall BHT's stock issue from Chapter 3. In that case, BHT issued 250 million shares of common stock with a par value of $1 per share for $6.50 per share. BHT recorded this stock issue (in millions) as follows:

Cash	1,625	
Common Stock		250
Paid-In-Capital		1,375

Sometimes firms issue common stock without a par (or stated) value, called **no par** stock. Here, the firm credits the full proceeds from stock issuance to the common stock account.

PREFERRED STOCK

Unless otherwise specified, preferred stock differs from common stock in three major respects:

1. Preferred stock does not convey voting rights.
2. Preferred stock dividends are generally set at a fixed percentage of the stock's par or stated value and must be paid before distributions to common stockholders.
3. Preferred stockholders stand ahead of common stockholders with respect to distributions in liquidation, but only receive the par or stated value of their holdings.

Sometimes preferred stock contracts contain other features:

◎ Preferred stock may be **cumulative,** meaning that if a firm does not declare a dividend in a given year, then the dividends accumulate (sometimes called *dividends in arrears*). Cumulative preferred stock dividends in arrears must be paid before any distributions to common stockholders. Note that one issue of preferred stock for Great Western in Exhibit 12.1 is a cumulative issue.

◎ Preferred stock may be participating. **Participating** preferred stock enables holders to receive dividends beyond a fixed percentage. Typically, participating preferred stock pays dividends on a pro-rata basis with common stock, after common stockholders receive a percentage dividend comparable to that of preferred stockholders.

◎ Preferred stock may be **callable** or **redeemable,** which means the issuing firm can buy back the stock at some prespecified price. Calling or redeeming the stock reduces the amount of future dividend payments that need to be made.

◎ Preferred stock may be **convertible** into common stock at a pre-specified price or exchange rate.

Exhibit 12.2

THE REAL WORLD

Hanover Direct, Inc.

Series A Cumulative Participating Preferred Stock, mandatory redemption at $50 per share ($70,000), 2,345,000 shares authorized, 1,530,829 shares issued at March 31, 2001 and 1,475,498 shares issued at December 30, 2000.

Hanover Direct, Inc.'s disclosure of its preferred stock in Exhibit 12.2 shows an issue that is cumulative, participating, and redeemable. Note that both the cumulative and participating features make the preferred stock more valuable to the stockholder. The redeemable feature, however, provides a constraint on the value of the preferred stock as it sets a cap on how high the value of the stock can go before it may be redeemed.

DISTRIBUTIONS TO STOCKHOLDERS

Recall from Chapter 6 that the value of a firm's equity may be expressed as the present value of its expected future cash dividends. This valuation approach assumes that the firm will eventually distribute cash to its stockholders either through periodic dividends, stock repurchases, or a liquidating distribution (often called a liquidating dividend). We review cash dividends and stock repurchases next.

> Many companies do not declare dividends, but instead reinvest the profits of the firm with the expectation that this will increase the firm's dividend-paying ability in the future.

CASH DIVIDENDS

A firm's board of directors initiates dividends. Typically, the board of directors declares a dividend payable on a certain date (referred to as the **date of declaration**) to stockholders of record as of a future date (referred to as the **date of record**). *Stockholders of record* are those investors who own shares at the end of the date of record. Should an investor sell the stock after this date, the *ex-dividend date,* then the new owner would not receive the dividend payment.

By declaring a dividend, a firm incurs an obligation in the form of dividends payable. This liability is reduced when the firm pays the dividend. To illustrate, suppose that BHT declares and later pays a cash dividend of 20 cents per share at the end of 20X1. BHT records these events (in millions) as follows (BHT had 250 million shares outstanding):

Retained Earnings	50	
Dividends Payable		50

Dividends Payable	50	
Cash		50

> An increase (decrease) in dividends may be interpreted by the market as good (bad) news. Raising dividends may avoid inefficient use of excess cash. Cutting dividends may imply financial difficulties.

If BHT's fiscal year ends after the firm declares the dividend but before BHT pays it, then BHT reports "Dividends Payable" as a liability on its balance sheet. Further, only dividends paid appear on the company's cash flow statement.

While rare, firms sometimes declare dividends in the form of assets other than cash. Distributions of assets are referred to as **property dividends** or as **dividends in kind.** For instance, a company holding marketable securities might distribute those securities as a dividend in kind to its own stockholders.

STOCK REPURCHASES

Some market observers suggest that firms also repurchase stock in an attempt to favorably influence price when management feels that its stock is undervalued and the firm plans to raise additional capital in the future by issuing stock (see Comment and Jarrell, *Journal of Finance*, 1991).

Firms also use other means to distribute cash to stockholders. One alternative is for a firm to repurchase its stock from investors via the stock market. The effects are similar, in that cash and stockholders' equity are reduced. The differences are that stock repurchases lower the number of shares outstanding and may change the composition of stockholders.

Stock repurchases may be motivated by the same factors that cause firms to pay cash dividends. However, firms may be motivated by other considerations. For example, a firm may repurchase shares to satisfy its employee stock ownership and option plans (we discuss these plans later in the chapter). Further, by repurchasing its shares rather than issuing new ones, a company avoids the transaction costs and additional information requirements that accompany public issuance of new shares.

A firm retires repurchased shares by canceling the stock certificates or, as is common practice, holds the shares for future reissue. In the latter case, the firm records the repurchased shares as treasury stock. **Treasury stock** is a contra-stockholders' equity account. Specifically, it has a debit balance and appears as a deduction in the stockholders' equity section of the balance sheet. This classification is logical in that by repurchasing its stock, the firm constructively contracts its size in terms of both assets and equity.

A firm values its treasury stock at its acquisition cost. If a firm later sells the treasury stock at a price that differs from its cost, then the firm treats the difference as an adjustment to paid-in capital. It would be inappropriate to treat this difference as income. However, if the firm resells the treasury stock at a price lower than its cost and the balance in paid-in capital is insufficient to fully absorb the loss then the portion of the loss in excess of the previous balance in paid-in capital reduces retained earnings. In no case would gains or losses related to treasury stock transactions be treated as components of income.

Exhibit 12.3 illustrates the accounting treatment of changes in treasury stock in the disclosures for The Dow Chemical Company during 2001. The amount received by Dow from sales of treasury stock and issuance of treasury stock to

Exhibit 12.3

THE REAL WORLD

The Dow Chemical Company

(in millions) Treasury Stock	2001	2000	1999
Balance at beginning of year	(2,625)	(2,932)	(3,100)
Purchases	(5)	(4)	(477)
Sales of treasury shares in open market	—	—	284
Issuance to employees and employee plans	218	311	361
Balance at end of year	(2,412)	(2,625)	(2,932)

employees and employee plans in 1999 was reported as $810 in the financial statements. The costs were reported in Exhibit 12.3 as $284 for the shares sold on the open market and $361 for the shares issued to employees, resulting in a total cost of shares of $645. This results in an increase in its "Additional Paid-In Capital" of $165 million (shown in Dow's Statement of Stockholders' Equity). Dow may have recorded these changes as follows:

Treasury Stock	477	
Cash		477

Cash	810	
Treasury Stock		645
Additional Paid-In-Capital		165

In addition to buying back shares from stockholders, the firm can also change the number of shares that are outstanding through the use of stock dividends and stock splits, considered next.

STOCK DIVIDENDS AND STOCK SPLITS

Firms distribute additional shares of stock to existing stockholders, in proportion to their present holdings, through **stock dividends** and stock splits. The accounting treatment often differs for these items, depending on how many shares are involved and whether par or stated value per share is altered. Let's take a closer look.

SMALL STOCK DIVIDENDS

Small stock dividends amount to less than 25 percent of shares issued and outstanding. A typical small stock dividend percentage is 5 percent. For small stock dividends, no change occurs in par or stated value. To account for them, firms capitalize retained earnings for the market value of the additional shares issued. In other words, firms reduce retained earnings by the market value of the additional shares issued, and increase common stock and additional paid-in-capital to reflect the par value of shares issued and any excess over par value, respectively.

For example, assume that BHT distributes a 5 percent stock dividend at the end of 20X2. The market price per share of BHT's stock at that date is $30. From Chapter 5 we know that BHT has 300 million shares outstanding at the end of 20X2. Therefore, a 5 percent stock dividend will result in the issuance of 15 million shares. Because this is a small stock dividend, BHT will capitalize the market value of these shares or $450 million (15 million shares × $30 per share).

BHT records the stock dividend (in thousands) as follows (remember that the par value of BHT's stock is $1 per share):

Retained Earnings	450	
Common Stock		15
Additional Paid-In-Capital		435

The rationale for issuing small stock dividends is unclear. Some view small stock dividends as a partial substitute for cash dividends. In this view, the recipient of a small stock dividend could sell the additional shares received for cash and therefore still hold the same number of shares as before. The result would be similar to a cash dividend. However, unlike a cash dividend, under a stock repurchase, the composition of shareholders would generally be changed. Differential tax treatments may also be a consideration. A gain, if any, on the sale of additional shares acquired through a stock dividend would generally be taxed as a capital gain, whereas dividends would generally be taxed as ordinary income.

LARGE STOCK DIVIDENDS

Stock dividends in general dilute the value of shares outstanding, as the value of the firm is allocated over a larger number of shares. For large stock dividends, this dilution effect is substantial. As a consequence, a large stock dividend may increase the demand for shares by lowering the market price to a range that allows smaller investors to acquire shares.

The accounting treatment for large stock dividends involves a reclassification of either additional paid-in capital as common stock or retained earnings as common stock (typically the case). The amount reclassified depends on the par value of the additional shares issued. For example, say that instead of a 5 percent stock dividend, BHT distributes a 100 percent stock dividend at the end of 20X2 without changing the par value of its stock. This would result in a distribution of 300 million shares, as 300 million were already outstanding. BHT records this event as follows (capitalizing only the par value of the stock issued):

Retained Earnings	300	
Common Stock		300

STOCK SPLITS

Stock splits (or split-ups) are similar to large stock dividends in the sense of increasing the number of shares outstanding. Furthermore, firms sometimes account for stock splits in exactly the same manner as a large stock dividend. However, a stock split differs from a stock dividend when the par value is changed. In particular, a stock split may involve an inversely proportional reduction of

The stock price per share of a company may have an effect on the marketability of the shares, as a smaller price per share makes the shares more affordable to a larger population of investors. In some cases, a company wishes to attract only high-wealth investors so the price per share is kept very high. For instance, the shares of Berkshire Hathaway traded at $93,750 in late-February 2004.

Stock dividends that reduce retained earnings may serve as signals of high future earnings prospects. Firms with low future earnings prospects might find it preferable to not declare such a dividend, thus revealing their lower future earnings prospects. The idea is that if the balance in retained earnings is sufficiently low, a firm with low future earnings prospects might conclude that reducing retained earnings would be too restrictive on future cash dividends (see Rankine and Stice, *Journal of Financial and Quantitative Analysis*, 1997).

Exhibit 12.4

THE REAL WORLD

Microsoft Corporation

Redmond, Wash.—Jan. 16, 2003—Microsoft Corp. today announced that its Board of Directors declared an annual dividend and approved a two-for-one split on Microsoft common stock. The annual dividend of $0.16 per share pre-split ($0.08 post-split) is payable March 7, 2003, to shareholders of record at the close of business on Feb. 21, 2003. As a result of the stock split, shareholders will receive one additional common share for every share held on the record date of Jan. 27, 2003.

"Declaring a dividend demonstrates the board's confidence in the company's long-term growth opportunities and financial strength. We are especially pleased to be able to return profits to our shareholders, while maintaining our significant investment in research and development and satisfying our long-term capital requirements," said John Connors, chief financial officer at Microsoft.

Upon completion of the split, the number of common shares outstanding will be approximately 10.8 billion. The additional shares will be mailed or delivered on or about Feb. 14, 2003, by the company's transfer agent, Mellon Investor Services. This is the ninth time Microsoft's common stock has split since the company's initial public offering on March 13, 1986. "We believe that the split, combined with an annual dividend, will make Microsoft stock even more attractive to a broader range of investors. We see enormous potential for growth in the software and technology sector, and remain committed to attracting investors who share this enthusiasm and take a long-term view of the company's growth opportunities," Connors said.

par value. For example, a two-for-one stock split may be accompanied by a reduction of par value to one-half of what that value had been prior to the split. If a firm reduces par value in this way, then the firm foregoes a formal accounting entry. No aggregate dollar amounts change in the accounts. Rather, the firm makes a memorandum entry to recognize the simultaneous changes in both the number of shares outstanding and par value, with no change in the total amount in the common stock account.

As with large stock dividends, firms use stock splits to place their stock in a more active trading range by reducing the market price. For example, in January 2003, Microsoft declared a two-for-one stock split in a press release (see Exhibit 12.4). Note the section where Microsoft discusses the increased marketability of its shares.

Exhibit 12.5 provides an example of a stock split announcement in the form of a stock dividend. A stock split and a stock dividend can have the same effect on the number of shares that are outstanding. For instance, a two-for-one split and a 100 percent stock dividend both have the effect of doubling the number of shares outstanding. The only real difference is that the stock dividend accounting requires the firm to move some amount of retained earnings into

Exhibit 12.5

THE REAL WORLD

The Progressive Corporation

Mayfield Village, Ohio—March 19, 2002—The Board of Directors of The Progressive Corporation today approved a three-for-one split of the Company's Common Shares, $1.00 par value, to be effected in the form of a stock dividend. In connection with the transaction, two additional Common Shares will be issued on April 22, 2002, for each Common Share held by shareholders of record as of the close of business on April 1, 2002. The purpose of the stock split is to increase the supply of the Company's Common Shares and to improve the liquidity of the stock.

the contributed capital accounts. This reduces the amount of retained earnings available to pay future dividends. However, because most large stock dividends are accounted for at their par value, the amount of this restriction of retained earnings is typically fairly small.

While the previous sections have focused on the issuance of stock to the investors, the next section addresses how stock can be used internally by the firm. The internal use of stock is typically to serve as an incentive to managers in the form of a stock option plan.

STOCK OPTIONS AND COMPENSATION

Stock options allow the purchase of stock at a prespecified price called the **exercise price,** during some prespecified interval of time. Generally, the value of a stock option depends on the market price of the underlying stock, the volatility of that market price, and the length of time until the option expires. Some stock options are written by investors and traded on a public exchange, such as the Chicago Board Options Exchange, and therefore, have a market price.

Firms increasingly use stock options to compensate their officers and other key employees. Theories vary about the rising popularity of stock options. One school of thought contends that stock options align the incentives of such individuals with those of stockholders. Because the value of a stock option increases with the market price of the stock, recipients of stock options should therefore work harder to maximize the value of the firm. This benefits the stockholders as well as the stock option recipients. However, recent scandals involving allegations of firm managers and investment houses attempting to artificially promote the firm's stock through questionable claims and accounting practices raise the question of whether compensation in the form of stock options may contribute to this behavior.

Another possible explanation for the popularity of stock options is that firm managers can hide the costs of stock options (compensation expense) to investors, who may ignore or underestimate their dilution effect. APB No. 25 and, more recently, SFAS No. 123 (FASB, SFAS No. 123, 1995) allow managers to avoid recognizing the costs of stock options as expenses on the income statement. However, in such cases these expenses must be disclosed on a *pro forma* basis in footnotes to financial statements.

Specifically, SFAS No. 123 establishes two acceptable procedures. Under one procedure, a firm estimates the value of stock options at the date it grants them and records that value as compensation expense in the accounting period containing that date. The firm records the offsetting credit to paid-in-capital. Later, if the option is exercised, then the firm records the sale of the stock at the exercise price plus the value recorded at the date of grant. If the option lapses without having been exercised, no further entry is made.

Note that at the writing of this book, the FASB has issued an exposure draft that would require firms to report stock options as compensation expense on their income statement. This is likely to be a contentious issue, and any decision in the short run may make the guidance in this section obsolete.

In addition to the financial reporting aspects of options, it should be noted that companies may incur tax savings that are larger than the expense recorded

(Dollars in millions except per share data)
Year ended December 31,

	2001	2000	1999
Sales and other operating revenues	$58,198	$51,321	$57,993
Cost of products and services	48,778	43,712	51,320
	9,420	7,609	6,673
Equity in income from joint ventures	93	64	4
General and administrative expense	2,389	2,335	2,044
Research and development expense	1,936	1,441	1,341
In-process research and development expense		557	
Gain on dispositions, net	21	34	87
Share-based plans expense	378	316	209
Special charges due to events of September 11, 2001	935		
Earnings from operations	3,896	3,058	3,170
Other income, principally interest	318	386	585
Interest and debt expense	(650)	(445)	(431)
Earnings before income taxes	3,564	2,999	3,324
Income taxes	738	871	1,015
Net earnings before cumulative effect of accounting change	2,826	2,128	2,309
Cumulative effect of accounting change, net	1		
Net earnings	$ 2,827	$ 2,128	$ 2,309

even if firms record an expense for the intrinsic value of the stock options. This is because the option value takes into account the uncertainty about future stock prices. For tax purposes, the IRS allows firms a tax deduction equal to the difference between the price at the exercise date and the exercise price. These tax deductions are recorded as reductions in taxes payable and direct adjustments to paid-in capital that only appear in the statement of changes in stockholders' equity.

Boeing Company's income statements from its 2001 annual report in Exhibit 12.6 provide an example of accounting recognition of stock option costs as compensation expenses. An appropriate journal entry (in millions) by Boeing to recognize the expense in 2001 might be as follows:

Share-Based Plans Expense	378	
Additional Paid-In-Capital		378

The vast majority of companies, however, do not recognize compensation expense related to stock options. These firms follow the second method allowed under SFAS No. 123; that is, they provide no formal accounting recognition of employee stock options until such time as the options are exercised.

Exhibit 12.7

THE REAL WORLD

Dole Food Company

The Company accounts for employee stock-based compensation related to the Option Plans under APB 25. As the Company's stock options were granted at or above market price on the date of grant, no compensation costs were recognized in the accompanying Consolidated Statements of Income for 2001, 2000, and 1999. Had compensation costs been determined under FAS 123, pro forma net income and net income per common share would have been as follows:

(In thousands)	2001	2000	1999
Net income	$148,053	$64,981	$44,530

The timing of news releases relative to executive stock option grants has been shown to be associated with the type of news conveyed by those releases. The value of options is augmented by market price increases that occur after the options are granted. Accordingly, executives have incentive to release bad (good) news before (after) options grants. (see Aboody and Kasznik, *Journal of Accounting and Economics*, 2000).

At that time, the firms simply record the exercise of previously unrecorded employee stock options as a sale of stock, possibly treasury stock, at the exercise price.

GAAP requires firms that do not recognize compensation expense to disclose additional information about the value of the options issued. In particular, a firm must provide a pro forma net income figure that includes options as a compensation expense. For example, Exhibit 12.7 illustrates a pro forma net income from Dole Food Company's 2001 annual report. Note that actual net income as reported on the company's income statement was (in thousands) $150,404, $67,655, and $48,544, for years 2001, 2000, and 1999, respectively.

As the Cognos case from the beginning of this chapter indicates, the effects of stock options can be significant. Exhibit 12.8 shows Cognos' full disclosure from its 2003 annual report. Note how significant the changes are relative to reported net income. Other disclosures required under SFAS No. 123 include details of options granted, exercised, cancelled, and lapsed along with exercise prices. Within the description of stock option plans, firms also include tenure requirements (how long the employee needs to work for the company before the options can be exercised) and vesting conditions (if the employee leaves the company, the employee still owns the option if they have become vested).

Generally, these supplemental disclosures allow the knowledgeable investor or analyst to determine the implied compensation expense associated with stock options. For example, Exhibit 12.9 shows a typical schedule of option activity for Archer Daniels Midland Company from its 2003 annual report. Note that

Exhibit 12.8

THE REAL WORLD

Cognos, Inc.

Pro Forma Computations for Stock Options

(Amounts in 000s)	2003	2002	2001
Net income (loss):			
As reported	$73,144	$19,408	$64,260
Add: Stock-based employee compensation included above	669	3,341	1,233
Less: Stock-based employee compensation using fair value based method	(27,808)	(28,808)	(21,393)
Pro forma	$46,005	$ (6,059)	$44,100

Exhibit 12.9

THE REAL WORLD

Archer Daniels
Midland Company

Stock option plans provide for the granting of options to employees to purchase common stock of the Company at market value on the date of grant. Options expire five to ten years after the date of grant. At June 30, 2003, there were 26 million shares available for future grants. Stock option activity during the years indicated is as follows:

	Number of Shares	Weighted Average Exercise Price per Share
(In thousands, except share amounts)		
Shares under option at June 30, 2000	10,965	$11.56
Granted	41	10.94
Exercised	(34)	9.27
Cancelled	(392)	12.23
Shares under option at June 30, 2001	10,580	11.54
Granted	2,632	12.54
Exercised	(724)	12.01
Cancelled	(1,907)	12.27
Shares under option at June 30, 2002	10,581	11.62
Granted	4,439	11.30
Exercised	(228)	9.32
Cancelled	(329)	12.75
Shares under option at June 30, 2003	14,463	11.54
Shares exercisable at June 30, 2003	5,445	11.40
Shares exercisable at June 30, 2002	3,705	11.55
Shares exercisable at June 30, 2001	3,311	$12.35

At June 30, 2003, the range of exercise prices and weighted average remaining contractual life of outstanding options was $8.33 to $14.84 and four years, respectively. The weighted average fair value of options granted during 2003, 2002, and 2001 are $3.20, $4.31, and $3.79, respectively.

at the end of the table, the weighted average fair value of the options for the year give the analyst an estimate of the amount of compensation expense implied by the granting of the options when combined with the number of options granted during the year.

One of the effects of stock options is to potentially increase the number of shares outstanding and thereby dilute the earnings per share of the firm. Other types of securities issued by the firm can have a similar effect if those securities are convertible into shares of common stock. In the next section, we consider the effects of these types of securities.

At the time of this writing, opponents of expensing stock options have been lobbying with the U.S. Congress to enact legislation that would bar a recent FASB proposed rule change to require such an accounting treatment.

CONVERTIBLE SECURITIES

Convertible securities include convertible debt and convertible preferred stock. Typically, convertible debt or preferred stock may be exchanged for common stock at some prescribed exchange rate. This provides investors with the prospect of sharing in the success of the firm while also enjoying priority over common stockholders until such time as they exercise the conversion privilege.

Although we focus on convertible debt in the discussion that follows, preferred stock follows a similar accounting treatment.

In effect, convertible debt is two securities in one. It is a debt instrument combined with an option. The interest rate on convertible debt is less than it would have been without the option to convert. Therefore, convertible debt is a popular means of raising capital when stock prices are increasing and alternative forms of debt are unavailable, or the cash flow drain to meet higher interest requirements is likely to inhibit growth.

Convertibles are often callable or redeemable by the issuing firm at a pre-specified call or redemption price. Such provisions enable the issuing firm to induce conversion and thereby limit the value of the option feature. Accounting for convertibles raises the issue of how to classify them on the balance sheet. Convertible debt derives some of its value from its debt characteristics and some from its equity characteristics through the option component. The difficulty therefore, lies in how to separate those elements. GAAP resolves this problem by requiring that firms classify convertible debt entirely as debt.

A similar situation occurs when a company issues detachable stock purchase warrants along with debt. A **stock purchase warrant** is like an option in that it enables the holder to buy a share of stock at a prespecified price on or before some prespecified date. The difference is that an investor may exercise the warrant without surrendering the debt. Moreover, stock warrants may have a discernible market value apart from the debt, making it easier to separate the value of the warrants from the value of the debt without the warrants for accounting purposes. Accordingly, under GAAP (AICPA, APB No. 14, 1969), firms classify the warrants as equity and the debt component as debt.

Firms face another accounting issue for convertible securities in recording a conversion when the market value of the stock issued differs from the book value of the convertible debt being retired. GAAP allows two acceptable accounting treatments. Under one treatment, a firm values the stock at its market value at the date of conversion, usually implying recognition of a loss. Under the second method, a firm values the stock at the book value of the debt, implying no loss recognition.

Exhibit 12.10 provides a description of convertible debt issued by Anadigics, Inc. during 2001, taken from the company's annual report. A journal entry to record the issuance of the company's convertible notes is:

Cash	100,000	
Convertible Notes		100,000

Exhibit 12.10

THE REAL WORLD

Anadigics, Inc.

On November 27, 2001, the Company issued $100,000 aggregate principal amount of 5 percent Convertible Senior Notes ("Convertible Notes") due November 15, 2006. The notes are convertible into shares of common stock at any time prior to their maturity or prior to redemption by the Company. The notes are convertible into shares of common stock at a rate of 47.619 shares for each $1,000 principal amount (convertible at a price of $21.00 per share), subject to adjustment.

Suppose that the notes above converted when the market value of a share is $23 (par value is $0.01/share). If the firm values the stock at its market price (note that 4,762 shares would be issued), then the following entry would be made:

Convertible Notes	100,000	
Loss on Conversion	9,524	
Common Stock		48
Additional Paid-In Capital		109,476

Alternatively, if Anadigics values the stock at the book value of the debt (net of issue costs that by maturity are fully amortized), then

Convertible Notes	100,000	
Common Stock		48
Additional Paid-In Capital		99,952

Although the second treatment fails to reflect the market price of stock issued when conversion takes place, investors could easily deduce any loss on conversion through reference to the market price of the stock at that time combined with the number of shares issued.

As we have seen in the last couple of sections, the numbers of shares of stock outstanding can be easily increased by the exercise of stock options or the conversion of convertible securities. In the next section, we discuss the effects of these types of securities on the calculation of earnings per share. Earnings per share is often one of the key metrics that analysts use in valuing a firm.

EARNINGS PER SHARE

Earnings per share (EPS), in its simplest form, is net income less preferred stock dividends, divided by a weighted average number of common shares outstanding during the year. EPS transforms earnings from a firm-wide measure of performance to a measure of performance for a single share of common stock. EPS is an especially prominent measure in part because of the popularity of the price-to-earnings (P/E) ratio to determine whether a firm may be mispriced relative to other comparable firms in the same industry. The P/E ratio can be thought of as a measure of the value of the firm per dollar of earnings. Consider a simple example such as an interest bearing account that pays 5 percent interest. Assume that an investor has $100 in such an account. The earnings are $5 annually. The P/E ratio for this account would be 20, representing the value per dollar of earnings. Of course, stocks are more complex because of the uncertain returns and risk. More sophisticated valuation models such as those discussed in Chapter 14 take these factors into account. However, some analysts use P/E ratios as screens. For example, companies with low P/E ratios may be more closely analyzed to assess whether they are undervalued by the market.

P/E ratios used in valuing the firm may be based on historical earnings from the most recent annual report or on earnings forecasts made by financial analysts. The former is called a trailing P/E ratio while the latter is called a leading P/E ratio. Researchers found that P/E ratios using two-year ahead analysts' earnings forecasts provided the more accurate estimates of market prices than other valuation methods including some more complicated approaches similar to those discussed in Chapter 14 (see Liu, Nissim, and Thomas, *Journal of Accounting Research,* 2002).

Because of its importance, financial analysts often forecast EPS. Typically, analysts forecast EPS one and two years into the future, along with an average growth rate in EPS for five years. However, computing EPS can be fairly complicated. One complication arises when a firm distributes a stock dividend or invokes a stock split. These events change the number of shares outstanding, but not the net assets used to produce income. In this case, EPS is calculated by using the number of shares outstanding after the stock dividend or stock split has transpired. EPS is then restated for all prior years in order to give effect to the greater number of shares. The restatement is necessary for comparability of EPS across years.

DILUTED EARNINGS PER SHARE

The previous calculations describe what is called **basic earnings per share.** This calculation, however, may give investors a distorted picture of earnings that accrue to the shares that they hold. That is, their interest in the firm and its earnings may be diluted (reduced) in the future if stock options or securities that are convertible into stock are later exercised or converted, respectively. This dilution occurs because the market price of the shares issued to the option or convertible security holder upon exercise generally exceeds the exercise price of the option or present value of the securities converted. One way to deal with the effects of potential dilution is to reduce earnings per share to reflect the expected effect. Such earnings per share are called **diluted earnings per share.**

For stock options, the general approach, called the **treasury stock method,** assumes that the options are exercised and that the proceeds received from the option holder are used to repurchase stock in the open market. The denominator of EPS increases by the number of shares issued and decreases by the number of shares that could have been repurchased. Given that the exercise price is lower than the market price, then more shares are issued than can be repurchased, thus lowering EPS.

For example, suppose that at the beginning of its first year, BHT grants 10 million stock options to its officers and key employees, giving them the right to purchase BHT's common stock at the market price of $6.50 per share at the date of grant. Assume that the average market price during the year is $10. Under the treasury stock method, we calculate the dilution effect as follows (in millions except for share prices):

Proceeds from exercise of options ($6.50 × 10)	$65
Shares repurchased from proceeds ($65/$10)	6.5
Shares added to denominator of EPS (10 − 6.5)	3.5

Recall from Chapter 3 that BHT's EPS before the effects of potentially dilutive securities was $1.66, based on net income of $416 million divided by 250 million shares of common stock issued and outstanding. Adding 3.5 million shares reduces EPS to $1.64.

For convertible debt, where the market value of the stock exceeds the price stated or implied by the terms of conversion, the approach assumes that the

When U.S. firms make significant investments in the stock of subsidiaries in other countries and are required to consolidate those subsidiaries (discussed in Chapter 13), they must translate the financial statements from their currency of record (i.e., the currency in which they record their transactions) to the U.S. dollar. This process results in foreign translation gains and losses, some of which go through the other comprehensive income account.

debt is converted to stock under the terms specified in the contract. The numerator increases by the interest expense that no longer would be due net of the income tax benefit of that expense. The denominator increases by the number of shares that would be issued "as if " the conversion occurred at the start of the year.

Again using BHT to illustrate, suppose that each $1,000 of notes issued at the start of the year 20X1 had been convertible into 50 shares of common stock, or 20 million shares in total if all notes were converted. The numerator of EPS therefore increases by $28 million dollars of interest that would not have been paid, while the denominator increases by the 20 million shares. Note that the interest expense should be adjusted to after tax but since we assumed no taxes in our BHT example we make no adjustment here. Taking both of these adjustments into effect, along with the 3.5 million shares added to the denominator due to options, would result in an EPS of $1.62.

RETAINED EARNINGS AND COMPREHENSIVE INCOME

We know from Chapter 3 that **retained earnings** represents the undistributed portion of accumulated net income to date. In this chapter, we have seen that distributions may come in the form of stock dividends as well as cash dividends. Reissuance of treasury stock at a loss too large to be absorbed by additional paid-in-capital also reduces retained earnings. Other transactions affecting retained earnings include prior-period adjustments related to accounting changes and corrections of previous accounting errors.

Another category of stockholders' equity is **accumulated comprehensive income.** This category includes certain transactions involving gains or losses that are not considered as part of net income. Common examples are unrealized holding gains and losses on marketable securities, and foreign currency translation. We consider the accounting treatment of marketable securities in Chapter 13. Foreign currency translation arises when companies have foreign subsidiaries that record their transactions in another currency and must convert (translate) those amounts into U.S. dollars to prepare consolidated financial statements (see Chapter 13 for a discussion of consolidation).

STATEMENT OF CHANGES IN STOCKHOLDERS' EQUITY

The statement of changes in stockholders' equity summarizes the transactions considered in this chapter. It bridges the gap between the income statement and changes in the stockholders' equity section of the balance sheet. For example,

(in thousands)	Common Shares	Stock Amount	Reinvested Earnings	Accumulated Other Comprehensive Loss	Total Shareholders' Equity
Balance July 1, 2000	632,296	$5,232,597	$1,325,323	($447,677)	$ 6,110,243
Comprehensive income					
Net earnings			383,284		
Other comprehensive loss				(16,738)	
Total comprehensive income					366,546
Cash dividends paid, $.19 per share			(125,053)		(125,053)
5% stock dividend	31,542	395,923	(395,923)		
Treasury stock purchases	(5,525)	(62,932)			(62,932)
Other	4,065	43,153	(274)		42,879
Balance June 30, 2001	662,378	5,608,741	1,187,357	(464,415)	6,331,683
Comprehensive income					
Net earnings			511,093		
Other comprehensive income				215,515	
Total comprehensive income					726,608
Cash dividends paid, $.20 per share			(130,000)		(130,000)
Treasury stock purchases	(12,818)	(184,519)			(184,519)
Other	433	11,929	(880)		11,049
Balance June 30, 2002	649,993	5,436,151	1,567,570	(248,900)	6,754,821
Comprehensive income					
Net earnings			451,145		
Other comprehensive income				81,942	
Total comprehensive income					533,087
Cash dividends paid, $.24 per share			(155,565)		(155,565)
Treasury stock purchases	(8,410)	(101,212)			(101,212)
Other	3,272	38,066			38,066
Balance June 30, 2003	644,855	$5,373,005	$1,863,150	($166,958)	$7,069,197

Exhibit 12.11
Consolidated Statements of Shareholders' Equity

THE REAL WORLD

Archer Daniels Midland Company

Exhibit 12.11 reflects many of the transactions considered in this chapter for Archer Daniels Midland Company. Note that Archer Daniels declared a 5 percent stock dividend in 2001, had treasury stock purchases every year, and showed significant reductions in accumulated other comprehensive loss over the most recent two years due largely to foreign currency translation adjustments. Note also that in the last two years the comprehensive income is a significant percentage of the reported net income. The "other" category is likely to be partially explained by the issuance of shares of stock via stock options plans.

SUMMARY AND TRANSITION

Stockholders' equity represents the residual interest in the firm's assets. Components of stockholders' equity include preferred and common stock accounts, additional paid-in-capital, retained earnings, accumulated comprehensive income, and treasury stock.

In this chapter, we considered a wide range of transactions affecting stockholders' equity. When a firm issues stock, it credits the par or stated value of the stock to a stock account, and the remainder of the amount received to additional paid-in-capital.

Repurchased stock that is not cancelled is called treasury stock. Treasury stock is deducted from stockholders' equity, consistent with its interpretation as a contraction of firm size. A common purpose for acquiring treasury stock is to service employee stock purchases and stock option plans. Firms treat gains and losses on subsequent resale of treasury stock as adjustments of additional paid-in-capital or, under certain conditions, retained earnings.

Firms distribute dividends to stockholders, which reduces retained earnings. Firms usually make dividends in the form of cash payments to stockholders, or, less commonly, in the form of additional shares of stock. Stock dividends increase the number of shares outstanding, thus diluting the value of each share. Stock splits also increase the number of shares outstanding and may be implemented either by reducing the stock's par value or as a stock dividend. The accounting treatment of large stock dividends or stock splits usually involves reclassifying additional paid-in capital as stock, such that the amount reported as stock corresponds to the par or stated value of shares outstanding. Small stock dividends involve reducing retained earnings for the market value of shares issued rather than additional paid-in capital.

Firms provide stock options as compensation to officers and key employees. Most firms account for stock options by estimating the value of options granted and recording this amount as compensation expense. GAAP requires disclosures of the effect that options would have on net income for firms that follow this accounting method.

Although convertible debt has some characteristics of both debt and equity, GAAP requires that firms classify these securities entirely as debt. Stock issued upon conversion may be valued for accounting purposes at either the book value of the debt converted or the market value of the stock issued.

Throughout this book we have pointed to the importance that the investment community places on earnings per share. In the simplest case, earnings per share is determined by dividing the number of shares outstanding into net income. However, the issuance or repurchase of stock, distribution of a stock dividend or stock split, and presence of potentially dilutive securities such as employee stock options or convertible debt complicate the calculation.

Finally, stockholders' equity includes a category called accumulated comprehensive income. Comprehensive income often arises from gains and losses on certain marketable securities and foreign currency translation. It completes the picture for events for which the income implications are debatable.

END OF CHAPTER MATERIAL

KEY TERMS

Accumulated Comprehensive Income

Basic Earnings per Share

Board of Directors

Callable Preferred

Contributed Capital

Convertible Preferred

Convertible Securities

Cumulative Preferred

Date of Declaration

Date of Record

Diluted Earnings per Share

Dividends in Kind

Earnings per Share

Exercise Price

No Par Stock

Other Comprehensive Income

Paid-In capital

Par Value

Participating Preferred

Preferred Stock

Property Dividends

Prospectus

Redeemable Preferred

Residual Interest

Retained Earnings

Stated Value

Stock Dividends

Stock Options

Stock Purchase Warrant

Stock Splits

Treasury Stock

Treasury Stock Method

Underwriting Agreements

Undistributed Income

ASSIGNMENT MATERIAL

REVIEW QUESTIONS

1. Describe the major components of owners' equity in a typical firm.

2. Describe what is meant by a prospectus and the role that is played by underwriters in the issuance of stock.

3. Discuss how preferred stock differs from common stock.

4. Briefly describe what each of the following features means in a preferred stock issue:

    a. Participating

    b. Cumulative

    c. Convertible

    d. Redeemable

5. Describe the process of declaring and paying a cash dividend, including information about the declaration date, date of record, and payment date.

6. Discuss the nature of a stock dividend and why GAAP makes a distinction between small and large stock dividends.

7. Compare and contrast a 100 percent stock dividend with a two-for-one stock split.

8. Describe why firms repurchase stock and how these purchases are recorded in the accounting system.

9. Discuss why companies issue employee stock options and what immediate and potential effects these options have on the financial results of the corporation.

10. Describe how convertible securities affect the financial statements at the date of conversion.

11. Why does GAAP require firms to compute both a basic and a diluted earnings per share?

12. Describe the calculation of basic earnings per share.

13. Describe the calculation of diluted earnings per share.

APPLYING YOUR KNOWLEDGE

14. Give journal entries for the following transactions:

   a. 10,000 shares of common stock with a par value of $10 per share are issued at $25 per share.

   b. 10,000 shares of no-par stock are issued at $25 per share.

   c. A dividend of $2 per share is declared for the common stockholders. The company is authorized to issue 25,000 shares; it has issued 10,000 shares, and it holds 2,000 shares in its treasury stock account.

   d. The dividend declared in part c is paid.

   e. The company purchased 500 of its own shares at a market price of $50 per share.

   f. Of the 500 shares purchased in part e, 300 shares are reissued at a price of $45 per share.

15. Give journal entries for the following transactions:

   a. A two-for-one stock split has been declared by a company that has 80,000 shares authorized, 50,000 shares issued, and 38,500 shares outstanding. The par value is $5 per share.

   b. A 10 percent stock dividend is declared when 40,000 shares are outstanding and the market value of each share is $30. The par value is $5 per share.

   c. Stock dividends declared in part b are satisfied with the issuance of stock.

   d. The company purchases 20,000 of its own shares at a market price of $100 per share.

   e. The company reissues all the shares acquired in part d at a loss of $75 per share. Prior to this transaction, the additional paid-in capital account had a credit balance of $1 million.

   f. Stock warrants priced at $10,000 are issued. The stock warrant holders are allowed to buy 10,000 shares at $50 per share within the next six months. The par value is $5 per share.

   g. Of the stock warrants issued in part f, 50 percent of the warrants are utilized to buy 5,000 shares at $50 per share.

16. The Timmerman Company has issued 50,000 shares having a par value of $10 each. Of the 50,000 shares issued, 45,000 shares are outstanding. The company has decided to issue stock dividends to its stockholders. The market price of each of the Timmerman Company's shares is $50. Give the journal entries for recording the issuance of the stock dividend if:

   a. The company decides to issue an 18 percent stock dividend.

   b. The company decides to issue a 30 percent stock dividend.

17. The following information relates to the owners' equity section of the Rogers Company (in thousands):

	12/31/X1	12/31/X2
Preferred Stock	$ 1,000	$1,000
Common Stock	5,000	?
Additional Paid-In Capital	2,500	?
Retained Earnings	3,750	4,400
Total Owners' Equity	$12,250	?

During 20X2, 10,000 shares of common stock having a par value of $10 each were issued at a price of $30 per share. Cash dividends of $750,000 and $100,000 were paid to common stockholders and preferred stockholders, respectively. The company acquired 15,000 shares of treasury stock during the year at $25 per share. Of these treasury shares, 5,000 were reissued under employee stock option plans at $22 per share.

Required:

a. Calculate the ending balance in common stock, additional paid-in capital, and treasury stock at the end of 20X2.

b. Calculate the amount of net income reported in 20X2.

18. Give the journal entries for the following owners' equity transactions of the Globe Apparel Company:

a. On January 10, 20X1, the articles of incorporation are filed with the state commission. The company is authorized to issue 100,000 shares of common stock having a par value of $50 per share and 50,000 shares of 10 percent cumulative preferred stock with a par value of $100 per share.

b. On January 12, 20X1, the company issues 50,000 shares of common stock at par value.

c. On January 15, 20X1, the assets of the Tritex Knits Company are acquired in exchange for 10,000 shares of common stock and 10,000 shares of 10 percent cumulative preferred stock. The market values of these shares approximate their par values on this date. The assets acquired and their relative fair market values are: land, $500,000; equipment, $250,000; inventory, $200,000; building, $500,000; and accounts receivable, $50,000.

d. On January 20, 20X1, 25,000 shares of 10 percent cumulative preferred stock are issued at par value.

e. No dividends are declared in 20X1.

f. On December 2, 20X2, preferred stock dividends are declared, payable on December 31, 20X2, to make the preferred stock current with regard to dividends in arrears.

g. On December 2, 20X2, a 10 percent stock dividend is declared for the common stockholders. The shares are issued on December 15, 20X2, when the market price per share is $75.

19. The Mattle Company was formed on January 1, 20X3, and the owners' equity section of the balance sheet on December 31, 20X3 appeared as follows:

Owners' Equity as of December 31, 20X3:

Common stock, $20 par value	$200,000
8% Preferred stock, $50 par value	250,000
Additional paid-in capital	205,000
Retained earnings	130,000
Less: treasury stock	25,000
Total owners' equity	$760,000

During the year, the following transactions took place:

● Common stock was issued at a price of $40 per share.

● Preferred stock was issued at par value.

● One thousand shares of treasury stock were acquired at $50 per share.

● A preferred stock dividend was declared and paid for during the year.

● A cash dividend of $5 per share was declared and paid to common stock-holders at year end.

● Some of the treasury stock was resold prior to year end.

The transactions just listed were the only capital stock transactions that occurred during the entire year. Given this information, answer the following questions:

a. How many shares of common stock were issued?

b. How many shares of preferred stock were issued?

c. How many shares are there in the treasury at year end?

d. How many shares of treasury stock were sold during the year, and what were the proceeds from the sale?

e. How much net income was reported during the year?

20. Explain why firms issue options, and discuss how they are reported in the financial statements.

21. Why might a company choose to issue debt that is convertible to common stock? What would you expect the interest rate on convertible debt to be relative to ordinary debt for the same company? Why?

22. Company X and Company Y are in the same industry. Company X has a P/E ratio of 20 while company Y has a P/E ratio of 15. Explain why the P/E ratios might differ.

○ USING REAL DATA

23. In 2002, Old Dominion Freight Line, Inc. declared a three-for-two split of its stock. It treated the transaction as a stock dividend. As of December 31, 2002, the company had 10,652,000 shares outstanding and a par value of $0.10 per share. What entry would be made by Old Dominion to record this transaction?

24. For three years, Southern Union Company has declared a 5 percent stock dividend each year. The company's fiscal year ends June 30. At the beginning of fiscal year 2003, Southern had 58,055,000 shares and a par value of $1. If the market price for Southern's shares was $17.86 at the time of the issuance, what entry would Southern make to record this dividend?

25. In fiscal year 2003 (ended December 31, 2003), PennRock Financial Services Corporation declard a 10 percent stock dividend. The number of shares outstanding for PennRock at the end of fiscal year 2002 was 17,544,000 at a par value of $1 per share. If the market price at the date of declaration was $12.40 per share, what entry would PennRock make to record the dividend?

26. In fiscal year 2003 (ended December 31, 2003), Hawthorne Financial Corporation declared a three-for-two stock split to be recorded as a 50 percent stock dividend. At the beginning of fiscal year 2003, Hawthorne had 11,082,000 shares outstanding and a par value of $0.01 per share. If the stock price at the date of declaration was $29.50 per share, what entry would be made to record this transaction?

27. On June 16, 2003, Tumbleweed, Inc. declared a reverse stock split for 1-for-5,000. Individuals otherwise entitled to receive less than one share would receive cash in the amount of $1.10 per share. As a result of this split, the number of investors holding stock in the company was reduced from approximately 900 to approximately 100.

    Required:

    a. Why might a company engage in such a transaction?

    b. What is the potential effect of this on the trading of the shares of this company on a stock exchange? (Prior to the split, the company traded on the Nasdaq SmallCap market.)

    c. Optional: Determine what the SEC reporting requirements would be for this company subsequent to the split.

28. One of the requirements to remain on the Nasdaq SmallCap Market is that a company must maintain a price of $1 or higher for 30 consecutive days. In April 2003, Onyx Software hit an all-time low of 56 cents per share and was in danger of being delisted.

    Required:

    a. How might Onyx use a stock split to avoid being delisted?

    b. Suppose that the company engaged in a one-for-four reverse stock split; what effect would this have on the company's stock price?

29. In 2003, Rayonier announced a three-for-two stock split and a 12.5 percent increase in the post-split dividend. Discuss the effect these announcements should have on the stock price of Rayonier.

30. In 2001, NeoPharm, Inc. declared at 10 percent stock dividend and in 2003 they declared a 15 percent stock dividend. The 15 percent stock dividend was treated as a stock split rather than a dividend. Describe how these two transactions would affect the owners' equity accounts of NeoPharm.

31. In May 2003, Oneida Ltd. (the world's leading manufacturer of flatware) suspended its common stock dividend indefinitely. This broke a 67-year record of paying consecutive quarterly dividends. By year end, Oneida had reported a loss of $99 million and in its January 31, 2004 10-K report provided a footnote that raised concerns about the company's ability to continue as a going concern. Serious doubt also existed with regard to whether lenders would require the company to immediately repay its debt, as the Company had violated interest coverage ratio, leverage ratio, and net worth covenants for the second and third quarter in fiscal year 2004 and at year end. Following is the balance sheet for Oneida Ltd. as it existed at the end of fiscal year 2003 on January 25, 2003.

ONEIDA LTD. Balance Sheet	1/25/2003	1/26/2002
Assets		
Cash	$ 2,653,000	$ 11,112,000
Receivables	78,006,000	76,099,000
Inventories	167,573,000	172,717,000
Other current assets	9,290,000	17,687,000
Total current assets	257,522,000	277,615,000
Property, plant, and equipment	102,366,000	108,534,000
Goodwill	133,944,000	131,796,000
Deferred income taxes	18,575,000	21,567,000
Other assets	12,713,000	4,390,000
Total assets	$525,120,000	$543,902,000
Liabilities		
Short-term debt	$ 8,510,000	$ 11,430,000
Accounts payable	25,711,000	24,848,000
Accrued liabilities	34,185,000	37,811,000
Current installments of long-term debt	6,406,000	3,956,000
Total current liabilities	74,812,000	78,045,000
Long-term debt	219,037,000	256,170,000
Accrued post-retirement liability	59,708,000	56,410,000
Accrued pension liability	23,496,000	15,206,000
Other liabilities	18,678,000	13,970,000
Total liabilities	395,731,000	419,801,000
Stockholders' Equity		
Cumulative 6% preferred stock—$25 par value; authorized 95,660 shares, issued 86,036 shares, callable at $30 per share	2,151,000	2,151,000
Common stock—$l.00 par value; authorized 48,000,000 shares, issued 17,836,571 and 17,809,235 shares	17,837,000	17,809,000
Additional paid-in capital	84,318,000	83,965,000
Retained earnings	68,407,000	60,638,000

	1/25/2003	1/26/2002
Accumulated other comprehensive loss	(19,190,000)	(16,328,000)
Less cost of common stock held in treasury; 1,285,679 shares	(24,134,000)	(24,134,000)
Stockholders' equity	129,389,000	124,101,000
Total liabilities and stockholders' equity	$525,120,000	$543,902,000

Required:

If the company were to decide it was not a going concern, what would be the effect of this decision on the ways that the company values:

a. Property, plant, and equipment

b. Goodwill

c. Deferred tax assets

d. Long-term debt

○ BEYOND THE BOOK

32. Find a company that repurchases its own stock using a web search (or use one assigned by your instructor). Examine the company's press releases to see why management says that they are repurchasing the stock. Do you agree with management's attributions? Explain.

33. Select a company with employee stock options (or use one assigned by your instructor). Determine

    a. the amount of compensation cost recorded related to the options and

    b. the amount of tax savings associated with option exercises.

    Discuss where you found this information and whether you believe that the disclosures are clear.

34. Select a company (or use one assigned by your instructor) that has convertible or redeemable debt. What are the terms for conversion? Does the company report different diluted earnings per share than basic? Why?

CHAPTER **13**

Intercorporate Investments

LEARNING OBJECTIVES

After reading this chapter, you should be able to:

1 Understand the classification of marketable securities and related variations in accounting treatments of gains and losses.

2 Construct entries for the equity method of accounting for investments in affiliates and related recognition of affiliate income.

3 Explain the rationale for and application of the purchase method of accounting for business acquisitions.

4 Describe the basic construction of consolidated balance sheets and issues pertaining to consolidation.

In June 2002, the SEC notified Amazon.com that it concluded its informal inquiry regarding the company's accounting treatment and disclosures for some of its strategic alliances. The SEC recommended no enforcement proceeding in connection with that inquiry. The informal inquiry, first disclosed by Amazon.com in October 2000, related to the revenue recognition, equity investments, and other accounting and disclosure matters pertaining to Amazon.com's commercial and stock purchase agreements with its partners in the Amazon Commerce Network.

An issue in the case of Amazon is accounting for barter transactions. Amazon receives shares of stock in privately held companies in return for providing advertising services. The approach, used by Amazon and approved by the SEC, involves estimating a fair value of stock received in order to measure revenue from the exchange (see Exhibit 13.1). In this chapter, we explore accounting for equity investments, along with other accounting issues related to intercorporate investments.

Exhibit 13.1
Excerpt from Footnotes to
Amazon's 2001 Annual
Report

THE REAL WORLD

Amazon.com

The initial cost of the Company's investments is determined based on the fair value of the investment at the time of its acquisition. The Company has received equity securities as consideration for services to be performed for the issuer under commercial agreements. In such cases, the Company has estimated the fair value of the equity securities received. For securities of public companies, the Company generally determines fair value based on the quoted market price at the time the Company enters into the underlying agreement, and adjusts such market price appropriately if significant restrictions on marketability exist. As an observable market price does not exist for equity securities of private companies, estimates of fair value of such securities are more subjective than for securities of public companies. For significant transactions involving equity securities in private companies, the Company obtains and considers independent, third-party valuations where appropriate. Such valuations use a variety of methodologies to estimate fair value, including comparing the security with securities of publicly traded companies in similar lines of business, applying price multiples to estimated future operating results for the private company, and estimating discounted cash flows for that company.

OVERVIEW OF INTERCORPORATE INVESTMENTS

Intercorporate investments are commonplace. Many companies acquire debt and equity securities issued by other companies. In some cases, the objective is to earn a return on excess funds until such time as those funds can be usefully invested for some other purpose. For example, a firm may acquire marketable securities in order to earn a return on funds obtained in advance of capital expenditures or debt repayments. In other cases, the objective is to exercise influence over customers or suppliers by holding a significant amount of their stock. A company may undertake more substantial investments in stock to acquire control of another firm. For example, business combinations, in which one firm acquires a majority of the common stock of another firm, may be used to achieve *vertical integration* with suppliers or customers, or *horizontal integration* with competitor firms. Vertical integration may allow a company to control much of the chain from acquiring resources to producing goods or services and ultimately marketing those outputs to final consumers. A principal advantage of vertical integration is the elimination of markups over cost at intermediate stages leading to more efficient production. Horizontal integration allows a company to obtain a larger share of the market for its product, possibly leading to economies of scale.

The accounting treatment of intercorporate investments varies with the objective of such investments, the level of ownership achieved, and the marketability of the securities acquired. Accounting standards currently classify intercorporate investments in three broad categories that reflect the percentage of ownership in common stock:

● **Passive minority ownership** Less than 20 percent ownership of common (voting) stock.

● **Active minority ownership** Between 20 percent and 50 percent ownership of common (voting) stock.

● **Majority ownership**   Greater than 50 percent ownership of common (voting) stock.

These classifications are somewhat arbitrary, and the FASB is currently considering what constitutes control in its deliberations. However, the idea underlying the percentage of voting stock as a criteria is that if a firm acquires less than 20 percent of another firm's common stock, the former generally does not intend to exercise significant influence over the latter's activities. Such acquisitions are commonly viewed as a productive use of funds in excess of the operational needs of the acquiring firm. Accordingly, the accounting treatment emphasizes the measurement of short-term returns, including appreciation in market prices. When ownership of common stock exceeds 20 percent, but not more than 50 percent, the investor has the ability to affect operating, investing, and financing decisions of the investee. This level of ownership suggests a long-term perspective and, hence, an accounting treatment less sensitive to temporary fluctuations in value. More than 50 percent ownership of common stock implies literal control of the investee's affairs. The accounting in this case considers the relevant reporting entity to be a combination of the investor and investee firms.

PASSIVE MINORITY OWNERSHIP

Passive minority investments are further classified as either held to maturity, trading, or available for sale securities. **Held to maturity securities** include debt securities that management intends to hold until their maturity date. **Trading securities** include debt and equity securities that management plans to sell in the near future. **Available for sale securities** include all remaining securities in the category of passive minority ownership. The accounting treatment afforded each class of securities relates to the rationale for investing in those securities, as we explain in the sections that follow.

HELD TO MATURITY DEBT SECURITIES

To account for held to maturity debt securities, a firm values them at cost and amortizes any discount or premium. The firm recognizes interest income in the income statement as accrued. Thus, interim price changes will not be realized if the debt is, in fact, held to maturity. In the view of the FASB, adjusting value for those changes would not serve a useful purpose.

Let's revisit the data from the BHT example in Chapter 11. Suppose that BHT sold the issued notes (issuance price of 386.75) to another company (the lender/investor). The lender (investor) records the initial investment in BHT notes (in thousands) as follows:

Investment in Held to Maturity Securities	386.75	
Cash		386.75

As we mentioned in Chapter 11, the issuing firm usually records the notes using a discount account. Purchasers of notes at a discount, however, typically do not create a separate account to record the discount. They simply report the net amount they paid for the notes in the investment account. As the notes mature, however, the purchasers amortize the discount in the same way as the issuing company. This amortization is reflected in the increase in the investment account, as shown here for the BHT example for the first interest payment:

Cash	28	
Investment in Held to Maturity Securities	2.94	
Interest Income		30.94

We can further illustrate the accounting procedures of notes issued at a discount using the somewhat more complex Champion Home Builders example from Chapter 11. In this case, Champion issued these notes for $148.6 million (face value $150 million), to yield 11.5 percent. If the lender had been another corporation, then the notes would have been viewed as an investment by the lending company. The lender would record the following entries to account for the initial purchase of these notes and the subsequent two interest payments in the first year (refer back to Chapter 11 for the calculation of these amounts):

Investment in Held to Maturity Securities	148,600,000	
Cash		148,600,000

Cash	8,437,500	
Investment in Held to Maturity Securities	107,000	
Interest Income		8,544,500

Cash	8,437,500	
Investment in Held to Maturity Securities	113,152	
Interest Income		8,550,652

If the notes were publicly traded, then it is also possible that the company purchased these debt securities on the open market rather than from the issuing firm. However, this would not affect the accounting treatment. The presence of a market raises the prospect of revaluing the investment at future report

Exhibit 13.2
Held to Maturity Securities

THE REAL WORLD

BMC Software

(In millions)	Fair Value	Unrecognized Gains	Unrecognized Losses	Amortized Cost
2001				
Maturities within 1 year:				
Municipal securities	$ 87.7	$ 0.6	$ –	$ 87.1
Corporate bonds	23.1	0.1	–	23.0
Euro bonds and other	18.9	–	–	18.9
Mortgage securities	2.1	–	–	2.1
Total maturities within 1 year	$131.8	$ 0.7	$ –	$131.1
Maturities from 1–5 years:				
Municipal securities	$275.2	$ 5.1	$ –	$270.1
Corporate bonds	167.2	4.3	(0.6)	163.5
Euro bonds and other	93.9	1.7	(0.1)	92.3
Mortgage securities	0.9	–	–	0.9
Total maturities from 1–5 years	$537.2	$11.1	$(0.7)	$526.8

dates to give effect to changes in fair value. Although the accounting treatment of held to maturity securities is not to record these changes, GAAP requires firms to provide supplemental footnote disclosures of fair values, as Exhibit 13.2 illustrates.

TRADING SECURITIES

Firms account for trading securities by valuing them at fair value (usually market value), and recording any changes in fair value as unrealized gains or losses to be included in net income. This treatment is called **mark-to-market** accounting. The procedure makes use of a **market adjustment account** to record changes to the asset trading securities, separate from their original historical cost. Commonly, the balance sheet suppresses this account. Only the net market value appears on that statement, with both historical cost and market value disclosed in a footnote. Firms, again, recognize any interest or dividend income on trading securities on an accrual basis in the income statement. A firm recognizes any realized gain or loss, as measured by the difference between book value inclusive of the market adjustment and selling price, at the time of sale. Industrial companies rarely engage in active trading of securities, but financial institutions, such as banks and insurance companies, often do. Therefore, you most often see the application of this method of accounting in financial institutions.

For example, suppose that in 2003 BHT purchases stocks issued by other companies for $500,000. It later sells shares costing $300,000 for $315,000. At year end, the market value of remaining shares is $240,000. BHT records these events (in thousands) as follows:

| Trading Securities | 500 | |
| Cash | | 500 |

Cash	315	
Realized Gain		15
Trading Securities		300

| Market Adjustment-Trading Securities | 40 | |
| Unrealized Gain | | 40 |

BHT's income statement will show both the realized gain of $15,000 and unrealized gain of $40,000. BHT's balance sheet will also report Trading Securities in the amount of $240,000.

Now assume that in 2004 BHT purchases no trading securities, sells trading securities costing $100,000 for $90,000, and realizes a year-end market value of the remaining trading securities of $95,000. BHT records the following journal entries (in thousands) for these events:

Cash	90	
Realized Loss	30	
Trading Securities		100
Market Adjustment-Trading Securities		20

| Unrealized Loss | 25 | |
| Market Adjustment-Trading Securities | | 25 |

After these entries, the balance in the Market Adjustment-Trading Securities account shows a credit of $5,000. The net book value of Trading Securities on the balance sheet is the market value of the remaining shares of $95,000.

AVAILABLE FOR SALE SECURITIES

Available for sale securities include passive investments for which management plans neither to hold them to maturity nor to actively trade them. Similar to the accounting treatment of trading securities, available for sale securities are also marked-to-market through the use of a market adjustment account.

However, the treatment of unrealized gains and losses differs. Rather than include such gains and losses in net income, firms accumulate them in stockholders' equity as part of other accumulated comprehensive income. Also, when a firm later sells these securities, then the firm realizes the accumulated unrealized gains or losses and includes them in net income.

Using the same events for BHT described previously, and ignoring any income tax effects, we illustrate the treatment that applies when the securities are classified as available for sale by the following journal entries (in thousands), first for 2003:

Securities Available for Sale	500	
Cash		500

Cash	315	
Realized Gain		15
Securities Available for Sale		300

Market Adjustment-Securities Available for Sale	40	
Unrealized Gain-Stockholders' Equity		40

Some accountants maintain that including fluctuations of asset values in net income better reveals the risks to which firms holding marketable securities are, in fact, exposed. However, disclosure of unrealized gains and losses in the statement of changes in stockholders' equity allows financial statement users to determine what net income would have been if these gains and losses had been included. The classification of securities as trading or available for sale is a management decision. Because of the fluctuation in earnings caused by trading securities, many firms classify all equity investments with less than 20 percent ownership as "available for sale."

The only accounting difference between securities classified as available for sale and those as trading (effects on deferred income taxes held aside) is that a firm treats unrealized gains and losses as direct adjustments to stockholders' equity (part of comprehensive income) instead of recognizing them as a component of net income.

BHT records the journal entries for 2004 as:

Cash	90	
Realized Loss	30	
Trading Securities		100
Market Adjustment-Securities Available for Sale		20

Unrealized Gain-Stockholders' Equity	25	
Market Adjustment-Securities Available for Sale		25

As this entry suggests, it is the net cumulative unrealized gain or loss on securities available for sale that is reflected as part of comprehensive income within stockholders' equity.

Exhibit 13.3 provides a real-world example of the accounting treatment of securities available for sale. Further information on changes in marketable

Exhibit 13.3

THE REAL WORLD

Hill Physicians

Marketable Securities:

Marketable securities consist principally of domestic debt and equity securities and money market funds. All marketable securities are classified as available for sale and are available to support current operations or to take advantage of other investment opportunities. These securities are stated at estimated fair market value based upon market quotes. Unrealized gains and losses are computed on the basis of specific identification and are included in shareholders' equity. Realized gains and losses are included in investment income in the accompanying statements of operations.

3. Marketable Securities

The composition of marketable securities, based on quoted market prices at December 31, 2001 and 2000, is as follows (in thousands):

| | 2001 | | 2000 | |
	Cost	Fair Value	Cost	Fair Value
Money market funds	$ 65	$ 65	$ 1,099	$ 1,099
Marketable equity securities	11,896	9,328	8,815	7,748
Marketable preferred stock	–	–	2,739	2,775
Marketable debt securities	7,065	6,944	5,649	5,645
Total	$19,026	$16,337	$18,302	$17,267

securities, available from Hill Physicians' Statement of Cash Flows and Statement of Changes in Stockholders' Equity, includes (in thousands) purchases of marketable securities, $14,774; proceeds from sales of marketable securities, $14,078; realized gain on sale of marketable securities, $28; and unrealized Loss on marketable securities, $1,654. We use this information to reconstruct the following summary journal entries for 2001 (in thousands):

Marketable Securities	14,774	
Cash		14,774

Cash	14,078	
Marketable Securities		14,050
Realized Gain		28

Unrealized Loss-Stockholders' Equity	1,654	
Marketable Securities		1,654

The realized gain is measured relative to original cost. We infer that the entry to record unrealized losses is net of the reversal of the implicit market adjustment balance that pertains to those securities that were sold. This treatment of a realized gain or loss differs from that for trading securities where, as mentioned previously, a firm measures any realized gain or loss relative to book value inclusive of market adjustments. Further, a firm reports any unrealized gains or losses on marketable securities available for sale, net of their income tax effect, as changes in comprehensive income within the statement of changes in stockholders' equity. However, in the case of Hill Physicians for 2001 (Exhibit 13.3), there were no income tax effects due to carryforward operating losses in that year. Carryforward losses imply that current income can be offset against previous tax losses, resulting in no taxes being paid.

NONMARKETABLE SECURITIES

Some firms make minority investments in equity securities of private companies, for which no market price exists. In these cases, a firm values the investments at cost (equivalent to fair value at the time of acquisition), reduced by what appear to be relatively permanent declines in fair value below cost. It may be difficult to determine costs in these cases, such as when Amazon acquired securities in barter transactions (see the chapter opener). Here, firms usually follow the general rule for asset exchanges (described in Chapter 9): employ the fair value of assets surrendered or the fair value of assets acquired, whichever is more objectively determinable. However, as noted earlier, Amazon traded future services for securities and applied valuation techniques such as price/earnings multiples of comparable companies or present values of discounted cash flows to estimate fair value.

VALUATION AND MARKETABLE SECURITIES

An interesting issue is how to deal with nonoperating assets, such as marketable securities, in valuing the firm. One approach separates marketable securities from operating assets for valuation purposes. Under this approach, the firm is valued as two components. The projected future free cash flows from operations, excluding interest or dividends received from investments in marketable securities, are used to value the operating component. The market value of marketable securities is then added to the present value of those free cash flows to estimate the value of the firm as a whole. Another approach reduces outstanding debt by the market value of marketable securities as if the firm used the marketable securities for this purpose. Yet another approach assumes that a firm converts marketable securities into cash, which the firm then uses to distribute a special dividend. The value of the firm would include this dividend.

ACTIVE MINORITY INVESTMENTS

Recall that active minority investments allow a firm sufficient ownership to influence the investment, production, and financing policies of the company in which it invests. The ability to influence these policies, however, raises the possibility of income manipulation, if income of the investing company for accounting purposes is measured by dividends received from the investee as it would be if the investment were valued at cost. Moreover, recall that ownership at these levels is presumed to be strategic and long-term in nature. As a result, temporary fluctuations in market value that would be measured under the mark-to-market method are not relevant for accounting purposes for active minority investments. Therefore, a different method of income recognition is needed for active minority investments.

To account for active minority investments, firms use the **equity method.** Under this method, a firm values the investment at cost, plus the investing company's share of undistributed earnings (earnings less dividends) reported by the investee. The firm increases its investment and recognizes income in the amount of the investing company's ownership percentage, multiplied by the net income reported by the investee. The firm decreases its investment by dividends received from the investee. Note that under the equity method dividends received do not affect the investing company's net income.

In many cases, the investing company pays more than the book value for its percentage interest in the investee. The reason for this is that the market value of the shares reflects the market value of the assets, less liabilities of the investee. The investee's book value likely reflects historical costs (especially for fixed assets) and may not reflect many intangible assets that provide value. Because reported income by the investee does not reflect these additional values, the investor must amortize the amount that it paid in excess of book value over time. Therefore, in addition to recognizing the investor's percentage of the investee's income, the firm also recognizes the amortization of the excess value. This amortization reduces the carrying value of the investment as well as net income reported.

Exhibit 13.4 illustrates accounting for equity method investments (called Associated Companies in its report) obtained from Lee Enterprises' 2001 annual report. The disclosure includes excerpts from Lee's balance sheet, statement of income, and statement of cash flows, respectively. Comparing "Equity in net income of Associated Companies" of $7,651 (all numbers in thousands) from the statement of income with "Distributions less than earnings of Associated Companies" of ($552), we deduce that dividends received from Associated Companies must be ($7,651 − 552) $7,099.

With no changes in the purchase or sale of shares of stock in associated companies, Lee Enterprises should have shown a net increase in its investment account for Associated Companies of $552. However, note the net decrease in the asset "Investment-Associated companies" of $215 ($18,940 − 19,155). During 2001, Lee evidently sold some of its shares in Associated Companies. While not explicitly disclosed, we deduce that Lee removed $767 ($552 + 215) from the account. In the journal entries that follow, we assume that Lee sold this investment for exactly the carrying value, as the firm reported no gain or loss for this item in the income statement. Note that if we remove the $767 from the account, the remaining net change in the account is an increase of $552. This is exactly the difference between the earnings from the Associated Companies and the dividends received. Finally, note the receivable from Associated Companies in the balance sheet. This receivable results from Associated Companies' unpaid dividends. Reconstructing journal entries (in thousands) to summarize these transactions, we have the following:

Recognition of income:

Investments in Associated Companies	7,651	
Equity in Net Income of Associated Companies		7,651

Exhibit 13.4

THE REAL WORLD

Lee Enterprises

(Thousands) September 30	2001	2000	
Receivable from associated companies	1,500	1,500	
Investments:			
Associated companies	18,940	19,155	
Other	13,585	15,021	
	32,525	34,176	

Year Ended September 30	2001	2000	1999
Operating revenue:			
Advertising	$284,124	$276,213	$264,392
Circulation	82,128	80,468	83,102
Other	67,250	65,455	57,114
Equity in net income of associated companies	7,651	9,377	9,238
	441,153	431,513	413,846

Year Ended September 30	2001	2000	1999
Cash provided by operating activities:			
Net income	$314,228	$ 83,663	$ 67,973
Less: discontinued operations	254,771	13,788	11,152
Income from continuing operations	59,457	69,875	56,821
Adjustments to reconcile income from continuing operations to net cash provided by operating activities of continuing operations:			
Depreciation and amortization	32,158	29,326	27,586
Losses (gains) on sales, or expected sales, of assets	6,233	(18,439)	(738)
Distributions less than earnings of associated companies	(552)	(2,891)	(2,220)
Change in assets and liabilities, net of effects from business acquisitions:			
Decrease (increase) in receivables	(654)	2,422	(3,491)
Decrease (increase) in inventories and other	113	3,751	(1,218)
Increase (decrease) in accounts payable, accrued expenses, and unearned income	(5,232)	8,357	(1,620)
Increase (decrease) in income taxes payable	6,449	2,421	(1,097)
Other	9,192	8,376	3,197
Net cash provided by operating activities	107,164	103,198	77,220

Recognition of dividends:

Cash (or Dividends Receivable)	7,099	
Investments in Associated Companies		7,099

Researchers found that adjustments to current year's earnings by firms required to adopt the equity method in place of the cost method positively correlated with both market price reactions to preliminary earnings announcements and analysts' forecast errors. This suggests that analysts did not previously learn that information from other sources (see Ricks and Hughes, *The Accounting Review*, 1985).

Recognition of sale of investment in Associated Companies (assuming sold at book value):

Cash	767	
Investment in Associated Companies		767

Some years ago, firms chose between the equity method of accounting for active minority investments and the cost method. Under the cost method, a firm made no entry to record its equity in the reported net income of affiliates. The dividends received were credited to an income account and included in net income. The FASB eliminated the cost method because it thought that the equity method provided more relevant information for investors and was less susceptible to earnings manipulation.

Some analysts have criticized companies who invest in companies and avoid consolidation by holding just slightly less than a controlling interest. Although the equity method does report earnings of the investee in proportion to the investment held, it suppresses disclosure of the assets and liabilities of the investee by netting these together in an investment account. This account provides no detail regarding the underlying assets and liabilities of the investee, leading some analysts to argue that companies heavily invested in equity method investees are hiding their underlying risk. An excerpt from the balance sheet of Coca-Cola, Inc. as of March 31, 2004 is shown in Exhibit 13.5 illustrates a typical disclosure.

Coca-Cola's equity method investments are over $5 billion and constitute over 23 percent of Coca-Cola's total assets. However, the assets and liabilities of these investments are not separately reflected in Coca-Cola's balance sheet. To the extent that the equity investments are also publicly traded (as is Coca-Cola Enterprises, Inc.), it is possible to recreate the balance sheet of Coca-Cola reflecting the investment on a pro forma consolidated basis. In addition, footnote disclosures of major asset and liability categories are provided by Coca-Cola in its footnotes.

Exhibit 13.5
Coca-Cola Disclosure of
Equity Method Investments

THE REAL WORLD

Coca-Cola, Inc.

Investments and Other Assets	3/31/2004
Equity method investments:	
Coca-Cola Enterprises, Inc.	1,347
Coca-Cola Hellenic Bottling Company S.A.	999
Coca-Cola FEMSA, S.A. de C.V.	691
Coca-Cola Amatil Limited	693
Other, principally bottling companies	1,619
Cost method investments, principally bottling companies	326
Other assets	3,281
	8,956

MAJORITY INVESTMENTS

As mentioned previously, majority investments are those in which the investing firm obtains over 50 percent of the voting common stock of the investee company. We often refer to the former as the *acquiring firm* and the latter as the *acquired firm*. These levels of investment imply control in that the acquiring firm's stockholders can dictate the acquired firm's activities through their ability to elect the latter firm's board of directors.

Frequently, majority investments involve acquiring 100 percent of the voting common stock. From an economic perspective, a controlling interest suggests that the firms involved are essentially a single entity. Accordingly, it is not surprising that GAAP requires that a single set of **consolidated financial statements** be prepared to reflect the financial position and changes in financial position of the combined entity as if it were one company.

Until 2002, firms used one of two accounting methods for majority investments: the purchase method and pooling method. At present, GAAP allows only the purchase method (although we discuss the pooling method below). Under the **purchase method,** a firm initially treats the investment as any other purchase of assets or stock. It is an exchange transaction for accounting purposes. The firm initially records the investment at its acquisition cost. If the investment is in the form of securities issued by the acquiring firm, the cost depends on the fair value of those securities. In turn, fair value reflects the market value, when a market exists in which those securities are actively traded. If the securities are not publicly traded, then the acquiring firm estimates fair value using suitable valuation techniques (see Chapter 14).

Exhibit 13.6 illustrates such an acquisition. In reading this announcement, the $780 (all amounts in millions) is the value of the assets Penn National acquired, except for Hollywood Casino's cash of $136. Therefore, the total assets acquired are $916 ($780 + 136). Penn National also agreed to take on the debt of Hollywood Casino. Therefore, the net amount that it paid is approximately $347 ($916 − 569). Penn National might record the purchase (in millions) as follows:

Investment in Subsidiary Company	347	
Cash		347

Exhibit 13.6

THE REAL WORLD

Penn National Gaming

Penn National Gaming, Inc. (PENN: Nasdaq) announced today that it has entered into a definitive agreement to acquire Hollywood Casino Corporation (HWD: AMEX) for total consideration of approximately $780 million. The total consideration is net of Hollywood Casino's cash and cash equivalents of approximately $136 million and includes approximately $569 million of long-term debt of Hollywood Casino and its subsidiaries. Under the terms of the agreement, Hollywood Casino will merge with a wholly-owned subsidiary of Penn National, and Hollywood Casino stockholders will receive cash in the amount of $12.75 per share at closing.

Exhibit 13.7
Breakdown of Purchase Price
in Business Acquisitions

Book value of net assets acquired
+ Markup of assets to fair value
= Fair value of net assets acquired
+ Excess of purchase price over fair value of net assets acquired, i.e., *goodwill*
= Purchase price of net assets acquired

Penn National must prepare consolidated financial statements for future financial reports. In place of the asset "Investment in Subsidiary Company," Penn National's consolidated balance sheet will include the assets and liabilities of Hollywood Casino.

SFAS No. 141 (FASB, SFAS No. 141, 2001) requires use of the purchase method for business combinations. Upon acquisition, a firm assigns the purchase price to the net assets acquired. The firm values specific assets at their fair values. Fair values may exceed book values of the acquired company, thus implying that depreciation charges in the future may be higher for the combined company than for the acquired company. Recall from Chapter 11 that any excess of the purchase price paid over the fair value of the net assets acquired is referred to as *goodwill*. Exhibit 13.7 provides a schedule showing the usual breakdown of the purchase price in a business acquisition.

Among the assets acquired may be intangibles that were not previously reported as assets by the acquired company. Some of these intangibles may be amenable to a reliable estimate of their fair value. If so, then the acquiring firm allocates part of the purchase price to those assets. For example, Exhibit 13.8 provides an excerpt from Abbot Laboratories' 2001 annual report, describing

Exhibit 13.8

THE REAL WORLD

Abbot Laboratories

On March 2, 2001, Abbott acquired, for cash, the pharmaceutical business of BASF, which includes the global operations of Knoll Pharmaceuticals, for approximately $7.2 billion. This acquisition was financed primarily with short- and long-term borrowings. The acquisition is accounted for under the purchase method of accounting. The allocation of the acquisition cost is as follows (in billions of dollars):

Acquired intangible assets, primarily product rights for currently marketed products	$3.5
Goodwill	2.4
Acquired in-process research and development	1.2
Deferred income taxes resulting primarily from nondeductible intangibles	(0.4)
Acquired net tangible assets	0.5
Total allocation of acquisition cost	$7.2

The acquisition cost has been allocated to intangible assets, goodwill, acquired in-process research and development, and net tangible assets based on an independent appraisal of fair values as of the date of acquisition. Product rights for currently marketed products will be amortized on a straight-line basis over 10 to 16 years (average 13 years), and goodwill was amortized in 2001 on a straight-line basis over 20 years. Acquired in-process research and development was charged to expense in 2001. The net tangible assets acquired consist primarily of property and equipment of approximately $630 million, trade accounts receivable of approximately $402 million, and inventories of approximately $275 million, net of assumed liabilities, primarily trade accounts payable and other liabilities.

its acquisition of Knoll Pharmaceuticals and the accounting treatment that it employed. Note that Abbot allocates the bulk of the purchase price to intangible assets, expensing acquired in-process R&D that has not reached technological feasibility.

SFAS 142 (FASB, SFAS No. 142, 2001) deals with the subsequent accounting treatment of intangible assets and goodwill. Among the specific assets acquired may be intangible assets that are subject to amortization over their economic lives. However, under this relatively new standard, goodwill is no longer subject to amortization. Rather, periodic assessments are made to determine if goodwill has become *impaired*. In general, a long-term asset is viewed as impaired if the sum of the estimated future cash flows from the asset is less than the carrying value of the asset. If the asset meets this test, a firm writes down the asset to its estimated fair market value.

In the case of goodwill, the test for impairment involves estimating the fair value of the entire acquired business unit and comparing that value to its book value at that time. If the fair value is less than the book value, then goodwill may be impaired. The next step is to estimate the fair value of specific assets in the business unit and compare that value to the fair value of the business unit as a whole. The difference is the implied fair value of goodwill. If this amount is less than the book value, then goodwill is written down. Once written down, goodwill is not revalued upward, even if the implied fair value increases in the future.

Although no longer permitted, many firms used the pooling of interests method before the FASB issued SFAS No. 141 (FASB, SFAS No. 141, 2001). The **pooling of interests method** only applied to acquisitions in which the acquiring firm issued shares of stock in exchange for virtually all of the acquired company's shares. Under this method, the assets and liabilities of the acquired firm are recorded at their book values rather than at their fair market values. The pooling method appealed to firms for a variety of reasons, one of which was that no adjustment of asset values to fair values or recognition of goodwill need be made. As a consequence, future earnings were not reduced by additional depreciation or amortization of goodwill. Furthermore, because assets were not revalued upward, the rate of return on assets did not suffer. Note that under the purchase method, assets were generally higher and income in future periods was generally lower, resulting in the return on assets ratio being lower in future years. Partly because of this, some companies went to great lengths to meet the criteria for the pooling of interests method.

Not surprisingly, the elimination of the pooling method was very controversial. Given that the opposition related to the negative effect on the combined companies' earnings of higher depreciation charges and goodwill amortization, a key element in the compromise reflected in the current policies was to change the standards such that goodwill was not to be amortized. An interesting issue is why firms were concerned about what appears to be an entirely cosmetic effect. Analysts could easily track the purchase price of combinations accounted

A case study on AT&T's efforts to meet the criteria for pooling of interests treatment for its acquisition of NCR estimates the cost of actions taken by AT&T in this regard to have been several hundred million dollars (Lys and Vincent, *Journal of Financial Economics*, 1995).

Research has linked the past choice of the pooling method to incentives contained in executive compensation plans and debt covenants. Firm managers recognized the effects that amortization of goodwill was likely to have in lowering their bonuses, as well as the increased probability that the firm might fail to reach a net-worth requirement to avoid technical default on the company's debt (see Aboody, Kasznik, and Williams, *Journal of Accounting and Economics*, 2001).

THINKING GLOBALLY

Pooling of interest continues to be allowed under IASB standards under certain circumstances.

for under the pooling method, and restate earnings as if the purchase method had been used. Nonetheless, by lobbying Congress, the opposition put enough pressure on the FASB and the SEC to force this result.

SPECIAL PURPOSE ENTITIES

We discussed the nature of special purpose entities (SPEs) in Chapter 11. Whether or not to consolidate special purpose entities has been a major issue for accounting regulators, particularly in light of the financial scandals that have plagued companies like Enron that made heavy use of SPEs. Generally, there is a presumption that SPEs should be consolidated unless there is a substantive investment by independent investors and that those investors exercise control over the SPE's affairs.

Meeting the independence requirement means that independent investors cannot be **related parties.** For example, an officer of the parent company is considered a related party. However, the guidelines for determining who is a related party are vague.

The FASB now requires consolidation of most special purpose entities (also called *variable interest entities*). The criteria applied by the FASB is that SPEs must be consolidated in the primary beneficiary's financial statements. This is a departure from the majority ownership criteria. The key issue is determining which entity bears the risks of the entity, not ownership of the voting stock.

SUMMARY AND TRANSITION

In this chapter, we considered accounting treatment of intercorporate investments. These investments can be usefully broken down by the percentage of common stock acquired. If the ownership percentage is less than 20 percent, it is assumed that the investing company does not exercise significant influence over the investee's affairs. Such investments are called passive minority investments. There are three categories of passive minority investments, depending on the intent of the investing company's management. Held to maturity securities are valued at amortized cost. Trading securities are valued at market value. Unrealized gains and losses on trading securities are recognized in net income. Available for sale securities are also valued at market value. However, firms record unrealized gains and losses as direct adjustments to a stockholders' equity account called comprehensive income. Firms measure realized gains and losses relative to original cost.

For investments for which 20 percent to 50 percent of common stock is acquired, it is assumed that the investing company has significant influence over the investee's affairs. Firms account for such investments using the equity method. Under this method, the firm values the investment at cost, plus the investing company's share of the undistributed earnings of the investee company. Accordingly, the firm increases the book value of the investment by the investing company's share of net income reported by the investee company and decreases it by dividends received from the investee company.

Investments in over 50 percent of the investee company's common stock give the investing company control. In these cases, the combination of the two companies is viewed as a single entity for accounting purposes. This means that the acquiring company must prepare consolidated financial statements. In preparing these statements, the acquiring company must employ the purchase method. Under this method, the firm values the net assets of the acquired company, including intangible assets not previously recorded as assets, at their fair value. The firm reports any excess of the purchase price paid over the fair value of the net assets acquired as goodwill. Goodwill is not subject to amortization. Rather, goodwill is periodically reviewed to determine if it has become impaired. Impaired means that the fair value has diminished and the asset should be written down.

APPENDIX CONSOLIDATION

In this appendix, we illustrate in Exhibit 13A.1 how the balance sheets of parties to a hypothetical business combination (Cintas and G&K Services) are consolidated for financial reporting purposes. Assume that Cintas acquires all of the

	Cintas 5/31/2001	G&K Services 6/30/2001	Elimination Entries	Consolidated
Asset				
Current assets:				
Cash and marketable securities	$ 110,229	$ 15,317		$ 125,546
Account receivables	244,450	66,911		311,361
Inventories	214,349	90,085		304,434
Uniforms in service and prepaid expenses	250,642	16,358		267,000
Total current assets	819,670	188,671		1,008,341
Property and equipment, net	702,132	225,965		928,097
Other assets	230,422	205,327	111,533	547,282
Investment in subsidiary	412,800		(412,800)	
Total assets	$2,165,024	$619,963		$2,784,987
Liabilities and Shareholders' Equity				
Liabilities:				
Long-term debt due in one year	$ 20,605	$ 59,220		$ 79,825
Accounts payable	42,495	18,622		61,117
Accrued liabilities	130,100	48,266		178,366
Long-term debt	220,940	163,459		384,399
Deferred taxes	106,769	29,129		135,898
Total liabilities	520,909	318,696		839,605
Shareholders' equity				
Common stock, net of comprehensive loss	469,785	22,295	(22,295)	469,785
Retained earnings	1,174,330	278,972	(278,972)	1,174,330
Total shareholders' equity	1,644,115	301,267		1,945,382
Total liabilities and shareholders' equity	$2,165,024	$619,963		$2,784,987

Exhibit 13A.1
Combined (Consolidated) Balance Sheets ($ in thousands)

common stock of G&K Services, one of its major rivals in the uniform rental business, in return for shares of its own stock. The exchange ratio is one share of Cintas common stock for two shares of G&K Services. This ratio reflects the approximate difference in market prices for their shares in the late spring of 2001. Given a market price of $40 for Cintas' shares, Cintas issues 10,320 shares of its common stock in return for all 20,640 shares of G&K Services outstanding at the time, implying a purchase price of $412,800 (thousand). Cintas records this transaction as follows:

Investment in G&K	412,800	
Common Stock		412,800

The financial statements shown in the first column of Exhibit 13A.1 have already been adjusted to show the effects of this hypothetical transaction.

Comparing the $412,800 to a book value for G&K Services of $301,267, we see that some assets of G&K Services had a fair value higher than their book value and/or that goodwill is involved. For simplicity, we assume that this excess amount is due to goodwill. The amount of goodwill is, therefore, $111,533 ($412,800 − 301,267).

Exhibit 13A.1 depicts the balance sheets of Cintas and G&K Services immediately after acquisition. For illustration purposes, we prepared Cintas' balance sheet as of May 31, 2001 (adjusted for the hypothetical acquisition of the shares of G&K), and G&K Services' balance sheet as of June 30, 2001, even though they differ by one month. If we added the columns for Cintas and G&K together, we would be double accounting for assets, liabilities, and owners' equity. Note that the investment in the G&K account represents 100 percent interest in the assets and liabilities of G&K, thus the double accounting for assets and liabilities. Also, note that the owners' equity accounts for G&K no longer represent outside owners of the company, as Cintas now holds these shares. If they are not eliminated, then we would be double accounting for the ownership interest (Cintas already recorded them in its books). To avoid the double accounting, we need to eliminate the investment in the G&K account as well as the owner's equity accounts of G&K.

To prepare consolidated statements, a firm creates a worksheet such as that shown in Exhibit 13A.1. Here, the financial statements of the parent company (Cintas) and the subsidiary (G&K) would be in the first two columns. A third column includes any adjusting entries to avoid double accounting and to allow for the preparation of the consolidated totals in the last column.

To eliminate the investment in the G&K account as well as the owners' equity accounts of G&K, the following entry is constructed on the worksheet:

Common Stock	22,295	
Retained Earnings	278,972	
Goodwill	111,533	
Investment in G&K		412,800

The elimination of the investment account against the owners' equity accounts does not balance. This difference is the amount that Cintas paid above the book value of the company. Earlier we concluded that this extra amount was due to an intangible asset, goodwill.

Having recognized goodwill in conjunction with the (hypothetical) purchase of G&K Services, Cintas now needs to test annually for possible goodwill impairment. If no impairment occurs, Cintas leaves goodwill unchanged on its consolidated balance sheet. Therefore, the effect of recognizing goodwill in these circumstances would have no effect on Cintas' future earnings.

Under the pooling of interests method, Cintas would have originally recognized the issuance of stock to purchase G&K at the book value of the shares acquired, or $301,267. Therefore, when Cintas constructs the elimination entry under this scenario, no difference occurs between the investment account and the owners' equity accounts, and no goodwill would be created.

END OF CHAPTER MATERIAL

KEY TERMS

Active Minority Ownership

Available for Sale Securities

Consolidated Financial Statements

Equity Method

Held to Maturity Securities

Majority Ownership

Market Adjustment Account

Mark-to-Market

Passive Minority Ownership

Pooling of Interests Method

Purchase Method

Related Parties

Trading Securities

ASSIGNMENT MATERIAL

REVIEW QUESTIONS

1. Describe the categories of investment securities that are identified under current GAAP.

2. Explain the accounting method used to account for available for sale securities.

3. Explain the accounting method used to account for trading securities.

4. Explain the accounting method used to account for held to maturity securities.

5. Explain the difference between the purchase and the pooling of interests methods.

6. Describe the entries made under the equity method.

7. Identify and briefly explain the major reasons a company might want to buy stock in another company.

8. Explain the nature of goodwill and how it arises in the context of an acquisition.

9. Briefly describe the requirements stated in GAAP for the accounting of long-term acquisitions of stock in other companies. In your description, make sure to identify the criteria used to distinguish the various accounting methods.

10. The equity method is sometimes referred to as a one-line consolidation. Explain.

11. Discuss what a consolidation is trying to accomplish.

○ APPLYING YOUR KNOWLEDGE

12. The following transactions relate to the TinCan Company. TinCan closes its books on December 31 each year.

Transaction:

March 25—TinCan purchased 1,500 shares of Meta-Solid Co. at $20 per share. It also paid fees to its stockbroker of $0.20 per share.

June 30—The market value of each share of Meta-Solid was $35.

August 15—Meta-Solid declared a dividend of $0.45 per share.

October 25—TinCan received dividend checks from Meta-Solid Co.

December 31—The market value of each share of Meta-Solid was $30.

February 18—500 shares of Meta-Solid Co. were sold at the prevailing market price of $29.50 per share. Brokerage fees were $0.15 per share.

a. Prepare journal entries for recording all the preceding transactions in the books of TinCan Company:

   1. Assuming that the securities are classified as trading securities.

   2. Assuming that the securities are classified as available for sale.

b. Discuss why management might choose to classify securities as available for sale rather than trading securities.

c. Would you expect the market to respond differently to the classification of the securities as trading securities or available for sale? Why or why not?

13. The Corona Company holds a portfolio of marketable equity securities classified as available for sale. The aggregate cost and market value of the entire portfolio in four years are as follows:

Dates	Aggregate Cost	Aggregate Market Value
Dec 31, 20X1	$250,000	$210,000
Dec 31, 20X2	300,000	280,000
Dec 31, 20X3	320,000	325,000
Dec 31, 20X4	350,000	345,000

Give the necessary journal entries for each year. The accounting period ends on December 31 each year.

14. The following information relates to the investment securities held by Trimex Corporation. The abbreviations used in the chart are HTM (Held to Maturity Securities), TR (Trading Securities), and AFS (Available for Sale Securities).

Security	Acquisition Date	Acquisition Cost	Date Sold	Selling Price	Market Value 12/31		
					19X1	19X2	19X3
A (HTM)	3/13/X1	$ 35,000			$ 38,000	$ 30,000	$33,000
B (TR)	6/24/X1	65,000	5/27/X3	$ 70,000	60,000	67,000	
C (AFS)	8/8/X1	95,000			88,000	100,000	90,000
D (AFS)	10/3/X1	100,000	6/30/X3	105,000	102,000	98,000	

Trimex closes its books on December 31 each year.

a. Make journal entries relating to these investment securities for each year.

b. Show how the investments would be presented on the income statement and balance sheet for each year.

15. The following information relates to the investment securities held by Rodman Corporation. The abbreviations used in the chart are HTM (Held to Maturity Securities), TR (Trading Securities), and AFS (Available for Sale Securities).

Security	Acquisition Date	Acquisition Cost	Date Sold	Selling Price	Market Value 12/31		
					20X4	20X5	20X6
A (AFS)	1/20/X4	$15,000			$12,000	$16,000	$17,500
B (HTM)	3/15/X4	44,000	4/8/X6	$48,000	42,000	45,000	
C (TR)	6/9/X4	65,000			63,000	61,000	68,000
D (TR)	11/12/X4	23,000	4/1/X5	19,000	25,000		

Rodman closes its books on December 31 each year.

a. Make journal entries relating to these investment securities for each year.

b. Show how the investments would be presented on the income statement and balance sheet for each year.

16. The balance sheet for Balderamma Company contained the following information on December 31, 20X2:

Available for Sale Securities (Cost—$100,000) $108,000

During 20X3, Balderamma sold available for sale securities costing $15,000 for $17,000 and purchased new securities for $30,000. As of December 31, 20X3, the market value of its portfolio of available for sale securities was $112,000.

a. Construct the journal entries that Balderamma would make to account for its available for sale securities in 20X3. Indicate how the income statement would be impacted by the transactions in 20X3.

b. How would your answer to part a change if the securities were classified as trading securities?

c. How would these securities be treated on the balance sheet and income statement if they were classified as held to maturity securities?

17. As a stock analyst, how might you adjust the income statement of a company that had all three types of investment securities (i.e., held to maturity, available for sale, and trading) to better reflect the results of the period?

18. Suppose that there is a management compensation plan at the XYZ Company that rewards managers based on achieving a certain level of reported net income. What incentives might management have to influence the assignment of a security to a held to maturity, available for sale, or trading classification?

19. As an auditor, what kind of evidence might you look for to support management's claim that a particular security should be classified as a held to maturity investment?

20. As a board member of the FASB, what arguments could you make to support treating the unrealized gains and losses from trading securities differently from those of available for sale securities?

21. Explain how the equity method works and why, in some cases, managers might prefer it to consolidation.

22. Wilston Company owns 40 percent of Abaco Co. Abaco reported the following information for 2003:

net income $3,000,000; Dividends paid $1,000,000.

Required:

Show the entries that Wilston would report at the end of 2003 related to its investment in Abaco.

USING REAL DATA

23. During 2003, Berkshire Hathaway disclosed the following acquisitions:

On May 23, 2003, Berkshire acquired McLane Company, Inc. (McLane) from Wal-Mart Stores, Inc. for cash consideration of approximately $1.5 billion. McLane is one of the nation's largest wholesale distributors of groceries and nonfood items to convenience stores, wholesale clubs, mass merchandisers, quick service restaurants, theaters, and others.

On August 7, 2003, Berkshire acquired all the outstanding common stock of Clayton Homes, Inc. (Clayton) for cash consideration of approximately $1.7 billion in the aggregate. Clayton is a vertically integrated manufactured housing company with 20 manufacturing plants, 306 company owned stores, 535 independent retailers, 89 manufactured housing communities, and financial services operations that provide mortgage services and insurance protection.

Required:

a. How should Berkshire account for these investments?

b. If these two acquisitions resulted in $650 million worth of goodwill, how would this goodwill affect the income statement in the period of acquisition and in the years subsequent to acquisition?

24. In 2000, Berkshire Hathaway acquired 9.9 percent of the outstanding shares of MidAmerican Energy Holdings Company. In its 2003 annual report,

Berkshire describes this transaction and subsequent acquisition of shares of preferred stock as follows:

> (3) Investments in MidAmerican Energy Holdings Company
>
> On March 14, 2000, Berkshire acquired 900,942 shares of common stock and 34,563,395 shares of convertible preferred stock of MidAmerican Energy Holdings Company (MidAmerican) for $35.05 per share, or approximately $1.24 billion in the aggregate. During March 2002, Berkshire acquired 6,700,000 additional shares of the convertible preferred stock for $402 million. Such investments currently give Berkshire about a 9.9 percent voting interest and an 83.7 percent economic interest in the equity of MidAmerican (80.5 percent on a diluted basis). Since March 2000, Berkshire and certain of its subsidiaries also acquired approximately $1,728 million of 11 percent nontransferable trust preferred securities, of which $150 million were redeemed in August 2003. Mr. Walter Scott, Jr., a member of Berkshire's Board of Directors, controls approximately 88 percent of the voting interest in MidAmerican.

While the convertible preferred stock does not vote generally with the common stock in the election of directors, the convertible preferred stock gives Berkshire the right to elect 20 percent of MidAmerican's Board of Directors. The convertible preferred stock is convertible into common stock only upon the occurrence of specified events, including modification or elimination of the Public Utility Holding Company Act of 1935 so that holding company registration would not be triggered by conversion. Additionally, the prior approval of the holders of convertible preferred stock is required for certain fundamental transactions by MidAmerican. Such transactions include, among others: a) significant asset sales or dispositions; b) merger transactions; c) significant business acquisitions or capital expenditures; d) issuances or repurchases of equity securities; and e) the removal or appointment of the Chief Executive Officer. Through the investments in common and convertible preferred stock of MidAmerican, Berkshire has the ability to exercise significant influence on the operations of MidAmerican.

Condensed consolidated statements of earnings of MidAmerican for each of the three years in the period ending December 31, 2003 are as follows. Amounts are in millions.

	2003	2002	2001
Revenues	$6,145	$4,968	$4,973
Costs and expenses:			
Cost of sales and operating expenses	3,944	3,189	3,522
Depreciation and amortization	610	526	539
Interest expense debt held by Berkshire	184	118	50
Other interest expense	727	640	443
	5,465	4,473	4,554
Earnings before taxes	680	495	419
Income taxes and minority interests	264	115	276
Net earnings	$ 416	$ 380	$ 143

Required:

a. Based on the percentage of ownership in MidAmerican, what method should Berkshire use to account for this investment? Justify your answer.

b. Regardless of your answer to part a, if Berkshire were to use the equity method to account for its investment in MidAmerican, what entries would be made during 2003 to account for this investment? MidAmerican disclosed that it paid preferred dividends of $170.2 million in 2003 and no common stock dividends.

25. In 2003, Berkshire Hathaway provided the following disclosures related to its fixed maturity and equity securities investments:

(4) Investments in fixed maturity securities

Investments in securities with fixed maturities as of December 31, 2003 and 2002 are shown below (in millions).

Dec-31-03	Amortized Cost	Unrealized Gains	Unrealized Losses	Fair Value
Insurance and other:				
Obligations of U.S. Treasury, U.S. government corporations and agencies	$ 2,019	$ 95	($ 5)	$ 2,109
Obligations of states, municipalities, and political subdivisions	4,659	241	0	4,900
Obligations of foreign governments	4,986	80	(26)	5,040
Corporate bonds and redeemable preferred stock	8,677	2,472	(23)	11,126
Mortgage-backed securities	2,802	145	(6)	2,941
	$23,143	$3,033	($60)	$26,116
Finance and financial products, available for sale:				
Obligations of U.S. Treasury, U.S. government corporations and agencies	$ 3,733	$ 320	$ 0	$ 4,053
Corporate bonds	704	79	0	783
Mortgage-backed securities	4,076	180	0	4,256
	$ 8,513	$ 579	$ 0	$ 9,092
Mortgage-backed securities, held to maturity	$ 563	$ 105	$ 0	$ 668

Dec-31-02	Amortized Cost	Unrealized Gains	Unrealized Losses	Fair Value
Insurance and other:				
Obligations of U.S. Treasury, U.S. government corporations and agencies	$ 9,091	$ 966	$ 0	$10,057
Obligations of states, municipalities, and political subdivisions	6,346	280	(1)	6,625
Obligations of foreign governments	3,813	92	(2)	3,903
Corporate bonds and redeemable preferred stock	10,120	1,041	(118)	11,043
Mortgage-backed securities	6,155	321	(8)	6,468
	$35,525	$2,700	($129)	$38,096
Finance and financial products, available for sale:				
Obligations of U.S. Treasury, U.S. government corporations and agencies	$ 3,543	$ 331	$ 0	$ 3,874
Corporate bonds	1,261	40	(10)	1,291
Mortgage-backed securities	10,202	299	0	10,501
	$15,006	$ 670	($ 10)	$15,666
Mortgage-backed securities, held to maturity	$ 1,019	$ 178	$ 0	$ 1,197

(5) Investments in equity securities

Data with respect to investments in equity securities are shown in the following table. Amounts are in millions.

	Cost	Unrealized Gains	Fair Value
Dec–31–03			
Common stock of:			
American Express Company	$1,470	$5,842	$ 7,312
The Coca-Cola Company	1,299	8,851	10,150
The Gillette Company	600	2,926	3,526
Wells Fargo & Company	463	2,861	3,324
Other equity securities	4,683	6,292	10,975
	$8,515	$26,772	$35,287
Dec–31–02			
Common stock of:			
American Express Company	$1,470	$ 3,889	$ 5,359
The Coca-Cola Company	1,299	7,469	8,768
The Gillette Company	600	2,315	2,915
Wells Fargo & Company	306	2,191	2,497
Other equity securities	5,489	3,335	8,824
	$9,164	$19,199	$28,363

(6) Realized investment gains (losses)

Realized investment gains (losses) are summarized in the following table (in millions).

	2003	2002	2001
Fixed maturity securities			
Gross realized gains	$2,715	$997	$ 536
Gross realized losses	−129	−287	−201
Equity securities and other			
Gross realized gains	2,033	791	1,522
Gross realized losses	−490	−583	−369
	$4,129	$918	$1,488

Required:

a. What amounts of gains and losses should appear on the income statement during 2003 related to the company's investments?

b. What amounts of unrealized gains and losses should appear in other comprehensive income in 2003?

c. What effect would the unrealized gains and losses have had on income in 2003 were they to be reported in net income? The reported net income in 2003 for Berkshire was $8,151 (million).

26. In 1990 Berkshire Hathaway had an investment in GEICO Corporation representing 48 percent of the voting rights of all GEICO shares outstanding at December 31, 1990. As described in a footnote to the annual report, Berkshire was precluded from voting its shares, and no officer or director was permitted to serve as a director of GEICO under an order of GEICO's domiciliary insurance supervisory authority. Berkshire accounted for its investment under the cost method (equivalent to the mark to market method in 2003). Justify Berkshire's method of accounting for its investment in GEICO in 1990.

27. In 2002, Craftmade International, Inc. changed the way it accounted for its two 50 percent-owned investees—Design Trends and PHI—to using the equity method of accounting rather than consolidation. Following you will find the original balance sheet and income statement from the 2001 annual report as well as the restated amounts.

Required:

a. Describe the effect of the change from the consolidation method to the equity method on the balance sheet and income statement.

b. Calculate the effect of the change on the debt/equity ratio of the company.

c. Calculate the effect of the change on the ROE and ROA of the company.

CRAFTMADE INTERNATIONAL, INC. Balance Sheet		
	06/30/2001	06/30/2000
Current assets:		
Cash	$ 1,638,000	$ 1,171,000
Accounts receivable, net of allowance of $150,000 and $236,000, respectively	19,215,000	17,610,000
Inventory	19,454,000	15,322,000
Deferred income taxes	758,000	462,000
Prepaid expenses and other current assets	1,149,000	918,000
Total current assets	42,214,000	35,483,000
Property and equipment, at cost:		
Land	1,535,000	1,535,000
Building	7,784,000	7,784,000
Office furniture, equipment, and other	5,651,000	2,297,000
Leasehold improvements	273,000	257,000
Total property and equipment, at cost	15,243,000	11,873,000
Less: accumulated depreciation	(3,102,000)	(2,410,000)
Total property and equipment, net	12,141,000	9,463,000
Other assets	39,000	24,000
Goodwill, net of accumulated amortization of 1,204,000 and 808,000, respectively	4,735,000	5,131,000
Total noncurrent assets	16,915,000	14,618,000
	$59,129,000	$50,101,000
Current liabilities:		
Note payable, current	$ 512,000	$ 470,000
Revolving lines of credit	20,600,000	17,600,000
Accounts payable	6,551,000	4,179,000

	06/30/2001	06/30/2000
Commissions payable	455,000	422,000
Income taxes payable	934,000	10,000
Accrued liabilities	2,929,000	1,540,000
Total current liabilities	31,981,000	24,221,000
Other noncurrent liabilities:		
Deferred income taxes	241,000	88,000
Note payable, long-term	8,076,000	8,588,000
Minority interest	1,049,000	245,000
Total liabilities	41,347,000	33,142,000
Stockholders' equity:		
Series A cumulative, convertible, callable preferred stock, $1.00 par value, 2,000,000 shares authorized; 32,000 shares issued	32,000	32,000
Common stock, $.01 par value, 15,000,000 shares authorized, 9,326,535 and 9,316,535 shares issued, respectively	93,000	93,000
Additional paid-in capital	12,683,000	12,453,000
Unearned deferred compensation	(108,000)	0
Retained earnings	25,886,000	22,654,000
Accumulated other comprehensive income	28,000	0
	38,614,000	35,232,000
Less: treasury stock, 3,429,477 and 3,116,177 common shares at cost, respectively, and 32,000 preferred shares at cost	(20,832,000)	(18,273,000)
Total stockholders' equity	17,782,000	16,959,000
Total liabilities and stockholders' equity	$59,129,000	$50,101,000

CRAFTMADE INTERNATIONAL, INC.
Income Statement

	06/30/2001	06/30/2000	06/30/1999
Net sales	$93,477,000	$85,499,000	$84,986,000
Cost of goods sold	63,120,000	59,182,000	57,862,000
Gross profit	30,357,000	26,317,000	27,124,000
Selling, general, and administrative expenses	17,598,000	15,787,000	15,051,000
Depreciation and amortization	1,088,000	874,000	805,000
Operating profit	11,671,000	9,656,000	11,268,000
Interest expense, net	2,219,000	1,645,000	1,293,000
Income before income taxes and minority interest	9,452,000	8,011,000	9,975,000
Provision for income taxes	2,811,000	2,583,000	3,336,000
	6,641,000	5,428,000	6,639,000
Minority interest	(1,954,000)	(1,148,000)	(950,000)
Net income	$ 4,687,000	$ 4,280,000	$ 5,689,000

CRAFTMADE INTERNATIONAL, INC.
Balance Sheet (Restated)

	06/30/2001	06/30/2000
Current assets:		
Cash	$ 723,000	$ 1,065,000
Accounts receivable, net of allowance of		
$150,000 and $236,000, respectively	13,308,000	15,857,000
Receivables from 50% owned investees	8,271,000	643,000
Inventory	12,650,000	12,776,000
Deferred income taxes	758,000	462,000
Prepaid expenses and other current assets	1,158,000	915,000
Total current assets	36,868,000	31,718,000
Property and equipment, net		
Land	1,535,000	1,535,000
Building	7,784,000	7,784,000
Office furniture and equipment	2,998,000	2,253,000
Leasehold improvements	253,000	237,000
	12,570,000	11,809,000
Less: accumulated depreciation	(2,900,000)	(2,397,000)
Total property and equipment, net	9,670,000	9,412,000
Goodwill, net of accumulated amortization of		
$1,204,000 and $808,000, respectively	4,735,000	5,131,000
Investment in 50% owned investees	1,049,000	255,000
Other assets	39,000	24,000
Total other assets	5,823,000	5,410,000
Total assets	$52,361,000	$46,540,000
Current liabilities:		
Note payable, current	$ 512,000	$ 474,000
Revolving line of credit	18,800,000	15,600,000
Accounts payable	4,124,000	3,104,000
Commissions payable	301,000	380,000
Income taxes payable	719,000	10,000
Accrued liabilities	1,806,000	1,337,000
Total current liabilities	26,262,000	20,905,000
Other noncurrent liabilities:		
Deferred income taxes	241,000	88,000
Note payable, long-term	8,076,000	8,588,000
Total liabilities	34,579,000	29,581,000
Stockholders' equity:		
Series A cumulative, convertible callable		
preferred stock, $1.00 par value, 2,000,000		
shares authorized; 32,000 shares issued	32,000	32,000
Common stock, $.01 par value, 15,000,000		
shares authorized, 9,326,535 and 9,316,535		
shares issued, respectively	93,000	93,000
Additional paid-in capital	12,683,000	12,453,000
Unearned deferred compensation	(108,000)	0
Retained earnings	25,886,000	22,654,000
Accumulated other comp. income	28,000	0
	38,614,000	35,232,000

	06/30/2001	06/30/2000
Less: treasury stock, 3,429,477 and 3,116,177 common shares at cost, and 32,000 preferred shares at cost	(20,832,000)	(18,273,000)
Total stockholders' equity	17,782,000	16,959,000
Total liabilities and stockholders' equity	$52,361,000	$46,540,000

CRAFTMADE INTERNATIONAL, INC.
Income Statement (Restated)

	06/30/2001	06/30/2000	06/30/1999
Net sales	$71,107,000	$75,098,000	$75,659,000
Cost of goods sold	48,727,000	53,070,000	52,235,000
Gross profit	22,380,000	22,028,000	23,424,000
Selling, general, and administrative expenses	14,235,000	13,955,000	13,396,000
Interest expense, net	1,786,000	1,494,000	1,154,000
Depreciation and amortization	899,000	867,000	798,000
Total Expenses	16,920,000	16,316,000	15,348,000
Income before equity in earnings of 50% owned investees and income taxes	5,460,000	5,712,000	8,076,000
Equity in earnings of 50% owned investees before income taxes	2,038,000	1,151,000	949,000
Income before income taxes	7,498,000	6,863,000	9,025,000
Provision for income taxes	2,811,000	2,583,000	3,336,000
Net income	$ 4,687,000	$ 4,280,000	$ 5,689,000

28. In March 2004, Service Corporation International (the world's largest provider of funeral and cemetery services) sold its funeral operations in France and then purchased a 25 percent equity interest in the acquiring company.

    Required:

    a. How should the company have accounted for its operation in France prior to the sale?

    b. How should the company account for its interest in the acquiring company after the sale?

29. In April 2004, Webb Interactive Services, Inc. sold a strategic interest in its primary subsidiary, Jabber. This transaction reduced Webb's interest in the company to 43 percent.

    Required:

    a. How should the company account for its investment in Jabber subsequent to the acquisition?

b. What effect will the accounting proposed in part a have on the balance sheet and income statement of Webb?

○ BEYOND THE BOOK

30. Obtain the financial statements for an insurance company or a bank and answer the following questions:

    a. What fraction of the assets of the company is in investments?

    b. What fraction of the investments is in securities that are classified as held to maturity, trading, and available for sale?

    c. What were the unrealized gains/losses for the company contained in the income statement?

    d. What were the unrealized gains/losses for the company contained in the other comprehensive income account?

    e. If the unrealized gains/losses for available for sale securities were to be included in the income statement, how would it have affected reported net income in the most recent period?

31. Go to the March 31, 2004 financial statements of Coca-Cola, Inc. and Coca-Cola Enterprises. Also find the stock price of each.

    a. Determine the market value of Coca-Cola's investment in Coca-Cola Enterprises as of December 31, 2003. How closely does the reported amount of Coca-Cola's investment in Coca-Cola Enterprises come to the market value?

    b. Does Coca-Cola's balance sheet reflect the risk of its underlying assets and liabilities? Why or why not?

CHAPTER 14

Introduction to Valuation Analysis

LEARNING OBJECTIVES

After reading this chapter, you should be able to:

1 Describe the projection of future financial statements based on operating forecasts.

2 Discuss the relationship between pro forma cash flow statements and changes in pro forma balance sheets.

3 Identify and apply the principal elements of the discounted cash flow (DCF) method of valuing equity.

4 Identify and apply the principal elements of the residual income (RI) method of valuing equity.

Many market observers believe that the substantial decline of market indexes in the years after 2000 (see Exhibit 14.1) resulted from inflated stock prices prior to the collapse of many Internet stocks. Some attribute the inflated stock prices before the decline, as Federal Reserve Chairman Alan Greenspan notes, to "irrational exuberance." The strong bull market of the 1990s seems to have been based, in part, on unrealistic expectations of future growth. Some contend that prices during this period reflected hype by stockbrokers and financial analysts, rather than fundamentals. *Fundamentals* refers to the economic and business factors that create value. An analysis of fundamentals begins with operating, investment, and financing data contained in a firm's financial statements. Using this data, along with their knowledge of the company and its industry, analysts may project pro forma financial statements from which they draw inputs to valuation methods. In this chapter, we consider how to estimate the value of a firm's equity from fundamental analysis.

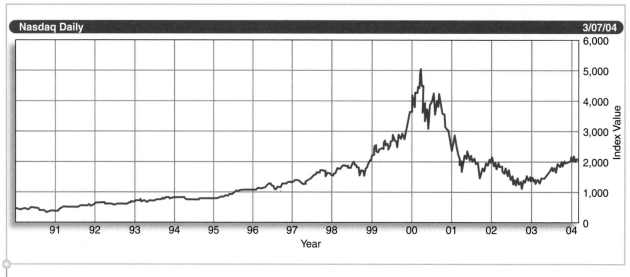

Exhibit 14.1

THE REAL WORLD

Nasdaq Composite
Index

OVERVIEW OF FUNDAMENTAL ANALYSIS METHODS

In this book, we underscore the main theme underlying the development of financial accounting: the use of financial accounting data in valuing (stockholders') equity. Analysts often use two approaches in valuing equity, the **discounted cash flow (DCF)** and **residual income (RI)** methods. Both approaches are consistent with valuing equity as the present value of its expected future dividends over the firm's entire remaining life. RI analysis focuses on accounting measures of earnings and book value taken directly from financial statements. As a result, although DCF analysis is the traditional approach, RI analysis continues to grow in popularity.

Both the DCF and RI approaches begin with the generation of **pro forma financial statements** over an appropriate time horizon, based on operating forecasts (such as those described in Chapter 6) and related predictions of investment and financing activities. Both approaches make use of pro forma income statements, balance sheets, and cash flow statements. Let's take a look at the construction of these pro forma statements.

PRO FORMA FINANCIAL STATEMENTS

PRO FORMA INCOME STATEMENTS

We begin by discussing typical assumptions made in forecasting the components of the pro forma income statement. Exhibit 14.2 shows the basic formulas used.

Exhibit 14.2
Pro Forma Income Statement

Sales (Forecast)

  − Cost of Goods Sold, Net of Depreciation (Percent of Sales)

  − Depreciation (Rate × Average Net PP&E)

  − Operating Expenses (Percent of Sales)

  − Interest Expense (Rate × Average Debt Outstanding)

Income before Taxes

Provision for Income Taxes (Rate × Income before Taxes)

Net Income

Sales Forecasting

The forecasting of sales plays a key role in pro forma statements. Many other income statement items (as well as balance sheet items) are often forecasted as a percentage of sales. Recall from Chapter 6 the techniques used to forecast sales, such as those that involve extrapolating recent trends.

Operating Expense Forecasting

Forecasting cost of goods sold and operating expenses often depends on historical percentages of sales, such as those found on common-size statements described in Chapter 6. However, depreciation expense is actually more closely aligned with the level of investment in property, plant, and equipment (PP&E) than the level of sales.

Depreciation is often embedded in the cost of goods sold (manufacturing firm) or in selling, general and administrative (SG&A) expense (retailer). As a result, the income statement often fails to itemize depreciation expense. Remember, however, that depreciation often appears on a firm's cash flow statement as an addback to net income in determining net cash from operations. One way to deal with this difficulty, therefore, is to remove depreciation from either cost of goods sold or SG&A as appropriate and then forecast the depreciation component separately. Notice in Exhibit 14.2 that cost of goods sold is stated net of depreciation for this reason. Manufacturing companies pose a particular challenge in forecasting depreciation as some depreciation cost may be capitalized in inventory.

> The percentages used in projecting cost of goods sold and operating expenses may be assumed to change over future years within the forecast horizon. For example, a firm may become more efficient over time, implying a decline in these percentages.

Depreciation Forecasting

Before we can forecast future depreciation, we need to project the levels of investment in PP&E, net of accumulated depreciation, upon which depreciation charges are usually based. (We discuss forecasting the level of net PP&E later in the chapter.) However, once we make that forecast, we assume the amount of depreciation expense to be a fixed percentage of the average balance of net PP&E during the forecast year. This common approach is consistent with a firm utilizing a declining balance method of depreciation (described in Chapter 9).

Interest Expense Forecasting

Similar to depreciation, projecting future interest expense first requires that we project future debt levels and estimate an effective interest rate. We estimate the effective interest rate from past interest charges, as a percent of past debt levels, or from footnote data on borrowing rates. (We discuss the forecasting of debt levels later in this chapter.)

Tax Expense Forecasting

Forecasting future income tax expense requires determining an effective tax rate to be applied to future income before taxes. We base the effective tax rate for this purpose on past income tax expense divided by income before income taxes, or an effective tax rate provided by footnote data.

Other Forecasting Items

We omit research and development (R&D) costs in our illustration. While these costs could also be projected based on sales, they are often not expected to change smoothly with sales. Accordingly, in some cases it might be more appropriate to forecast R&D costs as lump sums based on some historical pattern of their appearance on the income statement.

Past income statements also may include transitory components such as restructuring charges, discontinued operations, extraordinary items, and cumulative effects of accounting changes. These items are not expected to recur. Thus, we do not factor them into a forecast of future results.

PRO FORMA BALANCE SHEETS

In projecting future balance sheets, analysts commonly assume that required cash, current operating assets, net PP&E, and operating liabilities will each grow in fixed proportions to sales or revenues. As a result, we can work from the firm's balance sheet at the start of the forecast horizon, determine percentage relationships between the total account balances for each of these categories and sales, apply those percentages to future sales, and project changes in those totals (see Exhibit 14.3). Further, as we will discuss later in this section and as Exhibit 14.3 shows, analysts also often assume that debt remains a fixed proportion of net assets (net assets in this case refers to total assets less operating liabilities). Owners' equity then becomes a plug figure to balance the accounting equation.

Exhibit 14.3
Pro Forma Balance Sheet

Cash (Percent of Sales)

Current Operating Assets (Percent of Sales)

PP&E, Net (Percent of Sales)

Total Assets

Operating Liabilities (Percent of Sales)

Deferred Income Taxes (Percent of Sales)

Debt (Percent of Total Assets Less Operating Liabilities)

Stockholders' Equity

Total Liabilities and Stockholders' Equity

Plant, Property and Equipment

While we forecast net PP&E as a percentage of sales, we break down the projected change into two elements: depreciation that reduces net PP&E and capital expenditures that increase net PP&E. As discussed earlier, we assume that depreciation will be a fixed percentage of the average balance of net PP&E. Note that to estimate the historical depreciation rate, we need to know depreciation from at least the past year, and the beginning as well as the ending balance of net PP&E for that year.

Once we estimate the depreciation rate, we can apply it to the average of the beginning and ending balance of net PP&E for the past year to determine depreciation for the next (future) year. In turn, we determine capital expenditures for the year by subtracting depreciation from the ending balance of PP&E for the past year, and then subtracting the result from the projected ending balance for the next year. Or, we can add projected depreciation to the projected change in the balance of net PP&E (based on a percentage of sales) to determine projected capital expenditures.

Alternative Assumptions

Although it is convenient to project many operating assets and operating liabilities as percentages of sales or revenue, other possible assumptions may be made. For example, we can project inventories based on inventory turnover ratios involving cost of goods sold rather than sales. Property, plant, and equipment may not be projected to grow as smoothly as sales increase. Capital expenditures may be uneven over time. Even if sales are the principal driver of working capital and PP&E, the percentages may decline as the firm experiences economies of scale. Therefore, the appropriate assumptions depend on a careful analysis of past behavior and future plans.

Cash Forecasting

In some cases, a firm may have a large cash balance relative to the liquidity needs of its operating activities. It is generally inappropriate to assume that these large balances will persist indefinitely into the future. Instead, analysts make various assumptions concerning the treatment of such excess cash. One possibility simply assumes that a firm will reduce cash early in the forecast horizon, returning the excess cash to stockholders as dividends or stock repurchases. In this case the change in stockholders' equity on successive balance sheets should reconcile with the difference between net income and dividends on the intervening cash flow statements.

Effects of Intercorporate Investments

The presence of intercorporate investments poses many issues for the creation of pro forma financial statements. Recall from Chapter 13 that a firm may treat these investments as marketable securities under the mark-to-market method, as equity method investments, or eliminate them during the preparation of consolidated statements depending on the firm's ownership percentage. Under mark-to-market treatment, the current book value reflects the present value of future cash flows to be derived from such investments, suggesting that analysts consider these assets apart from the rest of the firm. For investments accounted for under the equity method, however, projecting future income and dividends in arriving at estimates of future value is more uncertain. Finally, with respect to investments leading to consolidation treatment, acquisitions often result in the creation of goodwill. Current accounting policy treats goodwill arising from such mergers and acquisitions as an asset not subject to amortization. Accordingly, it may be suitable to hold goodwill constant in future years, unless future mergers and acquisitions are projected. In that case, analysts would need an understanding of the firm's acquisition strategy.

Debt Forecasting

The mix of debt and stockholders' equity is referred to as the firm's **capital structure.** Capital structure affects the risk that stockholders face and hence the expected return they require to bear that risk. Analysts usually assume that the cost of equity capital is constant, implying a constant debt-to-total-capital (debt plus equity) ratio, where debt and equity are expressed in market value terms. Because both the DCF and RI valuation methods produce estimates that may differ from market values, the ratio of debt to total capital should be measured based on their relative estimated values in applying these methods. However, a common convention is to maintain a constant ratio in terms of book values of debt and equity. (We will revisit this issue later in the context of an example.)

As we indicated earlier in the forecasting of interest expense, once we forecast future debt levels, we can project future interest expense by determining the firm's interest rate from past interest expense as a percentage of average debt outstanding, and multiplying that rate by the average balance of debt. Alternatively, we can estimate an appropriate interest rate by using footnote data on recently issued debt (i.e., the marginal borrowing rate), or using such data to construct a weighted average of interest rates on debt currently outstanding.

Deferred Taxes

Interrelated with projecting future income tax expense is the consideration of deferred taxes. Here we simply treat deferred taxes on the balance sheet similar to current operating assets or operating liabilities (i.e., as a percentage of sales). Other assumptions are possible depending on more complex assumptions about tax timing differences.

Owners' Equity

We complete the construction of pro forma balance sheets by applying the accounting equation, thus implying the balance of stockholders' equity. Breaking down stockholders' equity into components such as paid-in capital and retained earnings is generally unnecessary.

PRO FORMA CASH FLOW STATEMENTS

With the current and future balance sheets now in hand, we can use the changes from one year to the next to project future cash flow statements, as shown in Exhibit 14.4. Following the indirect method described in Chapter 4, we start with projected net income, add back depreciation, subtract increases in current operating assets including deferred tax assets, and add increases in operating liabilities, including deferred tax liabilities, to obtain projected cash from

Exhibit 14.4
Pro Forma Cash Flow
Statement

Operating Activities:

Net Income (Pro Forma Income Statement)
+ Depreciation (Pro Forma Income Statement)
+ Deferred Income Taxes (Pro Forma Balance Sheets)
− Change in Current Operating Assets (Pro Forma Balance Sheets)
+ Change in Operating Liabilities (Pro Forma Balance Sheets)

Cash Provided by Operating Activities

Investment Activities:

− Capital Expenditures (Analysis of Change in net PP&E)

Cash Used for Investing Activities

Financing Activities:

+/− Change in Debt (Pro Forma Balance Sheets)
− Dividends or + Stock Issues (Analysis of Change in Stockholders' Equity)

Cash from Financing Activities

Change in Cash (Pro Forma Balance Sheets)

operating activities. In a simple case, cash for investing activities consists only of capital expenditures.

Cash from financing activities includes projected changes in debt and in stockholders' equity apart from net income. An increase in debt, for example, net borrowing, results in an increase in cash, whereas a decrease in debt results in a decrease in cash. An increase in stockholders' equity beyond net income such as from a net stock issuance results in an increase in cash. However, a decrease in stockholders' equity implies a cash outflow that we assume to be the payment of dividends. In the context of the valuation approaches considered here, a repurchase of stock results in the same net effect on cash flows as a dividend. Finally, there is an implicit assumption that a firm issues or repurchases stock at prices that reflect estimated values.

We are now ready to discuss how the pro forma cash flows/earnings are utilized within the DCF and the RI approaches.

DISCOUNTED CASH FLOW (DCF) APPROACH

The DCF method relies on data from pro forma cash flow statements to determine estimates of **free cash flows** to equity (originally discussed in Chapter 5) to stockholders over some specified forecast horizon. These estimates, along with an estimated terminal value (of free cash flows to equity beyond the specified forecast horizon), are then discounted at the rate of return required by stockholders to invest in the firm (called the equity **cost of capital**) to arrive at a present value. Dividing the present value of estimates of free cash flows to equity and terminal value by the number of shares of stock outstanding results in an **estimated value per share:**

$$\text{DCF Value/Share} = \frac{\text{NPV(Free Cash Flows + Terminal Value)}}{\text{Number of Shares}}$$

Next we discuss the various components of the calculation.

FREE CASH FLOWS

We construct free cash flows to equity holders from the cash flow statement. Specifically, free cash flows to equity holders consist of cash provided by operating activities, less cash used for investing activities, plus cash derived from debt financing activities, and less the required change in cash to sustain future operations:

Cash Flow Provided by Operations
− Cash Flow Used for Investment
+ Cash Flow from Debt Financing
− Change in Cash Needed to Maintain Operations
= Free Cash Flow

Although it might seem that we can forecast future free cash flows by projecting future cash flow statements alone, remember that the cash flow statement is a derivative of the other financial statements. Those statements also include assumptions regarding projected future operating, investment, and financing activities. Deriving the full set of pro forma financial statements thus serves as a check on the internal consistency of operating, investing, and financing activities assumed in arriving at the inputs to DCF analysis.

TERMINAL VALUE

Typically, analysts forecast detailed pro forma financial statements for a limited time horizon, even though the firm may continue indefinitely. This poses a problem of how to project free cash flows to equity holders beyond the last (terminal) year of this time horizon. The usual solution assumes that free cash flows beyond the terminal year grow at a constant rate (perhaps even zero). Analysts often select one of the following growth rates beyond the terminal year: zero, the inflation rate, or the rate of GNP growth. In this text, for simplicity we assume zero future growth.

Using an assumed zero growth rate, the free cash flows starting the year after the terminal year will be constant. From a time value of money perspective, this means that the free cash flows after the terminal year are a simple perpetuity, making the estimation of the terminal value relatively simple. Specifically, terminal value as of the terminal date equals the annual free cash flow beyond the terminal date divided by the cost of equity (the formula for the present value of a perpetuity). See Appendix B for a more complete discussion of perpetuities.

Choosing a terminal year involves assessing the firm's ability to generate a rate of return on new investment in excess of its cost of capital, in other words, to identify projects with a positive net present value. The principal factor in assessing this ability is competition. We expect that the discovery of new projects for which the firm would enjoy a competitive advantage leading to above-normal profits, cannot continue forever. Generally, above-normal profits will attract new firms, thereby increasing competition (and lowering profit margins) until such profits no longer exist. The presence of some firms that sustain a competitive advantage for a long time is consistent with uncertainty regarding the duration of such an advantage.

COST OF EQUITY

Cost of equity is defined as the rate of return required by potential equity investors of a firm. Analysts need to know what stockholders expect in order to estimate the value of the shares. Analysts use **asset-pricing models** to estimate the cost of equity. One of these commonly used models is called the **capital asset pricing model (CAPM).** The following equation describes the model, where "expected return" equals the cost of equity:

$$\text{Expected Return} = \text{Risk Free Return} + (\text{Beta} \times \text{Market Risk Premium})$$

The CAPM model starts with the rate of return that might be expected from a risk-free asset (e.g., a government-backed treasury bill or bond) and then adds an additional rate of return as compensation for the risk involved in the particular stock. In theory, some risk can be diversified away by investing in a large portfolio of stocks. Investing money in multiple stocks permits gains on investments in one stock to offset losses on another. However, the overall economy as reflected by stock and other asset markets has a level of risk that cannot be diversified away. The entire market may decline. The expected return required by investors for bearing market risk is called the **market risk premium.** The CAPM adjusts the expected market risk premium based on the sensitivity of the individual company's returns to returns on the overall market. The CAPM is a theoretical model. In order to use it in valuation estimates of the risk-free rate, the market risk premium and the sensitivity of the firm's return to market returns are needed. The risk-free rate usually used is the intermediate term U.S. government note or bond rate available from a variety of public sources. This can vary with general economic conditions. Measures of the market risk premium are difficult to determine reliably. In past years, historical long-term averages suggested a market risk premium of 7 to 8 percent. However, recent estimates are much lower. Most analysts now assume a market risk premium of 5 to 6 percent.

Some stocks' returns are more sensitive to swings in the economy as a whole (high covariance) than the returns from other stocks. Investors generally expect a higher rate of return from high-sensitivity stocks. The CAPM captures this sensitivity through a parameter known as beta. **Beta** is defined as the covariance of the individual firm's returns with returns on a portfolio of all stocks and other assets (the whole market), divided by the variance of the portfolio's returns.

Numerous sources of information provide estimates of betas for individual companies. (We utilize a published beta for the real example later in the chapter.)

However, we can also estimate beta by using a statistical procedure known as a regression model (in this context, called the *market model*). The regression model estimates the covariance between past returns on the firm's stock and returns on a market index, such as the value weighted average of returns on all stocks traded on the NYSE, divided by the variance of returns on the market index in the form of a coeffient to that index in the regression equation. Estimates of the market risk premium are generally available from commercial services.

EXAMPLE OF DCF ANALYSIS WITH DEBT FINANCING

In Chapter 6, we briefly illustrated the application of the DCF analysis to a simple example (Exhibit 6.8) in which we assumed that the firm had no debt. In this section, we modify that simple example to include debt into the capital structure. Exhibit 14.5 shows the pro forma financial statements for this modified example. Recall that valuation methods assume a constant ratio of debt to equity. Further, in principle this ratio should depend on the market or estimated value of the equity, not the book value. Accordingly, we construct the example so that the estimated value of equity relative to debt remains constant over the years of the firm's life. A quick look at the pro forma balance sheets

Exhibit 14.5
Valuation Example
Balance Sheet

	0	1	2	3	4
Cash	0	0	0	0	0
Investments	0	342	718	1,132	0
Equipment, Net	1,000	750	500	250	0
Total Assets	1,000	1,092	1,218	1,382	0
Debt	500	500	500	500	0
Common Stock	500	500	500	500	0
Retained Earnings	0	92	218	382	0
Total Liability & OE	1,000	1,092	1,218	1,382	0

Income Statement	1	2	3	4
Revenue	500	500	500	500
Depreciation	(250)	(250)	(250)	(250)
Interest Income	—	34	72	113
Interest Expense	(40)	(40)	(40)	(40)
Net Income	210	244	282	323

Cash Flow Statement	1	2	3	4
Net Income	210	244	282	323
Depreciation	250	250	250	250
Operating Cash Flow	460	494	532	573
(Purchase) Sell Investment	(342)	(376)	(414)	1,132
Repay Debt	0	0	0	(500)
Dividends	(118)	(118)	(118)	(1,205)
Change in Cash	0	0	0	0

	1	2	3	4
Operating Cash Flow	460	494	532	573
Investing Cash Flow	(342)	(376)	(414)	1,132
Debt Cash Flow	0	0	0	(500)
Free Cash Flow	118	118	118	1,205
PV Factor	0.902	0.813	0.733	0.661
Present Value	106	96	86	797
Total Present Value	1,085			

Exhibit 14.6
DCF Analysis

in the example reveals that the book value of equity grows over time, whereas the book value of the debt remains constant.

Note in Exhibit 14.5 that the company has a four-year life (the same as in the Chapter 6 example). The investment in equipment is exactly the same as in the previous example, as are the revenues and depreciation expenses reported. Equity obviously differs, consistent with the assumption that the investment in equipment is partially financed through the issuance of $500 of debt with an interest rate of 8 percent. The principal amount of debt remains constant over the four years, at the end of which the firm repays the principal.

On the income statement (Exhibit 14.5), this change in financing results in interest expense ($40) each period. The firm reinvests cash flows (not distributed as dividends) in investments that earn interest income at 10 percent. Therefore, we see interest income appear in years 2 through 4. Regarding equity, notice that the firm pays a fixed amount of dividends each period until the last period. In the last period, the firm repays the debt, converts any remaining investments into cash, and distributes the cash to the owners in the form of a liquidating dividend.

Exhibit 14.6 shows the calculation of the free cash flows to equity derived from the pro forma cash flow statements. For this example, we estimate the cost of equity to be 10.875 percent. The higher cost of equity (relative to that assumed in Chapter 6 where there was no debt) reflects the greater risk that stockholders face in the presence of debt. As Exhibit 14.6 shows, the estimated value of equity under all of these assumptions is $1,085.

Observe that in this simple example, free cash flows equal dividends, including a liquidating dividend in the last period. We can easily check that the present value of free cash flows at the start of each and every year is $1,085. This implies that the debt-to-equity ratio, as measured using estimated values of equity rather than book values, is 500/1,085 in each period until liquidation, thereby meeting the constant-ratio requirement. For example, at the start of period 2, the present value of future dividends is $(0.902 \times 118) + (0.813 \times 118) + (0.733 \times 1,205) = 1,085$. As a practical matter, it would be difficult to determine a dividend policy for a real company with an indefinite life that would produce the same estimated value of equity at the start of each year. Hence, we adopt the common convention of maintaining a constant leverage ratio in terms of book values in the applications later in this chapter.

RESIDUAL INCOME (RI) APPROACH

The RI approach uses the same operating forecasts, terminal year assumption, cost of capital, and pro forma financial statements as those employed under a DCF approach. The approaches differ, however, in the calculation of abnormal earnings in place of free cash flows to equity, and the addition of the book value of stockholders' equity from the latest historical balance sheet in arriving at the estimated value.

The RI approach relies on data from pro forma income statements and balance sheets to determine estimates of **abnormal earnings** (also called *residual income*) over some specified forecast horizon. Abnormal earnings are defined as net income reduced by a **capital charge** (determined by multiplying the beginning of the period book value of stockholders' equity by the equity cost of capital). These estimates of abnormal earnings, along with an estimated terminal value (of abnormal earnings beyond the specified forecast horizon), are then discounted at the equity cost of capital to arrive at a present value. The present value of estimates of abnormal earnings and terminal value are added to the beginning book value of stockholders' equity to estimate the total value of equity. Dividing that value by the number of shares outstanding results in an estimated value per share.

$$\text{RI Value/Share} = \frac{\text{NPV (Abnormal Earnings + Terminal Value)} + \text{Book Value}}{\text{Number of Shares}}$$

> Having managers maximize RI provides an incentive closely aligned with maximizing net present value of new investments, which has been an accepted norm in capital budgeting for many years.

We can also interpret the capital charge as a measure of **normal earnings.** In this sense, it is the amount investors would expect to earn if the firm reinvests in projects that yield the investor's required return. Thus, net income has two components, normal and abnormal earnings.

$$\text{Abnormal Earnings} = \text{Net Income} - \text{Capital Charge}$$

Note that in the absence of abnormal earnings, estimated value equals book value.

SIMPLE EXAMPLE CONTINUED

Returning to the simple example in Exhibit 14.6, Exhibit 14.7 shows the RI approach. We compute the capital charge by multiplying the cost of equity 10.875 percent times the book value of equity at the beginning of the period. Thus in the first period, the capital charge is $500 × 10.875 percent, or $55

Exhibit 14.7
RI Calculation

	1	2	3	4
Net Income	210	244	282	323
Capital Charge	(55)	(65)	(79)	(96)
Abnormal Earnings	155	179	203	227
Present Value Factor	0.902	0.813	0.733	0.661
Present Value	140	146	149	150
Total Present Value	585			
Book Value	500			
Value of Equity	1,085			

	1	2	3	4
Net Income	(40)	(6)	532	573
Capital Charge	(55)	(37)	(24)	(68)
Abnormal Earnings	(95)	(43)	508	505
Present Value Factor	0.902	0.813	0.733	0.661
Present Value	(86)	(35)	372	334
Total Present Value	585			
Book Value	500			
Value of Equity	1,085			

Exhibit 14.8
RI Calculations (Revised Depreciation Assumptions)

(some rounding occurs in certain entries in the table). Note that the RI method produces the same estimated value of equity as the DCF approach.

Under the RI approach, will a change in the accrual accounting choices make a difference, as a significant portion of the calculation is based on book values? The answer: the method produces the same net result regardless of the accrual choices. While this may seem counterintuitive, we illustrate using our example. Suppose we change the method of depreciating the equipment by shortening the life from four years to two years. Then net income would change in each year. Exhibit 14.8 illustrates RI, given that depreciation is now 500 in each of the first two years and zero after that. Note that while the net income changes, so does the capital charge. Note further that, as claimed earlier, the calculation continues to result in the same estimated value of equity.

APPLYING THE VALUATION APPROACHES

To more fully illustrate both the DCF and RI valuation approaches, we apply them to the BHT example from earlier chapters. Recall that the first step under either method is to project pro forma financial statements up to one year beyond the terminal year. We assume that the terminal year is 20X7, a five-year horizon, after which we expect no further sales growth. We also assume the following:

- Revenue growth rate will decline from approximately 23 percent in 20X2 to approximately 19 percent in 20X3. Revenues are expected to continue to decline until the terminal year, when we assume growth to be 0 percent.
- Cost of goods sold remains at 85 percent of sales, as in 20X2.
- SG&A expenses remain at 12.1 percent of sales, as in 20X2.
- Income taxes are 34 percent of gross income, as in 20X2.
- Cash, accounts receivable, inventories, prepaid expenses, net PP&E, and accounts payable remain at the same percentages of sales as at the end of year 20X2: approximately 2.7 percent, 8.3 percent, 10.0 percent, .8 percent, 1.7 percent, and 15.2 percent, respectively.
- Depreciation remains at the same 24.6 percent of average net PP&E, as in year 20X2 (150,000/(480,000 + 740,000)/2 = 150,000/610,000 = .246).

Income Statements for Biohealth, Inc.
($ in thousands)

	Year Ended 12/31/20X2	Year Ended 12/31/20X3	Year Ended 12/31/20X4	Year Ended 12/31/20X5	Year Ended 12/31/20X6	Year Ended 12/31/20X7	Year Ended 12/31/20X8
Sales Revenue	$43,850,000	$52,161,991	$60,072,049	$66,904,227	$71,977,042	$74,705,766	$74,705,766
Less: Cost of Goods Sold	(37,272,000)	(44,337,098)	(51,060,557)	(56,867,830)	(61,179,665)	(63,499,049)	(63,499,049)
Gross Profit	6,578,000	7,824,893	9,011,492	10,036,397	10,797,377	11,206,717	11,206,717
SG&A	(5,320,000)	(6,328,433)	(7,288,103)	(8,117,001)	(8,732,448)	(9,063,505)	(9,063,505)
Depreciation	(150,000)	(199,214)	(232,872)	(263,461)	(288,162)	(304,350)	(310,011)
Interest Expense	(85,000)	(130,968)	(153,096)	(173,206)	(189,445)	(200,087)	(203,809)
Income Taxes	(347,820)	(396,535)	(454,723)	(504,128)	(539,689)	(557,184)	(553,993)
Net Income	$ 675,180	$ 769,743	$ 882,698	$ 978,601	$ 1,047,633	$ 1,081,591	$ 1,075,399

Exhibit 14.9
BHT Pro Forma Income Statements

Balance Sheet for Biohealth, Inc.
($ in thousands)

	Year Ended 12/31/20X2	Year Ended 12/31/20X3	Year Ended 12/31/20X4	Year Ended 12/31/20X5	Year Ended 12/31/20X6	Year Ended 12/31/20X7	Year Ended 12/31/20X8
Assets							
Current Assets:							
Cash	$ 1,170,740	$ 1,392,660	$ 1,603,848	$ 1,786,259	$ 1,921,697	$ 1,994,550	$ 1,994,550
Accounts receivable	3,650,000	4,341,876	5,000,296	5,568,995	5,991,248	6,218,382	6,218,382
Inventory	4,400,000	5,234,042	6,027,754	6,713,309	7,222,326	7,496,132	7,496,132
Prepaid expenses	360,000	428,240	493,180	549,271	590,918	613,320	613,320
Total Current Assets	9,580,740	11,396,818	13,125,078	14,617,834	15,726,188	16,322,384	16,322,384
PPE (Net)	740,000	880,271	1,013,759	1,129,057	1,214,664	1,260,713	1,260,713
Total Assets	$10,320,740	$12,277,089	$14,138,837	$15,746,890	$16,940,852	$17,583,097	$17,583,097
Liabilities and Stockholders' Equity							
Liabilities:							
Accounts Payable	$ 6,671,000	$ 7,935,522	$ 9,138,897	$10,178,292	$10,950,031	$11,365,158	$11,365,158
Total Current Liabilities	6,671,000	7,935,522	9,138,897	10,178,292	10,950,031	11,365,158	11,365,158
Long-Term Debt	950,000	1,130,077	1,301,447	1,449,464	1,559,366	1,618,483	1,618,483
Total Liabilities	7,621,000	9,065,599	10,440,344	11,627,756	12,509,397	12,983,641	12,983,641
Stockholders' Equity:							
Paid-in Capital	2,250,000	2,562,386	2,820,770	2,987,954	3,028,938	2,916,807	2,638,278
Retained Earnings	449,740	649,104	877,722	1,131,180	1,402,517	1,682,649	1,961,178
Total Stockholders' Equity	2,699,740	3,211,490	3,698,493	4,119,134	4,431,455	4,599,456	4,599,456
Total Liabilities and Equity	$10,320,740	$12,277,089	$14,138,837	$15,746,890	$16,940,852	$17,583,097	$17,583,097

Exhibit 14.10
BHT Pro Forma Balance Sheets

Statements of Cash Flow for Biohealth, Inc.
($ in thousands)

	Year Ended 12/31/20X2	Year Ended 12/31/20X3	Year Ended 12/31/20X4	Year Ended 12/31/20X5	Year Ended 12/31/20X6	Year Ended 12/31/20X7	Year Ended 12/31/20X8
Cash Flow from Operating Activities:							
Net Income	$ 675,180	$ 769,744	$ 882,698	$ 978,602	$1,047,632	$1,081,592	$1,075,399
Depreciation	150,000	199,214	232,872	263,461	288,162	304,350	310,011
Funds From Operations	825,180	968,958	1,115,570	1,242,062	1,335,794	1,385,942	1,385,410
Increase in Receivables	(1,186,000)	(691,876)	(658,420)	(568,699)	(422,253)	(227,134)	0
Increase in Inventory	(480,000)	(834,042)	(793,712)	(685,555)	(509,017)	(273,806)	0
Increase in Other Current Assets	(360,000)	(68,240)	(64,940)	(56,091)	(41,647)	(22,402)	0
Increase in Accounts Payable	1,531,000	1,264,522	1,203,375	1,039,395	771,739	415,127	0
Cash Flow From Operating Activities	330,180	639,321	801,874	971,112	1,134,617	1,277,726	1,385,410
Cash Flow from Investing Activities:							
Capital Expenditures	(410,000)	(339,484)	(366,360)	(378,759)	(373,770)	(350,399)	(310,011)
Cash Flow From Investing Activities	(410,000)	(339,484)	(366,360)	(378,759)	(373,770)	(350,399)	(310,011)
Cash Flow from Financing Activities:							
Increase in Debt	550,000	180,077	171,370	148,018	109,901	59,117	0
Dividends Paid on Common	(500,000)	(570,380)	(654,079)	(725,144)	(776,295)	(801,460)	(796,870)
Net Issuance of Common Stock	625,000	312,386	258,385	167,183	40,984	(112,131)	(278,528)
Cash Flow From Financing Activities	675,000	(77,917)	(224,325)	(409,943)	(625,410)	(854,474)	(1,075,399)
Net Change in Cash	595,180	221,920	211,189	182,411	135,438	72,853	0
Beginning Cash Balance	575,560	1,170,740	1,392,660	1,603,848	1,786,259	1,921,697	1,994,550
Ending Cash Balance	$1,170,740	$1,392,660	$1,603,848	$1,786,259	$1,921,697	$1,994,550	$1,994,550

● Debt-to-total-debt and equity ratio of 26 percent remains constant, as at year end 20X2 (950,000/(950,000 + 2,699,740) = 950,000/3,649,740 = .260). Note that we maintain the constancy of the debt equity ratio based on the book value of the debt and equity in this case.

● Interest expense equals the average historical rate of 12.6 percent for 20X2 applied to the average balance of debt outstanding during the year (85,000/(400,000 + 950,000)/2 = 85,000/675,000 = .126).

● Dividends to stockholders remain at 74.1 percent of net income, as in 20X2.

Exhibit 14.11
BHT Pro Forma Cash Flow Statements

PRO FORMA STATEMENTS

Based on the assumptions above, we generated financial statements for the last historical year and the six forecasted years, on a pro forma basis (see Exhibits 14.9 through 14.11). We went one year beyond the terminal year

Cost of Equity 11% ($ in thousands)	Year Ended 12/31/20X3	Year Ended 12/31/20X4	Year Ended 12/31/20X5	Year Ended 12/31/20X6	Year Ended 12/31/20X7	Year Ended 12/31/20X8
Free Cash Flows	$ 257,995	$395,695	$557,961	$735,311	$913,591	$1,075,399
Terminal Value						$9,776,355
Present Value	$ 232,428	$321,155	$407,976	$484,372	$542,172	$5,801,787
Net Present Value	$7,789,890					
Outstanding Shares	250,000					
Estimated Value per Share	$ 31.16					

Exhibit 14.12
DCF Analysis of BHT

(20X7) to show how the statements stabilize to reflect the zero growth rate following that year. As Exhibit 14.11 indicates, the zero growth rate results in the absence of any further changes in operating working capital and the equivalence of depreciation and capital expenditures in 20X8, the year following the terminal year.

DCF ANALYSIS

From the pro forma statements, we extract free cash flows available to stockholders to construct the DCF estimate of value per share, as shown in Exhibit 4.12. We assume a cost of equity of 11 percent for BHT, which reflects the industry average for firms in the health products industry. We calculate the terminal value by dividing free cash flow in year 20X8 of $1,075,399 (assumed to remain constant for all future periods) by the cost of equity of 11 percent, treating it as a perpetuity. We then discount the terminal value in the same way as the other free cash flows.

RI ANALYSIS

For RI analysis, we begin with net income from the pro forma income statements, as shown in Exhibit 14.13. For the next step, we compute a capital charge by multiplying total stockholders' equity at the start of each forecast year by an assumed cost of capital of 11 percent. We then subtract the capital charge from net income to arrive at abnormal earnings.

We determine the terminal value in much the same manner as we would using the DCF approach. In this case, we assume the amount of abnormal earnings for the years after 20X7 to be the same, or the same amount as in 20X8 ($569,458). Therefore, they form a perpetuity. We then divide this constant amount by the cost of equity ($569,458/11% = $5,176,891). We then discount this amount along with the other abnormal earnings amounts. We again divide by the number of shares outstanding to produce an estimated value per share.

Cost of Equity 11% ($ in thousands)	Year Ended 12/31/20X3	Year Ended 12/31/20X4	Year Ended 12/31/20X5	Year Ended 12/31/20X6	Year Ended 12/31/20X7	Year Ended 12/31/20X8
Abnormal Earnings	$ 472,733	$529,434	$571,767	$594,527	$594,132	$ 569,458
Terminal Value						$5,176,891
Present Value	$ 425,921	$429,701	$418,071	$391,634	$352,588	$3,072,235
Net Present Value	$5,090,150					
Book Value 12/31/02	$2,699,740					
Total Value	$7,789,890					
Outstanding Shares	250,000					
Estimated Value per Share	$ 31.16					

Exhibit 14.13
RI Analysis of BHT

VALUING A REAL COMPANY

We now apply DCF and RI analyses to a real company, Cintas. As we discussed earlier, Cintas rents uniforms and provides other services to large and small businesses.

PRO FORMA STATEMENTS

We estimated a revenue growth rate of 19 percent by first fitting a time series analysis to the company's past revenue history. We then modified the result based on a review of growth predictions of financial analysts. To keep the presentation of pro forma financial statements concise, we arbitrarily assumed a five-year time horizon and zero growth rate beyond that date. We also made the following assumptions:

● Cost of rentals and other services continues its downward trend for one more year, resulting in cost of rentals and other services (CORS) set at 58 percent of revenues.

● SG&A expenses remain at the same percentage of sales, as in 2001. (Unlike BHT, we do not split out depreciation and amortization on the pro forma income statements.) As a result, we implicitly assume that higher repairs and maintenance costs charged to cost of goods sold offset the decline in depreciation and amortization as a percentage of revenue from employing a declining balance method.

● Cash and marketable securities, grouped together, remain at a constant percentage of revenue. We assume that "interest income and other" on the income statement is related to the average balance of cash and marketable securities during the year.

● We concluded that inventories were higher than usual at the end of 2001, so we reduced inventories as a percentage of revenues going forward from 17 percent to 14 percent.

Consolidated Statements of Income
($ in thousands)

	Year Ended 5/31/2001	Year Ended 5/31/2002	Year Ended 5/31/2003	Year Ended 5/31/2004	Year Ended 5/31/2005	Year Ended 5/31/2006	Year Ended 5/31/2007	Year Ended 5/31/2008
Revenue	$2,160,700	$2,571,233	$3,059,767	$3,641,123	$4,332,936	$5,156,194	$5,156,194	$5,156,194
Costs of rentals and other services	(1,264,433)	(1,491,315)	(1,774,665)	(2,111,851)	(2,513,103)	(2,990,593)	(2,990,593)	(2,990,593)
	896,267	1,079,918	1,285,102	1,529,272	1,819,833	2,165,602	2,165,602	2,165,602
SG&A expense	(528,354)	(628,741)	(748,202)	(890,360)	(1,059,529)	(1,260,840)	(1,260,840)	(1,260,840)
Interest expense	(15,119)	(15,416)	(18,157)	(21,607)	(25,712)	(30,598)	(33,252)	(33,252)
Interest Income and other	3,660	4,355	5,183	6,168	7,340	8,734	8,734	8,734
Income taxes	(134,003)	(165,454)	(196,961)	(234,384)	(278,917)	(331,911)	(330,913)	(330,913)
Net Income	$ 222,451	$ 274,662	$ 326,965	$ 389,088	$ 463,015	$ 550,987	$ 549,331	$ 549,331

Exhibit 14.14
Cintas' Pro Forma Income Statements

● Other operating working capital account balances, net property and equipment, and other assets remain at the same percentages of revenues.

● We calculate depreciation by applying a historically based declining balance rate of 19 percent to the average balance of net property and equipment.

● Debt to equity ratio remains constant, consistent with holding the cost of capital constant and computed interest expense by applying the company's current weighted average interest rate of 5.9 percent to the average outstanding debt during the ensuing year. As with BHT, we maintain this ratio on a book value basis.

● Deferred taxes remain at a constant percentage of revenue.

● We applied the past year's dividend payout ratio to projected earnings to determine future dividends.

● We interpret implied changes in common stock and other as either proceeds from new stock issues if a positive cash flow or stock repurchases if a negative cash flow, and, therefore, part of the free cash flows to equity for valuation purposes.

We generated pro forma financial statements for Cintas based on these assumptions, using the most recent historical year and six years on a pro forma basis, as shown in Exhibits 14.14 through 14.16. Cintas made some acquisitions in 2001, making it difficult to reconcile this statement with the changes in balance sheet accounts. As a result, we reconstructed a cash flow statement from changes in balance sheet accounts that suppresses these acquisitions as a lump-sum investment.

VALUATION ANALYSES

For the DCF and RI analyses, we estimated a cost of equity using the Capital Asset Pricing Model (CAPM). We utilized various information sources to determine the risk-free rate (5 percent) and the market risk premium (6 percent) at the date of this assessment. We obtained a beta of 0.941 from a commercial source. This results in a cost of equity of 10.65 percent (5% + .941 × 6%).

Consolidated Balance Sheets
($ in thousands)

	As of 5/31/2001	As of 5/31/2002	As of 5/31/2003	As of 5/31/2004	As of 5/31/2005	As of 5/31/2006	As of 5/31/2007	As of 5/31/2008
Assets								
Current Assets								
Cash and marketable securities	$ 110,229	$ 131,173	$ 156,095	$ 185,753	$ 221,047	$ 263,045	$ 263,045	$ 263,045
Account receivables	244,450	290,896	346,166	411,937	490,205	583,344	583,344	583,344
Inventories	214,349	208,784	248,453	295,659	351,834	418,683	418,683	418,683
Uniforms in service and prepaid expenses	250,642	298,264	354,934	422,372	502,622	598,120	598,120	598,120
Total current assets	819,670	929,116	1,105,648	1,315,721	1,565,708	1,863,193	1,863,193	1,863,193
Property and equipment, net	702,132	835,537	994,289	1,183,204	1,408,013	1,675,535	1,675,535	1,675,535
Other assets	230,422	274,202	326,301	388,298	462,074	549,868	549,868	549,868
	$1,752,224	$2,038,855	$2,426,238	$2,887,223	$3,435,795	$4,088,597	$4,088,597	$4,088,597
Liabilities and Shareholders' Equity								
Current debt	$ 20,605	$ 23,976	$ 28,531	$ 33,952	$ 40,403	$ 48,079	$ 48,079	$ 48,079
Accounts payable	42,495	50,120	59,643	70,975	84,460	100,508	100,508	100,508
Income taxes payable	57,703	68,667	81,713	97,239	115,714	137,700	137,700	137,700
Other current liabilities	130,100	154,819	184,235	219,239	260,895	310,465	310,465	310,465
Total current liabilities	250,903	297,581	354,122	421,405	501,472	596,751	596,751	596,751
Long-term debt	220,940	257,082	305,927	364,053	433,224	515,536	515,536	515,536
Deferred taxes	49,066	58,389	69,482	82,684	98,394	117,089	117,089	117,089
Total liabilities	520,909	613,051	729,531	868,142	1,033,089	1,229,376	1,229,376	1,229,376
Shareholders' Equity								
Common stock, net of comprehensive loss	56,985	22,710	21,286	19,592	17,575	15,175	(442,359)	(899,893)
Retained earnings	1,174,330	1,403,094	1,675,421	1,999,489	2,385,131	2,844,045	3,301,579	3,759,114
Total common equity	1,231,315	1,425,804	1,696,707	2,019,081	2,402,706	2,859,221	2,859,221	2,859,221
Total shareholders' equity	$1,752,224	$2,038,855	$2,426,238	$2,887,223	$3,435,795	$4,088,597	$4,088,597	$4,088,597

Exhibit 14.15
Cintas' Pro Forma Balance Sheets

Exhibits 14.17 and 14.18 show the DCF and RI calculations, respectively, in reaching an estimated value per share of $20.00 as of May 31, 2001.

Cintas' stock in May 2001 traded between $33.75 and $49.75. Over a broader range of time, from early 2000 to mid–2002, Cintas' stock traded over a range of approximately $23 to $56. The difference between these ranges and our estimate of $20.00 could be due to many factors. A leading possibility is that the market reasonably predicted positive growth beyond the five-year time horizon of our detailed operating forecasts. In fact, in March 2004, analysts (as reported on Yahoo! Finance) estimated an annual 15 percent growth rate for Cintas over the next five years, well into the time period beyond our estimation horizon.

Another consideration may be that investors envisioned the prospect of economies of scale as Cintas grows. These economies would be reflected in lower estimates of costs as a percentage of revenues and smaller investments in working capital and PP&E as percentages of revenues. We limited our time

Consolidation Statements of Cash Flows
($ in thousands)

	Year Ended 5/31/2001	Year Ended 5/31/2002	Year Ended 5/31/2003	Year Ended 5/31/2004	Year Ended 5/31/2005	Year Ended 5/31/2006	Year Ended 5/31/2007	Year Ended 5/31/2008
Cash Flow from Operating Activities:								
Net Income	$222,451	$274,662	$326,965	$389,088	$463,015	$550,987	$549,331	$549,331
Depreciation and amortization	122,873	146,219	174,001	207,060	246,402	293,219	293,219	293,219
Increase in accounts receivables	(18,715)	(46,446)	(55,270)	(65,771)	(78,268)	(93,139)	–	–
Increase in inventory	(49,443)	5,565	(39,669)	(47,206)	(56,175)	(66,849)	–	–
Increase in uniforms in service, etc	(29,635)	(47,622)	(56,670)	(67,437)	(80,251)	(95,498)	–	–
Increase in accounts payable	(8,481)	7,625	9,523	11,332	13,485	16,047	–	–
Increase in deferred taxes	8,459	20,287	24,141	28,728	34,185	40,681	–	–
Increase in accrued liabilities	11,902	24,719	29,416	35,005	41,655	49,570	–	–
Net cash provided by operating activities	259,411	385,008	412,435	490,797	584,049	695,019	842,550	842,550
Cash Flow from Investing Activities:								
Capital expenditures	(182,498)	(279,624)	(332,753)	(395,975)	(471,211)	(560,741)	(293,219)	(293,219)
Increase in other assets	(13,057)	(43,780)	(52,098)	(61,997)	(73,776)	(87,795)	–	–
Net cash used in investing activities	(195,555)	(323,404)	(384,851)	(457,972)	(544,987)	(648,536)	(293,219)	(293,219)
Cash Flow from Financing Activities:								
Increase in debt	(29,437)	39,512	53,401	63,547	75,621	89,989	–	–
Dividends	(37,173)	(45,898)	(54,638)	(65,019)	(77,373)	(92,074)	(91,797)	(91,797)
Changes in common stock and other	6,559	(34,275)	(1,424)	(1,695)	(2,017)	(2,400)	(457,534)	(457,534)
					–	–	–	–
Net cash flow from financing activities	(63,449)	(40,660)	(2,661)	(3,167)	(3,768)	(4,484)	(549,331)	(549,331)
Net change in cash	407	20,944	24,923	29,658	35,293	41,999	–	–
Cash and marketable securities at start	109,822	110,229	131,173	156,095	185,753	221,047	263,045	263,045
Cash and marketable securities at end	$110,229	$131,173	$156,095	$185,753	$221,047	$263,045	$263,045	$263,045

Exhibit 14.16
Cintas' Pro Forma Cash Flow Statements

horizon to simplify the presentation of pro forma financial statements. If we extend the analysis to include a longer time horizon, allow for additional growth, and introduce some modest cost efficiencies, then our analysis provides an estimate within the actual trading range of Cintas stock.[1] Finally, it is also possible that the market overpriced Cintas at the valuation date.

[1]Specifically, we assumed declining sales growth beyond five years of 18.5 percent, 16 percent, 14 percent, 11 percent, 7 percent, and 3.5 percent thereafter. This results in an estimate of $33.94. Trimming SG&A to 24 percent and cash requirements to 3 percent of sales, the estimate becomes $36.31.

10.65%						
Cost of Equity	Year Ended 5/31/2002	Year Ended 5/31/2003	Year Ended 5/31/2004	Year Ended 5/31/2005	Year Ended 5/31/2006	Year Ended 5/31/2007
Free Cash Flows	$ 80,173	$56,062	$66,714	$79,389	$94,473	$ 549,331
Terminal Value						$5,158,038
Present Value	$ 72,456	$45,789	$49,245	$52,961	$56,957	$3,109,764
Net Present Value	$3,387,173					
Outstanding Shares	169,371					
Estimated Value per Share	$ 20.00					

Exhibit 14.17
DCF Analysis for Cintas Corporation

THE REAL WORLD
Cintas Corporation

10.65%						
Cost of Equity ($ in thousands)	Year Ended 5/31/2002	Year Ended 5/31/2003	Year Ended 5/31/2004	Year Ended 5/31/2005	Year Ended 5/31/2006	Year Ended 5/31/2007
Stockholders' Equity 1/1	$1,231,315	$1,425,804	$1,696,707	$2,019,081	$2,402,706	$2,859,221
Net Income	274,662	326,965	389,088	463,015	550,987	549,331
Capital Charge	131,135	151,848	180,699	215,032	255,888	304,507
Abnormal Earnings	143,527	175,117	208,389	247,983	295,099	244,824
Terminal Value						$2,298,817
Present Value	$ 129,713	$ 143,029	$ 153,823	$ 165,431	$ 177,914	$1,385,949
Net Present Value	$2,155,858					
Book Value 5/31/2001	$1,231,315					
Total Value	$3,387,173					
Outstanding Shares	169,371					
Estimated Value per Share	$ 20.00					

Exhibit 14.18
RI Analysis for Cintas Corporation

THE REAL WORLD
Cintas Corporation

Several other complications occur when applying DCF and RI analyses to real companies, which we disregarded in valuing Cintas. For instance, Cintas issues stock options to compensate employees, which has a potential dilutive effect on value per share. We could adjust for this effect by employing a pro forma earnings number disclosed in a required footnote, or by estimating the value of options outstanding at the valuation date and subtracting that amount from our estimate. Applying the latter approach lowers our estimated value per share by approximately $0.30.

We also did not project components of comprehensive income, but simply combined accumulated comprehensive items to stockholders' equity. We did not distinguish future capital expenditures for property and equipment from future business acquisitions. Here, though, it appears that Cintas has completed acquisitions related to its main line of business. An alternative way to deal with how we treated marketable securities would be to separate them from operating activities, not forecast future income from these investments, value them at quoted market prices, and add that value to the present value of free cash flows to equity (arising purely from operating activities) to estimate the value of the equity as a whole. We used an average interest rate on debt instead of forecasting specific future borrowings or estimating marginal borrowing rates at the valuation date. And we could have applied forecasting techniques to major business segments rather than to the firm as a whole. We conjecture that, in this case, allowing for these refinements likely would not have materially altered the estimate.

VALUATION AND PRICING MULTIPLES

Pricing multiples, such as the price-to-earnings ratio we discussed in Chapter 6, are popular with investors as a short-cut to valuing companies or to assess the reasonableness of estimates derived from more complicated methods such as DCF or RI. Investors compute these ratios using recent reported values of earnings per share (called **trailing P/E ratios**) or using forecasts of earnings per share provided to the public by financial analysts (called **forward P/E ratios**). For example, Cintas' trailing P/E ratio in September 2002 (based on actual earnings per share through the first quarter of fiscal year 2002 of $1.36 and a market price of $41.61) was 29.94, while its forward P/E ratio (based on analysts' consensus forecast at that time of $1.57) was 26.50. Reversing the order, we take the P/E ratio as given and estimate value by multiplying that ratio by the latest report or forecast of earnings per share.

We assess the viability of a DCF or RI estimate of value by using that estimate, along with earnings per share, to compute a value-to-earnings ratio. We can then compare that ratio to P/E ratios of similar firms or the industry as a whole. For example, Cintas has two major competitors, ARAMARK and G&K Services. ARAMARK is not very comparable because of its various diversified activities. However, G&K Services is reasonably similar to Cintas. G&K Services' trailing P/E ratio in September 2002 was 18.02, an amount considerably lower than that of Cintas. In fact, it is closer to our estimated value-to-earnings ratio (albeit as of May 2002) of 16.20. Investors may conclude that Cintas may have been overpriced. However, a closer look at G&K Services' profit margin (6.12 percent) and return on equity (11.7 percent) suggests that it was not performing as well as Cintas (10.09 percent and 16.8 percent, respectively).

We can also compare Cintas' ratios with those for the Diversified Services industry. The industry's trailing P/E ratio was 33.18 in September 2002. Putting it all together, it appears that our estimated value is too low, probably because of an overly conservative estimate of revenue growth beyond the next five years.

Other common pricing multiples include price-to-sales (P/S), price-to-cash flow (P/CF), and price-to-book value (P/B) of stockholders' equity. Investors often use price-to-sales for startup companies that have negative earnings in their early years. Comparing Cintas to G&K Services and the Diversified Services industry at September 2002, we see somewhat similar orderings to those we saw for P/E ratios: Cintas (2.98, 20.00, and 4.97, respectively), G&K (1.10, 9.44, and 2.11, respectively), and Diversified Services (1.24, 17.59, and 2.97, respectively).

There are many caveats to simple multiples as valuation devices. The unwary user of such methods might fail to distinguish changes in ratios that result from accounting changes, or changes in accounting estimates from changes in

Valuation Marginalia
A recent academic study found that a forward P/E ratio based on analysts' forecasts of earnings two years out outperformed other multiples and RI-type estimates in minimizing pricing errors (Liu, Nissim, and Thomas, *Journal of Accounting Research*, 2002).

operating efficiency. Multiples may not capture economies of scale and scope. Different multiples reflect different judgments as to the factors that may contribute to a firm's value. Even if several multiples are available, it is unclear how investors should combine the information contained in those ratios.

SUMMARY AND TRANSITION

This chapter laid out the essential ingredients of the two principal approaches toward valuing the firm from fundamentals: discounted cash flow (DCF) and residual income (RI). Both of these approaches begin with generating forecasts of operating revenues and expenses. Combining these forecasts with assumptions regarding levels of working capital; property, plant, and equipment; and debt required to sustain future operations leads to the construction of pro forma financial statements extending forward to a terminal date. A terminal date is projected, beyond which either cash flows or earnings can be reasonably portrayed as a perpetuity.

Under DCF, free cash flows to equity are extracted from the pro forma cash flow statements over a specified forecast horizon and projected as a perpetuity beyond that horizon. Free cash flows to equity are the subtotal of cash provided by operating activities, less cash used for investments, plus net borrowings from lenders; or the cash flows available to stockholders. These cash flows are discounted to a present value employing the cost of equity capital. That cost of capital may be estimated from asset pricing models such as the capital asset pricing model (CAPM). Dividing the present value of the free cash flows by the number of shares outstanding results in an estimated value per share.

RI begins with net income from the pro forma income statements and is projected as a perpetuity beyond the specified forecast horizon (terminal year). A capital charge is computed by multiplying the firm's equity cost of capital by the beginning book value of stockholders' equity. Deducting the capital charge from net income leads to abnormal earnings. Abnormal earnings are discounted at the cost of capital. The present value of abnormal earnings is added to the beginning book value of stockholders' equity to obtain a total estimated value. Dividing by the number of shares outstanding results in an estimated value per share.

Pricing multiples are often employed either as a check on estimates obtained from DCF or RI or as simple valuation models in their own right. Although this approach to valuing the firm is crude and subject to distortions caused by accounting, P/E ratios, based on forecasts of earnings per share and intelligently applied, perform remarkably well in explaining market prices.

The principal focus in our treatment of valuation from fundamental analysis has been on the mechanics of generating pro forma statements, taking what's needed from those statements, and calculating present values. However, realize that the estimates of firm value produced by these methods are only as good as the quality of the inputs. As we saw, revenues often play a primary role in generating pro forma financial statements from which free cash flows or abnormal earnings are derived. Accordingly, considerable thought should go into the projection of revenues, such as consideration of the company's business strategy, an appropriate extrapolation of past data, an assessment of the competition, and industry and economy outlooks.

END OF CHAPTER MATERIAL

KEY TERMS

Abnormal Earnings

Asset Pricing Models

Beta

Capital Asset Pricing Model (CAPM)

Capital Charge

Capital Structure

Cost of Capital

Discounted Cash Flow (DCF) Method

Estimated Value per Share

Expected Market Risk Premium

Forecasting

Forward P/E Ratio

Free Cash Flow

Normal Earnings

Pro Forma Financial Statements

Residual Income (RI) Method

Terminal Value

Trailing P/E Ratio

ASSIGNMENT MATERIAL

REVIEW QUESTIONS

1. Describe the general approach to valuation used in the discounted cash flow method.

2. Describe the general approach to valuation used in the residual income method.

3. Discuss how a pro forma income statement would be calculated.

4. Discus how a pro forma balance sheet would be calculated.

5. Describe how free cash flows are calculated for a firm.

6. How is terminal value generally determined for the discounted cash flow method?

7. Describe how the cost of equity is determined using the capital asset pricing model.

8. Describe how abnormal earnings are calculated under the residual income model.

9. Describe what trailing and forward P/E mean.

● APPLYING YOUR KNOWLEDGE

10. If the beta of the ABC Company is 1.15 what would the cost of equity be for ABC if the current market risk-free rate is 3 percent and the expected market risk premium is 6 percent?

11. Suppose that the free cash flow to equity for the Helman Company for the first year beyond the ten-year time horizon to the terminal date was estimated by an analyst to be $150,000 per year. Further assume that the analyst estimates that the Helman Company will have zero growth beyond ten years and that the cost of equity for Helman is 14 percent. What would the analyst estimate to be the terminal value for Helman Company at the end of the ten-year horizon?

12. The following table shows the estimates of free cash flow for the Barber Company. Assume that year 8 is the terminal year and that free cash flows after year 9 are assumed to be constant at the year 9 level. If the cost of equity for Barber is estimated to be 15 percent, what is the estimated market value of the equity of Barber?

Year	1	2	3	4	5	6	7	8	9
Free Cash Flow	1,000	1,050	1,103	1,158	1,216	1,276	1,340	1,407	1,477

13. The Clark Company's most recent income statement and balance sheet are shown below. Make the following assumptions: Sales are forecasted to increase by 5 percent during each of the next five years. CGS and Operating Expenses are to remain at the same percent of sales over the next five years as in the most recent year. Depreciation is estimated using the declining balance method at a rate based on the most recent year's depreciation as a percent of the beginning balance of PP&E ($36,000 at the start of the most recent year). PP&E is expected to increase proportionally to sales. Interest expense is computed at a rate based on the most recent year's interest expense as a percent of the beginning balance of debt ($24,000) at the start of the most recent year). The debt to equity ratio is to remain constant based on book value at the end of the most recent year.

Sales	$190,000	Assets	
CGS	140,000	Assets Other Than PP&E	$ 60,000
		PP&E	40,000
Gross Margin	50,000	Total Assets	$100,000
Depreciation	4,000		
Operating Expenses	32,000	Liabilities and Owners' Equity	
Interest Expense	1,200	Liabilities Other Than Debt	$ 30,000
Income before Taxes	12,800	Debt	30,000
Income Taxes	4,480	Owners' Equity	40,000
Net Income	$ 8,320	Total Liabilities and Owners' Equity	$100,000

Required:

Prepare pro forma income statements for the next five years.

14. Assume the same facts as in problem 13.

Required:

Prepare pro forma balance sheets for the next five years.

15. Assume the same facts as in problem 13.

Required:

Prepare pro forma cash flow statements for the next five years. Using data from those cash flow statements, determine free cash flows to equity for the next five years. Assuming that sales are expected to remain constant (zero growth) after the next five years, determine free cash flows to equity for the sixth year. Estimate the value of equity using the discounted cash flow method.

USING REAL DATA

16. In Chapter 2 of this book we discussed the situation Polaroid faced in late 2000 with a significant decline in its quarterly sales. If you were an analyst in late 2000, discuss how Polaroid's decline in quarterly sales might affect an estimate of Polaroid's value per share.

17. In a press release in April 2004, Amazon.com reported profits for the first quarter that beat the expectations of analysts. In the same report, however, the company reported considerable lower gross profit margins. Discuss how these reports might affect an estimate of Amazon's value per share.

18. In April 2004 Callaway Golf reported first quarter net income of 64 cents a share that was short of analysts' concensus forecast of 70 cents a share. Comment on the sensitivity of stock prices failing to meet analysts' forecasts.

19. Ligand Pharmaceuticals, Inc. missed its first quarter expectations for sales of its pain-relief drug Avinza in 2004. Explain how this event might affect forecasts of future quarterly sales and, ultimately, estimates of firm value. Indicate your assumptions regarding how future sales depend on current sales.

20. Estimate the value of a share of Paccar's common stock employing the data provided by the company's income statement for 2003 and its balance sheets for 2002 and 2003. Make the following assumptions:

○ Net sales and revenue are expected to grow at a rate of 9 percent in 2004 and to decline by 0.4 percent per year until the terminal year 2013. No sales growth is expected beyond 2013.

○ Cost of sales and revenue, SG&A, and provision for losses are expected to remain at the same percentages of net sales and revenue as they were in 2003.

○ Depreciation expense is estimated as a percentage of the average balance of PP&E, net.

- Interest expense is estimated as a percentage of the average balance of both current and long-term debt.
- Investment Income is estimated as a percentage of the average balance of cash and cash equivalents.
- Income taxes are estimated to remain at the same percentage of total income before taxes as in 2003.
- All current assets; PP&E, net; accounts payable and accrued expenses; deferred revenues; and deferred taxes are expected to remain at the same percentages of net sales and revenues as in 2003.
- Goodwill is assumed to be constant for all future periods.
- Current and long-term debt is assumed to remain at a constant percentage of total assets less operating liabilities.
- Dividends payable are expected to be zero starting in 2004.
- Beta is 1.031, and the risk-free rate and market risk premium are 4 percent and 5 percent, respectively.

Historical Income Statement
PACCAR, INC. Income Statement
(in $ millions)

	2003
Net Sales and Revenues	$8,194.9
Cost of Sales and Revenues	6,464.5
SG&A	417.9
Provision for Losses	28.6
Depreciation Expense	267.5
Interest Expense	252.2
Subtotal	764.2
Investment Income	41.3
Total Income Before Taxes	805.5
Income Taxes	279.0
Net Income	$ 526.5

Historical Balance Sheets
PACCAR, INC. Balance Sheet
(in $ millions)

	2002	2003
Assets		
Current Assets		
Cash and cash equivalents	$1,308.3	$1,724.1
Accounts receivable, net of allowance	5,063.9	5,474.0
Inventory	310.6	334.5
Total Truck and Other Current Assets	6,682.8	7,532.6
PP&E, net	1,683.9	1,974.9
Goodwill and other, net	222.9	347.1
Total Assets	$8,589.6	$9,854.6

	2002	2003
Liabilities and Stockholders' Equity		
Current Liabilities		
Accounts payable and accrued expenses	$1,275.2	$1,461.2
Dividends payable	71.4	140.1
Current debt	2,047.5	2,270.8
Total Current Liabilities	3,394.1	3,872.1
Long-term debt	1,551.7	1,556.8
Deferred revenues	516.4	560.4
Deferred taxes, net	526.7	618.9
Total Liabilities	5,988.9	6,608.2
Stockholders' Equity		
Total Stockholders' Equity	2,600.7	3,246.4
Total Liabilities and Stockholders' Equity	$8,589.6	$9,854.6

BEYOND THE BOOK

21. For a public company of your choice, find out what analysts currently forecast earnings to be for the next year. (Use public data to find an estimate.) Using the residual income method, and assuming that forecasted earnings for the next year will continue indefinitely as a perpetuity, estimate the value of your selected company using the residual income method. You will need to find an estimate of the company's beta as well as its earnings. You will also need to know the book value of equity as of the most recent balance sheet date. For purposes of this exercise, assume a risk-free interest rate of 4 percent and a market risk premium of 6 percent.

22. Select a company of your choice or use one assigned by your instructor. Using the methods discussed in this chapter, estimate the company's value.

Adjusting Entries

Many economic events that require recognition are signaled by some direct artifact of the event, such as cash being received or paid, checks being cut, orders received, inventory being shipped, and so on. However, there are some events that require recognition that do not have such direct artifacts. For instance, there is no direct signal at the end of the period that indicates that plant, property, and equipment needs to be depreciated or that interest needs to be accrued on a loan. These types of events require the accountant to recognize them and to make adjusting entries. Adjusting entries are thus a specific and important component of accrual accounting.

Adjusting entries are also generally required for transactions in which prepaid assets or accrued liabilities are created. For example, with prepaid insurance, the first entry is to record the cash payment which was signaled when the cash was paid. At the end of the period, the accountant would have to think about whether all of the prepaid insurance had been used up by that point and then make the appropriate adjusting entry. For accrued expense such as wages payable, an adjusting entry would be made at the end of the year to reflect wages earned but not yet paid.

Adjusting entries are made at the end of the fiscal period to make sure that revenues, expenses, assets, and liabilities are appropriately accounted for under accrual-basis accounting. Common adjusting entries include:

1. Accruing of interest receivable (interest income) and interest payable (interest expense)
2. Accruing expiration of various prepaid assets that are "used up" over time, such as prepaid insurance
3. Accruing revenue earned during a period that had been collected in advance such as magazine subscriptions
4. Recording depreciation expense for a particular time period

> Unethical management might intentionally underestimate discretionary or estimated expenses such as warranty costs in order to try to meet analysts' forecasts or internal performance targets. One role of the audit function is to examine the reasonableness of assumptions used in making the estimates that serve as the basis for many adjustments. To the extent that investors understand this potential manipulation and fully process the information provided them, they are likely to see through the efforts to manage earnings via inappropriate adjustments and will discount the price of the stock of firms that do so.

5. Recording various estimated expenses such as warranties and estimated uncollectible accounts

Real businesses have many adjusting entries to make each time that books are closed. They can have a significant impact on earnings. By their nature, certain adjusting entries involve estimation (for instance, warranty expenses) and require making a number of assumptions (for instance, the useful life and salvage value estimate used in the depreciation calculation). There may also be different allowable methods that can be used according to GAAP (for instance, several methods of calculating depreciation expense are permitted).

Because management must exercise judgment in the assumptions used and the estimates made in adjusting entries, there is always a concern by investors and auditors that management may have an incentive to inappropriately exercise their judgment to their own benefit. For instance, they might try to overstate earnings to meet an earnings target tied to a bonus payment. Given the size of certain adjustments, this could have a material effect on the outcome. The role of adjusting entries in financial reporting cannot be overestimated.

ILLUSTRATION OF ADJUSTING ENTRIES

Because adjusting entries are specific to each individual company, it is not practical to illustrate every possible adjustment a company might make to its books. The following information covers four representative adjusting entries that might be made by BHT. Recall the BHT example used in Chapter 3 and assume that BHT is closing its books at the end of the first quarter of 20X2 (March 31). The following information is available about BHT prior to closing the books.

1. BHT pays interest annually on December 31 on the $400 million note borrowed at the end of 20X0. Recall that the note carries an interest rate of 7 percent and that BHT would therefore pay $28 million in interest expense on December 31, 20X1.

2. BHT has subleased a portion of its warehouse space to another business starting on January 1, 20X2. The lessee paid BHT $36 million for 6 months rent on January 1, 20X2. BHT recorded the cash received and a credit to Unearned Rent as follows on January 1, 20X2:

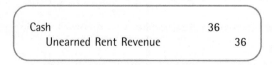

Cash	36	
Unearned Rent Revenue		36

3. BHT recognizes depreciation expense on the fixtures for the quarter ending March 31, 20X2 in the amount of $15 million (three months of depreciation). Recall that BHT uses the straight-line depreciation method and annually records $60 million in depreciation expense.

4. Starting on January 1, 20X2, BHT agrees to provide explicit warranty coverage on the products it sells. BHT estimates product warranty costs on product sales for the period January 1 through March 31, 20X2 to be $20 million. By March 31, 20X2, it has received no claims against this warranty.

5. On March 31, 20X2, BHT owes $4 million in accrued wages.

6. On January 1, 20X2, BHT paid $12 million for a one-year insurance policy covering the period January 1, 20X2 through December 31, 20X2. The insurance policy was recorded as Prepaid Insurance on January 1.

The appropriate adjusting entries for this scenario are as follows:

Transaction #	Account		
1.	Interest expense	7	
	Interest payable		7
2.	Unearned rent revenue	18	
	Rent revenue		18
3.	Depreciation expense	15	
	Accumulated depreciation		15
4.	Warranty expense	20	
	Warranty liability		20
5.	Wage expense	4	
	Wages payable		4
6.	Insurance expense	3	
	Prepaid insurance		3

In entry 1, the amount of interest expense is for one quarter of the year and is therefore one quarter of the annual amount or $7 million ($400 million × 7 percent × .25). In entry 2, half of the six-month rental period has passed as of March 31, so half of the rent should be recognized as having been earned. Entries 3 through 5 require no additional calculation. In entry 6, the annual premium of $12 million is assumed to be used up on a pro-rata basis (i.e., equal amounts each month). Therefore, $1 million is used up each month and this means that for the quarter, $3 million should be expensed. Note that each of the previous transactions affects a revenue or an expense account as well as an asset or liability. Also, none of the transactions involves cash.

APPENDIX **B**

Time Value of Money

To gain an appreciation for the time value of money, consider the following situation. Robin, a college student on a reasonably tight budget, would like to raise some cash. She has a compact disc player that she would like to sell. John and Samantha have made her separate offers to buy the CD player. John has offered her $300 today. Samantha has made a higher offer, $330, but she will not have the cash for another two months. Regardless of what offer Robin accepts, she has agreed to exchange the CD player today. Which offer should Robin accept? Before you read on, come to some decision about what you think Robin should do and why.

There are numerous reasons why Robin might accept John's or Samantha's offer. John's offer is attractive because she gets the cash immediately. This may be important because she may need to eat. If she has run out of money, it may not be feasible to wait two months to collect from Samantha, even though she is offering more money. Another reason that John's offer is attractive is that collecting the cash presents no risk. John will hand over the cash as Robin hands over the CD. With Samantha's offer, there is some possibility that Robin will never be paid the $330.

A third reason for accepting John's offer is that if Robin doesn't have to use the money to live, she can invest the $300 today and have more than $300 two months from now. For this reason, it is inappropriate to compare the $300 offer directly with the $330 offer. It is more appropriate to compare what the $300 would be worth two months from now with the $330 offer. In the terminology of the time value of money, the $300 is a **present value** and the $330 is a **future value.** To compare them on a dollar-for-dollar basis, Robin would have to calculate either what the $300 would be worth in two months (its future value) or what the $330 would be worth today (its present value).

Assume that Robin takes the approach of calculating what the $300 offer would be worth two months from now. How much the $300 will generate will depend on what investment opportunities are available to her. For instance, suppose that the best she can do is invest at 10% interest. The $300 could earn $5 in two months ($300 × 10% × 2/12). She would, therefore, have $305 at the end of two months. This is clearly less than the $330 that Samantha is offering, which makes Samantha's offer more attractive. But Robin might also want to consider the riskiness of her investment compared to the risk that Samantha won't pay. For instance, if she invests in wildcat oil wells (a risky investment) and no oil is found, her $300 investment may be lost. In this case, it may be more risky to invest than to accept the risk that Samantha won't pay.

The advantage of Samantha's offer is clearly that it is for more money. Compared with the next best investment she can make (invest at 10%), it is clearly superior (assuming that accepting Samantha's offer and investing have similar risks). To make the offers equivalent on a dollar-for-dollar basis, Robin would have to be able to earn a 60% return on her $300 investment ($300 × 60% × 2/12 = $30).

A firm faces many decisions similar to this example where cash flows occur at different periods of time under various alternatives. The only way to compare the dollar amounts adequately is to use time value of money concepts and computations. One standard approach is to calculate the present value of all alternatives and then compare them. All other things being equal, the firm would choose the option that produced the highest present value. Unfortunately, all other things are not usually equal. As our example points out, there may be differences in the risk associated with the alternatives. It may also be that the firm has objectives other than maximizing the present value; that is, it may need to spend its money in other ways to survive, just as Robin may need to get the cash immediately in order to eat. A firm, for instance, may have a loan coming due, may need cash immediately, and cannot wait to receive cash in the future.

Decisions comparing the present value of alternatives are not the subject of this book. The accountant generally is faced with recording the results of the decisions already made by management or providing data for management to make those decisions. Time value of money considerations enter into the accountant's work when a present-value method is used to record the results of a particular transaction. There are at least two situations in which present-value methods are used under GAAP. The first situation is in the accounting for liabilities. Most liabilities are carried on the firm's books at their net present value under GAAP. Interest on these liabilities is then recorded over time based on time value of money calculations. The second situation in which present values are used is in the accounting for long-term receivables. These receivables, on the books of a lender, are the mirror image of the long-term liabilities that appear on the books of a borrower.

FUTURE VALUE

In the example of Robin and the CD player, the future value of an amount was calculated based on the present value, an assumed interest rate, and the time period between the present and future dates. There are many contexts in which a firm or an individual has to make a future-value calculation of this type. For instance, if you are saving money for a future purchase, like a car or a house, you would like to know how long it will take to accumulate the appropriate amount (the future value) based on the amount deposited in a savings account and the rate of interest offered. In a corporate context, a firm might like to know whether it will have sufficient funds available from its investments to pay a liability that comes due at some future date.

To illustrate the calculation of a future value, consider a simple example. Suppose that $100 is invested in a bank savings account that pays interest at a 10% annual rate. (Interest rates are always stated as an annual rate unless otherwise indicated.) How much will be in the savings accounts at the end of the year? The simple answer is $110. The calculation of the interest is as follows:

$$\text{Interest} = \text{Principal} \times \text{Interest Rate} \times \text{Time}$$
$$= \$100 \times 10\%/\text{year} \times 1 \text{ year} = \$10$$

In addition to calculating the interest, we could also represent the ending balance in the account with an equation. The amount at the end of the period could be calculated using the following formula:

$$\text{Ending Balance} = \text{Beginning Balance} + \text{Interest}$$
$$= \text{Beginning Balance} + (\text{Principal} \times \text{Interest Rate} \times \text{Time})$$
$$= \$100 + (\$100 \times .1/\text{year} \times 1 \text{ year}) = \$110$$

Another way to express the relationship is to use the terminology of the time value of money. The *principal* is the *present value,* and the *interest rate* is sometimes referred to as the **discount rate.** The *beginning balance* is the same as the *present value,* and the *ending balance* is the *future value.* The formula to calculate the ending balance (future value) is then:

Calculation of Ending Balance—First Year:

$$\text{Ending Balance} = \text{Beginning Balance} + (\text{Principal} \times \text{Interest Rate} \times \text{Time})$$

If we let:

$$PV = \text{Present Value}$$
$$FV = \text{Future Value}$$
$$r = \text{Discount rate per period}$$

then:

$$FV = PV + (PV \times r \times 1)$$

Simplifying this yields:

$$FV = PV \times (1 + r)$$
$$= \$100 \times (1 + .1) = \$110$$

How much will be in the account at the end of the second year? The answer depends on whether the interest that was earned in the first year is left in the account or withdrawn and whether the bank then pays interest on the interest that is left in the account. If the bank does not add the interest to the principal before it calculates the interest in the following period, then the interest calculation is said to be one of **simple interest.** In the case of simple interest, the interest earned in the second period will be the same as the first period as long as the principal is not changed. In most situations involving more than one year, simple interest is not used. Most banks would calculate **compound interest,** which means that the interest earned in one period is added to the principal and then earns interest in the next period. The standard assumption used in all the discussion that follows is that interest is not withdrawn at the end of the period and is compounded. In our example, this means that the $110 that existed at the end of the first year then earns interest in the second year, producing $11 in interest ($110 × 10%) for an ending balance of $121. The formulation for the situation in the second year would be (the time variable is dropped at this point and is assumed to be one year):

Calculation of Ending Balance—Second Year:

$$\text{Ending Balance} = \text{Beginning Balance} + (\text{Principal} \times \text{Interest Rate})$$

If we let:

$$PV = \text{Present Value}$$

$$FV_i = \text{Future Value}$$

where i represents the year

$$r = \text{Discount rate per year}$$

then:

$$FV_2 = FV_1 \times (1 + r)$$

where FV_1 is the value at the end of the year 1. Substituting for FV_1 from the equation shown earlier, we get:

$$FV_2 = \left[PV \times (1 + r) \right] \times (1 + r)$$

$$= PV \times (1 + r)^2$$

$$= \$100 \times (1 + .1)^2 = \$121$$

This result can be generalized to N years into the future so that the relationship between present and future values is as follows:

Future-Value Formula: $FV_N = PV \times (1 + r)^N$

This formula applies to what is known as *lump sum amounts,* that is, single cash flows. The future value of a single amount, at the present value (PV), N years into the future, at an interest rate of r per year, can then be calculated by applying this formula.

Note that, in the future-value formula, the last term on the right is only a function of r and N. This last term is called a **future-value factor** and can be summarized in a two-way table with values of r on one dimension and values of N on the other. These factors, which are sometimes called *future value of $1 factors,* are provided in Table B-1 at the end of the appendix. The term $FV_{r,N}$

will be used to represent future value of $1 factors. The formula can then be expressed in terms of the factors as:

Future-Value Formula: $FV_N = PV \times FV_{r,N}$

Suppose that $1,000 is deposited in a savings account today at 12%. What amount will be available in the account by the end of five years, assuming interest is compounded at the end of each year? Using the preceding formula, the factor from the table for $N = 5$ and $r = 12\%$ is used and plugged into the formula:

Future-Value Formula: $FV_5 = \$1,000 \times FV_{12\%,5}$
$= \$1,000 \times 1.76234 = \$1,762.34$

COMPOUNDING PERIODS

In the previous examples, an annual period for compounding interest was used in the computations. Interest can be compounded more often than annually; in fact, most banks compound interest more often than once a year. Some compound it quarterly, some monthly, some daily, and some even compound it on what is known as a continuous basis. How does changing the compound period affect the calculation?

To incorporate a different compounding period into the future-value formulas (and the present-value formulas discussed later), the number of periods N and the interest rate per period r are adjusted to reflect the appropriate compounding period. For instance, in the example of the future-value calculation in which $1,000 was deposited at 12%, compounded annually for five years, suppose that the problem is changed so that interest is compounded semiannually (twice a year). There would now be two compounding periods per year and, therefore, a total of 10 periods over the five years. The interest rate per period would then be adjusted to 6% per period (12%/2 periods per year). The calculation would then be:

Future-Value Formula: $FV_{10} = \$1,000 \times FV_{6\%,10}$
$= \$1,000 \times 1.79085 = \$1,790.85$

Note that the future value is larger when interest is compounded more often (it was $1,762.34, compounded annually). This should make sense because the interest has a greater chance to earn interest itself.

To provide a comparison of the effects of different compounding periods, consider the data in Exhibit B-1, which show the effects of changing the compounding period on a $1 investment for one year. You can see from Exhibit B-1 that the future value increases as the compounding period increases in frequency. The continuous compounding formula will not be discussed because

Exhibit B-1
Effects of Compounding
Periods

Assumptions:

Investment (PV) = $1

Yearly interest rate = 12%

Investment period = 1 year

Compounding Period	r(%)	N	Factor	Future Value
Yearly	12	1	1.12000	$1.12
Semiannually	6	2	1.12360	$1.1236
Quarterly	3	4	1.12551	$1.12551
Monthly	1	12	1.12683	$1.12683
Continuously	a	a	1.12750	$1.12750

[a]The continuous method calculates the ending value of e, where e is the base of the natural logarithms.

it is not used often for accounting purposes. It provides the maximum improvement in return that can be obtained based on changes in the compounding period. On a yearly basis, it is clear that the compounding period affects the return on the investment: yearly compounding yields a 12% return, and monthly compounding yields a 12.683% return. Both investments are based on a 12% interest rate but different compounding periods. The 12% is generally referred to as the **nominal interest rate** and the 12.683% as the **effective interest rate.** Because of differences in the compounding periods, banks in the United States are required to disclose effective interest rates (known as the annual percentage rate or APR) as well as nominal interest rates on the products they offer.

PRESENT VALUE

The calculation of a present value from a future value is simple once the future-value formula is known. Simply rearrange the future-value formula so that the present value appears on one side and the rest of the formula appears on the other. The present-value formula would then be:

$$\text{Present-Value Formula:} \quad PV = FV_N \times \left[1/(1 + r)^N\right]$$

Note again that the second term on the right side of the equation depends only on r and N. Table B-2 at the end of the appendix provides a listing of these present value of $1 factors. The term $PV_{r,N}$ is used to represent the present value of $1 factors. The formula can then be written as:

$$\text{Present-Value Formula:} \quad PV = FV_N \times PV_{r,N}$$

This formula can be used in situations in which the future value is known and the present-value information is needed. For instance, if $1,000 is needed five years from now and you want to know how much should be deposited in the bank today at 8%, compounded annually, to have the $1,000 by then, the calculation would be:

Present-value formula: $PV = \$1,000 \times PV_{8\%,5}$
$$= \$1,000 \times 0.68058 = \$680.58$$

Note that the present-value factors are simply the reciprocals of the future-value factors. Two tables of these factors are not really needed since one can be easily derived from the other by taking the reciprocal.

MULTIPLE CASH FLOWS

The foregoing discussion dealt only with single present values and single future values. In many contexts, however, more than one cash amount is involved. For instance, if the accountant is to record the present value of a loan that is to be repaid with monthly payments over five years, there will be a total of 60 payments. Multiple cash flows can be handled using the formulas that have been derived here. In a present-value problem, the present-value formula derived could simply be applied to each of the cash flows separately and then added together to get the total present value. Future values could be handled in a similar fashion.

ANNUITIES

A special and simplifying situation occurs if the multiple cash flows are equal. This is a fairly common occurrence in business. For instance, most loans are structured such that the payments are the same. Many lease agreements also call for equal payments over an extended period of time.

A stream of cash flows in which the amounts are the same is called an *annuity.* Annuities are characterized in two ways. The first is how many payments are included. The second is the timing of the payments, in particular, the timing of the first in the series of payments. An annuity in which the first cash flow (payment) comes at the end of the first time period is known as an *ordinary annuity.* It is also sometimes referred to as an **annuity in arrears.** Most equal-payment loans are structured as ordinary annuities. The first payment comes a month after the loan is made.

An annuity in which the first payment comes at the beginning of the first time period is called an *annuity due,* or sometimes an **annuity in advance.** Most rent agreements and leases are structured as annuities in advance.

Annuities in which the first payment is delayed beyond the end of the first period are referred to as **deferred annuities.** Some annuities are structured so that there is no terminal date; that is, the payments are theoretically paid forever. Such annuities are called **perpetuities,** and they can either be *in advance* or *in arrears.*

ANNUITIES IN ARREARS (ORDINARY ANNUITIES)

The present or the future value of an annuity in arrears can be calculated by applying the formulas developed earlier to each of the payments, separately and then adding them together. A more efficient way is to take into consideration the simplifications that result when the payments are equal.

Consider the situation of an annuity in arrears for N periods. The following time line represents the pattern of payments (referred to as PMT):

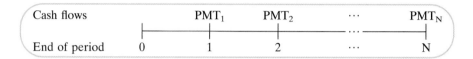

To develop an equation to calculate the present value of the annuity, start by creating a formula for the sum of the individual cash payments using the formula developed earlier. The equation would be as follows:

$$\text{Total present value} = PV_1 + PV_2 + \cdots + PV_N$$

where PV_i is the present value of payment i. Substituting the formula for each PV_i:

$$\text{Total present value} = (PMT_1 \times PV_{r,1}) + (PMT_2 \times PV_{r,2}) + \cdots + (PMT_N + PV_{r,N})$$

Now recognize that $PMT_1 + PMT_2 = \cdots = PMT_N = PMT$, and simplify the preceding equation:

$$\text{Total present value} = PMT \times (PV_{r,1} + PV_{r,2} + \cdots + PV_{r,N})$$

Note that the last term (i.e., the sum of the present-value factors) is a function of only the interest rate and the number of periods. It is, therefore, a **present-value factor** *for an annuity in arrears*. It can be expressed in a simplified formula (which will not be derived) as:

Present value of an annuity in arrears factor:
$$PV_{A,r,N} = (PV_{r,1} + PV_{r,2} + \cdots + PV_{r,N})$$
$$= \frac{\left[1 - (1 + r)^{-N}\right]}{r}$$
where $PV_{A,r,N}$ is the annuity in arrears factor for N periods at r% interest.

The formula for the present value of an annuity in arrears can then be expressed as:

Present value of an annuity in arrears formula: $PV = PMT \times PV_{A,r,N}$

The present value of an annuity in arrears factors appear in Table B-3 at the end of the appendix. To illustrate the usage of this formula, assume that the payments on a loan are $300 a month for three years at an interest rate of 12%. Calculate the present value of these payments (i.e., the principal of the loan). Note that since the loan requires monthly payments, the compounding period is, implicitly, monthly. To calculate the present value, the following calculation would be made:

> Present value of an annuity in arrears formula:
> $$PV = \$300 \times PV_{A,1\%,36}$$
> $$= \$300 \times 30.10751 = \$9,032.25$$

The present value of an annuity in arrears formula can also be rearranged to calculate the payments required to pay off a loan, given the principal of the loan, the interest rate, and the number of payment periods. Suppose that you want to borrow \$15,000 to buy a car. The bank will lend you money for three years at 12%, with monthly payments. The calculation is:

> Annuity in arrears payment formula: $PMT = PV/PV_{A,1\%,36}$
> $$= \$15,000/30.10751 = \$498.21/month$$

The future value of an annuity can also be calculated using the formula derived for the lump sum amounts. Again, because of the unique nature of annuities, a simplified formula exists for calculating the future value of an annuity in arrears. The formula is as follows:

> Future value of an annuity in arrears factor:
> $$FV_{A,r,N} = (FV_{r,1} + FV_{r,2} + \cdots + FV_{r,N})$$
> $$= \frac{[(1 + r)^N - 1]}{r}$$
> where $FV_{A,r,N}$ is the future value of an annuity in arrears factor for N periods at r% interest.

The future value of an annuity in arrears formula then becomes:

> Future value of an annuity in arrears formula: $FV_N = PMT \times FV_{A,r,N}$

The future value of an annuity in arrears factors appear in Table B-4 at the end of this appendix.

To use this formula, suppose that you were able to save \$100 each month out of your paycheck. You deposit this amount at the end of each month in a savings account that pays interest at 12%, compounded monthly. You want to know how much you will have accumulated in the savings account at the end of two years. This is a future-value question that can be solved as follows:

> $$FV_N = PMT \times FV_{A,r,N}$$
> $$FV_{24} = \$100 \times FV_{A,1\%,24}$$
> $$FV_{24} = \$100 \times 26.97346 = \$2,697.35$$

In another situation, you might want to know how much you must save every month to accumulate a certain amount in the future. Suppose that you want to save $10,000 for a down payment on a house. You want to accumulate it over a five-year period, and you can invest your money at 8%, compounded quarterly. How much must you deposit at the end of each quarter to accumulate the $10,000? The solution can be found by rearranging the future value of an annuity in arrears formula to allow you to calculate the payment:

$$PMT = FV_N / FV_{A,r,N}$$
$$PMT = FV_{20} / FV_{A,2\%,20}$$
$$= \$10{,}000 / 24.29737 = \$411.57 \text{ per quarter}$$

ANNUITIES IN ADVANCE

An *annuity in advance* differs from an annuity in arrears only in that the first payment is made at the beginning of the first period rather than at the end. The same total number of payments are made. The following time line shows the pattern of payments for an N-period annuity in advance.

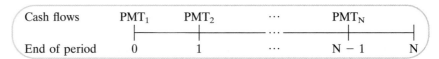

Cash flows	PMT_1	PMT_2	$\cdots$	PMT_N	
End of period	0	1	$\cdots$	N − 1	N

Notice that the first payment comes at the beginning of period 1 and the last payment comes at the beginning of period N.

A present-value factor for an annuity in advance can be derived in the same way as the one developed for the annuity in arrears factor. However, knowledge of the annuity in arrears factors will be used to calculate the present value of the annuity in advance problem.

The trick to using the annuity in arrears factors in an annuity in advance problem is to make the annuity in advance problem look like an annuity in arrears problem. To do this, look at the N-period annuity in advance time line and cover up the first cash flow. This leaves N-1 remaining cash flows, the first of which comes at the end of the first period. This is an annuity in arrears problem for N-1 periods. You already know how to find this present value. The present value of the cash flow that was covered up is equal to the payment itself since it comes at time zero. Therefore, if this payment is added to the present value of the annuity in arrears for N-1 periods, the present value of the annuity in advance is obtained. In a formula, this relationship can be shown as follows:

$$PV \text{ annuity} = PV \text{ of first cash flow} + PV \text{ or remaining N-1 cash flows in advance}$$
$$= PMT + (PMT \times PV_{A,r,N-1})$$

This can then be simplified as follows:

$$PV \text{ annuity in advance} = PMT \times (PV_{A,r,N-1} + 1)$$

The last term in this expression (in parentheses) is the factor for an annuity in advance problem. Note that you multiply this factor by the payment to get the present value. Therefore, the conversion of present value of annuity in arrears factors to present value of annuity in advance factors is to take the present value of annuity in arrears factor for one less period (N-1) and add 1. In many annuity in arrears factor tables (including Table B-3), this conversion is stated in a footnote to the table.

A similar conversion can be made for the future-value factors. The trick, in this case, for making the problem look like an annuity in arrears problem is to add one cash flow. This extra cash flow appears in the diagram below as PMT*.

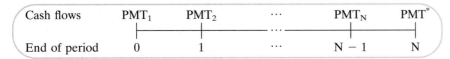

Cash flows	PMT_1	PMT_2	$\cdots$	PMT_N	PMT^*
End of period	0	1	$\cdots$	N − 1	N

The diagram now shows N + 1 payments, which could be viewed as an annuity in arrears if you start at time period −1. You could then use the future value of an annuity in arrears factors to calculate the future value of this annuity at time N. Then, recognizing that the future value of PMT* is equal to PMT, you could subtract PMT from the future value of the annuity, which would leave the future value of the annuity in advance. In a formula, this is expressed as follows:

$$\text{FV annuity} = \text{FV of N + 1 cash flows} - \text{FV of cash flow at time N in advance}$$
$$= (\text{PMT} \times FV_{A,r,N+1}) - \text{PMT}$$

This can then be simplified to:

$$\text{FV annuity in advance} = \text{PMT} \times (FV_{A,r,N+1} - 1)$$

The conversion is, therefore, to take the annuity in arrears factor for one more period (N + 1) and subtract 1. Again, this conversion appears in the footnote to Table B-4.

Consider a problem in which a company decides to rent a piece of equipment for five years. It will make yearly payments of $1,000 each, in advance. If the firm can invest its money at 10%, how much would it have to put in the bank today to allow it to make the payments from the bank account? In other words, what is the present value of the payments the firm has to make? This is an annuity in advance problem. It can be solved as follows:

$$\text{PV annuity in advance} = \text{PMT} \times (PV_{A,r,N-1} + 1)$$
$$= \$1,000 \times (PV_{A,10\%,4} + 1)$$
$$= \$1,000 \times (3.16987 + 1) = \$4,169.87$$

PERPETUITIES

A perpetuity is a special case of an annuity since it has no ending date (the cash flows continue forever). In this case, the formula for the present value simplifies even more and becomes:

$$\text{PV perpetuity in arrears} = \text{PMT}/r$$
$$\text{PV perpetuity in advance} = \text{PMT} + (\text{PMT}/r) = \text{PMT}(1 + 1/r)$$

As an example of the use of a perpetuity calculation, consider the problem of trying to establish the appropriate price to acquire another firm. While there are several ways analysts may estimate the value of a firm, as discussed in Chapter 14, one approach is to estimate the free cash flows that would occur in the future and discount them using an appropriate discount rate. A rough estimate can be made if the analyst estimates the average amount of free cash flow the firm generates each year. Using this estimate and assuming that the firm can continue to generate this level of free cash flows forever, the present value can be calculated using the perpetuity formula. For instance, if you estimate that the firm can generate $100,000 a year in free cash flow for the foreseeable future and you estimate that 10% is an appropriate discount rate for the riskiness of the firm, then the market value of the firm should be the present value of the perpetuity of cash flows. This would be $1 million ($100,000/10%).

INTERNAL RATES OF RETURN

In the formulas and problems discussed earlier, we were interested in calculating the present value, the future value, or the payments, given information about the number of periods and the interest rate. We treated the interest rate as having been given in these problems. In some situations, the interest rate is not explicitly given but is implicit in the structure of the cash flows. For instance, a non-interest-bearing note would state the proceeds from the note (the original principal) and the amount due at maturity. No interest rate would be stated in the contract. The interest, of course, is the difference between the proceeds at issuance and the amount repaid at maturity. To calculate the implicit interest rate, consider the following example.

Suppose that a firm issues a note (i.e., borrowed money) for $1,000 that requires repayment in two years at $1,210. The $1,000 is the present value of the loan, and the $1,210 is the future value. The interest paid over the life of the note is $210, but no explicit interest rate is stated. The interest rate could be calculated by making some assumptions about how interest is compounded and making use of the formulas derived earlier. Suppose it is assumed that interest is compounded annually. This means that there are two periods between the present value and the future value. The interest rate can then be found using the present-value formula for a lump sum:

Present-value formula: $PV = FV_N \times [1/(1 + r)^N]$
$$\$1{,}000 = \$1{,}210 \times [1/(1 + r)^2]$$

To solve for r in the preceding equation, two strategies may be employed. The first is to solve the quadratic equation for r. This requires that you know how to solve a quadratic equation. While many readers may know how to solve this equation, imagine the situation where $N = 15$ rather than $N = 2$. The equation then becomes much more difficult. The second approach to solving this equation is to make a guess at the appropriate value for r and then compare the right side of the equation to the left side. If the right side is higher, then you know that the r you picked was too low. You then try a higher value of r and recalculate the right side. You continue to iterate this process until the right side equals the left side. When they are equal, you have found the interest rate that equates the future value with the present value. This rate is known as the **internal rate of return.**

If you have only the formula or the tables to work with, the calculation of the internal rate of return is probably best done using the iteration procedure. If, on the other hand, you have access to a sophisticated calculator or a

$$PV = FV_N \times PV_{r,N}$$

$$\$1,000 = \$1,210 \times PV_{r,2}$$

Interest Rate, %	Value of Right–Hand Side	Decision
8	$\$1,210 \times 0.85734 = \$1,037$	Rate too low
12	$\$1,210 \times 0.79719 = \$965$	Rate too high
10	$\$1,210 \times 0.82645 = \$1,000$	Correct Rate

computer with a spreadsheet package, the calculation of the internal rate of return is usually a built-in function. You simply have to plug in the cash flows and invoke the built-in function. This is a much more efficient way to solve for the internal rate of return than the iterative procedure.

To illustrate the iterative procedure, Exhibit B-2 presents the calculation of the internal rate of return for the problem just posed. The initial guess is 8%.

SUMMARY PROBLEM

As a final example, consider a situation with multiple sets of cash flows. Suppose that a firm wants to borrow money from a lender. The firm wants to borrow the money for seven years. The firm has determined that it can afford to make periodic payments of $75 at the end of each six months (a small dollar amount is used in the example, but you can add more zeros to make the amounts larger and more realistic). The firm also agrees to make a large payment (sometimes called a *balloon payment*) of $1,000 (in addition to the last $75 payment) at the end of the seven years.

Under the conditions outlined earlier, what would the lender be willing to lend to the company? The lender would have to determine what the payments would be worth based on an appropriate interest rate. Suppose the lender wants to earn 12%. The lender would present-value the cash flows to be received from the firm at the 12% discount rate. The present value will then tell the lender what amount can be lent in order to result in a return on the investment of 12%.

The loan is structured such that there are to be 14 payments (7 years × 2 payments per year) of $75 each and a final payment of $1,000 at the end of the 14 six-month periods. This is an annuity in arrears and a lump sum. The interest rate per period is 6%. The present value of the cash flows is calculated as follows:

$$
\begin{aligned}
PV &= PV \text{ (annuity in arrears)} + PV \text{ (lump-sum)} \\
&= PMT \times PV_{A,r,N} + FV_N \times PV_{r,N} \\
&= \$75 \times PV_{A,6\%,14} + \$1,000 \times PV_{6\%,14} \\
&= \$75 \times 9.29498 + \$1,000 \times 0.44230 \\
&= \$697.12 + 442.30 = \$1,139.42
\end{aligned}
$$

The $1,139.42 is the amount the lender should be willing to lend the firm. If the lender lends this amount to the firm and receives the $75 periodic payments and the $1,000 at the end, the lender will have earned 12% (compounded semi-annually). The preceding calculation is exactly the same as the one used to calculate the price of a bond or note.

Periods	0.50%	0.75%	1.00%	1.50%	2.00%	3.00%	4.00%	5.00%	6.00%	7.00%	8.00%
1	1.00500	1.00750	1.01000	1.01500	1.02000	1.03000	1.04000	1.05000	1.06000	1.07000	1.08000
2	1.01003	1.01506	1.02010	1.03023	1.04040	1.06090	1.08160	1.10250	1.12360	1.14490	1.16640
3	1.01508	1.02267	1.03030	1.04568	1.06121	1.09273	1.12486	1.15763	1.19102	1.22504	1.25971
4	1.02015	1.03034	1.04060	1.06136	1.08243	1.12551	1.16986	1.21551	1.26248	1.31080	1.36049
5	1.02525	1.03807	1.05101	1.07728	1.10408	1.15927	1.21665	1.27828	1.33823	1.40255	1.46933
6	1.03038	1.04585	1.06152	1.09344	1.12616	1.19405	1.26532	1.34010	1.41852	1.50073	1.58687
7	1.03553	1.05370	1.07214	1.10984	1.14869	1.22987	1.31593	1.40710	1.50363	1.60578	1.71382
8	1.04071	1.06160	1.08286	1.12649	1.17166	1.26677	1.36857	1.47746	1.59385	1.71819	1.85093
9	1.04591	1.06956	1.09369	1.14339	1.19509	1.30477	1.42331	1.55133	1.68948	1.83846	1.99900
10	1.05114	1.07758	1.10462	1.16054	1.21899	1.34392	1.48024	1.62889	1.79085	1.96715	2.15892
11	1.05640	1.08566	1.11567	1.17795	1.24337	1.38423	1.53945	1.71034	1.89830	2.10485	2.33164
12	1.06168	1.09381	1.12683	1.19562	1.26824	1.42576	1.60103	1.79586	2.01220	2.25219	2.51817
13	1.06699	1.10201	1.13809	1.21355	1.29361	1.46853	1.66507	1.88565	2.13293	2.40985	2.71962
14	1.07232	1.11028	1.14947	1.23176	1.31948	1.51259	1.73168	1.97993	2.26090	2.57853	2.93719
15	1.07768	1.11860	1.16097	1.25023	1.34587	1.55797	1.80094	2.07893	2.39656	2.75903	3.17217
16	1.08307	1.12699	1.17258	1.26899	1.37279	1.60471	1.87298	2.18287	2.54035	2.95216	3.42594
17	1.08849	1.13544	1.18430	1.28802	1.40024	1.65285	1.94790	2.29202	2.69277	3.15882	3.70002
18	1.09393	1.14396	1.19615	1.30734	1.42825	1.70243	2.02582	2.40662	2.85434	3.37993	3.99602
19	1.09940	1.15254	1.20811	1.32695	1.45681	1.75351	2.10685	2.52695	3.02560	3.61653	4.31570
20	1.10490	1.16118	1.22019	1.34686	1.48595	1.80611	2.19112	2.65330	3.20714	3.86968	4.66096
24	1.12716	1.19641	1.26973	1.42950	1.60844	2.03279	2.56330	3.22510	4.04893	5.07237	6.34118
36	1.19668	1.30865	1.43077	1.70914	2.03989	2.89828	4.10393	5.79182	8.14725	11.42394	15.96817
48	1.27049	1.43141	1.61223	2.04348	2.58707	4.13225	6.57053	10.40127	16.39387	25.72891	40.21057
60	1.34885	1.56568	1.81670	2.44322	3.28103	5.89160	10.51963	18.67919	32.98769	57.94643	101.2571
120	1.81940	2.45136	3.30039	5.96932	10.76516	34.71099	110.6626	348.9120	1088.188	3357.788	10252.99
240	3.31020	6.00915	10.89255	35.63282	115.8887	1204.853	12246.20	1.22E+05	1.18E+06	1.13E+07	1.05E+08
360	6.02258	14.73058	35.94964	212.7038	1247.561	41821.62	1.36E+06	4.25E+07	1.29E+09	3.79E+10	1.08E+12

(continued)

Table B-1
Future Value of $1

Periods	9.00%	10.00%	11.00%	12.00%	13.00%	14.00%	15.00%	16.00%	18.00%	20.00%	25.00%
1	1.09000	1.10000	1.11000	1.12000	1.13000	1.14000	1.15000	1.16000	1.18000	1.20000	1.25000
2	1.18810	1.21000	1.23210	1.25440	1.27690	1.29960	1.32250	1.34560	1.39240	1.44000	1.56250
3	1.29503	1.33100	1.36763	1.40493	1.44290	1.48154	1.52088	1.56090	1.64303	1.72800	1.95313
4	1.41158	1.46410	1.51807	1.57352	1.63047	1.68896	1.74901	1.81064	1.93878	2.07360	2.44141
5	1.53862	1.61051	1.68506	1.76234	1.84244	1.92541	2.01136	2.10034	2.28776	2.48832	3.05176
6	1.67710	1.77156	1.87041	1.97382	2.08195	2.19497	2.31306	2.43640	2.69955	2.98598	3.81470
7	1.82804	1.94872	2.07616	2.21068	2.35261	2.50227	2.66002	2.82622	3.18547	3.58318	4.76837
8	1.99256	2.14359	2.30454	2.47596	2.65844	2.85259	3.05902	3.27841	3.75886	4.29982	5.96046
9	2.17189	2.35795	2.55804	2.77308	3.00404	3.25195	3.51788	3.80296	4.43545	5.15978	7.45058
10	2.36736	2.59374	2.83942	3.10585	3.39457	3.70722	4.04556	4.41144	5.23384	6.19174	9.31323
11	2.58043	2.85312	3.15176	3.47855	3.83586	4.22623	4.65239	5.11726	6.17593	7.43008	11.64153
12	2.81266	3.13843	3.49845	3.89598	4.33452	4.81790	5.35025	5.93603	7.28759	8.91610	14.55192
13	3.06580	3.45227	3.88328	4.36349	4.89801	5.49241	6.15279	6.88579	8.59936	10.69932	18.18989
14	3.34173	3.79750	4.31044	4.88711	5.53475	6.26135	7.07571	7.98752	10.14724	12.83918	22.73737
15	3.64248	4.17725	4.78459	5.47357	6.25427	7.13794	8.13706	9.26552	11.97375	15.40702	28.42171
16	3.97031	4.59497	5.31089	6.13039	7.06733	8.13725	9.35762	10.74800	14.12902	18.48843	35.52714
17	4.32763	5.05447	5.89509	6.86604	7.98608	9.27646	10.76126	12.46768	16.67225	22.18611	44.40892
18	4.71712	5.55992	6.54355	7.68997	9.02427	10.57517	12.37545	14.46251	19.67325	26.62333	55.51115
19	5.14166	6.11591	7.26334	8.61276	10.19742	12.05569	14.23177	16.77652	23.21444	31.94800	69.38894
20	5.60441	6.72750	8.06231	9.64629	11.52309	13.74349	16.36654	19.46076	27.39303	38.33760	86.73617
24	7.91108	9.84973	12.23916	15.17863	18.78809	23.21221	28.62518	35.23642	53.10901	79.49685	211.7582
36	22.25123	30.91268	42.81808	59.13557	81.43741	111.8342	153.1519	209.1643	387.0368	708.8019	3081.488
48	62.58524	97.10723	149.7970	230.3908	352.9923	538.8065	819.4007	1241.505	2820.567	6319.749	44841.55
60	176.0313	304.4816	524.0572	897.5969	1530.053	2595.919	4383.999	7370.201	20555.14	56347.51	652530.4
120	30987.02	92709.07	274636.0	805680.3	2.34E+06	6.74E+06	1.92E+07	5.43E+07	4.23E+08	3.18E+09	4.26E+11
240	9.60E+08	8.59E+09	7.54E+10	6.49E+11	5.48E+12	4.54E+13	3.69E+14	2.95E+15	1.79E+17	1.01E+19	1.81E+23
360	2.98E+13	7.97E+14	2.07E+16	5.23E+17	1.28E+19	3.06E+20	7.10E+21	1.60E+23	7.45E+25	3.20E+28	7.72E+34

Table B-1
Future Value of $1
(Continued)

Periods	0.50%	0.75%	1.00%	1.50%	2.00%	3.00%	4.00%	5.00%	6.00%	7.00%	8.00%
1	0.99502	0.99256	0.99010	0.98522	0.98039	0.97087	0.96154	0.95238	0.94340	0.93458	0.92593
2	0.99007	0.98517	0.98030	0.97066	0.96117	0.94260	0.92456	0.90703	0.89000	0.87344	0.85734
3	0.98515	0.97783	0.97059	0.95632	0.94232	0.91514	0.88900	0.86384	0.83962	0.81630	0.79383
4	0.98025	0.97055	0.96098	0.94218	0.92385	0.88849	0.85480	0.82270	0.79209	0.76290	0.73503
5	0.97537	0.96333	0.95147	0.92826	0.90573	0.86261	0.82193	0.78353	0.74726	0.71299	0.68058
6	0.97052	0.95616	0.94205	0.91454	0.88797	0.83748	0.79031	0.74622	0.70496	0.66634	0.63107
7	0.96569	0.94904	0.93272	0.90103	0.87056	0.81309	0.75992	0.71068	0.66506	0.62275	0.58349
8	0.96089	0.94198	0.92348	0.88771	0.85349	0.78941	0.73069	0.67684	0.62741	0.58201	0.54027
9	0.95610	0.93496	0.91434	0.87459	0.83676	0.76642	0.70259	0.64461	0.59190	0.54393	0.50025
10	0.95135	0.92800	0.90529	0.86167	0.82035	0.74409	0.67556	0.61391	0.55839	0.50835	0.46319
11	0.94661	0.92109	0.89632	0.84893	0.80426	0.72242	0.64958	0.58468	0.52679	0.47509	0.42888
12	0.94191	0.91424	0.88745	0.83639	0.78849	0.70138	0.62460	0.55684	0.49697	0.44401	0.39711
13	0.93722	0.90743	0.87866	0.82403	0.77303	0.68095	0.60057	0.53032	0.46884	0.41496	0.36770
14	0.93256	0.90068	0.86996	0.81185	0.75788	0.66112	0.57748	0.50507	0.44230	0.38782	0.34046
15	0.92792	0.89397	0.86135	0.79985	0.74301	0.64186	0.55526	0.48102	0.41727	0.36245	0.31524
16	0.92330	0.88732	0.85282	0.78803	0.72845	0.62317	0.53391	0.45811	0.39365	0.33873	0.29189
17	0.91871	0.88071	0.84438	0.77639	0.71416	0.60502	0.51337	0.43630	0.37136	0.31657	0.27027
18	0.91414	0.87416	0.83602	0.76491	0.70016	0.58739	0.49363	0.41552	0.35034	0.29586	0.25025
19	0.90959	0.86765	0.82774	0.75361	0.68643	0.57029	0.47464	0.39573	0.33051	0.27651	0.23171
20	0.90506	0.86119	0.81954	0.74247	0.67297	0.55368	0.45639	0.37689	0.31180	0.25842	0.21455
24	0.88719	0.83583	0.78757	0.69954	0.62172	0.49193	0.39012	0.31007	0.24698	0.19715	0.15770
36	0.83564	0.76415	0.69892	0.58509	0.49022	0.34503	0.24367	0.17266	0.12274	0.08754	0.06262
48	0.78710	0.69861	0.62026	0.48936	0.38654	0.24200	0.15219	0.09614	0.06100	0.03887	0.02487
60	0.74137	0.63870	0.55045	0.40930	0.30478	0.16973	0.09506	0.05354	0.03031	0.01726	0.00988
120	0.54963	0.40794	0.30299	0.16752	0.09289	0.02881	0.00904	0.00287	0.00092	0.00030	0.00010
240	0.30210	0.16641	0.09181	0.02806	0.00863	0.00083	0.00008	0.00001	8.4E−07	8.9E−08	9.5E−09
360	0.16604	0.06789	0.02782	0.00470	0.00080	0.00002	7.4E−07	2.4E−08	7.8E−10	2.6E−11	9.3E−13

(continued)

Table B-2
Present Value of $1

Periods	9.00%	10.00%	11.00%	12.00%	13.00%	14.00%	15.00%	16.00%	18.00%	20.00%	25.00%
1	0.91743	0.90909	0.90090	0.89286	0.88496	0.87719	0.86957	0.86207	0.84746	0.83333	0.80000
2	0.84168	0.82645	0.81162	0.79719	0.78315	0.76947	0.75614	0.74316	0.71818	0.69444	0.64000
3	0.77218	0.75131	0.73119	0.71178	0.69305	0.67497	0.65752	0.64066	0.60863	0.57870	0.51200
4	0.70843	0.68301	0.65873	0.63552	0.61332	0.59208	0.57175	0.55229	0.51579	0.48225	0.40960
5	0.64993	0.62092	0.59345	0.56743	0.54276	0.51937	0.49718	0.47611	0.43711	0.40188	0.32768
6	0.59627	0.56447	0.53464	0.50663	0.48032	0.45559	0.43233	0.41044	0.37043	0.33490	0.26214
7	0.54703	0.51316	0.48166	0.45235	0.42506	0.39964	0.37594	0.35383	0.31393	0.27908	0.20972
8	0.50187	0.46651	0.43393	0.40388	0.37616	0.35056	0.32690	0.30503	0.26604	0.23257	0.16777
9	0.46043	0.42410	0.39092	0.36061	0.33288	0.30751	0.28426	0.26295	0.22546	0.19381	0.13422
10	0.42241	0.38554	0.35218	0.32197	0.29459	0.26974	0.24718	0.22668	0.19106	0.16151	0.10737
11	0.38753	0.35049	0.31728	0.28748	0.26070	0.23662	0.21494	0.19542	0.16192	0.13459	0.08590
12	0.35553	0.31863	0.28584	0.25668	0.23071	0.20756	0.18691	0.16846	0.13722	0.11216	0.06872
13	0.32618	0.28966	0.25751	0.22917	0.20416	0.18207	0.16253	0.14523	0.11629	0.09346	0.05498
14	0.29925	0.26333	0.23199	0.20462	0.18068	0.15971	0.14133	0.12520	0.09855	0.07789	0.04398
15	0.27454	0.23939	0.20900	0.18270	0.15989	0.14010	0.12289	0.10793	0.08352	0.06491	0.03518
16	0.25187	0.21763	0.18829	0.16312	0.14150	0.12289	0.10686	0.09304	0.07078	0.05409	0.02815
17	0.23107	0.19784	0.16963	0.14564	0.12522	0.10780	0.09293	0.08021	0.05998	0.04507	0.02252
18	0.21199	0.17986	0.15282	0.13004	0.11081	0.09456	0.08081	0.06914	0.05083	0.03756	0.01801
19	0.19449	0.16351	0.13768	0.11611	0.09806	0.08295	0.07027	0.05961	0.04308	0.03130	0.01441
20	0.17843	0.14864	0.12403	0.10367	0.08678	0.07276	0.06110	0.05139	0.03651	0.02608	0.01153
24	0.12640	0.10153	0.08170	0.06588	0.05323	0.04308	0.03493	0.02838	0.01883	0.01258	0.00472
36	0.04494	0.03235	0.02335	0.01691	0.01228	0.00894	0.00653	0.00478	0.00258	0.00141	0.00032
48	0.01598	0.01031	0.00668	0.00434	0.00283	0.00186	0.00122	0.00081	0.00035	0.00016	0.00002
60	0.00568	0.00328	0.00191	0.00111	0.00065	0.00039	0.00023	0.00014	0.00005	0.00002	1.5E−06
120	0.00003	0.00001	3.6E−06	1.2E−06	4.3E−07	1.5E−07	5.2E−08	1.8E−08	2.4E−09	3.1E−10	2.3E−12
240	1.0E−09	1.2E−10	1.3E−11	1.5E−12	1.8E−13	2.2E−14	2.7E−15	3.4E−16	5.6E−18	9.9E−20	5.5E−24
360	3.4E−14	1.3E−15	4.8E−17	1.9E−18	7.8E−13	3.3E−21	1.4E−22	6.2E−24	1.3E−26	3.1E−29	1.3E−35

Table B-2
Present Value of $1
(Continued)

Periods	0.50%	0.75%	1.00%	1.50%	2.00%	3.00%	4.00%	5.00%	6.00%	7.00%	8.00%
1	0.99502	0.99256	0.99010	0.98522	0.98039	0.97087	0.96154	0.95238	0.94340	0.93458	0.92593
2	1.98510	1.97772	1.97040	1.95588	1.94156	1.91347	1.88609	1.85941	1.83339	1.80802	1.78326
3	2.97025	2.95556	2.94099	2.91220	2.88388	2.82861	2.77509	2.72325	2.67301	2.62432	2.57710
4	3.95050	3.92611	3.90197	3.85438	3.80773	3.71710	3.62990	3.54595	3.46511	3.38721	3.31213
5	4.92587	4.88944	4.85343	4.78264	4.71346	4.57971	4.45182	4.32948	4.21236	4.10020	3.99271
6	5.89638	5.84560	5.79548	5.69719	5.60143	5.41719	5.24214	5.07569	4.91732	4.76654	4.62288
7	6.86207	6.79464	6.72819	6.59821	6.47199	6.23028	6.00205	5.78637	5.58238	5.38929	5.20637
8	7.82296	7.73661	7.65168	7.48593	7.32548	7.01969	6.73274	6.46321	6.20979	5.97130	5.74664
9	8.77906	8.67158	8.56602	8.36052	8.16224	7.78611	7.43533	7.10782	6.80169	6.51523	6.24689
10	9.73041	9.59958	9.47130	9.22218	8.98259	8.53020	8.11090	7.72173	7.36009	7.02358	6.71008
11	10.67703	10.52067	10.36763	10.07112	9.78685	9.25262	8.76048	8.30641	7.88687	7.49867	7.13896
12	11.61893	11.43491	11.25508	10.90751	10.57534	9.95400	9.38507	8.86325	8.38384	7.94269	7.53608
13	12.44615	12.34235	12.13374	11.73153	11.34837	10.63496	9.98565	9.39357	8.85268	8.35765	7.90378
14	13.48871	13.24302	13.00370	12.54338	12.10625	11.29607	10.56312	9.89864	9.29498	8.74547	8.24424
15	14.41662	14.13699	13.86505	13.34323	12.84926	11.93794	11.11839	10.37966	9.71225	9.10791	8.55948
16	15.33993	15.02431	14.71787	14.13126	13.57771	12.56110	11.65230	10.83777	10.10590	9.44665	8.85137
17	16.25863	15.90502	15.56225	14.90765	14.29187	13.16612	12.16567	11.27407	10.47726	9.76322	9.12164
18	17.17277	16.77918	16.39827	15.67256	14.99203	13.75351	12.65930	11.68959	10.82760	10.05909	9.37189
19	18.08236	17.64683	17.22601	16.42617	15.67846	14.32380	13.13394	12.08532	11.15812	10.33560	9.60360
20	18.98742	18.50802	18.04555	17.16864	16.35143	14.87747	13.59033	12.46221	11.46992	10.59401	9.81815
24	22.56287	21.88915	21.24339	20.03041	18.91393	16.93554	15.24696	13.79864	12.55036	11.46933	10.52876
36	32.87102	31.44681	30.10751	27.66068	25.48884	21.83225	18.90828	16.54685	14.62099	13.03521	11.71719
48	42.58032	40.18478	37.97396	34.04255	30.67312	25.26671	21.19513	18.07716	15.65003	13.73047	12.18914
60	51.72556	48.17337	44.95504	39.38027	34.76089	27.67556	22.62349	18.92929	16.16143	14.03918	12.37655
120	90.07345	78.94169	69.70052	55.49845	45.35539	32.37302	24.77409	19.94268	16.65135	14.28146	12.49878
240	139.58077	111.14495	90.81942	64.79573	49.56855	33.30567	24.99796	19.99984	16.66665	14.28571	12.50000
360	166.79161	124.28187	97.21833	66.35324	49.95992	33.33254	24.99998	20.00000	16.66667	14.28571	12.50000

(continued)

Table B-3
Present Value of an Annuity
in Arrears

Periods	9.00%	10.00%	11.00%	12.00%	13.00%	14.00%	15.00%	16.00%	18.00%	20.00%	25.00%
1	0.91743	0.90909	0.90090	0.89286	0.88496	0.87719	0.86957	0.86207	0.84746	0.83333	0.80000
2	1.75911	1.73554	1.71252	1.69005	1.66810	1.64666	1.62571	1.60523	1.56564	1.52778	1.44000
3	2.53129	2.48685	2.44371	2.40183	2.36115	2.32163	2.28323	2.24589	2.17427	2.10648	1.95200
4	3.23972	3.16987	3.10245	3.03735	2.97447	2.91371	2.85498	2.79818	2.69006	2.58873	2.36160
5	3.88965	3.79079	3.69590	3.60478	3.51723	3.43308	3.35216	3.27429	3.12717	2.99061	2.68928
6	4.48592	4.35526	4.23054	5.11141	3.99755	3.88867	3.78448	3.68474	3.49760	3.32551	2.95142
7	5.03295	4.86842	4.71220	4.56376	4.42261	4.28830	4.16042	4.03857	3.81153	3.60459	3.16114
8	5.53482	5.33493	5.14612	4.96764	4.79877	4.63886	4.48732	4.34359	4.07757	3.83716	3.32891
9	5.99525	5.75902	5.53705	5.32825	5.13166	4.94637	4.77158	4.60654	4.30302	4.03097	3.46313
10	6.41766	6.14457	5.88923	5.65022	5.42624	5.21612	5.01877	4.83323	4.49409	4.19247	3.57050
11	6.80519	6.49506	6.20652	5.93770	5.68694	5.45273	5.23371	5.02864	4.65601	4.32706	3.65640
12	7.16073	6.81369	6.49236	6.19437	5.91765	5.66029	5.42062	5.19711	4.79322	4.43922	3.72512
13	7.48690	7.10336	6.74987	6.42355	6.12181	5.84236	5.58315	5.34233	4.90951	4.53268	3.78010
14	7.78615	7.36669	6.98187	6.62817	6.30249	6.00207	5.72448	5.46753	5.00806	4.61057	3.82408
15	8.06069	7.60608	7.19087	6.81086	6.46238	6.14217	5.84737	5.57546	5.09158	4.67547	3.85926
16	8.31256	7.82371	7.37916	6.97399	6.60388	6.26506	5.95423	5.66850	5.16235	4.72956	3.88741
17	8.54363	8.02155	7.54879	7.11963	6.72909	6.37286	6.04716	5.74870	5.22233	4.77463	3.90993
18	8.75563	8.20141	7.70162	7.24967	6.83991	6.46742	6.12797	5.81785	5.27316	4.81219	3.92794
19	8.95011	8.36492	7.83929	7.36578	6.93797	6.55037	6.19823	5.87746	5.31624	4.84350	3.94235
20	9.12855	8.51356	7.96333	7.46944	5.02475	6.62313	6.25933	5.92884	5.35275	4.86958	3.95388
24	9.70661	8.98474	8.34814	7.78432	7.28288	6.83514	6.43377	6.07263	5.45095	4.93710	3.98111
36	10.61176	9.67651	8.87859	8.19241	7.59785	7.07899	6.62314	6.22012	5.54120	4.99295	3.99870
48	10.93358	9.89693	9.03022	8.29716	7.67052	7.12960	6.65853	6.24497	5.55359	4.99921	3.99991
60	11.04799	9.96716	9.07356	8.32405	7.68728	7.14011	6.66515	6.24915	5.55529	4.99991	3.99999
120	11.11075	9.99989	9.09088	8.33332	7.69230	7.14286	6.66667	6.25000	5.55556	5.00000	4.00000
240	11.11111	10.00000	9.09091	8.33333	7.69231	7.14286	6.66667	6.25000	5.55556	5.00000	4.00000
360	11.11111	10.00000	9.09091	8.33333	7.69231	7.14286	6.66667	6.25000	5.55556	5.00000	4.00000

*To compute the present value factor for an annuity in advance, use the arrears factor for one less period and add 1.

Table B-3
Present Value of an Annuity
in Arrears (Continued)

Periods	0.50%	0.75%	1.00%	1.50%	2.00%	3.00%	4.00%	5.00%	6.00%	7.00%	8.00%
1	1.00000	1.00000	1.00000	1.00000	1.00000	1.00000	1.00000	1.00000	1.00000	1.00000	1.00000
2	2.00500	2.00750	2.01000	2.01500	2.02000	2.03000	2.04000	2.05000	2.06000	2.07000	2.08000
3	3.01502	3.02256	3.03010	3.04522	3.06040	3.09090	3.12160	3.15250	3.18360	3.21490	3.24640
4	4.03010	4.04523	4.06040	4.09090	4.12161	4.18363	4.24646	4.31013	4.37462	4.43994	4.50611
5	5.05025	5.07556	5.10101	5.15227	5.20404	5.30914	5.41632	5.52563	5.63709	5.75074	5.86660
6	6.07550	6.11363	6.15202	6.22955	6.30812	6.46841	6.63298	6.80191	6.97532	7.15329	7.33593
7	7.10588	7.15948	7.21354	7.32299	7.43428	7.66246	7.89829	8.14201	8.39384	8.65402	8.92280
8	8.14141	8.21318	8.28567	8.43284	8.58297	8.89234	9.21423	9.54911	9.89747	10.25980	10.63663
9	9.18212	9.27478	9.36853	9.55933	9.75463	10.15911	10.58280	11.02656	11.49132	11.97799	12.48756
10	10.22803	10.34434	10.46221	10.70272	10.94972	11.46388	12.00611	12.57789	13.18079	13.81645	14.48656
11	11.27917	11.42192	11.56683	11.86326	12.16872	12.80780	13.48635	14.20679	14.97164	15.78360	16.64549
12	12.33556	12.50759	12.68250	13.04121	13.41209	14.19203	15.02581	15.91713	16.86994	17.88845	18.97713
13	13.39724	13.60139	13.80933	14.23683	14.68033	15.61779	16.62684	17.71298	18.88214	20.14064	21.49530
14	14.46423	14.70340	14.94742	15.45038	15.97394	17.08632	18.29191	19.59863	21.01507	22.55049	24.21492
15	15.53655	15.81368	16.09690	16.68214	17.29342	18.59891	20.02359	21.57856	23.27597	25.12902	27.15211
16	16.61423	16.93228	17.25786	17.93237	18.63929	20.15688	21.82453	23.65749	25.67253	27.88805	30.32428
17	17.69730	18.05927	18.43044	19.20136	20.01207	21.76159	23.69751	25.84037	28.21888	30.84022	33.75023
18	18.78579	19.19472	19.61475	20.48938	21.41231	23.41444	25.64541	28.13238	30.90565	33.99903	37.45024
19	19.87972	20.33868	20.81090	21.79672	22.84056	25.11687	27.67123	30.53900	33.75999	37.37896	41.44626
20	20.97912	21.49122	22.01900	23.12367	24.29737	26.87037	29.77808	33.06595	36.78559	40.99549	45.76196
24	25.43196	26.18847	26.97346	28.63352	30.42186	34.42647	39.08260	44.50200	50.81558	58.17667	66.76476
36	39.33610	41.15272	43.07688	47.27597	51.99437	63.27594	77.59831	95.83632	119.1209	148.9135	187.1021
48	54.09783	57.52071	61.22261	69.56522	79.35352	104.4084	139.2632	188.0254	256.5645	353.2701	490.1322
60	69.77003	75.42414	81.66967	96.21465	114.0515	163.0534	237.9907	353.5837	533.1282	813.5204	1253.213
120	163.8793	193.5143	230.0387	331.2882	488.2582	1123.700	2741.564	6958.240	18119.80	47954.12	128149.9
240	462.0409	667.8869	989.2554	2308.854	5744.437	40128.42	306130.1	2.43E+06	1.97E+07	1.61E+08	1.31E+09
360	1004.515	1830.743	3494.964	14113.59	62328.06	1.39E+06	3.39E+07	8.50E+08	2.15E+10	5.41E+11	1.35E+13

(continued)

Table B-4
Future Value of an Annuity
in Arrears

Periods	9.00%	10.00%	11.00%	12.00%	13.00%	14.00%	15.00%	16.00%	18.00%	20.00%	25.00%
1	1.00000	1.00000	1.00000	1.00000	1.00000	1.00000	1.00000	1.00000	1.00000	1.00000	1.00000
2	2.09000	2.10000	2.11000	2.12000	2.13000	2.14000	2.15000	2.16000	2.18000	2.20000	2.25000
3	3.27810	3.31000	3.34210	3.37440	3.40690	3.43960	3.47250	3.50560	3.57240	3.64000	3.81250
4	4.57313	4.64100	4.70973	4.77933	4.84980	4.92114	4.99338	5.06650	5.21543	5.36800	5.76563
5	5.98471	6.10510	6.22780	6.35285	6.48027	6.61010	6.74238	6.87714	7.15421	7.44160	8.20703
6	7.52333	7.71561	7.91286	8.11519	8.32271	8.53552	8.75374	8.97748	9.44197	9.92992	11.25879
7	9.20043	9.48717	9.78327	10.08901	10.40466	10.73049	11.06680	11.41387	12.14152	12.91590	15.07349
8	11.02847	11.43589	11.85943	12.29969	12.75726	13.23276	13.72682	14.24009	15.32700	16.49908	19.84186
9	13.02104	13.57948	14.16397	14.77566	15.41571	16.08535	16.78584	17.51851	19.08585	20.79890	25.80232
10	15.19293	15.93742	16.72201	17.54874	18.41975	19.33730	20.30372	21.32147	23.52131	25.95868	33.25290
11	17.56029	18.53117	19.56143	20.65458	21.81432	23.04452	24.34928	25.73290	28.75514	32.15042	42.56613
12	20.14072	21.38428	22.71319	24.13313	25.65018	27.27075	29.00167	30.85017	34.93107	39.58050	54.20766
13	22.95338	24.52271	26.21164	28.02911	29.98470	32.08865	34.35192	36.78620	42.21866	48.49660	68.75958
14	26.01919	27.97498	30.09492	32.39260	34.88271	37.58107	40.50471	43.67199	50.81802	59.19592	86.94947
15	29.36092	31.77248	34.40536	37.27971	40.41746	43.84241	47.58041	51.65951	60.96527	72.03511	109.6868
16	33.00340	35.94973	39.18995	42.75328	46.67173	50.98035	55.71747	60.92503	72.93901	87.44213	138.1085
17	36.97370	40.54470	44.50084	48.88367	53.73906	59.11760	65.07509	71.67303	87.06804	105.9306	173.6357
18	41.30134	45.59917	50.39594	55.74971	61.72514	68.39407	75.83636	84.14072	103.7403	128.1167	218.0446
19	46.01846	51.15909	56.93949	63.43968	70.74941	78.96923	88.21181	98.60323	123.4135	154.7400	273.5558
20	51.16012	57.27500	64.20283	72.05244	80.94683	91.02493	102.4436	115.3797	146.6280	186.6880	342.9447
24	76.78981	88.49733	102.1742	118.1552	136.8315	158.6586	184.1678	213.9776	289.4945	392.4842	843.0329
36	236.1247	299.1268	380.1644	484.4631	618.7493	791.6729	1014.346	1301.027	2144.649	3539.009	12321.95
48	684.2804	960.1723	1352.700	1911.590	2707.633	3841.475	5456.005	7753.782	15664.26	31593.74	179362.2
60	1944.792	3034.816	4755.066	7471.641	11761.95	18535.13	29219.99	46057.51	114189.7	281732.6	2.61E+06
120	344289.1	927080.7	2.50E+06	6.71E+06	1.80E+07	4.81E+07	1.28E+08	3.39E+08	2.35E+09	1.59E+10	1.70E+12
240	1.07E+10	8.59E+10	6.86E+11	5.41E+12	4.22E+13	3.24E+14	2.46E+15	1.84E+16	9.92E+17	5.04E+19	7.25E+23
360	3.31E+14	7.97E+15	1.88E+17	4.36E+18	9.87E+19	2.19E+21	4.73E+22	1.00E+24	4.19E+26	1.60E+29	3.09E+35

*To compute the annuity in advance factor, use the arrears factor for one more period and subtract 1.

Table B-4
Future Value of an Annuity in Arrears (Continued)

ASSIGNMENT MATERIAL

○ APPLYING YOUR KNOWLEDGE

1. SBEG Inc. has some excess cash that they want to invest for five years. They can either deposit the $25,000 in a money market bank account and earn 9%, compounded annually, or deposit at a bank that pays 8%, compounded quarterly. What should they do?

2. Tom and Mary Kay plan to buy a house in three years. They will need $15,000 for the down payment. How much must they deposit today if they can earn 8% interest, compounded in each of the following ways?

   a. Annually

   b. Semiannually

   c. Quarterly

3. a. Ann Marie is saving to buy a car. She plans to deposit $50 at the end of each month into an account that pays 6%, compounded monthly. How much will she have for a down payment in two years?

   b. If she uses the amount arrived at in part a to put a down payment on a $15,000 car, how much will her monthly payments be? The loan is at 12% for four years, and the payments will come at the end of the month.

4. The law firm of Cohen, Rayburn & Nisbet is considering the acquisition of computers for their offices. They plan to lease (rent) a system. The lease (rent) payments of $2,000 are due the first of the month. They have signed an 18-month contract, and the first payment was due on signing. If the firm is able to invest at 9% annually, how much do they need today to ensure that the lease payments will be paid?

5. Today is your daughter's fourteenth birthday. You anticipate that she will go to college and will enter college on her eighteenth birthday. She will need $10,000 at the end of each of the four years, once school has begun. You plan to make a deposit one year from today into an account paying 12% annually and to make three more identical deposits, one in each year until she starts college. To reach your goal, what must the annual deposits be?

6. Hiranandani Inc. has issued bonds that pay $100 at the end of each year indefinitely. If you require a 12% rate of return (i.e., the discount rate is 12%), what is the value of such a bond?

7. Karen is the lucky winner of $1 million in the state lottery. Before taxes are removed, she will receive 20 annual payments of $50,000 each, starting today. She can earn 8% on this money. What is the present value of her winnings?

8. Mr. Hussein wants to buy a house that costs $180,000. He is evaluating the possibilities of how to pay for the house and has come up with the following alternatives. Calculate the monthly payments that Mr. Hussein will have to make under each alternative.

   a. 20% down, monthly payments, maturity 30 years, rate 12%

   b. 10% down, monthly payments, maturity 20 years, rate 9%

   c. 0% down, monthly payments, maturity 10 years, rate 9%

9. Mr. Gramling takes out a three-year graduated-payment loan. The monthly payments under this loan are as follows:

Year 1: $100/month

Year 2: $125/month

Year 3: $150/month

If interest rates are currently 12%, how much did Mr. Gramling borrow, given the payments that are to be made?

10. Ms. Bedard wants to establish a scholarship at her alma mater that will pay out $4,800 a year indefinitely in monthly installments. The first monthly installment of the award is to be paid immediately. How much will she have to donate if the school can invest at 9% compounded monthly?

11. How does the answer to question 10 change if the first monthly installment is to be paid one month after the initial donation?

12. You want to go through law school, for which you will need $9,000 per year for four years, starting next year. Your parents agree to support you in this endeavor and decide to deposit an amount of money today that is sufficient to provide the four payments. They can deposit the amount in an account that pays 8%, compounded annually.

   a. Calculate the amount that your parents should deposit.

   b. Calculate the amount that will be left in the account after the first withdrawal.

13. A finance company advertises that it will pay a lump sum of $8,115 at the end of six years to an investor who deposits $1,000 annually (at the end of the year) for six years. Calculate the interest rate that is implicit in this offer.

14. On your retirement, you deposit $100,000 in a bank that pays 10% annual interest. Calculate how much you will be able to withdraw at the end of each year to deplete the fund in exactly 10 years.

15. Mr. Scott is considering two investment alternatives:

   a. A bond that costs $1,000 today and makes annual interest payments of $75 at the end of each year for the next three years and a final payment of $1,075 at the end of year 4.

   b. A zero coupon bond that costs $735.03 today and pays back $1,000 at the end of year 4.

   Which alternative should Mr. Scott take and why?

16. A manufacturing company is considering an option to sell a machine via a lease. The machine cost the company $100,000. The lease agreement requires lease payments to be made at the beginning of the month for three years, with the title to the machine passing to the buyer at the end of the lease term. If the manufacturers want to earn a return of 9%, what monthly payments must the firm set for the lease?

17. SBT Company wants to establish a fund that will be used to meet a $900,000 commitment at the end of 10 years. The company plans to deposit a fixed amount in the fund each year for 10 years beginning today. The company estimates that the assets in the fund will earn a return of 9%. Calculate the annual contribution that SBT should make to the fund.

18. You have just won $1 million in the lottery. This amount will be paid to you in yearly installments of $50,000 for 20 years. You are expecting to receive the first check today. If you can invest this money at 10%, how much are your winnings worth today?

19. Suppose that an investment company offers you a contract that will pay you and your heirs $750 a year for your lifetime and that of your heirs. If your next best alternative is to invest at 8%, how much should you be willing to invest in this contract?

Comprehensive Case and Chico's 10K Report Fiscal 2002

A MESSAGE FROM OUR CEO TO OUR SHAREHOLDERS

I would like to open with my heartfelt thanks to the tremendous Chico's team and all the customers and stockholders who have embraced our dream. Last year I reported that fiscal 2001 had been our best year in terms of financial, operational, and management accomplishments and that we had set very aggressive goals for fiscal 2002. These goals included opening our newly-acquired distribution facility while transitioning out of the distribution portion of our existing Ft. Myers facilities, preparing for an early fiscal 2003 roll out of our new concept (which was later named Pazo) and to add at least an additional 64 Chico's stores by year end. I'm happy to report that we accomplished all of the above, as well as other initiatives, in fiscal 2002. I'd like to review with you the financial results for fiscal 2002, go over our key accomplishments during this very productive year, and finally set some goals for fiscal 2003.

Fiscal 2002 continued our strong sales and earnings growth trends as we saw sales increase 40% to just over $531 million, while earnings per share increased by 54% to close the year at $0.78 per share versus $0.50 per share for the previous year (adjusted for our 2 for 1 split in July last year). Our same stores sales were up double digits for each of the four quarters, we ended the year with our highest gross margin since 1995 at over 60%, and we achieved our highest operating margin in our history of just over 20%. On the balance sheet side, we funded over $25 million of one-time capital expenditures for our new distribution center and our Pazo and software initiatives, we paid off the mortgage on our Ft. Myers headquarters facility, and, at the same time, we managed to add over $46 million to our cash and marketable securities balances. Our inventory balances remain strong at $65 per sq. ft., which is in the same range we have experienced in ten of the last eleven quarters since back in the second quarter of fiscal 2000 when we adopted the initiative to raise the number of apparel units per square foot in our stores. Lastly, our net book value rose by over $96 million to end the year at over $240 million.

During fiscal 2002 we planned for a launch of the Pazo division in early fiscal 2003, and I am pleased to say that we successfully opened our first ten Pazo test stores in March 2003. With no advertising and little promotion, we have already seen a strong, positive reaction from our target customer. We look forward to reacting to this customer's desires and we're committed to a continued enhancement, as and when necessary, of the Pazo brand. For example, we've already added a size two to our four to fourteen size range and we are making subtle changes to our display fixtures to better highlight the clothing, shoes, and accessories.

As I stated last year, we acquired a 230,000 square foot distribution facility north of Atlanta, Georgia in early 2002. During fiscal 2002 we successfully installed state-of-the-art material handling equipment, hired an all new staff in Georgia, installed best-of-breed software from Manhattan Associates, transitioned all distribution activities to Georgia in the third and fourth quarters, and transitioned out of the distribution operations in our Ft. Myers headquarters facility. This fiscal year we will convert our Ft. Myers distribution center to office space and move our Pazo team from rented facilities into their own new headquarters that we recently acquired adjacent to our existing Chico's headquarters. On our software initiatives, we are still targeting a late year conversion of our existing back office systems (all merchandising, production, sourcing, sales audit, and financial applications) to systems we believe will help to provide part of the foundation for our "bridge to a billion" that we have talked about in the past.

Our Passport Club membership steadily increases as we continue building the Chico's brand. Last year our permanent membership rose by approximately 240,000 members, or almost 60%, while our preliminary membership jumped by approximately 774,000 members, or 50%. Our Passport members accounted for over 90% of our sales last year, with over 70% coming from our permanent members. We continue to offer exciting promotions to our permanent members in an effort to maintain their interest. Beyond that, we plan to increase our circulation of catalogs from approximately 18 million last year to over 27 million this year and significantly increase our television advertising as we continue our penetration of the baby boomer apparel market. Although the catalogs are primarily designed to increase our store visits, they also provide the impetus for our call center which handles direct sales from the internet and catalog and where sales increased to just over $16 million in fiscal 2002 from just over $10 million in fiscal 2001.

Looking forward, our current plan for fiscal 2003 is to open 70–75 net new stores, of which a minimum of 10 will carry the Pazo brand. We believe that the Chico's brand, as it stands now, should allow us to operate between 550 and 650 Chico's stores (we are currently at 391 Chico's stores) and a yet-to-be determined amount of Pazo stores. We have also identified yet another opportunity as we have begun to explore possibilities in extending the Chico's brand into intimates and activewear. Already, we have been successfully testing some intimate wear in our outlets and we are very pleased with this spring's test of activewear in our front line stores. We have also hired an experienced product development manager for this new, yet unnamed concept, and plan at this point to test this concept in 6 to 10 stores in fiscal 2004. The hope is that this new concept will be able to leverage the Chico's brand and take advantage of our Passport database of over 3 million customers who already know and love the Chico's brand. We remain committed to providing our

Chico's customers with the quality and value that have made Chico's so successful and to offering this same quality and value as a key element in each of our new concepts.

Lastly, we have begun the transition of my duties as I approach retirement in early 2004. Scott Edmonds, our President and COO, has been working directly with our Chief Merchandising Officer and our Senior Vice President of Marketing, while Charlie Kleman, our CFO, has been working directly with our CIO in an effort to effect an orderly transition of these activities. Although Helene and I plan to retire from our day-to-day activities early next year, we will be monitoring Chico's, both as Board members and dedicated Founders, to help ensure that the vision and values are maintained at the same levels. Helene and I believe the Chico's brand has only now begun to be recognized. We look forward to partnering with the Chico's management team and its directors to take advantage of the tremendous growth potential that we see both now and in the future.

As always, keep your eye on Chico's.

Sincerely,

/s/ Marvin J. Gralnick

Marvin J. Gralnick, CEO April 18, 2003

Financial Highlights	Fiscal Year Ended				
	February 1, 2003 (52 Weeks)	February 2, 2002 (52 Weeks)	February 3, 2001 (53 Weeks)	January 29, 2000 (52 Weeks)	January 30, 1999 (52 Weeks)
	(Dollars in thousands except per share data)				
STATEMENT OF INCOME DATA:					
Net Sales	$531,108	$378,085	$259,446	$155,002	$106,742
Income from Operations	106,793	67,536	45,363	24,806	15,134
Net Income	66,759	42,187	28,379	15,489	9,139
Basic Earnings Per Share (1)	0.80	0.52	0.36	0.20	0.13
Diluted Earnings Per Share (1)	0.78	0.50	0.35	0.19	0.12
BALANCE SHEET AND OPERATING DATA:					
Total Assets	$301,544	$186,385	$117,807	$ 70,316	$ 49,000
Long-Term Debt	—	5,022	5,150	5,222	5,294
Other Noncurrent Liabilities	6,551	2,922	2,008	1,617	1,419
Stockholders' Equity	240,133	143,495	85,321	52,641	34,303
# of Stores (at end of period):					
Company-owned	366	300	239	191	154
Franchised	12	11	11	9	8
Total	378	311	250	200	162

(1) Restated to give retroactive effect for the 2 for 1 stock split payable in July 2002, the 3 for 2 stock split payable in January 2002, the 3 for 2 stock split payable in May 2001 and the 2 for 1 stock split payable in January 2000.

MANAGEMENT'S DISCUSSION AND ANALYSIS OF FINANCIAL CONDITION AND RESULTS OF OPERATIONS

The following discussion and analysis should be read in conjunction with the Company's consolidated financial statements and notes thereto.

GENERAL

Chico's FAS, Inc. (together with its subsidiaries, the "Company") is a specialty retailer of exclusively designed, private label, sophisticated, casual-to-dressy clothing, complementary accessories and other non-clothing gift items under the Chico's and Pazo brand names.

The Chico's brand, which began operations in 1983, focuses on women who are 35 years old and up with moderate and higher income levels. The styling is relaxed, figure-flattering and designed for easy care. Pazo, which opened its first 10 test stores in March 2003, focuses on women in the 25–40 age group with moderate income. Its offerings are more diverse, including casual, active wear, intimate apparel and casual career. The Pazo brand intends to be more fashion forward with a European feel that is more fashionable.

Since the Company opened its first store in 1983 principally selling folk art, its retail store system, now selling principally women's apparel, has grown to 378 stores as of February 1, 2003, of which 366 are Company-owned stores and 12 are franchised stores. Over the last five fiscal years, the Company has opened 243 new Company-owned stores and acquired two stores from franchisees, and one franchisee has opened five new franchised stores. Of the new Company-owned stores, 66 were opened in fiscal 2002 (year ended February 1, 2003), 64 were opened in fiscal 2001, 51 were opened in fiscal 2000, 40 were opened in fiscal 1999, and 22 were opened in fiscal 1998. During this same time period, the Company closed 11 Company-owned stores and no franchised stores closed. The Company plans to open a minimum of 70–75 net new Company-owned stores (including at least 10 Pazo stores, the Company's new concept store) in the fiscal year ending January 31, 2004. In addition, the Company is evaluating certain existing Company-owned store locations, including stores with leases coming up for renewal, and is considering the possibility of closing between one and three existing Company-owned stores in fiscal 2003.

RESULTS OF OPERATIONS

The following table sets forth, for each of the respective periods indicated, certain operating statement data and the percentage of the Company's net sales represented by each line item presented.

	Fiscal Year Ended (000's)					
	February 1, 2003 (52 Weeks)	%	February 2, 2002 (52 Weeks)	%	February 3, 2001 (53 Weeks)	%
Net sales by company stores	$508,492	95.8%	$362,443	95.9%	$252,168	97.2%
Net sales by catalog and Internet	16,070	3.0	10,203	2.7	2,656	1.0
Net sales to franchisees	6,546	1.2	5,439	1.4	4,622	1.8
NET SALES	531,108	100.0	378,085	100.0	259,446	100.0

	Fiscal Year Ended (000's)					
	February 1, 2003 (52 Weeks)	%	February 2, 2002 (52 Weeks)	%	February 3, 2001 (53 Weeks)	%
Cost of goods sold	209,770	39.5	153,937	40.7	108,671	41.9
GROSS PROFIT	321,338	60.5	224,148	59.3	150,775	58.1
General, administrative and store operating expenses	199,495	37.6	146,611	38.8	99,757	38.4
Depreciation and amortization	15,050	2.8	10,001	2.6	5,655	2.2
INCOME FROM OPERATIONS	106,793	20.1	67,536	17.9	45,363	17.5
Interest income, net	883	0.2	507	0.1	409	0.1
INCOME BEFORE INCOME TAXES	107,676	20.3	68,043	18.0	45,772	17.6
Provision for income taxes	40,917	7.7	25,856	6.8	17,393	6.7
NET INCOME	$ 66,759	12.6%	$ 42,187	11.2%	$ 28,379	10.9%

FIFTY-TWO WEEKS ENDED FEBRUARY 1, 2003 COMPARED TO THE FIFTY-TWO WEEKS ENDED FEBRUARY 2, 2002

Net Sales. Net sales by Company-owned stores for the fifty-two weeks ended February 1, 2003 (the current period) increased by $146.0 million, or 40.3%, over net sales by Company-owned stores for the comparable fifty-two weeks ended February 2, 2002 (the prior period). The increase was the result of a comparable Company store net sales increase of $48.3 million, or 13.5%, and $97.7 million additional sales from new stores not yet included in the Company's comparable store base (net of sales of $1.0 million from three stores closed in the previous fiscal year).

Net sales by catalog and Internet for the current period increased by $5.9 million, or 57.5%, compared to net sales by catalog and Internet for the prior period. The increase was believed to be principally attributable to the increased number of catalog mailings and additional television spots in the current year versus the prior period.

Net sales to franchisees for the current period increased by approximately $1.1 million, or 20.4%, compared to net sales to franchisees for the prior period. The increase in net sales to franchisees was primarily due to a net increase in purchases by the franchisees, and to a lesser degree, to the opening of a new franchise location by an existing franchisee.

Gross Profit. Gross profit for the current period was $321.3 million, or 60.5% of net sales, compared with $224.1 million, or 59.3% of net sales, for the prior period. The increase in the gross profit percentage primarily resulted from improved initial merchandise markups on new products, and a significant improvement in the gross profit percentage experienced in the Company's outlet division. To a lesser degree, this increase in gross profit percentage resulted from decreased freight and inventory shrinkage costs as well as from leveraging costs associated with the Company's product development and merchandising operations (which costs are included in the Company's cost of goods sold), and net of a slight increase in markdowns as a percent of sales and an overall increase in outlet net sales as a percent of overall sales. Although the gross profit percentage in the outlet division has improved, outlet net sales still tend to have a substantially lower gross profit margin than sales at the Company's front line stores. The increase in outlet net sales as a percent of net sales and the increase in gross profit percentage in this division results primarily from the change in outlet strategy implemented by the Company in the prior fiscal year.

General, Administrative and Store Operating Expenses. General, administrative and store operating expenses increased to $199.5 million, or 37.6% of net sales, in the current period from $146.6 million, or 38.8% of net sales, in the prior period. The increase in general, administrative and store operating expenses was, for the most part, the result of increases in store operating expenses, including associate compensation, occupancy and other costs associated with additional store openings, and to a lesser degree, an increase in marketing expenses. The decrease in these expenses as a percentage of net sales was principally due to decreases in store payroll and bonuses as a percentage of sales, and to a lesser degree, to leverage associated with the Company's fiscal 2002 same store sales increase of 13.5%.

Depreciation and Amortization. Depreciation and amortization increased to $15.1 million, or 2.8% of net sales, in the current period from $10.0 million, or 2.6% of net sales, in the prior period. The increase in depreciation and amortization was principally due to capital expenditures related to new, remodeled and expanded stores, which have tended to be greater on a per store basis than capital expenditures for previously opened stores. The higher capital expenditures per store for new stores is attributable largely to a growth in the average square footage for the newer stores.

Interest Income, Net. The Company had net interest income during the current period of approximately $883,000 versus approximately $507,000 in the prior period. The increase in net interest income was primarily a result of the Company's increased cash and marketable securities position, partially offset by lower interest rates.

Net Income. As a result of the factors discussed above, net income increased 58.2% to $66.8 million in the current period from net income of $42.2 million in the prior period. The income tax provision represented an effective rate of 38% for the current and prior period.

FIFTY-TWO WEEKS ENDED FEBRUARY 2, 2002 COMPARED TO THE FIFTY-THREE WEEKS ENDED FEBRUARY 3, 2001

Net Sales. Net sales by Company-owned stores for the fifty-two weeks ended February 2, 2002 (fiscal 2001 or the current period) increased by $110.3 million, or 43.7%, over net sales by Company-owned stores for the fifty-three weeks ended February 3, 2001 (fiscal 2000 or the prior period). The increase was the result of a comparable Company store net sales increase of $42.1 million, and $68.2 million additional sales from the new stores not yet included in the Company's comparable store base (net of sales of $1.8 million from six stores closed in fiscal 2001 and fiscal 2000, and net of $5.3 million sales from the additional week in the prior year versus the current year).

Net sales from the Company's call center (website and catalog sales), which began operations in late May 2000, increased by $7.5 million in the current period compared to the short year of selling in fiscal 2000.

Net sales to franchisees for the current period increased by approximately $817,000, or 17.7%, compared to net sales to franchisees for the prior period. The increase in net sales to franchisees was primarily due to a net increase in purchases by the franchisees as a whole, and the opening by an existing franchisee of two additional franchised stores in fiscal 2000, net of the additional week in the prior period.

Gross Profit. Gross profit for the current period was $224.1 million, or 59.3% of net sales, compared with $150.8 million, or 58.1% of net sales, for the prior period. The increase in the gross profit percentage primarily resulted from an improvement in the Company's initial markup on goods, offset, in part, by slightly higher markdowns as a percent of sales in the current period versus the prior period. To a lesser degree, the increase in the gross profit percentage resulted from leveraging costs associated with the Company's product development and merchandising areas, which costs are included in the Company's cost of goods sold.

General, Administrative and Store Operating Expenses. General, administrative and store operating expenses increased to $146.6 million, or 38.8% of net sales, in the current period from $99.8 million, or 38.4% of net sales, in the prior period. The increase in general, administrative and store operating expenses was, for the most part, the result of increases in store operating expenses, including store compensation, occupancy and other costs associated with additional store openings, and to a lesser degree, an increase in marketing expenses. The increase in these expenses as a percentage of net sales was principally due to an increase in direct store expenses related to costs associated with the Company's new cash register rolled out in the first half of fiscal 2001 and an increase in direct marketing expenses as a percentage of net sales, comprising 3.4% of net sales in the current period, versus 2.7% of net sales in the prior period, net of leverage associated with the Company's 17.1% comparable Company store sales increase for the current period.

Depreciation and Amortization. Depreciation and amortization increased to $10.0 million, or 2.6% of net sales in the current period from $5.7 million, or 2.2% of net sales, in the prior period. The increase in depreciation and amortization was principally due to capital expenditures related to new, remodeled and expanded stores as well as capital expenditures related to the new cash registers and the addition to the Company's Headquarters facility which opened in early 2001. The increase as a percentage of net sales was principally due to the new cash registers and the Headquarters expansion.

Interest Income, Net. The Company had net interest income during the current period of approximately $507,000 versus approximately $408,000 in the prior period. The increase in net interest income was primarily a result of the Company's increased cash and marketable securities position throughout most of the year, net of decreased interest rates earned on cash and marketable securities.

Net income.   As a result of the factors discussed above, net income increased 48.7% to $42.2 million in the current period from net income of $28.4 million in the prior period. The income tax provision represented an effective rate of 38.0% for the current and prior period.

COMPARABLE COMPANY STORE NET SALES

Comparable Company store net sales increased by 13.5% in the 52 weeks ended February 1, 2003 (fiscal 2002) when compared to the comparable prior period. Comparable Company store net sales data is calculated based on the change in net sales of currently open Company-owned stores that have been operated as a Company store for at least thirteen months, including stores that have been expanded or relocated within the same general market area (approximately five miles).

The comparable store percentage reported above includes 44 stores that were expanded or relocated within the last two fiscal years by an average of 882 net selling square feet. If the stores that were expanded and relocated had been excluded from the comparable Company-owned store base, the increase in comparable Company-owned store net sales would have been 11.8% for fiscal 2002 (versus 13.5% as reported). The Company does not consider the effect to be material to the overall comparable store sales results and believes the inclusion of expanded stores in the comparable store net sales to be an acceptable practice, consistent with the practice followed by the Company in prior periods and by many other retailers.

The Company believes that the increase in comparable Company store net sales in the current fiscal year resulted from the continuing effort to focus the Company's product development, merchandise planning, buying and marketing departments on Chico's target customer. The Company also believes that the look, fit and pricing policy of the Company's product was in line with the needs of the Company's target customer, and that the increase in comparable store sales was also fueled by a coordinated marketing plan, which includes national and regional television advertising, national magazine advertising, increased direct mailings of catalogs, a larger database of existing customers for such mailings and the success of the Company's loyalty club (the "Passport Club"). To a lesser degree, the Company believes the increase was due to continued store-level training efforts associated with ongoing training programs and continuing strong sales associated with several styles of clothing produced from a related group of fabrics newly introduced by the Company in the fourth quarter of fiscal 1998.

The following table sets forth for each of the quarters of the previous five fiscal years, the percentage change in comparable store net sales at Company-owned stores from the comparable period in the prior fiscal year:

	Fiscal Year Ended				
	2/1/03	2/2/02	2/3/01	1/29/00	1/30/99
FULL YEAR	13.5%	17.1%	34.3%	23.3%	30.3%
First Quarter	13.2%	27.7%	30.9%	22.6%	31.7%
Second Quarter	11.6%	17.4%	34.3%	17.2%	23.0%
Third Quarter	18.2%	7.0%	39.1%	26.9%	28.5%
Fourth Quarter	11.0%	17.9%	32.2%	26.5%	38.5%

LIQUIDITY AND CAPITAL RESOURCES

The Company's primary ongoing capital requirements are for funding capital expenditures for new, expanded, relocated and remodeled stores and merchandise inventories. Also, during fiscal 2002, the Company experienced the need for capital to address the acquisition and equipping of the Company's new distribution center, the remodeling of the space at the Company's Ft. Myers headquarters that previously had been used for distribution, and the acquisition and installation of new software packages as more fully described in the Company's Form 10-K for the fiscal year ended February 1, 2003.

During the current fiscal year (fiscal 2002) and the prior fiscal year (fiscal 2001), the Company's primary source of working capital was cash flow from operations of $108.8 million and $65.5 million, respectively. The increase in cash flow from operations of $43.3 million was primarily due to an increase in net income of $24.6 million, an increase in the tax benefit of options exercised of $14.4 million, an increase in accounts payables and accrued liabilities of $20.0 million in the current period versus an increase of $9.6 million in the prior period, and an increase in depreciation and amortization of $5.7 million. These increases were offset by an increase in inventories in the current year of $16.0 million versus an increase of $4.5 million in the prior period. The year-over-year increases in accounts payable and inventories are due to a planned increase in inventory levels in the current period versus the prior period due to strong unplanned January sales in the prior period and a general reduction in inventories last year due to concerns over the effect of terrorist attacks.

The Company invested $64.7 million in the current fiscal year in capital expenditures primarily associated with the acquisition and costs of equipping its new distribution center in Georgia and modify its existing distribution center in Florida ($14.0 million), the acquisition and initial installation costs associated with new software packages ($10.3 million) and, the costs associated with the establishment of Pazo concept stores (including costs incurred to date on unopened Pazo stores) and the acquisition of additional land and a 12,000 square foot building, which property is adjacent to the Company's headquarters in Ft. Myers, Florida and is to be used as the Pazo headquarters ($2.2 million), and with the balance attributable primarily to new, relocated, remodeled and expanded Chico's Company stores. During the same period in the prior fiscal year, the Company invested $37.4 million primarily for capital expenditures associated with the opening of new, relocated, remodeled and expanded Company stores.

During the current fiscal year, fourteen of the Company's eighteen officers and two of its three independent directors exercised an aggregate of 3,495,628 stock options (split-adjusted) at prices ranging from $0.36 to $10.84 (split-adjusted) and several employees and former employees exercised an aggregate of 179,264 (split-adjusted) options at prices ranging from $0.36 to $10.84 (split-adjusted). Also, during this period, the Company sold 29,296 and 18,315 shares of common stock during the July and September offering periods under its employee stock purchase plan at prices of $15.44 and $15.09, respectively. The proceeds from these issuances of stock, exclusive of the tax benefit realized by the Company, amounted to approximately $7.2 million.

The Company invested $50.7 million, net, in marketable securities and repaid its existing mortgage of $5.2 million in the current year. In the prior year, the Company invested $26.2 million in marketable securities and repaid $66,000 of its indebtedness.

In September 2002, the Company entered into a replacement unsecured revolving credit facility with Bank of America, N.A., expanding the maximum available commitment from $25 million to $45 million, extending the maturity to June 2005 and increasing the letter of credit sublimit of the facility from $22 million to $35 million.

The following table summarizes the Company's contractual obligations at February 1, 2003:

	Total	Less Than 1 Year	1–3 Years	4–5 Years	After 5 Years
Long-term debt	$ —	$ —	$ —	$ —	$ —
Short-term borrowings	—	—	—	—	—
Operating leases	217,177,000	33,279,000	65,052,000	53,407,000	65,439,000
Non-cancelable purchase commitments	24,865,000	23,800,000	1,065,000	—	—
TOTAL CONTRACTUAL COMMITMENTS	$242,042,000	$57,079,000	$66,117,000	$53,407,000	$65,439,000

At February 1, 2003 and February 2, 2002, the Company did not have any relationship with unconsolidated entities or financial partnerships, which certain other companies have established for the purpose of facilitating off-balance sheet arrangements or other contractually narrow or limited purposes. Therefore, the Company is not materially exposed to any financing, liquidity, market or credit risk that could arise if the Company had engaged in such relationships.

As more fully described in "Item 1" beginning on page 14 of the Company's Annual Report on Form 10-K for the fiscal year ended February 1, 2003, the Company is subject to ongoing risks associated with imports. The Company's reliance on sourcing from foreign countries causes the Company to be exposed to certain unique business and political risks. Import restrictions, including tariffs and quotas, and changes in such tariffs or quotas could affect the importation of apparel generally and, in that event, could increase the cost or reduce the supply of apparel available to the Company and have an adverse effect on the Company's business, financial condition and/or results of operations. The Company's merchandise flow could also be adversely affected by political instability in any of the countries in which its goods are manufactured, by significant fluctuations in the value of the U.S. dollar against applicable foreign currencies and by restrictions on the transfer of funds.

The Company plans to open a minimum of approximately 70–75 net Company-owned new stores (which includes a minimum of 10 Pazo stores) in fiscal 2003, of which 23 were opened as of April 18, 2003. The Company believes that the liquidity needed for its planned new store growth, continuing remodel/expansion program, continued remodeling of the space in the Company's Ft. Myers headquarters previously used for distribution, continued installation of new software packages, rollout of its new concept stores on a test basis in fiscal 2003, and maintenance of proper inventory levels associated with this growth will be funded primarily from cash flow from operations and its strong existing cash and marketable securities balances. The Company further believes that this liquidity will be sufficient, based on the above, to fund anticipated capital needs over the near-term. Given the Company's existing cash and marketable securities balances and the capacity included in its bank credit facilities, the Company does not believe that it would need to seek other sources of financing to conduct its operations or pursue its expansion plans even if cash flow from operations should prove to be less than anticipated or if there should arise a need for additional letter of credit capacity due to establishing new and expanded sources of supply, or if the Company were to increase the number of new Company stores planned to be opened in future periods.

SEASONALITY AND INFLATION

Although the operations of the Company are influenced by general economic conditions, the Company does not believe that inflation has had a material effect on the results of operations during the current or prior periods. The Company does not consider its business to be seasonal.

CERTAIN FACTORS THAT MAY AFFECT FUTURE RESULTS

This annual report may contain certain "forward-looking statements" within the meaning of Section 27A of the Securities Act of 1933, as amended, and Section 21E of the Securities Exchange Act of 1934, as amended, which reflect the current views of the Company with respect to certain events that could have an effect on the Company's future financial performance. The statements may address items such as future sales, gross profit expectations, planned store openings, closings and expansions, future comparable store sales, future product sourcing plans, inventory levels, planned capital expenditures and future cash needs. In addition, from time to time, the Company may issue press releases and other written communications, and representatives of the Company may make oral statements which contain forward-looking information.

These statements, including those in this annual report and those in press releases or made orally, may include the words "expects," "believes," and similar expressions. Except for historical information, matters discussed in such oral and written statements, including this annual report, are forward-looking statements. These forward-looking statements are subject to various risks and uncertainties that could cause actual results to differ materially from historical results or those currently anticipated. These potential risks and uncertainties include the financial strength of retailing in particular and the economy in general, the extent of financial difficulties that may be experienced by customers, the ability of the Company to secure and maintain customer acceptance of Chico's styles, the propriety of inventory mix and sizing, the quality of merchandise received from vendors, the extent and nature of competition in the markets in which the Company operates, the extent of the market demand and overall level of spending for women's private label clothing and related accessories, the adequacy and perception of customer service, the ability to coordinate product development with buying and planning, the ability of the Company's suppliers to timely produce and deliver clothing and accessories, the changes in the costs of manufacturing, labor and advertising, the rate of new store openings, the buying public's acceptance of the Company's new store concept, the performance, implementation and integration of management information systems, the ability to hire, train, energize and retain qualified sales associates and other employees, the availability of quality store sites, the ability to hire and train qualified managerial employees, the ability to effectively and efficiently establish and operate catalog and Internet sales, the ability to secure and protect trademarks and other intellectual property rights, the ability to effectively and efficiently integrate and operate the newly acquired facility, risks associated with terrorist activities and other risks. In addition, there are potential risks and uncertainties that are peculiar to the Company's reliance on sourcing from foreign vendors, including the impact of work stoppages, transportation delays and other interruptions, political or civil instability, foreign currency fluctuations, imposition of and changes in tariffs and import and export controls such as import quotas, changes in governmental policies in or towards foreign countries and other similar factors.

The forward-looking statements included herein are only made as of the date of this Annual Report. The Company undertakes no obligation to publicly update or revise any forward-looking statements, whether as a result of new information, future events or otherwise.

CRITICAL ACCOUNTING POLICIES AND ESTIMATES

The Company's discussion and analysis of its financial condition and results of operations are based upon the Company's consolidated financial statements, which have been prepared in accordance with accounting principles generally accepted in the United States of America. The preparation of consolidated financial statements requires the Company to make estimates and judgments that affect the reported amounts of assets, liabilities, revenues and expenses, and related disclosure of contingent assets and liabilities. On an ongoing basis, the Company evaluates its estimates, including those related to customer product returns, inventories, income taxes, insurance reserves, contingencies and litigation. The Company bases its estimates on historical experience and on various other assumptions that are believed to be reasonable under the circumstances, the results of which form the basis for making judgments about the carrying values of assets and liabilities that are not readily apparent from other sources. Actual results may differ from these estimates under different assumptions or conditions.

The Company believes the following critical accounting policies affect its more significant judgments and estimates used in the preparation of its consolidated financial statements.

Inventory Valuation

The Company identifies potentially excess and slow-moving inventories by evaluating turn rates and inventory levels in conjunction with the Company's overall growth rate. Excess quantities are identified through evaluation of inventory ageings, review of inventory turns and historical sales experiences, as well as specific identification based on fashion trends. Further, exposure to inadequate realization of carrying value is identified through analysis of gross margins and markdowns in combination with changes in the fashion industry. The Company provides lower of cost or market reserves for such identified excess and slow-moving inventories.

Inventory Shrinkage

The Company estimates its expected shrinkage of inventories between physical inventory counts by applying historical chain-wide average shrinkage experience rates to the related periods' sales volume. The historical rates are updated on a regular basis to reflect the most recent physical inventory shrinkage experience.

Sales Returns

The Company's policy is to honor customer returns at all times. Returns after 30 days of the original purchase, or returns without the original receipt, qualify for store credit only. The Company will, in certain circumstances, offer full customer refunds either after 30 days or without a receipt. The Company estimates its reserve for likely customer returns based on the average refund experience in relation to sales for the related period.

Self-Insurance

The Company is self-insured for certain losses relating to workers' compensation, medical and general liability claims. Self-insurance claims filed and claims incurred but not reported are accrued based upon management's estimates of the aggregate liability for uninsured claims incurred using insurance industry benchmarks and historical experience. Although management believes it has the ability to adequately accrue for estimated losses related to claims, it is possible that actual results could significantly differ from recorded self-insurance liabilities.

QUANTITATIVE AND QUALITATIVE DISCLOSURES ABOUT MARKET RISK

The market risk of the Company's financial instruments as of February 1, 2003 has not significantly changed since February 2, 2002. The Company is exposed to market risk from changes in interest rates on its indebtedness. The Company's exposure to interest rate risk relates in part to its revolving line of credit with its bank; however, as of February 1, 2003, the Company did not have any outstanding borrowings on its line of credit and, given its strong liquidity position, does not expect to utilize its line of credit in the foreseeable future except for its continuing use of the letter of credit facility portion thereof.

NEWLY ISSUED ACCOUNTING PRONOUNCEMENTS

In June 2002, the Financial Accounting Standards Board (FASB) issued Statement of Financial Accounting Standards (SFAS) No. 146, "Accounting for Costs Associated with Exit or Disposal Activities" (SFAS 146). The standard requires companies to recognize costs associated with exit or disposal activities when they are incurred rather than at the date of a commitment to an exit or disposal plan. SFAS 146 is effective for exit or disposal activities that are initiated after December 31, 2002. The adoption of SFAS 146 did not have a significant impact on the Company's financial position or results of operations.

In November 2002, the FASB issued FASB Interpretation No. 45, "Guarantor's Accounting and Disclosure Requirements for Guarantees, Including Indirect Guarantees of Indebtedness of Others" (FIN 45). FIN 45 elaborates on the existing disclosure requirements for most guarantees, including loan guarantees such as standby letters of credit. It also clarifies that at the time a company issues a guarantee, the company must recognize an initial liability for the fair value, or market value, of the obligations it assumes under that guarantee and must disclose that information in its interim and annual financial statements. FIN 45 is effective on a prospective basis to guarantees issued or modified after December 31, 2002. The disclosure requirements of FIN 45 are effective for financial statements of interim or annual periods ending after December 15, 2002. The adoption of FIN 45 did not have a significant impact on the Company's financial position or results of operations.

In December 2002, the FASB issued SFAS 148, "Accounting for Stock-Based Compensation, Transition and Disclosure" (SFAS 148). SFAS 148 amends SFAS 123, to provide alternative methods of transition to the fair value method of accounting for stock-based employee compensation. In addition, SFAS 148 amends the disclosure provisions of SFAS 123. SFAS 148 does not amend SFAS 123 to require companies to account for their employee stock-based awards using the fair value method. However, the disclosure provisions are required for all companies with stock-based employee compensation, regardless of whether they utilize the fair value method of accounting described in SFAS 123 or the intrinsic value method described in APB 25. The Company adopted the disclosure provisions of SFAS 148 during the year ended February 1, 2003.

CONTROLS AND PROCEDURES

Within the 90 days prior to the date of this report, an evaluation was earned out under the supervision and with the participation of the Company's management, including its Chief Executive Officer and Chief Financial Officer, of the effectiveness of the design and operation of the Company's disclosure controls and procedures pursuant to Exchange Act Rule 13a-14. Based upon that evaluation, the Chief Executive Officer and Chief Financial Officer concluded that the Company's disclosure controls and procedures are effective in timely alerting them to material information relating to the Company (including its consolidated subsidiaries) required to be included in the Company's periodic SEC filings. There were no significant changes in the Company's internal controls or in other factors that could significantly affect these controls subsequent to the date of their evaluation.

LEGAL PROCEEDINGS

The Company was named as defendant in a suit filed in September 2001 in the Superior Court for the State of California for the County of Orange. This suit, Carmen Davis vs. Chico's FAS, Inc., was filed by the plaintiff, seeking to represent all other Company assistant store managers, sales associates and hourly employees in California from September 21, 1997 to the present. The Company responded by seeking to dismiss the complaint and strike selected claims in order to either eliminate the litigation or gain greater clarity as to the basis for the plaintiff's action. In response, the plaintiff filed an amended complaint on February 15, 2002, which differs in a number of material respects from the original complaint. The amended complaint alleged that the Company failed to pay overtime wages and failed to provide rest breaks and meal periods. The action sought "class action" status and sought unspecified monetary damages.

Following preliminary settlement discussions, the parties attended a mediation on October 14, 2002, at which the parties reached a settlement on a class-wide basis. The settlement provides for a common fund out of which settlement awards to class members and the costs of the settlement will be paid. The parties prepared a settlement agreement, which was lodged with the Court. The settlement agreement states that the settlement is not an admission of liability and that the Company continues to deny liability for any of plaintiff's claims. Subsequent to year end, the Court heard the plaintiff's motion for preliminary approval of the settlement. The Court granted the motion and ordered that the parties give notice of the settlement to the class members. Once notice is given, class members will have sixty days to file claim forms to participate in the settlement or to file exclusion forms to opt out of the settlement. On September 16, 2003, the Court will hold a settlement fairness hearing for the purpose of determining whether to give final approval to the settlement. If final approval is given, and no appeals challenging the settlement are filed, the Company will pay the settlement sums to class members who have filed valid claims and also will pay amounts owing for attorney's fees, costs and other expenses of the settlement. The settlement provides for a release of all covered claims by class members who do not opt out of the settlement. The Company does not believe the outcome of this will have a material impact on the Company's results of operations or financial condition.

Chico's is not a party to any other legal proceedings, other than various claims and lawsuits arising in the normal course of the Company's business, none of which the Company believes should have a material adverse effect on its financial condition or results of operations.

TRADING AND DIVIDEND INFORMATION

The following table sets forth, for the periods indicated, the range of high and low sale prices for the Common Stock, as reported on the New York Stock Exchange and Nasdaq National Market System.(1)

FOR THE FISCAL YEAR ENDED FEBRUARY 1, 2003	High(2)	Low(2)
Fourth Quarter (November 3, 2002–February 1, 2003)	$23.73	$16.83
Third Quarter (August 4, 2002–November 2, 2002)	21.09	13.02
Second Quarter (May 5, 2002–August 3, 2002)	21.00	13.26
First Quarter (February 3, 2002–May 4, 2002)	18.99	14.40
FOR THE FISCAL YEAR ENDED FEBRUARY 2, 2002	High(2)	Low(2)
Fourth Quarter (November 4, 2001–February 2, 2002)	$15.29	$ 9.50
Third Quarter (August 5, 2001–November 3, 2001)	13.00	6.83
Second Quarter (May 6, 2001–August 4, 2001)	12.84	8.66
First Quarter (February 4, 2001–May 5, 2001)	10.45	6.86

(1) On April 11, 2001, the Company commenced its trading on the New York Stock Exchange.

(2) Adjusted for the 2 for 1 stock split payable in July 2002, the 3 for 2 stock split payable January 2002 and the 3 for 2 stock split payable in May 2001.

The Company does not intend to pay any cash dividends for the foreseeable future and intends to retain earnings, if any, for the future operation and expansion of the Company's business. Any determination to pay dividends in the future will be at the discretion of the Company's Board of Directors and will be dependent upon the Company's results of operations, financial condition, contractual restrictions and other factors deemed relevant by the Board of Directors.

The approximate number of equity security holders of the Company is as follows:

Title of Class	Number of Record Holders As of April 18, 2003
Common Stock, par value $.01 per share	1,080

REPORT OF INDEPENDENT CERTIFIED PUBLIC ACCOUNTANTS

Board of Directors and Shareholders Chico's FAS, Inc.

We have audited the accompanying consolidated balance sheet of Chico's FAS, Inc. and subsidiaries as of February 1, 2003, and the related consolidated statements of income, stockholders' equity and cash flows for the year then ended. These financial statements are the responsibility of the Company's management. Our responsibility is to express an opinion on these financial statements based on our audit. The financial statements of Chico's FAS, Inc. and subsidiaries as of February 2, 2002 and for each of the two years in the period then ended, were audited by other auditors who have ceased operations and whose report dated March 4, 2002, expressed an unqualified opinion on those statements before the common stock split restatement adjustments described in Note 1.

We conducted our audit in accordance with auditing standards generally accepted in the United States. Those standards require that we plan and perform the audit to obtain reasonable assurance about whether the financial statements are free of material misstatement. An audit includes examining, on a test basis, evidence supporting the amounts and disclosures in the financial statements. An audit also includes assessing the accounting principles used and significant estimates made by management, as well as evaluating the overall financial statement presentation. We believe that our audit provides a reasonable basis for our opinion.

In our opinion, the financial statements referred to above present fairly, in all material respects, the consolidated financial position of Chico's FAS, Inc. and subsidiaries at February 1, 2003, and the consolidated results of their operations and their cash flows for the year then ended, in conformity with accounting principles generally accepted in the United States.

As discussed above, the financial statements of Chico's FAS, Inc. and subsidiaries as of February 2, 2002, and for each of the two years in the period then ended were audited by other auditors who have ceased operations. As described in Note 1, in the fiscal year ended February 1, 2003, the Company's Board of Directors approved a two-for-one common stock split, and all references to number of shares and per share information in the financial statements have been adjusted to reflect the common stock split on a retroactive basis. We audited the adjustments that were applied to restate the number of shares and per share information reflected in the financial statements for the years ended

February 2, 2002 and February 3, 2001. Our procedures included (a) agreeing the authorization for the two-for-one common stock split to the Company's underlying records obtained from management, and (b) testing the mathematical accuracy of the restated number of shares, basic and diluted earnings per share and other applicable disclosures such as stock options. In our opinion, such adjustments are appropriate and have been properly applied. However, we were not engaged to audit, review, or apply any procedures to the financial statements of the Company for the years ended February 2, 2002 and February 3, 2001 other than with respect to such adjustments and, accordingly, we do not express an opinion or any other form of assurance on the financial statements for the years ended February 2, 2002 and February 3, 2001 taken as a whole.

Tampa, Florida, February 28, 2003

REPORT OF INDEPENDENT CERTIFIED PUBLIC ACCOUNTANTS

THIS REPORT OF INDEPENDENT CERTIFIED PUBLIC ACCOUNTANTS IS A COPY OF A REPORT PREVIOUSLY ISSUED BY ARTHUR ANDERSEN LLP AND HAS NOT BEEN REISSUED BY ARTHUR ANDERSEN LLP. THE INCLUSION OF THIS PREVIOUSLY ISSUED ANDERSEN REPORT IS PURSUANT TO THE "TEMPORARY FINAL RULE AND FINAL RULE REQUIREMENTS FOR ARTHUR ANDERSEN LLP AUDITING CLIENTS," ISSUED BY THE U.S. SECURITIES AND EXCHANGE COMMISSION IN MARCH 2002. NOTE THAT THIS PREVIOUSLY ISSUED ANDERSEN REPORT INCLUDES REFERENCES TO CERTAIN FISCAL YEARS, WHICH ARE NOT REQUIRED TO BE PRESENTED IN THE ACCOMPANYING CONSOLIDATED FINANCIAL STATEMENTS AS OF AND FOR THE YEARS ENDED FEBRUARY 1, 2003.

To Chico's FAS, Inc. and Subsidiaries:

We have audited the accompanying consolidated balance sheets of Chico's FAS, Inc. (a Florida corporation) and subsidiaries as of February 2, 2002, and February 3, 2001, and the related consolidated statements of income, stockholders' equity and cash flows for the fiscal years ended February 2, 2002, February 3, 2001, and January 29, 2000. These financial statements are the responsibility of the Company's management. Our responsibility is to express an opinion on these financial statements based on our audits.

We conducted our audits in accordance with auditing standards generally accepted in the United States. Those standards require that we plan and perform the audit to obtain reasonable assurance about whether the financial statements are free of material misstatement. An audit includes examining, on a test basis, evidence supporting the amounts and disclosures in the financial statements. An audit also includes assessing the accounting principles used and significant estimates made by management, as well as evaluating the overall financial statement presentation. We believe that our audits provide a reasonable basis for our opinion.

In our opinion, the financial statements referred to above present fairly, in all material respects, the financial position of Chico's FAS, Inc. and subsidiaries as of February 2, 2002, and February 3, 2001, and the results of their operations and their cash flows for the fiscal years ended February 2, 2002, February 3, 2001, and January 29, 2000, in conformity with accounting principles generally accepted in the United States.

Tampa, Florida, March 4, 2002

Chico's FAS, Inc. and Subsidiaries
Consolidated Balance Sheets

Assets	February 1, 2003	February 2, 2002
CURRENT ASSETS:		
Cash and cash equivalents	$ 8,753,089	$ 13,376,864
Marketable securities	91,195,175	40,428,675
Receivables, less allowances for sales returns of $304,000 and $293,000, respectively	2,226,068	2,083,470
Inventories	44,907,504	28,905,066
Prepaid expenses	6,222,526	3,796,798
Deferred taxes	7,125,000	4,400,000
Total current assets	160,429,362	92,990,873
PROPERTY AND EQUIPMENT:		
Land and land improvements	5,166,394	2,870,111
Building and building improvements	19,667,654	12,424,784
Equipment, furniture and fixtures	71,769,250	41,752,754
Leasehold improvements	78,792,080	57,259,004
Total property and equipment	175,395,378	114,306,653
Less accumulated depreciation and amortization	(36,686,235)	(23,000,701)
Property and equipment, net	138,709,143	91,305,952
DEFERRED TAXES	92,000	1,166,000
OTHER ASSETS, NET	2,313,242	922,535
	$301,543,747	$186,385,360

Liabilities and Stockholders' Equity		
CURRENT LIABILITIES:		
Accounts payable	$ 28,488,471	$ 18,054,137
Accrued liabilities	26,200,081	16,585,157
Current portion of debt and deferred liabilities	171,217	306,876
Total current liabilities	54,859,769	34,946,170
NONCURRENT LIABILITIES:		
Long-term debt, excluding current portion	—	5,022,499
Deferred liabilities	6,550,856	2,921,760
Total noncurrent liabilities	6,550,856	7,944,259
Commitments and Contingencies		
STOCKHOLDERS' EQUITY:		
Common stock, $.01 par value; 200,000,000 shares authorized and 85,282,321 and 81,581,318 shares issued and outstanding, respectively	852,823	815,813
Additional paid-in capital	63,985,702	34,226,490
Retained earnings	175,109,145	108,350,203
Accumulated other comprehensive income	185,452	102,425
Total stockholders' equity	240,133,122	143,494,931
	$301,543,747	$186,385,360

The accompanying notes are an integral part of these consolidated balance sheets.

Chico's FAS, Inc. and Subsidiaries
Consolidated Statements of Income

	Fiscal Year Ended		
	February 1, 2003	February 2, 2002	February 3, 2001
Net sales by company stores	$508,492,490	$362,443,217	$252,168,208
Net sales by catalog and Internet	16,070,061	10,202,908	2,656,156
Net sales to franchisees	6,545,594	5,439,215	4,621,532
NET SALES	531,108,145	378,085,340	259,445,896
Cost of goods sold	209,770,101	153,937,579	108,670,577
GROSS PROFIT	321,338,044	224,147,761	150,775,319
General, administrative and store operating expenses	199,495,043	146,610,788	99,757,264
Depreciation and amortization	15,049,746	10,001,087	5,654,582
INCOME FROM OPERATIONS	106,793,255	67,535,886	45,363,473
Interest income, net	882,687	507,145	408,146
INCOME BEFORE INCOME TAXES	107,675,942	68,043,031	45,771,619
Income tax provision	40,917,000	25,856,000	17,393,000
NET INCOME	$ 66,758,942	$ 42,187,031	$ 28,378,619
PER SHARE DATA:			
Net income per common share—basic	$ 0.80	$ 0.52	$ 0.36
Net income per common and common equivalent share—diluted	$ 0.78	$ 0.50	$ 0.35
Weighted average common shares outstanding—basic	83,308,829	80,365,350	78,083,786
Weighted average common and common equivalent shares outstanding—diluted	86,032,052	83,778,336	81,665,394

The accompanying notes are an integral part of these consolidated statements.

Chico's FAS, Inc. and Subsidiaries
Consolidated Statements of
Stockholders' Equity

	Common Stock		Additional Paid-in Capital	Retained Earnings	Accumulated Other Comprehensive (Loss) Income	Total
	Shares	Par Value				
BALANCE, JANUARY 29, 2000	77,078,412	$770,784	$14,109,739	$ 37,784,553	$(24,334)	$ 52,640,742
Net income	—	—	—	28,378,619	—	28,378,619
Unrealized gain on marketable securities, net	—	—	—	—	71,580	71,580
Comprehensive income						28,450,199

	Common Stock		Additional Paid-in Capital	Retained Earnings	Accumulated Other Comprehensive (Loss) Income	Total
	Shares	Par Value				
Issuance of common stock	1,668,758	16,688	1,526,456	–	–	1,543,144
Stock option compensation	–	–	70,156	–	–	70,156
Tax benefit of stock options exercised	–	–	2,617,000	–	–	2,617,000
BALANCE, FEBRUARY 3, 2001	78,747,170	787,472	18,323,351	66,163,172	47,246	85,321,241
Net income	–	–	–	42,187,031	–	42,187,031
Unrealized gain on marketable securities net	–	–	–	–	55,179	55,179
Comprehensive income						42,242,210
Issuance of common stock	2,834,148	28,341	7,674,495	–	–	7,702,836
Stock option compensation	–	–	44,644	–	–	44,644
Tax benefit of stock options exercised	–	–	8,184,000	–	–	8,184,000
BALANCE, FEBRUARY 2, 2002	81,581,318	815,813	34,226,490	108,350,203	102,425	143,494,931
Net income	–	–	–	66,758,942	–	66,758,942
Unrealized gain on marketable securities, net	–	–	–	–	83,027	83,027
Comprehensive income						66,841,969
Issuance of common stock	3,701,003	37,010	7,210,212	–	–	7,247,222
Tax benefit of stock options exercised	–	–	22,549,000	–	–	22,549,000
BALANCE, FEBRUARY 1, 2003	85,282,321	$852,823	$63,985,702	$175,109,145	$185,452	$240,133,122

The accompanying notes are an integral part of these consolidated statements.

Chico's FAS, Inc. and Subsidiaries
Consolidated Statements
of Cash Flows

	Fiscal Year Ended		
	February 1, 2003	February 2, 2002	February 3, 2001
CASH FLOWS FROM OPERATING ACTIVITIES:			
Net income	$ 66,758,942	$ 42,187,031	$ 28,378,619
Adjustments to reconcile net income to net cash provided by operating activities—Depreciation and amortization, cost of goods sold	1,093,486	405,787	323,162
Depreciation and amortization, other	15,049,743	10,001,087	5,654,582
Stock option compensation	–	44,644	70,156
Deferred tax benefit	(1,651,000)	(1,816,000)	(606,000)

	Fiscal Year Ended		
	February 1, 2003	February 2, 2002	February 3, 2001
Tax benefit of options exercised	22,549,000	8,184,000	2,617,000
Deferred rent expense, net	1,481,689	882,873	406,971
Loss from disposal of property and equipment	1,314,696	1,445,078	393,970
(Increase) decrease in assets—			
Receivables, net	(142,598)	915,440	(1,292,249)
Inventories	(16,002,438)	(4,510,904)	(9,559,362)
Prepaid expenses	(2,425,728)	(1,542,449)	(1,585,654)
Other assets, net	735,079	(292,305)	(109,821)
Increase in liabilities—			
Accounts payable	10,434,334	4,302,375	7,769,078
Accrued liabilities	9,612,266	5,285,805	6,706,248
Total adjustments	42,048,529	23,305,431	10,788,081
Net cash provided by operating activities	108,807,471	65,492,462	39,166,700
CASH FLOWS FROM INVESTING ACTIVITIES:			
Purchases of marketable securities	(134,918,633)	(56,396,476)	(30,131,458)
Proceeds from sale of marketable securities	84,235,160	30,244,500	29,977,045
Purchases of property and equipment	(64,741,870)	(37,436,496)	(40,468,993)
Net cash used in investing activities	(115,425,343)	(63,588,472)	(40,623,406)
CASH FLOWS FROM FINANCING ACTIVITIES:			
Proceeds from issuance of common stock	7,247,222	7,702,836	1,543,144
Principal payments on debt	(5,155,500)	(66,000)	(72,000)
Deferred finance costs	(97,625)	(78,080)	(81,250)
Net cash provided by financing activities	1,994,097	7,558,756	1,389,894
Net (decrease) increase in cash and cash equivalent	(4,623,775)	9,462,746	(66,812)
CASH AND CASH EQUIVALENTS, Beginning of period	13,376,864	3,914,118	3,980,930
CASH AND CASH EQUIVALENTS, End of period	$ 8,753,089	$ 13,376,864	$ 3,914,118
SUPPLEMENT DISCLOSURES OF CASH FLOW INFORMATION:			
Cash paid for interest	$ 284,739	$ 610,384	$ 893,811
Cash paid for income taxes	$ 19,200,379	$ 17,657,563	$ 15,839,172

The accompanying notes are an integral part of these consolidated statements.

CHICO'S FAS, INC. AND SUBSIDIARIES NOTES TO CONSOLIDATED FINANCIAL STATEMENTS FEBRUARY 1, 2003

BUSINESS ORGANIZATION

The accompanying consolidated financial statements include the accounts of Chico's FAS, Inc., a Florida corporation, and its wholly-owned subsidiaries. The Company operates as a specialty retailer of exclusively designed, private label casual clothing and related accessories. The Company sells its products through traditional retail stores, catalog, a small franchise network and via the Internet at www.chicos.com. As of February 1, 2003, the Company's retail store system consisted of 378 stores located throughout the United States, 366 of which are owned and operated by the Company, and 12 of which are owned and operated by franchisees.

FISCAL YEAR

The Company has a 52–53 week fiscal year ending on the Saturday closest to January 31. The fiscal years ended February 1, 2003, February 2, 2002, and February 3, 2001 contained 52, 52 and 53 weeks, respectively.

FRANCHISE OPERATIONS

A summary of the changes in the number of the Company's franchise stores as compared to total company-owned stores as of February 1, 2003, and February 2, 2002, and for the fiscal years then ended is as follows:

	Fiscal Year Ended	
	February 1, 2003	February 2, 2002
Franchise stores opened	1	—
Franchise stores in operation at fiscal year-end	12	11
Company-owned stores at fiscal year-end	366	300

PRINCIPAL OF CONSOLIDATION

The consolidated financial statements include the accounts of the Company and its wholly-owned subsidiaries. All significant intercompany balances and transactions have been eliminated in consolidation.

MANAGEMENT ESTIMATES

The preparation of financial statements in conformity with accounting principles generally accepted in the United States requires management to make estimates and assumptions that affect the reported amounts of assets and liabilities and disclosure of contingent assets and liabilities at the date of the financial statements and the reported amounts of revenues and expenses during the reporting period. Actual results could differ from those estimates. Significant estimates and assumptions made by management primarily impact the following key financial areas:

Inventory Valuation

The Company identifies potentially excess and slow-moving inventories by evaluating turn rates and inventory levels in conjunction with the Company's overall growth rate. Excess quantities are identified through evaluation of inventory ageings, review of inventory turns and historical sales experiences, as well as specific identification based on fashion trends. Further, exposure to inadequate realization of carrying value is identified through analysis of gross margins and markdowns in combination with changes in the fashion industry. The Company provides lower of cost or market reserves for such identified excess and slow-moving inventories.

Inventory Shrinkage

The Company estimates its expected shrinkage of inventories between physical inventory counts by applying historical chain-wide average shrinkage experience rates to the related periods' sales volume. The historical rates are updated on a regular basis to reflect the most recent physical inventory shrinkage experience.

Sales Returns

The Company's policy is to honor customer returns at all times. Returns after 30 days of the original purchase, or returns without the original receipt, qualify for store credit only. The Company will, in certain circumstances, offer full customer refunds either after 30 days or without a receipt. The Company estimates its reserve for likely customer returns based on the average refund experience in relation to sales for the related period.

Self-Insurance

The Company is self-insured for certain losses relating to workers' compensation, medical and general liability claims. Self-insurance claims filed and claims incurred but not reported are accrued based upon management's estimates of the aggregate liability for uninsured claims incurred using insurance industry benchmarks and historical experience. Although management believes it has the ability to adequately accrue for estimated losses related to claims, it is possible that actual results could significantly differ from recorded self-insurance liabilities.

RECLASSIFICATIONS

Reclassifications of certain prior-year balances were made in order to conform to the current-year presentation.

CASH AND CASH EQUIVALENTS

Cash and cash equivalents includes cash on hand and in banks with original maturities of three months or less.

MARKETABLE SECURITIES

Marketable securities are classified as available-for-sale securities and are carried at fair value, with the unrealized holding gains and losses, net of income taxes, reflected as a separate component of stockholders' equity until realized. For the purposes of computing realized and unrealized gains and losses, cost is determined on a specific identification basis.

INVENTORIES

Fabric inventories of approximately $2,466,000 and $2,400,000 as of February 1, 2003, and February 2, 2002, respectively, are recorded at the lower of cost, using the first-in, first-out (FIFO) method, or market. All other inventories consisting of merchandise held for sale are recorded at the lower of cost, using the last-in, first-out (LIFO) method, or market. If the lower of FIFO or market method had been used for all inventories, inventories would have been approximately $638,000 and $1,578,000 higher as of February 1, 2003, and February 2, 2002, respectively, than those reported in the accompanying consolidated balance sheets. Purchasing, merchandising, distribution and product development costs are expensed as incurred, and are included in the accompanying consolidated statements of income as a component of cost of goods sold.

PROPERTY AND EQUIPMENT

Property and equipment is stated at cost. Depreciation of property and equipment is provided on a straight-line basis over the estimated useful lives of the assets. Leasehold improvements are depreciated over the lesser of the useful lives of the assets or the lease terms. The Company's property and equipment is depreciated using the following estimated useful lives:

	Estimated Useful Lives
Land and land improvements	35 years
Building and building improvements	20–35 years
Equipment, furniture and fixtures	2–10 years
Leasehold improvements	3–10 years or term of lease, if shorter

Maintenance and repairs of property and equipment are expensed as incurred, and major improvements are capitalized. Upon retirement, sale or other disposition of property and equipment, the cost and accumulated depreciation or amortization are eliminated from the accounts, and any gain or loss is charged to operations.

ACCOUNTING FOR THE IMPAIRMENT OF LONG-LIVED ASSETS

Long-lived assets are reviewed periodically for impairment if events or changes in circumstances indicate that the carrying amount may not be recoverable. If expected future undiscounted cash flows from operations are less than their carrying amounts, an asset is determined to be impaired, and a loss is recorded for the amount by which the carrying value of the asset exceeds its fair value.

INCOME TAXES

The Company follows the liability method, which establishes deferred tax assets and liabilities for the temporary differences between the financial reporting bases and the tax bases of the Company's assets and liabilities at enacted tax rates expected to be in effect when such amounts are realized or settled. Net deferred tax assets, whose realization is dependent on taxable earnings in future years, are recognized when a greater than 50 percent probability exists that the tax benefits will actually be realized sometime in the future.

FAIR VALUE OF FINANCIAL INSTRUMENTS

The Company's financial instruments consist of cash and cash equivalents, marketable securities, short-term trade receivables and payables and in the prior year, long-term debt instruments. The carrying values of cash and cash equivalents, marketable securities, trade receivables and trade payables equal current fair value. The terms of the Company's long-term debt agreements, as amended, include variable interest rates, which approximate current market rates.

REVENUE RECOGNITION

Retail sales by Company stores are recorded at the point of sale and are net of estimated customer returns. Retail sales by catalog and Internet are recorded when shipments are made to catalog and Internet customers and are net of estimated customer returns. Net sales to franchisees are recorded when merchandise is shipped to franchisees and are net of estimated returns.

STORE PRE-OPENING COSTS

Operating costs (including store set-up, rent and training expenses) incurred prior to the opening of new stores are expensed as incurred and are included in general, administrative and store operating expenses in the accompanying consolidated statements of income.

ADVERTISING COSTS

Costs associated with advertising are charged to expense when the advertising occurs. During the fiscal years ended February 1, 2003, February 2, 2002, and February 3, 2001, advertising costs of approximately $18,811,000, $12,816,000 and $7,051,000, respectively, are included in general, administrative and store operating expenses.

STOCK-BASED COMPENSATION PLANS

As allowed by Statement of Financial Accounting Standards (SFAS) No. 123, "Accounting for Stock-Based Compensation" (SFAS 123), the Company has elected to account for its stock-based compensation plans under the intrinsic value method of accounting prescribed by Accounting Principles Board (APB) Opinion No. 25, "Accounting for Stock Issued to Employees" (APB 25). Accordingly, the Company does not recognize compensation expense for stock option grants when the exercise price of the option equals or exceeds the market price of the Company's common stock on the date of grant. The Company has adopted the pro forma disclosure requirements of SFAS 123 and SFAS 148. See Note 7.

COMMON STOCK SPLITS

During the fiscal years ended February, 1, 2003 and February 2, 2002, the Board of Directors (the Board) declared three common stock splits (collectively, the Stock Splits). On April 19, 2001, the Board declared a three-for-two stock split of the Company's common stock, payable in the form of a stock dividend on May 16, 2001, to shareholders of record as of the close of business on May 2, 2001. On December 19, 2001, the Board declared a three-for-two stock split of the Company's common stock, payable in the form of a stock dividend on January 18, 2002, to shareholders of record as of the close of business on December 31, 2001. On June 27, 2002, the Board declared a two-for-one stock split of the Company's common stock, payable in the form of a stock dividend on July 29, 2002, to shareholders of record as of the close of business on July 15, 2002. Accordingly, all historical weighted average share and per share amounts and all references to the number of common shares elsewhere in the consolidated financial statements and notes thereto have been restated to reflect the Stock Splits. Par value remains unchanged at $0.01.

NET INCOME PER COMMON AND COMMON EQUIVALENT SHARE

SFAS No. 128, "Earnings per Share" (SFAS 128), requires companies with complex capital structures that have publicly held common stock or common stock equivalents to present both basic and diluted earnings per share (EPS) on the face of the income statement. As provided by SFAS 128, basic EPS is based on the weighted average number of common shares outstanding and diluted EPS is based on the weighted average number of common shares outstanding plus the dilutive common equivalent shares outstanding during the period.

The following is a reconciliation of the denominators of the basic and diluted EPS computations shown on the face of the accompanying consolidated statements of income as restated for the Stock Splits:

	Fiscal Year Ended		
	February 1, 2003	February 2, 2002	February 3, 2001
Weighted average common shares outstanding—basic	83,308,829	80,365,350	78,083,786
Dilutive effect of stock options outstanding	2,723,223	3,412,986	3,581,608
Weighted average common and common equivalent shares outstanding—diluted	86,032,052	83,778,336	81,665,394

The following options were outstanding as of the end of the fiscal years but were not included in the computation of diluted EPS because the options' exercise prices were greater than the average market price of the common shares:

| | Fiscal Year Ended | | |
	February 1, 2003	February 2, 2002	February 3, 2001
Number of options	523,800	373,000	1,026,000
Exercise price	$18.30–$21.42	$10.66–$13.34	$7.31–$7.72
Expiration date	June 25, 2012– December 16, 2012	May 23, 2010– January 2, 2012	August 7, 2010– October 30, 2010

NEWLY ISSUED ACCOUNTING PRONOUNCEMENTS

In June 2002, the Financial Accounting Standards Board (FASB) issued SFAS No. 146, "Accounting for Costs Associated with Exit or Disposal Activities" (SFAS 146). The standard requires companies to recognize costs associated with exit or disposal activities when they are incurred rather than at the date of a commitment to an exit or disposal plan. SFAS 146 is effective for exit or disposal activities that are initiated after December 31, 2002. The adoption of SFAS 146 did not have a significant impact on the Company's financial position or results of operations.

In November 2002, the FASB issued FASB Interpretation No. 45, "Guarantor's Accounting and Disclosure Requirements for Guarantees, Including Indirect Guarantees of Indebtedness of Others" (FIN 45). FIN 45 elaborates on the existing disclosure requirements for most guarantees, including loan guarantees such as standby letters of credit. It also clarifies that at the time a company issues a guarantee, the company must recognize an initial liability for the fair value, or market value, of the obligations it assumes under that guarantee and must disclose that information in its interim and annual financial statements. FIN 45 is effective on a prospective basis to guarantees issued or modified after December 31, 2002. The disclosure requirements of FIN 45 are effective for financial statements of interim or annual periods ending after December 15, 2002. The adoption of FIN 45 did not have a significant impact on the Company's financial position or results of operations.

In December 2002, the FASB issued SFAS 148, "Accounting for Stock-Based Compensation Transition and Disclosure" (SFAS 148). SFAS 148 amends SFAS 123, to provide alternative methods of transition to the fair value method of accounting for stock-based employee compensation. In addition, SFAS 148 amends the disclosure provisions of SFAS 123. SFAS 148 does not amend SFAS 123 to require companies to account for their employee stock-based awards using the fair value method. However, the disclosure provisions are required for all companies with stock-based employee compensation, regardless of whether they utilize the fair value method of accounting described in SFAS 123 or the intrinsic value method described in APB 25. The

Company adopted the disclosure provisions of SFAS 148 during the year ended February 1, 2003.

Marketable securities classified as available-for-sale consist of the following:

	February 1, 2003	February 2, 2002
Municipal bonds, cost	$91,009,723	$40,326,250
Municipal bonds, fair value	91,195,175	40,428,675
Unrealized gain	$ 185,452	$ 102,425

During the fiscal years ended February 1, 2003, February 2, 2002 and February 3, 2001, realized gains of approximately $5,900, $500 and $5,000, respectively, were recognized on sales of the Company's marketable securities and are included in interest income, net in the accompanying consolidated statements of income. At February 1, 2003, approximately 26 percent of the Company's marketable securities mature within one year, 7 percent between one and two years and the remainder by 2032.

Accrued liabilities consisted of the following:

	February 1, 2003	February 2, 2002
Allowance for estimated customer returns, gift certificates and store credits outstanding	$10,136,121	$ 5,598,777
Accrued payroll, bonuses and severance costs	8,004,105	6,203,882
Other	8,059,855	4,782,498
	$26,200,081	$16,585,157

The Company's income tax provision consisted of the following:

	Fiscal Year Ended		
	February 1, 2003	February 2, 2002	February 3, 2001
Current:			
Federal	$37,399,000	$24,394,000	$15,820,000
State	5,169,000	3,278,000	2,179,000
Deferred:			
Federal	(1,451,000)	(1,603,000)	(492,000)
State	(200,000)	(213,000)	(114,000)
Total income tax provision	$40,917,000	$25,856,000	$17,393,000

The reconciliation of the income tax provision based on the U.S. statutory federal income tax rate (35 percent) to the Company's income tax provision is as follows:

	Fiscal Year Ended		
	February 1, 2003	February 2, 2002	February 3, 2001
Tax expense at the statutory rate	$37,687,000	$23,815,000	$16,020,000
State income tax expense, net of federal tax benefit	3,230,000	2,041,000	1,369,000
Other	—	—	4,000
Total income tax provision	$40,917,000	$25,856,000	$17,393,000

Deferred tax assets and liabilities are recorded due to different carrying amounts for financial and income tax reporting purposes arising from cumulative temporary differences. These differences consist of the following as of February 1, 2003, and February 2, 2002:

	February 1, 2003	February 2, 2002
Assets:		
Accrued liabilities and allowances	$ 5,505,000	$2,897,000
Lease obligations	1,738,000	1,176,000
Inventories	1,577,000	1,431,000
Other	860,000	207,000
	9,680,000	5,711,000
Liabilities:		
Property and equipment	(2,463,000)	(145,000)
	$ 7,217,000	$5,566,000

Debt and deferred liabilities consisted of the following:

	February 1, 2003	February 2, 2002
Line of credit	$ —	$ —
Mortgage note	—	5,155,500
Deferred rent	4,574,666	3,095,635
Deferred compensation	2,147,407	—
Total debt and deferred liabilities	6,722,073	8,251,135
Less current portion	(171,217)	(306,876)
	$6,550,856	$7,944,259

During the fiscal year ended February 3, 2001, the Company entered into a two-year unsecured revolving credit facility (the Credit Facility), whereby the Company was able to borrow up to $25 million. The Credit Facility consisted of a $10 million line of credit and $15 million in reserves for letters of credit (see Note 6). During the fiscal year ended February 2, 2002, the Company amended the Credit Facility, to (i) increase the reserve for letters of credit from $15 million to $20 million and lower the line of credit from $10 million to $5 million and (ii) extend the Mortgage Note through February 2012, as more fully described below. In September 2002, the Company entered into a replacement unsecured revolving credit facility replacing the existing Credit Facility, expanding the maximum available commitment from $25 million to $45 million, extending the maturity to June 2005 and increasing the letter of credit sublimit of the facility to $35 million. All borrowings under the Credit Facility bear interest at the LIBOR rate, plus an additional amount ranging from 0.80 percent to 2.90 percent adjusted quarterly based on the Company's performance per annum (a combined 2.14 percent at February 1, 2003). The Company is also required to pay, quarterly in arrears, a commitment fee of 0.10 percent per annum on the average daily unused portion of the Line. There are no compensating balance requirements associated with the Credit Facility.

The Credit Facility contains certain restrictions regarding additional indebtedness, business operations, liens, guaranties, transfers and sales of assets, and transactions with subsidiaries or affiliates. In addition, the Company must comply with certain quarterly restrictions (based on a rolling four-quarters basis) regarding net worth, leverage ratio, fixed charge coverage and current ratio requirements. The Company was in compliance with all covenants at February 1, 2003.

The Mortgage Note was financed with a bank, initially bearing interest at the bank's prime rate plus 0.5 percent. During the fiscal year ended February 3, 2001, in connection with the closing of the Credit Facility, the Company amended the Mortgage Note to provide that the existing indebtedness would bear interest under the same provision as that in the Credit Facility and the restrictive covenants would be modified to be the same as those in the Credit Facility. The Mortgage Note was secured by a first priority mortgage on land, land improvements and certain building and equipment. During December 2001, the Company amended the Mortgage Note to extend the balloon payment due date from 2003 to February 2012. The monthly payments were increased from $6,000 principal plus interest to $11,083 principal plus interest, beginning February 2002. Monthly principal payments thereafter increase annually by 6 percent each February through 2011. In December 2002, the Company repaid the outstanding balance on the Mortgage Note of $5,049,862.

Deferred rent represents the difference between actual operating lease obligations due and operating lease expense, which is recorded by the Company on a straight-line basis over the terms of its leases.

Deferred compensation represents the deferred compensation liability payable to participants of the Chico's FAS, Inc. Deferred Compensation Plan (the "Deferred Plan"). See Note 8.

The Company leases retail store space and various office equipment under operating leases expiring in various years through the fiscal year ending 2013. Certain of the leases provide that the Company may cancel the lease if the Company's retail sales at that location fall below an established level, while certain leases provide for additional rent payments to be made when sales exceed a base amount. Certain operating leases provide for renewal options for periods from three to five years at their fair rental value at the time of renewal. In the normal course of business, operating leases are generally renewed or replaced by other leases.

Minimum future rental payments under noncancellable operating leases (including leases with certain minimum sales cancellation clauses described below and exclusive of common area maintenance charges and/or contingent rental payments based on sales) as of February 1, 2003, are approximately as follows:

Fiscal Year Ending	Amount
January 31, 2004	$ 33,279,000
January 29, 2005	33,679,000
January 28, 2006	31,373,000
February 3, 2007	28,716,000
February 2, 2008	24,691,000
Thereafter	65,439,000
	$217,177,000

As mentioned previously, a majority of the Company's new store operating leases contain cancellation clauses that allow the leases to be terminated at the Company's discretion, if certain minimum sales levels are not met within the first few years of the lease term. The Company has not historically exercised many of these cancellation clauses and, therefore, has included the full lease terms of such leases in the above table. For the fiscal years ended February 1, 2003, February 2, 2002, and February 3, 2001, total rent expense under the Company's operating leases was approximately $42,204,000, $30,818,000 and $21,185,000, respectively, including common area maintenance charges of approximately $5,206,000, $3,560,000 and $2,511,000, respectively, other rental charges of approximately $5,014,000, $3,406,000 and $2,473,000, respectively, and contingent rental expense of approximately $3,970,000, $3,431,000 and $2,437,000, respectively, based on sales.

At February 1, 2003, the Company had approximately $22,766,000 in commercial letters of credit outstanding (see Note 5), which had arisen in the normal course of business due to foreign purchase commitments.

The Company was named as defendant in a suit filed in September 2001 in the Superior Court for the State of California for the County of Orange. This suit, Carmen Davis vs. Chico's FAS, Inc., was filed by the plaintiff, seeking to represent all other Company assistant store managers, sales associates and hourly employees in California from September 21, 1997 to the present. The Company responded by seeking to dismiss the complaint and strike selected claims in order to either eliminate the litigation or gain greater clarity as to the basis for the plaintiff's action. In response, the plaintiff filed an amended complaint on February 15, 2002, which differs in a number of material respects from the original complaint. The amended complaint alleged that the Company failed to pay overtime wages and failed to provide rest breaks and meal periods. The action sought "class action" status and sought unspecified monetary damages. Following preliminary settlement discussions, the parties attended a mediation on October 14, 2002, at which the parties reached a settlement on a class-wide basis. The settlement provides for a common fund out of which settlement awards to class members and the costs of the settlement will be paid. The parties prepared a settlement agreement, which was lodged with the Court. The settlement agreement states that the settlement is not an admission of liability and that the Company continues to deny liability for any of plaintiff's claims. Subsequent to year end, the Court heard the plaintiff's motion for preliminary approval of the settlement. The Court granted the motion and ordered that the parties give notice of the settlement to the class members. Once notice is given, class members will have sixty days to file claim forms to participate in the settlement or to file exclusion forms to opt out of the settlement. On September 16, 2003, the Court will hold a settlement fairness hearing for the purpose of determining whether to give final approval to the settlement. If final approval is given, and no appeals challenging the settlement are filed, the Company will pay the settlement sums to class members who have filed valid claims and also will pay amounts owing for attorney's fees, costs and other expenses of the settlement. The settlement provides for a release of all covered claims by class members who do not opt out of the settlement. The Company does not believe the outcome of this will have a material impact on the Company's results of operations or financial condition.

Chico's is not a party to any other legal proceedings, other than various claims and lawsuits arising in the normal course of the Company's business, none of which the Company believes should have a material adverse effect on its financial condition or results of operations.

1992 STOCK OPTION PLAN

During fiscal year 1992, the Board approved a stock option plan (the 1992 Plan), which reserved approximately 1,210,000 shares of common stock for future issuance under the 1992 Plan to eligible employees of the Company. The per share exercise price of each stock option is not less than the fair market value of the stock on the date of grant or, in the case of an employee owning more than 10 percent of the outstanding stock of the Company and to the extent incentive stock options, as opposed to nonqualified stock options, are issued, the price is not less than 110 percent of such fair market value. Also, the aggregate fair market value of the stock with respect to which incentive stock options are exercisable for the first time by an employee in any calendar year may not exceed $100,000. Options granted under the terms of the 1992 Plan generally vest evenly over three years and have a 10-year term. As of February 1, 2003, approximately 13,000 nonqualified options are outstanding under the 1992 Plan.

1993 STOCK OPTION PLAN

During fiscal year 1993, the Board approved a stock option plan, as amended in fiscal 1999 (the 1993 Plan), which reserved approximately 7,010,000 shares of common stock for future issuance under the 1993 Plan to eligible employees of the Company. The terms of the 1993 Plan are essentially the same as the 1992 Plan. As of February 1, 2003, approximately 3,945,000 nonqualified options are outstanding under the 1993 Plan.

INDEPENDENT DIRECTORS' PLAN

In October 1998, the Board approved a stock option plan (the Independent Directors' Plan), which reserved 1,257,500 shares of common stock for future issuance to eligible independent directors of the Company. Options granted under the terms of the Independent Directors' Plan and these individual grants vest after six months and have a 10-year term. As of February 1, 2003, 402,500 shares had been granted under the Independent Directors' Plan. Since 1993 and prior to adoption of the Independent Directors' Plan, four independent directors of the Company had been granted a total of 651,000 nonqualified options through individual grants at exercise prices ranging from $0.93 to $1.42. Subsequent to the adoption of the Independent Directors' Plan, three independent directors of the Company were granted 135,000 nonqualified stock options through individual grants at exercise prices of $4.29 per share. As of February 1, 2003, approximately 534,000 of these individual grant nonqualified options and options under the Independent Directors' Plan are outstanding.

OMNIBUS STOCK AND INCENTIVE PLAN

In April 2002, the Board approved the Chico's FAS, Inc. Omnibus Stock and Incentive Plan (the Omnibus Plan), which reserved 4,862,640 shares of common stock for future issuance to eligible employees and directors of the Company. The Omnibus Plan provides for awards of nonqualified stock options, incentive stock options, restricted stock awards and restricted stock units. No new grants will be made under the Company's existing 1992 Plan, 1993 Plan or Independent Directors' Plan, and such existing plans will remain in effect only for purposes of administering options that were outstanding thereunder on the date the Omnibus Plan was approved by the Company's stockholders. As of February 1, 2003, approximately 520,000 nonqualified options are outstanding under the Omnibus Plan.

EXECUTIVE OFFICERS' SUPPLEMENTARY STOCK OPTION PROGRAM

During the fiscal year ended February 3, 2001, the Board approved an executive officers' supplementary stock option program (the Executive Officers' Program), which reserved 375,000 shares of common stock for future issuance to eligible executive officers of the Company. Options granted under the terms of the Executive Officers' Program vest after three years and have a 10-year term. As of February 1, 2003, all 375,000 shares have been granted under the Executive Officers' Program at exercise prices ranging from $3.40 to $5.10. Of the 375,000 shares granted, 45,000 shares were granted at exercise prices below fair market value. The granting of these shares resulted in stock compensation expense of approximately $45,000 and $70,000 in the accompanying consolidated financial statements for the fiscal years ended February 2, 2002, and February 3, 2001, respectively. No compensation expense was recorded for the fiscal year ended February 1, 2003. At February 1, 2003, there were no options outstanding under the Executive Officers' Program.

AGGREGATE STOCK OPTION ACTIVITY

As of February 1, 2003, 5,011,600 nonqualified options are outstanding at a weighted average exercise price of $8.75 per share, and 4,342,840 remain available for future grants. Of the options outstanding, 2,275,095 options are exercisable.

Stock option activity for the fiscal years ended February 1, 2003, February 2, 2002, and February 3, 2001, was as follows:

| | Fiscal Year Ended | | | | | |
| | February 1, 2003 | | February 2, 2002 | | February 3, 2001 | |
	Number of Options	Weighted-Average Exercise Price	Number of Options	Weighted-Average Exercise Price	Number of Options	Weighted-Average Exercise Price
Outstanding, beginning of period	7,251,228	$ 3.66	8,712,158	$2.40	7,721,812	$1.14
Granted	1,435,266	16.66	1,927,000	8.84	2,700,000	5.02
Exercised	(3,653,392)	1.78	(2,579,780)	2.21	(1,586,044)	0.76
Canceled or expired	(21,500)	5.09	(808,152)	7.07	(123,610)	2.09
Outstanding, end of period	5,011,600	8.75	7,251,226	3.66	8,712,158	2.40
Options exercisable, end of period	2,275,095	5.87	4,167,668	1.64	5,004,298	1.15

The following table summarizes information about stock options as of February 1, 2003:

| | Options Outstanding | | | Options Exercisable | |
Ranges of Exercise Prices	Number Outstanding	Weighted-Average Remaining Contractual Life (Years)	Weighted-Average Exercise Price	Number Exercisable	Weighted-Average Exercise Price
$ 0.36–$ 2.49	495,828	3.58	$ 0.88	495,828	$ 0.88
$ 2.50–$ 4.99	1,358,006	6.96	3.08	988,001	3.12
$ 5.00–$ 9.99	1,369,500	8.04	8.27	339,500	8.16
$10.00–$21.42	1,788,266	9.08	15.61	451,766	15.64
	5,011,600	8.56	8.75	2,275,095	5.87

EMPLOYEE STOCK PURCHASE PLAN

The Company has a noncompensatory employee stock purchase plan (ESPP) under which substantially all fulltime employees are given the right to purchase up to 800 shares of the common stock of the Company two times a year at a price equal to 85 percent of the value of the stock immediately prior to the beginning of each exercise period. During the fiscal years ended February 1, 2003, February 2, 2002, and February 3, 2001, approximately 48,000, 260,000 and 82,000 shares, respectively, were purchased under the ESPP. The Company recognized no compensation expense for the issuance of these shares.

SFAS NO. 123, "ACCOUNTING FOR STOCK-BASED COMPENSATION"

The Company accounts for its stock-based compensation plans under APB 25 and, accordingly, does not recognize compensation expense based on the fair value method of accounting as provided under SFAS 123. If the Company had elected to recognize compensation cost based on the fair value of all options granted beginning in fiscal year 1995, net income would have been reduced to the pro forma amounts indicated in the table below.

For pro forma disclosure purposes, the fair value of each option granted has been estimated as of the grant date using the Black-Scholes option pricing model with the following weighted average assumptions: risk-free interest rate of 4.8, 5.1 and 6.3 percent for the fiscal years ended February 1, 2003, February 2, 2002, and February 3, 2001, respectively, expected life of seven years, no expected dividends, and expected volatility of 68, 73 and 74 percent for the fiscal years ended February 1, 2003, February 2, 2002, and February 3, 2001, respectively. The weighted average fair value of options granted during the fiscal years ended February 1, 2003, February 2, 2002, and February 3, 2001, was $11.63, $8.84 and $4.09, respectively. Options granted under the 1992 Plan and 1993 Plan generally vest ratably over three years. All other options were either exercisable generally after six months or vested ratably over three years. The term of all options granted is 10 years.

	Fiscal Year Ended		
	February 1, 2003	February 2, 2002	February 3, 2001
Net income:			
As reported	$66,758,942	$42,187,031	$28,378,619
Pro forma	58,063,247	37,372,941	26,382,313
Net income per common share—basic:			
As reported	$ 0.80	$ 0.52	$ 0.36
Pro forma	0.70	0.47	0.34
Net income per common and common equivalent share—diluted:			
As reported	$ 0.78	$ 0.50	$ 0.35
Pro forma	0.67	0.45	0.32

The Company has a 401(k) defined contribution employee benefit plan (the Plan) covering substantially all employees. Employees' rights to Company-contributed benefits vest over two to six years of service, as specified in the Plan. Under the Plan, employees may contribute up to 20 percent of their annual compensation, subject to certain statutory limitations. The Company has elected to match employee contributions at 33 1/3 percent on the first 6 percent of the employees' contributions and can elect to make additional contributions over and above the mandatory match. Effective January 1, 2003, the Plan has been amended for the Company to match employee contributions at 50 percent on the first 6 percent of the employees' contributions. For the fiscal years ended February 1, 2003, February 2, 2002, and February 3, 2001, the Company's costs under the Plan were approximately $935,000, $425,000 and $283,000, respectively.

In April 2002, the Company adopted the Chico's FAS, Inc. Deferred Compensation Plan (the "Deferred Plan") to provide supplemental retirement income benefits for a select group of management employees. Eligible participants may elect to defer up to 80 percent of their salary and 100 percent of their bonuses pursuant to the terms and conditions of the Deferred Plan. The Deferred Plan generally provides for payments upon retirement, death or termination of employment. In addition, the Company may make employer contributions to participants under the Deferred Plan. To date, no Company contributions have been made under the Deferred Plan. The amount of the deferred compensation liability payable to the participants is included in "deferred liabilities" on the consolidated balance sheet. A portion of these obligations are funded through the establishment of trust accounts held by the Company on behalf of the management group participating in the plan. The trust accounts are reflected in "other assets" in the accompanying consolidated balance sheet.

	Net Sales	Gross Profit	Net Income	Net Income Per Common Share– Basic	Net Income Per Common and Common Equivalent Share Diluted
FISCAL YEAR ENDED FEBRUARY 1, 2003:					
First quarter	$130,453,641	$81,464,050	$19,777,283	$0.24	$0.23
Second quarter	125,068,123	75,478,555	16,388,288	0.20	0.19
Third quarter	137,260,963	82,375,696	15,543,679	0.19	0.18
Fourth quarter	138,325,418	82,019,743	15,049,692	0.18	0.17
FISCAL YEAR ENDED FEBRUARY 2, 2002:					
First quarter	$ 93,233,012	$56,291,716	$12,379,128	$0.16	$0.15
Second quarter	89,492,217	53,684,549	11,090,613	0.14	0.13
Third quarter	93,978,124	55,542,287	8,899,660	0.11	0.11
Fourth quarter	101,381,987	58,629,209	9,817,630	0.12	0.12
FISCAL YEAR ENDED FEBRUARY 3, 2001:					
First quarter	$ 56,692,814	$33,928,820	$ 7,475,922	$0.10	$0.09
Second quarter	60,638,316	34,994,364	7,377,426	0.09	0.09
Third quarter	68,990,473	40,669,142	7,820,096	0.10	0.09
Fourth quarter	73,124,293	41,182,993	5,705,175	0.07	0.07

COMPREHENSIVE CASE

Attached are Chico's FAS, INC. AND SUBSIDIARIES financial statements and related footnotes contained in their 10K report dated February 1, 2003. Case requirements based on the information disclosed in these statements and notes are listed below:

RECEIVABLES:

1. Calculate the company's receivables turnover ratio.
2. Explain why receivables turnover is typically higher for specialty clothiers such as Chico than for department stores.
3. Determine from the contra-asset allowances for sales returns whether estimated sales returns for the year were higher or lower for the past year than actual returns.
4. Suppose that merchandise shipped to franchisees was shipped on consignment. Explain how this might affect the timing of revenue recognition.

INVENTORIES:

1. Suppose that all the company's inventories were valued for accounting purposes at the lower of FIFO cost or market. Determine what cost of goods sold would have been in that case.
2. Suggest an explanation for why the company's LIFO reserves declined while inventory levels increased during the past year.
3. Describe how one might determine the market value employed by the company in determining the lower of cost or market for inventories.

PROPERTY AND EQUIPMENT:

1. Determine how much of the combined amounts shown as depreciation and amortization on the cash flow statement represent depreciation.
2. Reconstruct a journal entry summarizing the disposal of property and equipment during the year.
3. Estimate the average remaining useful life of the company's property and equipment at year end.
4. Comment the conservatism evident in the company's accounting policy for property and equipment. Compare this policy with Great Britain's policies for similar assets.

ACCRUED LIABILITIES:

1. Explain why the company maintains a reserve for customer returns, etc. in the form of an accrued liability as well as in the form of a contra-asset.

2. Suppose that the company's consistent policy had been to not accrue payroll, bonuses, and severance costs. Determine the effect on income from operations.

DEFERRED TAXES:

1. Estimate the company's effective income tax rate for the past year.
2. Reconstruct a journal entry summarizing the company's income tax provision for the past year.
3. A significant portion of deferred taxes arises from accrued liabilities and allowances. Explain.
4. Comment on why deferred taxes appear on the company's balance sheet as both a current asset and a non-current asset.

OTHER ASSETS:

1. Other assets include deferred finance costs. Explain the rationale for this treatment of finance costs.
2. Other assets also include deferred compensation as does the deferred liabilities. Comment on circumstances that could produce this result.
3. Determine the amortization of other assets recorded during the year.

DEBT:

1. Reconstruct a journal entry summarizing the retirement of the company's mortgage note during the year.
2. Comment on where the funds used to retire the mortgage note appear to have been obtained.
3. The company refers to the LIBOR rate in describing the terms of its credit facility. Define LIBOR.
4. The company increased the principal component of its mortgage payments before the mortgage note was retired. Explain in general terms how this would affect amounts recognized as interest expense.

LEASES:

1. Discuss the accounting rationale for the company's recognition of the difference between actual operating lease obligations due and operating lease expense as a deferred liability.
2. Suppose that the amounts shown as minimum future rental payments under non-cancellable leases were capitalized as a lease obligation. Assuming an implicit interest rate of 5 percent and payments after 2008 were equally spread over three years, determine the present value of that obligation.

3. Comment on the effect of capitalizing leases as described in problem 2 on the company's leverage ratio.

4. Describe the criteria for classifying leases as capital leases versus operating leases and suggest an accounting incentive for structuring leases that do not meet those criteria.

COMMON STOCK:

1. Reconstruct a journal entry summarizing the issuance of common stock during the year.

2. During the year, the company implemented a two-for-one stock split by reclassifying additional paid-in capital as common stock retroactively for all preceding years. Comment on what the company's objective might have been.

3. Estimate the opportunity cost of stock options exercised during the year assuming an average market price equal to the exercise price of options granted during the year.

4. Comment on why the vast majority of companies chose the intrinsic value method of accounting for stock options before the recent spate of accounting scandals.

5. The company's stock options are nonqualified. Explain what this means and indicate the effects on stockholders' equity as a consequence during the past year.

MARKETABLE SECURITIES:

1. Analyze the changes in marketable securities as they appear on the company's balance sheet from the start to the end of the past year.

2. Suppose that the company had classified marketable securities as trading securities rather than as securities available for sale since the company's inception. Indicate how the company's balance sheet at year-end and income statement for the past year would differ.

3. Comment on the rationale for the difference in accounting policies for trading securities and securities available for sale.

ARTICULATION OF STATEMENTS:

Create "T" accounts for each item appearing on the comparative balance sheets for the last two years. Enter the beginning and ending balances for those items. Reconstruct entries to those accounts that summarize changes in those balances during the year and that reconcile with items appearing on the cash flow statement and statement of stockholders' equity.

FINANCIAL RATIOS:

Compute each of the financial ratios identified in the text for the past year. Comment on the limitations of computing ratios for just a single year and company.

VALUING EQUITY:

Apply the residual income method for valuing equity based on data contained in the company's balance sheets for the past two years and income statement for the most recent year in generating pro forma statements. Assume the following:

The net sales growth rate of the past year will continue for five (5) years with zero growth beyond that point.

Cost of goods sold net of depreciation and amortization and general, administrative, and store expenses will remain at the same percentages of net sales as for the most recent year. (Note that the amount of depreciation and amortization included in cost of goods sold appears on the cash flow statement.)

Depreciation and amortization are expected to remain at the same percentages of average property and equipment, net and other assets, net as for the most recent year.

The income tax rate is expected to be the same as the effective tax rate for the most recent year.

Ending balances of all assets, net other than marketable securities are expected to remain at the same percentages of net sales as for the most recent year.

Ending balances of all liabilities are expected to remain at the same percentages of net sales as for the most recent year. (Note that there is no outstanding debt as of February 1, 2003, implying a pure equity firm going forward.)

The balance of marketable securities is expected to remain constant at its present amount, and interest income on those securities is expected to remain at the same percentage of marketable securities as for the most recent year. (Note that interest income on the income statement is net of interest expense and that an estimate of interest expense would be interest paid as disclosed below the formal cash flow statement.)

The company's estimated cost of equity capital is 10 percent.

APPENDIX D

Journal References

David Aboody, Ron Kasznik, "CEO stock option awards and the timing of corporate voluntary disclosures," *Journal of Accounting & Economics,* Amsterdam: Feb 2000, Vol. 29, Iss. 1, pg. 73.

David Aboody, Ron Kasznik, Michael Williams, "Purchase versus pooling in stock-for-stock acquisitions: Why do firms care?", *Journal of Accounting & Economics,* Amsterdam: Jun 2000, Vol. 29, Iss. 3, pg. 261.

Robert Comment, Gregg A. Jarrell, "The Relative Signaling Power of Dutch-Auction and Fixed-Price Self-Tender Offers and Open-Market Share Repurchases," *The Journal of Finance,* Cambridge: Sep 1991, Vol. 46, Iss. 4, pg. 1243, 29 pgs.

Kirsten M. Ely, "Operating lease accounting and the market's assessment of equity risk," *Journal of Accounting Research,* Chicago: Autumn 1995, Vol. 33, Iss. 2, pg. 397, 19 pgs.

John S. Hughes, Jennifer L. Kao, Michael Williams, "Public Disclosure of Forward Contracts and Revelation of Proprietary Information," *Review of Accounting Studies,* Boston: Dec 2002, Vol. 7, Iss. 4, pg. 459.

John S. Hughes, William E. Ricks, "Accounting for Retail Land Sales: Analysis of a Mandated Change," *Journal of Accounting & Economics,* Amsterdam: Aug 1984, Vol. 6, Iss. 2, pg. 101, 32 pgs.

Patricia J. Hughes, Eduardo Schwartz, John Fellingham, "The LIFO/FIFO Choice: An Asymmetric Information Approach," *Journal of Accounting Research,* Chicago, 1988, Vol. 26, pg. 41.

Stephanie Lenway, Judy Rayburn, "An Investigation of the Behavior of Accruals in the Semiconductor Industry: 1985," *Contemporary Accounting Research,* Toronto: Fall/automme 1992, Vol. 9, Iss. 1, pg. 237, 15 pgs.

Jing Liu, Doron Nissim, Jacob Thomas, "Equity valuation using multiples," *Journal of Accounting Research,* Chicago: Mar 2002, Vol. 40, Iss. 1, pg. 135, 38 pgs.

Thomas Lys, Linda Vincent, "An analysis of value destruction in AT&T's acquisition of NCR," *Journal of Financial Economics,* Amsterdam: Oct/Nov 1995, Vol. 39, Iss. 2,3, pg. 353, 26 pgs.

Jeff L. Payne, Wayne B. Thomas, "The implications of using stock-split adjusted I/B/E/S data in empirical research," *The Accounting Review,* Sarasota: Oct 2003, Vol. 78, Iss. 4, pg. 1049, 19 pgs.

Graeme Rankine, Earl K. Stice, "The market reaction to the choice of accounting method for stock splits and large stock dividends," *Journal of Financial and Quantitative Analysis,* Seattle: Jun 1997, Vol. 32, Iss. 2, pg. 161, 22 pgs.

William E. Ricks, John S. Hughes, "Market Reactions to a Non-Discretionary Accounting Change: The Case of Long-Term Investments," *The Accounting Review,* Sarasota: Jan 1985, Vol. 60, Iss. 1, pg. 33, 20 pgs.

Douglas J. Skinner, Richard G. Sloan, "Earnings Surprises, Growth Expectations, and Stock Returns or Don't Let an Earnings Torpedo Sink Your Portfolio," *Review of Accounting Studies,* Boston: Jun–Sep 2002, Vol. 7, Iss. 2–3; pg. 289.

Amy Patricia Sweeney, "Debt-covenant violations and managers' accounting responses," *Journal of Accounting & Economics,* Amsterdam: May 1994, Vol. 17, Iss. 3, pg. 281, 28 pgs.

Financial Accounting Standards Board References

Below is a listing of the Statement of Financial Accounting Standards (SFAS) and the Statement of Financial Accounting Concepts Statements (SFAC). They are listed in reverse order of their adoption. Full text of the statements can be found at the FASB's website at http://www.fasb.org/st/. In addition, the opinions of the AICPA's Accounting Principles Board (APB) follow those of the FASB.

STATEMENTS OF FINANCIAL ACCOUNTING STANDARDS (SFAS)

Statement No. 150
Accounting for Certain Financial Instruments with Characteristics of both Liabilities and Equity
(Issue Date 5/03)

Statement No. 149
Amendment of Statement 133 on Derivative Instruments and Hedging Activities
(Issue Date 4/03)

Statement No. 148
Accounting for Stock-Based Compensation—Transition and Disclosure—An amendment of FASB Statement No. 123
(Issue Date 12/02)

Statement No. 147
Acquisitions of Certain Financial Institutions—An amendment of FASB Statements No. 72 and 144 and FASB Interpretation No. 9
(Issue Date 10/02)

Statement No. 146
Accounting for Costs Associated with Exit or Disposal Activities
(Issue Date 6/02)

Statement No. 145
Rescission of FASB Statements No. 4, 44, and 64, Amendment of FASB Statement No. 13, and Technical Corrections
(Issue Date 4/02)

Statement No. 144
Accounting for the Impairment or Disposal of Long-Lived Assets
(Issue Date 8/01)

Statement No. 143
Accounting for Asset Retirement Obligations
(Issue Date 6/01)

Statement No. 142
Goodwill and Other Intangible Assets
(Issue Date 6/01)

Statement No. 141
Business Combinations
(Issue Date 6/01)

Statement No. 140
Accounting for Transfers and Servicing of Financial Assets and Extinguishments of Liabilities—A replacement of FASB Statement No. 125
(Issue Date 9/00)

Statement No. 139
Rescission of FASB Statement No. 53 and amendments to FASB Statements No. 63, 89, and 121
(Issue Date 6/00)

Statement No. 138
Accounting for Certain Derivative Instruments and Certain Hedging Activities—An amendment of FASB Statement No. 133
(Issue Date 6/00)

Statement No. 137
Accounting for Derivative Instruments and Hedging Activities—Deferral of the Effective Date of FASB Statement No. 133—An amendment of FASB Statement No. 133
(Issue Date 6/99)

Statement No. 136
Transfers of Assets to a Not-for-Profit Organization or Charitable Trust That Raises or Holds Contributions for Others
(Issue Date 6/99)

Statement No. 135
Rescission of FASB Statement No. 75 and Technical Corrections
(Issue Date 2/99)

Statement No. 134
Accounting for Mortgage-Backed Securities Retained after the Securitization of Mortgage Loans Held for Sale by a Mortgage Banking Enterprise—An amendment of FASB Statement No. 65
(Issue Date 10/98)

Statement No. 133
Accounting for Derivative Instruments and Hedging Activities
(Issue Date 6/98)

Statement No. 132 (revised 2003)
Employers' Disclosures about Pensions and Other Postretirement Benefits— An amendment of FASB Statements No. 87, 88, and 106
(Issue Date 12/03)

Statement No. 132
Employers' Disclosures about Pensions and Other Postretirement Benefits— An amendment of FASB Statements No. 87, 88, and 106
(Issue Date 2/98)

Statement No. 131
Disclosures about Segments of an Enterprise and Related Information
(Issue Date 6/97)

Statement No. 130
Reporting Comprehensive Income
(Issue Date 6/97)

Statement No. 129
Disclosure of Information about Capital Structure
(Issue Date 2/97)

Statement No. 128
Earnings per Share
(Issue Date 2/97)

Statement No. 127
Deferral of the Effective Date of Certain Provisions of FASB Statement No. 125—An amendment to FASB Statement No. 125
(Issue Date 12/96)

Statement No. 126
Exemption from Certain Required Disclosures about Financial Instruments for Certain Nonpublic Entities—An amendment to FASB Statement No. 107
(Issue Date 12/96)

Statement No. 125
Accounting for Transfers and Servicing of Financial Assets and Extinguishments of Liabilities
(Issue Date 6/96)

Statement No. 124
Accounting for Certain Investments Held by Not-for-Profit Organizations
(Issue Date 11/95)

Statement No. 123
Accounting for Stock-Based Compensation
(Issue Date 10/95)

Statement No. 122
Accounting for Mortgage Servicing Rights—An amendment of FASB Statement No. 65
(Issue Date 5/95)

Statement No. 121
Accounting for the Impairment of Long-Lived Assets and for Long-Lived Assets to Be Disposed Of
(Issue Date 3/95)

Statement No. 120
Accounting and Reporting by Mutual Life Insurance Enterprises and by Insurance Enterprises for Certain Long-Duration Participating Contracts—An amendment of FASB Statements 60, 97, and 113 and Interpretation No. 40
(Issue Date 1/95)

Statement No. 119
Disclosure about Derivative Financial Instruments and Fair Value of Financial Instruments
(Issue Date 10/94)

Statement No. 118
Accounting by Creditors for Impairment of a Loan-Income Recognition and Disclosures—An amendment of FASB Statement No. 114
(Issue Date 10/94)

Statement No. 117
Financial Statements of Not-for-Profit Organizations
(Issue Date 6/93)

Statement No. 116
Accounting for Contributions Received and Contributions Made
(Issue Date 6/93)

Statement No. 115
Accounting for Certain Investments in Debt and Equity Securities
(Issue Date 5/93)

Statement No. 114
Accounting by Creditors for Impairment of a Loan—An amendment of FASB Statements No. 5 and 15
(Issue Date 5/93)

Statement No. 113
Accounting and Reporting for Reinsurance of Short-Duration and Long-Duration Contracts
(Issue Date 12/92)

Statement No. 112
Employers' Accounting for Postemployment Benefits—An amendment of FASB Statements No. 5 and 43
(Issue Date 11/92)

Statement No. 111
Rescission of FASB Statement No. 32 and Technical Corrections
(Issue Date 11/92)

Statement No. 110
Reporting by Defined Benefit Pension Plans of Investment Contracts—An amendment of FASB Statement No. 35
(Issue Date 8/92)

Statement No. 109
Accounting for Income Taxes
(Issue Date 2/92)

Statement No. 108
Accounting for Income Taxes—Deferral of the Effective Date of FASB Statement No. 96—An amendment of FASB Statement No. 96
(Issue Date 12/91)

Statement No. 107
Disclosures about Fair Value of Financial Instruments
(Issue Date 12/91)

Statement No. 106
Employers' Accounting for Postretirement Benefits Other Than Pensions
(Issue Date 12/90)

Statement No. 105
Disclosure of Information about Financial Instruments with Off-Balance-Sheet Risk and Financial Instruments with Concentrations of Credit Risk
(Issue Date 3/90)

Statement No. 104
Statement of Cash Flows—Net Reporting of Certain Cash Receipts and Cash Payments and Classification of Cash Flows from Hedging Transactions—An amendment of FASB Statement No. 95
(Issue Date 12/89)

Statement No. 103
Accounting for Income Taxes—Deferral of the Effective Date of FASB Statement No. 96—An amendment of FASB Statement No. 96
(Issue Date 12/89)

Statement No. 102
Statement of Cash Flows—Exemption of Certain Enterprises and Classification of Cash Flows from Certain Securities Acquired for Resale—An amendment of FASB Statement No. 95
(Issue Date 2/89)

Statement No. 101
Regulated Enterprises-Accounting for the Discontinuation of Application of FASB Statement No. 71
(Issue Date 12/88)

Statement No. 100
Accounting for Income Taxes—Deferral of the Effective Date of FASB Statement No. 96—An amendment of FASB Statement No. 96
(Issue Date 12/88)

Statement No. 99
Deferral of the Effective Date of Recognition of Depreciation by Not-for-Profit Organizations—An amendment of FASB Statement No. 93
(Issue Date 9/88)

Statement No. 98
Accounting for Leases: Sale-Leaseback Transactions Involving Real Estate, Sales-Type Leases of Real Estate, Definition of the Lease Term, and Initial Direct Costs of Direct Financing Leases—An amendment of FASB Statements No. 13, 66, and 91 and a rescission of FASB Statement No. 26 and Technical Bulletin No. 79-11
(Issue Date 5/88)

Statement No. 97
Accounting and Reporting by Insurance Enterprises for Certain Long-Duration Contracts and for Realized Gains and Losses from the Sale of Investments
(Issue Date 12/87)

Statement No. 96
Accounting for Income Taxes
(Issue Date 12/87)

Statement No. 95
Statement of Cash Flows
(Issue Date 11/87)

Statement No. 94
Consolidation of All Majority-owned Subsidiaries—An amendment of ARB No. 51, with related amendments of APB Opinion No. 18 and ARB No. 43, Chapter 12
(Issue Date 10/87)

Statement No. 93
Recognition of Depreciation by Not-for-Profit Organizations
(Issue Date 8/87)

Statement No. 92
Regulated Enterprises—Accounting for Phase-in Plans—An amendment of FASB Statement No. 71
(Issue Date 8/87)

Statement No. 91
Accounting for Nonrefundable Fees and Costs Associated with Originating or Acquiring Loans and Initial Direct Costs of Leases—An amendment of FASB Statements No. 13, 60, and 65 and a rescission of FASB Statement No. 17
(Issue Date 12/86)

Statement No. 90
Regulated Enterprises—Accounting for Abandonments and Disallowances of Plant Costs—An amendment of FASB Statement No. 71
(Issue Date 12/86)

Statement No. 89
Financial Reporting and Changing Prices
(Issue Date 12/86)

Statement No. 88
Employers' Accounting for Settlements and Curtailments of Defined Benefit Pension Plans and for Termination Benefits
(Issue Date 12/85)

Statement No. 87
Employers' Accounting for Pensions
(Issue Date 12/85)

Statement No. 86
Accounting for the Costs of Computer Software to Be Sold, Leased, or Otherwise Marketed
(Issue Date 8/85)

Statement No. 85
Yield Test for Determining whether a Convertible Security is a Common Stock Equivalent—An amendment of APB Opinion No. 15
(Issue Date 3/85)

Statement No. 84
Induced Conversions of Convertible Debt—An amendment of APB Opinion No. 26
(Issue Date 3/85)

Statement No. 83
Designation of AICPA Guides and Statement of Position on Accounting by Brokers and Dealers in Securities, by Employee Benefit Plans, and by Banks as Preferable for Purposes of Applying APB Opinion 20—An amendment of FASB Statement No. 32 and APB Opinion No. 30 and a rescission of FASB Interpretation No. 10
(Issue Date 3/85)

Statement No. 82
Financial Reporting and Changing Prices: Elimination of Certain Disclosures— An amendment of FASB Statement No. 33
(Issue Date 11/84)

Statement No. 81
Disclosure of Postretirement Health Care and Life Insurance Benefits
(Issue Date 11/84)

Statement No. 80
Accounting for Futures Contracts
(Issue Date 8/84)

Statement No. 79
Elimination of Certain Disclosures for Business Combinations by Nonpublic Enterprises—An amendment of APB Opinion No. 16
(Issue Date 2/84)

Statement No. 78
Classification of Obligations That Are Callable by the Creditor—An amendment of ARB No. 43, Chapter 3A
(Issue Date 12/83)

Statement No. 77
Reporting by Transferors for Transfers of Receivables with Recourse
(Issue Date 12/83)

Statement No. 76
Extinguishment of Debt—An amendment of APB Opinion No. 26
(Issue Date 11/83)

Statement No. 75
Deferral of the Effective Date of Certain Accounting Requirements for Pension Plans of State and Local Governmental Units—An amendment of FASB Statement No. 35
(Issue Date 11/83)

Statement No. 74
Accounting for Special Termination Benefits Paid to Employees
(Issue Date 8/83)

Statement No. 73
Reporting a Change in Accounting for Railroad Track Structures—An amendment of APB Opinion No. 20
(Issue Date 8/83)

Statement No. 72
Accounting for Certain Acquisitions of Banking or Thrift Institutions—An amendment of APB Opinion No. 17, an interpretation of APB Opinions 16 and 17, and an amendment of FASB Interpretation No. 9
(Issue Date 2/83)

Statement No. 71
Accounting for the Effects of Certain Types of Regulation
(Issue Date 12/82)

Statement No. 70
Financial Reporting and Changing Prices: Foreign Currency Translation—An amendment of FASB Statement No. 33
(Issue Date 12/82)

Statement No. 69
Disclosures about Oil and Gas Producing Activities—An amendment of FASB Statements 19, 25, 33, and 39
(Issue Date 11/82)

Statement No. 68
Research and Development Arrangements
(Issue Date 10/82)

Statement No. 67
Accounting for Costs and Initial Rental Operations of Real Estate Projects
(Issue Date 10/82)

Statement No. 66
Accounting for Sales of Real Estate
(Issue Date 10/82)

Statement No. 65
Accounting for Certain Mortgage Banking Activities
(Issue Date 9/82)

Statement No. 64
Extinguishments of Debt Made to Satisfy Sinking-Fund Requirements—An amendment of FASB Statement No. 4
(Issue Date 9/82)

Statement No. 63
Financial Reporting by Broadcasters
(Issue Date 6/82)

Statement No. 62
Capitalization of Interest Cost in Situations Involving Certain Tax-Exempt Borrowings and Certain Gifts and Grants—An amendment of FASB Statement No. 34
(Issue Date 6/82)

Statement No. 61
Accounting for Title Plant
(Issue Date 6/82)

Statement No. 60
Accounting and Reporting by Insurance Enterprises
(Issue Date 6/82)

Statement No. 59
Deferral of the Effective Date of Certain Accounting Requirements for Pension Plans of State and Local Governmental Units—An amendment of FASB Statement No. 35
(Issue Date 4/82)

Statement No. 58
Capitalization of Interest Cost in Financial Statements That Include Investments Accounted for by the Equity Method—An amendment of FASB Statement No. 34
(Issue Date 4/82)

Statement No. 57
Related Party Disclosures
(Issue Date 3/82)

Statement No. 56
Designation of AICPA Guide and Statement of Position (SOP) 81-1 on Contractor Accounting and SOP 81-2 Concerning Hospital-Related Organizations as Preferable for Purposes of Applying APB Opinion 20—An amendment of FASB Statement No. 32
(Issue Date 2/82)

Statement No. 55
Determining whether a Convertible Security is a Common Stock Equivalent— An amendment of APB Opinion No. 15
(Issue Date 2/82)

Statement No. 54
Financial Reporting and Changing Prices: Investment Companies—An amendment of FASB Statement No. 33
(Issue Date 1/82)

Statement No. 53
Financial Reporting by Producers and Distributors of Motion Picture Films
(Issue Date 12/81)

Statement No. 52
Foreign Currency Translation
(Issue Date 12/81)

Statement No. 51
Financial Reporting by Cable Television Companies
(Issue Date 11/81)

Statement No. 50
Financial Reporting in the Record and Music Industry
(Issue Date 11/81)

Statement No. 49
Accounting for Product Financing Arrangements
(Issue Date 6/81)

Statement No. 48
Revenue Recognition When Right of Return Exists
(Issue Date 6/81)

Statement No. 47
Disclosure of Long-Term Obligations
(Issue Date 3/81)

Statement No. 46
Financial Reporting and Changing Prices: Motion Picture Films
(Issue Date 3/81)

Statement No. 45
Accounting for Franchise Fee Revenue
(Issue Date 3/81)

Statement No. 44
Accounting for Intangible Assets of Motor Carriers—An amendment of Chapter 5 of ARB No. 43 and an interpretation of APB Opinions 17 and 30
(Issue Date 12/80)

Statement No. 43
Accounting for Compensated Absences
(Issue Date 11/80)

Statement No. 42
Determining Materiality for Capitalization of Interest Cost—An amendment of FASB Statement No. 34
(Issue Date 11/80)

Statement No. 41
Financial Reporting and Changing Prices: Specialized Assets—Income-Producing Real Estate—A supplement to FASB Statement No. 33
(Issue Date 11/80)

Statement No. 40
Financial Reporting and Changing Prices: Specialized Assets—Timberlands and Growing Timber—A supplement to FASB Statement No. 33
(Issue Date 11/80)

Statement No. 39
Financial Reporting and Changing Prices: Specialized Assets—Mining and Oil and Gas—A supplement to FASB Statement No. 33
(Issue Date 10/80)

Statement No. 38
Accounting for Preacquisition Contingencies of Purchased Enterprises—An amendment of APB Opinion No. 16
(Issue Date 9/80)

Statement No. 37
Balance Sheet Classification of Deferred Income Taxes—An amendment of APB Opinion No. 11
(Issue Date 7/80)

Statement No. 36
Disclosure of Pension Information—An amendment of APB Opinion No. 8
(Issue Date 5/80)

Statement No. 35
Accounting and Reporting by Defined Benefit Pension Plans
(Issue Date 3/80)

Statement No. 34
Capitalization of Interest Cost
(Issue Date 10/79)

Statement No. 33
Financial Reporting and Changing Prices
(Issue Date 9/79)

Statement No. 32
Specialized Accounting and Reporting Principles and Practices in AICPA Statements of Position and Guides on Accounting and Auditing Matters—An amendment of APB Opinion No. 20
(Issue Date 9/79)

Statement No. 31
Accounting for Tax Benefits Related to U.K. Tax Legislation Concerning Stock Relief
(Issue Date 9/79)

Statement No. 30
Disclosure of Information about Major Customers—An amendment of FASB Statement No. 14
(Issue Date 8/79)

Statement No. 29
Determining Contingent Rentals—An amendment of FASB Statement No. 13
(Issue Date 6/79)

Statement No. 28
Accounting for Sales with Leasebacks—An amendment of FASB Statement No. 13
(Issue Date 5/79)

Statement No. 27
Classification of Renewals or Extensions of Existing Sales-Type or Direct Financing Leases—An amendment of FASB Statement No. 13
(Issue Date 5/79)

Statement No. 26
Profit Recognition on Sales-Type Leases of Real Estate—An amendment of FASB Statement No. 13
(Issue Date 4/79)

Statement No. 25
Suspension of Certain Accounting Requirements for Oil and Gas Producing Companies—An amendment of FASB Statement No. 19
(Issue Date 2/79)

Statement No. 24
Reporting Segment Information in Financial Statements That Are Presented in Another Enterprise's Financial Report—An amendment of FASB Statement No. 14
(Issue Date 12/78)

Statement No. 23
Inception of the Lease—An amendment of FASB Statement No. 13
(Issue Date 8/78)

Statement No. 22
Changes in the Provisions of Lease Agreements Resulting from Refundings of Tax-Exempt Debt—An amendment of FASB Statement No. 13
(Issue Date 6/78)

Statement No. 21
Suspension of the Reporting of Earnings per Share and Segment Information by Nonpublic Enterprises—An amendment of APB Opinion No. 15 and FASB Statement No. 14
(Issue Date 4/78)

Statement No. 20
Accounting for Forward Exchange Contracts—An amendment of FASB Statement No. 8
(Issue Date 12/77)

Statement No. 19
Financial Accounting and Reporting by Oil and Gas Producing Companies
(Issue Date 12/77)

Statement No. 18
Financial Reporting for Segments of a Business Enterprise: Interim Financial Statements—An amendment of FASB Statement No. 14
(Issue Date 11/77)

Statement No. 17
Accounting for Leases: Initial Direct Costs—An amendment of FASB Statement No. 13
(Issue Date 11/77)

Statement No. 16
Prior Period Adjustments
(Issue Date 6/77)

Statement No. 15
Accounting by Debtors and Creditors for Troubled Debt Restructurings
(Issue Date 6/77)

Statement No. 14
Financial Reporting for Segments of a Business Enterprise
(Issue Date 12/76)

Statement No. 13
Accounting for Leases
(Issue Date 11/76)

Statement No. 12
Accounting for Certain Marketable Securities
(Issue Date 12/75)

Statement No. 11
Accounting for Contingencies: Transition Method—An amendment of FASB Statement No. 5
(Issue Date 12/75)

Statement No. 10
Extension of "Grandfather" Provisions for Business Combinations—An amendment of APB Opinion No. 16
(Issue Date 10/75)

Statement No. 9
Accounting for Income Taxes: Oil and Gas Producing Companies—An amendment of APB Opinions No. 11 and 23
(Issue Date 10/75)

Statement No. 8
Accounting for the Translation of Foreign Currency Transactions and Foreign Currency Financial Statements
(Issue Date 10/75)

Statement No. 7
Accounting and Reporting by Development Stage Enterprises
(Issue Date 6/75)

Statement No. 6
Classification of Short-Term Obligations Expected to Be Refinanced—An amendment of ARB No. 43, Chapter 3A
(Issue Date 5/75)

Statement No. 5
Accounting for Contingencies
(Issue Date 3/75)

Statement No. 4
Reporting Gains and Losses from Extinguishment of Debt—An amendment of APB Opinion No. 30
(Issue Date 3/75)

Statement No. 3
Reporting Accounting Changes in Interim Financial Statements—An amendment of APB Opinion No. 28
(Issue Date 12/74)

Statement No. 2
Accounting for Research and Development Costs
(Issue Date 10/74)

Statement No. 1
Disclosure of Foreign Currency Translation Information
(Issue Date 12/73)

STATEMENTS OF FINANCIAL ACCOUNTING CONCEPTS (SFAC)

Concepts Statement No. 7
Using Cash Flow Information and Present Value in Accounting Measurements
(Issue Date 2/00)

Concepts Statement No. 6
Elements of Financial Statements—A replacement of FASB Concepts Statement No. 3 (incorporating an amendment of FASB Concepts Statement No. 2)
(Issue Date 12/85)

Concepts Statement No. 5
Recognition and Measurement in Financial Statements of Business Enterprises
(Issue Date 12/84)

Concepts Statement No. 4
Objectives of Financial Reporting by Nonbusiness Organizations
(Issue Date 12/80)

Concepts Statement No. 3
Elements of Financial Statements of Business Enterprises
(Issue Date 12/80)

Concepts Statement No. 2
Qualitative Characteristics of Accounting Information
(Issue Date 5/80)

Concepts Statement No. 1
Objectives of Financial Reporting by Business Enterprises
(Issue Date 11/78)

ACCOUNTING PRINCIPLES BOARD (APB) OPINIONS, AICPA

APB Opinion No. 1 1962
New Depreciation Guidelines and Rules

APB Opinion No. 2 1962
Accounting for the Investment Credit

APB Opinion No. 3 1963
The Statement of Source and Application of Funds

APB Opinion No. 4 1964
Accounting for the Investment Credit

APB Opinion No. 5 1964
Reporting of Leases in Financial Statement of Lessee

APB Opinion No. 6 1965
Status of Accounting Research Bulletins (Amendment of ARB No. 43)

APB Opinion No. 7 1966
Reporting the Results of Operations

APB Opinion No. 8 1966
Accounting for the Cost of Pension Funds

APB Opinion No. 9 1966
Reporting the Results of Operations

APB Opinion No. 10 1966
Omnibus Opinion

APB Opinion No. 11 1967
Accounting for Income Taxes

APB Opinion No. 14 1969
Accounting for Convertible Debt and Debt Issued with Stock Purchase Warrants

APB Opinion No. 15 1969
Earnings per Share

APB Opinion No. 16 1970
Business Combinations

APB Opinion No. 17 1970
Intangible Assets

APB Opinion No. 18 1971
The Equity Method of Accounting for Investments in Common Stock

APB Opinion No. 19 1971
Reporting Changes in Financial Position

APB Opinion No. 20 1971
Accounting Changes

APB Opinion No. 21 1971
Interest on Receivables and Payables

APB Opinion No. 22 1972
Disclosure of Accounting Policies

APB Opinion No. 23 1972
Accounting for Income Taxes—Special Areas

APB Opinion No. 24 1972
Accounting for Income Taxes—Equity Method Investments

APB Opinion No. 25 1972
Accounting for Stock Issued to Employees

APB Opinion No. 26 1972
Early Extinguishment of Debt

APB Opinion No. 28 1973
Interim Financial Reporting

APB Opinion No. 29 1973
Accounting for Nonmonetary Transactions

APB Opinion No. 30 1973
Reporting the Results of Operations

APB Opinion No. 31 1973
Disclosure of Lease Commitments by Lessees

Glossary

Abnormal earnings   The difference between actual earnings and expected earnings where expected earnings are typically calculated as the expected rate of return times the net assets of the firm.

Accelerated Cost Recovery System (ACRS)   A system of depreciation that is a part of the tax code in the United States.

Accelerated depreciation   A method of depreciation that allocates higher expenses to the earlier years of an asset's life than does the straight-line method.

Accounting cycle   The sequence of steps that occurs in the recording of transactions and events in the accounting system.

Accounting equation   The equation that represents the equality maintained in any accounting system between assets, liabilities, and owners' equity. The equation is Assets = Liability + Owners' Equity.

Accounts payable   The liability that results when the firm buys goods or services on credit. It represents the obligation to pay cash to the supplier.

Accounts payable turnover   The number of times that accounts payable are replaced during the accounting period. It is usually calculated as the cost of goods sold divided by the average accounts payable.

Accounts receivable   The asset that results when a customer buys goods or services on credit. It represents the right to receive cash from the customer.

Accounts receivable turnover   The number of times that accounts receivable are replaced during the accounting period. It is calculated as the sales divided by the average accounts receivable.

Accrual basis   The accounting basis used by almost all corporations that recognizes revenues and expenses in the period in which they are earned or incurred and not in the period in which the cash inflow or outflow occurs.

Accrual concept   A fundamental concept in accounting that revenues are recognized in the period in which they are earned and expenses are recognized in the period in which they are incurred, regardless of when the associated cash flows are received or paid.

Accrual entry   In the context of pension accounting, this is the entry to accrue pension cost and create the pension obligation.

Accrued   A term used to describe either expenses or revenues indicating that these items are recognized in the financial statements regardless of whether they have resulted in cash flows.

Accrued expense   An expense that has been incurred and recognized in the financial statements but has not yet been paid for.

Accrued interest receivable   An asset that results when interest revenue is recognized in the period in which it has been earned but has not yet been received in cash.

Accrued liability   A liability that results from an accrued expense.

Accumulated Benefit Obligation (ABO)   The present value of the pension obligations under a defined benefit plan. The calculation includes all necessary actuarial assumptions but does not assume any escalation of salaries.

Accumulated comprehensive income   An account in owners' equity that accumulated the owners' equity effect of items that are classified in comprehensive income but are excluded from reported net income.

Accumulated depreciation   The total depreciation that has been taken on an asset to a particular point in time.

Active minority ownership   A classification of the investment in the stock of other companies where the acquiring company has between 20 and 50 percent ownership interest.

Actuary   A professional trained in statistical methods who can make reasonable estimates of pension costs.

Additional paid-in capital   The excess of the issuance price of stock over its par value.

Adjunct account   An account that adds to a related account; that is, it has the same type of balance as the related account. An example of this type of account is the premium on bonds payable account.

Adjusted Current Earnings (ACE)   A term used in the U.S. tax code for the earnings number used to calculate the alternative minimum tax.

Adjusted trial balance   A listing of the account balances after adjusting entries are made but before the closing entries are made.

Adjusting entry   An entry made at the end of the period to record an event or transaction that has not been recorded during the current accounting period. Events or transactions that are not signaled in any other way are recorded through adjusting entries.

Advances on sales   The title of a liability account that represents cash received from the customer prior to the delivery of the goods or services being sold. It represents the firm's obligation to provide those goods or services in the future.

Aging of accounts receivable method   A method used to estimate the amount of accounts receivable that will not be collected. The estimate is prepared by categorizing the receivables into age groups (30 days overdue, 60 days overdue, etc.) and estimating the probabilities that the receivables in each group will not be collected.

AICPA   The American Institute of Certified Public Accountants, the professional association of certified public accountants in the United States.

Allowance for doubtful accounts   A contra asset account that contains an estimate of the amount of accounts receivable that are not likely to be collected. It is contra to the accounts receivable account.

Allowance method   A method used to value accounts receivable by estimating the amount of accounts receivable that will not be collected in the future.

Alternative Minimum Tax (AMT)   A tax computed in the U.S. tax code that establishes a minimum tax a corporation has to pay regardless of the deductions that are allowed based on various accounting methods.

Amortization   The allocation of the cost of intangible assets to expense over their useful lives.

Amortization of discount   The systematic reduction of the discount account balance over the life of a bond. The reduction of the discount account each period adds to the interest expense recorded during the period.

Amortization of premium   The systematic reduction of the premium account balance over the life of a bond. The reduction of the premium account each period reduces the interest expense recorded during the period.

Annuity   A series of cash flows in which the same amount is to be received or paid every period.

APB   The Accounting Principles Board, an organization formed by the AICPA to set accounting standards immediately prior to the formation of the Financial Accounting Standards Board (FASB).

Articles of incorporation   A document filed with state regulatory authorities when a business incorporates in that state. The articles include, among other items, the authorized number of shares, as well as the par or stated value of the stock that is to be issued.

Articulate   A concept in accounting that refers to the interconnectedness of the financial statements such that changes in one statement (for instance, the cash flow statement) explain changes in another statement (for instance, the balance in cash on the balance sheet).

Asset Depreciation Ranges (ADR)   Guidelines for useful lives for property, plant, and equipment that were defined in the tax code prior to the adoption of the Accelerated Cost Recovery System (ACRS).

Asset purchase An acquisition of assets from another company in which the acquiring company purchases the assets directly rather than buying a controlling interest in the stock of the other company. Title to the assets passes to the acquiring company.

Asset-pricing models Theoretical models that explain the prices and/or the returns that result from investments in the stock of a company. The most commonly used asset-pricing model is the Capital Asset Pricing Model or CAPM.

Assets Elements of the balance sheet that have probable future value and are owned or controlled by the firm.

Auditing Standards Board The regulatory body in the United States that establishes auditing standards for auditors.

Auditor A professionally trained accountant who examines the accounting records and statements of the firm to determine whether they fairly present the financial position and operating results of the firm in accordance with GAAP.

Authorized shares The maximum number of shares that a corporation is authorized to issue under its articles of incorporation.

Available for sale securities A classification of passive investment securities. All actively traded securities that do not fit into the classification of trading securities or held-to-maturity securities are classified as available for sale.

Average cost of capital The average cost of obtaining funds, usually in the context of a regulated utility.

Bad debts Those accounts receivable not likely to be collected.

Balance sheet A financial statement showing the asset, liability, and owners' equity account balances of the firm.

Balance sheet equation The equation that describes the relationship between assets, liabilities, and owners' equity. It is as follows: Assets = Liabilities + Owners' Equity

Basic earnings per share A ratio that describes the earnings for a period relative to the number of shares of common stock outstanding. In the simplest case, it is calculated as earnings divided by the average number of shares outstanding.

Basket purchase A purchase of assets in which more than one asset is acquired for a single purchase price.

Best efforts basis The basis on which underwriters sometimes sell bonds for firms. The underwriter makes its "best effort" to sell the bonds but if they cannot be sold, the bonds are returned to the firm.

Beta A parameter in the Capital Asset Pricing Model (CAPM) that describes the sensitivity of a given stock's price movement to changes in the overall price of the market portfolio.

Black-Scholes Model A theoretical model used to price options.

Board of directors The governing body of a corporation elected by the shareholders to represent their ownership interest.

Bond A long-term borrowing of a firm that is evidenced by a bond certificate. The borrowing is characterized by a face value, coupon rate, and maturity date.

Bond covenants Restrictions placed on a firm that issues bonds. The restrictions usually apply to the ability of the firm to pay dividends or require that the firm maintain certain minimum ratios.

Bond indenture A document that describes all of the parameters, features, and conditions of a public bond issue of a firm.

Bond market A market in which bonds of firms are actively traded.

Book value The value of an asset or liability carried on a firm's books. For property, plant, and equipment, this value is the original cost of the asset less the accumulated depreciation of the asset.

Book value per share A ratio that compares the total book value of a company's net assets to the number of shares of common stock outstanding. It is calculated as the net book value at the end of a period divided by the number of shares outstanding at the same point in time.

Books The accounting records of the firm. Usually this term refers to the records reported to shareholders rather than to any other body, such as the tax authority.

Call option An option that gives the holder the right to buy shares of stock at a fixed price stated in the contract.

Callable preferred Preferred stock that has a provision for the company to retire (call) the stock at a set price at some specified point in time.

CAP Committee on Accounting Procedures, a committee of the AICPA that sets accounting standards prior to the Accounting Principles Board (APB).

Capital A general term that refers to the long-term sources of funding for the firm. Capital typically consists of owners' equity (stock) and long-term debt.

Capital account   An account used in a partnership to record the investment and accumulated earnings of each partner.

Capital Asset Pricing Model (CAPM)   A model that describes the relationship between the return on a stock and the return of the market and the risk-free rate.

Capital asset turnover   A ratio describing the conversion of capital assets into revenues. It is calculated as revenues divided by average capital assets.

Capital charge   The expected earnings used in calculating abnormal earnings. It is calculated as the cost of equity times the net assets of the firm.

Capital expenditures   The cash outflows a firm incurs to acquire new plant, property, and equipment.

Capital lease   A lease that the lessee must record as an asset and a related borrowing as if the transaction represented the purchase of the asset.

Capital stock   Synonym for common stock.

Capital structure   A term that describes the sources of funding for the firm from long-term sources.

Capitalizable cost   A cost that can be recorded as an asset on the financial statements rather than being expensed immediately.

Cash basis accounting   The accounting basis used by some entities in which revenues and expenses are recognized when the cash inflow or outflow occurs.

Cash discount   A reduction in the amount that has to be paid on an account payable if payment is made within a specified time limit.

Cash flow statement   A financial statement that shows the cash flows of the firm during the accounting period categorized into operating, investing, and financing activities.

Cash ratio   A short-term liquidity ratio that compares the cash balance of the firm with the current liabilities.

Chart of accounts   A listing of the names of the accounts used in the accounting system.

Classified balance sheet   A balance sheet in which the assets and liabilities are listed in liquidity order and are categorized into current and noncurrent sections.

Clean opinion   An audit opinion that states that the financial statements present fairly the financial position and operating results of the firm in conformity with GAAP.

Close the books   The process by which the firm makes closing entries to complete one accounting period and sets the balances in the accounts to start the next period.

Closing entries   Entries made at the end of the accounting period to transfer the balances from the temporary income statement and dividend accounts to the retained earnings account.

Collateral   Something of value that is pledged against a debt. If the borrower defaults on the debt, the lender receives title to the collateral.

Collateral trust bond   A bond that provides marketable securities as collateral in the event of default by the firm.

Commercial paper   A short-term borrowing in which the lender is another corporation.

Commitments   Obligations that a company has agreed to but that do not yet meet the recognition criteria under GAAP.

Common size balance sheet   A balance sheet in which each line item on the balance sheet is computed as a percent of total assets.

Common size data   Data that are prepared from the financial statements (usually the income statement and balance sheet) in which each element of the financial statement is expressed as a percentage of some denominator value. On the income statement, the denominator value is usually the sales revenues for the period and, on the balance sheet, the denominator is the total assets for the period.

Common size income statement   An income statement in which each line item is computed as a percent of total revenues.

Common stock   The stock issued by a corporation to its owners.

Common stock equivalents   Shares of common stock that would be issued upon exercise of convertible securities or options. Common stock equivalents are used to calculate the earnings per share of a firm under certain assumptions about which of the convertible securities or options are likely to be converted.

Common stockholders' equity   The section of the balance sheet that describes the balances of the owners' equity accounting. It represents the residual value of the firm that belongs to owners.

Comparability   A quality of accounting information that improves the ability of financial statement readers to compare different sets of financial statements.

Completed contract method   A method of revenue recognition used in the construction industry in which the revenues from a contract are recognized only when the contract is completed.

Compounding of interest   Interest computed by adding the interest earned in one period to the balance in the account and multiplying by the interest rate. The interest earned in one period then earns interest itself in the next period.

Compound interest depreciation A depreciation method that calculates the depreciation expense for a period by the change in the present value of the asset.

Comprehensive income A term used in the FASB's conceptual framework to describe all changes in the owners' equity accounts except the initial investment by owners and the withdrawals by owners in the form of dividends.

Concepts statements A set of statements enacted by the FASB that sets forth the concepts and principles that guide them as they set new accounting standards.

Conceptual framework The framework set out in the concepts statements of the FASB to guide them as they set new accounting standards.

Conservatism A concept in accounting that generally indicates that losses should be recognized as soon as they can be estimated but gains should be postponed until most of the uncertainty is resolved.

Consistency A quality of accounting information that requires consistent application of accounting principles across time.

Consolidated financial statements Financial statements that represent the combined financial results of a parent company and its subsidiaries.

Consolidating working papers A worksheet that adjusts the financial statements of a parent and its subsidiaries so that the statements can be combined to show the consolidated financial statements.

Consolidation An accounting method that firms are required to use to represent their ownership in other companies when the percentage ownership exceeds 50 percent. The method requires the preparation of consolidated financial statements.

Contingencies Events or transactions whose effects on the financial statements depend on the outcome of some future event.

Contingent liability A liability of a firm that is contingent on some future event, such as the resolution of a lawsuit.

Contingent losses A loss of the firm that is contingent on some future event.

Continuing operations The operations of the firm that are expected to continue into the future.

Contra-asset account An account used to record reductions in a related asset account. An example is accumulated depreciation.

Contributed capital The capital that is provided by owners through the issuance of shares of stock. It is represented by the sum of the common stock and paid-in capital accounts.

Controlling interest The percentage ownership of a subsidiary that a parent company must have in order to control the actions of the subsidiary. In the absence of other evidence, an ownership interest of greater than 50 percent is presumed to represent a controlling interest.

Convertible bond A bond that is convertible under certain conditions into shares of common stock.

Convertible preferred stock Preferred stock that is exchangeable or convertible into a specified number of shares of common stock.

Convertible securities Securities, either stocks or bonds, that can be exchanged (converted) for shares of common stock.

Corporation A form of business in which the owners have limited liability and the business entity is taxed directly. Owners receive distributions from the entity in the form of dividends.

Cost accounting A branch of accounting that studies how cost information is used internally within the firm.

Cost of capital The return that owners of common stock expect to receive.

Cost of goods sold The expense that is recorded for the inventory sold during the period.

Cost recovery method A method of revenue recognition based on cash collections in which no profits are recognized from a sale until the cash collected equals the costs of the item sold. Cash collected subsequent to the recovery of all costs is considered pure profit.

Cost/benefit constraint A constraint set forth in the concepts statements of the FASB that states that the cost of implementing a new accounting standard should be less than the benefits that will be derived.

Coupon payment The periodic payments made by a bond. The payments are typically made semiannually. The amount is calculated by multiplying the face value of the bond by the coupon rate.

Coupon rate A rate specified in a bond used to determine the coupon payments that are made by the bond.

Credit An entry made to the right side of an account or a reference to the right side of an account.

Creditors Individuals or entities that are owed something by the firm.

Credits Right-hand side entries that are made to the accounting system.

Cross-sectional analysis A type of financial statement analysis in which one company is compared with other companies either within the same industry or across industries.

Cumulative effect of changes in accounting principles An income statement item that reflects the cumulative difference in income that results from converting from one accounting principle to another. The net amount is reported in income in the period of change and is shown net of tax.

Cumulative preferred stock Preferred stock that accumulates dividends that are not declared from one period to the next. These accumulated dividends, called dividends in arrears, must be paid before a dividend can be declared for common stockholders.

Current asset An asset that will be turned into cash or consumed within the next year or operating cycle of the firm.

Current installments of long-term debt A current liability that represents the portion of long-term debt that comes due in the next year.

Current liability A liability that will require the use of cash or will be replaced by another current liability within the next year or operating cycle of the firm.

Current portion of long-term debt That portion of long-term debt that is within one year of being due.

Current ratio A measure of the short-term liquidity of the firm. It is measured as the ratio of the current assets of the firm divided by the current liabilities.

Cyclical business A business that is subject to significant swings in the level of its activity, such as seasonal businesses, like Christmas tree farms.

Date of declaration The date the board of directors votes to declare a dividend. On this date, the dividend becomes legally payable to stockholders.

Date of record The date on which a stockholder must own the stock in order to receive the dividend from a share of stock.

Debenture A bond that is issued with no specific collateral.

Debit An entry made to the left side of an account or a reference to the left side of an account.

Debt covenants Restrictions stated in a bond indenture agreement meant to protect the interest of the bond holders.

Debt for equity swap A transaction in which debt securities are exchanged for equity securities.

Debt/equity ratios Measures of the leverage of the firm. There are numerous definitions of these ratios, but all of them attempt to provide a comparison of the amount of debt in the firm compared to the amount of equity.

Decelerated depreciation A method of depreciation that allocates lower expenses to the earlier years of an asset's life than the straight-line method does.

Declining balance depreciation A family of methods of depreciation that calculate the depreciation each period by multiplying a declining balance rate of depreciation by the declining balance in the asset account (its remaining book value).

Declining balance percent (DB%) A percent that characterizes a particular member of the declining balance family of depreciation methods. The percent is used to determine the declining balance rate of depreciation.

Declining balance rate The rate of depreciation used for a particular member of the declining balance family of depreciation methods. The rate is determined by multiplying the declining balance percent by the straight-line rate for the asset.

Defeasance of debt The legal retirement of debt.

Deferral method A method of computing deferred taxes in which the tax expense to stockholders is calculated by multiplying the enacted tax rates by the income before taxes reported to stockholders. The entry to the deferred tax account is then the difference between this expense and the taxes owed to the taxing authority on the company's tax return.

Deferred expense An expense that has already required the outflow of cash but has not yet met the recognition criteria for reporting it in the income statement. Deferred expenses are generally reported as assets.

Deferred revenues Revenues that have already resulted in the inflow of cash but have not yet met the recognition criteria for reporting in the income statement. Deferred revenues are generally reported as liabilities.

Deferred tax An asset or liability account that arises under U.S. GAAP when there is a difference between the revenues or expenses reported to the tax authority and the stockholders of the firm.

Deferred taxes Accounts used to reconcile the differences between the taxes reported to the taxing authority (taxes payable) and those reported to stockholders (tax expense).

Defined benefit plan A pension plan that specifies the benefits retirees will receive upon retirement. The benefits are usually determined based on the number of years of service and the highest salary earned by the employee.

Defined contribution plan A pension plan that specifies how much the firm will contribute to the pension fund of its employees. No guarantee is made of the amount that will be available upon retirement.

Depletion method A method used to allocate the cost of natural resources to expense over the useful life of the resource.

Depreciable cost The portion of the cost of a noncurrent asset, such as plant or equipment, that is to be depreciated over its useful life. The depreciable cost is equal to the original cost of the asset less its estimated salvage value.

Depreciable value A synonym for depreciable cost.

Depreciated cost The amount of the cost of an asset that remains after it has been depreciated. It is the same as the book value of the asset.

Depreciation The expense taken each period based on the use of a noncurrent asset, such as plant or equipment. Depreciation is a process that uses a systematic and rational method, such as the straight-line method, to allocate the cost of a noncurrent asset to each of the future years of its useful life.

Diluted earnings per share An earnings per share calculation that takes into consideration all securities that are potentially convertible into shares of common stock.

Direct costs Costs that are directly associated with the production of inventory units. Examples would be direct material and labor costs.

Direct method A method of calculating the cash from operations of a firm in which the direct gross cash receipts and payments are determined.

Direct write-off method A method of recognizing bad debts. Bad debt expense is recognized under this method at the time the account receivable is written off.

Discontinued operations Operations of the firm that are being phased out and will, therefore, not continue in the future.

Discount A term used to indicate that a bond is sold or issued at a value below its face value.

Discount rate The interest rate used in the calculation of the time value of money.

Discounted Cash Flow Model (DCF) A model of estimating the price of a company's stock that discounts estimated future free cash flows of the firm.

Diversification A reason for acquiring ownership in another company. Diversification typically implies that the new company acquired is in a business very different from the current business of the company. The idea is to find a business that is countercyclical to the firm's current business.

Dividend declaration An action by the board of directors of a corporation that makes payment of a dividend a legal obligation of the firm.

Dividends Payments made to owners that represent a return on their investment in the firm. Dividends are paid only after they are declared by the board of directors.

Dividends declared A distribution of assets (usually cash) to the owners of a corporation. The board of directors of the corporation votes to formally declare the distribution, at which point it becomes a legal obligation of the corporation. The distribution of cash occurs at a date specified at the time of declaration.

Dividends in arrears Dividends on cumulative preferred stock that have not yet been declared from a prior year.

Dividends in kind Dividends that are paid with some other asset than cash.

Double Declining Balance Depreciation (DDB) A particular member of the declining balance family of depreciation methods that is characterized by a 200 percent declining balance percent.

Double entry accounting system An accounting system that maintains the equality of the balance sheet equation. Each entry requires that equal amounts of debits and credits be made.

Doubtful accounts Accounts receivable that are unlikely to be collected due to a default on the part of the customer.

Drawing account An account used in a partnership to record the cash withdrawals by partners.

Dual entry accounting system Synonym for the double entry accounting system.

Early extinguishment of debt The retirement of debt prior to its scheduled maturity date.

Early retirement of debt See early extinguishment of debt.

Earned A term used to indicate that the firm has completed its earnings process sufficiently to allow the recognition of the revenues from the sale.

Earnings The profits generated by a firm during a specified time period. Earnings are determined by subtracting the expenses from the revenues of the firm.

Earnings per share A ratio calculated by dividing the earnings for the period by the average number of shares outstanding during the period.

Earnings statement The financial statement that reports the revenues and expenses of the firm.

Elimination entry A working paper consolidating entry that eliminates the balance in the investment in a subsidiary account against the owners' equity accounts of the subsidiary. At the same time, if the price paid by the parent company exceeds the book value of the subsidiary's owners' equity section, excess fair market value of the net assets acquired and goodwill are recognized as part of the entry.

Employee stock option An option granted to an employee to buy stock at a fixed price, usually as part of an incentive compensation plan.

Employee Stock Option Plan (ESOP) A benefit plan for employees that buys shares of the company's stock and then grants these shares to employees based on the requirements of the plan.

Entry market The market from which goods or materials enter the firm; sometimes referred to as the wholesale market.

Equity A term used to describe the sum of liabilities and owners' equity; sometimes also used to refer simply to the owners' equity section, which can lead to some confusion in the use of this term.

Equity in subsidiary's earnings An account used in a parent company's books to record its share of the subsidiary's net income for the period using the equity method.

Equity method An accounting method that firms are required to use to represent their ownership in other companies when the percentage ownership is between 20 percent and 50 percent. In addition, this method is often used in parent-only statements to account for the investment in a subsidiary greater than 50 percent. In this case, the account will be eliminated when consolidated financial statements are prepared.

ERISA (Employees' Retirement Income Security Act) An act of the federal government that regulates employee retirement funds and, among other things, specifies how much must be set aside each period to fund the retirement plan.

Estimated value per share The result of calculating the estimated value of a firm's stock and then dividing by the number of shares outstanding.

Excess fair market value The difference between the fair market value and book value of the assets of a subsidiary company whose stock is acquired by a parent company. The difference is measured at the date of acquisition.

Ex-dividend day A date specified in the stock market on which the stock is sold without the most recently declared dividend.

Executory contracts Contracts in which both the buyer and the seller must perform in the future.

Exercise price The price per share that is required to be paid by the holder of a stock option upon exercise.

Exit market The market in which goods exit the firm; sometimes also referred to as the retail market.

Expenses The resources used in the production of revenues by the firm; representing decreases in the owners' wealth.

Experience gains/losses The gains and losses that result from investments made by pension funds.

Expiration date In the context of stock options, the date on which the option holder must either exercise the option or lose it.

Explanatory language opinion An audit opinion that is unqualified but requires some additional explanation beyond that expressed in a clean opinion.

Extraordinary item A gain or loss appearing on the income statement that meets two criteria: (1) it is unusual and (2) it is infrequent.

Face value A value specified in a bond that determines the cash payment that will be made on the maturity date of the bond. The face value is also used to determine the periodic coupon payments made by the bond.

Factor An entity that buys accounts receivable from a firm.

Factoring receivables The process of selling the accounts receivable of a firm.

Fair market value The value of an asset or liability based on the price that could be obtained from, or paid to, an independent third party in an arm's-length transaction.

FASB Financial Accounting Standards Board, the regulatory body that currently sets accounting standards in the United States.

Feedback value A quality of accounting information that gives it relevance to decision makers. The information provides information on previous decisions.

FIFO A cost flow assumption that assigns the cost of the first unit into the firm to the first unit sold (first-in, first-out).

Financial accounting The study of the accounting concepts and principles used to prepare financial statements for external users.

Financial Accounting Standards Board (FASB) The regulatory organization in the United States that sets accounting policy.

Financial leverage A ratio that measures the amount of debt in the capital structure of the firm relative to the total assets of the firm.

Financial reporting books The accounting records that are summarized and reported to owners and other users via the annual report.

Financial statement analysis The process of analyzing the financial performance of a firm using its major financial statements.

Financing activities Activities of the firm in which funds are raised to support the other activities of the firm. The two major ways to raise funds are to issue stock or borrow money.

Financing lease A lease in which the lessor buys an asset and immediately leases the asset to a customer. The lessor is not the manufacturer of the asset. The lease would qualify as a capital lease to the lessee. The title to the asset may or may not pass to the lessee at the end of the lease term.

Financing receivable A receivable from a customer that is represented by a contract to make payments over time including interest.

Finished goods inventory An inventory account that contains the cost of units that have been completed and are awaiting sale.

First-in, First-out Method (FIFO) A method of tracking inventory costs where the unit costs of the first units purchased are the first ones to be reported in cost of goods sold.

Fiscal year The year over which a firm reports its financial results in its annual report.

FISH An acronym (first-in, still-here) that describes the ending inventory units with the LIFO cost flow assumption.

Fixed costs Costs that are incurred by the firm that do not vary with the volume of production or sales.

Flow statement A statement that describes certain types of inflows and outflows of the firm. The cash flow statement and the income statement are both examples of this type of statement.

FOB Free on board. Refers to the point at which title passes to goods in shipment, either the shipping point or the destination.

Forecasting The process of estimating future financial results such as future revenues or expenses.

Foreign-denominated debt Borrowing of a firm that must be repaid in a foreign currency.

Forward P/E ratio A price-to-earnings ratio calculated based on the current price of a share of stock and the forecasted earnings per share of the firm.

Free cash flow A cash flow measure that is computed as cash flow from operations, less cash flows used for investing activities, plus cash flows from debt financing activities, and less the increase in cash required to sustain operations.

Full costing method A method of accounting for the drilling and exploration costs of an oil exploration company in which all costs of exploration are capitalized and amortized without regard to the success or failure of individual wells.

Fully diluted earnings per share An earnings per share calculation for a firm that has issued convertible securities. It assumes the worst-case scenario that all convertible securities are converted, resulting in the lowest possible earnings per share value.

Fully funded Refers to a pension plan in which the pension plan assets equal the projected benefit obligation.

Funding entry In the context of pensions, this is the entry made to show the cash payment made to the pension plan to fund the obligation.

Funds A term used to describe a set of assets and liabilities used in a funds flow statement. Common definitions of funds include cash and working capital.

Funds flow statement A flow statement that describes the sources and uses of funds during the period.

Future sum A term used in the time value of money that represents a cash flow that occurs at some point in the future.

Future value A term used in the time value of money that represents the value of a series of or a single cash flow at some point in the future.

Future value factor A time value of money factor that converts a present value to a future value. The amount of the factor depends on the number of periods and the interest rate.

GAAP Generally Accepted Accounting Principles.

General partners The partners that have unlimited liability in a limited partnership.

Generally Accepted Accounting Principles (GAAP) The accounting principles that U.S. firms are required to follow in preparing their financial statements.

Going-concern assumption An assumption made in GAAP that the firm for which the financial statements are being prepared will continue to exist into the foreseeable future.

Goods available for sale The units of inventory available to be sold during the period. These units include those available from the beginning inventory plus those produced during the current period.

Goodwill An intangible asset that arises when a parent company acquires ownership in a subsidiary company and pays more for the shares of stock than the fair market value of the underlying net assets at the date of acquisition.

Held to maturity securities A classification of investments in bonds or notes that a firm has both the intent and capability to hold until maturity.

Historical cost A valuation attribute or method that values assets at the price paid to obtain those assets.

Horizontal integration A type of merger or acquisition in which a parent company buys a competitor firm in order to gain a larger market share or to expand the company's markets geographically.

Identifiable net assets The assets and liabilities that can be specifically identified at the date of a merger or acquisition. Some of the identifiable assets may not have been recorded on the subsidiary's book, such as patents and trademarks.

Income from continuing operations A subcategory of income that results from all continuing operations.

Income summary account An account used to summarize all the temporary income statement accounts prior to their being closed to retained earnings.

Indenture agreement An agreement that accompanies the issuance of a bond specifying all the terms and restrictions of the borrowing.

Indirect costs Costs incurred in the production process that are only indirectly associated with a particular unit. Supervisory and maintenance labor costs are examples.

Indirect method A method of calculating the cash from operations of a firm in which the net income number is adjusted for all noncash revenues or expenses to convert it from an accrual basis to its cash basis equivalent.

Input market Another name for the entry market, the market from which goods or materials enter the firm.

Installment method A method of revenue recognition based on cash collections in which each payment received is viewed as part profit and part recovery of costs. A fraction of each payment received is recorded as profit.

In-substance defeasance of debt The retirement of debt by placing assets in trust, the proceeds of which are used to make the remaining payments on the debt. The debt is not legally retired.

Intangible assets A nonphysical noncurrent asset that provides the firm with some probable future benefit.

Interest capitalization The recording of interest as a part of the construction cost of an asset.

Interest coverage A ratio that measures the capability of a firm to meet its interest obligations. It is calculated as the net income before interest and taxes divided by interest.

Inter-temporal A term that refers to financial comparisons made over time.

In-the-money option An option that would be worth something if exercised immediately.

Inventory shrinkage The losses of inventory due to spoilage, damage, thefts, and so forth.

Inventory turnover The number of times that inventory is replaced during the accounting period. It is calculated as the cost of goods sold divided by the average inventory.

Investee A company whose stock is being acquired by another company (the investor).

Investing activities The activities of the firm involved with long-term investments, primarily investments in property, plant, and equipment and in the stock of other companies.

Investment banker The intermediary that arranges the issuance of a bond in the public debt market on behalf of a firm. The investment banker sells the bonds to its clients before the bond is traded in the open market.

Investor A company that acquires shares of another company's stock as an investment.

Issued at a discount Bonds or notes that are issued at a price below their maturity value.

Issued at a premium Bonds or notes that are issued at a price above their maturity value.

Issued at par Bonds or notes that are issued at their maturity value.

Issued shares The shares of stock of a corporation that have been issued.

Journal A place where transactions and events are originally recorded in the accounting system.

Journal entry An entry made to the journal to record a transaction or event.

Just-in-time production A method of production in which inventory is produced "just in time" to be sold or to be used in the next stage of production. Inventories using these methods are, therefore, kept to a minimum.

Large stock dividend A stock dividend that meets the criterion for treatment as a large stock dividend. The criterion states that the cutoff is between 20 percent and 25 percent of the outstanding shares. The dividend is recorded at the par value of the shares issued.

Last-in, First-out Method (LIFO) An inventory tracking method in which the unit costs of the last units purchased are the first to appear in the cost of goods sold.

Lease agreement An agreement between a lessee and a lessor for the rental or purchase of an asset, or both.

Lease term The period or term over which a lessee makes payments to a lessor in a lease.

Ledger A place where transactions and events are summarized in account balances. Entries are recorded in the ledger by a process known as posting.

Lessee The party or entity that is borrowing or purchasing the asset in a lease.

Lessor The party or entity that is selling or lending the asset in a lease.

Leverage The use of debt in a firm to improve the return to the owners.

Leverage lease A lease in which a third party provides some of the financing to allow the lessor to buy the asset that is then leased to the lessee. Payments from the lease are then used to repay the third party as well as to pay the lessor.

Leveraged ESOP An employee stock ownership plan that is financed through a borrowing. The proceeds from the borrowing are used to buy shares for the ESOP.

Liability An element of the balance sheet characterized by a probable future sacrifice of resources of the firm.

Liability method A method of computing deferred taxes in which the balance in the deferred tax account is calculated based on a pro forma tax calculation of future years and future tax rates. The tax expense reported to stockholders is then determined based on the calculated deferred tax amount and the taxes owed to the taxing authority.

LIFO A cost flow assumption that assigns the cost of the last unit purchased by the firm to the first unit sold (last-in, first-out).

LIFO liquidation A LIFO liquidation occurs when a layer of inventory that existed at the beginning of an accounting period is sold during the period, thereby decreasing the level of inventory. The costs (old and sometimes very old) associated with the layer sold are, therefore, reported as a part of cost of goods sold.

LIFO reserve An account used to carry the differences between the valuation of inventory on a LIFO basis and that on a FIFO basis. The account would be a contra-account to the inventory account carried on a FIFO basis.

Limited liability A feature of common stock ownership that restricts the liability of owners to the amount they have invested in the corporation.

Limited partners The partners in a limited partnership that have limited liability.

Limited partnership A partnership that allows some partners to have limited liability (limited partners) and others to have unlimited liability (general partners).

Liquidation In the context of an acquisition, this term means that the company acquired ceases to exist as a legal company and that all title to the assets of the acquired company pass to the acquiring company.

Liquidity A quality of an asset that describes how quickly it can be converted into cash.

Liquidity Order The order in which assets and liabilities are listed in a classified balance sheet. Assets that will be converted into cash the quickest are listed first as are liabilities that will require cash the quickest.

LISH An acronym (last-in, still-here) that describes the ending inventory units using the FIFO cost flow assumption.

Loss contingencies Estimated losses that rely upon some future event (such as a lawsuit).

Lower of cost or market A valuation method that reports the value of an asset at the lower of its historical cost or its current market value.

Majority ownership An investment in the stock of another company that represents more than 50 percent of the outstanding shares of stock of the company.

Management The individuals responsible for running or managing the firm.

Management accounting The study of the preparation and uses of accounting information by the management of the firm.

Marginal tax rate The tax rate that applies to the next dollar of income earned. The rate depends on the level of income and how graduated the tax rules are.

Market adjustment account An account that is used to keep track of changes in the market value of either trading or available for sale securities.

Market risk premium The difference between the actual return on the market portfolio and the expected market return as used in the capital asset pricing model (CAPM).

Marketable equity securities Ownership securities that actively trade in a market.

Marketable securities Ownership or debt securities that actively trade in a market.

Mark-to-market A method of accounting for investments in marketable securities that are classified as trading or available for sale securities. The investment account is adjusted to market value at the end of each period.

Matching concept A concept in accounting that requires all expenses related to the production of revenues to be recorded during the same time period as the revenues. The expenses are said to be matched with the revenues.

Materiality A concept in auditing stating that auditors should be concerned only with items that are large enough to have a significant effect in the evaluation of the presentation of the financial results of a company.

Maturity date A date specified in a bond that determines the final payment date of the bond.

Memorandum entry An entry made to record a stock split. No amounts are affected; only the record of the number of shares and of par value is changed by the entry.

Minority interest The stockholders, other than the parent company, of a subsidiary company who own less than 50 percent of the stock of the company.

Minority shareholders Synonym for minority interest.

Modified Accelerated Cost Recovery System (MACRS) A system of depreciation that is part of the current tax code of the United States and that defines asset categories and the allowable deductions for those categories.

Monetary An attribute of an asset or liability that indicates that the asset or liability represents a fixed number of monetary units.

Monetary liability A liability that is fixed in terms of the number of currency units it represents.

Monetary unit The nominal units used to measure assets and liabilities. The monetary unit used is usually the local currency unit (such as the U.S. dollar).

Mortgage bond A bond that provides some type of real asset as collateral in the event of default by the firm.

Multistep income statement An income statement in which revenues and expenses from different types of operations of the firm are shown in separate sections of the statement.

Mutually unexecuted contract A contract between two entities in which neither entity has performed its part of the agreement.

Negative goodwill A credit balance account that results from an acquisition in which a parent company pays less than the fair market value of the net assets of the acquired company, the acquired noncurrent assets (other than long-term investments) have been reduced to zero, and a credit is still needed to balance the entry.

Net asset The assets of the firm less the liabilities.

Net book value The carrying value of an asset on the books of a company.

Net income Synonym for earnings.

Net of tax A term that describes how an income statement item might be reported. The item would be shown on the statement minus the tax effect of the item. This type of presentation is reserved for discontinued operations, extraordinary items, and cumulative effects.

Net Operating Losses (NOLs) Losses that are reported for tax purposes.

Net present value The value today of an amount or series of amounts to be received in the future.

Net realizable value A selling price of a unit of inventory less any costs necessary to complete and sell the unit.

Neutrality A quality of accounting information indicating that the methods or principles applied should not depend on the self-interest of the firm being measured but be neutral with regard to the potential outcomes of the firm.

No Par Stock Stock that is issued with no stated par value. All of the original proceeds are credited to the common stock account.

Nominal Accounts A term used to describe the balance sheet accounts of the firm.

Noncurrent A term used to refer to an asset or liability that is not classified as current.

Noncurrent asset/liability Assets or liabilities that do not fit the definition of current assets and liabilities.

Nonmonetary An attribute of an asset or liability that indicates that the asset or liability does not represent a fixed number of monetary units.

Nonmonetary asset An asset that is not fixed in terms of the number of monetary units it represents. Examples include inventory or property, plant, and equipment.

Nonmonetary exchange An exchange of goods or services in which the assets or liabilities exchanged are not cash.

No-par stock Common stock that has no par value associated with it.

Normal earnings Expected earnings that are used in the calculation of abnormal earnings in the Residual Income Model. They are calculated as the capital charge times the net assets of the firm.

Note A long-term borrowing that has an initial maturity of less than seven years.

Notes payable Obligations of the firm that are represented by a contract to make payments over time to a lender along with interest.

Notes receivable An asset that represents the right of the holder of the note to receive a fixed set of cash payments in the future.

One-line consolidation The equity method is referred to as a one-line consolidation method because it produces the same net results as the full consolidation method except that the results are shown in a single line on the balance sheet (the investment account) and in a single line on the income statement (the equity in subsidiary's earnings).

Operating activities The activities of the firm that involve the sales of goods and services to customers.

Operating forecasts Forecasts of the operating results of the firm, both income and cash flow.

Operating lease A lease in which the lessee does not record an asset and related obligation but treats the lease as a mutually unexecuted contract. Lease expense is then recognized as payments are made per the lease contract. Or, a lease that does not meet the criteria as a capital lease. No entry is made at lease signing, and lease expense is recognized over time as cash payments are made.

Operating leverage The replacement of variable costs with fixed costs in the operation of the firm. If sufficient volume of sales is achieved, the investment in fixed costs can be very profitable.

Option A contract that grants the holder an option to engage in certain types of transactions. In the case of stock options, the contract usually grants the holder the right to buy (call option) or sell (put option) shares of the stock at a fixed price (striking price).

Originating differences The initial differences between book and tax reporting that arise in the accounting for the transactions of the firm. When these differences reverse themselves, the reversals are referred to as reversing differences.

Other comprehensive income Income items that are considered part of comprehensive income but not reported income.

Other Postemployment Benefits (OPEB) Benefits provided to retirees other than pensions. These benefits are typically health-care or life insurance benefits.

Out-of-the-money option An option that would be worthless if exercised immediately because the market value is less than the exercise price.

Output market Another name for the exit market, the market in which inventory exits the firm.

Outstanding shares The number of shares of a corporation that are held by individuals or entities outside the corporation (i.e., does not include treasury shares).

Overfunded Refers to a pension plan in which the plan assets exceed the projected benefit obligation.

Overhead costs Costs incurred in the production of units of inventory that are considered indirect costs.

Owners The individuals or entities that hold shares of stock in a corporation.

Owners' equity The section of the balance sheet that represents the owners' wealth; equivalent to the assets less the liabilities.

Paid-in capital The additional amount paid above par value by owners at the initial issuance to acquire the stock of a company.

Par A term used to indicate that a bond is sold or issued at its face value.

Par value A value per share of common stock that is set in the articles of incorporation. When stock is issued, the proceeds from the issuance are split between the par value account and the paid-in capital account.

Parent company A company that acquires more than 50 percent of another company. The acquired company is referred to as a subsidiary.

Parent-only books The accounting records of a parent company not combined with its subsidiary's records as in the consolidated financial statements. The parent typically records the investment in its subsidiary using the equity method on the parent-only books.

Partially executed contract A contract between two entities in which one or both of the parties has performed a portion of its part of the agreement.

Participating preferred stock Preferred stock that can also participate in dividends declared beyond the level specified by the preferred stock, that is, beyond the fixed dividend payout specified in the preferred stock contract.

Partnership A form of business in which the owners have unlimited legal liability and the business entity is not taxed directly, but the income from the entity passes through to the owners' individual tax returns.

Partnership agreement An agreement between the partners in a partnership that specifies how the individual partners will share in the risks and rewards of ownership of the partnership entity.

Passive investment An investment by one company in another company in which the acquiring company has no capability of controlling or influencing the decisions of the acquired company.

Passive minority ownership A classification of investments in which the company owns less than 20 percent of the outstanding shares of stock.

Payment date The date on which a dividend payment is actually made.

Pension A plan that provides benefits to employees upon retirement.

Percentage of completion method A method of revenue recognition used in the construction industry in which a percentage of the profits that are expected to be realized from a given project are recognized in a given period, based on the percentage of completion of the project. The percentage complete is typically measured as the fraction of costs incurred to date relative to the total estimated costs to complete the project.

Percentage of sales method A method of estimating the bad debt expense of a firm by estimating the expense as a percentage of the credit sales for the period.

Periodic inventory system An inventory system in which cost of goods sold is determined by counting ending inventory, assigning costs to these units, and then subtracting the ending inventory value from the sum of the beginning inventory plus purchases for the period.

Periodic method A method of calculating cost of goods sold in which the company keeps track of purchases during the period and then backs into the cost of goods sold amount by counting ending inventory, assigning costs to the ending inventory, and then using purchases and beginning inventory to calculate cost of goods sold.

Permanent accounts Accounts whose balance carries over from one period to the next. All balance sheet accounts are considered permanent accounts.

Permanent differences Differences between book and tax reporting that never reverse themselves; that is, they are "permanent." For example, tax-exempt income would be reported for book purposes but would never be reported for tax purposes because it is exempt.

Perpetual inventory system An inventory system in which the cost of goods sold is determined at the time of sale of the unit.

Perpetual method A method of calculating cost of goods sold in which the company records the cost of goods sold at the time of sale.

Pledging The process by which a firm commits the collections from its accounts receivable to repay a loan. The accounts receivable serve as collateral for the loan.

Pooling on interests method An accounting method used in acquisitions involving a stock swap. The underlying concept of the method is that the ownership groups of the two companies are pooled together and, therefore, there is no basis on which to revalue the assets and liabilities of the two companies. In consolidation, the assets and liabilities are combined at their book values at the date of acquisition.

Posting A synonym for posting to the ledger.

Posting to the ledger The process of transferring the information recorded in a journal entry to the ledger system.

Predictive value A quality of accounting information that makes the information relevant to decision makers. Its relevance stems from its ability to predict the future.

Preemptive right The right of stockholders to share proportionately in new issuances of shares of common stock.

Preferred stock An ownership right in which the owner has some preference as to dividends; that is, if dividends are declared, the preferred stockholder receives them first. Other rights that normally are held by common stockholders may also be changed in preferred stock; for instance, many issues of preferred stock are nonvoting.

Premium A term used to indicate that a bond is sold or issued at a value above its face value.

Present value A time value of money term that represents the value today of future cash flows.

Present value depreciation A depreciation method that calculates the depreciation expense for a period by the change in the present value of the asset.

Present value factor A factor used to convert a future amount to a present value. The amount of the factor depends on the number of periods and the interest rate.

Price/earnings ratio A performance ratio that compares the market price per share of a stock with the earnings per share.

Prior period adjustment An adjustment to financial statements because of an error or mistake in a prior period. If the error involves the income statement in the prior period, the adjustment is made by debiting or crediting the beginning balance in retained earnings.

Private placement A borrowing arranged privately between two corporations or entities.

Privately held company A company whose shares are held by a few individuals and do not trade in an active stock market.

Pro forma An "as-if" calculation of financial results. In this chapter, the pro forma calculation is that of the deferred tax differences with the liability method.

Pro forma earnings An earnings statement that is based on projected future results.

Pro forma statements A set of financial statements that is based on projected future results.

Pro rata consolidation theory A theory of consolidation in which minority interest is given no credit in the consolidated financial statements. The portion of assets and liabilities of the subsidiary company owned by the minority interest is ignored in the preparation of the consolidated financial statements. The consolidated financial statements then contain the parent's share of the book value and the excess fair market value and goodwill of the subsidiary. This method is also known as the proprietary theory.

Product costs Costs incurred by the firm in the production of inventory.

Profit The difference between the revenues and the expenses recognized during the period; also a synonym for net income.

Profit margin The difference between the revenues from sales and the cost of goods sold.

Profit margin ratio A performance measure that compares the after-tax but before-interest return (income) earned by the firm with the revenues of the firm.

Projected Benefit Obligation (PBO) The present value of the pension obligations under a defined benefit plan. The calculation includes all necessary actuarial assumptions and an assumption with regard to the escalation of salaries.

Promissory note A document in which the issuer of the note agrees to pay fixed amounts to the holder of the note at some point in the future.

Property dividend A dividend that is satisfied with the transfer of some type of property rather than cash.

Prospective analysis A financial statement analysis of a firm that attempts to look forward in time to predict future results.

Prospectus A document filed with the SEC by a corporation when it wants to issue public debt or stock.

Provision for doubtful accounts A synonym for bad debt expense.

Provision for taxes A synonym for tax expense.

Public bond market A market in which bonds are publicly traded.

Publicly traded corporations A company whose shares are traded in a public stock market.

Purchase commitment A contract between two entities in which one entity agrees to buy goods or services from another entity, but neither party has executed the contract.

Purchase method An accounting method used to record the acquisition of another company. The acquisition is treated as a purchase, and the assets and liabilities acquired are measured at their cost. Since this is typically a basket purchase, the cost is allocated to the individual assets and liabilities on the basis of their relative fair market values.

Purchasing power An attribute of an asset that measures its ability to be exchanged for goods and services.

Put option An option that provides the holder with the option to sell something at a fixed price (striking price).

Qualified opinion An audit opinion that finds some exception to the fair presentation of the financial results.

Quick ratio   A measure of the short-term liquidity of a firm. It is calculated by dividing the current assets less inventories (and, in some cases, prepaid items) by the current liabilities.

Rate of depreciation   A ratio or percentage that describes the amount of depreciation that may be taken during a given period. For straight-line depreciation, the rate is the reciprocal of the number of years of useful life (1/N).

Raw materials inventory   An inventory account that contains the costs of the raw materials purchased for use in the production process of the firm.

Realized (realizable)   A term indicating that revenues have been received in cash or claims to cash.

Realized gain/loss   A gain or loss from the sale of an asset or liability that is the result of a completed transaction (in general, it means that cash or an agreement to pay cash has been exchanged).

Realized holding gain   A gain that results from the sale of a unit of inventory that had been held during a period of time during which prices increased. The profits that result from the change in price are the portion referred to as a holding gain.

Realized/realizable   A revenue recognition criteria, which means that the cash to be received from the sale has been received or is very easily obtained.

Receivables turnover   A ratio that measures the efficiency with which the firm collects its accounts receivables. It is calculated by dividing sales by the average receivables.

Recourse   A provision in agreements to sell receivables in which the buyer of the receivables has the right to return the receivable to the seller if the buyer cannot collect the receivable.

Recovery (accounts receivable)   The reinstatement and collection of an account receivable that was previously written off.

Redeemable preferred stock   Preferred stock that can be bought back (redeemed) by the corporation under certain conditions and at a price stated in the prospectus.

Related parties   Entities related to the firm, typically through ownership interest, which also engage in transactions with the firm.

Relevance   A quality of accounting information indicating that the information should be relevant to the decisions of the user.

Reliability   A quality of accounting information indicating that the information should be reliable to be of use to decision makers.

Replacement cost   The current price at which a unit of inventory can be replaced by the firm.

Reporting books   Synonym for financial reporting books.

Representational faithfulness   A quality of accounting information indicating that the information should accurately represent the attribute or characteristic that it purports to represent.

Resale value   The market value of an asset in the market in which it can be sold.

Residual claim   A claim on the assets of the firm by the owners. It is residual in that the claims of liability holders must be met before the owners' claims can be met.

Residual Income (RI) Method   A valuation method that estimates the value of the firm by discounting the abnormal earnings of the firm and adding this value to the book value of the firm.

Retained earnings   Earnings that are retained within the firm and not paid out to owners in the form of dividends.

Retrospective analysis   A financial statement analysis of a firm that looks only at historical data.

Return on Assets (ROA)   A measure of performance that measures the return on the investment in assets of the firm. It is calculated by dividing the net income, after tax but before interest, by the average total assets of the firm during the accounting period. The ratio can be split into the profit margin ratio and the total asset turnover ratio.

Return on Capital (ROC)   An overall performance measure that calculates the return on total long-term capital (both debt and equity) of the firm. It is calculated as the net income before interest (net of taxes) divided by the average long-term capital.

Return on Equity (ROE)   A measure of performance that measures the return on the investment made by owners. It is calculated by dividing the net income less dividends paid to preferred stockholders by the average owners' equity during the accounting period.

Revenue   The selling price of a good or service recorded on the income statement.

Revenue recognition   The policy that determines when revenues are to be recognized in the income statement under GAAP.

Revenue recognition criteria   Criteria established within GAAP that stipulate when revenues should be recognized in the financial statements.

Revenues   Inflows of resources to the firm that result from the sales of goods and/or services.

Reversing differences Timing or temporary differences that are reversals of previously recognized originating differences.

Sale on account A sale in which the seller receives a promise to pay at a later date from the buyer.

Sales allowances Adjustments to the selling price of a good or service such as for goods that are damaged.

Sales returns Sales that are returned by the customer for credit.

Sales revenue The amount of sales recognized during the accounting period based on the revenue recognition criteria.

Sales-type lease A lease in which the lessor is the manufacturer of the asset and the lease is a vehicle to sell the asset to the lessee. The lessor treats the transaction as a sale and records profit on the sale at the time the contract is signed. The lessee records the lease as a capital lease.

Salvage value The estimate of the value of an asset at the end of its useful life, made at the time of purchase of the asset.

SAS Statement of Auditing Standards.

SEC Securities and Exchange Commission.

Securities and Exchange Commission (SEC) A federal agency that governs the reporting requirements for firms that issue shares of stock to the public. The SEC also has the power to set accounting policies for these firms.

Securitization A process by which various types of assets, such as accounts receivable, are aggregated together and sold via a security interest in the ownership of the proceeds from the collection of those assets.

Senior debenture A general borrowing of the firm that has priority over other types of long-term borrowings in the event of bankruptcy.

SFAC Statement of Financial Accounting Concepts.

SFAS Statement of Financial Accounting Standards.

Shareholders' equity Synonym for owners' equity.

Simple interest Interest that is calculated by multiplying the interest rate in the agreement by the principal involved. Interest earned in one period does not earn interest in a subsequent period.

Single-step income statement An income statement in which all revenues are listed in one section and all expenses in a second section.

Small stock dividend A stock dividend that meets the criterion for treatment as a small stock dividend. The criterion states that the cutoff is between 20 percent and 25 percent of the outstanding shares. The dividend is recorded at the market value of the shares issued.

Sole proprietorship A form of business in which there is a single owner (sole proprietor). This form is characterized by unlimited liability to the owner and its exemption from corporate taxation.

Special Purpose Entities (SPEs) Entities that are created for some special purpose such as the securitization of receivables or the conduct of research and development. The company forming such an entity often retains some amount of ownership interest in the entity.

Specific identification method A method of assigning costs to units of inventory in which the cost of a unit can be specifically identified from the records of the firm.

Stated value A value per share of common stock set in the articles of incorporation.

Statement of cash flows A statement that describes the inflows and outflows of cash during a specified period of time.

Statement of changes in financial position Synonym for funds flow statement.

Statement of changes in stockholders' equity A financial statement that reports on all of the changes in the stockholders' equity accounts during the year.

Statement of earnings A financial statement that reports the revenues and expenses of the firm.

Statement of Financial Accounting Standards (SFAS) Statements of Financial Accounting Standards are the official pronouncements of the FASB that establish generally accepted accounting standards in the United States.

Statement of financial position Synonym for balance sheet.

Stock A certificate that represents ownership in a corporation.

Stock acquisition An acquisition of another company that is accomplished through the acquisition of shares of stock of the acquired company. The acquired company continues as a separate legal entity.

Stock appreciation right A right given to employees that allows them to profit from increases in the value of the underlying stock without having to own the stock.

Stock dividend A distribution of additional shares of common stock to owners. Existing owners receive shares in proportion to the number of shares they already own.

Stock option An option typically granted to employees that allows them to obtain shares of stock at a fixed price at certain points in time.

Stock purchase warrant A right to purchase additional shares of stock at a fixed price typically attached to other kinds of securities such as bonds.

Stock rights A right granted to existing stockholders to buy shares in proportion to the amount already held.

Stock split A distribution of new shares of common stock to owners. The new shares take the place of existing shares, and existing owners receive new shares in proportion to the number of old shares they already own.

Stock swap An acquisition in which an acquiring company swaps shares of its stock for the shares of the acquired company's stock.

Stockholders' equity The accounts on the balance sheet that represent that stockholders' interest in the net assets of the firm.

Straight-line depreciation A depreciation method that calculates the amount of depreciation expense for each period by dividing the depreciable cost by the estimated number of years of useful life.

Straight-line rate The rate of depreciation for the straight-line method; calculated as the reciprocal of the number of years of useful life ($1/N$).

Subchapter S corporation A form of business organization that is characterized by limited liability but exemption from corporate taxation.

Subordinated debenture A general borrowing of the firm that has a lower priority than senior debentures in the event of bankruptcy.

Subsidiary A company acquired by another company (the parent) for more than 50 percent of its outstanding shares.

Successful efforts method A method of accounting for the drilling and exploration costs of an oil exploration company in which the costs of exploration are capitalized and amortized only for successful wells.

Summary account An account used to summarize the income before taxes in a given accounting period. Individual revenue and expense items are transferred to this account for the purpose of determining income before taxes, and the net balance is eventually closed to retained earnings.

Sum-of-the-Years' Digits Depreciation (SYD) A method of depreciation in which the depreciable cost of an asset is allocated to years of useful life based on a ratio known as the sum-of-the-years'

digits ratio. The ratio is calculated by dividing the digits of the years in reverse order by the sum of the years' digits.

Sum-of-the-years' digits ratio A ratio used to calculate depreciation in the sum-of-the-years' digits method; calculated by dividing the digits of the years in reverse order by the sum of the years' digits.

Syndicate A group of underwriters that collectively helps a firm sell its bonds.

T-account A device used to represent a ledger account.

Tangible asset An asset that has a physical form but, under GAAP, includes all current assets regardless of physical form.

Tax books The accounting records the firm keeps to report to the taxing authority.

Tax loss carryback A provision in the U.S. tax code that allows a firm to carry back tax losses for up to three years to recover tax paid in those prior years.

Tax loss carryforward A provision in the U.S. tax code that allows a firm to carry forward tax losses for up to 15 years to offset positive income and avoid paying taxes on that income.

Tax provision A synonym for tax expense.

Taxing authority An agency that assesses and collects taxes from the firm.

Temporary accounts Accounts used to keep track of information temporarily during an accounting period. Balances in these accounts are eventually transferred to a permanent account at the end of the period using a closing entry.

Temporary differences Differences that arise in the accounting for the transactions of a firm between the tax rules and the GAAP rules. The differences are restricted to those that only involve timing issues, that is, the period in which the items are reported. The term is used in the liability method of computing deferred taxes.

Terminal value In the Discounted Cash Flow Model (DCF) it is the value of the company that is estimated at the end of the investment horizon.

Time value of money A concept in accounting that the value of a dollar depends on the time period in which it is received. In general, the notion is that a dollar received today is worth more than a dollar received tomorrow because the dollar received today can earn interest.

Timeliness A quality of accounting information indicating that information must be timely in order to be relevant to decision makers.

Times interest earned ratio A measure of long-term liquidity of a firm. It measures the ability of the firm to make its interest payments. It is calculated by dividing the income before interest and taxes by the interest expense.

Time-series analysis A financial statement analysis in which data are analyzed over time.

Timing differences Differences that arise in the accounting for the transactions of a firm between the tax rules and the GAAP rules. The differences are restricted to those that only involve timing issues, that is, the period in which the items are reported. The term is used in the deferral method of computing deferred taxes.

Tombstone ad An advertisement that indicates the essential terms of an initial bond issuance.

Total asset turnover A measure of performance of a firm that shows the number of dollars of sales that are generated per dollar of investment in total assets. It is calculated by dividing the sales revenue by the average total assets for the accounting period.

Trade receivable An account receivable that results from a transaction with another business entity in the normal conduct of trade.

Trading on equity A synonym for leverage.

Trading securities A classification of marketable securities. Securities that are actively traded are placed in this classification.

Trailing P/E ratio A price earnings ratio that is calculated based on the current price per share and the latest reported earnings per share.

Transaction analysis The process by which the accountant decides what accounts are affected and by how much they are affected by an economic transaction or event.

Transactions An economic event in which there is some type of economic exchange with the firm that affects its accounts.

Transition gain/loss A gain or loss that exists at the date when a firm first converts to the requirements of SFAS No. 87 (pensions). A gain exists if the plan is overfunded at the date of transition, and a loss exists if the plan is underfunded. The transition gain/loss is amortized into income over an extended period of time.

Treasury stock Shares of stock repurchased by a corporation and held internally. The shares may be resold at any time.

Treasury stock method A method used in the computation of diluted earnings per share. The method applies to situation where, on a pro forma basis, the firm would expect to receive cash upon the conversion of securities into stock, such as stock options. The cash expected to be received is then assumed to be used to repurchase shares of stock in the open market to prevent further dilution of the earnings per share.

Trial balance A listing of the account balances.

Trial balance phase A phase in the preparation of financial statements in which the temporary accounts still contain income statement and dividend information from the period and have not been closed out to retained earnings.

Troubled debt restructuring The renegotiation of the terms of a debt agreement when the debtor is financially distressed.

Trustee An entity legally separate from the firm that is entrusted with assets of the firm. A typical example would be to assign a trustee to manage the pension assets of the firm.

Unclassified balance sheet A balance sheet that does not classify assets and liabilities into current and noncurrent categories.

Uncollectible accounts Accounts receivable that are deemed to be uncollectible. The point at which they are uncollectible is generally established by company policy.

Underfunded A pension plan in which the plan assets are less than the projected benefit obligation.

Underwriter An investment bank that arranges and agrees to sell the initial issuance of a company's bonds.

Underwriting agreements The agreement between a company and an underwriter (typically an investment bank) that governs the terms and conditions of the sale of a company's bonds or stock.

Undistributed income Income earned by the firm that has not been distributed in the form of dividends.

Unearned revenues Cash receipts from customers that have not yet met the criteria for revenue recognition.

Unguaranteed residual value The value of an asset at the end of the lease term of the asset when the asset reverts back to the lessor.

Uniform Partnership Act An act that has been passed by all states specifying standard partnership agreement terms in the event that a partnership does not have a partnership agreement.

Unit-of-measure assumption An assumption made under GAAP that all transactions should be measured using a common unit, the U.S. dollar.

Units-of-production method A method of depreciation that allocates the depreciable cost of the asset to the years of its useful life as a function of the volume of production for the period.

Unlimited liability A characteristic of sole proprietorships and partnerships that means owners are personally responsible for the liabilities incurred by the business entity.

Unqualified opinion Synonym for clean opinion.

Unrealized gain/loss A gain or loss recognized in the financial statements that has not resulted in the receipt of cash or the right to receive cash.

Useful life The estimate of the expected life over which an asset will be used.

Valuation allowance An account used to hold the adjustments necessary to lower the carrying value of the marketable securities account from historical cost to market value when the market value is lower.

Value in sale The value of an asset if the intent is to sell the asset.

Value in use The value of an asset if the intent is to use the asset rather than sell it.

Verifiability The capability of accounting information to be verified by an independent measurer.

Vertical integration A type of merger or acquisition in which a parent company buys a supplier or a customer firm in order to assure a supply of raw materials or a market for its end product.

Vesting An event by which employees are granted pension benefits even if they leave the employ of the company.

Warrant A contract that allows the holder to acquire new shares of common stock upon exercise of the warrant. A fixed price is stated in the warrant and is the price that the holders have to pay for each share of stock.

Warranty liabilities Liabilities that result from the guarantees provided by the company regarding the performance of its products that are sold to customers.

Weighted Average Cost of Capital (WACC) The average cost of obtaining capital from debtholders and owners. It is weighted by the proportion of capital obtained from these two sources.

Weighted average costing A method of assigning costs to units of inventory in which each unit is assigned the average cost of the units available for sale during the period.

Wholesale market Another name for the entry market.

Widely held stock Stock of a company that is held by a large number of individuals or institutions such that no one stockholder has significant influence on the decisions of the company.

Working capital The difference between the current assets and the current liabilities.

Working capital turnover A ratio that measures the efficiency with which the firm uses its working capital to produce sales. It is measured by dividing sales by the average working capital for the period.

Work-in-process inventory An inventory account used to accumulate the various costs of producing a unit of inventory while the unit is in the production process. The three major costs included are those for raw materials, labor, and overhead.

Write-off The process by which an account receivable is removed from the books of a firm when it is deemed to be uncollectible.

Zero-coupon notes Notes that are issued by a firm that carry a zero percent coupon payment.

Index